Financial Markets, Financial Institutions and Financial Services

Second Edition

FOREWORD
Manoj Mittal
MD & CEO
IFCI Limited

SANDEEP GOEL
Professor
Accounting and Finance
Management Development Institute Gurgaon
Gurugram

PHI Learning Private Limited
Delhi-110092
2023

₹ **1150.00**

FINANCIAL MARKETS, FINANCIAL INSTITUTIONS AND FINANCIAL SERVICES, Second Edition
Sandeep Goel

ISBN-978-81-963789-7-4 (Print Book)
ISBN-978-81-963789-6-7 (e-Book)

Published by Asoke K. Ghosh, PHI Learning Private Limited, Rimjhim House, 111, Patparganj Industrial Estate, Delhi-110092 and Printed by Mudrak, D-61, Sector 63, Noida, U.P.-201301.

About the Author

Dr. Sandeep Goel is a Senior Professor in the area of Accounting and Finance at Management Development Institute (MDI) Gurgaon. He holds 'Double Doctorate', one in Finance; and another in Accounting from Faculty of Management Studies (FMS), University of Delhi. He did his Hons. in Commerce from Shri Ram College of Commerce (SRCC), University of Delhi and Master's degree in Commerce with specialisation in Finance from Department of Commerce, Delhi School of Economics, University of Delhi.

He has over 25 years of industry and academic experience in key positions in organizations/institutions; including Shri Ram Group, University of Delhi and MDI Gurgaon. He also has hands on experience in the family business in business compliance and financial management functions.

He sits as an Independent Director on the Board of Machino Plastics Ltd., Gurugram, a Suzuki JV. He is a Visiting Professor to the Faculty of Management, University of Lodz, Poland. He offers a popular course, 'Financial Markets' to second year students of MBA at MDI.

He has got an extensive international experience in different parts of the world; including the US, Europe, Canada and Asia. His cross-national research and training experience includes Duke University, US; Sapienza University of Rome, Italy; Frankfurt School of Finance and Management, Germany; and Ontario College for Research and Development, University of Toronto, Canada.

He is a Management Trainer and Consultant to Organizations like Bata, Encore, Federal-Mogul Goetze (India) Ltd., SOS Village International, Cairn India, National Banking Institute (Nepal), Druk Holdings (Bhutan), UltraTech Cements, ONGC, IOCL, Jindal, LIC, BEL, IGL, TIL, Ester Industries, and Armed Forces. He has conducted and delivered over 200 MDPs/Training Programs at senior levels for the organizations and trained more than 5,000 executives over the years. These mainly include *Finance for Non-Finance Executives, Forensic Analytics, Fraud Risk Management, Independent Director's and Corporate Governance and Enhancing Financial Skills Using Excel.* He has executed a number of consultancy assignments, the major ones include *Assessment of Employees for Promotion Exercise* for IFCI Ltd., *Evaluation of Bid* for Municipal Corporation Gurugram, *Corporate Governance* for IOCL, *Feasibility Study for Increasing Coin Production* at SPMCIL, *Financial Management* of Bata, *Accounting Application for SAP Professionals* of Ester Industries, and *Financial Leadership* of TIL.

He is a prolific writer and has authored 12 books, including highly acclaimed books *Finance for Non-Finance People and Corporate Governance: Theory and Practice.* He has published more than 75 research articles in national and international journals of repute. His cases have been published by *Ivey Publishing, Asia Case Research Centre, and Emerald Emerging Markets Case Studies.*

His interest areas are *Financial Reporting and Analysis, Corporate Finance, Forensic Accounting, Fraud Risk Management and Corporate Governance.* He has been the Financial Columnist to 'Purchase' (A Publication of Indian Purchase.com).

He has been conferred with Award for Excellence in Research, 2015–16 and Award for Excellence in Teaching, 2015–16 at MDI.

Contents

PART IV FEE-BASED CLASS

PART V CUSTOMER CENTRICITY

APPENDICES: TIME VALUE OF MONEY TABLES

Foreword

As per the International Monetary Fund (IMF), India is to remain the fastest-growing major economy in the world despite global headwinds. It said that India will grow at 6.1 per cent in 2023 before picking up to 6.8 per cent in 2024 fuelled by resilient domestic demand. This growth has been backed by a safe, efficient, innovative and well-regulated financial system which has rapidly evolved over last few years and has kept pace with the changing needs of the economy. This has been possible due to regular thrust on policy reforms as well as regulatory interventions, inter-alia, in the areas of financial inclusion, market efficiency and transparency. In the recent years, there has been a big push on creation of enabling environment through use of technology to reach to the masses, novation in products and offering, setting up of specialised institutions, etc. The game changer trinity of Jan Dhan accounts, Aadhar and Mobile linkage have eased the access of financial and payment services to all especially the poor and the disadvantaged. The Unified Payment Interface [UPI] is now making waves on foreign shores. Certain new initiatives such as account aggregator framework are also catching up fast and building a fintech revolution. These are but very few examples of technology interventions in financial sector. A lot more is happening in the Indian financial system at this time. Financing to create climate resilience and to mitigate the effects of climate change will take centre stage in the remaining part of this decade. Startups are not just limited to top metros but are also emerging from Tier-III and IV towns as well and have access to funds through various routes. In sum, these are exciting times for India; more so for the financial sector.

Given the dynamic changes in the Indian financial sector, there is a need for financial literature and pedagogies to keep pace with the developments in industry.

Dr. Sandeep Goel has catered to this requirement through this book by lucidly blending basic financial concepts and corporate practices with the latest trends and developments in the country's financial system. Dr. Goel is a senior faculty at MDI Gurgaon, a premier business school in India promoted by IFCI, about 50 years back.

He has more than 25 years of industry and academic experience and has authored many books.

I had the privilege of going through this book at the draft stage. The book is well-designed, easy to read and adequately covers the financial system in India; with a global outlook. The book comprehensively presents the three key inter-related constituents of the Indian financial system, viz. *financial markets, financial institutions and financial services*. This book introduces the reader to each of these constituents at a steady pace with relevant illustrations, case studies, quantitative models and real-world examples to give the reader an immersive experience. The Instructor's Manual and Students' Learning Material are supplements that enrich the book and make it an useful read.

Though the book is primarily designed for postgraduate and undergraduate students of management and allied disciplines, it is equally useful to anyone who wants to build conceptual foundation and gain clarity on the Indian financial system. It may also serve as a handbook for ready reference by professionals associated with the financial industry. I commend and congratulate Dr. Goel on the publication of the new version of this book '**Financial Markets, Financial Institutions and Financial Services**'. My best wishes to him for his endeavours.

Manoj Mittal
MD & CEO
IFCI Limited

The Second Edition

I take immense pride in presenting to the readers the second completely revised edition of my successful textbook: **Financial Markets, Financial Institutions and Financial Services.** The basic organizational structure, topical coverage, readability, and useful instructional cases and examples that marked the success of the first edition have been retained. The key features of the revision are highlighted below.

Introduction of New Chapter

A new chapter has been added into the book, keeping in view the recent trends and practices in the financial system as follows:

Chapter 3: "Risk Management in Banks" has been added under Financial Frontiers Part, explaining the risk management system in banking sector.

Chapter-wise Additions/Revisions

The chapter-wise additions/revisions are listed as under:

Chapter 1: 'Regulatory Framework of the Pension Funds' has been added in REGULATORY FRAMEWORK OF INDIAN FINANCIAL SYSTEM.

Chapter 2: 'IMPS' as a new financial facility has been added in KEY BANKING APPLICATIONS.
Revision of 'Financial Performance Analysis of SBI' case for current data of 2022.

Chapter 4: 'New Scale-based Regulation of NBFCs in India' has replaced the older legislation.

Chapter 5: 'Significance of Money Market' has been added as a new topic.

Chapter 7: Revision of 'Analysis of Financial Performance of LIC' case for current data of 2022.

Chapter 8: 'Growth of Mutual Funds Industry in India' has been completely amended in EVOLUTION OF MUTUAL FUNDS.
The topic, 'CATEGORIES OF MUTUAL FUNDS' has been thoroughly reoriented.

Chapter 9: 'RBI's Regulation of Conduct of Plastic Card Business' has been added as a new topic.

Chapter 12: 'The latest amendments in the Factoring Regulation Act, 2011', issued in 2022 have been incorporated under "REGULATORY FRAMEWORK OF FACTORING".
'Practice Exercises' have been added in the chapter with Solutions in the Instructor's Manual.

Chapter 13: 'RBI (Securitisation of Standard Assets) Directions, 2021' have been added in REGULATORY FRAMEWORK OF SECURITISATION IN INDIA.

Chapter 14: 'Practice Exercises' have been added in the chapter with Solutions in the Instructor's Manual.

Addition of Review Cases

"Case exercises" as part of brain-storming application and for value-added learning have been added in the chapters in the last.

Further, all chapters, including Instructor's Manual and Students' Learning Material have been thoroughly advanced and updated to reflect the current data, status, and practices in the domain of *financial markets, management of financial institutions, and finaneial services industry in India in particular, and world at large.* I hope that these enrichments will enhance the value of the book.

Preface

In the last few years, India has emerged as one of the fastest growing economies in the world. India has been categorized with nations like Brazil, Russia, China and South Africa (BRICS Nations) who are going to be the prime drivers of world economy in the next few decades. Since the time India first opened its gates to foreign investment in 1991, there has been a complete turnaround. Now, the traditional Hindu rate of growth is a thing of past and clocking 8%–9% GDP growth rate is the common norm.

India makes for one of the fastest growing nations in the entire world. Even during the global recession, India had managed to perform far better than other nations. Right from banking system to financial regularities, the country has thrived on discipline and out-performance. The booming Indian economy resulted in widespread growth and arrival of new industries. The most sparkling phenomenon is in the form of financial markets of India. The last decade particularly has seen significant changes in the Indian financial markets in terms of institutions and instruments as well as the regulatory framework, obviously for good. Institutions, such as Venture funds and Credit rating agencies have changed the functioning of the Indian financial system and paved new ways for global outreach along with other financial institutions. The financial services sector is a key contributor to India's GDP and is the second largest component after trade, hotels, transport and communication all combined together.

Present book

In the light of inevitable significance of financial system worldwide, particularly in India, the present book is an attempt to throw light on the financial markets, financial institutions and financial services offered by these financial institutions in India. The objective is to help the readers to understand the concept and practices of these three inter-related facets of the financial system in a clearer and better perspective and also to make them aware of the emerging issues and challenges of the sector.

Various aids like Figures, Tables, Illustrations, Discussion questions, and Case studies have been included in the book to facilitate learning. Examples and cases of real world organizations have been discussed. I hope all these features will make the book more interesting and useful to the readers.

The book contains current concepts, corporate practices, recent trends, and current data of the Indian financial system. An attempt has been made to cover the possible aspects of financial system in depth.

Highlights

- Updated and Comprehensive Coverage
- Current Data
- Global Trends and Recent Practices
- Solved Problems and Practice Exercises
- Corporate Case Studies
- Summary Points
- Key Terms
- Objective Questions
- Short Questions
- Critical Thinking Questions
- Descriptive Questions
- Project Exercises
- Review Cases
- Instructor's Manual and Students' Learning Material

'Instructor's Manual' and 'Learning Material' for students are available at https://www.phindia.com/financial_markets_institutions_and_services_sandeep_goel, which comprise PowerPoint Presentations, Additional Cases, Relevant Readings, Quizzes (MCQs) and Solutions to Practice Exercises.

Target Audience

The book is primarily designed for the postgraduate and undergraduate students of management and business administration, and allied disciplines of commerce, finance, economics and others.

It is highly recommended for courses, like:

- Financial Markets
- Financial Markets and Institutions
- Management of Financial Services
- Merchant Banking and Financial Services
- Indian Financial System

Business managers may also be benefited with the detailed discussion on the issues of the financial system in India. In fact, it is of interest to anyone dealing with the nitty-gritty of the financial sector in business and other sectors, who do not have prior knowledge base or required expertise on the subject.

Organization of the book

To create conceptual clarity and connect readers to financial system practices in a suitable fashion, the chapters have been logically organised, meeting the requirement of modern approach of teaching. The book has been divided into five parts with 19 chapters in total.

Though there is no real distinction between financial markets, institutions and services and they all are inter-woven aspects of the financial system, but for facilitating better understanding of the readers, they have been classified under Part I, Part II, Part III, Part IV and Part V. Part I 'Introduction' presents an overview of the financial system in India. Part II 'Financial frontiers' discusses banking, its risk management, and non-banking financial companies' mechanism, money market and capital market. Part III 'Fund-based class' includes those forces which involve exchange of funds at their levels. The forces which are advisory in nature and act as facilitators have been clubbed under Part IV 'Fee-based class'. The last part, Part V 'Customer centricity' highlights the essence of marketing of financial services.

Part I 'Introduction' with Chapter 1 on 'Financial System' is introductory in nature. It discusses Indian financial system, types of financial institutions, instruments and intermediaries, recent developments in global financial system, the concept of financial services and regulatory framework of financial services.

Part II 'Financial Frontiers' discusses two key constituents of the financial system. Chapter 2 entitled 'Banking: Products, Services and Functioning' provides an overview of the evolution of banking industry, types of banks, banking products and reforms in the banking sector with a financial analysis of SBI. Chapter 3 entitled 'Risk Management in Banks' discusses the risk management process and system in banks. Chapter 4 entitled 'Non-Banking Financial Companies' analyses the concept and rationale of non-banking financial companies along with their regulatory framework. Chapter 5 entitled 'Money Market' reviews the Indian money market and its instruments. Chapter 6 entitled 'Capital Market' discusses the capital instruments, recent trends and emerging challenges in these markets.

Part III 'Fund-based Class' includes those forces which involve exchange of funds either directly or indirectly. Chapter 7 entitled 'Insurance' contains a discussion on growth of insurance industry, types of insurance products and emerging issues in Insurance Industry. It also analyses the financial performance of LIC. Chapter 8 entitled 'Mutual Funds' gives an overview of the development phase of mutual funds in India, types of mutual funds products and recent trends in mutual fund industry. Chapter 9 entitled 'Plastic Money' discusses in detail the functioning of plastic money in India. Chapter 10 entitled 'Home Loans' contains a discussion on evolution of home loan industry, types of home loan products and innovative concepts in home loans. Chapter 11 entitled 'Leasing and Hire Purchase' discusses types of leasing services and the interrelationship between leasing and hire purchase. Chapter 12 entitled 'Factoring and Forfaiting' talks about mechanics of factoring services and bills financing and forfaiting flow in India. Chapter 13 entitled 'Securitisation' discusses the conceptual framework of securitisation, its types and practicalities. Chapter 14 entitled 'Venture Capital' throws light on mechanics of venture capital and regulatory framework of venture capital in India.

Part IV 'Fee-based Class' includes those forces which are primarily facilitating the operations and are advisory in nature. Chapter 15 entitled 'Merchant Banking/ Investment Banking and Depositories' overviews merchant banking and its distinction with investment banking, along with the bouquet of services provided by them. It also elaborates on the types of depositories in India. Chapter 16 entitled 'Credit Rating' discusses credit rating services in India. Chapter 17 entitled 'Corporate Restructuring' discusses forms of corporate restructuring and valuation techniques used in M&A. Chapter 18 entitled 'Barter Exchange' provides an overview of the economics of barter and bartering in India.

Part V 'Customer Centricity' is the concluding part. Chapter 19 entitled 'Marketing of Financial Services' discusses the essentiality of marketing of financial services.

I am confident that the readers will find this new edition of the book truly valuable in terms of its quality and presentation. Any constructive comments and suggestions for improving the contents of the book will be highly appreciated, and are welcome at *sandeepgoel18@rediffmail.com or phi@phindia.com.*

SANDEEP GOEL

Acknowledgements

I wish to thank God Almighty for everything in life! The work would be incomplete if I do not acknowledge my parents' contribution. They have been a constant source of inspiration for me and have always stood by me through thick and thin. My wife provided her unstinted support and encouragement in completing the book. My daughter Maanya is my soul whose smile always keeps me going in life.

I am indebted to Sh. Manoj Mittal, MD & CEO, IFCI Limited for obliging me most willingly by writing the Foreword for the book.

I am also thankful to the entire team of PHI Learning, Delhi for their tremendous support and whole-hearted cooperation at all stages of publication of this book. Mr. Asoke K. Ghosh, CMD of PHI Learning and Ms. Babita Mishra, Editorial Coordinator deserve special mention and credit for being instrumental in supporting me at every stage of this book and the edition.

Last, but not the least, I gratefully express my gratitude to the following fellow academic colleagues and professional associates for providing their valuable suggestions and inputs for the refinement of the book, and adopting it for their courses and programs.

- **Dr. Robert C. Rickards,** *Professor of Accounting, Harz University of Applied Sciences, Germany*
- **Dr. J.P. Singh,** *Professor of Finance, Indian Institute of Technology Roorkee*
- **Dr. Ram Kumar Kakani,** *Director and Professor of Finance & Accounts, Indian Institute of Management Raipur*
- **Dr. N.K. Gupta,** *Professor of Commerce, Ramjas College, University of Delhi*
- **Ms. Pooja Mahajan,** *General Manager, IFCI Ltd., New Delhi*
- **Dr. Niti Nandini Chatnani,** *Professor of Finance, Indian Institute of Foreign Trade, New Delhi*
- **Dr. Mayank Joshipura,** *Professor of Finance and Accounting, NMIMS University, Mumbai*

- **Mr. Vinod Kumar Makhija,** *Advisor, IFCI Ltd., New Delhi*
- **Dr. Anand Sharma,** *Professor of Finance and Accounting, Central University of Haryana, Mahendergarh*
- **Dr. Joshy Jacob,** *Associate Professor of Finance and Accounting, Indian Institute of Management Ahmedabad*
- **Mr. Vivek Bhatia,** *Management Consultant, Delhi*
- **Dr. Neelam Rani,** *Associate Professor of Finance & Control, Indian Institute of Management Shillong*
- **Dr. Ashish Varma,** *Associate Professor of Finance, Institute of Management Technology, Ghaziabad*
- **Dr. Chetan G.K.,** *Associate Professor of Finance, Management Development Institute Murshidabad*
- **Mr. Manek Narang,** *Director, Alphas Strategic Advisory LLP, Gurugram*
- **Dr. Samveg Patel,** *Associate Professor of Finance and Accounting, NMIMS University, Mumbai*
- **Dr. Nimisha Kapoor,** *Associate Professor of Finance, University of Lucknow*
- **Dr. Vishakha Bansal,** *Assistant Professor of Finance & Control, Indian Institute of Management Shillong*
- **Dr. Dushyant Ashok Mahadik,** *Assistant Professor of Finance, National Institute of Technology, Rourkela*
- **Dr. Sarveshwar Kumar Inani,** *Assistant Professor of Finance and Accounting, O.P. Jindal Global University, Sonipat*
- **Dr. Rahul Pramani,** *Assistant Professor of Finance, Flame University, Pune*

SANDEEP GOEL

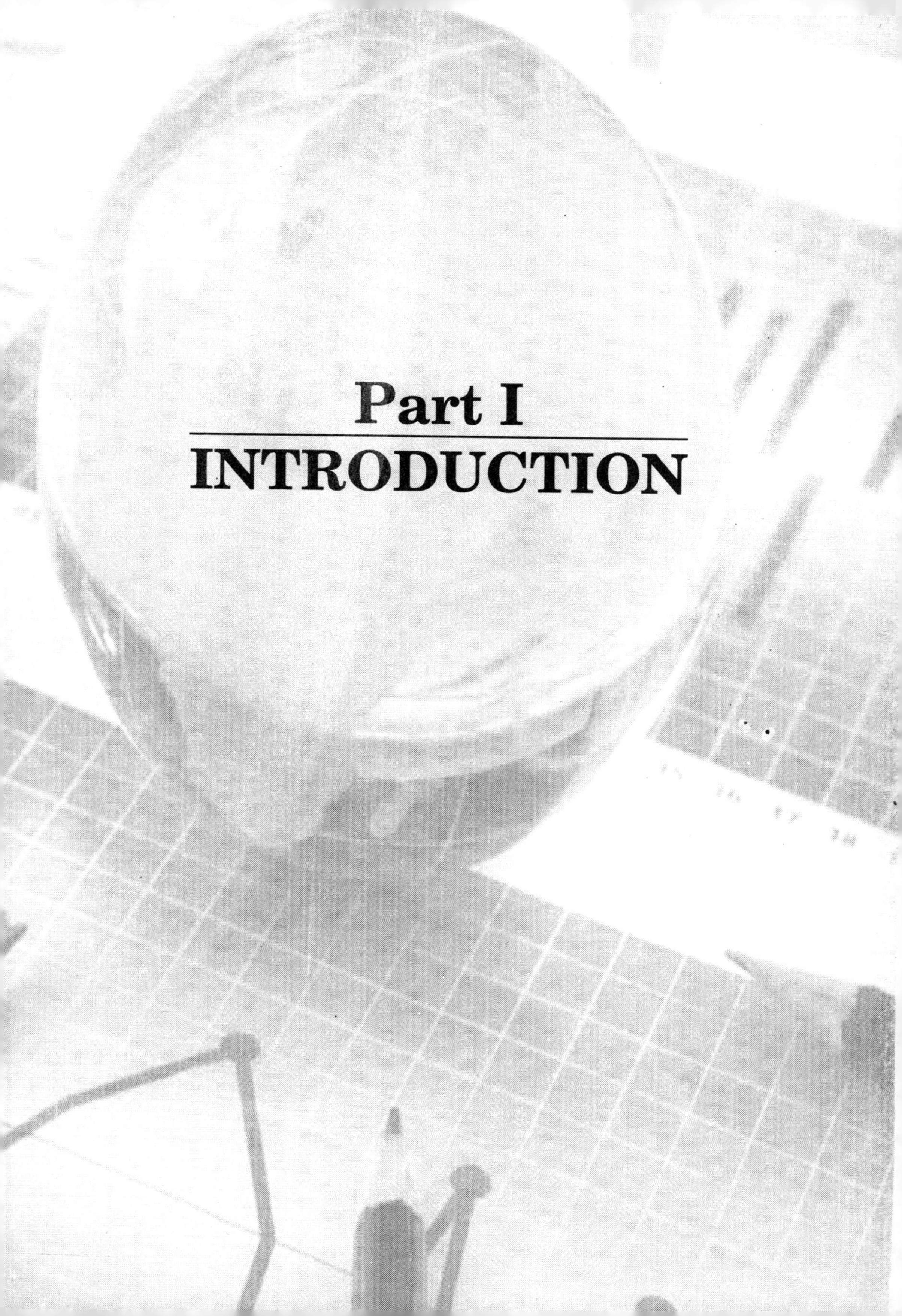

Part I

INTRODUCTION

CHAPTER 1

Financial System

If you don't have a functioning financial system the world economy won't be revived. All the major economies have their responsibility to assist at a pace which is required to clean up the balance sheet of the banking system and to ensure that credit flows are resumed.

— **Manmohan Singh**

LEARNING OBJECTIVES

This chapter discusses the following:

- Financial system and its constituents
- Growth and organisation of Indian financial system
- Components of Indian financial system
- Key innovations in the Indian financial system
- Concept of financial services
- Regulatory framework of financial system in India

INTRODUCTION

A financial system in any country provides the necessary lubricant to its economy. It acts as a link between the savers and the investors, thereby facilitating the flow of savings into industrial investment and stimulating capital formation, which is indispensable for the speedy economic development of the country.

Both savers and investors are important in the process of capital formation, because the act of investment is usually confined to a special class of businessmen who possess the requisite technical and market information and temperament to use it. On the other hand, the activity of savings is largely diffused between innumerable individuals who lack the skill and capacity for active investment. Hence, the transferred process is crucial for facilitating economic growth. Besides, there are geographical and technical limitations that inhibit the process of investment. This gap is filled by the financial system which promotes the process of capital formation by bringing together the supply of savings and the demand for investible funds.

FINANCIAL SYSTEM: NATURE AND SCOPE

A *financial system* consists of a set of individuals and institutions which trade in various instruments in the respective markets, and the supervisory bodies responsible for their regulation (Figure 1.1). The end-users of the system are the people and firms who desire to lend or borrow. A financial system performs the following functions:

- Facilitates lending and borrowing (*outer flows*).
- Enables wealth-holders to invest their savings in the form of accumulated wealth through financial markets (*inner flows*).
- Provides a payment mechanism (*middle flows*).
- Provides specialist services such as insurance and pensions.

In nutshell, a financial system is a composite of financial institutions, financial markets and financial instruments.

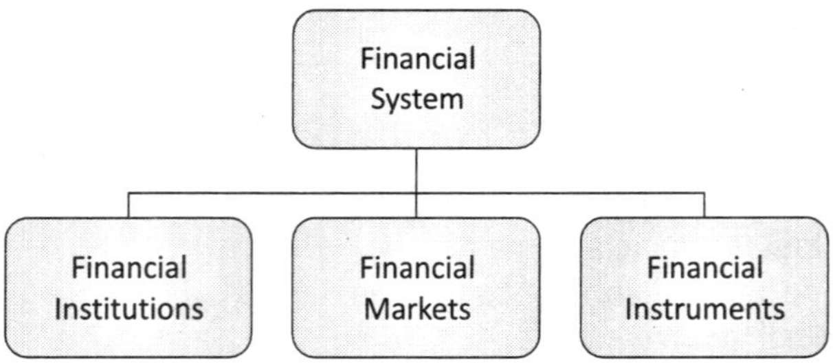

Figure 1.1 Financial system

Financial Institutions

Financial institutions take different forms and offer a wide range of products and services. They are all affected directly or indirectly by each other.

Financial institutions are bodies or firms which perform functions at three different levels.

On the **first level**, they are 'regulatory' in nature which supervise the functioning of financial system.

On the **second level**, they become 'intermediary' which means acting as middlemen between two parties. The parties here are usually called *lenders* and *borrowers* or sometimes *surplus sectors (units)*, and *deficit sectors (units)*.

On the **third level**, they are 'non-intermediary' and provide various forms of direct lending to people who are willing to borrow for their industrial or developmental needs. Hence, they are also called *term lending institutions*.

The Structure of Financial Markets

Based on the nature of funds which are their stock-in-trade, the financial markets are classified into—(i) Money market, and (ii) Capital/Securities market. The financial markets are also categorized into—(i) Primary market, and (ii) Secondary market, as per the issuance process.

Money and Capital Markets

A *money market* is a market where short-term debt instruments (maturity of less than one year) are traded. *Capital market* is a market for long-term funds.

Primary and Secondary Markets

A *primary market* is the one where new issues of a security, both debt and equity, are sold to initial buyers. It is also called '**new issue market**'. A *secondary market* is a financial market where securities that have been previously issued can be resold.

Financial Instruments

Financial instrument is a real or a virtual document representing a legal agreement involving some sort of monetary value. In today's financial market, financial instruments can be generally classified as *equity-based* (representing ownership of the asset), or *debt-based* (representing a loan made by an investor to the owner of the asset). Foreign exchange and derivative instruments comprise another, unique types of instrument.

EVOLUTION OF INDIAN FINANCIAL SYSTEM

Over the years, the Indian financial system has developed at a tremendous pace and has become broad-based. The growth of financial system in India can be discussed under three heads:

Phase I: Pre-Independence

The Indian financial system, before independence, was a colonial economy under the British rule. It was a traditional model with low savings and industrial output. As a result, the rate of economic growth was very low. It was a "close-ended system".

Phase II: Post-Independence (Up to 1991)

The Indian financial system evolved during this phase as a part of planned economic development by the government of India. The objective of India's development strategy was to establish a socialistic pattern of society through economic growth with self-reliance, social justice and alleviation of poverty. These objectives were to be achieved within a democratic political framework using the mechanism of a mixed economy where both public and private sectors co-exist. India initiated planning for national economic development with the establishment of the Planning Commission. The aim of the First Five-Year Plan (1951–56) was to raise domestic savings for growth and to help the economy resurrect itself from colonial rule. Five-year plans were introduced to achieve the much desired growth. Resources were now being channelised from the surplus to deficit sectors. Nationalization of large banks took place in 1969 and 1980. Among non-banking financial intermediaries, Development Finance Institutions (DFIs) paced up the required lending to the industrial sectors of the economy. Regulatory and legal system was strengthened in the form of Capital Issues (Control) Act (1947), Companies Act (1956), Securities Contracts (Regulation) Act (1956) and Foreign Exchange Regulation Act (FERA) in 1973. The major developments during this phase could be grouped as following:

(i) Nationalisation of banks and other institutions.
(ii) Setting up of development banks.
(iii) Broad-based financial system with a mix of banking, insurance and mutual funds.
(iv) Investors' protection with the help of an effective legislative system.

Phase III: Post-Liberalisation (After 1991)

This phase witnessed a radical restructuring of the economic system consisting of industrial deregulation, liberalisation of policies relating to foreign direct investment, public enterprise reforms, trade liberalisation, reforms of taxation system, and reforms of the financial sector.

Improving financial soundness and credibility of banks was a part of banking reforms undertaken by the RBI. Regarding Non-Bank Finance Companies (NBFCs), the Reserve Bank of India issued several measures aimed at encouraging disciplined NBFCs which run on sound business principles.

The reforms in the financial markets focused on removing the structural weaknesses and developing the markets on sound lines. In the area of capital market, the Securities and Exchange Board of India (SEBI) was set up in 1992 to protect the interests of investors in securities and to promote development and regulation of the securities market. SEBI issued guidelines for primary markets, stipulating access to capital market to improve the quality of public issues, allotment of shares, private placement, book building, take-over of companies and venture capital. In the area of secondary markets, measures were taken to control volatility and transparency in dealings by modifying the "badla system". Insider regulations were laid down to protect the integrity of markets. Introduction of screen-based online trading, dematerialising shares by setting up depositories and trading in derivative securities (stock index futures) further added to the strengthening of the financial system. The Foreign Exchange Management Act (FEMA), 1999 was implemented, replacing FERA and making way for new foreign exchange management regime. The Companies Act (2013) was introduced with the objective of meeting the changed national, international and economic environment and to accelerate the expansion and growth of the economy in India. The Act was passed for improving reforms and corporate governance, and to overhaul the previous companies law, the Companies Act, 1956.

Since the liberalisation of the economy in 1992–93 and the initiation of reform measures, the financial system became market-oriented. There was a sea change in the institutional and regulatory environment of the Indian financial system during this period.

ORGANISATION OF INDIAN FINANCIAL SYSTEM

The Indian financial system is broadly classified into two groups—Organised sector and Unorganised sector.

Organised Indian Financial System

The organised financial system comprises of an impressive network of banks and other financial and investment institutions, which together function in fairly developed capital and money markets, and deal in a range of financial instruments. With around two-third share in the total assets in the financial system, banks play an important role. Of late, Indian banks have also diversified into areas such as merchant banking, mutual funds, leasing and factoring.

The organised financial system comprises of the following sub-systems:

- Commercial Banking system
- Development Banking system
- Insurance and Mutual funds
- Money markets
- Capital markets

*These sub-systems are broadly grouped into **financial institutions**, **financial markets** and **financial instruments** in India, as explained in the introductory part. They are discussed in detail in the next section.*

Unorganised Indian Financial System

The unorganised financial system comprises of relatively less controlled moneylenders, indigenous bankers, lending brokers, traders, etc. This part of the financial system is not directly amenable to control by the Reserve Bank of India (RBI). There are a host of financial companies, investment companies, and chit funds, etc. which are also not regulated by the RBI or the government in a systematic manner. However, they are governed by rules and regulations and are, therefore within the orbit of the monetary authorities.

INDIAN FINANCIAL INSTITUTIONS

The financial institutions in India are divided in three categories—Regulatory institutions, the Intermediaries, and the Non-intermediaries.

Regulatory Institutions

The regulators are assigned with the job of governing all the divisions of the Indian financial system. These regulatory institutions are responsible for maintaining transparency in the operations of the institutions under their supervision.

The regulatory bodies of the financial institutions, sector-wise, in India are:

- Banking Sector: Reserve Bank of India (RBI)
- Stock Market: Securities and Exchange Board of India (SEBI)
- Insurance Sector: Insurance Regulatory and Development Authority (IRDA)
- Pension Fund Regulatory and Development Authority (PFRDA)

There are specific regulatory institutions which control a particular service or commodity, like:

- Forward Markets Commission
- Central Board of Direct Taxes (CBDT)
- Central Board of Excise & Customs

Intermediaries

Apart from the regulatory bodies, there are intermediaries acting as middlemen between depositors (lenders) and borrowers that include the banking and non-banking financial institutions (Box 1.1). Financial intermediaries bring them together and mobilise savings of the savers into investments by lending them to borrowers.

Some of these financial institutions in India are:

Banking

- State Bank of India (SBI)
- Punjab National Bank (PNB)
- Axis Bank
- HDFC Bank

These banking institutions of India play a major role in the economy of the country. They are the providers of depository and transaction services which are the major sources for creating money. They extend loans and other credit facilities to the clients.

Non-banking

- Life Insurance Corporation of India (LIC)
- General Insurance Corporation of India (GIC)
- Unit Trust of India (UTI)

The non-banking financial institutions including the insurance companies, pension funds, etc. provide an alternative source of saving to an investor than banking.

BOX 1.1: CLASSIFICATION OF INTERMEDIARY FINANCIAL INSTITUTIONS

These intermediaries can be classified as follows:

Banking

- Retail banks
- Investment banks
- Overseas banks

Non-banking

- Insurance companies
- Pension funds
- Investment trusts
- Building societies

Non-Intermediaries

There are a number of specialised financial institutions in India that have been incorporated for a definite purpose. These are institutions which were established for the industrial development of the country under a special act of the parliament and for this reason, they are also called as *NBSFOs* (*Non-Banking Statutory Financial Organizations*) *or DFIs* (*Development Financial Institutions*). These institutions include the housing finance companies, merchant banks, debt collection companies, etc.

They were primarily set up as term lending institutions; many of them have diversified over the years into other areas, e.g., Industrial Development Bank of India (IDBI) had moved into commercial banking and in 2005, the institution was merged with its commercial division, IDBI Bank. Presently, IDBI Bank Limited is an Indian private sector bank providing financial and banking services.

Some of the specialised financial institutions in India are:

- Industrial Finance Corporation of India (IFCI)
- Export-Import Bank of India (EXIM Bank)
- National Bank for Agriculture and Rural Development (NABARD)
- Small Industries Development Bank of India (SIDBI)

Apart from these, there are several other financial institutions that exist in the country. These are stock-brokers and sub-brokers, portfolio managers, investment advisors, underwriters, foreign institutional investors, etc. and either act as intermediary or non-intermediary. They are profit maximisers and their profit arises from charging interest on the borrowers at a rate which exceeds the amount lent to them.

FINANCIAL MARKETS IN INDIA

The most significant component of the financial system comprises of financial markets which perform a crucial function in the savings-investment process as facilitating organisations. They are not sources of finance but they are a link between the savers and investors, both individual as well as institutional.

The most common way of classifying markets is on the basis of types of securities issued—Money and Capital markets.

Money Market

Money market, as already discussed, is a market for dealing in monetary assets of short-term nature, generally less than one year. It refers to that segment of the financial market which enables the raising of short-term funds for meeting temporary shortages of cash and obligations, and the temporary deployment of excess funds for earning returns. So, a firm or a bank with temporary surplus funds would purchase a money market instrument to earn interest and meet its liquidity requirement. The major participants in the money market in India are the Reserve Bank of India (RBI) and other commercial banks.

Money market organisation/structure comprises of a number of interrelated sub-markets, that is, Call market, Treasury-Bills market, Commercial Bills market, Commercial Papers (CPs) market, Certificate of Deposits (CDs) market, Money Market Mutual Funds (MMMFs) and Repo (repurchase) market, and so on.

Capital Market

It is a market for long-term financial instruments. These long-term instruments include company shares, government bonds and corporate bonds. Company shares are considered to have an infinite life. Corporate and government bonds are issued with maturities, ranging from over one year to thirty years. Its focus is on financing of fixed investment in contrast to money market which is the institutional source of working capital finance. The main participants in the capital market are corporate, foreign institutional investors, mutual funds, insurance organisations and individuals.

Another way of classifying markets is on the basis of time of issue of securities: Primary and Secondary markets.

Primary Market/New Issue Market (NIM)

The NIM deals in new securities, i.e., securities which are offered to the investors for the first time. Capital formation occurs in the NIM as it supplies additional funds to the corporate directly. It does not have any organisational setup located in any particular place, and is recognised only by the specialist institutional services that it tenders to the lenders/borrowers (buyers/sellers) of capital funds at the time of any particular operation.

Secondary Market/Stock Exchange (SE)

The SE is a market for old/existing securities, that is, for those who are already issued and granted SE quotation/listing. Most trading in financial markets takes place on secondary markets (as wealth-holders rotate their portfolios), yet it is the primary markets that facilitate the financing of investment projects by firms. The existence of a secondary market enhances the flow of liquidity in a system. It plays only an indirect role in industrial financing by providing liquidity to investments already made. It has a physical existence and is located in a particular geographical area.

The behaviour of SEs as reflected in the prices of listed securities has a significant bearing on the level of activity in the NIM in terms of its response to issues of capital. Similarly, the prices of new issues are generally influenced by the price movements in the stock markets.

During over last twenty years, a new market has emerged in the form of ***Derivatives market****, which is a trade-off between the traditional markets.*

Derivatives Market

Derivatives were introduced in India in the year 2000. These can be used both for hedging (protecting oneself against financial risks) as well as for speculation.

Instruments whose value is derived from the price of some underlying assets like securities, commodities, bullions, currency, interest level, stock market index, etc. are known as *Derivatives*. In simpler form, derivatives are financial security such as future or option whose value is derived in part from the value and characteristics of another security, the underlying asset.

When a person invests in derivatives, the underlying asset is usually a stock, bond, commodity or currency. He bets that the value derived from the underlying asset will increase or decrease by a certain amount within a certain fixed period of time.

Futures and *options* are two commonly traded types of derivatives. The owner of a *futures contract* is obligated to buy or sell the asset. On the other hand, an *option contract* gives the owner the right to buy or sell an asset at a set price on or before a given date.

Other examples of derivatives are *warrants* and *convertible bonds* (similar to shares, implying they are assets) but derivatives are usually contracts. Beyond this, the range of derivatives is only limited by the imagination of investment banks. It is likely that any person, who has funds invested, an insurance policy or a pension fund, is exposed to derivatives—willingly or unwillingly.

Box 1.2 gives the description of a Foreign Exchange Market.

BOX 1.2: FOREX MARKET

Forex (Foreign Exchange) market is a market wherein participants can buy, sell, exchange or speculate on currencies.

It is primarily an inter-bank market that took shape in 1971 when global trade shifted from fixed exchange rates to floating ones. The origin of the foreign exchange market in India could be traced back to the year 1978 when banks in India were permitted to undertake intra-day trade in foreign exchange*.

Besides, banking institutions, investment management firms, retail brokers and investors also trade in. This is a set of transactions among forex market participants involving an exchange of specified sums of money in a currency unit of any given nation for currency of another nation, at an agreed rate, as of any specified date. During exchange, the exchange rate of one currency to another currency is determined simply by supply and demand exchange to which both parties agree. It is basically a type of derivative market only.

* http://rbidocs.rbi.org.in/rdocs/PublicationReport/Pdfs/77577.pdf.

FINANCIAL INSTRUMENTS: ASSETS IN INDIA

The third component of the organisation of the financial system is financial assets or instruments (securities). The financial instruments, that financial markets have in India, can be broadly classified into Government Securities (G-Secs) and Industrial Securities.

Government Securities (G-Secs)

In India, G-Secs are issued by the Central Government, State Governments and Semi-Government authorities such as Municipalities, State Electricity Boards and Public Sector Corporations. The Central and State Governments raise money through these securities to finance the creation of new infrastructure as well as to meet their current cash needs. Since these are issued by the government, the risk of default is minimal and therefore, interest rates on these securities often serve as a benchmark for the level of interest rates in the economy. Other issuers may price their offerings by 'marking up' this benchmark rate to reflect the credit risk specific to them.

These securities may have maturities ranging from *five to twenty years* and are fixed income securities which pay interest every six months. The Reserve Bank of India manages the issues of the securities. These securities are sold in the primary market mainly through the auction mechanism. The RBI notifies issue of a new tranche of securities and the prospective buyers submit their bids. The RBI decides to accept bids based on a cut-off price.

Industrial Securities

These are securities issued by the corporate sector to finance their long-term and working capital requirements. Major instruments that fall under industrial securities are:

- Equity shares
- Debentures and Bonds
- Preference shares
- Mutual funds
- Deposits
- Commercial Papers (CPs)

KEY INNOVATIONS IN THE INDIAN FINANCIAL SYSTEM

This section discusses some of the important developments in the Indian financial environment that took place during over last two decades, such as Globalisation, Securitisation, Financial engineering, and e-Finance in the Indian perspective.

Globalisation

After liberalization in 1991, the Indian financial system has gone really global. Since 1992, the Indian corporate houses can directly access the overseas financial markets. This can be done through issue of Global Depository Receipts (GDRs) and American Depository Receipts (ADRs) for raising equity finance, and External Commercial Borrowing (ECB) for debt finance. Similarly, the Foreign Institutional Investors (FIIs) can now directly invest in the Indian Securities. Foreign Direct Investment (FDI) regulations have been considerably liberalised.

Securitisation

The process of securitisation allows an entity to raise fresh capital on the security of its existing assets. *For example,* a banking company may group a part of its existing assets (outstanding home loans) into a single pool, and raise fresh capital on the security of this pool. Due to the lower default rate on home loans, it is easier to raise money on the security of these loans.

Financial Engineering

This involves the designing of innovative products to suit the specific needs of the investors. *For example,* Unit linked insurance plans were introduced to suit the needs of policy-holders who aspire a market return with the safety of insurance. So, they have both the risk and investment elements of life insurance into a single product.

e-Finance

During the last few years, there has been a tremendous increase in online trading. The investor can now trade by himself and keep a track of his investments through computer networks without depending upon the brokers. The IT System has greatly facilitated e-finance.

CONCEPT OF FINANCIAL SERVICES

Financial services can be defined as "the products and services offered by financial institutions to meet the financial needs of the consumers". There are different types of financial services like lending money for different purposes, providing insurances, depository services, mortgage services, investment services, credit rating services and many more. In terms of earning, financial services are the largest growing industries in the world.

Financial services basically deal with banks, insurance companies, credit card companies, stock brokerages or money management firms, and consumer finance companies.

Banks

These are one of the biggest financial services companies of the world. There are different types of banks in the world. Some of these are *commercial banks, investment banks, etc.* Banks provide a number of financial services to the clients and these services include depository services, lending services, credit card facilities, etc. These services are provided for both the individuals and the commercial sector.

Insurance Companies

Insurance companies provide the clients with risk coverage services. These services are designed to cover a number of risks that are related to an individual's life, property and the like. These services are not only designed to provide security but at the same time are designed to provide regular income to the clients in the form of the insurance plans. Insurance policies are broadly divided into *Life Insurance* and *General Insurance.*

Intermediaries or Advisory Services Companies

These companies are also called *money management firms* and are basically involved in providing investment services to the clients. There are a number of factors like returns from the investment, security of the investment and several other risk factors that are involved with the investments. These companies are designed to provide advice to the investors in selecting the right investment options that suit their investment plans and also the risk-tolerance capacity. At the same time, the intermediaries or advisory services companies are handling the investor's money and investing it according to the client's choice.

These companies also provide services like asset management, hedge funds, custody services, etc.

Credit Rating Agencies

The credit rating agencies are those firms that evaluate different types of companies. These ratings are based on a number of factors like their performance, the risk factors involved, shareholders' satisfaction, customer facilitation, etc.

Consumer Finance Companies

Consumer finance companies serve individuals by providing personal loans, auto loans, and mortgages, as well as payday loans, cash advances, and credit cards.

FINANCIAL SERVICES IN INDIA

In the last few years, India has emerged as one of the most rapidly growing economies in the world. Since the time India first opened its gates to foreign investment (FDI & FII), there has been a complete turn-around. India has a diversified financial sector undergoing rapid expansion, both in terms of strong growth of existing financial services firms and new entities entering the market. The financial services sector has been an important contributor to the country's Gross Domestic Product (GDP). Along with real estate and professional services, it accounted for 22.05% share in India's GDP in 2020–21. This has been the largest contribution in the services sector's share of 53.89% to nation's GDP.[1] Financial service sector share in India's *market capitalisation* increased to 24% in FY21 from 6% in FY01.[2]

Even in 2008, the year of global recession, India had managed to perform far better than other nations on account of its sound financial system.

Financial services in India have grown phenomenally, from standing up in long queues in banks for several hours to open a savings account or to get the passbook updated to a finger-tip service.

There is a complete bouquet of financial services available at a much affordable cost including brokerage, financial advisory, personal banking, mutual funds, auto and home loans, equity market trading, private equity and others.

Market Size

The country's financial services sector consists of capital markets, insurance sector and non-banking financial companies (NBFCs). India's gross national savings (GDS) as a percentage of Gross Domestic Product (GDP) stood at 30.73% in 2020. India's Ultra High Net Worth Individuals (UHNWIs) is likely to expand by 63% in the next five years. It is expected to have 6.11 lakh HNWIs in 2025.

India's Mutual Fund industry has experienced immense growth. In May 2021, the mutual fund industry crossed over 10 crore folios. As of July 2022, AUM managed by the mutual fund industry stood at ₹37.75 trillion (US$ 474.87 billion), and the total number of accounts stood at 135.6 million. Another crucial component of India's financial industry is the insurance industry. The insurance industry has been expanding at a fast pace. The total first-year premium of life insurance companies reached US$ 40.1 billion in FY22. In FY23 (until May 2022) non-life insurance sector premiums

1. https://statisticstimes.com/economy/country/india-gdp-sectorwise.php
2. https://www.ibef.org/industry/financial-services-india

reached at ₹36,680.69 crore (US$ 4.68 billion). India's insurance market is expected to reach US$ 250 billion by 2025.

In FY22, US$ 14.55 billion was raised across 127 initial public offerings (IPOs). The number of companies listed on the NSE increased from 135 in 1995 to 2,012 by FY22 and total companies listed on BSE and NSE combined were 6,819 by the year.

According to the statistics by the Futures Industry Association (FIA), a derivatives trade association, the National Stock Exchange of India Ltd. (NSE) emerged as the world's largest derivatives exchange in 2020 in terms number of contracts traded.

India's market capitalization had surged by 37% from October 2021, it was at US$ 3.46 trillion. Indian stock market rally made investors ₹72 lakh crore (US$ 953.68 billion) in 2021.[3]

REGULATORY FRAMEWORK OF INDIAN FINANCIAL SYSTEM

There are multiple regulators for the Indian financial system. The regulatory framework of financial system in India can be examined in terms of respective Bills, Acts and other legislative policies made by the Parliament and Judicial precedents.

Regulation of Banking and Non-Banking Finance Companies (NBFCs)

There is a comprehensive mechanism for the regulation of Banking and NBFCs started with two fundamental Acts:

- Reserve Bank of India Act, 1934 which governs the Reserve Bank functions.
- Banking Regulation Act, 1949 which governs the financial sector.

There are other acts which are discussed as under:

Acts Governing Banking Operations

- Companies Act, 2013 and earlier 1956 govern banks as companies.
- Banking Companies (Acquisition and Transfer of Undertakings) Act, 1970/1980 relates to nationalisation of banks.
- Negotiable Instruments Act, 1881.

Acts Governing Individual Institutions

- State Bank of India Act, 1954.
- The Industrial Development Bank (Transfer of Undertaking and Repeal) Act, 2003.
- The Industrial Finance Corporation (Transfer of Undertaking and Repeal) Act, 1993.
- National Bank for Agriculture and Rural Development Act, 1981.
- National Housing Bank Act, 1987.
- Deposit Insurance and Credit Guarantee Corporation Act, 1961.

Acts Governing Specific Functions

- Public Debt Act, 1944 governs the government debt market.
- Securities Contract (Regulation) Act, 1956 regulates government securities market.

3. https://www.ibef.org.op. cit.

- Indian Coinage Act, 1906 governs currency and coins.
- Foreign Exchange Management Act, 1999 governs trade and foreign exchange market.
- Payment and Settlement Systems Act, 2007 provides for regulation and supervision of payment systems in India.

Regulatory Framework for Insurance Industry

The Insurance Industry is regulated by Insurance Regulatory and Development Authority of India (IRDA) Act, 1999. This Act provides for the establishment of an authority to protect the interests of holders of insurance policies, to regulate, promote and ensure orderly growth of an insurance industry and for matters connected therewith or incidental thereto, and further to amend the Insurance Act, 1938, the Life Insurance Corporation Act, 1956 and the General Insurance Business (Nationalisation) Act, 1972.

Regulation of Indian Capital Market (Stock Market)

The capital market is regulated by the Capital Markets Division of the Department of Economic Affairs, Ministry of Finance. The division is responsible for formulating the policies related to the orderly growth and development of the securities markets (that is, shares, debt and derivatives) as well as protecting the interest of the investors.

The five main legislations governing the Indian capital market are:

1. Capital Issues (control) Act, 1947.
2. The Indian Companies Act, 2013 and 1956, which set out rules and regulations for the corporate sector.
3. The Securities Contracts (Regulation) Act, 1956, which provides for regulation of transactions in securities through control over stock exchange.
4. The SEBI Act, 1992 which was established to protect investors, and develop and regulate securities market.
5. The Depositories Act, 1996 which provides for electronic maintenance and transfer of ownership of demat securities.
6. Securities and Exchange Board of India (Listing Obligations and Disclosure Requirements) Regulations, 2015 which enables transparency and fair disclosures by all listed entities in India.

Regulatory Framework of the Forex Market

The Forex market is governed by the FEMA Act, 1999 which came into force from 1st June 2000 to facilitate external trade and regulate the working of foreign exchange market in India.

Regulatory Framework of the Pension Funds

The Government of India through a resolution on 23rd August, 2003, established Interim Pension Fund Regulatory & Development Authority (PFRDA) to promote, develop and regulate pension sector in India.

The contributory pension system was notified by the Government on 22nd December, 2003, now named the National Pension System (NPS) with effect from the 1st January, 2004. The NPS was subsequently extended to all citizens of the country w.e.f. 1st May, 2009 including self-employed professionals and others in the unorganized sector on a voluntary basis. Subsequently, Pension Fund Regulatory and Development Authority (PFRDA) Act was passed on 19th September, 2013 and the same was notified on 1st February, 2014. It regulates NPS, subscribed by employees of Governmenrt of India, State Governments and by employees of private institutions/ organizations and unorganized sectors.[4]

CASE STUDY

The Performance Saga of Indian Financial System

It is a known fact that financial system is the backbone of any economy. A sound financial system is considered one that has five key components—(a) sound public finances and public debt management, (b) stable monetary arrangements, (c) sound banking system, (d) a central bank to stabilize domestic finances and manage international financial relations, and (e) well-developed securities markets. Such a well-developed financial system is vital for mobilizing capital domestically, thereby promoting country's economic development and growth. Also, it makes an economy global and raises its standard to an international arena by attracting foreign investors. To make the financial system stronger and more efficient, emphasis must be placed on incentive-based financial sector reforms, that is, on setting up a system of rewards and penalties. To support such a system, a good infrastructure (including the legal, regulatory, and supervisory frameworks) should be the responsibility of government. But, the reforms have to be backed up by the society as well.

Performance of a financial system is a dynamic concept, which is expressed as the ability of the system to react to changing global economic and technological conditions. The soundness of a system is usually reflected in the superiority of its resource base and performance outcomes. Human capital, the capabilities, innovativeness, and long-term vision are also needed for growth in the long run and to gain edge over others. An efficient financial system facilitates linkage between mobilization and use of resources, which accelerates the process of economic growth. Therefore, a financial system which relies on a wide array of national products, and is quick to adapt to the changing economic scenario outside, is able to carry out this function because it increases its efficiency by offering a broader and flexible array of services to the benefits of all the stakeholders.

To place India's financial system in the light of the above discussion, it has to be studied at all possible parameters of economic development. The organisation of the Indian financial system before independence was a traditional model with low savings and industrial production. It evolved after Independence as a part of planned economic development by the Government of India. The objective of India's development strategy was to establish a socialistic pattern of society through economic growth with self- reliance, social justice and alleviation of poverty. These objectives were to be achieved within a democratic framework using the mechanism of a mixed-economy

4. https://www.pfrda.org.in

where both public and private sectors co-exist. The Post-Liberalisation phase witnessed a radical restructuring of the economic system consisting of deregulation of industrial sector, policy liberalisation relating to foreign direct investment, public sector reforms, strengthening of taxation system, trade liberalisation and financial sector reforms.

POINTS TO REMEMBER

- A financial system acts as a link between the savers and investors.
- Financial system comprises of financial institutions, financial markets and financial instruments.
- A money market is a market where short-term debt instruments are traded.
- A capital market is a market for long-term financial instruments.
- A primary market is for new issues of a security. It is also called 'New Issue market'.
- A secondary market is a financial market in which securities that have been previously issued can be resold.
- The Indian financial system evolved during post-independence phase and witnessed developments like—(i) Nationalisation of banks and other institutions, (ii) Setting up of development banks, (iii) Broad-based financial system, and (iv) Investors' protection.
- The Post 1991 (Liberalisation) phase witnessed a radical restructuring of the economic system consisting of industrial deregulation, liberalisation of policies and financial sector reforms. The Securities and Exchange Board of India (SEBI) was set up in 1992 to protect the interests of investors and regulate the securities market.
- The Indian financial system is classified into two broad groups—(i) organised sector, and (ii) unorganised sector.
- The regulatory bodies of the financial institutions in India are—(a) Banking Sector: Reserve Bank of India (RBI), (b) Stock Market: Securities and Exchange Board of India (SEBI), (c) Insurance Sector: Insurance Regulatory and Development Authority (IRDA), and (d) Pension Fund Regulatory and Development Authority (PFRDA).
- The intermediary institutions act as middle-men between depositors and borrowers.
- Non-Intermediary institutions are specialised financial institutions in India that have been incorporated for a definite purpose of the industrial development of the country, under a special act of the Parliament. Hence, they are also called as NBSFOs (Non-Banking Statutory Financial Organizations) or DFIs (Development Financial Institutions), like Industrial Development Bank of India (now IDBI Bank Ltd.), Export-Import Bank of India (EXIM Bank), etc.
- The financial markets are classified into—(i) Money markets and (ii) Capital markets. The financial markets are also categorized into—(i) Primary markets and (ii) Secondary markets, as per the issuance process. In over last twenty years, a new market has come out in the form of Derivatives market.

- Money market organisation/structure comprises of a number of interrelated sub-markets, that is, Call market, Treasury-bills market, Commercial bills market, Commercial papers (CPs) market, Certificate of Deposits (CDs) market, Money market Mutual Funds (MMMFs) and Repo (repurchase) market.
- Derivatives Market comprise of instruments whose value is derived from the price of some underlying assets like securities, commodities, bullion, currency, interest level, stock market index, etc.
- There are two major types of derivative contracts—futures and options.
- Forex (Foreign Exchange) market is one which facilitates the exchange of currencies.
- It took shape in 1971 and is a part of derivatives segment only.
- The third component of the organisation of the financial system is financial assets/ instruments (securities). The financial instruments in India can be broadly classified into Government Securities (G-Secs) and Industrial Securities.
- Government Securities (G-Secs) are issued by the Central Government, State Governments and Semi-Government authorities such as Municipalities, State Electricity Boards and Public-sector Corporations.
- Industrial Securities are securities issued by the corporate sector to finance their long-term and working capital requirements. Major instruments that fall under industrial securities are Equity shares, Debentures and Bonds, Preference shares, Mutual funds and Deposits.
- Globalisation started in 1990s. Since 1992, the Indian corporate houses are permitted to directly access the overseas financial markets through the issue of Global Depository Receipts (GDRs), American Depository Receipts (ADRs) to access equity finance, or through External Commercial Borrowing (ECB) to access debt finance.
- Securitisation is the process that allows borrowers to directly enter the capital market without any involvement of the financial intermediaries.
- Financial Engineering refers to the design of innovative products to suit the specific needs of the lenders as well as the borrowers.
- e-Finance refers to the growth of online trading.
- Financial services can be defined as the products and services offered by financial institutions to meet the financial needs of the consumers.
- The regulatory framework of financial services in India can be examined in terms of respective Bills, Acts and other legislative policies made by the Parliament and Judicial precedents. Regulation of Banking and Non-Banking Finance Companies (NBFCs) is done by Reserve Bank of India Act, 1934 and Banking Regulation Act, 1949.
- Regulatory Framework for Insurance Industry is governed by Insurance Regulatory and Development Authority of India (IRDA) Act, 1999.
- Regulation of Indian Capital Market (Stock Market) is governed by Capital Issues (Control) Act, 1947, The Indian Companies Act, 2013 and 1956, The Securities Contracts (Regulation) Act, 1956, The SEBI Act, 1992, The Depositories Act, 1996 and SEBI (LODR) Regulations, 2015.

- Regulatory Framework in the Forex Market is governed by the FEMA Act, 1999.
- Regulation of the Pension Funds is governed by Pension Fund Regulatory and Development Authority (PFRDA) Act, 2013.

KEY TERMS

- **Financial system** is a composite of financial institutions, financial markets and financial instruments.
- **Financial institutions** are bodies which perform triple-level functions of regulatory, intermediary, and non-intermediary nature.
- **Financial markets** are the platform which brings savers and borrowers together.
- **Money market** is a market for short-term debt instruments (maturity of less than one year).
- **Capital market** is a market for long-term financial instruments.
- **Primary market** is the place of new security issues, both debt and equity.
- **Secondary market** is a financial market for trading existing securities.
- **Financial instrument** is a real or a virtual document representing a legal agreement with a monetary value.
- **Derivatives** are instruments whose value is derived from the price of some underlying assets like securities, commodities, bullion, currency, interest level, stock market index, etc.
- **Forex (Foreign Exchange) market** is an inter-bank market.
- **Financial services** can be defined as the products and services offered by financial institutions to meet the financial needs of the consumers.

EXERCISES

Objective Questions

1. **Tick the correct answer:**

   (a) The primary function of the financial system is to:
   (i) Mobilize the funds (ii) Allocate the funds
   (iii) Generate return on funds (iv) All of the above

   (b) Capital market is:
   (i) Internal in nature (ii) External in nature
   (iii) Both of the above (iv) None of the above

   (c) Equity share is:
   (i) Voting security (ii) No voting security
   (iii) Debt security (iv) None of the above

(d) Primary Market is concerned with:
(i) First time issues (ii) Second time issues
(iii) Subsequent issues (iv) None of the above

(e) Derivatives are:
(i) Futuristic (ii) Historical
(iii) Present (iv) None of the above

Answers: (a) iv (b) ii (c) i (d) i (e) i.

2. Fill in the blanks:

(a) The hybrid security issued by a company is ....
(b) Financial system comprises of ...., ..., and ....
(c) .... is responsible for financial sector reforms in India.
(d) Equity always has a risk of ....
(e) .... allow tax benefits to the company.
(f) Non-intermediaries are also called ....
(g) .... are non-standardized derivatives.

Answers:

(a) Preference share
(b) Financial institutions, financial markets and financial instruments
(c) RBI
(d) Non-payment of dividend
(e) Debenture and Bond
(f) NBSFOs/DFIs
(g) Forwards

3. True or False

(a) Derivatives are speculative in nature.
(b) Debt is the safest instrument.
(c) In a future contract, there is a reverse gear.
(d) Financial services are tangible in nature.
(e) SEBI regulates the mutual funds industry in India.
(f) Commercial paper is a short-term debt instrument.
(g) Treasury bills are issued by RBI.
(h) Insurance companies are intermediary institutions.

Answers: (a) True (b) True (c) False (d) False
(e) True (f) True (g) True (h) True

Short Questions

1. What are the key functions of the financial system?
2. State one difference between money market and capital market?
3. Distinguish between primary market and secondary market?

4. What is future and option?
5. Define a financial asset.
6. What is underwriting?

Critical Thinking Questions

1. "Financial intermediaries bridge the gap between fund-providers and fund-allocators". Explain.
2. "Indian financial system has evolved by leaps and bounds". Justify.
3. "Financial services are not merely confined to depositing a cheque". Elaborate with suitable illustrations.
4. "Derivatives have changed the definition of investments in the present times". Discuss.
5. "The real stakeholders of the financial system are savers". Prove this statement.
6. "Preference share is a hybrid instrument". Explain.
7. "The global recession of late has not left anyone untouched. But, India has still managed to perform in this global turmoil". Discuss.
8. "Financial services industry is considered to be more volatile than any other industry". Do you agree? Give reasons.

Descriptive Questions

1. Describe the constituents of financial system. Highlight their role in the process of economic development.
2. What are the regulatory financial institutions in India?
3. Discuss the different types of owned instruments.
4. What are the various financial services which are operating in India?
5. Explain the different types of derivative instruments.
6. What are the various ways of classifying financial markets?
7. Explain the key innovations that have redefined the financial system in India.
8. What are the major issues and challenges faced by the Indian financial services industry?

PROJECT EXERCISE

Strengthening the Financial Systems of Developing Countries

A financial system is the backbone of any economy, and therefore, it must be strong and efficient enough to tackle any uncertainty. Take a project on the "financial system" in a developing country, say India or China, and discuss whether it is strong and efficient enough for the development of the economy? Suggest the possible steps to be initiated and implemented, both at the government and public level, to make financial systems stronger in developing countries, particularly in the context of the country selected for discussion.

REVIEW CASE

Mechanics of Financial Markets for Kapoors

Financial market is not an ordinary market where you buy regular commodities but a special place where one can trade in different securities. Securities get a buyer on the one hand and the seller on the other hand on a common platform—this helps in easy conversion of securities into cash. In a sound economy, the money trapped in the houses should come out and flow in the form of investments and should have the capability to attain the maximum value. One wonders how the economy of a company can grow without the existence of financial market.

The development of a country is mainly judged by its system of transferring finance from the sector where it is in surplus to the sector where it is needed the most. To give strength to the economy, the Securities and Exchange Board of India (SEBI) regularly undertakes measures to develop the securities market. A financial company named 'Dhan Varsha Ltd.' provides Kapoor family an opportunity to deposit their money into its "Cash scheme" to deposit their money time for a definite return in the form of monthly interest. Closeby, there is a stock exchange, Mr. Ravi Kapoor, the head of the family, goes there and buys securities. He is of the opinion that in this way they will be able to earn more return on the saved money though the risk is also there.

Issues for Discussion:

(i) Identify the types of financial markets and their functions discussed in the above case.
(ii) How does a bank perform its role in the financial process?
(iii) What is the role of the stock market in the process of financial intermediation?
(iv) Financial system has become more organized and streamlined and contribute to the growth of an economy. Throw light on this.
(v) How financial soundness and credibility of financial markets are improved by SEBI as part of financial sector reforms?
(vi) Has Mr. Kapoor made the right decision? Examine.

REFERENCES

Buckle, M. and Thompson, J.L. (1998). *The UK Financial System*, 3rd ed., Manchester University Press.

Brearley, R., Myers, S.C., and Marcus, A.J. (1995). *Fundamentals of Corporate Finance*, McGraw-Hill.

Goldsmith, R.W. (1965). *The Flow of Capital Funds in the Post-War Economy*, New York, Columbia.

Howells, P. and Bain, K. (1998). *The Economics of Money, Banking and Finance*, Longman, Harlow.

Smith, P.F. (1971). *Economics of Financial Institution and Markets*, Richard D. Irwin, Illinois.

www.ibef.org

www.irda.gov.in

www.pfrda.org.in

www.rbi.org

www.sebi.gov.in

www.statisticstimes.com

Part II

FINANCIAL FRONTIERS

CHAPTER 2

Banking: Products, Services and Functioning

There is an expression, "Cash is king". In bad times, it's perfectly fine to put your cash in a bank, although return rates are low, they are stable.

— Donald Trump

LEARNING OBJECTIVES

This chapter discusses the following:

- Concept of a bank
- Principles of banking
- Growth of Indian banking
- Indian banking reforms
- Present picture and structure of Indian banking industry
- Role and functions of RBI
- Tools of monetary control
- Functions of commercial banks
- Comparative picture of scheduled and non-scheduled banks
- Types of banking
- Banking ombudsman scheme
- Key banking applications
- Financial performance analysis of SBI

INTRODUCTION

Banks act as the prime source for mobilising savings of investors into profitable channels. Also, they act as fund providers to diverse fields for speedy economic development of the country. The banks in India have come a long way from the traditional set up to the modern banking era. The face of Indian banking sector changed irreversibly after liberalisation in the early 1990s—after the advent of the private sector banks or the new generation banks, as they are often called. Till then, banking was government-centric and quite limited. Despite the post 1991 economic reforms in India which liberalised the banking sector and brought it to the world standards, the journey is still far from ever.

The new generation banks are customer-centric, focused and driven. They have specialists and in-house expertise to cater to diverse groups. As a consequence, banking has become functionally segmented—*retail banking, corporate banking, branch banking, merchant banking, personal banking and treasury*. This mushrooming of private sector and foreign banks has resulted in an enormous competition for public sector banks in India. In this race, there is a wide range of products and services available to a common investor to choose from, as supply outstrips demand. This is a healthy trend for any economy.

CONCEPT OF BANK

A *bank* is a financial institution where you can deposit your money and borrow when you need. Banks provide a system for easily transferring money from one person or business to another. Using banks and the services they offer, saves us an incredible amount of time, and ensures that our funds "pass hands" in a legal and structured manner.

A bank is defined as a commercial institution licensed as a receiver of deposits and giver of loans both short-term and long-term. Section 5(b) of the Banking Regulation Act, 1949 defines banking as "the accepting for the purpose of lending or investment, of deposits from the public, repayable on demand or otherwise, and withdrawal by cheque, draft, order or otherwise".[1*] Section 5(c) defines a banking company as "any company which transacts the business of banking in India".[2]

Banking, therefore, involves:

- Borrowing of money
- Lending of money, with or without security
- Discounting bills of exchange, hundis, promissory notes, whether transferable or negotiable or not
- Collecting and transmitting money, warrants, debentures, scrips and other financial securities
- Issuing of drafts, letters of credit, travellers' cheques and circulars notes

1. http://fiuindia.gov.in/relatedacts-bankingregu.htm.

* Glimpses of the Banking Regulation Act, 1949 are given in the Instructor's manual.

2. http://fiuindia.gov.in.ibid.

- Buying and selling of foreign exchange including bank notes
- Buying and selling of bullion and currency
- Underwriting, commissioning and dealing in shares, debentures, securities and investments of all kinds
- Providing safe deposit vaults
- Undertaking guarantee and indemnity business
- Acting as agents for any government, or local authority or any other person(s).

Box 2.1 explains banking in the American concept.

BOX 2.1: BANKING IN US CONTEXT

The banking system in US is regulated both at federal and state level. The central bank of US is called the *Federal Reserve System* which was established under the Federal Reserve Act. Its function is to regulate all the financial activities and formulate policies. It also actively participates in the maintenance of financial stability and provides financial assistance to depository institutions. Some of the activities of central bank are private, some are public, and they work independently.

PRINCIPLES OF BANKING

The basic principles of banking which guide the business of banking are discussed below:

Principle of Intermediation

Banks are called *financial intermediaries* because they invest or lend funds of depositors who themselves are unable to lend their funds. They assume the credit risk arising from default by the borrower.

Principle of Liquidity

A bank must keep a certain portion of its 'deposit liabilities' in liquid form so as to be able to repay the same on demand or maturity dates to the depositors.

This principle is reinforced by the regulatory requirements of the RBI that every bank has to maintain deposits with the RBI as Cash Reserve Ratio (CRR) and Statutory Liquidity Ratio (SLR), wherein, every bank has to invest in gilts/government and other approved securities.

Principle of Profitability

Banking business, like any other, has to be profitable in order to sustain the required growth. The interest earned by a bank on its lending operations should be higher than the interest paid by the bank on its deposit operations.

The absolute size of a bank's Gross/Operating/Net Profit considered with ratios like Return on Assets (ROA) and Return on Capital Employed (ROCE) are the true financial indicators of a bank's profits.

Principle of Solvency

A bank's financial soundness is judged by analyzing its financial trend of a couple of years and comparing the relevant ratios (e.g. capital adequacy ratio, standard assets ratio and provisions to non-performing assets ratio) with other banks.

Principle of Trust

Trustworthiness is a function of a bank's good track record over a fairly long period of time, in terms of liquidity, profitability, financial soundness, and its record of meeting its commitments to all concerned parties.

GROWTH OF BANKING IN INDIA

The Indian banking system has grown over centuries in various phases as described below:

Phase I (Pre-Independence)

Banking in India originated in the last decades of the 18th century. The first banks were The General Bank of India which started in 1786, and the Bank of Hindustan, both of which are now defunct. The East India Company established Bank of Bengal (1809), Bank of Bombay (1840) and Bank of Madras (1843) as independent units and called them *Presidency Banks*. These three banks were amalgamated in 1920 and the Imperial Bank of India was established which started as a private shareholders' bank, mostly consisting of Europeans shareholders. The then Imperial Bank of India is today's State Bank of India (SBI) which is the largest and the oldest bank existing in India.

Besides, in 1865, Allahabad Bank was established first time exclusively by Indians; in 1894, Punjab National Bank Ltd. was set up. Between 1906 and 1913, Bank of India, Central Bank of India, Bank of Baroda, Canara Bank, Indian Bank, and Bank of Mysore were set up. The Reserve Bank of India came into existence in 1935.

Phase II (Post-Independence)

India's independence marked the end of a regime of the laissez faire for the Indian banking. The Industrial Policy Resolution adopted by the government resulted into greater involvement of the State in different segments of the economy including banking and finance. The major steps to regulate banking included:

- The Reserve Bank of India, India's central banking authority, was nationalised on January 1, 1949 under the terms of the Reserve Bank of India (Transfer to Public Ownership) Act, 1948.
- In 1949, the Banking Regulation Act was enacted which empowered the RBI to regulate, control, and inspect the banks in India.
- The Banking Regulation Act also provided that no new bank or branch of an existing bank could be opened without a license from the RBI, and no two banks could have common directors.

In 1955, the government nationalised the Imperial Bank of India, as mentioned above (now known as SBI) with extensive banking facilities on a large scale, especially in rural and semi- urban areas. SBI is the largest Indian Bank with 1/4th market share, serves over 45 crore customers through its vast network of over 22,000 branches. SBI acts as the principal agent of RBI and handles banking transactions of the Union and State Governments all over the country. Seven banks, forming subsidiaries of SBI, were nationalised in 1960. Fourteen major commercial banks in the country were nationalised in 1969 followed by 7 more banks in 1980. Thus, over 80% of banking is under Government control. By 1960s, the Indian banking industry had become an important tool to facilitate the development of the Indian economy.

Phase III (Post-Liberalisation)

In the early 1990s, the Narasimha Rao government embarked on a policy of liberalisation, licensing a small number of private banks. It saw the advent of private banks in India like HDFC Bank, ICICI Bank and Axis Bank (earlier UTI Bank), and foreign banks like City Bank (Citibank) and HSBC Bank. This move reenergised the banking sector in India. It saw a strong contribution from all the three sectors of banks, namely, *government banks, private banks and foreign banks.*

The growth of Indian banking industry as discussed above is presented in Figure 2.1.

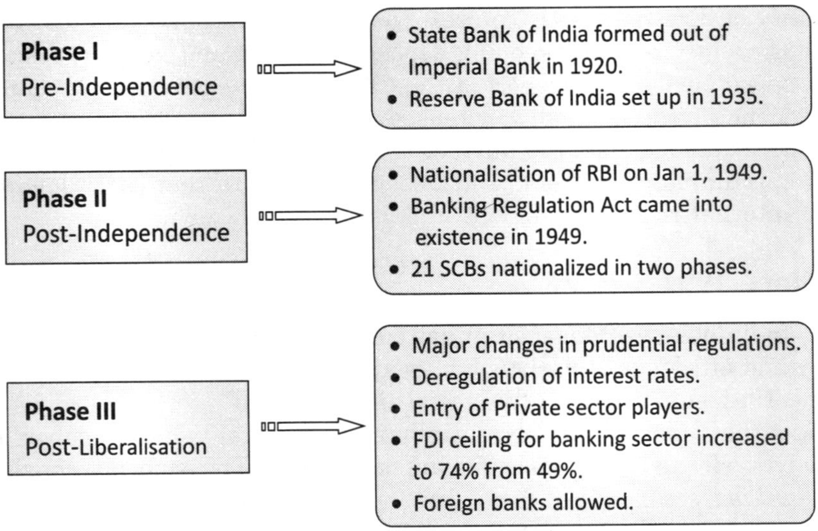

Figure 2.1 Growth of Indian Banking

BANKING REFORMS IN INDIA

The Indian banking system's reform program was widely ranged. They are discussed as follows:

Reforms Pre-1991

Prior to the reforms starting from 1991 onwards, India's financial sector had long been characterised as highly regulated and financially repressed. The prevalence of reserve requirements, interest rate controls, and allocation of financial resources to priority sectors increased the degree of financial repression which adversely affected the country's financial resource mobilisation and allocation. After Independence in 1947, the government took the view that loans extended by colonial banks were biased towards working capital for trade and large firms. Moreover, it was perceived that banks should be utilised to assist India's planned development strategy by mobilising financial resources to strategically important sectors.

Reflecting these views, all large private banks were nationalised in two stages—*the first in 1969, and the second in 1980.* Subsequently, quantitative loan targets were imposed on these banks to expand their networks in rural areas and they were directed to extend credit to priority sectors. These nationalised banks were then increasingly used to finance fiscal deficits. Although non-nationalised private and foreign banks were allowed to coexist with public-sector banks at that time, their activities were highly restricted through entry regulations and strict branch licensing policies. Thus, their activities remained negligible.

The first wave of financial liberalisation took place in the second half of the 1980s, in the form of interest rate deregulation. Prior to this period, almost all interest rates were administered and influenced by budgetary concerns and the degree of concessionality of directed loans. To preserve some profitability, interest rate margins were kept sufficiently large by keeping deposit rates low and non-concessional lending rates high. Based on the 1985 report of the Chakravarty Committee[3*], coupon rates on government bonds were gradually increased to reflect demand and supply conditions. During the period 1969–1991, the number of banks slightly increased, and many banks remained unprofitable, inefficient, and unsound owing to their poor lending strategy and lack of internal risk management under government ownership.

Reforms Since 1991

Since 1991, India has been engaged in banking sector reforms aimed at increasing the profitability and efficiency of various banks at an extended level. New Economic Policy (NEP), June 1991 emphasised a 'Financial liberalisation'.

Following the report of the Narasimham Committee[4] in November 1991, more comprehensive reforms took place during that year. The reforms consisted of—*(a) a shift of banking sector supervision from intrusive micro-level intervention towards economically viable credit decisions; (b) a reduction of the CRR and SLR; (c) interest rate and entry deregulation; and (d) adoption of prudential norms.* Further, in 1992, the RBI issued guidelines for income recognition, asset classification and provisioning, and also adopted the Basle Accord capital adequacy standards. The government also established the Board of Financial Supervision in the Reserve Bank of India and

3. http://www.yourarticlelibrary.com/2788/some-important-recommendations-made-by-chakravarty-committee.
* The Report of Chakravarty Committee is given in the Instructor's manual.
4. The Report of Narasimham Committee is given in the Instructor's manual.

recapitalised public-sector banks in order to give banks sufficient financial strength and enable them to access capital markets. In 1993, the Reserve Bank of India permitted private entry into the banking sector, provided that new banks were well capitalised and technologically advanced, and at the same time prohibited cross-holding practices with industrial groups. The Reserve Bank of India also imposed some restrictions on new banks with respect to opening branches, with a view to maintain the franchise value of existing banks.

As a result of the reforms, the number of banks increased rapidly. In 1991, there were 27 public-sector and 26 domestic private banks with 60,000 branches, 24 foreign banks with 140 branches, and 20 foreign banks with a representative office. Between January 1993 and March 1998, 24 new private banks (9 domestic and 15 foreign) entered the market; the total number of scheduled commercial banks, excluding specialised banks such as the Regional Rural Banks rose from 75 in 1991/92 to 99 in 1997/98. While the CRR and SLR, interest rate policy, and prudential norms have always been applied uniformly to all commercial banks, the RBI treated foreign banks differently with respect to the regulation that requires a portion of credit to be allocated to priority sectors. In 1998, the Narasimham Committee II[5] recommended a convergence of developing financing institutions with commercial banks or non-bank financial institutions and an adoption of the integrated system of regulation and supervision.

Therefore, India's reform program included:

1. *Liberalisation.* Allowing foreign and private banks in the Indian banking sector to coexist, dismantling the complex system of interest rate controls, eliminating prior approval of the RBI for large loans, and reducing the statutory requirements to invest in government securities.

2. *Gradual privatisation.* Indian Government did not engage in a drastic privatisation of public-sector banks. Rather, it chose a gradual approach towards restructuring these banks by enhancing competition through entry deregulation of foreign and domestic banks. Housing Development Finance Corporation Limited (HDFC) was amongst the first one to receive an 'in principle' approval from the Reserve Bank of India (RBI) to set up a bank in the private sector. The 1994 amendment of the Banking Act allowed banks to raise private equity upto 49% of paid-up capital. Consequently, public-sector banks, which used to be fully owned by the government prior to the reform, were now allowed to increase non-government ownership.

3. *Measures to increase financial soundness.* Introducing capital adequacy requirements and other prudential norms for banks, and strengthening banking supervision.

4. *Measures for increasing competition.* More liberal licensing of private banks and freer expansion by foreign banks.

5. *Diversification of banking activities.* RBI permitted commercial banks to engage in diverse activities such as securities related transactions (for example, underwriting, dealing and brokerage), foreign exchange transactions and leasing activities. The 1991 reforms lowered the CRR and SLR, enabling banks to diversify their activities.

5. The Report of Narasimham Committee II is given in the Instructor's manual.

These steps have produced actual positive outcomes. There has been a sharp reduction in the share of non-performing assets in the portfolio and more than 90% of the banks now meet the relevant capital adequacy standards.

PRESENT PICTURE OF INDIAN BANKING SECTOR

In line with the ongoing policy reforms and recommendations of noted committees, the major features of the present Indian banking sector can be grouped as follows:

A Mix of Public and Private Sector Banks

There is a healthy mix of public and private (national and foreign) banks in India. For the year 2022 there were 142 commercial banks in India, comprising of 12 public sector banks, 42 private sector banks (including local area banks, small banks, and payments banks) and 45 foreign banks. This excluded Regional Rural Banks (RRBs).[6]

Prudential Accounting Norms for Banks

The RBI persevered with the on-going process of strengthening prudential accounting norms with the objective of improving the financial soundness of banks and to bring them at par with international standards.

Asset Liability Management (ALM) System

The RBI advised banks to set up an internal asset Liability committee (ALCO) at the top management level to oversee its implementation. As per the guidelines, banks and such institutions are required to prepare statements on liquidity gaps and interest rate sensitivity at regular intervals.

Risk Management

Banks would put in place loan policies approved by their board of directors, covering the methodologies for measurement, monitoring and control of credit risk. Banks have to evaluate their portfolios on an on-going basis, rather than at a time close to the balance sheet date. Regarding, off-balance sheet exposures, the current and potential credit exposures may be measured on a daily basis. Banks also fix a definite timeframe for moving over to the Value-at-Risk (VaR) and duration approaches for the measurement of "interest rate risk".

Better Transparency

Banks disclose the following additional information in 'Notes to Accounts' in the balance sheets from the accounting year ending on March 31—*(i) maturity pattern of loans and advances, investment securities, deposits and borrowings; (ii) foreign currency assets and liabilities; (iii) movements in NPAs, and (iv) lending to sensitive sectors as defined by the Reserve Bank from time to time.*

Technological Advancement

In India, banks as well as other financial entities have entered the domain of

6. https://m.rbi.org.in/commonperson/English/Scripts/BanksInIndia.aspx#SCB

information technology and computer networking. A satellite-based Wide Area Network (WAN) would provide a reliable communication framework for the financial sector. The Indian Financial Network (INFINET) was inaugurated in June 1999. It is based on satellite communication using VSAT technology that would enable faster connectivity within the financial sector.

STRUCTURE OF INDIAN BANKING INDUSTRY

The Indian banking system is headed by the apex bank of the country, i.e., RBI, and comprises of the following institutions:

1. Commercial Banks
   (a) Nationalised Banks
   (b) Private Banks
   (c) Foreign Banks
   (d) Regional Rural Banks (RRBs)
2. Financial Institutions/Specialised Banks
3. Cooperative Banks
   (a) State Co-operative Banks (SCBs)
   (b) District Central Co-operative Banks (DCCBs)

These are classified in Figure 2.2.

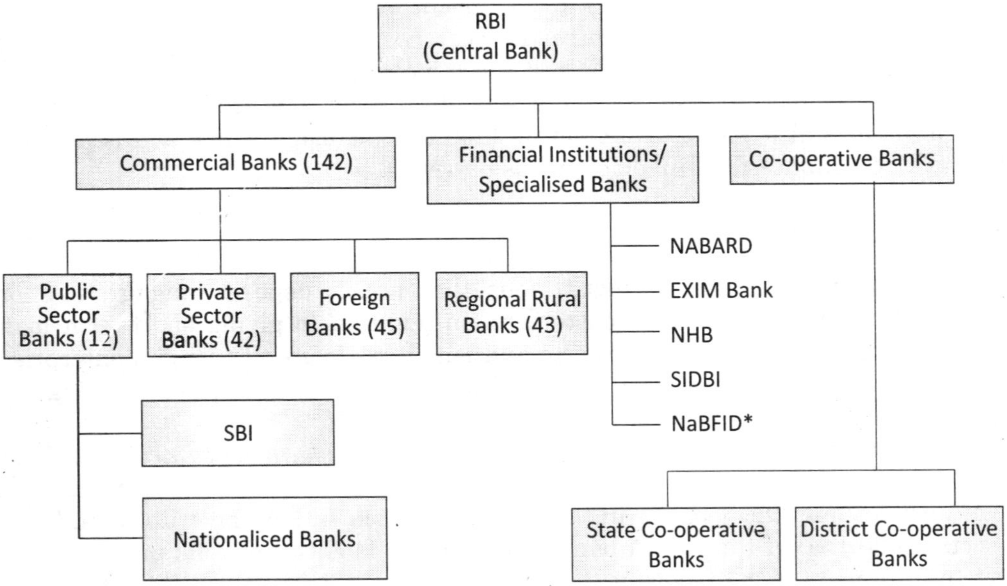

Figure 2.2 Indian Banking Structure

Notes: The above data is as available on November, 2022.
*NaBFID has been set up as a DFI and shall be regulated and supervised as an AIFI by the Reserve Bank under Sections 45L and 45N of the RBI Act, 1934.

Source: https://m.rbi.org.in/commonperson/English/Scripts/BanksInIndia.aspx#SCB

RBI—The Central Bank

Reserve Bank of India is the Central Bank of India. It was established on 1 April 1935 during the British Raj in accordance with the provisions of the Reserve Bank of India Act, 1934. Following India's independence in 1947, the RBI was nationalised in the year 1949.

It is entrusted with the functions of guiding and regulating the banking system of the country. Being the apex bank of the country, it does not deal with the general public. It acts essentially as Government's banker, maintaining deposit accounts of all other banks and advancing money to other banks, when needed. It provides guidance to other banks whenever they face any problem. It is, therefore, known as the *Banker's Bank*.

RBI maintains the record of government revenues and expenditures under various heads. It also advises the government on monetary and credit policies and decides on the interest rates for bank deposits and bank loans. In addition to this, foreign exchange rates are also determined by RBI.

Another important function of RBI as the central bank is the issuance of currency notes and regulating their circulation in the country by different methods. No other bank than the central bank can issue currency.

RBI plays an important part in the development strategy of the Government of India. It is a member bank of the Asian Clearing Union. The general superintendence and direction of the RBI is entrusted with the 15-member-strong Central Board of Directors—the Governor (currently Mr. Shaktikanta Das), four Deputy Governors, ten government-nominated directors to represent important elements from India's economy, and four directors to represent local boards headquartered at Mumbai, Kolkata, New Delhi and Chennai. Each of these local boards consists of five members who represent regional interests, as well as the interests of co-operative and indigenous banks. The RBI is also active in promoting financial inclusion policy and is a leading member of the Alliance for Financial Inclusion (AFI).

Commercial Banks

Commercial banks are banking institutions that accept deposits and grant short-term loans and advances to their customers. In addition to giving short-term loans, commercial banks also give medium-term and long-term loans to business enterprises. Nowadays, some of the commercial banks also provide housing loans on a long-term basis to individuals.

Commercial banks are either scheduled or non-scheduled. A *scheduled bank* is one whose name is included in the Second Schedule to the RBI Act, 1934[7] (Box 2.2). RBI, in turn, includes only those banks in this schedule which satisfy the criteria laid down vide section 42(6) (a) of the Act. A bank is entitled to facilities of refinance from RBI, subject to fulfilment of the following conditions laid down in Section 42(6) of the Act[8]:

- It must have paid-up capital and reserves of an aggregate value of not less than five lakhs of rupees; and

7. Glimpses of the RBI Act, 1934 are given in the Instructor's manual.
8. http://rbidocs.rbi.org.in/rdocs/Publications/PDFs/RBIA1934170510.pdf.

- It must satisfy RBI that its affairs are not being conducted in a manner detrimental to the interests of its depositors.

Non-scheduled banks in India mean "a banking company as defined in Clause (c) of Section 5 of the Banking Regulation Act, 1949 (10 of 1949)[9], which is not a scheduled bank".

The classification of commercial banks into scheduled and non-scheduled categories that was introduced at the time of establishment of RBI in 1935, has been extended during the last few decades to include state cooperative banks, primary urban cooperative banks, and RRBs. The RBI is authorised to exclude the name of any bank from the Second Schedule if the bank, having been given suitable opportunity to increase the value of paid-up capital and improve deficiencies, goes into liquidation or ceases to carry on banking activities.

BOX 2.2: STRUCTURE OF SCHEDULED COMMERCIAL BANKS

The composition of the board of directors of a scheduled commercial bank shall consist of a wholetime chairman. Section 10A of the Banking Regulation Act, 1949* provides that not less than 51% of the total number of members of the board of directors of a banking company shall consist of persons, who shall have special knowledge or practical experience in respect of one or more of the matters including accountancy, agriculture and rural economy, banking, cooperation, economics, finance, law, small-scale industry, or any other matter the special knowledge of, and practical experience in, which would, in the opinion of the RBI, be useful to the banking company. Out of the aforesaid number of directors, not less than two shall be persons having special knowledge or practical experience in respect of agriculture and rural economy, co-operation or small-scale industry.

Besides the above, the board of the scheduled bank shall consist of the directors representing workmen and officer employees. The Reserve Bank of India and the Central Government also have the right to appoint their nominees into the board of the banks.

Commercial banks mainly are of three types: Public sector banks, Private sector banks and Foreign banks.

* https://www.pnbindia.in/.Ibid.

Public Sector Banks

These are banks where the majority stake is held by the Government of India or the RBI. The state bank group and nationalised banks are together referred to as the *Public Sector Banks* (*PSBs*). *Examples of public sector banks are:* State Bank of India, Union Bank of India, Bank of Baroda, Dena Bank, etc.

1. *State bank group:* This consists of the State Bank of India (SBI) and associate banks of SBI. The Reserve Bank of India (RBI) owns the majority share of SBI and some associate banks of SBI. SBI has 17 local head offices each governed by a board of directors under the supervision of a central board. The board of directors and their committees hold monthly meetings while the executive committee of each central board meets every week.

9. https://www.pnbindia.in/Upload/En/BANK%20REGULATION%20ACT.pdf.

2. ***Nationalised banks:*** In 1969, the government arranged the nationalisation of 14 scheduled commercial banks in order to expand the branch network, followed by six more in 1980. A merger reduced the number from 20 to 19. Nationalised banks are wholly owned by the government, although some of them have made public issues. In contrast to the state bank group, nationalised banks are centrally governed, that is, they are controlled by their respective head offices. Thus, there is only one board for each nationalised bank and meetings are less frequent (generally, once a month).

Private Sector Banks

In case of private sector banks, majority of share capital of the bank is held by private individuals. These banks are registered as companies with limited liability. *For example Axis Bank Ltd., HDFC Bank Ltd., ICICI Bank Ltd., IDFC First Bank Ltd., etc.*

Foreign Banks

These banks are registered and have headquarters in a foreign country but operate their branches in our country. *Some of the foreign banks operating in our country are Hong Kong and Shanghai Banking Corporation (HSBC), Citibank, American Express Bank, Standard Chartered Bank, and so on.* The number of foreign banks operating in our country has increased since the financial sector reforms of 1991.

Regional Rural Banks

Regional Rural Banks (RRBs) were established during 1976–1987 with a view to develop the rural economy. Each RRB is owned jointly by the Central Government, concerned State Government and a sponsoring public sector commercial bank. RRBs provide credit to small farmers, artisans, small entrepreneurs and agricultural labourers.

Cooperative Banks

These are established under the Cooperative Societies Acts of different states. Cooperative banks have a three-tier setup, with state cooperative bank at the apex, district central cooperative banks at district level, and primary cooperative societies at rural level. Only some of the sections of the Banking Regulation Act of 1949 (fully applicable to commercial banks) are applicable to cooperative banks, resulting in only partial control of cooperative banks by RBI.

Cooperative banks function on the principle of cooperation and not entirely on commercial parameters. *For example, The Surat People's Co-operative Bank Ltd. Gujarat and New India Co-operative Bank Ltd., Mumbai.*

Financial Institutions/Specialised Banks

Business often requires medium and long-term capital for purchase of machinery and equipment, using latest technology, or for expansion and modernisation. Such financial assistance is provided by Development Banks. They also undertake other development measures like subscribing to the shares and debentures issued by companies, in case of under subscription of the issue by the public. *Industrial Finance Corporation of India (now IFCI Ltd.), State Financial Corporations (SFCs) are examples of development banks, set up in India.*

Development Financial Institutions (DFIs) were established to resolve market failures in developing economies and shortage of long-term investments. The first DFI to be established was the Industrial Finance Corporation of India (IFCI) in 1948, and was followed by SFCs at state level set up under a special statute. In 1955, Industrial Credit and Investment Corporation of India (ICICI) was set up in the private sector with foreign equity participation. This was followed by Industrial Development Bank of India (IDBI) in 1964, set up as a subsidiary of RBI. The same year saw the founding of the first mutual fund in the country, the Unit Trust of India (UTI). A wide variety of financial institutions (FIs) have been established, for example, National Bank for Agriculture and Rural Development (NABARD), Export Import Bank of India (EXIM Bank), National Housing Bank (NHB), and Small Industries Development Bank of India (SIDBI), which serve as apex banks in their specified areas of responsibility and concern. The three institutions that dominate the term-lending market in providing financial assistance to the corporate sector are IDBI, IFCI, and ICICI.

Banks such as EXIM Bank cater to the requirements and provide overall support for setting up business in specific areas of activity, like credit for foreign trade, global finance, etc. Therefore, they are referred to as *specialised banks.*

The Government owns insurance companies, including Life Insurance Corporation of India (LIC) and General Insurance Corporation (GIC). Subsidiaries of GIC also provide substantial equity and loan assistance to the industrial sector, while UTI, though a mutual fund, conducts similar operations. RBI also set up the Discount and Finance House of India Ltd. (DFHI) in April 1988 in partnership with SBI and other banks to deal with money market instruments and provide liquidity to money markets by creating a secondary market for each instrument. Major shares of DFHI are held by SBI.

Liberalisation of economic policy since 1991 has highlighted the urgent need to improve infrastructure in order to provide services of international standards. Infrastructure is woefully inadequate for the efficient handling of the foreign trade sector, power generation, communication, etc. The Infrastructure Development Finance Company Ltd. (IDFC) was set up in 1997 to meet specialised financing needs. To nurture the growth of private capital flows, IDFC seeks to unbundle and mitigate the risks that investors face in infrastructure and creates an efficient financial structure at institutional and project levels. IDFC works on commercial orientation, innovations in financial products, rationalising the legal and regular framework, creation of a long-term debt market, and best global practices on governance and risk management in infrastructure projects.

Therefore, Indian banking has evolved leaps and bounds and is undoubtedly, taking the Indian flag to scaling heights in the international arena day by day. Still, there is a long way to go. The 'customer-centric approach' cannot be denied. In fact, there should be a trade-off between business-centric and customer-centric approaches. The final banking superstructure is yet to be erected in the framework of financial liberalisation approach.

ROLE AND FUNCTIONS OF RBI

Being the apex bank of the country, RBI plays an important role in the development of the nation. Its role and key functions are discussed below:

1. *Issuing notes:* The RBI has the sole authority to issue, circulate, withdraw and exchange currency notes. The basic objective is to give the public adequate supplies of currency notes and coins and in good quality. RBI has issued and put in circulation, notes in the denomination of ₹2, 5, 10, 20, 50, 100, 200, 500 and 2000, except ₹1 and other coins, which are issued by Government of India, but put into circulation by the RBI.

The RBI with the Issue Departments of its Regional Offices across India oversees currency management. This is achieved through a wide network of more than 3000 currency chests of commercial banks., where new and re-issuable notes are stored. The currency chests are kept in custody of various banking groups who function as agents of the RBI.

2. *Government's banker:* RBI acts as a banker to the Central and State Governments. In this role, it provides them banking services of deposits, withdrawal of funds, making payments and receipts, collection and transfer of funds, and management of public debt.

The RBI charges commission for managing the public debt and interest on overdrafts from the concerned Governments.

3. *Bankers' bank:* RBI, like all other central banks, acts as a 'banker's bank'. The commercial and state/urban co-operative banks which are scheduled banks (appearing in the Second Schedule of the RBI Act) have to maintain stipulated reserves in cash and in approved securities as a percentage of their Demand and Time Liabilities (DTL).

RBI can also change its bank rate to regulate the cost of bank credit and thereby, indirectly, its volume. It also acts as a 'lender of the last resort'.

4. *Banks' supervision and regulation:* From November 1993, the RBI's supervisory function has been separated from its traditional central banking functions. The Reserve Bank of India performs this function under the guidance of the Board for Financial Supervision[10] (BFS) (Box 2.3). The Board was constituted in November 1994 as a committee of the Central Board of Directors of the Reserve Bank of India.

5. *Development of financial system:* RBI performs the most important role of development agency of Indian economy. Therefore, it has created specialized financial institutions for:

(a) *Industrial finance*: Industrial Development Bank of India (IDBI) 1964, Small Industries Development Bank of India (SIDBI), 1989.

(b) *Agricultural credit*: National Bank for Agriculture and Rural Development (NABARD), 1981.

(c) *Export-import finance:* Export-Import Bank of India (EXIM Bank), 1981.

(d) *Deposits Insurance Corporation of India* (1961): It later became Deposit Insurance and Credit Guarantee Corporation of India (DICGC).

---

10. http://www.rbi.org.in/scripts/AboutusDisplay.aspx.

BOX 2.3: BOARD FOR FINANCIAL SUPERVISION (BFS)

In 1994, Board of Financial Supervision (BFS) was established to oversee and undertake the consolidated supervision of the Indian Financial System, comprising not only commercial and state cooperative banks, but also the All-India Financial Institutions (AIFIs) and Non-banking Finance Companies (NBFCs).

Constitution

The BFS is chaired by the Governor of RBI and is constituted by co-opting four Directors from the Central Board as Members. The Deputy Governors of the Reserve Bank are ex-officio members. One Deputy Governor, traditionally, the Deputy Governor in charge of supervision, is nominated as the Vice-Chairman of the Board.

BFS Meetings

The Board is required to meet normally once every month. It considers inspection reports and other supervisory issues placed before it by the supervisory departments. BFS, through the Sub-Committee, also aims at upgrading the quality of the statutory audit and internal audit functions in banks and financial institutions. The Sub-committee is chaired by the Deputy Governor in charge of supervision and includes the three Deputy Governors and two Directors of the Central Board as Members. The BFS oversees the functioning of Department of Banking Supervision (DBS), Department of Non- Banking Supervision (DNBS), and Department of Co-operative Bank Supervision (DCBS), and gives directions on the regulatory and supervisory issues.

Functions

Some of the initiatives taken by BFS include:

- Restructuring of the system of bank inspections,
- Introduction of off-site surveillance,
- Strengthening of the role of statutory auditors, and
- Strengthening of the internal defences of supervised institutions.

Current Focus

- Supervision of financial institutions,
- Consolidated accounting,
- Legal issues in bank frauds,
- Divergence in assessments of non-performing assets, and
- Supervisory rating model for banks.

6. *Exchange control:* The RBI is responsible for maintaining stability of the external value of the national currency—the Indian Rupee.

The FERA (1973) which has been replaced by the Foreign Exchange Management Act, 1999 (FEMA) provisions, would now guide RBI in this regard. The RBI performs the following tasks:

(i) It administers foreign exchange control through its Exchange Control Department. It authorizes banks, specified branches and other dealers, called *Authorized Dealers* (*ADs*), to execute the prescribed kinds of foreign exchange transactions.

(ii) The RBI manages the exchange rate between Indian Rupee and foreign currencies, by buying and selling foreign exchange to/from the Authorized Dealers and by other means.

(iii) The RBI manages the foreign exchange reserves of the country and maintains reserves in the form of gold and foreign securities, which are issued by the foreign Governments and the international financial institutions.

7. ***Monetary and credit policy:*** RBI formulates, implements and monitors the monetary policy of the country in order to maintain price stability and ensure adequate flow of credit to productive sectors.

RBI controls money supply, volume of bank credit and the cost of bank credit (via Bank Rate), thereby controlling the overall money supply in the economy.

TOOLS OF MONETARY CONTROL

RBI uses its monetary policy for controlling inflationary (i.e. rate of growth of prices) or deflationary (rate of fall of prices) situation in the economy by using one or more of the following tools of monetary control:

Bank Rate

The *Bank Rate,* also referred to as the *discount rate*, is the rate of interest which a central bank charges on the loans and advances to a commercial bank.

Repo Rate

It is the rate at which banks can acquire funds from RBI by selling the securities and at the same time agreeing to repurchase them at a later date at a predetermined price [this facility is for short-term measure and to fill gaps between demand and supply of money in a bank].

So, borrowing against securities is *repo rate*, and simple borrowing is *bank rate*.

Reverse Repo Rate

It is the rate which is paid by RBI to banks on deposit of funds with RBI [a reduction in the repo rate will help banks to get money at a cheaper rate].

Cash Reserve Ratio (CRR)

CRR refers to the cash that all banks are required to maintain with RBI as a certain percentage of their Net Demand and Time Liabilities (NDTL). In order to meet these liabilities in time (i.e., to keep liquidity), a bank has to keep the regulatory cash reserve with RBI. Every scheduled bank shall maintain in India with the Reserve Bank, an average daily balance, the amount of which shall not be less than four per cent of the bank's total NDTL in India as on the last Friday of the second preceding fortnight.

If a bank fails to maintain the prescribed CRR at prescribed intervals, penal interest is levied on the shortfall by adjustment from the interest receivable on balances with the RBI.

Statutory Liquidity Ratio (SLR)

It refers to the liquid reserve requirement of banks, in addition to CRR. SLR is maintained by all banks (scheduled) in the form of cash-in-hand, gold and unencumbered approved securities. They shall maintain in 'SLR assets', the value of which shall not, at the close of business on any day, be less than 18 per cent and not exceeding 40 per cent of their total net demand and time liabilities in India as on the last Friday of the second preceding fortnight in accordance with the method of valuation specified by RBI from time to time.

Increase in SLR results in the reduction of the lending capacity of banks by preempting certain portion of their NDTL for Government or other approved securities. This has a deflationary impact on the economy, not only by reducing the supply of loanable funds of banks, but also by increasing the lending rates in the face of an increasing demand for bank credit. The reverse phenomenon happens in case of a slash in SLR.

Key figures:

- Bank Rate = 6.50%
- Repo Rate = 6.25%
- Reverse Repo Rate = 3.35%
- CRR = 4.50%
- SLR = 18.00%

(*Source:* RBI, As on 28th December 2022)

Open Market Operations (OMO)

This refers to the sale or the purchase of Government securities (of Central or State Governments or both) by the RBI in the open market with a view to increase or decrease the liquidity in the banking system, thereby affecting the loanable funds with banks (Box 2.4).

BOX 2.4: LIQUIDITY ADJUSTMENT FACILITY (LAF)

Liquidity Adjustment Facility (LAF) is a facility extended by the RBI to SCBs and primary dealers to avail liquidity in case of requirement or park excess funds with RBI on an overnight basis against the collateral of government securities. Basically, LAF enables liquidity management on a day-to-day basis. It is a monetary tool which consists of repo and reverse repo operations. The interest rate in LAF is fixed by RBI from time to time.

Credit Ceiling

In this operation, RBI directs the commercial banks that loans will be given up to a certain limit. Here, commercial bank will be stringent in advancing loans to the public. They will allocate loans to limited sectors. *Few example of credit ceiling are agriculture sector advances, priority sector lending, etc.*

Credit Authorization Scheme

Under this instrument of credit regulation, RBI, as per the guidelines, authorizes the banks to advance loans to desired sectors.

Moral Suasion

Moral Suasion is a request by the RBI to the commercial banks to take the required action and measures with the trend of the economy. RBI may request commercial banks not to give loans for unproductive purpose which does not add to economic growth but increases inflation.

Selective Credit Control (SCC)

RBI issues Selective Credit Control (SCC) directives, under Sections 21 and 35A of Banking Regulation Act, with an objective to prevent speculative holding of essential commodities which results in a rise in their prices. The RBI's general guidelines on SCC are:

(i) Banks should not grant the customers dealing in SCC commodities, any credit facilities (including those against book debts/receivables or even collateral securities like insurance policies, shares, stocks and real estate) that would directly or indirectly defect the purpose of the SCC directives.

(ii) Credit limits against each commodity covered by SCC Directives should be segregated and the SCC restrictions be applied.

FUNCTIONS OF COMMERCIAL BANKS

Having understood the structure of Indian banking, more light shall be thrown on commercial banks since they are the core of the banking industry. The functions of commercial banks are divided into two categories—Primary functions, and Secondary functions including agency functions.

Primary Functions

The primary functions of a commercial bank include:

(a) Accepting deposits, and
(b) Granting loans and advances

Accepting Deposits

The most important activity of a commercial bank is to mobilise deposits from the public. People who have surplus income and savings find it convenient to deposit the amounts with banks. Depending upon the nature of deposits, funds deposited with banks also earn interest. Thus, deposits with the bank grow along with the interest earned.

Basically, deposits are either demand deposits or time deposits. *Demand deposits* are those which are repayable on demand and do not have a maturity. *Time deposits* are repayable only on due maturity.

1. *Demand deposits:* Demand deposits are of three types—Current account, Saving account and Call deposits.

(i) *Current account:* Current Accounts are basically meant for businessmen for working capital operations and are not used for the purpose of investment or savings. There is no interest which is paid by banks but they impose certain service charges on such accounts. These account holders may avail overdraft facility as per the bank's policy.

These deposits are the most liquid deposits and there are no limits for number of transactions or the amount of transactions in a day. Most of the current accounts are opened in the name of firm/company.

(ii) *Savings account:* These accounts are one of the most popular deposits for individual accounts. Such account holders earn interest on their balance in the accounts. Savings accounts are flexible in nature as they provide flexibility for deposits and withdrawal of funds from the account.

Most of the banks have rules for the maximum number of withdrawals in a period and the maximum amount of withdrawal. Till 24th October 2011, the interest on saving bank accounts was regulated by RBI and it was fixed at 4.00% on daily balance basis. However, w.e.f. 25th October 2011 RBI has deregulated Saving Fund account interest rates and now banks are free to decide the same within certain conditions imposed by RBI. Although Public Sector Banks still pay around 3–4% rate of interest, some private banks are paying higher.

For example, AU Small Finance Bank w.e.f. October 10, 2022 is now giving an interest rate of 7.00% on saving account balances between INR 25 lacs and less than INR 1 crore.[11]

Yes Bank gives a higher return than most of the banks of 5.5% p.a. on savings account.[12]

From the financial year 2012–13, interest earned upto ₹10,000 in a financial year on saving bank accounts is exempted from tax.

(iii) *Call deposits:* These deposits are maintained by banks for a specific period of time with other banks. Generally, they are kept overnight and are interest earning.

2. *Time deposits:* Time deposits are of two types which are discussed as follows:

Recurring Deposit Account (RD Account): These are a special kind of Term Deposits and are suitable for people who do not have lump sum amount of savings, but are ready to save a small amount every month. Under this scheme, the person has to deposit a fixed amount of money every month. Such deposits earn interest on the amount already deposited at the same rates as are applicable for Fixed Deposits/Term Deposits. Recurring Deposit accounts normally have maturities generally ranging from 12 months to 120 months. *For example,* SBI's RD account.[13]

Some of the key features of RD account are:

- Monthly deposits of minimum ₹100 and there is no maximum limit.
- Minimum period is 12 months; maximum is 120 months.

1. https://www.livemint.com/money/personal-finance/9-banks-offering-from-7-to-7-50-interest-rates-on-savings-accounts-in-2022-11668854400032.html
2. https://www.yesbank.in/personal-banking/yes-individual/savings-account
3. http://www.sbi.co.in/user.htm.

- Rate of interest as applicable to the bank's TDR/STDR for the period of the RD.
- Loan/Overdraft upto 90% available against the balance in RD account.
- TDS benefits.

Fixed Deposit Account (FD Account): Fixed deposit schemes are offered by banks with a wide range of tenures, from 7 days to 10 years. Here, the depositor invests a lump sum amount for a fixed term, based on his requirement. At the end of maturity, he gets his principle with interest. He also has an option to get his interest annually. The rate of interest for Fixed Deposits differs from bank to bank. Generally, private sector and foreign banks offer a higher rate of interest.

Hybrid or flexi deposits: These are a combination of demand and fixed deposits. Most banks in India offer a hybrid between savings and fixed deposit accounts that can help you boost the returns on your savings accounts. These hybrid accounts are commonly referred to as *Flexi-Deposit schemes*. They help you enjoy high returns of a fixed deposit on surplus money in your savings account. Therefore, these accounts not only provide liquidity like a simple savings account but also provide high returns like fixed deposit accounts.

For example, iWish—Flexible Recurring Deposit of ICICI Bank. iWish is a unique flexible Recurring Deposit that lets you save for your goals as and when you have the funds and earn better interest rates just like a Fixed Deposit.[14]

Grant of Loans and Advances

The second important function of a commercial bank is to grant loans and advances which are given to members of the public and to the business community at a higher rate of interest than allowed by banks on various deposit accounts. The rate of interest charged on loans and advances varies depending upon the purpose, period and the mode of repayment. The difference between the rate of interest allowed on deposits and the rate charged on the loans is the main source of a bank's income.

1. *Loans:* A loan is granted for a specific time period. Generally, commercial banks grant short-term loans but term loans (loan for more than a year), may also be granted. The borrower may withdraw the entire amount in lump sum or in instalments. However, interest is charged on the full amount of loan. Loans are generally granted against the security of certain assets. A loan may be repaid either in lump sum or in instalments.

Modes of short-term financial assistance: Banks grant short-term financial assistance by way of cash credit, overdraft and bill discounting.

Cash credit: Cash credit is an arrangement where the bank allows the borrower to draw amounts upto a specified limit. The amount is credited to the account of the customer which can be withdrawn as and when he requires. Interest is charged on the amount actually withdrawn. Cash credit is granted as per agreed terms and conditions with the customers.

---

14. http://www.icicibank.com/Personal-Banking/account-deposit/personal-banking-accounts-deposits.html.

Overdraft: Overdraft is also a credit facility granted by a bank. A customer who has a current account with the bank is allowed to withdraw more than the amount of credit balance in his account. It is a temporary arrangement. Overdraft facility with a specified limit is allowed either on the security of assets, or on personal security, or both.

Discounting of bills: Banks provide short-term finance by discounting bills, that is, making payment of the amount before the due date of the bills after deducting a certain rate of discount. The customer gets the funds without waiting for the date of maturity of the bills. In case any bill is dishonoured on the due date, the bank can recover the amount from the customer.

Advances: An advance is a credit facility provided by the bank to its customers. It differs from loan in the sense that loans may be granted for a longer period, but advances are normally granted for a short period of time. Further, the purpose of granting advances is to meet the day-to-day requirements of business. The rate of interest charged on advances varies from one bank to another. Interest is charged only on the amount withdrawn and not on the sanctioned amount.

Secondary Functions

Besides the primary functions of accepting deposits and lending money, banks perform a number of other functions which are called *secondary functions*. These are as follows:

- Issuing letters of credit, travellers cheques, circular notes and the like,
- Undertaking safe custody of valuables, important documents, and securities by providing safe deposit vaults or lockers,
- Providing customers with facilities of foreign exchange,
- Transferring money from one place to another, and from one branch to another branch of the bank,
- Acting as a guarantor on behalf of customers, for making payments for purchase of goods, machinery, vehicles, etc.
- Agency functions for customers to manage and protect their property or issue and redeem their securities,
- Collecting and supplying business information,
- Issuing demand drafts and pay orders, and
- Providing reports on the creditworthiness of customers.

SCHEDULED AND NON-SCHEDULED BANKS—A COMPARISON

In the preceding section, we had discussed various banking products. Now, let us have a comparative picture of these products offered by a scheduled bank vis-a-vis non-scheduled bank in India.

The non-scheduled banks selected for the comparison, as per RBI's list[15], include the following:

15. http://rbidocs.rbi.org.in/rdocs/Content/pdfs/nonschedulecoop.pdf.

Adarsh Co-operative Bank Ltd., Jaipur

Adarsh Co-operative Bank Ltd. was established on 5th September 1972 to promote financial cooperation among low income group members of society. The bank was registered under provisions of Rajasthan Co-operative Society Act, 1965. Initially it operated in the adjoining districts of Jalore, Pali, Udaipur later in Jaipur and Ajmer districts of Rajasthan. As on date all the 46 branches stand computerized and the bank has also achieved highest growth rate amongst the cooperative banks in Northern India.[16]

The Andhra Bank Employees' Co-operative Bank Ltd., Hyderabad

The Andhra Bank Employees' Co-operative bank is a brainchild of the employees of Andhra Bank. The Andhra Bank Employees' Co-op. Credit Society Ltd. got registered on 11 October 1949 and the society started functioning from 12 June 1952. Its central office shifted from Machilipatnam to Hyderabad in the year 1977. The bank is one of the top 10 Urban Co-operative banks of the country[17].

The Baroda City Co-operative Bank Ltd., Ahmedabad

The Baroda City Co-operative Bank Ltd was established in 1927 in Vadodara Gujarat State. It has 8 branches, all of them are operating with Core Banking Solution (CBS).[18]

The City Co-operative Bank Ltd., Mumbai

It is a Mumbai-based bank with 8 branches in Mumbai and 2 branches in Thane district. The bank has consistently made profit[19].

Comparative Return on Fixed Deposits

Table 2.1 depicts the comparison between SBI and Adarsh Co-op. Bank for interest offered on term deposits.

TABLE 2.1 Interest Rates on Fixed Deposits of SBI and Adarsh Co-operative Bank (As on 28th December 2022)

Normal	*SBI*	*Adarsh Co-operative Bank*	*Senior Citizen*	*SBI*	*Adarsh Co-operative Bank*
Up to 364 days	5.75%	7.50%	Up to 364 days	6.25%	8.00%
365 days, less than 2 years	6.75%	6.25%	365 days, less than 2 years	7.25%	6.75%

16. https://adarshco-operativebank.com
17. http://www.abecoopbank.com.
18. http://bccbank.coop
19. http://www.citycoopbank.com.

Normal	*SBI*	*Adarsh Co-operative Bank*	*Senior Citizen*	*SBI*	*Adarsh Co-operative Bank*
2 years, less than 3 years	6.75%	6.50%	2 years, less than 3 years	7.25%	7.00%
3 years, less than 5 years	6.25%	6.25%	3 years, less than 5 years	6.75%	6.75%
5 years to 10 years	6.25%	6.00%	5 years to 10 years	7.25%	6.50%

Notes: 1. SBI's Interest Rates are on Domestic term deposits Below ₹2 crore.
2. Interest rates of Adarsh Co-operative Bank for senior citizen are also for single deposit of ₹35 lacs and above.

From the table above, one can find out that for Term Deposits, Adarsh bank (non-scheduled bank) is offering higher return over SBI (scheduled bank) for both type of customers, normal and senior citizens in the first year, and that too, on shortest term deposits.

In case of term deposit non-scheduled banks may offer higher rate of interest over scheduled banks but, there is also a risk factor associated with non-scheduled banks due to less compliance. The scheduled banks are completely monitored under Reserve Bank of India Act, 1934.

TYPES OF BANKING

Over the years, Indian banking has assumed many shapes and sizes and has not been confined to mere accepting of deposits and granting of loans.

There are various forms of banking which are prevalent nowadays and they are discussed below:

Retail Banking

With growing household incomes, the Indian retail financial services market has high growth potential. The key dimensions of the retail banking include:

- Customer focus
- Wide range of products
- Customer convenience
- Widespread distribution
- Strong processes
- Prudent risk management

Retail banking is often used interchangeably with branch banking. The fee income that banks earn while extending commercial banking services to retail customers includes retail loan processing fees, credit card and debit card fees, transaction banking fees, and fees from distribution of third-party products. Cross-selling of the entire range of credit and investment products and banking services to customers is often a key aspect of the retail strategy.

Retail banking products on the liability side include all types of deposit accounts, and on the assets side include mortgages and loans (personal, housing, educational, etc).

Aggregate deposits of All-India SCB's as on March, 2022 were ₹1,70,08,795 crore[20].

Private Banking

It is also called *Personal banking* or *Exclusive banking*. *Wealth Management* is another term coined for this. It basically aims at providing personalized services to selected customers, identified as per their income groups. These customers are categorized as 'High Net Worth Individual (HNWI) clients. In addition to high net worth resident Indians, Non-Resident Indians (NRIs) form a major chunk of the customer base for personal wealth management industry in India.

Wealth management is an investment advisory discipline that incorporates financial planning, investment portfolio management and a number of aggregated financial services. HNWIs, small business owners and families who desire the assistance of a credentialed financial advisory specialist call upon wealth managers to coordinate retail banking, estate planning, legal resources, tax professionals and investment management.

Corporate Banking

Corporate banking is also called *Wholesale banking* or *Business banking* and is primarily oriented towards corporates. Corporate business covers project finance including infrastructure finance, cross-border finance, working capital loans, non-fund based working capital products and other fee-based services, including foreign exchange products, documentary credits (such as letter of credit or LC) and guarantees to business enterprises.

Most of the banks classify wholesale banking into mid-corporate and large corporate as a part of their internal policy. A large portion of wholesale banking business comes from off balance sheet businesses. Hedging solutions form a significant portion of exposures coming from corporate. Hence, wholesale banking clients are strategic for the banks with the view to gain other businesses from them. Corporate banking is largely dominated by famous Indian banks *like SBI, ICICI Bank, IDBI Bank, Punjab National Bank and Central Bank of India.*

Merchant Banking/Investment Banking

As per SEBI (Merchant Bankers) Rules, 1992[21] and SEBI (Merchant Bankers) Regulations, 1992[22], *merchant banking service* is any service provided in relation to issue management either by making arrangements regarding selling, buying or subscribing securities as manager, consultant, advisor or rendering corporate advisory service in relation to such issue management. In addition, merchant banking services

20. https://dbie.rbi.org.in/DBIE/dbie.rbi?site=publications#!18
21. http://www.sebi.gov.in/acts/act09main1.html.
22. http://www.sebi.gov.in/acts/Merchantbankers.pdf.

also include advisory services on corporate restructuring, debt or equity restructuring, loan restructuring, etc. Fees are charged by the merchant banker for rendering these services.

On the other hand, the term *Investment banking* is an umbrella term for a range of activities and has a much broader perspective referring to all types of capital market activities. Investment banking includes not only merchant banking but also other related capital market activities such as stock trading, market making, broking and asset management as well as specialized corporate advisory services in the areas of mergers and acquisitions, project advisory, and business and financial advisory. Investment banking has a large number of Indian and foreign players *like Kotak Bank, Citi Bank, Goldman Sachs and Merrill Lynch.*

Cross-border banking services like issue management of ECBs, GDRs/ADRs/IDRs, providing foreign currency loans, import financing/export financing, leasing, factoring/forfaiting form a very significant part of merchant banking.

Universal Banking

It refers to the provision of a wide range of financial services by an organization, under one roof, e.g. commercial banking, merchant banking (or investment banking), mutual funds and insurance—all by one bank. In India, the Narasimham Committee Report, 1991* emphasised the importance of universal banking. It advised to consolidate (bring together) the banking industry through mergers and integration of financial activities, i.e. it advised a combination of all banking and financial activities. Now, almost all leading commercial banks besides primary functions, are acting as universal banks for multi-diverse needs of the depositors.

E-Banking

E-banking refers to electronic banking which is an e-business in the banking industry. It is also referred to as *Online Banking* or *Virtual Banking*. Today, everybody wants services at his/her fingertips which is a result of the growing expectations of bank's customers. It involves information technology based banking. Under this system, the banking services are delivered by way of a computer-controlled system where the customers do not have to visit the bank's premises. Some of the popular e-banking services include *internet banking, telephone banking, ATMs, etc.*

It works both ways as the operating cost per unit services is lower for the banks and it offers convenience to customers as they are not required to be physically present at a bank's premises.

BANKING OMBUDSMAN SCHEME

This scheme came into force in 2006 by RBI and extends to the whole of India. It applies to all the banking businesses in India[23]. This implies that there is independent external machinery for resolving customer grievances in cases where the same are not satisfied with the bank's decision on their complaints.

* The Report of Narasimham Committee I is given in the Instructor's manual.
23. http://rbidocs.rbi.org.in/rdocs/Content/PDFs/67933.pdf.

The RBI Governor appoints Banking Ombudsman for various regions from amongst people of high repute and calibre in legal, banking, financial services, public administration or management sectors.

Following kinds of complaints are considered under the Banking Ombudsman Scheme:

1. ***Complaints concerning deficiency in banking services:*** For example, non-payment or inordinate delay in payment/collection of cheques, failure to honour a guarantee or letter of credit commitment by a bank, fraudulent withdrawals from the accounts, etc.

2. ***Complaints concerning loans:*** These relate to non-observance of RBI directive on interest rates, or other matters concerning loans, delay in sanction of loans, etc.

3. ***Complaints concerning deficiency in banking services:*** For example, non-payment or inordinate delay in payment/collection of cheques, failure to honour a guarantee or letter of credit commitment by a bank, fraudulent withdrawals from the accounts, etc.

4. ***Complaints concerning loans:*** These relate to non-observance of RBI directive on interest rates, or other matters concerning loans, delay in sanction of loans, etc.

5. ***Limit on the amount of compensation as specified in an Award:*** The amount, if any, to be paid by the bank to the complainant by way of compensation for any loss suffered by the complainant, is limited to the amount arising directly out of the act or omission of the bank or ₹10 lacs, whichever is lower.

Further, the Banking Ombudsman may award compensation not exceeding ₹1 lac to the complainant only in the case of complaints relating to credit card operations for mental agony and harassment. The Banking Ombudsman will take into account the loss of the complainant's time, expenses incurred by the complainant, and the harassment and mental anguish suffered by the complainant while passing such award.

6. ***Further recourse available:*** If a customer is not satisfied with the decision passed by the Banking Ombudsman, he can approach the appellate authority against the Banking Ombudsman's decision. Appellate authority is vested with the Deputy Governor of RBI. He can also explore any other recourse available to him as per the law. The bank also has the option to file an appeal before the appellate authority under the scheme.

KEY BANKING APPLICATIONS

Magnetic Ink Character Recognition (MICR)

'MICR' is s a character recognition technology used primarily by the banking industry to facilitate the processing of cheques. The MICR has a distinct code structure. MICR characters are printed in special typefaces with a magnetic ink or toner, usually on the bottom strip of the cheque leaf.

There are 15 numbers in total. The first six numeric digits (numbers) denote the serial number of the cheque. In the next band, there are nine numbers. These are as follows:

(i) The first three numbers represent the city (for e.g. Mumbai is 400).
(ii) The next three numbers represent the bank (for e.g. American Express is 031).
(iii) The next three numbers represent the branch.

RTGS

It stands for 'Real Time Gross Settlement', and can be defined as the continuous (real-time) settlement of fund transfers individually on an order-by-order basis. *Real Time* means the processing of instructions is done immediately when they are received, not later. *Gross Settlement* means the settlement of funds transfer occurs individually (on an instruction-by-instruction basis). Since the funds settlement takes place in the books of the Reserve Bank of India, the payments are final and irrevocable. The RTGS system is the fastest possible inter-bank money transfer facility available through secure banking channels in India.

NEFT

'National Electronic Funds Transfer' (NEFT) is a nation-wide payment system which facilitates one-to-one funds transfer. Under this scheme, individuals, firms and corporates can electronically transfer funds from any bank branch to any individual, firm or corporate having an account with any other bank branch in the country. The maximum limit of these cash remittances is ₹50,000 per transaction (Table 2.2).

NEFT is an electronic fund transfer system which settles transactions in standard batches, whereas in RTGS, the transactions are settled individually.

TABLE 2.2 Minimum/maximum amount for RTGS/NEFT transactions under Retail Internet Banking and Corporate Internet Banking

Type	*Minimum*	*Maximum*
RTGS	₹2 lac	No limit
NEFT	No limit	No limit

IMPS

'Immediate Payment Service' (IMPS) refers to the instant payment, inter-bank electronic fund transfer service for India. For transferring funds real time and 24×7×365 interbank was a major challenge faced in banking industry. Only NEFT and RTGS were available to user for fund transfer during banking hours.

With the above context in mind, National Payments Corporation of India (NPCI) launched Immediate Payment Service on 22nd November 2010.

IMPS provides robust and real time fund transfer which offers an instant, 24×7, interbank electronic fund transfer service that could be accessed on multiple channels like Mobile, Internet, ATM, SMS. IMPS is an emphatic service which allow transferring of funds instantly within banks across India which is not only safe but also economical. Currently on IMPS, 677 members are live which includes banks and PPIs. This facility is provided by NPCI through its existing NFS switch.

The eligible criteria for the Banks who can participate in IMPS is that the entity should have valid banking or prepaid payment instrument license from Reserve Bank of India to participate in IMPS.[24]

SWIFT

'SWIFT' code is a standard format of Bank Identifier Codes (BIC) and it is a unique identification code for a particular bank. These codes are used at the time of transferring money between banks, particularly for international wire transfers. Banks also used codes for exchanging other messages between them.

The SWIFT code consists of 8 or 11 characters. When an 8-digit code is given, it refers to the primary office.

- First 4 characters: bank code (only letters)
- Next 2 characters: country code (only letters)
- Next 2 characters: location code (letters and digits)
- Last 3 characters: branch code, optional (letters and digits)

The registrations of SWIFT Codes are handled by *Society for Worldwide Interbank Financial Telecommunication (SWIFT)* with headquarters located in Belgium.

FINANCIAL PERFORMANCE ANALYSIS OF STATE BANK OF INDIA

In this section, we shall analyze the financial performance of State Bank of India to understand the financial indicators and focus areas of a banking company. State Bank of India is the largest bank in India in terms of revenue and market capitalization. It is a public sector bank with head office in Mumbai and came into existence on 1st July 1955, by the merger of Imperial Bank of India along with other state-owned and state-associated banks. The financial performance analysis of SBI makes the readers aware about the financial challenges and issues in a banking sector company. SBI is primarily governed by the Banking Regulation Act, 1949, in addition to the Companies Act, 1956 and 2013, being a corporate.

I. Financial Statements' Insight

The financial statements of State Bank of India are discussed here to have a complete idea of the relevant financial indicators of a banking company. Table 2.3 presents the financial statements of SBI. (*Source*: https://sbi.co.in/Accessed on 2nd January 2023).

Table 2.3(a) presents the balance sheet of SBI as at 2022.

24. https://www.npci.org.in/what-we-do/imps/product-overview

TABLE 2.3(a) Balance Sheet of SBI as at 31st March, 2022 (000s omitted)

Particulars	31.03.2022 (₹)	31.03.2021 (₹)
Capital and Liabilities		
Capital	89,24,612	89,24,612
Reserves & Surplus	2,79,19,55,989	2,52,98,27,285
Deposits	40,51,53,41,227	36,81,27,70,796
Borrowings	4,26,04,33,798	4,17,29,76,988
Other Liabilities and Provisions	2,29,93,18,428	1,81,97,96,631
Total	**49,87,59,74,054**	**45,34,42,96,312**
Assets		
Cash and Balances with RBI	2,57,85,92,071	2,13,20,15,363
Balances with Banks and money at call and short notice	1,36,69,31,140	1,29,83,71,731
Investments	14,81,44,54,698	13,51,70,52,051
Advances	27,33,96,65,929	24,49,49,77,911
Fixed Assets	37,70,81,583	38,41,92,419
Other Assets	3,39,92,48,633	3,51,76,86,837
Total	**49,87,59,74,054**	**45,34,42,96,312**
Contingent Liabilities	20,07,08,34,406	17,06,94,99,117
Bills for Collection	77,73,01,234	56,51,61,188

Funding Pattern

1. ***Net Worth:*** The equity-based capital witnesses a rise of over 10%, i.e. around ₹26212.87 crores in the net worth of SBI, and reserves and surplus account for the major contribution. It is a good sign in terms of internal strength of an organization.

2. ***Reserves:*** The important sub-heads under reserves are:

- Statutory reserves: compulsorily to be maintained as per Banking law and Company law.
- Capital reserves.
- Share premium.
- Investment fluctuation reserve.
- Foreign currency translation reserve: SBI has a lot of assets and liabilities which are denominated in foreign currency. These assets are investments which may have to be marked to market on the balance sheet date. While doing so, the bank may face a loss in the foreign exchange as on the date of preparing the balance sheet and thus, this loss is not written off in the P&L account but is reduced from reserves directly and vice-versa in case of profits.
- Revenue and other reserves.
- Revaluation reserve

The total reserves have increased during the year and a major portion of this is because of increase in investment fluctuation reserve.

3. ***Deposits:*** The components of Deposits are:

- Demand deposits
- Saving deposits
- Term deposits

If we notice, there has been a growth in the total sources of funds. Deposits grew by almost 11%. What improved was the Savings deposits' margin of the bank. This determines the bank's ability to raise cheap deposits as these accounts give low interest.

4. ***Borrowings:*** Borrowings are different from deposits in that deposits are collected in the course of business, and borrowings are like loans taken by the bank. Borrowings include:

- Borrowings from RBI
- Borrowings from other banks and institutions
- Debt instruments

The borrowings of the bank increased by 3% and we notice that SBI has a lower reliance on external borrowings and specifically borrowings from outside India.

5. ***Other liabilities and provisions:*** Other liabilities and provisions have also increased by 26%, not a major concern being short-term in nature. They basically include bills payable, inter-office adjustments, etc.

Utilization Trend

1. ***Cash and Balances:*** These include cash in hand majorly with RBI for the purpose of maintaining CRR.

2. ***Balances with Banks and Money-at-call:*** It includes balances with other banks and call money for liquidity.

3. ***Investments:*** These mainly include investments in government securities and other approved securities to meet SLR requirements, holding of equity shares and debentures of other companies and investments in subsidiaries and/or joint ventures.

4. ***Advances:*** A major portion of this, i.e. 90%, is towards advances in India. Bills purchased, Term loans, cash credits and overdraft facilities account for the major advances.

5. ***Fixed Assets:*** Fixed Assets include premises, furniture and fixtures, assets under construction, etc.

6. ***Other Assets:*** Other Assets majorly comprise of inter-office adjustments, interest accrued and deferred tax assets.

The application of funds has been mainly contributed by advances and investments, followed by balances with RBI and banks and call money.

Contingent Liabilities: One important point about banking industry is the amount of Contingent Liabilities. For SBI, it has increased by 18% in the current year. Most of these contingent liabilities are due to the outstanding amount on forward exchange contracts. The other few reasons for the contingent liabilities include acceptances, guarantees and obligations.

Table 2.3(b) presents the P/L statement of SBI for 2022.

TABLE 2.3(b) Profit and Loss Account of SBI for the year ended 31st March 2022 (000s omitted)

Particulars	31.03.2022 (₹)	31.03.2021 (₹)
I. Income		
Interest earned	2,75,45,72,904	2,65,15,06,338
Other Income	40,56,39,140	43,49,63,747
Total	**3,16,02,12,044**	**3,08,64,70,085**
II. Expenditure		
Interest expended	1,54,74,97,043	1,54,44,06,333
Operating expenses	93,39,75,152	82,65,22,235
Provisions and contingencies	36,19,80,044	51,14,36,823
Total	**2,84,34,52,239**	**2,88,23,65,391**
III. Profit		
Net profit for the year	31,67,59,805	20,41,04,694
Add: Profit/(Loss) brought forward	(3,60,08,446)	(10,49,83,021)
Total	**28,07,51,359**	**9,91,21,673**
IV. Appropriations		
Transfer to Statutory Reserve	9,50,27,942	6,12,31,408
Transfer to Capital Reserve	53,81,524	1,46,51,242
Transfer to Investment Fluctuation Reserve	4,64,78,702	1,92,81,963
Transfer to Revenue and other Reserves	1,16,84,400	42,67,060
Dividend for the current year	6,33,64,742	3,56,98,446
Balance carried over to Balance Sheet	5,88,14,049	(3,60,08,446)
Total	**28,07,51,359**	**9,91,21,673**

Income Trend

The income of the bank has increased by just around 3% (YOY) despite higher interest rates, majorly due to slow down in the credit market. The positive part is that there has been majorly an increase in the interest income. A major reason for the bank's increasing net profit margin as compared to last year is because of its improving operating efficiency, and manpower and employee efficiency.

Expenses

Interest expense has increased marginally mainly because of the cost of funds available in the market at reasonable rates and no prominent change in interest rates by RBI. SBI has shown good operational efficiency by reducing total expenses as compared to last year.

Profitability

The net profit crossed ₹30,000 crores and increased by 55% to ₹31,675.98 crores. The increase in total income has outperformed expenses by reduction in them.

Table 2.3(c) presents the Cash flow statement of SBI for 2022.

TABLE 2.3(c) Cash Flow Statement of SBI for the year ended 31st March 2022 (000s omitted)

Particulars	31.03.2022 (₹)	31.03.2021 (₹)
Cash Flow from Operating Activities:		
Net Profit/(Loss) before Taxes	43,42,18,536	27,54,11,161
Adjustments for:		
Depreciation on Fixed Assets	3,24,85,858	3,31,75,525
(Profit)/Loss on sale of Fixed Assets	1,68,660	2,85,817
(Profit)/Loss on revaluation of Investments	26,32,788	—
(Profit) on sale of Investments in Subs./JVs/Associates	—	(1,53,97,330)
Loss on sale of Investments in Subs./JVs/Associates	1,29,261	—
Provision for diminution in fair value & NPAs	14,08,68,454	27,24,43,502
Provision on Standard Assets	4,67,70,392	3,78,97,838
Provision on non-performing Investments	3,44,00,987	3,01,44,966
Other provisions	2,24,81,481	9,96,44,051
Income from investment in Subs./JVs/Associates	(71,83,749)	(64,28,622)
Interest charged on Capital Instruments	5,45,19,800	5,78,25,198
	76,14,92,468	**78,50,02,106**
Adjustments for:		
Increase/(Decrease) in Deposits	37,02,57,0431	4,39,65,63,453
Increase/(Decrease) in Borrowings other than Capital Instruments	5,06,49,809	92,13,55,347
(Increase)/Decrease in Investments other than investments in Subs./JVs/Associates	(1,32,64,61,469)	(3,05,56,44,158)
(Increase)/Decrease in Advances	(2,98,55,56,472)	(1,51,45,25,806)
Increase/(Decrease) in other Liabilities	40,37,52,717	16,51,63,543
(Increase)/Decrease in other Assets	5,58,30,680	(77,53,13,847)
Taxes refund/(Taxes paid)	(7,81,23,634)	(2,39,45,246)
Net cash generated from/(used in) Operating Activities A	**58,41,54,530**	**89,86,55,392**
Cash Flow from Investing Activities		
Purchase of Investments in Subs./JVs/Associates	(87,84,710)	(2,23,49,750)
Sale of Investments in Subs./JVs/Associates	8,09,757	3,42,066
Profit on sale of Investments in Subs./JVs/Associates	—	1,53,97,330
(Loss) on sale of Investments in Subs./JVs/Associates	(1,29,261)	—
Income from Investments in Subs./JVs/Associates	71,83,749	64,28,623
(Increase) in Fixed Assets	(2,71,53,118)	(3,44,06,473)
Decrease in Fixed Assets	19,46,406	10,45,608
Net cash generated from/ (used in) Investing Activities B	**(2,61,27,177)**	**(3,35,42,596)**

Particulars	31.03.2022 (₹)	31.03.2021 (₹)
Cash Flow from Financing Activities		
Issue of Capital Instruments	13,97,40,000	27,43,10,000
Redemption of Capital Instruments	(10,29,33,000)	(16,84,78,380)
Interest paid on Capital Instruments	(5,28,83,702)	(4,95,05,299)
Dividend paid	(3,56,98,446)	—
Net cash generated from/(used in) Financing Activities C	**(5,17,75,148)**	**5,63,26,321**
Effect of Exchange Fluctuation on Translation Reserve D	**88,83,912**	**(20,22,077)**
Net Increase/(Decrease) in Cash & Cash Equivalents (A + B + C + D)	**51,51,36,117**	**91,94,17,040**
Cash and Cash Equivalents as at 1st April	**3,43,03,87,094**	**2,51,09,70,054**
Cash and Cash Equivalents as at 31st March	**3,94,55,23,211**	**3,43,03,87,094**

An interesting point to be noted in the banking industry is that though most of the banks have high profits, they have a decreasing cash inflow, majorly due to decline in inflow from operating activities during 2021–22.

SBI's reducing cash flow from operating activities indicates a most constant credit/deposit ratio. Further, total cash flows of SBI for the year have been on a lower side, indicating declining liquidity.

II. Financial Appraisal

Here, SBI is analyzed with regard to company analysis and then industry analysis, using financial ratios to find out its financial performance at a more intrinsic level. (https://www-aceanalyser-com/ Accessed on 2nd January 2023).

A. Company Analysis

Profitability Appraisal

1. ***Net profit margin*** **(%):** Net profit margin aims to find the net amount that is available after all expenses, as a percentage of revenue earned. Here, revenue is 'interest earned'. In simple terms, it can be said that this ratio calculates the amount of revenue that is converted into net profit. It is calculated as:

$$\frac{\text{Net profit}}{\text{Turnover}}$$

TABLE 2.4(a) PAT Margin (%)

	2020–21	2021–22
SBI	7.70	11.50

Explanation: Net profit margin has shown an increase for SBI because of higher growth in interest earned (Table 2.4a).

2. ***Net interest margin*** **(%):** This is the ratio which determines the difference between the interest income earned and the cost of borrowed capital (Table 2.4b). It examines how efficiently the interest is generated on the average earning assets. A bank's prime focus is to increase this net interest margin. It is computed as:

$$\frac{\text{Investment Returns} - \text{Interest Expense}}{\text{Average Earning Assets}}$$

TABLE 2.4(b) Net Interest Margin (%)

	2020–21	2021–22
SBI	2.67	2.62

Explanation: Net interest margin for SBI is expected to be growing in the future than other banks in India due to increasing trend of the low-cost deposits and retail deposits in their total funding.

Return Generation

3. ***Return on capital employed*** **(%):** It is an indicator of how profitable a company is relative to its total capital employed (Table 2.5a). ROCE gives an idea as to how efficiently management is using its funds to generate earnings. It is calculated as:

$$\frac{\text{EBIT}}{\text{Capital Employed}}$$

TABLE 2.5(a) ROCE (%)

	2020–21	2021–22
SBI	11.65	13.18

Explanation: ROCE for SBI has shown an increasing trend, indicating the efficient utilisation of funds during the period.

4. ***Return on net worth/Return on equity*** **(%):** It is the ratio of net income after taxes to end of the year net worth (Table 2.5b). This ratio indicates the return on stockholder's total equity. It is determined as:

$$\frac{\text{Net Profit after Tax}}{\text{Net Worth}}$$

TABLE 2.5(b) RONW/ROE (%)

	2020–21	2021–22
SBI	9.94	13.92

Explanation: There has been a good increase in the RONW/ROE for the period for SBI. This is an indication of prosperity for shareholders.

5. *Earnings per share* (₹): This ratio determines the earnings available to an individual shareholder (Table 2.5c). It shows the growth prospects of a company. It is calculated as:

$$\frac{\text{Net Profit}}{\text{Number of Equity Shares}}$$

TABLE 2.5(c) EPS (₹ per Share)

	2020–21	2021–22
SBI	22.87	35.49

Explanation: EPS has shown a tremendous rise for SBI, indicating an efficient employment of shareholders' funds and generating them an increasing return.

6. *Dividend per share* (₹): It indicates the amount of profit that is distributed as dividend to shareholders (Table 2.5d). It is computed as:

$$\frac{\text{Dividend}}{\text{Number of Equity Shares}}$$

TABLE 2.5(d) DPS (₹ per Share)

	2020–21	2021–22
SBI	4.00	7.10

Explanation: SBI has distributed higher dividend to shareholders in the current year as compared to last year from ₹4 to ₹7 per share.

Liquidity

7. *Credit: Deposit ratio* (%): This ratio helps determine how much funds of the banks are used for giving out credit (Table 2.6a). It is calculated as:

$$\frac{\text{Loans}}{\text{Deposits}}$$

TABLE 2.6(a) Credit Margin (%)

	2020–21	2021–22
SBI	66.54	67.48

Explanation: This helps us understand what percentage of the funds is being used by the bank in its core activities. If a bank is using lesser funds in giving out credit, which means it is focusing on all other activities and not on its core activity. SBI is moving ahead on this front which reflects its emphasis on core banking activities.

8. *CASA ratio* (%): This ratio tells us the percentage of deposits which come in the form of current account and saving account. It is important to know this ratio as these funds which come in the form of current and saving account deposits are available at a very low cost to the bank and thus, reduce the interest cost of the bank. *For example,* current account has an interest earning rate of anywhere between 0–1% and savings from 3–5% (Table 2.6b).

It is calculated as:

$$\frac{\text{Current Accounts + Saving Accounts}}{\text{Total deposits}}$$

TABLE 2.6(b) CASA Margin (%)

	2020–21	2021–22
SBI	45.40	44.52

Explanation: There is a marginal decrease in the CASA ratio of SBI, showing a decline in retail banking.

Asset Quality

9. *Net NPAs to net advances* (%): Non-Performing Assets (NPAs) are the advances which have become uneven and these are not expected to pay back the loans and advances taken by them. The ratio shows what percentage of net advances have become NPAs (Table 2.7). This ratio helps to find the quality of assets and is computed as:

$$\frac{\text{Net NPA}}{\text{Net Advances}}$$

TABLE 2.7 NPA Margin (%)

	2020–21	2021–22
SBI	1.50	1.02

Explanation: Banks try to keep this ratio to a minimum possible because NPAs cut profits as well as reduce the customer base of the bank. The decrease in non-performing assets indicates higher level of efficiency in the loan portfolio.

Solvency

10. *Capital adequacy ratio* (%): CAR is a measure of the ability of a bank to meet its credit risk, operational risk, etc. It is measured by dividing total capital by risk weighted assets. In accordance with Basel-III norms, it is given in Table 2.8(a).

TABLE 2.8(a) Capital Adequacy Margin (%)

	2020–21	2021–22
SBI	13.74	13.83

BOX 2.5: DEBT TO EQUITY RATIO VS CAPITAL ADEQUACY RATIO

Debt to Equity in banking industry is quite high because of the high debts that these companies owe. Unlike other industries where high D/E ratio indicates bad long-term liquidity, the business of the banks is carried out due to debts. Therefore, D/E ratio is not really relevant for the banking industry. Instead, 'Capital adequacy ratio' is relevant for solvency for the banking industry.

Tier-I Capital (%): Equity of Capital adequacy is divided into two parts—Tier-I capital and Tier-II capital. Tier-I capital mainly includes equity issued, and reserves and surplus. Tier-II capital includes preference shares and subordinated debt, etc. (Table 2.8b).

TABLE 2.8(b) Tier-I Capital Margin (Basel III) (%)

	2020–21	2021–22
SBI	11.44	11.42

Explanation: As per the capital adequacy guidelines of RBI under Basel III, a bank is required to maintain a minimum ratio of total capital to risk weighted assets (CRAR) of 9.0%, with minimum Tier-I capital ratio of 7%. SBI is well above the statutory requirements. Higher the capital adequacy ratio, the better it is for lenders as the losses are well covered for them. SBI's ratio above 11% is a sign that there is enough space to cover any addition of riskier assets to the company's balance sheet.

Tier-II Capital (%): As mentioned above, Tier-II capital includes preference shares and subordinated debt, and others.

TABLE 2.8(c) Tier-II Capital Margin (Basel III) (%)

	2020–21	2021–22
SBI	2.30	2.41

Explanation: As per RBI's guidelines in accordance with Basel III, a bank should have a total capital (combined Tier-I and Tier-II capital) ratio of at least 9% of RWAs on an ongoing basis. Thus, within the minimum CRAR of 9%, Tier-II capital can be admitted maximum up to 2%. SBI's combined capital is higher than the statutory requirements.

Valuation

11. *Book value per share* (₹): This aims to find the net worth available to a common shareholder. It is the real value of a share (Table 2.9a) and it is calculated as:

$$\frac{\text{Net Worth}}{\text{Number of Equity Shares}}$$

TABLE 2.9(a) BV (₹ per Share)

	2020–21	2021–22
SBI	258.05	287.64

Explanation: Book value per share has shown an increasing trend for SBI, indicating a rising internal strength of the company. In the case of banking business where most of the liabilities and assets are more liquid than in any other industry, the book value tells the value of the share if the company were to be liquidated.

12. *P/E ratio*: This ratio indicates the market reaction to the earnings of a company (Table 2.9b). It is calculated as:

$$\frac{\text{Market Price}}{\text{Earnings per Share}}$$

TABLE 2.9(b) P/E Ratio

	2020–21	2021–22
SBI	15.93	13.90

Explanation: Price-earnings ratio has declined for SBI despite an increasing EPS. This signifies the market reaction on an unfavourable side to the earnings of the company in the short-run.

B. Industry Analysis

Interest Earning

The core earnings' analysis of SBI vis-a-vis to industry in terms of interest margin is discussed in Table 2.10.

TABLE 2.10 Interest Margin

	2020–21		2021–22	
	SBI	*Industry*	*SBI*	*Industry*
Net Interest Margin (%)	2.67	4.03	2.62	3.89

Explanation: SBI is the largest commercial bank in India. The said fact reflects in its interest ratios. Its interest margin of almost constant around 3% during the years shows sound core competency. It is lower than the industry, which can be looked into by the bank.

Return Generation

In the long run, the ultimate factor is efficient utilisation of resources and return generated on them. The return efficiency of SBI with regard to the industry is analyzed in Table 2.11.

TABLE 2.11 Return Generation

	2020–21		2021–22	
	SBI	*Industry*	*SBI*	*Industry*
ROA (%)	0.48	0.34	0.67	0.60
ROE (%)	9.94	5.60	13.92	9.21

Explanation: The utilisation of resources by SBI as compared to industry does not need any explanation. It is very much evident that SBI is the deciding factor in industry in terms of efficiency of resources. Its ROA is higher than industry with 0.48% and 0.67% for both the years. Return on equity is also much higher than industry for 2021 and 2022 at 9.94% and 13.92%. As shareholders are the real owners of any company, this indicator is very good for future prospects.

Final Observation

SBI has been performing well, and has the ability to raise funds at a lower cost. The interest income earned as a percentage of the total income is around the industry and thus, the net profit as a percentage of total income for SBI is on a growing trend. SBI Retail Banking has been its core focus and hence, it has always maintained such a high CASA ratio, except in the current year. On the cash front, an interesting point to be noted in the banking industry is that though most of the banks have high profits, many banks have a negative cash inflow due to operating activities. This is not true of SBI for the year 2021–22 though it has declined. This is a sign of concern, yet reasonable.

Policy Suggestions

Financial strength is the key to any sector, in particular the banking sector, being the backbone of an economy. Though SBI has been performing well, still to improve the situation further, it is suggested that:

- The chief strength of the Indian banking industry is the regulatory system, which has enabled India to carve a place for itself in the global banking scene. Therefore, the regulatory system of Indian banks should be more strengthened to ensure stability, soundness, and efficiency of the financial sector.
- There should be a 'lessening quality of the loan portfolio'. Although there was a general deterioration in the quality of the loan portfolio of the banks, the extent of the deterioration varied substantially among individual banks. Overall, these indicators call for an eye to watch.
- There should be an adequate level of short-term and long-term financing. There is always a need for the development of financial structure and policies to provide both types of financing. A major issue is the apparent mismatch between the type

of funds required by the private sector and those provided by the financial system. Thus, the issue is more one of the 'types' of funds rather than the 'lack' of funds.

- As for the commercial banking sector, the major objective is to promote the viability of the banking system while preserving competitiveness and sound financial environment. The mobilisation of financial savings should be in a way which is consistent with the stability of the financial system. Stability in this context refers to the ability of the financial system to withstand disturbances, including those that may arise internally.
- Reporting and accounting standards and practices should be more streamlined, particularly in private sector banks. An improvement of accounting and disclosure practice would enhance transparency in financial markets.

CASE STUDY

Lending Rationale

This case study discusses the debt trap faced by a working couple and the grievance mechanism pursued thereof.

Mr. and Mrs. Sharma both were school teachers in a leading private school of Delhi, India. As advised by their close friend, they opened a current account with their local bank and started using its overdraft facility for their daily needs. In past, they had taken a personal loan due to some emergency, which was continuing.

In April 2014, they found themselves in a greater financial difficulty due to non-payment of salary by their school because of a financial crunch. They visited their bank seeking help and explained their situation to the branch manager, who released a fresh loan to them, based on their regularity. However, the rate of interest was higher than the existing loan.

They used the loan to support their monthly expenses and requested the branch manager to clear their overdraft out of the proceeds of the loan. However, to their surprise, at the end of the month they were served the bank notice to pay the overdraft. They visited the bank again to explain the position and found that the bank had not cleared the couple's overdraft. The bank's branch manager assured them that it would be done but with processing charges. They agreed with no choice.

Their worries did not end here. In October, they were again served the bank notice to clear the recent loan. The couple got furious as the branch manager had promised the loan for two years. When they complained to the branch manager, they were threatened with dire consequences.

As a last resort, they complained to the Ombudsman India, stating they were trapped in this debt by the branch manager in the name of help and were threatened now.

The ombudsman, India found the branch manager's behaviour unprofessional and unethical. Moreover, the ombudsman was concerned about his role in exploiting the couple with new debt at higher rates and not utilizing the proceeds for clearing their overdraft.

The ombudsman ordered the bank to refund the bank charges on the overdraft clearance and increase the tenure of the existing loan further to enable the couple to pay it. The ombudsman also advised Mr. and Mrs. Sharma not to blindly rely on such advice in future.

POINTS TO REMEMBER

- A bank is a financial institution where you can deposit your money and borrow when you need.
- The basic principles of banking which guide the business of banking are: (i) Principle of Intermediation, (ii) Principle of Liquidity, (iii) Principle of Profitability, (iv) Principle of Solvency, and (v) Principle of Trust.
- Growth of Indian banking can be divided into three phases:

  Phase I (Pre-Independence): Banking in India originated in the last decades of the 18th century. The first banks were The General Bank of India which started in 1786, and the Bank of Hindustan, both of which are now defunct. The East India Company established Bank of Bengal (1809), Bank of Bombay (1840) and Bank of Madras (1843) as independent units and called them Presidency Banks. These three banks were amalgamated in 1920 and the Imperial Bank of India was established which started as private shareholders' bank.

  Phase II (Post-Independence): The Reserve Bank of India, was nationalised on January 1, 1949. In 1949, the Banking Regulation Act was enforced which empowered the RBI to regulate, control, and inspect the banks in India. In 1955, the government nationalised the Imperial Bank of India which came to be known as SBI. Seven banks forming subsidiaries of SBI were nationalised in 1960. Fourteen major commercial banks in the country were nationalised in 1969 followed by 7 more banks in 1980.

  Phase III (Post-Liberalisation): In the early 1990s, the Narasimha Rao government embarked on a policy of liberalisation, licensing a small number of private banks. It saw the advent of private banks in India like HFDC Bank, ICICI Bank and Axis Bank (earlier UTI Bank), and foreign banks like City Bank and HSBC Bank.
- Indian banking reforms are:

  Indian Banking reforms pre-1991: After Independence, all large private banks were nationalised in two stages—the first in 1969, and the second in 1980.

  Indian Banking reforms since 1991: New Economic Policy (NEP), June 1991 emphasised on financial liberalisation. Following the report of the Narasimham Committee in November 1991, more comprehensive reforms took place in that year. The reforms consisted of—a shift of banking sector supervision from intrusive micro-level intervention towards economically viable credit decisions; a reduction of CRR and SLR; interest rate and entry deregulation; and adoption of prudential norms. The government also established the Board of Financial Supervision in the Reserve Bank of India and recapitalised public-sector banks. In 1993, the RBI permitted private entry into the banking sector. Therefore, the reforms comprised of—(i) liberalisation, (ii) gradual privatisation, (iii) measures to increase financial soundness, (iv) measures for increasing competition, and (v) diversification of banking activities.

- The present Indian banking sector is characterised by a mix of Public and Private Sector Banks, Prudential Accounting Norms for Banks, Asset Liability Management (ALM) system, risk management, better transparency and technological advancement.
- The structure of Indian banking industry has RBI as the apex bank of the country and comprises of these institutions—Commercial banks, Financial Institutions/ Specialised banks, and Cooperative banks.
- RBI is the central bank of India. It acts essentially as government's banker, maintaining deposit accounts of all other banks and advancing money to these banks, when needed.
- Commercial banks are banking institutions that accept deposits and grant short-term loans and advances to their customers. Commercial banks are either *scheduled* or *non-scheduled*. A scheduled bank is one whose name is included in the Second Schedule to the RBI Act, 1934. Non-scheduled bank in India "means a banking company as defined in Clause (c) of Section 5 of the Banking Regulation Act, 1949 (10 of 1949), which is not a scheduled bank". Commercial banks are of three types—Public sector banks, Private sector banks and Foreign banks.
- Public sector banks are banks where the majority stake is held by the Government of India or the RBI. The State Bank group and nationalised banks are together referred to as the public sector banks (PSBs).
- Private sector banks have majority of share capital of the bank held by private individuals.
- Foreign banks are registered and have their headquarters in a foreign country but operate their branches in our country.
- Regional Rural Banks (RRBs) were established during 1976–1987 with a view to develop the rural economy. Each RRB is owned jointly by the Central Government, the concerned State Government and a sponsoring public sector commercial bank.
- Cooperative banks are established under the Cooperative Societies Acts of different states. Cooperative banks have a three-tier setup, with state cooperative bank at the apex, central/district cooperative banks at district level, and primary cooperative societies at rural level.
- Financial Institutions/Specialised banks are the banks which were set up for a special purpose. They provide financial assistance for expansion and growth of a business. They are also referred to as Development Financial Institutions (DFIs).
- RBI's role and key functions are—Issuing notes, Government's banker, Bankers' bank, Banks' supervision and Regulation, Development of financial system, Exchange control, and Monetary and credit policy.
- RBI uses following tools of monetary control to stabilise the economy: Bank rate, Repo rate, Reverse repo rate, Cash reserve ratio (CRR), Statutory liquidity ratio (SLR), Open market operations, Credit ceiling, Credit authorization scheme, Moral suasion, Selective credit control (SCC).
- The primary functions of a commercial bank include—accepting deposits, and grant of loans and advances.

- Current accounts are basically meant for businessmen for working capital operations and there is no interest on these accounts.
- Savings account holders earn interest on their balance in the accounts. These accounts are flexible in nature.
- Call deposits are maintained by banks with other banks for a period of time.
- Recurring deposit accounts are a special kind of term deposits and are suitable for people who do not have lump sum amount of savings, but are ready to save a small amount every month.
- Fixed deposit account has the depositor investing a lump sum amount for a fixed term, based on his requirement.
- Hybrid or Flexi deposits are a combination of demand and fixed deposits.
- Cash credit is an arrangement wherein the bank allows the borrower to draw amounts upto a specified limit.
- Overdraft is also a credit facility granted by banks. A customer who has a current account with the bank is allowed to withdraw more than the amount of credit balance in his account.
- Discounting of bills is a facility where banks provide short-term finance by making payment of the credit sales before the due date of the bills after deducting a certain rate of discount.
- Retail banking includes customer focus and a wide range of products.
- Private banking basically aims at providing personalized services to selected customers, identified as per their income groups.
- Corporate banking is also called Wholesale banking or Business banking, and is primarily oriented towards corporate.
- Merchant banking/Investment banking are services provided in relation to issue management, advisory services on corporate restructuring, debt restructuring, loan restructuring, etc.
- Universal banking refers to the provision of a wide range of financial services by an organization under one roof.
- E-banking refers to electronic banking.
- Banking Ombudsman Scheme came into force in 2006 by RBI and extends to the whole of India. It applies to all the banking businesses in India. There is independent external machinery for resolving customer grievances in cases where the same are not satisfied with the bank's decision on their complaints.

KEY TERMS

- **Bank** is a commercial institution licensed as a receiver of deposits and giver of loans—both short- and long-term.
- **Commercial banks** are banking institutions that accept deposits and grant short-term loans and advances to their customers.

- **Scheduled bank** is one whose name is included in the Second Schedule to the RBI Act, 1934.
- **Bank rate** is the rate of interest at which a central bank provides the loans and advances to a commercial bank.
- **Repo rate** is the rate at which banks can borrow funds from RBI by selling the securities.
- **Reverse repo rate** is the rate which RBI pays to banks on Deposit of funds with RBI.
- **Cash Reserve Ratio (CRR)** refers to the cash that all banks have to maintain with RBI as a percentage of their deposits.
- **Statutory Liquidity Ratio (SLR)** refers to the liquid reserve requirement of banks maintained in the form of cash-in-hand.
- **Demand deposits** are those which are repayable on demand and do not have a maturity.
- **Time deposits** are repayable only on due maturity.
- **Merchant banking** is any service provided in relation to issue management or advisory services.
- **Universal banking** refers to the provision of a wide range of financial services by an organization, under one roof.
- **Non-Performing Asset (NPA)** is a loan where the interest remains due for at least 90 days.
- **Capital Adequacy Ratio (CRAR)** is the ratio of Capital fund to risk weighted assets.

EXERCISES

Objective Questions

1. **Tick the correct answer:**

(a) The main focus of banks is:
(i) Profitability (ii) Efficiency of operations
(iii) Risk management (iv) All of the above

(b) Demand deposit is payable on
(i) Maturity (ii) Requirement
(iii) Bank's discretion (iv) None of the above

(c) Banking Regulation Act got enacted in:
(i) 1949 (ii) 1947
(iii) 1950 (iv) 1955

(d) Scheduled bank is one which is:
(i) Trader with RBI (ii) Affiliated with RBI
(iii) Associated with RBI (iv) None of the above

(e) DFIs stand for:
   (i) Development Fund Institutions
   (ii) Development Financial Institutions
   (iii) Donation Fund Institutions
   (iv) None of the above

Answers: (a) iv (b) ii (c) i (d) iv (e) ii

2. Fill in the blanks:

(a) RBI Act came out in ....
(b) Interest income is the balance of .... , over ....
(c) .... is a zero interest account.
(d) Loan given by bank is an......... .
(e) CASA stands for ....
(f) Specialised institutions are also called ....
(g) .... is a ratio of liquidity with banks.

Answers:

(a) 1934
(b) Interest income, interest expenses
(c) Current account
(d) Asset
(e) Current account and Savings account
(f) NBSFOs/DFIs
(g) Statutory liquidity ratio

3. True or False

(a) A commercial bank is always scheduled.
(b) Cash reserve ratio is a ratio of liquid reserves with banks.
(c) Cash credit and overdraft are different.
(d) Tier–I is the secondary capital.
(e) Banking Ombudsman Scheme is meant for HNIs.
(f) RTGS is for offline payment.
(g) Capital adequacy ratio is used for testing solvency of banks.

Answers: (a) False (b) False (c) True (d) False
(e) False (f) False (g) True

Short Questions

1. State the different principles for banks.
2. List the key functions of Reserve Bank of India.
3. What are core operations of a bank?
4. Distinguish between Repo rate and Reverse repo rate.
5. Explain universal banking.
6. ABC bank has a dip in capitalization ratio to 7%. What does this mean?
7. What is private banking?

Critical Thinking Questions

1. "Reserve Bank of India acts as promoter and regulator of the Indian banking system". Explain.
2. "Commercial banks are the backbone of banking in India". Justify.
3. "Merchant banking is now an inevitable segment of the banking sector". Examine.
4. "Liberalisation era has been a landmark period in the history of Indian banking". Discuss with examples.
5. "Depositors are the real beneficiaries of the banking system". Critique.
6. "Fixed deposit is blocked money". Examine in the light of emerging banking products for fixed deposits.
7. "Financial system has undergone a significant change over the last twenty years regarding advent of outside participation". Discuss how foreign players have contributed to the existing banking sector in India.

Descriptive Questions

1. Explain the organizational structure of banking industry in India.
2. Discuss the tools of monetary control adopted by RBI.
3. Discuss the different types of deposits offered by banks.
4. What are the various types of banking at global level?
5. Explain the different functions of commercial banks in detail.
6. What are the major challenges faced by public sector banks as compared to private and foreign banks in India?

PROJECT EXERCISE

Analyzing Banking Performance

Take the financial statements of a leading private sector bank for the last two years and analyze its financial performance on the relevant parameters as discussed in the chapter. Comment upon its viability and determine its present standing in the Indian banking industry. Also, throw light on the emerging issues and challenges faced by the bank in the context of foreign participation in the sector.

REVIEW CASE

Wise and Fool's Banking Dilemma

Mrs. Wise and Mr. Fool started their own business of manufacturing candles and lights with a seed capital of ₹5 million. They had a profit of ₹20,000 in the first year out of which the core composition was only 40%. In the second and third year, they had a profit of ₹40,000 and ₹80,000, respectively. Their core composition of profits was still below 50%. The trend seemed to be more or less same in the future as well. In the fourth year, they thought to expand their business. For this, they needed another ₹15 million. To meet the same, they applied for a loan from the bank at 9.5% compounded annual interest. The Indian economy was going through an inflationary phase and this is why RBI had hiked the repo rate from 8.5% to 9%. The present CRR was 5% and the SLR was 24%.

They applied to a nearby bank in the hope that they would get locational advantage in getting the loan. The bank had an eligibility requirement for the borrowers:

- The borrower should be an Indian National.
- In case of a business house, the average net profit for the last three should be minimum ₹30,000.
- Should have sufficient fixed assets, free of charge, to offer as security for the loans.
- The top management of the firm should not have any court case going against them.
- They must have minimum credit rating as prescribed by the bank.

It further said that it would be up to the banks to consider a deserving case of loan despite not fulfilling the above requirements in complete.

Regarding repayment of loan, it stated that if the borrower was not able to pay off within the scheduled time, extension of time for payment might be permitted for a maximum period of 2 years. An interest concession of 0.25% might be provided by the bank, if interest is serviced during the due period without any failure. As a loan applicant, the bank required their financial documents of the last 3 years. Since they did not have an account with the bank, they had to undergo a verification process for the loan. For this, the bank would be charging processing fee. The fee was ₹1,000 on a loan upto ₹5 million. They were under a dilemma whether to take loan due to fixed burden of interest and hypothecation requirements or to use the internal funds they had with them and wait for some more time? One of their relatives advised them to borrow from bank for tax benefits. They were also suggested to go for restructuring of debts in future to reduce the burden of interest payments and to change the bank's PLR. Another relative suggested to borrow but to go for zero EMI in the initial years.

Issues for Discussion

(i) What financial documents did they have to submit?

(ii) How does the Repo rate determine the PLR?

(iii) How does CRR and SLR affect the liquidity of a bank?

(iv) Determine their capacity to repay the interest.

(v) What is restructuring of debts? How does it affect the interest burden and risk element?

(vi) What is zero EMI concept?

(vii) What is hypothecation clause?

(viii) Advise them on the best possible alternative.

REFERENCES

Allen, Franklin and Douglas, Gale (2000), *Comparing Financial Systems,* The MIT Press.

Demirgüç-Kunt, Asli and Huizinga, Harry (1997), "Determinants of commercial bank interest margins and profitability: Some international evidence", *World Bank Policy Research Working Paper No. 1,900.*

Joshi, Vijay and I.M.D., Little (1996), *India's Economic Reforms: 1991–2001,* Oxford: Clarendon Press.

Palfreman, D. and Ford, O. (1985), Elements of Banking 1 and 2, Estover: Macdonald & Evans Publications.

Patil, R.H. (2001), "Broadbasing and deepening the bond market in India", A paper presented at the Asian Development Bank Institute/Wharton Seminar titled *Regulatory Differences between Banks and Securities Markets: Implications for Crisis Prevention and Management*, 26–27 July.

Sinkey, J.F. (2002), *Commercial Bank Financial Management*, PHI Learning, New Delhi.

www.aceanalyser.com

www.adarshco-operativebank.com

www.abecoopbank.com

www.bccbank.coop

www.citycoopbank.com

www.fiuindia.gov.in

www.icicibank.com

www.livemint.com

www.npci.org.in

www.pnbindia.in

www.rbi.org.in

www.sbi.co.in

www.sebi.gov.in

www.yesbank.in

www.yourarticlelibrary.com

CHAPTER 3

Risk Management in Banks

The essence of investment management is the management of risks, not the management of returns.

— **Benjamin Graham**

LEARNING OBJECTIVES

This chapter discusses the following:

- Meaning of risk management
- Types of risks and their management
- Basel norms
- Capital adequacy ratio rationale
- Prudential norms of banking in India
- RBI's guidelines for banking industry regulation

INTRODUCTION

Just like any other business, banks face a myriad of risks. However, given the importance the banking sector has on the entire economy, the risk management weighs heavier than they do on most other industries. Banks must prioritize risk management and need to have a clear, formalized risk management plan in order to stay ahead of the various critical risks they face every day. With proper implementation of a plan, banks ultimately can better allocate time and resources towards key areas of consideration. Risk management in banks goes far beyond compliance, as it serves as a roadmap for improving performance by revealing key dependencies and control effectiveness. In the banking industry, managing risks is the most effective option and critically necessary for internationally serving the financial system in a healthy manner.

Banks not only provide financial services, they also act as a "middleman" in the transactions, and this dual role causes various kinds of risks to the banks. Therefore, there are multiple issues related to risk management process in banking which need to be addressed rationally and systematically, such as: What kind of events can harm banking business and to what extent? What kind of actions should be taken by the institutions in order to manage those risks? The ideal risk management process starts with the identification of the potential losses or risk and continues by assessing or measuring those issues. Risk management in banking has been transformed over the past decade, largely in response to regulations that emerged from the global financial crisis and the fines levied in its wake. But important trends are afoot that suggest risk management will experience even more sweeping change in the next decade. The change expected in the risk function's operating model illustrates the magnitude of what lies ahead. Today, about 50 percent of the function's staff are dedicated to risk-related operational processes such as credit administration, while 15 percent work in analytics. McKinsey research suggests that by 2025, these numbers will be closer to 25 and 40 percent, respectively.[1]

WHAT IS RISK MANAGEMENT?

Risk management in banking is theoretically defined as "the logical development and execution of a plan to deal with potential losses". Usually, the focus of the risk management practices in the banking industry is to manage an institution's exposure to losses or risk and to protect the value of its assets.

In general banking business is regarded as risky business. Economic theory suggests that there are two economic units—*surplus unit* and *deficit unit*—and these economic units prefer to use financial institutions (intermediaries) to transfer the necessary funds to each other. Certainly, this process increases the importance of the financial intermediaries in the economy, but also poses some risks to these institutions. Banks have to usually manage those risks are part of their normal operations. These risks are related to a bank's credits, liquidity, trading, earnings, and solvency issues.

If banks do not address the risks, this can lead to significant losses for the institution and the economy as whole. There have been many banking crises around the world in previous decades. Now, countries have implemented risk management practices to deal with these crises.

The risk management process can be described with the following three steps:

1. Identifying and assessing the potential risk in the banking business.
2. Developing and executing an action plan to deal with and manage these activities that incur potential losses.

1. https://www.mckinsey.com/capabilities/risk-and-resilience/our-insights/the-future-of-bank-risk-management

3. Continuously reviewing and reporting the risk management practices after they have been put into action/operation.

The overall purpose of the risk management process is to evaluate the potential losses or risks for the banks in the future and to take precautions to deal with these potential problems when they occur.[2]

TYPES OF RISKS AND MANAGEMENT

However cautious banks might be in sanctioning loans, and banking practices some losses would always occur. In short, risk is an inherent element of banking industry worldwide. They encounter various types of *financial* and *non-financial risks*. These risks are highly interdependent and one area of risk can have ramifications for a range of other risk categories. Thus, top management of banks should give considerable importance to improve the ability to identify, measure, monitor and control the overall level of risks undertaken.

There are three main categories of risks—*Credit Risk, Market Risk* and *Operational Risk*, depicted in Figure 3.1.

Figure 3.1 Risk chart

1. Credit Risk

Credit Risk is the risk of non-payment by the bank's borrower. There is always a possibility that the borrower would default in his commitments to pay, resulting in losses to the bank. These losses could be in the form of complete default or partial default, or others. This is the reason why credit risk management is an integral

2. Turgut, Tursoy. (2018). Risk management process in banking industry, Munich Personal RePEc *Archive,* 30 April, https://mpra.ub.uni-muenchen.de/86427/1/MPRA_paper_86427.pdf

part of risk management which aims at minimizing the risk and maximizing bank's risk adjusted rate of return by assuming and maintaining credit exposure within the acceptable parameters.

Another variant of credit risk is "counterparty risk". The counterparty risk arises from non-performance of the trading partners. The non-performance may arise from counterparty's refusal/inability to perform due to adverse price movements or from external constraints that were not anticipated by the principal. The counterparty risk is generally viewed as a transient financial risk associated with trading rather than standard credit risk.

Credit risk management[3]

The *management of credit risk* should receive the top management's attention and the process should encompass:

(a) Measurement of risk through credit rating/scoring;
(b) Quantifying the risk through estimating expected loan losses, i.e. the amount of loan losses that bank would experience over a chosen time horizon (through tracking portfolio behaviour over 5 or more years) and unexpected loan losses, i.e. the amount by which actual losses exceed the expected loss (through standard deviation of losses or the difference between expected loan losses and some selected target credit loss quantile);
(c) Risk pricing on a scientific basis; and
(d) Controlling the risk through effective *Loan Review Mechanism* and *portfolio management.*

The credit risk management process should be articulated in the bank's Loan Policy, duly approved by the Board. Each bank should constitute a high level Credit Policy Committee, also called 'Credit Risk Management Committee' or 'Credit Control Committee' etc. to deal with issues relating to credit policy and procedures and to analyse, manage and control credit risk on a bank wide basis.

Credit Risk Management encompasses a host of management techniques, which help the banks in mitigating the adverse impacts of credit risk:

(i) Credit approving authority
(ii) Prudential limits
(iii) Risk rating and pricing
(iv) Portfolio management
(v) Loan review mechanism (LRM)

2. Market Risk

It is the expected loss to bank's earnings and capital due to changes in the market variables. It is the risk that directly affects on/off balance sheet items on account of movements in equity and interest rate markets, currency exchange rates, and commodity prices. Market risk takes the form of:

1. Liquidity risk
2. Interest rate risk

3. Risk Management Systems in Banks, https://rbidocs.rbi.org.in/rdocs/notification/PDFs/9492.pdf

3. Foreign exchange rate (Forex) risk
4. Commodity price and equity price risk

Market risk management[4]

Managing market risk is a comprehensive process of measuring, monitoring and managing liquidity, interest rate, foreign exchange, and equity as well as commodity price risk of a bank using techniques, like *scenario analysis and stress testing.*

Management of market risk should be the major concern of top management of banks. The Boards should clearly articulate market risk management policies, procedures, prudential risk limits, review mechanisms and reporting and auditing systems. The policies should address the bank's exposure on a consolidated basis and clearly articulate the risk measurement systems that capture all material sources of market risk and assess the effects on the bank. The operating prudential limits and the accountability of the line management should also be clearly defined.

The Asset-Liability Management Committee (ALCO) should function as the top operational unit for managing the balance sheet within the performance/risk parameters laid down by the Board.

(i) *Liquidity Risk:* Liquidity planning is an important facet of risk management framework in banks. 'Liquidity' is the ability to efficiently accommodate deposit and other liability decreases, as well as, fund loan portfolio growth and the possible funding of off-balance sheet claims.

The liquidity risk of banks arises from funding of long-term assets by short-term liabilities, thereby making the liabilities subject to rollover or refinancing risk. "Liquidity management" is to put in place an effective liquidity management policy, which should spell out the funding strategies, liquidity planning under alternative scenarios, prudential limits, liquidity reporting/reviewing, etc.

(ii) *Interest Rate Risk:* Interest Rate Risk (IRR) refers to potential impact on Net Interest Income (NII) or Net Interest Margin (NIM) or Market Value of Equity (MVE), caused by unexpected changes in market interest rates.

The management of Interest Rate Risk should be one of the critical components of market risk management in banks. The regulatory restrictions in the past had greatly reduced many of the risks in the banking system. Deregulation of interest rates has, however, exposed them to the adverse impacts of interest rate risk. The NII or NIM of banks is dependent on the movements of interest rates. Any mismatches in the cash flows (fixed assets or liabilities) or repricing dates (floating assets or liabilities), expose banks' NII or NIM to variations. The earning of assets and the cost of liabilities are now closely related to market interest rate volatility.

(iii) *Forex Risk:* Forex risk is the risk that a bank may suffer losses as a result of adverse exchange rate movements during a period in which it has an open position, either spot or forward, or a combination of the two, in an individual foreign currency. In the forex business, banks also face the risk of default of the counterparties or settlement risk.

---

4. *Risk Management Systems in Banks,* https://rbidocs.rbi.org.in.op.cit.

Forex Risk Management Measures include: 1. Set appropriate limits—open positions and gaps. 2. Clear-cut and well-defined division of responsibility between front, middle and back offices. The top management should also adopt the VaR approach to measure the risk associated with exposures. Reserve Bank of India has introduced two statements, viz. Maturity and Position (MAP) and Interest Rate Sensitivity (SIR) for measurement of forex risk exposures. Banks should use these statements for periodical monitoring of forex risk exposures.

3. Operational Risk

Risks due to human error, financial fraud and operational inefficiencies are again a possible threat to the banks. The fiascos of AIG, Lehman Brothers are an example of the losses on account of operational risk. Therefore, *operational risk* is the risk of loss arising from inadequate or failed internal processes, people and systems, and corporate governance or from external events. Generally, operational risk is defined as any risk, which is not categorized as market or credit risk.

Operational risk has some sort of link between credit and market risks. An operational problem with a business transaction could trigger a credit or market risk.

Operational risk management[5]

Managing operational risk is becoming an important feature of sound risk management practices in modern financial markets in the wake of phenomenal increase in the volume of transactions, high degree of structural changes and complex support systems. In order to mitigate this, sound internal control and internal audit systems are required.

There is no uniformity of approach in measurement of operational risk in the banking system. Measuring operational risk requires both estimating the probability of an operational loss event and the potential size of the loss. It relies on risk factor that provides some indication of the likelihood of an operational loss event occurring. The process of operational risk assessment needs to address the likelihood (or frequency) of a particular operational risk occurring, the magnitude (or severity) of the effect of the operational risk on business objectives and the options available to manage and initiate actions to reduce/mitigate operational risk.

Indian banks have so far not evolved any scientific methods for quantifying operational risk.

Box 3.1 presents a brief of ALM.

BOX 3.1: ASSET LIABILITY MANAGEMENT

The "Asset Liability Management" (ALM) is a part of the overall risk management system in the banks. It refers to the examination of all the assets and liabilities simultaneously on a continuous basis with a view to ensure a proper balance between funds mobilization and their deployment with respect to their maturity, cost, yield, and risk exposure.

The risk metric is presented in Figure 3.1.

5. *Risk Management Systems in Banks,* https://rbidocs.rbi.org.in.op.cit.

BASEL NORMS

Basel guidelines refer to broad supervisory standards formulated by the Basel Committee on Banking Supervision (BCBS). This committee was set up in 1974 under the auspices of Bank of International Settlement (BIS). BIS is headquartered in Basel, Switzerland.

Box 3.2 gives an overview of BIS and BCBS.

BOX 3.2: BIS-BCBS

Bank of International Settlement (BIS) set up BCBS, which is a committee of central banks of G-10 countries, with an objective of developing standards and establishing a framework for bank supervision, and for strengthening the financial stability throughout the world.

This set of agreement by the BCBS, which mainly focuses on risks to banks and the financial system are also called *Basel accord*. The purpose of the accord is to ensure that financial institutions have enough capital on account to meet obligations and absorb unexpected losses.

Basel I

In 1988, BCBS introduced the first Basel capital accord, Basel I. It focused on the credit and market risks to calculate the minimum capital adequacy ratio. It requires the assets of banks to be classified in one of the five categories and assigning them appropriate risk weight. Under Basel I, risk weight parameter was fixed at 0, 20, 50, or 100%.

The minimum capital requirement was fixed at 8% of Risk Weighted Assets (RWA). RWA means assets with different risk profiles. *For example,* an asset backed by collateral would carry lesser risks as compared to personal loans, which have no collateral. India adopted Basel I guidelines in 1999.

Basel II

This was developed by BCBS as an aftermath of financial crisis of 1999 spreading from East Asia to Brazil, Russia, and beyond. In 2004, Basel II guidelines were published by BCBS, which were considered to be the refined and reformed versions of Basel I accord. Under Basel II, the Basel committee improved the credit risk calculation with the weight classes for the type of instruments and also added "operational risk" as a third type of risk into the calculation of the minimum capital adequacy ratio calculation. The main objective of Basel II was to keep banks safe by requiring them to match the size of their capital cushion to the riskiness of their loans and securities.

The guidelines were based on three parameters. Banks should maintain a minimum capital adequacy requirement of 8% of risk assets; banks should develop a better risk management system for managing all the three types of risks and increased disclosure requirements; and banks need to mandatorily disclose their risk exposure, etc. to the central bank.

Basel I provided the framework for the method of calculating the necessary capital for banks to compensate for future potential losses, and the Basel II provided and improved the old version by including other risks with the pillar issues. The Basel II provided a three-pillar framework for the risk management procedure. These three pillars are: "a minimum capital requirement", "supervision", and "market discipline". (This is described under Basel III.)

Basel II norms in India were implemented by RBI on 31st March 2009.

Capital structure

Though total minimum regulatory capital required were same in both Basel I and II, i.e. 8% of RWA, there was a distinct qualitative change in the required capital under Basel II accord. The capital required is divided in two categories:

Tier-I: Capital

It is the capital which is first readily available to protect the unexpected losses. It is the core measure of a bank's financial strength from a regulator's point of view.

Tier-I capital consists of:

- Paid-Up Capital (Common Stock), Statutory Reserves and other disclosed free reserves.
- Perpetual Non-Cumulative Preference Shares (PNCPS) eligible for inclusion subject to laws in force from time to time.
- Innovative Perpetual Debt Instruments (IPDI)
- Capital Reserves

Tier-II: Capital

It is the supplementary capital which is second readily available to protect the unexpected losses.

Tier-II capital consists of:

- Undisclosed Reserves
- Revaluation Reserves
- General Provisions and Loss Reserves
- Hybrid Debt Capital Instruments
  - (i) Debt Capital Instruments
  - (ii) Perpetual Cumulative Preference Shares (PCPS)/Redeemable Non-Cumulative Preference Shares (RNCPS)/Redeemable Cumulative Preference Shares (RCPS)
- Subordinated Debt
- Investment Reserve Account

Tier-II capital cannot be more than 100% of total Tier-I capital for the purpose of compliance with the norms.[6]

Basel III

In December 2010, Basel III guidelines were released, which were revised in June 2011.

6. https://rbidocs.rbi.org.in/rdocs/content/pdfs/FBSEIII020512_I.pdf

These guidelines were introduced in response to the financial crisis of 2008. There was a need to further strengthen the system as banks in the developed economies were under-capitalized, over-leveraged and had a greater reliance on short-term funding. Also, the quantity and quality of capital under Basel II tend to be insufficient to avoid any further risk. The basic objective was to improve the banking sector's ability to absorb shocks arising from financial and economic stress, whatever the source, thus reducing the risk of spillover from the financial sector to the real economy.

Key Principles of Basel III

Basel III norms aim at promoting a more sound banking system by focusing on four vital banking parameters, viz. *capital, leverage, risk coverage and liquidity*. The Basel III transitional arrangements intended to cover the period 2017–2028 by the BIS.

1. ***Minimum capital:*** The Basel III accord raised the minimum capital requirements for banks from 2% in Basel II to 4.5% of common equity, as a percentage of the bank's risk-weighted assets. There is also an additional 2.5% buffer capital requirement that brings the total minimum requirement to 7%. As of 2015, the Tier-I capital requirement increased from 4% in Basel II to 6% in Basel III. The 6% includes 4.5% of Common Equity Tier-I and an extra 1.5% of additional Tier-I capital.

2. ***Leverage ratio:*** Basel III introduced a non-risk-based leverage ratio to serve as a backstop to the risk-based capital requirements. Banks are required to hold a leverage ratio in excess of 3%. The non-risk-based leverage ratio is calculated by dividing Tier-I capital by the average total consolidated assets of a bank.

3. ***Liquidity:*** Basel III introduced the usage of two liquidity ratios—the 'Liquidity Coverage Ratio' and the 'Net Stable Funding Ratio'.

The Liquidity Coverage Ratio requires banks to hold sufficient highly liquid assets that can withstand a 30-day stressed funding scenario as specified by the supervisors. The Liquidity Coverage Ratio mandate was introduced in 2015 at only 60% of its stated requirements with expected increase by 10% each year till 2019.

The Net Stable Funding Ratio (NSFR) requires banks to maintain stable funding above the required amount of stable funding for a period of one year of extended stress. The NSFR was designed to address liquidity mismatches.[7]

BOX 3.3: BASEL III IN INDIA

The Basel III capital regulations were implemented in India with effect from April 1, 2013 and have been fully implemented as on October 1, 2021. Banks have to comply with the regulatory limits and minima as prescribed under Basel III capital regulations, on an ongoing basis.[8] Further, on a review, the parallel run and prudential floor for implementation of Basel II vis-à-vis Basel I have been discontinued.[9]

7. https://corporatefinanceinstitute.com/resources/risk-management/basel-iii
8. https://rbidocs.rbi.org.in/rdocs/content/pdfs/12MCBaselIII05042022_A.pdf
9. https://rbidocs.rbi.org.in/rdocs/notification/PDFs/114BI010714FL.pdf

In accordance with Basel III norms, Indian banks will have to maintain their capital adequacy ratio at 9% as against the minimum recommended requirement of 8%.

Under Basel III, with a view to improving the quality of capital, the Tier-I capital predominantly consists of Common Equity. The qualifying criteria for instruments to be included in Additional Tier-I capital outside the Common Equity element as well as Tier-II capital were strengthened.[10]

Basel Framework (Basel Pillars)

Though specific regulatory provisions in individual Basel recommendations, i.e. I, II and III, are different from each other, the "basic pillars" in Basel III continue to be same of the Basel II capital adequacy framework, as follows:

Pillar 1: Minimum capital requirement

- Based on Credit risk, Market risk and Operational risk
- Measured by Standard/Internal models—Internal Rating Based (IRB) approach, Basic Indicator Approach (BIA), The Standardised Approach (TSA) and Advanced Measurement Approach (AMA)

Pillar 2: Supervisory review and evaluation process

- Evaluate bank's capital adequacy strategies
- Certify internal models
- Additional capital adjustments

Pillar 3: Market discipline

- Information disclosures
- Core and Supplementary

CAPITAL ADEQUACY RATIO

Capital adequacy ratio (CAR) is a specialized ratio used by banks to determine the adequacy of their capital keeping in view their risk exposures. Banking regulators require a minimum capital adequacy ratio so as to provide the banks with a cushion to absorb losses before they become insolvent. This improves stability in financial markets and protects deposit-holders.

It is defined as the ratio of "Capital fund/Risk weighted assets". It is the measure of a bank's financial strength expressed by the ratio of its capital (net worth and other funds) to its risk-weighted credit exposure (loans).

As mentioned above, Basel Committee on Banking Supervision of the BIS develops rules related to capital adequacy which member countries are expected to follow. It was first introduced in 1988 under Basel I. This ratio also, also known as the "Cooke Ratio", determines the minimum percentages for the capital to be a safety net for the potential losses from the asset activities.

10. https://rbidocs.rbi.org.in/rdocs/content/pdfs.op.cit.

Capital Adequacy Ratio (CRAR/CAR) is generally calculated as:

$$\frac{\text{Tier-I Capital} + \text{Tier-II Capital}}{\text{Total Risk Weighted Assets}}$$

As per Basel III, bank should compute capital ratio in the following manner[11]:

$$\text{Total Capital (CRAR\#)} = \frac{\text{Eligible Total Capital}}{\text{Credit Risk RWA* + Market Risk RWA + Operational Risk RWA}}$$

* RWA = Risk Weighted Assets

\# Capital to Risk Weighted Asset Ratio

1. *Components of Capital:* Total regulatory capital will consist of the sum of the following categories:

(i) Tier-I Capital (going-concern capital)

   (a) Common Equity Tier-I

   (b) Additional Tier-I

(ii) Tier-II Capital (gone-concern capital)

2. *Limits and Minima*

(i) As a matter of prudence, it has been decided that scheduled commercial banks (excluding LABs and RRBs) operating in India shall maintain a minimum total capital (MTC) of 9% of total risk weighted assets (RWAs), i.e. capital to risk weighted assets (CRAR). This will be further divided into different components as described hereunder, from (ii) to (viii):

(ii) Common Equity Tier-I (CET-I) capital must be at least 5.5% of risk-weighted assets (RWAs) on an ongoing basis.

(iii) Tier-I capital must be at least 7% of RWAs on an ongoing basis. Thus, within the minimum Tier-I capital, Additional Tier-I capital can be admitted maximum at 1.5% of RWAs.

(iv) Total Capital (Tier-I Capital plus Tier-II Capital) must be at least 9% of RWAs on an ongoing basis. Thus, within the minimum CRAR of 9%, Tier-II capital can be admitted maximum up to 2%.

(v) If a bank has complied with the minimum Common Equity Tier-I and Tier-I capital ratios, then the excess Additional Tier-I capital can be admitted for compliance with the minimum CRAR of 9% of RWAs.

(vi) In addition to the minimum Common Equity Tier-I capital of 5.5% of RWAs, banks are also required to maintain a capital conservation buffer (CCB) of 2.5% of RWAs in the form of Common Equity Tier-I capital. Details of operational aspects of CCB have been furnished in paragraph 15. Thus, with full implementation of capital ratios and CCB the capital requirements are summarised as follows:

---

11. https://rbidocs.rbi.org.in/rdocs/content/pdfs/12MCBaselIII05042022.op.cit.

TABLE 3.1 Capital Requirements under Basel III

S. No.	*Regulatory Capital*	*As % to RWAs*
(i)	Minimum Common Equity Tier-I Ratio	5.5
(ii)	Capital Conservation Buffer (comprised of Common Equity)	2.5
(iii)	Minimum Common Equity Tier-I Ratio plus Capital Conservation Buffer [(i) + (ii)]	8.0
(iv)	Addit ional Tier-I Capital	1.5
(v)	Minimum Tier-I Capital Ratio [(i) + (iv)]	7.0
(vi)	Tier-II Capital	2.0
(vii)	Minimum Total Capital Ratio (MTC) [(v) + (vi)]	9.0
(viii)	Minimum Total Capital Ratio plus Capital Conservation Buffer [(vii) + (ii)]	11.5

(vii) For the purpose of reporting Tier-I capital and CRAR, any excess Additional Tier-I (AT-I) capital and Tier-II (T-II) capital will be recognised in the same proportion as that applicable towards minimum capital requirements. This would mean that to admit any excess AT-I and T-II capital, the bank should have excess CET1 over and above 8% (5.5% + 2.5%).

(viii) It would follow from above in cases where the a bank does not have minimum Common Equity Tier-I + capital conservation buffer of 2.5% of RWAs as required but, has excess Additional Tier-I and/or Tier-II capital, no such excess capital can be reckoned towards computation and reporting of Tier-I capital and Total Capital.

'CRAR' Computation

Most banks in India have a capital adequacy of more than 12%. SCBs remained well capitalised, with a CRAR (16.7%) as on March, 2022.[12] A bank with higher capital adequacy is considered safer because if its loans go faulty, it can make up for it from its net worth.

Note: For risk weights Calculation of Capital Charge for Credit Risk as defined by RBI, visit Annex 6, https://rbidocs.rbi.org.in/rdocs/content/pdfs/87MD27102021_AN6.pdf.

EXAMPLE: *CRAR Computation*

Assets	*Value*	*Risk weights (%)*
1. Cash, balances with RBI	100 crores	0
2. Claims on commercial banks	20 crores	20
3. All other investments	10 crores	100
4. Loans and Advances*	50 crores	100
5. Other Assets—Premises, etc.	20 crores	100
Total	**200 crores**	

*These are the loans granted to public sector undertakings of Govt. of India.

12. Financial Institutions, 30 June 2022, https://www.rbi.org.in/Scripts/PublicationReportDetails.aspx?UrlPage=&ID=1209

The bank's Tier-I capital and Tier-II capital are ₹8 crores and ₹5 crores, respectively.

Solution: Bank's total capital = ₹8 crores + ₹5 crores = ₹13 crores.

Assets	*Value (in ₹)*	*Risk weights (%)*	*Value to be taken for CRAR*
1. Cash, balances with RBI	100 crores	0	0
2. Claims on commercial banks	20 crores	20	4 crores
3. All other investments	10 crores	100	10 crores
4. Loans and Advances*	50 crores	100	50 crores
5. Other Assets – Premises, etc.	20 crores	100	20 crores
Total	**200 crores**		**84 crores***

* Risk-weighted exposures = ₹100 crores × 0% + ₹20 crores × 20% + ₹10 crores × 100% + ₹50 crores × 100% + ₹20 crores × 100 = ₹84 crores.

$$\text{Capital Adequacy Ratio} = \frac{₹\ 13 \text{ crores}}{₹\ 84 \text{ crores}} = 15.48\%$$

PRUDENTIAL NORMS OF BANKING IN INDIA

These are the norms laid down by the RBI to ensure that banks are prudent while investing and do not become risky. Commercial banks have to follow these norms to protect the interests of the customers.

In line with the international practices and as per the recommendations made by the Narasimham Committee* on the financial system, the Reserve Bank of India introduced, in a phased manner, prudential norms for **income recognition, asset classification and provisioning pertaining to advances** of the banks in order to have greater consistency and transparency in the published accounts. [RBI's Master Circular on Prudential Norms consolidates instructions on the above matters issued dated April 1, 2022.][13]

The policy of *income recognition* should be objective and based on record of recovery rather than on any subjective considerations.

Likewise, the *classification of assets* of banks has to be done on the basis of objective criteria which would ensure a uniform and consistent application of the norms.

Also, the *provisioning* should be made on the basis of the classification of assets based on the period for which the asset has remained non-performing and the availability of security and the realisable value thereof.

* The Report of Narasimham Committee II is given in Chapter 2 in the Instructor's manual.

13. https://rbidocs.rbi.org.in/rdocs/notification/PDFs/15MCIRACP0104202272A68328898841D488D7CC79E35C5F73.PDF [The complete Master Circular is given in the Instructor's manual.]

I. Basic Guidelines

1. *Non-performing Assets:* An asset, including a leased asset, becomes non-performing when it ceases to generate income for the bank. A non-performing asset (NPA) is a loan or an advance where:

(i) interest and/or instalment of principal remain 'overdue' for a period of more than 90 days in respect of a term loan.
(ii) the account remains 'out of order' in respect of an Overdraft/Cash Credit (OD/CC), as explained below.
(iii) the bill remains overdue for a period of more than 90 days in the case of bills purchased and discounted.
(iv) the instalment of principal or interest thereon remains overdue for two crop seasons for short duration crops.
(v) the instalment of principal or interest thereon remains overdue for one crop season for long duration crops.
(vi) the amount of liquidity facility remains outstanding for more than 90 days, in respect of a securitisation transaction undertaken in terms of the Reserve Bank of India (Securitisation of Standard Assets) Directions, 2021.
(vii) in respect of derivative transactions, the overdue receivables representing positive mark-to-market value of a derivative contract, if these remain unpaid for a period of 90 days from the specified due date for payment.

2. *'Out of Order' status:* A CC/OD account shall be treated as 'out of order' if:

(i) The outstanding balance in the CC/OD account remains continuously in excess of the sanctioned limit/drawing power for 90 days, or
(ii) The outstanding balance in the CC/OD account is less than the sanctioned limit/drawing power but there are no credits continuously for 90 days, or the outstanding balance in the CC/OD account is less than the sanctioned limit/drawing power but credits are not enough to cover the interest debited during the previous 90 days period.

3. *'Overdue' status:* Any amount due to the bank under any credit facility is 'overdue' if it is not paid on the due date fixed by the bank. The borrower accounts shall be flagged as overdue by the banks as part of their day-end processes for the due date, irrespective of the time of running such processes.

II. Income Recognition

1. *Income Recognition Policy:* The policy of income recognition has to be objective and based on the record of recovery. Therefore, the banks should not charge and take to income account interest on any NPA. This will apply to Government guaranteed accounts also.

However, interest on advances against *Term Deposits, National Savings Certificates (NSCs), Kisan Vikas Patras (KVPs) and life insurance policies* may be taken to income account on the due date, provided adequate margin is available in the accounts.

Fees and commissions earned by the banks as a result of renegotiations or rescheduling of outstanding debts should be recognized on an accrual basis over the period of time covered by the renegotiated or rescheduled extension of credit.

In cases of loans where moratorium has been granted for repayment of interest, income may be recognized on accrual basis for accounts which continue to be classified as 'standard'.

Income recognition norms for loans towards projects under implementation involving deferment of DCCO shall be subject to the prescribed instructions and that for loans against gold ornaments and jewellery for non-agricultural purposes shall be subject to the prescribed instructions.

- On Accrual Basis, if the asset is Standard
- On Cash Basis if the asset is Substandard

2. *Reversal of income:* If any advance, including bills purchased and discounted, becomes NPA, the entire interest accrued and credited to income account in the past periods, should be reversed if the same is not realised. This will apply to Government guaranteed accounts also.

If loans with moratorium on payment of interest (permitted at the time of sanction of the loan) become NPA after the moratorium period is over, the capitalized interest, if any, corresponding to the interest accrued during such moratorium period need not be reversed.

In respect of NPAs, fees, commission and similar income that have accrued should cease to accrue in the current period and should be reversed with respect to past periods, if uncollected.

Leased Assets—The *finance charge* component of finance income [as defined in 'AS 19 Leases'] on the leased asset which has accrued and was credited to income account before the asset became non-performing, and remaining unrealised, should be reversed or provided for in the current accounting period.

III. Asset Classification

1. *Categories of NPAs:* Banks are required to classify non-performing assets further into the following three categories based on the period for which the asset has remained non-performing and the realisability of the dues:

(i) Substandard Assets
(ii) Doubtful Assets
(iii) Loss Assets

Substandard Assets

With effect from March 31, 2005, a substandard asset would be one, *which has remained NPA for a period less than or equal to 12 months.* Such an asset will have well defined credit weaknesses that jeopardise the liquidation of the debt and are characterised by the distinct possibility that the banks will sustain some loss, if deficiencies are not corrected.

Doubtful Assets

With effect from March 31, 2005, an asset would be classified as doubtful *if it has remained in the substandard category for a period of 12 months.* A loan classified as doubtful has all the weaknesses inherent in assets that were classified as substandard, with the added characteristic that the weaknesses make collection or liquidation in full,—on the basis of currently known facts, conditions and values—highly questionable and improbable.

Loss Assets

A loss asset is one *where loss has been identified by the bank or internal or external auditors or the RBI inspection, but the amount has not been written off wholly.* In other words, such an asset is considered uncollectible and of such little value that its continuance as a bankable asset is not warranted although there may be some salvage or recovery value.

So, a Standard Asset is a non-NPA account.

IV. Provisioning

In conformity with the prudential norms, provisions should be made on the non-performing assets on the basis of classification of assets into prescribed categories:

Loss Assets

Loss assets should be written off. If loss assets are permitted to remain in the books for any reason, 100% of the outstanding should be provided for.

Doubtful Assets

100% of the extent to which the advance is not covered by the realisable value of the security to which the bank has a valid recourse and the realisable value is estimated on a realistic basis.

Regarding the secured portion, provision may be made on the following basis, at the rates ranging from 25% to 100% of the secured portion, depending upon the period for which the asset has remained doubtful:

Period for which the advance has remained in 'doubtful' category	*Provision requirement (%)*
Upto one year	25
One to three years	40
More than three years	100

Substandard Assets

A general provision of 15% on total outstanding should be made without making any allowance for ECGC guarantee cover and securities available.

Standard Assets

(i) The provisioning requirements for all types of standard assets are given below. Banks should make general provision for standard assets at the following rates for the funded outstanding on global loan portfolio basis:

(a) Farm Credit to agricultural activities, individual housing loans and Small and Micro Enterprises (SMEs) sectors at 0.25%;
(b) Advances to Commercial Real Estate (CRE) Sector at 1.00%;
(c) Housing loans extended at teaser rates;
(d) Restructured advances;
(e) Advances restructured and classified as standard at 5%;
(f) All other loans and advances not included in (a)–(f) above at 0.40%.

(ii) The provisions on standard assets should not be reckoned for arriving at net NPAs.

GUIDELINES ISSUED BY RBI FOR THE REGULATION OF BANKING INDUSTRY

1. *Management oversight, policy/operational guidelines:* The management of a primary dealer should bear the primary responsibility for ensuring maintenance of appropriate standards of conduct and adherence to proper procedures by the entity. Primary Dealers (PD) should frame and implement suitable policy guidelines on securities transactions. Operational procedures and controls in relation to the day-to-day business operations should also be worked out and put in place to ensure that operations in securities are conducted in accordance with sound and acceptable business practices. With the approval of respective Boards, the PDs should clearly lay down broad objectives to be followed while undertaking transactions in securities on their own account and on behalf of clients. They should precisely define the authority to put through deals, and the procedure to be followed while putting through deals. PDs should adhere to prudential exposure limits, policy regarding dealings with brokers, systems for management of various risks, guidelines for valuation of the portfolio and the reporting systems. While laying down such policy guidelines, the Primary Dealers should strictly observe RBI's instructions on the following:

- Ready forward deals
- Transactions through SGL account
- Internal controls/Risk management system
- Dealings through brokers
- Accounting standards
- Audit, review and reporting

(*Any other instructions issued from time to time.*)

The internal policy guidelines on securities transactions framed by the PD, duly certified by its management to the effect that they are in accordance with the RBI guidelines and have been put in place, may be perused by the Statutory Auditors and commented upon as to the conformity of the guidelines with the instructions/guidelines issued by RBI. The effectiveness of the policy and operational guidelines should be periodically evaluated.

2. Prohibition of short selling of securities: The primary dealers should not put through any sale transaction without actually holding the security in its portfolio, i.e. under no circumstances, a PD should hold an oversold position in any security.

3. ***Concurrent audit of securities transactions:*** Securities transactions should be separately subjected to a concurrent audit by internal/external auditors to the extent of 100% and the results of the audit should be placed before the CEO (Chief Executive Officer)/CMD (Chief Managing Director) of the PD once every month. The compliance wing should monitor the compliance on an ongoing basis, with the laid down policies and prescribed procedures, the applicable legal and regulatory requirements, the deficiencies pointed out in the audits and should report directly to the management.

4. ***All problem exposures where security of doubtful value, diminution of value to be provided for:*** which are not backed by any security or backed by security of doubtful value should be fully provided for.

5. ***Provision for suits under litigation:*** Even in cases where a PD has filed suit against another party for recovery, such exposures should be evaluated and provisions should be made to the satisfaction of auditors.

6. ***Claims against the PD to be taken note of and provisions made:*** Any claim against the PD should also be taken note of and provisions should be made to the satisfaction of auditors.

7. ***Problem exposures to be reflected clearly in the Profit and Loss Account:*** The profit and loss account should reflect the problem exposures, if any, as also the effect of valuation of portfolio, as per the instructions issued by the RBI, if any, from time to time. The report of the statutory auditors should contain a certification to this effect.

8. ***Business through brokers and contract limits for approved brokers:*** A disproportionate part of the business should not be transacted through only one or a few brokers. PDs should fix aggregate contract limits for each of the approved brokers. A limit of 5%, of total transactions (both purchase and sales) entered into by a PD during a year should be treated as the aggregate upper contract limit for each of the approved brokers. This limit should cover both—the business initiated by a PD, and the business offered/brought to the PD by a broker. PDs should ensure that the transactions entered into through individual brokers during a year normally do not exceed this limit. However, the norm would not be applicable to PD's dealings through other Primary Dealers.

9. ***Investments in and Underwriting of Shares, Debentures and PSU Bonds and Investments in Units of Mutual Funds Guidelines:*** PDs should formulate, within the above parameters, their own internal guidelines, as approved by their Board of Directors, on securities transactions either by directly subscribing or through secondary market with counter-party or counter-party group, including norms to ensure that excessive exposure against any single counter-party or group or product is avoided and that due attention is given to the maturity structure and the quality of such transactions. The PDs will also need to take into account the fact that such securities are subject to risk weight and that necessary depreciation has to be fully provided for.

10. ***Material changes in circumstances:*** The PDs should report any material changes in circumstances such as change in the ownership structure, business profile, organisation, etc. affecting the conditions of licensing as PD to the RBI immediately.

CASE STUDY

Risk Management @ Bandhan Bank

The banking sector is one of the important sectors for the economic and social development of a country. The key area that makes up an effective banking organization is its 'Risk Management'.

Bandhan Bank Limited started its banking operations on August 23, 2015 and got listed on March 29th, 2018 on NSE and BSE. In accordance with Basel III Disclosures as on March 31, 2022, Bandhan Bank Limited aims to operate within an effective risk management framework to actively manage all the material risks faced by the Bank, in a manner consistent with the Bank's risk appetite.

Following is the Capital Adequacy status and Risk Process and Governance of Bandhan Bank.

1. *Capital Adequacy:* The Bank has a process for assessing its overall capital adequacy as per its risk profile and strategy for maintaining its capital levels. The objective is to ensure that the Bank has adequate capital to support all risks inherent to its business and an appropriate capital buffer based on its business activities. The Bank identifies, assesses and manages comprehensively all risks that it is exposed to through sound governance and control practices, robust risk management framework and an elaborate process for capital calculation and planning.

In line with the Basel III guidelines which are effective since April 01, 2013, the Bank has calculated its capital ratios as per the extant RBI guidelines. The main focus of Basel III norms is on the quality and quantity of Tier-I capital and these regulatory requirements are currently met with the quantum of capital available with the Bank. The Pillar I Risk Weighted Assets (RWA) Calculation covers the following risks:

(i) Credit Risk
(ii) Market Risk
(iii) Operational Risk

As on March 31, 2022, the Bank had a total capital of ₹18,234.23 crore, out of which Tier-I capital stood at ₹17,136.82 crore. The Capital to Risk Assets Ratio (CRAR) of the Bank stood at 20.10% against regulatory requirement of 11.50%. The Bank has in place the Internal Capital Adequacy Assessment Process (ICAAP) wherein, all risks relevant to the bank are identified and the risk factors are stressed to measure the capital requirement for such risk.

2. *Risk Exposure and Assessment:* The Bank follows calculated risk-taking, where risks are known, and are within the risk limits arising from the Board approved risk appetite. Also while evaluating the risks, the associated returns are also considered.

3. *Risk Governance Model:* The Bank has established a robust system for directing and controlling the management of various risks within and across the Bank. This governance model defines three key roles:

- Business that take, manage, and assess risk;
- Risk Management that provide risk appetite, governing policies, analysis, monitoring, and reporting; and
- Internal Audit that provide independent inspection and assurance.

4. ***Risk Governance Framework:*** The Bank is of the view that the role of risk management should not be biased by consideration of profits or performance evaluation and should be in line with regulatory guidelines and international good practices. The risk governance framework has been designed taking this into account. The risk governance framework provides guidance on adopting a more holistic approach to manage risk, emphasizing four related elements:

- Developing the corporate risk profile;
- Establishing a risk function that manages risk in an integrated manner;
- Practicing integrated risk management; and
- Ensuring continuous risk monitoring.

The risk management system of the Bank is well supported by the detailed roles and responsibilities within the Bank.

Source: https://bandhanbank.com/sites/default/files/202206/BaselIII_Disclosures_as_on_March_31st_2022.pdf

POINTS TO REMEMBER

- Risk management in banking is defined as "the logical development and execution of a plan to deal with potential losses".
- Risk management in banks is a process to mitigate credit risk, market risk and operational risk.
- Credit risk is the risk of non-payment by the bank's borrower.
- Credit risk management encompasses a host of management techniques, which help the banks in mitigating the adverse impacts of credit risk: *(i) Credit approving authority, (ii) Prudential limits, (iii) Risk rating and pricing, (iv) Portfolio management, and (v) Loan review mechanism (LRM).*
- Market risk is the expected loss to bank's earnings and capital due to changes in the market variables.
- Managing market risk is a comprehensive process of measuring, monitoring and managing *liquidity risk, interest rate risk (IRR), and foreign exchange risk, and commodity price and equity price risk.*
- Operational risk is the risk due to human error, financial fraud and operational inefficiencies.
- There is no uniformity of approach in measurement of operational risk in the banking system. Indian banks have so far not evolved any scientific methods for quantifying operational risk.
- The Asset Liability Management (ALM) is a part of the overall risk management system in the banks. It refers to the examination of all the assets and liabilities simultaneously on a continuous basis with a view to ensure a proper balance between mobilization of funds and their deployment.

- Basel norms refer to broad supervisory standards formulated by the Basel Committee on Banking Supervision (BCBS).
- Basel I was introduced in 1988. It focused on credit and market risks. The minimum capital requirement was fixed at 8% of Risk Weighted Assets (RWA). India adopted Basel I guidelines in 1999.
- Basel II commenced in 2004. The guidelines were based on three parameters. Banks should maintain a minimum capital adequacy requirement of 8% of risk assets; banks were required to develop and use better risk management techniques in monitoring and managing all the three types of risks; and increased disclosure requirements.
- The capital required under Basel II is divided into Tier-I capital and Tier-II capital
- Basel III guidelines were released in 2010. These guidelines were introduced in response to the financial crisis of 2008. In accordance with Basel III norms, Indian banks will have to maintain their capital adequacy ratio at 9% as against the minimum recommended requirement of 8%.
- The "basic pillars" in Basel III continue to be same of the Basel II capital adequacy framework, comprising of 3 Pillars.
- Capital Adequacy Ratio is defined as the ratio of Capital fund/risk weighted assets. It is the measure of a bank's financial strength expressed by the ratio of its capital to its risk-weighted credit exposure (loans). The Reserve Bank of India (RBI) currently prescribes a minimum capital of 9% of risk-weighted assets, which is higher than the internationally prescribed capital of 8%.
- Prudential norms are norms laid down by the RBI to ensure that banks are prudent while investing and do not become risky.
- Non-performing Asset is an asset which ceases to generate income for the bank for at least a quarter.
- Income recognition is done on accrual-basis if the asset is Standard, and on cash-basis, if the asset is Substandard.
- Banks are required to classify non-performing assets into three categories based on the period for which the asset has remained non-performing and the realisability of the dues: (i) Substandard Assets, (ii) Doubtful Assets, and (iii) Loss Assets.
- Provisioning Norms are—1. Loss assets: Loss assets should be written off. 2. Doubtful assets: 100% of the extent to which the advance is not covered by the realisable value of the security. 3. Substandard assets: Provision of 15% on total outstanding. 4. Standard assets: General provision at the standard rates for the funded outstanding on global loan portfolio basis.

KEY TERMS

- **Risk Management** refers to the logical development and execution of a plan to deal with potential losses.

- **Credit Risk** is the risk of non-payment by the bank's borrower.
- **Market Risk** is the expected loss to bank's earnings and capital due to changes in the market variables.
- **Liquidity Risk** is from funding of long-term assets by short-term liabilities, thereby making the liabilities subject to rollover or refinancing risk.
- **Interest Rate Risk (IRR)** refers to potential impact on Net Interest Income (NII) or Net Interest Margin (NIM) or Market Value of Equity (MVE), caused by unexpected changes in market interest rates.
- **Foreign Exchange Rate (Forex) Risk** is the risk that a bank may suffer losses as a result of adverse exchange rate movements during a period.
- **Operational Risk** is the risk of loss arising from inadequate or failed internal processes, people and systems, and corporate governance or from external events.
- **Asset Liability Management (ALM)** refers to the examination of all the assets and liabilities simultaneously on a continuous basis with a view to ensure a proper balance between funds mobilization and their deployment.
- **Capital Adequacy Ratio (CRAR)** is the ratio of Capital fund to risk weighted assets.
- **Non-performing Asset (NPA)** is a loan where the interest remains due for at least 90 days.

EXERCISES

Objective Questions

1. Tick the correct answer:

(a) There are three main categories of risks—Credit risk, Market risk, and:

(i) Quality risk (ii) Parity risk
(iii) Operational risk (iv) None of the above

(b) Interest Rate Risk impacts Net Interest:

(i) Income (ii) Value
(iii) Factor (iv) Index

(c) Basel III introduced a:

(i) Financial ratio (ii) Leverage ratio
(iii) Physical ratio (iv) Operation Ratio

(d) Indian banks will have to maintain their capital adequacy ratio at:

(i) 7% (ii) 7.5%
(iii) 8% (iv) 9%

(e) How many Basel Pillars are there?

(i) 1 (ii) 2
(iii) 3 (iv) 4

Answers: (a) iii (b) i (c) ii (d) iv (e) iii

2. Fill in the blanks:

(a) Basel III guidelines got released in ....
(b) The Basel III capital regulations were implemented in India in ....
(c) Tier-II is the .... capital.
(d) Income recognition is done on Accrual Basis, if the asset is ....
(e) NPAS are classified into .... categories.
(f) .... assets should be written off.

Answers:

(a) 2010
(b) 2013
(c) Secondary
(d) Standard
(e) Three
(f) Loss

2. True or False

(a) Operational risk has link between credit and market risks.
(b) Bank of International Settlement is headquartered in Paris.
(c) Basel II divides the capital in two categories.
(d) CAR is also known as the "Cooke Ratio".
(e) Most banks in India have a capital adequacy of more than 12%.
(f) An asset becomes non-performing when it ceases to generate income for the bank.
(g) The policy of income recognition has to be based on the record of recovery.

Answers: (a) True (b) False (c) True (d) True (e) True
(f) True (g) True

Short Questions

1. Define risk management in banks?
2. State the different types of risk exposures for banks.
3. What do you mean by Asset Liability Management in a bank?
4. What are capital adequacy norms for banks?
5. What is an NPA?
6. State the different types of capital requirement under Basel III norms.

Critical Thinking Questions

1. "Risk management in banks is one of the most technical area". Do you agree? Given reason.
2. "Banks not only provide financial services, they also act as a "middleman" in the transactions". Discuss their dual role performance.
3. "Market risk is a culmination of various sub-categories of risks". Elaborate.

4. "Operational risk management is an internal issue of the banks". Justify.
5. "Financial risk management in banking industry has become more systematic than before". Throw light on this.
6. "Capital adequacy ratio is an important tool in the risk management systems of banks". Prove.

Descriptive Questions

1. Explain the process of risk management in banks.
2. What are the different types of risks faced by banks worldwide? Discuss in detail.
3. How Basel III is an improvement over older Basel norms? Critique.
4. Discuss in brief, the prudential norms relating to banks.
5. Outline the main guidelines of RBI for the regulation of banking industry.
6. How financial soundness and credibility of banks were improved by RBI as part of risk management systems?
7. Can India's banking sector be categorized as risk free sector? Examine.

PROJECT EXERCISE

Assessment of Risk in Banking

Study the Basel III norms and analyse their current progress about how they attempt to reduce the gap in conflicting point of views between the existing banking practices at the global level, and in India. Determine the implementation of resolutions adopted by the Indian banks thereof, focussing on different aspects of risk assessment, keys for effective risk management, and the challenges and impact of implementing them.

REVIEW CASE

IFB's Data Solution

Indian Forex Bank (IFB) was founded on 10th February 1975 with the main objective of specializing in foreign exchange business in banking, and to take the Bank across the globe. It had migrated its different core banking systems at IFB New York, London, Singapore, and Hong Kong and offices to a new Core Banking Solution (CBS). The 4 foreign offices of the bank hence intended to engage a technology partner for implementing a Data Archival and Retrieval Solution for archiving data of its existing Core Banking and other legacy systems. This was a part of the Risk Management process of the bank, as directed by the top management.

IFB planned to implement the archival solution at its primary data-centre at Mumbai, India. It selected Techno's FinSol™ Data Archival & Retrieval Solution (FinDAR™) for implementing it separately for each overseas branch. In India, with the help of new model, they migrated from earlier CBS to new CBS. This ensured that separate access was maintained for respective foreign branches and would also take care of any local data protection requirements holistically. The bank could now fulfill its commitment to sound banking system internally and offering more hi-tech advanced services to the customers.

Issues for Discussion

(i) What is the key issue with IFB?
(ii) Why did IBF decide to move to new CBS?
(iii) How did the new model help the bank in risk management?
(iv) Discuss the benefits post implementation of FinDAR model.
(v) Explain the role of data management in overall risk managements of banks.

REFERENCES

Allen, Franklin and Douglas, Gale (2000), *Comparing Financial Systems,* The MIT Press.

Caprio, Gerald and Maria Soledad Martinez-Peria (2000), "Avoiding disaster: policies to reduce the risk of banking crises", Discussion Paper, Egyptian Center for Economic Studies, Egypt.

Sinkey, J.F. (2002), *Commercial Bank Financial Management*, PHI Learning, New Delhi.

Turgut, Tursoy. (2018). Risk management process in banking industry, *Munich Personal RePEc Archive,* 30 April, https://mpra.ub.uni-muenchen.de/86427/1/MPRA_paper_86427.pdf

www.bandhanbank.com

www.corporatefinanceinstitute.com

www.mckinsey.com

www.rbi.org

CHAPTER

4

Non-Banking Financial Companies

As a company, we have to very transparent. We are in a business very related to finance, and I want this company to last long, and I want this company to be audited by everyone.

— Jack Ma

LEARNING OBJECTIVES

This chapter discusses the following:

- Concept and scope of non-banking financial company
- Classification of non-banking financial companies
- Distinction between bank and non-banking financial company
- Rationale of non-banking financial companies
- Regulation of non-banking financial companies, including regulatory structure, prudential and governance guidelines
- Issues and challenges of non-banking financial companies

INTRODUCTION

Non-Banking Financial Companies (NBFC) play a crucial role in the economy, offering their financial services in urban as well as rural areas; varying from granting loans for growth of new ventures to monetary advices like chit-reserves and insurance. They supplement the role of the banking sector in meeting the increasing financial needs of the corporate sector, delivering credit to the unorganized sector and to small local borrowers. Hence, they have become a very important part of our nation's Gross

Domestic Product and alone count for 12.5% raise in Gross Domestic Product of the country.[1]

Most people prefer NBFCs over banks on account of better efficiency and flexibility in meeting their financial requirements. Many of them experiment with their products too and therefore find a favour with the consumers. But, there is a risk element attached to them as they are not fully regulated like banks. Most of these NBFCs are involved in high-risk lending, and they often lend to small and medium-sized businesses, which are classified as high-risk assets. As of October 01, 2022, there were 9,506 non-banking financial companies (NBFCs) registered with the Reserve Bank of India[2]. In December, RBI released a list of 16 upper layer non-banking finance companies (NBFC-ULs) that must adhere to enhanced regulation. This list included names, like: *LIC Housing Finance, Bajaj Finance, Mahindra and Mahindra Financial Services, Shriram Transport, Tata Sons, L&T Finance, Indiabulls Housing Finance, Piramal Capital and Housing Finance, and others.*[3]

NON-BANKING FINANCIAL COMPANY: CONCEPT AND SCOPE

Non-Banking Financial Companies (NBFC) are entities that provide financial services and banking facilities but do not meet the legal definition of a Bank, though they are covered under the Banking regulations laid down by the Reserve Bank of India. NBFCs are financial intermediaries engaged in the business of accepting deposits and delivering credit and play an important role in channelizing the scarce financial resources to capital formation.

"A Non-Banking Financial Company (NBFC) is a company which is registered under the Companies Act, 1956 and engaged in the business of loans and advances, acquisition of shares/stocks/bonds/debentures/securities issued by Government or local authority or other marketable securities of a like nature, leasing, hire-purchase, insurance business, chit business. It also includes a 'residuary non-banking company', i.e. Non-banking institution which is a company and has principal business of receiving deposits under any scheme or arrangement in one lump sum or in instalments by way of contributions or in any other manner."[4]

Financial activity as "principal business" for NBFC

Financial activity as principal business means:

(a) when a company's financial assets constitute more than 50 per cent of the total assets, and

(b) income from financial assets constitute more than 50 per cent of the gross income.

A company which fulfils both these criteria will be registered as NBFC by RBI.

1. https://www.nelito.com/blog/the-top-10-nbfcs-in-india.html, March 2021.
2. NBFCs, https://rbi.org.in/Scripts/BS_NBFCList.aspx
3. https://www.livemint.com/industry/banking/rbi-names-16-leading-nbfcs-in-its-upper-layer-list-11664561762908.html, September 30, 2022.
4. https://www.rbi.org.in/Scripts/FAQView.aspx?Id=92.

So, NBFC is a financial institution which is into the business of lending or investment or collecting money under any scheme or arrangement. It excludes any institution which undertakes its principal business as agriculture activity, industrial activity, trading and purchase or sale of immovable properties.

It may also be mentioned that Mortgage Guarantee Companies have been notified as Non-Banking Financial Companies under Section 45 I (f) (iii) of the RBI Act, 1934.

BOX 4.1: SYSTEMICALLY IMPORTANT NBFCs

NBFCs whose asset size is of ₹500 cr or more as per last audited balance sheet are considered as 'systemically important NBFCs'. The activities of such NBFCs are considered to have an impact on the financial stability of the overall economy.

Registration of NBFCs

In accordance with the Section 45-IA of the RBI Act, 1934, every non-banking financial company to commence or carry on business of a non-banking financial institution must satisfy the following conditions:

(i) it should be a company registered under the Companies Act, 1956 or under Companies Act, 2013,

(ii) it should obtain a certificate of registration from the Bank, and

(iii) it must have a 'net owned funds' of ₹ two crore.

BOX 4.2: OWNED FUND AND NET OWNED FUNDS

'Owned Fund' means sum total of the paid-up equity capital, convertible preference shares, free reserves, balance in share premium account and capital reserves representing surplus arising out of sale proceeds of asset. It excludes reserves created by revaluation of asset, after deducting therefrom accumulated balance of loss, deferred revenue expenditure and other intangible assets.

'Net Owned Fund' is Owned Fund minus investments of such company in shares of its subsidiaries, companies in the same group and all other NBFCs, and the book value of debentures, bonds, outstanding loans and advances including hire purchase and lease finance made to and deposits with subsidiaries and companies in the same group, to the extent it exceeds 10% of the owned fund.

However, certain categories of NBFCs which are regulated by other regulators are exempted from the requirement of registration with RBI:

(i) Venture capital fund/Merchant banking companies/Stock exchanges/Stock-broking companies registered with SEBI,

(ii) Insurance company holding a valid certificate of registration issued by IRDA,

(iii) Nidhi companies as notified under Section 620A of the Companies Act, 1956,

(iv) Chit companies as defined in clause (b) of Section 2 of the Chit Funds Act, 1982.[5]

5. https://www.rbi.org.in/Scripts/FAQView.aspx?Id=92.

The Core Investment Companies with asset size of less than ₹100 crore, and those with asset size of ₹100 crore and above but not accessing public funds are exempted from registration with the RBI.[6]

CLASSIFICATION OF NON-BANKING FINANCIAL COMPANIES

In accordance with RBI's regulation, NBFCs are broadly categorized in terms of the following:

(a) *The type of liabilities:*

(i) Deposit-taking NBFCs (NBFCs-D) and
(ii) Non-Deposit-taking NBFCs (NBFCs-ND)

Non-deposit NBFCs by their size can be further classified into "systemically important" (NBFCs-ND-SI) and "non-systematically important"/other non-deposit holding companies (NBFCs-ND). NBFCs-ND-SI are with asset size more than ₹500 crore and NBFCs-ND are with asset size less than ₹500 crore.

The NBFCs-ND-SI category accounted for around 86 per cent of the total assets of the NBFC sector at end-March 2022. Although the category is largely populated by non-government companies, a few large government-owned NBFCs hold a substantial share of the assets of the NBFCs-ND-SI sub-sector.[7]

Figure 4.1 depicts an overview of the non-banking financial companies in India regulated by RBI, and categorised "based on liabilities".

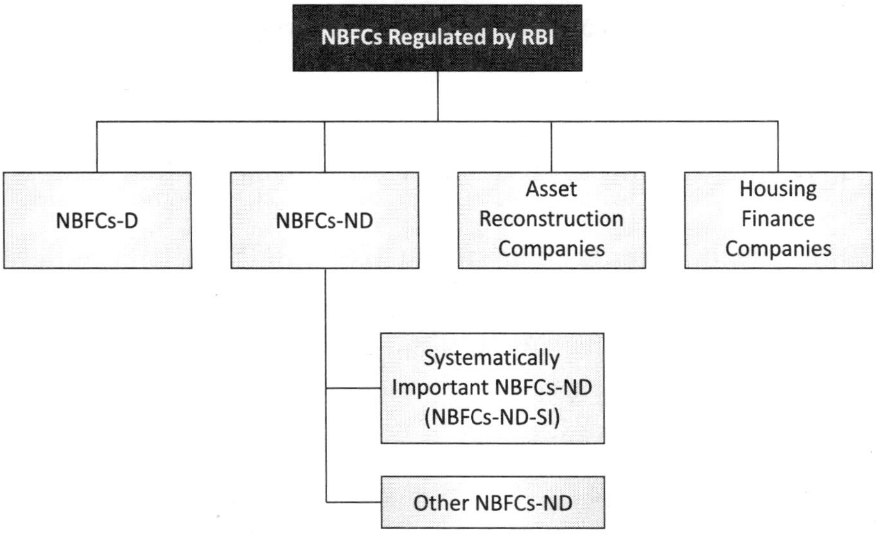

Figure 4.1 Structural of NBFCs under RBI's Regulation

6. https://www.rbi.org.in/op. cit.
7. https://rbidocs.rbi.org.in/rdocs/Publications/PDFs/0RTP20212225730A6FC708454BB270AC1705CCF178.PDF

(b) *The kind of activity they conduct:* The different types of NBFCs regulated by RBI, and classified on the "basis of activity" are explained below.

1. **Investment and Credit Company (ICC):** It means a financial institution carrying on as its principal business of providing finance whether by making loans or advances or otherwise for any activity. It is primarily into lending and investment.

   Examples: Bajaj Finance Ltd. and Sundaram Finance Ltd.

2. **NBFC-Infrastructure Finance Company (NBFC-IFC):** It is a non-banking finance company which finances the infrastructure sector, and
   (a) which deploys at least 75 per cent of its total assets in infrastructure loans,
   (b) has a minimum Net Owned Funds of ₹300 crore,
   (c) has a minimum credit rating of 'A' or equivalent, and
   (d) a CRAR of 15%.

   Examples: Indian Railway Finance Corporation Ltd. and Power Finance Corporation Ltd.

3. **Core Investment Company (CIC):** It refers to a financial institution which carries on as its principal business of the acquisition of securities. It comprises of investment in equity shares, preference shares, debt, or loans of group companies.

   Examples: Bandhan Financial Services Ltd. and Equitas Holdings Ltd.

4. **NBFC-Infrastructure Debt Fund (NBFC-IDF):** NBFC-IDF is a company registered as NBFC to facilitate the flow of long-term debt into post commencement operations in infrastructure projects which have completed at least one year of satisfactory performance. IDF-NBFC raise resources through issue of Rupee or Dollar denominated bonds of minimum 5 year maturity.

   Examples: Kotak Infrastructure Debt Fund Limited and L&T Infra Debt Fund Limited.

5. **NBFC-Micro Finance Institution (NBFC-MFI):** NBFC-MFI is a non-deposit taking NBFC providing collateral free small ticket loans to economically disadvantaged groups. It has not less than 85% of its assets in the nature of qualifying assets which satisfy the following criteria:
   - loan disbursed by an NBFC-MFI to a borrower with a rural household annual income not exceeding ₹1,00,000 or urban and semi-urban household income not exceeding ₹1,60,000;
   - loan amount does not exceed ₹50,000 in the first cycle and ₹1,00,000 in subsequent cycles;
   - total indebtedness of the borrower does not exceed ₹1,00,000;
   - tenure of the loan not to be less than 24 months for loan amount in excess of ₹15,000 with prepayment without penalty;
   - loan to be extended without collateral;

- aggregate amount of loans, given for income generation, is not less than 50 per cent of the total loans given by the MFIs;
- loan is repayable on weekly, fortnightly or monthly instalments at the choice of the borrower.

Examples: Madura Micro Finance Limited and Sahayog Microfinance Limited.

6. **NBFC-Factor:** NBFC-F is engaged in the business of factoring. It deals with acquisition of receivables of an assignor or extending loans against the security interest of the receivables at a discount. The financial assets in the factoring business should constitute at least 50 per cent of its total assets and its income derived from factoring business should not be less than the 50 per cent of its gross income.

   Examples: IFCI Factors Ltd. and Canbank Factors Ltd.

7. **NBFC-Non-Operative Financial Holding Company (NBFC-NOFHC):** It is financial institution through which promoter / promoter groups will be permitted to set up a new bank. It's a wholly-owned Non-Operative Financial Holding Company (NOFHC) which will hold the bank as well as all other financial services companies regulated by RBI or other financial sector regulators, to the extent permissible under the applicable regulatory prescriptions.

   Examples: IDFC Financial Holding Company Limited and Bandhan Financial Holdings Limited.

8. **Mortgage Guarantee Company (MGC):** It is financial institution whose at least 90% of the business turnover is mortgage guarantee business or at least 90% of the gross income is from mortgage guarantee business and net owned fund is ₹ 100 crore.

9. **NBFC-Account Aggregator (NBFC-AA):** It is into collecting and providing information about a customer's financial assets in a consolidated, organised, and retrievable manner to the customer or others as specified by the customer.

   Example: AA Cookiejar Technologies Private Limited.

10. **NBFC-Peer to Peer Lending Platform (NBFC-P2P):** It provides an online platform to bring lenders and borrowers together to help mobilise funds.

    Examples: Creditech Solutions Private Limited and Peerfintech Solutions Private Limited.

11. **Housing Finance Company (HFC):** This financial institution provides financing for housing to individuals, co-operative societies and corporate bodies to support housing activity in the country.

Figure 4.2 presents an overview of the non-banking financial companies in India regulated by "other regulators".

The NBFCs 'Regulated by Others' are discussed in the respective chapters in detail.

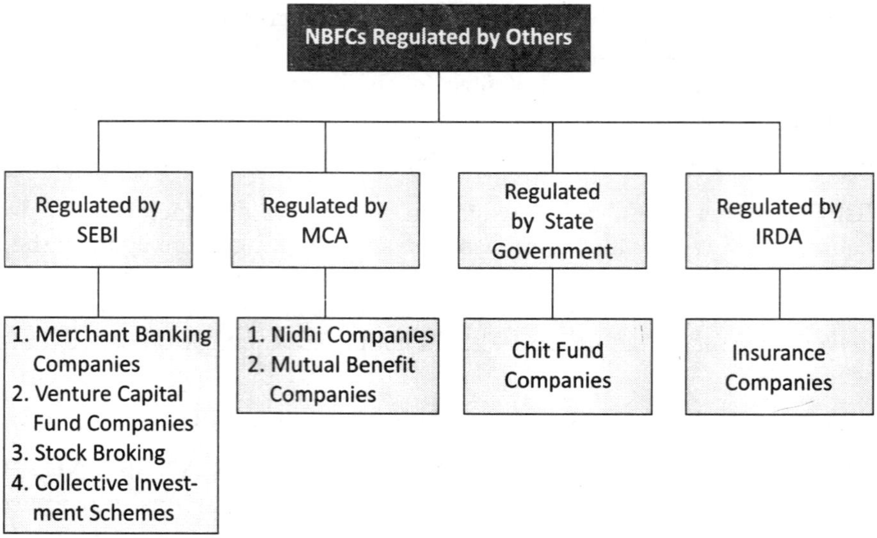

Figure 4.2 Structural of NBFCs under Others' Regulation

DISTINCTION BETWEEN BANK AND NON-BANKING FINANCIAL COMPANY

Both Banks and NBFCs deal with public and the role of NBFCs of accepting deposits and lending is similar to that of banks; however there are a few differences as given in Table 4.1.

TABLE 4.1 Distinction between Bank and NBFC

	Bank	*NBFC*
1. Bank license	Required	Not required
2. Demand deposit	Can accept demand deposits	Cannot accept demand deposits
3. Cheque facility	Can provide cheque facilities	Cannot provide cheque facilities
3. Payment and settlement system	Form part of the payment and settlement system	Do not form part of the payment and settlement system and cannot issue cheques drawn on itself
4. Deposit and insurance facility	Deposit insurance facility of 'Deposit Insurance and Credit Guarantee Corporation' is available to depositors of banks	Deposit insurance facility of 'Deposit Insurance and Credit Guarantee Corporation' is not available to depositors of NBFCs
5. Maintenance of reserve ratios	Required to maintain reserve ratios (CRR, SLR, etc.)	Not required to maintain reserve ratios (CRR, SLR, etc.)

RATIONALE OF NON-BANKING FINANCIAL COMPANIES

The role and presence of Non-Banking Financial Companies (NBFCs) is critical in a country and would boost the economy in the right direction. Their significance is discussed below:

- **Size of the sector:** The NBFC sector has grown considerably in the last few years despite the slowdown and COVID in the economy. In terms of year-over-year growth rate, the NBFC sector beat the banking sector in respective years between 2015 and 2022. Its average growth rate during the period has been 16%. This shows, it is significantly contributing to the economy all these years.[8]

  The growing importance of the NBFC sector in the Indian financial system is reflected in the consistent rise of NBFCs' credit as a proportion to GDP as well as in relation to credit extended by scheduled commercial banks.

  The share of NBFCs' credit in GDP (at current market prices) increased steadily from just 8.9% as at end-March, 2015 to 12.3% as at end-March, 2022; while the share of bank assets declined from 59.3% to 51.6% during the same period (Table 4.2).[9]

TABLE 4.2 NBFCs' Credit vis-à-vis SCBs' Credit and GDP (At end-March)

Year / *Ratio*	2015	2016	2017	2018	2019	2020	2021	2022
NBFCs' Credit to GDP Ratios (%)	8.9	9.6	9.6	11.5	12.1	12.3	13.6	12.3
SCBs' Credit to GDP Ratios (%)	59.3	57.3	52.7	51.2	51.2	51.3	54.6	51.6

Source: Report on Trend and Progress of Banking in India 2021–22.

- **Business concentration:** NBFCs differ with banks not only in terms of size and sophistication of operations but also in terms of activities they undertake. NBFC would include not only entities which are part of large multinational groups, but also small players with assets around ₹25 lakhs.

  The business concentration in terms of total assets increased from ₹35,04,335 crore during 2020–21 to ₹38,40,921 crore during 2021–22 (Table 4.3), despite greater competition in financial sector as compared with banking sector. This shows an increasing outreach in the market.

- **Profitability:** NBFCs are more profitable than the banking sector due to lower costs. This helps them in offering cheaper loans to customers. As a result, NBFCs' income growth is on an increasing side with more customers opting for NBFCs. NBFCs' income grew at a higher rate in 2021–22 than a year ago, primarily driven by fund-based income of NBFCs-ND-SI and NBFCs-D.

  Overall, expenditure of the sector declined due to lower provisions and decrease in interest expenses on bank loans and inter-corporate deposits. The result was a sizable growth in net profit. Net profit increased phenomenally

8. https://rbidocs.rbi.org.in/rdocs/Publications/PDFs/0RTP20212225730A6FC708454BB270AC1705CCF178. op. cit.
9. https://rbidocs.rbi.org.in/rdocs/Publications.ibid.

from ₹41,578 crore in 2020–21 to ₹61,843 crore in 2021–22 (Table 4.3), indicating Y-o-Y growth over 40 per cent.

- **Infrastructure lending:** NBFCs contribute largely to the economy by lending to infrastructure projects, which are very important to a developing country like India. These projects require large amount of funds, and have a long gestation period of generating profits. Therefore, being riskier projects they might not be favourable with banks for lending. In the last few years, NBFCs have contributed significantly in infrastructure lending.
- **Promoting inclusive growth:** Non-Banking Financial Companies (NBFCs) play an important role in promoting inclusive growth in the country, by catering to the diverse financial needs of bank excluded customers. They cater to a wide variety of customers—both in urban and rural areas, finance projects of small-scale companies, and provide small-ticket loans for affordable housing projects. All these help in promoting an inclusive growth in the country.

TABLE 4.3 Financial Performance of NBFCs (Amount in ₹ crore)

Items	2020–21	2021–22
A. Income	3,56,252	3,76,563
B. Expenditure	3,00,373	2,94,928
C. Net Profit	41,578	61,843
D. Total Assets	35,04,335	38,40,921

Source: Report on Trend and Progress of Banking in India 2021–22.

REGULATION OF NON-BANKING FINANCIAL COMPANIES

NBFCs are deeply interconnected with the entities in the financial sector and have a considerable influence on the financial system. Thus, they require a strong regulation to address various risks for facilitating smoother compliance and strengthen governance standards.

In keeping with the principle of proportionality, the Reserve Bank had released the revised regulatory framework for NBFCs, **SCALE BASED REGULATION** on October 22, 2021.[10] Thereby narrowing the regulatory arbitrage between banks and large NBFCs while preserving operational flexibility. This was an effort by RBI to ensure a level playing field for all NBFCs and increase their growing participation in the Indian economy.

The key provisions of the revised regulatory framework of NBFCs are explained below.

1. *Structural Changes for NBFCs:* Regulatory structure for NBFCs shall comprise of four layers based on their size, activity, and perceived riskiness. NBFCs in the lowest layer shall be known as NBFC-Base Layer (NBFC-BL). NBFCs in middle layer

10. *Scale Based Regulation (SBR),* https://www.rbi.org.in/Scripts/NotificationUser.aspx?Id=12179&Mode=0 [The Complete Revised Regulatory Framework for NBFCs is given in the Instructor's manual.]

and upper layer shall be known as NBFC-Middle Layer (NBFC-ML) and NBFC-Upper Layer (NBFC-UL) respectively. The Top Layer is ideally expected to be empty and will be known as NBFC-Top Layer (NBFC-TL).

- **Base Layer.** The Base Layer shall comprise of (a) non-deposit taking NBFCs below the asset size of ₹1000 crore and (b) NBFCs undertaking the following activities—(i) NBFC-Peer to Peer Lending Platform (NBFC-P2P), (ii) NBFC-Account Aggregator (NBFC-AA), (iii) Non-Operative Financial Holding Company (NOFHC) and (iv) NBFCs not availing public funds and not having any customer interface.
- **Middle Layer.** The Middle Layer shall consist of (a) all deposit taking NBFCs (NBFC-Ds), irrespective of asset size, (b) non-deposit taking NBFCs with asset size of ₹1000 crore and above and (c) NBFCs undertaking the following activities (i) Standalone Primary Dealers (SPDs), (ii) Infrastructure Debt Fund-Non-Banking Financial Companies (IDF-NBFCs), (iii) Core Investment Companies (CICs), (iv) Housing Finance Companies (HFCs) and (v) Infrastructure Finance Companies (NBFC-IFCs).
- **Upper Layer.** The Upper Layer shall comprise of those NBFCs which are specifically identified by the Reserve Bank as warranting enhanced regulatory requirement based on a set of parameters and scoring methodology. The top ten eligible NBFCs in terms of their asset size shall always reside in the upper layer, irrespective of any other factor.
- **Top Layer.** The Top Layer will ideally remain empty. This layer can get populated if the Reserve Bank is of the opinion that there is a substantial increase in the potential systemic risk from specific NBFCs in the Upper Layer. Such NBFCs shall move to the Top Layer from the Upper Layer.

2. *Regulatory Changes*

(a) *Net Owned Fund:* Regulatory minimum Net Owned Fund (NOF) for NBFC-ICC, NBFC-MFI and NBFC-Factors shall be increased to ₹10 crore. The following glide path is provided for the existing NBFCs to achieve the NOF of ₹10 crore:

NBFCs	*Current NOF*	*By March 31, 2025*	*By March 31, 2027*
NBFC-ICC	₹2 crore	₹5 crore	₹10 crore
NBFC-MFI	₹5 crore (₹2 crore in NE Region)	₹7 crore (₹5 crore in NE Region)	₹10 crore
NBFC-Factors	₹5 crore	₹7 crore	₹10 crore

However, for NBFC-P2P, NBFC-AA, and NBFCs with no public funds and no customer interface, the NOF shall continue to be ₹2 crore. It is clarified that there is no change in the existing regulatory minimum NOF for NBFCs—IDF, IFC, MGCs, HFC, and SPD.

(b) *NPA Classification:* The extant NPA classification norm stands changed to the overdue period of **more than 90 days** for all categories of NBFCs. A glide path is provided to NBFCs in Base Layer to adhere to the 90 days NPA norm as under

NPA Norms	*Timeline*
>150 days overdue	By March 31, 2024
>120 days overdue	By March 31, 2025
>90 days	By March 31, 2026

Explanation: The glide path will not be applicable to NBFCs which are already required to follow the 90-day NPA norm.

(c) *Experience of the Board:* Considering the need for professional experience in managing the affairs of NBFCs, at least one of the directors shall have relevant experience of having worked in a bank/NBFC.

(d) *Ceiling on IPO Funding:* There shall be a ceiling of ₹1 crore per borrower for financing subscription to Initial Public Offer (IPO). NBFCs can fix more conservative limits.

3. *Capital Guidelines:* Regulatory changes under SBR applicable to NBFC-ML and NBFC-UL

(a) *Internal Capital Adequacy Assessment Process (ICAAP):* NBFCs are required to make a thorough internal assessment of the need for capital, commensurate with the risks in their business. This internal assessment shall be on similar lines as ICAAP prescribed for commercial banks under Pillar 2 (Basel III Capital Regulations dated July 01, 2015). While Pillar 2 capital will not be insisted upon, NBFCs are required to make a realistic assessment of risks. Internal capital assessment shall factor in credit risk, market risk, operational risk and all other residual risks as per methodology to be determined internally. The methodology for internal assessment of capital shall be proportionate to the scale and complexity of operations as per their Board approved policy. The objective of ICAAP is to ensure availability of adequate capital to support all risks in business as also to encourage NBFCs to develop and use better internal risk management techniques for monitoring and managing their risks. This will facilitate an active dialogue between the supervisors and NBFCs on the assessment of risks and monitoring as well as mitigation of the same.

Additional regulatory changes under SBR applicable to NBFC-UL

(b) *Common Equity Tier-I:* In order to enhance the quality of regulatory capital, NBFC-UL shall maintain Common Equity Tier-I capital of at least 9 per cent of Risk Weighted Assets.

(c) *Leverage:* In addition to the CRAR, NBFC-UL will also be subjected to leverage requirement to ensure that their growth is supported by adequate capital, among other factors. A suitable ceiling for leverage will be prescribed subsequently for these entities as and when necessary.

(d) *Differential standard asset provisioning:* NBFC-UL shall be required to hold differential provisioning towards different classes of standard assets.

4. *Prudential Guidelines:* Regulatory changes under SBR applicable to NBFC-ML and NBFC-UL

(a) *Concentration of credit / investment:* The extant credit concentration limits prescribed for NBFCs separately for lending and investments shall be merged into a single exposure limit of 25% for single borrower/party and 40% for single group of borrowers/parties. Further, the concentration limits shall be determined with reference to the NBFC's Tier-I capital instead of their Owned Fund. The revised norms are indicated in the table below:

Existing limit (as a percentage of Owned Fund)				*Revised limit (as a percentage of Tier I Capital)*	
	Lending	*Ivestmnet*	*Total*		*Exposure*
Single borrower/ party	15	15	25	Single borrower/party	25
Single group of borrowers/parties	25	25	40	Single group of borrowers/parties	40

NBFC-UL shall follow these norms till Large Exposure Framework is put in place for them. Extant instructions on concentration norms for different categories of NBFC, other than the changes indicated above, will continue to remain applicable.

(b) *Sensitive Sector Exposure (SSE):* Exposure to capital market (direct and indirect) and commercial real estate shall be reckoned as sensitive exposure for NBFCs. NBFCs shall fix Board-approved internal limits for SSE separately for capital market and commercial real estate exposures. Dynamic vulnerability assessments of various sectors and their likely impact on business, as evaluated periodically, should help NBFCs determine such internal exposure limits. While the Board is free to determine various sub-limits within the overall SSE internal limits, the following are specifically prescribed:

- (i) A sub-limit within the commercial real estate exposure ceiling shall be fixed internally for financing land acquisition.
- (ii) Ceiling on IPO Funding.

Housing Finance Companies shall continue to follow specific regulation on sensitive sector exposure, as are currently applicable in terms of Direction—Non-Banking Financial Company—Housing Finance Company (Reserve Bank) Directions, 2021.

(c) *Regulatory restrictions on loans:* NBFCs shall be subject to regulatory restrictions in respect of the following:

- (i) Granting loans and advances to directors, their relatives and to entities where directors or their relatives have major shareholding.
- (ii) Granting loans and advances to Senior Officers of the NBFC.
- (iii) While appraising loan proposals involving real estate, NBFCs shall ensure that the borrowers have obtained prior permission from government/local governments other statutory authorities for the project, wherever required. To ensure that the loan approval process is not hampered on account of this, while the proposals could be sanctioned in normal course, the disbursements shall be made only after the borrower has obtained requisite clearances from the government authorities.

BOX 4.3: PROMPT CORRECTIVE ACTION (PCA) FRAMEWORK

The Reserve Bank has extended its Prompt Corrective Action (PCA) framework applicable to banks, to NBFCs in the middle and upper layers so as to undertake remedial measures in a timely manner if vital financial parameters breach the prescribed thresholds. PCA framework is also applicable to NBFCs in the top layer (NBFC-TL). However, the top layer is currently empty. PCA framework is not applicable to government NBFCs, Standalone Primary Dealers (SPDs), Housing Finance Companies (HFCs) and NBFCs not accepting/not intending to accept public funds.

In case of NBFCs-ND-SI and NBFCs-D, capital adequacy ratio (CRAR), Tier-I capital ratio and net non-performing assets (NNPA) ratio are the key indicators for monitoring in PCA Framework.

RT for NBFCs is presented below.

Risk Thresholds (RT) defined under PCA Framework for NBFCs-D and NBFCs-ND

Indicator	*RT-1*	*RT-2*	*RT-3*
CRAR	Less than the regulatory minimum of 15 per cent but greater than or equal to 12 per cent.	Less than 12 per cent but greater than or equal to 9 per cent.	Less than 9 per cent.
Tier-1 Capital Ratio	Less than the regulatory minimum of 10 per cent but greater than or equal to 8 per cent.	Less than 8 per cent but greater than or equal to 6 per cent	Less than 6 per cent.
NNPA Ratio	Greater than 6 per cent but less than or equal to 9 per cent.	Greater than 9 but less than or equal to 12 per cent.	Greater than 12 per cent.

Source: Report on Trend and Progress of Banking in India 2021–22.
Note: The complete PCA Framework is given in the Instructor's Manual.

5. *Governance Guidelines:* Regulatory changes under SBR applicable to NBFC-BL

(a) *Risk Management Committee:* In order that the Board is able to focus on risk management, NBFCs shall constitute a Risk Management Committee (RMC) either at the Board or executive level. The RMC shall be responsible for evaluating the overall risks faced by the NBFC including liquidity risk and will report to the Board.

(b) *Disclosures:* Disclosure requirements shall be expanded, inter alia, to include types of exposure, related party transactions, loans to Directors/Senior Officers and customer complaints.

(c) *Loans to directors, senior officers and relatives of directors:* NBFC-BL shall have a Board approved policy on grant of loans to directors, senior officers and relatives of directors and to entities where directors or their relatives have major shareholding.

(d) *Key Managerial Personnel:* Except for directorship in a subsidiary, Key Managerial Personnel shall not hold any office (including directorships) in any other NBFC-ML or NBFC-UL. A timeline of two years is provided with effect from October 01, 2022 to ensure compliance with these norms. It is clarified that they can assume directorship in NBFC-BLs.

(e) *Independent Director:* Within the permissible limits in terms of Companies Act, 2013, an independent director shall not be on the Board of more than three NBFCs (NBFC-ML or NBFC-UL) at the same time. Further, the Board of the NBFC shall ensure that there is no conflict arising out of their independent directors being on the Board of another NBFC at the same time. A timeline of two years is provided with effect from October 01, 2022 to ensure compliance with these norms. There shall be no restriction to directorship on the Boards of NBFC-BLs, subject to applicable provisions of Companies Act, 2013.

(f) *Disclosures:* NBFCs shall, in addition to the existing regulatory disclosures, disclose the following in their Annual Financial Statements, with effect from March 31, 2023:

(i) Corporate Governance report containing composition and category of directors, shareholding of non-executive directors, etc.

(ii) Disclosure on modified opinion, if any, expressed by auditors, its impact on various financial items and views of management on audit qualifications.

(iii) Items of income and expenditure of exceptional nature.

(iv) Breaches in terms of covenants in respect of loans availed by the NBFC or debt securities issued by the NBFC including incidence/s of default.

(v) Divergence in asset classification and provisioning above a certain threshold to be decided by the Reserve Bank.

(g) *Chief Compliance Officer:* In order to ensure an effective compliance culture, it is necessary to have an independent compliance function and a strong compliance risk management framework in NBFCs. NBFCs are, therefore, required to appoint a Chief Compliance Officer (CCO), who should be sufficiently senior in the organization hierarchy. NBFCs shall put in place a Board approved policy laying down the role and responsibilities of the CCO with the objective of promoting better compliance culture in the organization.

(h) *Compensation guidelines:* In order to address issues arising out of excessive risk taking caused by misaligned compensation packages, it has been decided that NBFCs shall put in place a Board approved compensation policy. The guidelines shall at the minimum include, (a) constitution of a Remuneration Committee, (b) principles for fixed/variable pay structures, and (c) malus/clawback provisions. The Nomination and Remuneration Committee shall ensure that there is no conflict of interest.

(i) *Other Governance matters:* NBFCs shall comply with the following:

(i) The Board shall delineate the role of various committees (Audit Committee, Nomination and Remuneration Committee, Risk Management Committee or any other Committee) and lay down a calendar of reviews.

(ii) NBFCs shall formulate a whistle blower mechanism for directors and employees to report genuine concerns.

(iii) The Board shall ensure good corporate governance practices in the subsidiaries of the NBFC.

(j) *Core Banking Solution:* NBFCs with 10 and more branches are mandated to adopt Core Banking Solution. A glide path of 3 years with effect from October 01, 2022 is being provided.

ISSUES AND CHALLENGES FOR NON-BANKING FINANCIAL COMPANIES

NBFCs are criticized for issues like unprofessionalism, poor customer orientation and one-sided approach. Thus, the following issues need to be addressed by the NBFC industry in order to strengthen their position.

Customer Protection

This is one of the major challenges for the NBFC industry. Protection of customers against unfair, deceptive or fraudulent practices has become top priority for them internationally. RBI has been receiving numerous complaints against charging of exorbitant interest rates, raising of surrogate deposits in the name of non-convertible debentures, preference shares, etc. Aggressive practices in improper possessing of automobiles in the case of auto loans and opaque practices in selling the underlying gold jewellery in case of gold loans are grabbing the attention of regulator due to relatively more complaints. NBFCs are often found not to practice Fair Practices Code (FPC) in letter and spirit. A responsive and proper grievance redressal mechanism is required to address these issues.

Improvement in Corporate Governance

To become real winners, business transparency is inevitable for any financial entity and so in case of NBFCs. They need to adopt good corporate governance practices. RBI has already prescribed a governance code for NBFCs as part of their best practices. This includes constitution of Audit, Nomination and Risk Management Committees, and disclosure and transparency norms.

Capacity Building

NBFCs struggle on account of lack of professionally trained staff which is also a major reason of customer grievance. They, on both individual and collective basis, need to work towards building capacity base as it is the quality of staff which largely determines the health of the sector.

Innovation in Products and Services

The modernisation of financial services is happening very fast. NBFCs have to design innovative products to suit the client and market conditions, else they will be obsolete by other players in the system.

ATMs Reach

NBFCs have significant business presence in semi-urban and rural centres, they should explore business potential by setting ATMs in such areas.

Single Representative Body for the Industry

In the case of NBFCs, there are multiple representative bodies such as 'Finance Industry Development Council (FIDC) for Assets and Loan Financing Companies, 'Association of Gold Loan Companies (AGLOC) for Gold Loan NBFCs, etc. In addition, there are RBI's guidelines for 'Self-Regulatory Organisation for Micro Finance Institutions'. In the interests of harmonious and balanced development of the sector, NBFCs should think of establishing one representative body for the entire sector with an adequate representation of all the segments.[11]

CASE STUDY

Sahara's NBFC in Blue

The registration certificate of Sahara India Financial Corporation, a Lucknow-headquartered non-banking finance company, was cancelled by the Reserve Bank of India (RBI) with effect from September 3, 2015[12]. This had put a stop on transacting its business. It was registered in December 1998.

The step was taken by RBI in the light of several alleged irregularities and violation of financial rules and regulations by Sahara. Sahara Group had a long-running regulatory and legal battle with the Securities and Exchange Board of India.

In 2013, the central bank had barred Sahara India Financial Corporation from accepting fresh deposits from the public for violation of the prescribed guidelines. The NBFC had over 25 million depositors, who have 42.5 million accounts, with a cumulative deposit base of around ₹ 18,000 crore. The violations were related to maintenance of directed investments, payment of minimum interest rate, asset-liability management guidelines, and know-your-customer (KYC) norms. Another violation pertained absence of information at the time of maturity of deposits[13].

The group chairman Subrata Roy got behind the bars on account of this. The registration of Sahara Mutual Fund was also cancelled as the entity failed to qualify as "fit and proper" any more to run business.

As per the verdict of the Supreme Court, the Sahara group owed around ₹ 36,000 crore to bond investors which was supposed to be deposited in nine instalments.

---

11. https://www.indiainfoline.com/article/market-currency/nbfcs-to-become-real-game-changers-rbi-114020503871_1.html
12. https://economictimes.indiatimes.com/industry/banking/finance/rbi-cancels-sahara-india-financial-corporations-nbfc-registration/articleshow/48959450.cms
13. http://www.business-standard.com/article/finance/rbi-sahara-may-meet-again-over-nbfc-issue-108061701010_1.html.

POINTS TO REMEMBER

- A Non-Banking Financial Company (NBFC) is a company which is registered under the Companies Act, 1956 and engaged in the business of loans and advances, acquisition of shares/stocks/bonds/debentures/securities or other marketable securities of a like nature, leasing, hire-purchase, insurance business, chit business. It also includes a 'residuary non-banking company', i.e. non-banking institution which is a company and has principal business of receiving deposits under any scheme or arrangement. Financial activity as "principal business" means: (a) when a company's financial assets constitute more than 50 per cent of the total assets, and (b) income from financial assets constitute more than 50 per cent of the gross income.
- In accordance with the Section 45-IA of the RBI Act, 1934, every non-banking financial company to commence or carry on business of a non-banking financial institution must satisfy the following conditions: (a) it should be a company registered under the companies Act, 1956 or under Companies Act, 2013, (b) it should obtain a certificate of registration from the Bank, and (c) it must have a 'net owned funds' of ₹2 crore.
- NBFCs are broadly categorized into (a) *deposit-taking* and (b) *non-deposit-taking NBFCs*. Non-deposit NBFCs by their size can be further classified into systemically important (NBFC-ND-SI) and other non-deposit holding companies (NBFC-ND). NBFC-ND-SI are with asset size more than ₹ 500 crore and NBFC-ND are with asset size less than ₹ 500 crore.
- Investment and Credit Company (ICC) means a financial institution carrying on as its principal business of providing finance.
- NBFC-Infrastructure Finance Company (NBFC-IFC) is a non-banking finance company which finances the infrastructure sector.
- Core Investment Company (CIC) refers to a financial institution which carries on as its principal business of the acquisition of securities.
- NBFC-Infrastructure Debt Fund (NBFC-IDF) is a company registered as NBFC to facilitate the flow of long-term debt into post commencement operations in infrastructure projects.
- NBFC-Micro Finance Institution (NBFC-MFI) is a non-deposit taking NBFC providing collateral free small ticket loans to economically disadvantaged groups.
- NBFC-Factor is engaged in the business of factoring.
- NBFC-Non-Operative Financial Holding Company (NBFC-NOFHC) is financial institution through which promoter/promoter groups will be permitted to set up a new bank.
- Mortgage Guarantee Company (MGC) is financial institution whose at least 90% of the business turnover is mortgage guarantee business or at least 90% of the gross income is from mortgage guarantee business and net owned fund is ₹100 crore.

- NBFC-Account Aggregator (NBFC-AA) is into collecting and providing information about a customer's financial assets in a consolidated, organised, and retrievable manner to the customer.
- NBFC-Peer to Peer Lending Platform (NBFC-P2P) provides an online platform to bring lenders and borrowers together to help mobilise funds.
- Housing Finance Company (HFC) is a financial institution provides financing for housing to individuals, co-operative societies and corporate bodies to support housing activity in the country.
- The role of NBFCs of accepting deposits and lending is similar to that of banks; however there are a few differences among them. Banks can accept demand deposits, while NBFCs cannot accept them. Banks form part of the payment and settlement system but NBFCs do not form its part. Banks provide the deposit insurance facility to their depositors but this facility is not available to the depositors of NBFCs.
- The significance of NBFCs can be discussed in terms of (a) *size of the sector,* (b) *business concentration*, (c) *profitability*, (d) *infrastructure lending*, and (e) *promoting inclusive growth.*
- RBI had released the revised regulatory framework for NBFCs, Scale Based Regulation on October 22, 2021.
- NBFCs are criticized for issues like unprofessionalism, poor customer orientation and one-sided approach. Their key challenges include, (a) customer protection, (b) improvement in corporate governance, (c) capacity building, (d) innovation in products and services, (e) ATMs reach, and (f) single representative body for the industry.

KEY TERMS

- **Non-Banking Financial Company (NBFC)** is a financial institution which is into the business of lending or investment or collecting money under any scheme or arrangement.
- **Systemically Important NBFCs** are those NBFCs whose asset size is of ₹500 crore or more as per last audited balance sheet.
- **Owned Fund** means sum total of the paid-up equity capital, convertible preference shares, free reserves, balance in share premium account and capital reserves.
- **Net Owned Fund** is Owned Fund minus investments of such company in shares of its subsidiaries, companies in the same group and all other NBFCs, and the book value of debentures, bonds, outstanding loans and advances and deposits with subsidiaries and companies in the same group.
- **Investment and Credit Company (ICC)** is a financial institution carrying on as its principal business of providing finance.
- **NBFC-Infrastructure Finance Company (NBFC-IFC)** is a non-banking finance company which finances the infrastructure sector.

- **Core Investment Company (CIC)** refers to a financial institution which carries on as its principal business of the acquisition of securities.
- **NBFC-Infrastructure Debt Fund (NBFC-IDF)** is a company registered as NBFC to facilitate the flow of long-term debt into post commencement operations in infrastructure projects.
- **NBFC-Micro Finance Institution (NBFC-MFI)** is a non-deposit taking NBFC providing collateral free small ticket loans to economically disadvantaged groups.
- **NBFC-Factor** is engaged in the business of factoring.
- **NBFC-Non-Operative Financial Holding Company (NBFC-NOFHC)** is financial institution through which promoter/promoter groups will be permitted to set up a new bank.
- **Mortgage Guarantee Company (MGC)** is financial institution whose at least 90% of the business turnover is mortgage guarantee business or at least 90% of the gross income is from mortgage guarantee business and net owned fund is ₹100 crore.
- **NBFC-Account Aggregator (NBFC-AA)** is into collecting and providing information about a customer's financial assets in a consolidated, organised, and retrievable manner to the customer.
- **NBFC-Peer to Peer Lending Platform (NBFC-P2P)** provides an online platform to bring lenders and borrowers together to help mobilise funds.
- **Housing Finance Company (HFC)** is a financial institution provides financing for housing to individuals, co-operative societies and corporate bodies to support housing activity in the country.

EXERCISES

Objective Questions

1. **Tick the correct answer:**

   (a) NBFCs stand for:
   - (i) Non-banking financial companies
   - (ii) Non-banking fund companies
   - (iii) Non-banking financial corporations
   - (iv) None of the above

   (b) Systematically important NBFCs are:
   - (i) whose asset size is ₹ 5 cr
   - (ii) whose asset size is ₹ 500 cr or more
   - (iii) whose asset size is ₹ 100 cr or more
   - (iv) whose asset size is ₹ 10 cr or more

   (c) NBFCs are regulated by:
   - (i) RBI
   - (ii) RBI and Others
   - (iii) SEBI
   - (iv) None of the above

(d) All NBFCs are divided into how many layers?
 (i) 2 (ii) 3
 (iii) 4 (iv) None of the above

Answers: (a) i (b) ii (c) ii (d) iii

2. Fill in the blanks:

(a) NBFC is a .... institution.
(b) The Board Committees required for NBFCs are: audit committee, nomination committee and ....
(c) Every NBFC is required to make a provision for standard assets at .... of the outstanding.
(d) The requirement of minimum net owned fund for NBFC is ....

Answers:
(a) financial
(b) risk management committee
(c) 0.40%
(d) ₹200 lakh

3. True or False

(a) Non-Banking Financial Companies are entities that provide financial services and banking facilities.
(b) NBFC includes any institution whose principal business is agriculture activity.
(c) Mortgage Guarantee Companies have been notified as Non-Banking Financial Companies.
(d) Core Investment Company is a financial institution whose principal business is the acquisition of securities.
(e) NBFC–Non-Operative Financial Holding Company is financial institution through which promoter/promoter groups get permitted to set up a new bank.

Answers: (a) True (b) False (c) True (d) True (e) True

Short Questions

1. What is non-banking financial company?
2. What is meant by financial activity as "principal business" for NBFC?
3. Distinguish between Bank and NBFC.
4. Explain owned funds and net owned funds.
5. Differentiate between deposit and non-deposit accepting NBFCs.
6. State the layers of NBFCs categorization.

Critical Thinking Questions

1. "Systemically important NBFCs are considered to have an impact on the financial stability of the overall economy." Explain.

2. "The regulation of NBFCs has scope for improvement". Discuss.
3. "Corporate governance and disclosure norms for NBFCs are a step towards their consolidation". Prove.
4. "NBFCs have their own cup of issues and challenges". Elaborate.
5. "NBFCs are popular only in semi-urban and rural sections of the society". Critique.

Descriptive Questions

1. Discuss the rationale of non-banking financial companies.
2. What are the various categories of non-banking financial companies?
3. Explain the prudential norms applicable to NBFCs.
4. Comment on the future prospects of NBFCs in India.
5. Outline the key elements of the RBI's 'fit and proper criteria for directors' prescribed by RBI for NBFCs.

PROJECT EXERCISE

Analysis of NBFCs Mechanism

Choose any two categories of NBFCs. Study their products, services, organizational structure and management. Highlight the major differences and the suggest the areas of improvement required for them in particular and NBFC industry in general for future growth.

REVIEW CASE

Doll Drummed NBFC!

Hi-Fi Financial Company Ltd.'s management was in state of shock. They were summoned by the banking regulator on account of financial discrepancies in their state of affairs. The company was a leading non-banking financial company in northern India. It was into the business of financing two wheelers and its major customer segment was lower middle class.

This summon was a serious blow to the company's big dreams of going for initial public offering. A group of customers had filed a complaint to the Supreme Court about company's shadow clauses in the financing agreements which were undisclosed to them. One of the clause was about arbitrary swing in the interest rate from second year.

The company had over 10 million customers, with around 25% market share of asset financing in the two-wheeler segment.

Issues for Discussion

(i) Why Hi-Fi Financial Company was summoned by the banking regulator?

(ii) What impact Hi-Fi NBFC summon will have on Indian NBFC industry?

(iii) What redressal mechanism is available to customers in such case?

(iv) What steps should be taken by the regulators in improving corporate governance practices of NBFCs?

REFERENCES

Financial regulations in India need to have uniform standard, January 15, 2010, www.financialexpress.com.

Non-Banking Finance Companies: The Changing Landscape, ASSOCHAM India, 2016, https://www.pwc.in/assets/pdfs/publications/2016/non-banking-finance-companies-the-changing-landscape.pdf

www.business-standard.com

www.economictimes.indiatimes.com

www.indiainfoline.com

www.livemint.com

www.nelito.com

www.rbi.org.in

CHAPTER 5

Money Market

Cash, in savings accounts, short-term CDs or money market deposits, is great for an emergency fund.

— Suze Orman

LEARNING OBJECTIVES

This chapter discusses the following:

- Structure of financial markets in India
- Money market and its objectives
- Types of money market instruments
- Pricing of T-bills
- Money market instruments in India
- Significance of money market

INTRODUCTION

The Indian financial market is one of the oldest in the world and is considered to be the fastest-growing and best among all the markets of the emerging economies. While the need for long-term financing is met by the capital market, money market deals with short-term finance.

The Indian money market is a monetary system that involves the lending and borrowing of short-term funds. Financial institutions employ money market instruments for financing short-term monetary requirements of various sectors such as agriculture, finance and manufacturing. Indian money market has seen exponential growth since liberalization in 1992. It has exhibited the required maturity and flexibility over the past two decades. Decision of the government to permit the operation of private-sector banks has provided much needed healthy competition in the money market resulting in fair amount of improvement in its performance.

Reserve Bank of India (RBI)—the central bank of the country, plays the major role in regulating and controlling the Indian money market. The intervention of RBI is varied—curbing crisis situations by reducing the Cash Reserve Ratio (CRR) or infusing more money in the economy.

Money market is one of the most significant mechanisms of any developing financial system. It plays a key role in banks' liquidity management and the transmission of monetary policy. By providing the appropriate instruments and partners for liquidity trading, money market allows the refinancing of short- and medium-term positions and facilitates the mitigation of business' liquidity risk. The development of the money market smoothes the progress of financial intermediation and boosts lending to the economy, hence improving the country's economic and social welfare. Therefore, the development of the money market is in all stakeholders' interests: the banking system, the Central Bank and the economy, on the whole.

STRUCTURE OF FINANCIAL MARKETS

Financial markets are the common platform which bring individuals, companies and government together to meet their financing needs by engaging in buying and selling of securities. They are regulated by the securities regulator in India, i.e. Securities and Exchange Board of India (SEBI), the Central Bank of India, and the Reserve Bank of India (RBI), according to the type of market.

As discussed in Chapter 1, financial markets are classified into money market and capital market, depending upon the maturity of funds. *Money market* is the market for short-term funds, whereas *Capital market* is the market for long-term funds. Financial market is also classified as Primary market (New Issues Market) and the Secondary market [Old (Existing) Issues Market]. This classification is done on the basis of the process of issue of the instruments. In *primary market*, newly issued stocks and bonds are exchanged, and in the *secondary market*, trade of existing stocks and bonds takes place. The primary market helps to raise fresh capital in the market whereas in the secondary market, the buying and selling (trading) of capital market instruments takes place.

Capital market, on the basis of the types of institutions involved, can be classified into various categories such as the Government Securities market or Gilt-edged market and Industrial Securities market.

Figure 5.1 will help us in understanding the organisational structure of the Indian financial market.

RBI: Reserve Bank of India

Reserve Bank of India is the apex bank of India. It is entrusted with the responsibility of regulating the banking system of the country. It also looks after the money market of the country, especially the treasury bills which are issued by them on behalf of the Government of India.

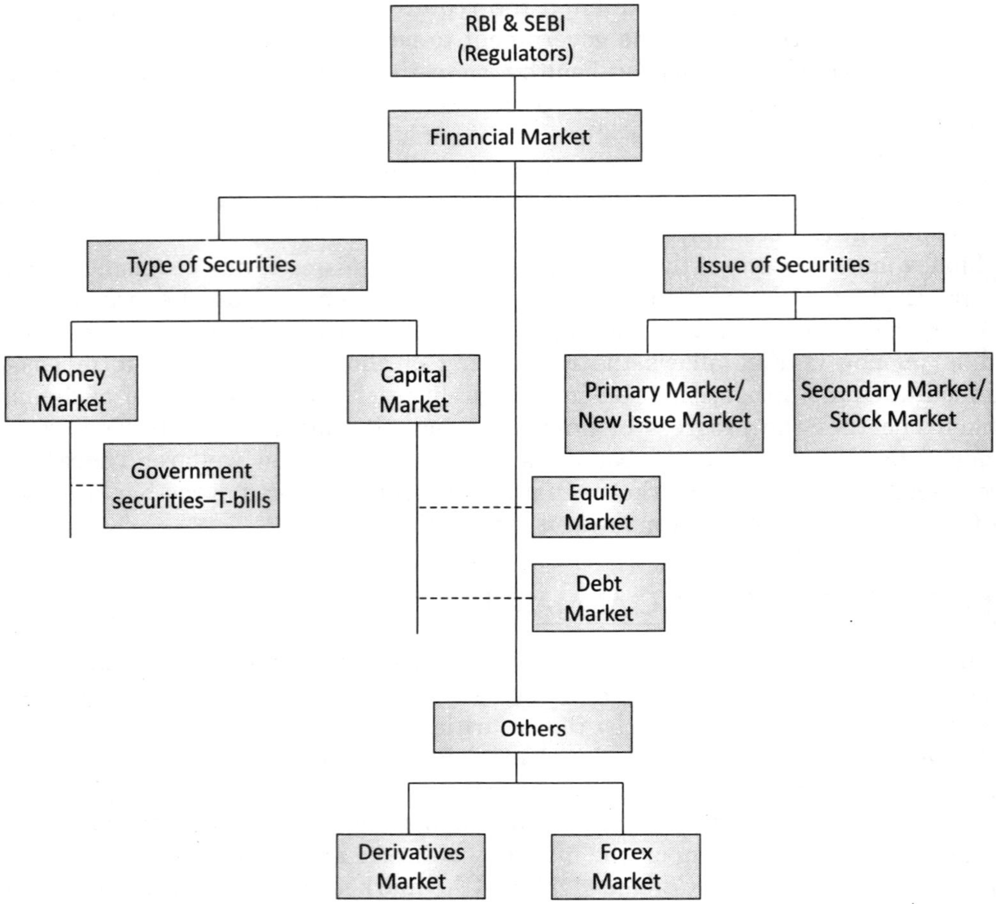

Figure 5.1 Indian Financial Market

SEBI: Securities and Exchange Board of India

SEBI as a regulatory body was established under SEBI Act, 1992. Its regulatory jurisdiction extends over corporate in the issuance of capital and transfer of securities, in addition to all intermediaries and persons associated with securities market. It can conduct enquiries, audits and inspection of all concerned and adjudicate offences under the Act. It has powers to register and regulate all market intermediaries and also to penalize them in case of violations of the provisions of the Act, Rules and Regulations made thereunder. SEBI has full autonomy and authority to regulate and develop an orderly securities market.

Money Market

The categorisation of financial markets into money and capital markets is essentially based on the maturity of the claims traded in each of them. Money markets are mainly wholesale markets (large size transactions) where firms and financial institutions manage their short-term liquidity needs.

Money market is a market for debt securities that pay off in the short-term, usually less than one year, *for example,* the market for 90-days treasury bills. This market encompasses the trading and issuance of short-term non-equity debt instruments, like treasury bills, commercial papers, discounted bills, certificates of deposits, etc.

It is the place where large financial institutions, dealers and government participate and meet out their short-term cash needs. They usually borrow and lend money with the help of instruments or securities to generate liquidity. Due to highly liquid nature of securities and their short-term maturities, money market is also known as liquid market.

Objectives of Money Market

The broad objectives of a money market are:

- To provide an equilibrium between short-term surpluses and deficiencies
- To act as a focal point of RBI (central bank) for influencing liquidity in the economy, and
- To provide a reasonable access to the users of short-term funds to meet their requirements at realistic or reasonable price/cost.

MONEY MARKET INSTRUMENTS

Following are the money market instruments:

Money Market at Call and Short Notice

Call market is the most liquid market. The loans made in this market are of the shortest term—overnight and are repayable on demand. Money at short notice is repayable within 14 days of serving a notice. The major participants are banks and All India Financial Institutions as permitted by RBI.

It is basically an inter-bank market, wherein those banks which are facing a short-term cash deficit, borrow funds from the cash surplus banks for maintaining their CRR, making huge payments, etc. The rate of interest is market-driven and depends on the liquidity position in the banking system. The market is over the telephone.

Treasury Bills (T-bills)

Treasury bills are short-term government securities and are one of the safest money market instruments as they are issued by RBI on behalf of the Central Government. Therefore, they are zero-risk instruments, and hence yield low returns. They are traded in both primary and secondary markets.

They come with the maturities of 3-month, 6-month and 1-year. At present, the Government of India issues three types of treasury bills through auctions, namely, 91 days, 182 days and 364 days.

They are issued at a discounted price, i.e. less than their face-value and redeemed at full. So, the difference between the purchase price and the maturity value is the interest earned by the buyer of the instrument. The purchase price of the T-bill is determined by auction mechanism.

Calculation of Yield of Treasury Bill

It is calculated as per the formula given below:

$$\text{Yield} = \left(\frac{100 - P}{P}\right) \times \left(\frac{365}{D}\right) \times 100$$

wherein

P = Purchase price
D = Days to maturity

Illustration

Suppose that the price of 91 days treasury bill at the time of issue is ₹98.20, the yield on the same would be:

$$\text{Yield} = \left(\frac{100 - 98.20}{98.20}\right) \times \left(\frac{365}{91}\right) \times 100 = 7.34\%$$

Pricing of T-bills

Following graphs show the fluctuations in the rate of return of treasury bills over a period of 10 years, including the year of global recession 2007–08. The x-axis shows the years and the y-axis shows the rate of interest. The treasury bills rates are highest for 91 days T-bills and lowest for 364 days T-bills. The demand for T-bills is the pricing mechanism; demand itself is affected by the rate of return that investors can get from other securities. At the time of recession, when the market sentiment is down and stock markets are erratic, demand for treasury bills increases. The reason for this is that they have the least chance of default and are safe liquid assets.

Moreover, if not high return, at least the principal amount of investment is saved. Hence, high demand leads to high price as a result of which the yield on T-bills fall, since price and yield are negatively related. This trend can be seen in Figure 5.2(a–d) during the period 2007–08 when Lehman Brothers crisis unfolded.

(a) Upto 14 Days

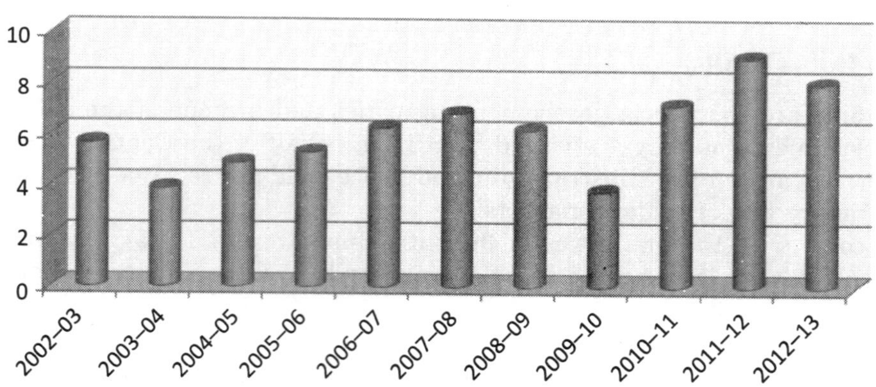

Source: http://www.rbi.org.in/scripts/PublicationsView.aspx?id=15307

Figure 5.2(a) (Contd.)

(b) 15–91 Days

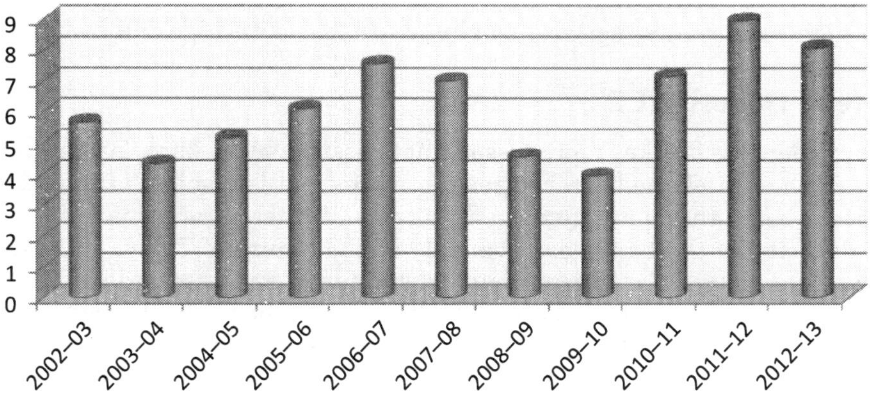

Source: http://www.rbi.org.in/scripts/PublicationsView.aspx?id=15307A.

(c) 92–182 Days

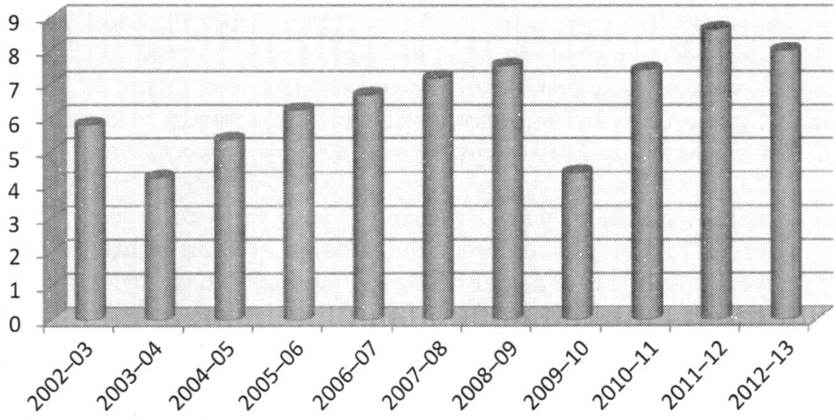

Source: http://www.rbi.org.in/scripts/PublicationsView.aspx?id=15307Ac.

(d) 183–364 Days

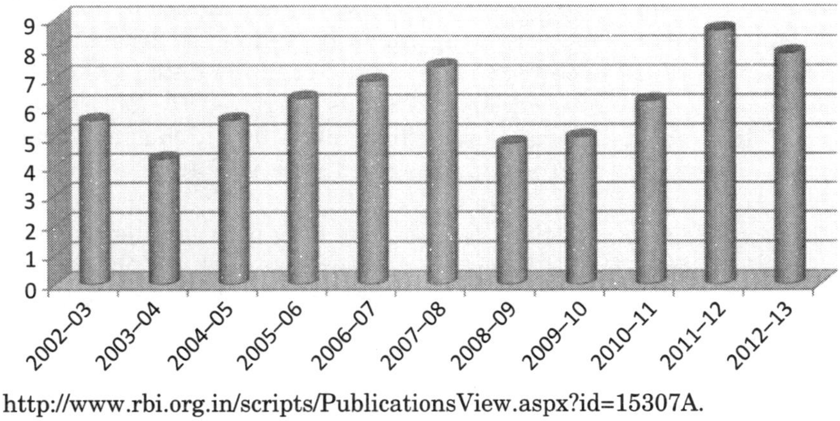

Source: http://www.rbi.org.in/scripts/PublicationsView.aspx?id=15307A.

Figure 5.2(b)–(d) Trend of T-bills

Another notable trend is the increase in the rate of interest since the year 2010. This can be because of the high rate of inflation that the country was experiencing. Periods of high rate of inflation are usually associated with high interest rates.

Certificate of Deposits (CDs)

Certificate of deposit is like a promissory note issued by a bank in the form of a certificate which entitles the bearer to receive interest. It is a short-term bank deposit. The certificate bears the maturity date, fixed rate of interest and the value.

These deposits by the banks are available in the tenure of 7 days to 1 year. They can be issued to individuals, corporations, trusts, funds and associations. The returns on certificate of deposits are higher than T-bills because they carry higher level of risk. They are issued in denominations of ₹5 lakh and in the multiples of ₹5 lakh thereafter.

Commercial Papers (CPs)

Commercial paper is a short-term, unsecured promissory note issued by corporate and financial institutions at a discounted price like T-bills.

CPs are issued by the corporates to finance their working capital needs. These are issued for short-term maturities, at a discount and redeemed at face-value. Only those companies who have a good credit standing are able to access funds through this instrument, since they are unsecured. The rate of interest is market-driven and depends on the current liquidity position and the creditworthiness of the issuing company.

They have a fixed maturity period ranging from 7 days to 1 year. The return on commercial papers is higher as compared to T-bills on account of higher risk element. They need to have a credit rating as per SEBI's guidelines. These securities are actively traded in secondary market and are issued in denominations of ₹5 lakh and in the multiples of ₹5 lakh thereafter.

Repurchase Agreements (Repo) and Reverse Repurchase Agreements (Reverse Repo)

Repo and Reverse Repo are short-term instruments which enable collateralized short-term borrowing and lending through sale/purchase in debt instruments.

A *Repo* is an instrument for borrowing funds by selling securities to an investor with an agreement to repurchase them at a pre-determined date in the future at an agreed price which includes interest for the funds borrowed. A *Reverse Repo* is the opposite of repo. It is an instrument for lending funds by purchasing securities with an agreement to resell them at a mutually agreed date in future, at an agreed price which includes interest for the funds lent.

Repo or Reverse Repo transactions can be done only between the parties approved by RBI and allowed only for RBI-approved securities such as State and Central government securities, T-bills, PSU bonds and corporate bonds. They are usually traded for overnight borrowing.

Banker's Acceptance

Banker's acceptance is a short-term investment plan created by non-financial firms, backed by a guarantee from the bank. It is like a bill of exchange stating a buyer's promise to pay the seller a certain specified amount at a certain date, and the bank guarantees that the buyer will pay the seller this amount at a future date.

Firms with strong credit rating can draw such a bill. These securities come with maturities between 30 and 180 days, and the most common term for these instruments is 90 days. Companies use these negotiable instruments to finance imports, exports and other trades.

Discounted Bills/Commercial Bills

Bills of exchange are a short-term, negotiable, and liquidating instrument with low risk. They are issued by the seller (drawer) to the buyer (drawee) for the value of the goods delivered to him which are encased with the bank for a fee.

They are generally used by business houses to finance their working capital needs against credit sales. Banks can also get such bills re-discounted by financial institutions such as LIC, UTI, ICICI and others. The maturity period of the bills varies from 30 days, 60 days or 90 days, depending on the credit extended in the industry.

Inter-Corporate Deposits (ICDs)

It is an unsecured, inter-corporate loan. Corporates having surplus funds lend to other corporates. Since, the cost of funds for a corporate is much higher than that for a bank, the rates in this market are higher than those in the other markets. Also, as ICDs are unsecured, the risk inherent is high and this is also the reason for higher rates.

Inter-Bank Participation Certificates (IBPCs)

They were introduced in 1988 by RBI with two types—one on risk-sharing basis, and the other without risk-sharing. These are strictly inter-bank instruments confined to scheduled commercial banks, including regional rural banks. These instruments are used only to obviate short-term liquidity problems by some banks by parting with the standard assets[1].

Money Market Mutual Funds (MMMFs)

A money market fund is a mutual fund that invests solely in money market instruments. Money market instruments are short-term form of debt and are very liquid. Treasury bills constitute the major part of money market instruments. Money market mutual funds were introduced in India in April 1991 to provide an additional short-term avenue to investors and to bring money market instruments within the reach of individuals. The minimum lock-in period is 15 days.[2]

1. http://rbidocs.rbi.org.in/rdocs/PublicationReport/Pdfs/77574.pdf.
2. http://rbidocs.rbi.org.in/rdocs/PublicationReport/Pdfs.ibid.

An overview of money market instruments in India is given in Table 5.1.

TABLE 5.1 Money Market Instruments in India

Instruments	*Tenor*	*Major participants*
1. Call money	Overnight	SCBs (excluding RRBs), Cooperative banks, Primary Dealers (PDs)
2. Notice money	2 to 14 days	
3. Term money	15 days to 1 year	Banks, All India FIIs, PDs
4. Treasury bills	91, 182 and 364 days	Banks, FIIs, PDs, Insurance companies and other non-bank entities
5. Certificate of deposit (1989)	Minimum 7 days	SCBs (excluding RRBs and Local Area Banks) and Select All India FIIs
6. Commercial paper (1990)	Minimum 7 days	Corporates, All India FIIs and PDs
7. Repurchase agreements/Reverse repurchase agreements (1992)	1 day to 1 year	Banks, All India FIIs, PDs, Insurance companies, Mutual funds, and listed Corporate
8. Banker's acceptance	1 month to 6 months	Banks and FIs
9. Bills discounting	Need-based	Banks, Select All India FIIs, PDs, Insurance Companies and Mutual funds
10. Inter-corporate deposits	Flexible	Corporates
11. Inter-bank participation certificates (1988)	91 to 180 days	SCBs
12. Money market mutual funds (1991)	1 day to 1 year	Banks, Select All India FIIs, Insurance companies and Mutual funds

Note: Year in parentheses denotes the year of introduction of the instrument.

SIGNIFICANCE OF MONEY MARKET

Money market is the backbone of any economy. Its relevance can be attributed to the following factors:

1. Effective Banking System: A developed money market not only helps in the effective functioning of a central bank, but also facilitates effective implementation of its monetary policy.

It provides the commercial banks with facilities for temporarily employing their surplus funds in liquid assets. The banks can get back the funds quickly, in times of need, by resorting to the money market. It enables commercial banks to meet their statutory requirements of cash reserve ratio (**CRR**) and Statutory Liquidity Ratio (**SLR**) by utilizing the money market mechanism.

2. Liquidity in the Economy: It is through the money market that surplus fund subsidizes the move to shortfall territories. This aids in handling liquidity emergencies in the country. The money market's most crucial purpose is to fill this liquidity void.

Money market serves as a true indicator of the monetary state of an economy.

3. Source of Finance to the Government: Money market helps the Government to raise short-term funds by floating treasury bills in the market. In the absence of a developed money market, the Government would be forced to print and issue more currency or borrow from the central bank; which would result in an increase in prices and the bring an inflationary trend in the economy.

4. Development of Capital Market: Money market decides the short-term interest rates which ultimately influence the long-term interest and the resource mobilization in capital market. This helps the financial markets as new investors flocked in to benefit from the better interest rates.

Ultra-defined monetary policies of central bank and high liquidity lead to the equity market's strong performance and its rally gets broad-based.

5. Development of Trade and Industry: A well developed money market is an important source of financing trade and industry, as it meets short-term financing requirements promptly. Through discounting operations and commercial papers, it finances the working capital requirements of trade and industry and facilities their development.

CASE STUDY

Elite Money Market Account

IndiWise Credit Ltd. is one of the leading financial cooperative banks in India with its head office at Delhi.

In 2008, IndiWise Credit wanted to raise funds to meet their growing requirements. However, they did not want to go through the traditional way of certificates at above market rates. The prime reason was the narrow margins. Secondly, they wanted to retain deposits that were flowing out to the emerging foreign banks and online financial institutions because of interest rates.

Therefore, they introduced an Elite high rate/high minimum balance money market account, as per the reports of the research team, on October 24, 2008.

Their research team demonstrated that each account would have approximately double the balance than the minimum required balance. Therefore, IndiWise set the minimum balance for their account at ₹50,000 with an interest rate of 7% Annual Percentage Yield (APY). They set a goal of ₹20 lacs in deposits within the account.

Thereafter, they advertised this new account scheme in all the leading national newspapers. They also informed all the existing money market account holders over ₹40,000 with an offer to open this elite account at 0% processing charges.

Outcome

This project was a huge success. At the end of December 2008, within a span of two months, the statistics were as follows:

• Number of accounts	55
• Balance of all Elite Money Market accounts	₹ 25,50,075
• Average balance of each account	₹ 46,365
• Average profit per account	₹ 4,80,000

IndiWise Credit's M.D. was finally happy, as they could get the required funds at a much lesser cost than the traditional deposits. Additionally, their customer base had increased which took their bank to new heights.

POINTS TO REMEMBER

- Financial markets are classified into money market and capital market, depending upon the maturity of funds. *Money market* is the market for short-term funds, whereas *Capital market* is the market for long-term funds.
- Financial market is also classified as Primary market (New Issues Market) and the Secondary market (Old [Existing] Issues Market). This classification is done on the basis of the process of issue of the instruments.
- Reserve Bank of India is the apex bank of India. It also looks after the money market of the country.
- SEBI, as a regulatory body, was established under SEBI Act, 1992. Its regulatory jurisdiction extends over corporates in the issuance of capital and transfer of securities, etc.
- Call market is the most liquid market. It is repayable on demand, and money at short notice is repayable within 14 days of serving a notice.
- Treasury Bills (T-bills) are short-term government securities.
- Certificate of Deposits (CDs) is like a promissory note issued by a bank.
- Commercial Papers (CPs) is a short-term unsecured promissory note issued by corporate and financial institutions at a discounted price.
- Repurchase Agreements (Repo) or Reverse Repurchase Agreements (Reverse Repo) are short-term loans that buyers and sellers agree upon for selling and repurchasing at a later date.

- Banker's Acceptance is like a short-term investment plan created by a non-financial firm, backed by a bank guarantee.
- Bills of exchange are a short-term, negotiable, and liquidating instrument with low risk.
- Inter-Corporate Deposits (ICDs) are an unsecured, inter-corporate loan.
- Inter-Bank Participation Certificates (IBPCs) are strictly inter-bank instruments confined to scheduled commercial banks.
- Money Market Mutual Funds (MMMFs) are mutual funds that invest solely in money market instruments.
- Money market is the backbone of any economy and its relevance can be attributed to the following factors: (i) effective banking system, (ii) liquidity in the economy, (iii) financing to the government, (iv) development of capital market, and (v) development of trade and industry.

KEY TERMS

- **Financial market** is the common platform where all the parties come together to meet their financing needs.
- **Money market** is the market for short-term funds, usually less than one year.
- **Liquid market** is the money market which deals in highly liquid nature of securities with short-term maturities.
- **Treasury bills** are short-term government securities issued by RBI on behalf of Central Government.
- **Certificate of deposit** is like a promissory note issued by a bank in the form of a certificate which entitles the bearer to receive interest.
- **Commercial paper** is the short-term unsecured promissory note issued by corporates and financial institutions at a discounted price.

EXERCISES

Objective Questions

1. **Tick the correct answer:**

(a) Financial markets are regulated by:

(i) SEBI (ii) RBI
(iii) Both SEBI and RBI (iv) None of the above

(b) Discounted bills arise only in case of:

(i) Cash sales (ii) Credit sales
(iii) Credit purchases (iv) None of the above

(c) Call market is:
(i) Inter-bank market (ii) Inter-country market
(iii) Inter-household market (iv) None of the above

(d) Commercial paper is:
(i) Short-term (ii) Short-term debt
(iii) Short-term debt at discount (iv) All of the above

(e) Treasury bills are:
(i) Government securities (ii) Corporate securities
(iii) Credit securities (iv) None of the above

Answers: (a) iii (b) ii (c) i (d) iv (e) i

2. Fill in the blanks:

(a) Money market is meant for ....
(b) Certificate of deposit is like a ....
(c) Repurchase agreements are .... loans.
(d) Banker's acceptance is backed by a guarantee from the ....
(e) A .... is a mutual fund that invests solely in money market instruments.

Answers:

(a) Short-term funds
(b) Promissory note
(c) Short-term
(d) Bank
(e) Money market fund

3. True or False

(a) Call market is the most liquid market.
(b) Commercial paper is a long-term equity instrument.
(c) Treasury bills are issued by SEBI.
(d) Certificate of deposits pay a higher rate of interest than T-bills.
(e) Repurchase agreements are always between the banks.

Answers: (a) True (b) False (c) False (d) True (e) True

Short Questions

1. What are T-bills?
2. Explain commercial papers.
3. Differentiate between money market and capital market.
4. What is discounting of bills?

Critical Thinking Questions

1. "Government securities are considered to be risk-free instruments". Examine.
2. "Certificate of deposits are like a promissory note". Discuss.
3. "Money market is also referred to as banking market". Elaborate.
4. "Money market is only meant for meeting working capital requirements". Do you agree?
5. "Money market in India is still at a developing stage". Justify.

Descriptive Questions

1. Discuss various types of financial markets.
2. How has money market in India changed over the past twenty years?
3. Comment on the future prospects of Indian money market.
4. Explain the relevance of money market in an economy.

PROJECT EXERCISE

Relevance of Money Market

Choose any developed country and compare its money market with India, a developing nation. Highlight the major differences and the areas of improvement regarding the structure and regulatory framework which can be learnt by India for future development.

REVIEW CASE

Starter's Scratch!

Stewart had heard it is better to park your funds in government securities of short-term nature for rotating your money faster and earning decent return at the same time. He had little money, ₹20,000 but did not have any knowledge in which instruments he should invest in. He had seen his friend making good money by investing in stocks which tempted him to try out that side as well. Like everyone's wife, his wife cautioned him, being a lower middle-class family.

He thought of approaching a wealth advisor for the same. The wealth advisor advised against short-term instruments. He was back to the square one.

As a financial expert, advice Stewart:

(i) Which market is suited best for him?

(ii) How should he build his portfolio?

(iii) What instruments in money market should he invest in?

(iv) Should he stick to one portfolio or should he experiment?

(v) Is timing important for money market investment?

REFERENCES

Financial Regulation and Financial Inclusion—Speech by Deputy Governor, Reserve Bank of India, June 11, 2010, indiamicrofinance.com.

Financial regulations in India need to have a uniform standard, January 15, 2010, www.financialexpress.com.

Wellyn, David T. Lle (2006), "Institutional Structure of Financial Regulation and Supervision", The Basic Issues, www.worldbank.org.

www.rbi.org.in

www.sebi.gov.in

CHAPTER

6

Capital Market

Most people get interested in stocks when everyone else is. The time to get interested is when no one else is. You can't buy what is popular and do well.

— Warren Buffett

LEARNING OBJECTIVES

This chapter discusses the following:

- SEBI's role and functions
- Growth of Indian capital market
- Structure and instruments of capital market: Equity market and Debt market
- Risks in stock market
- Under-development saga of bond market in India
- Types of financial markets: Primary market, Secondary market, Derivatives market and Forex market
- IPO process
- Capital market reforms
- Stock exchanges in India
- Factors for investment in capital markets
- Concept and mechanism of circuit-breakers
- Regulatory framework of financial markets

INTRODUCTION

The capital market in India has come a long way in the past decade and a half, in terms of economic reforms, making India one of the world's largest equity markets.

There are around 7,000 companies listed on the Indian stock exchanges with over 20 million shareholders. The Indian capital market is significant in terms of degree of development, volume of trading and its tremendous growth potential.

Theoretically, the capital market facilitates allocation of resources efficiently, which involves quick dissemination of information and reaction to it. The process of capital market regulation ensures that important guidelines are issued concerning how primary dealers (brokers) should operate with regard to mode of operation, conduct, litigation, amount of business to be handled, risk management, internal control and the like. The essence of the argument in it is that the occurrence and reoccurrence of such security scams and financial scandals can be attributed to a failure of corporate governance in finance, despite the existence of a functioning regulatory authority empowered with the legal sanctions.

Therefore, challenges remain, especially in the areas of institutional and business environment, such as the elements outside the direct control of financial policy-makers. In the light of financial crisis, much attention is being paid to systemic risks and inter-connectedness of markets. These result into new regulatory priorities like more extensive overview of large financial conglomerates and the creation of a macro-prudential regulator.

SEBI: SECURITIES MARKET REGULATOR

Capital market in India is regulated by the "Securities and Exchange Board of India" (SEBI). SEBI came into existence under the SEBI Act, 1992. It regulates the corporate for the issuance of capital and transfer of securities.

SEBI consists of the following members:

1. A Chairperson,
2. Two members, i.e. Officers from the Union Finance Ministry,
3. One member from amongst the officials of the Reserve Bank of India, and
4. Five other members nominated by the Central Government, of whom at least three shall be whole-time members.

The general superintendence, direction and management of the affairs of SEBI vests in a Board of Members, which exercises all powers and conducts all activities which may be exercised or done by SEBI.

Functions of SEBI

SEBI has been set up primarily for protecting the interests of the investors in securities, and to promote and regulate the securities market by the necessary measures. Following are the key functions of SEBI:

1. Regulating the functioning of stock exchanges in India,
2. Registering and regulating the working of all those who are associated with securities markets in any manner, including stock-brokers, sub-brokers, share transfer agents, merchant bankers, underwriters, portfolio managers, investment advisers and such other intermediaries,

3. Registering and regulating the working of the depositories, participants, custodians of securities, foreign institutional investors, credit-rating agencies and such other intermediaries as SEBI may, by notification, specify in this behalf,
4. Registering and regulating the working of venture capital funds and collective investment schemes including mutual funds,
5. Promoting and regulating self-regulatory organizations,
6. Prohibiting fraudulent and unfair trade practices relating to securities markets,
7. Promoting investors' education and training of intermediaries of securities markets,
8. Prohibiting insider trading in securities (Box 6.1),
9. Regulating substantial acquisition of shares and take-over of companies,
10. Performing such functions and exercising according to Securities Contracts (Regulation) Act, 1956, as may be delegated to it by the Central Government,
11. Performing such other functions as may be prescribed.

BOX 6.1: INSIDER TRADING CASE

Hindustan Lever Ltd. vs. SEBI (1998) was one of the first cases where SEBI took action on grounds of 'insider trading'. SEBI's charges were triggered off by HLL's purchase of 8 lac shares of Brooke Bond Lipton India Ltd. (BBLIL) from the Unit Trust of India (UTI, 1996–97 income: ₹7,481 crore) at ₹350.35 per share. This transaction took place on March 25, 1996, before the HLL-BBLIL merger was announced on April 19, 1996. A day after the announcement of the merger, the BBLIL scrip quoted at ₹405, thereby leading to a notional gain of ₹4.37 crore for HLL, which then cancelled the shares bought*.

HLL was held liable by SEBI for insider trading. According to SEBI, HLL had full knowledge of the impending merger and misused the unpublished price-sensitive information to its advantage. However, the Securities Appellate Tribunal reversed the order on the ground that the information was not price-sensitive as it was reported in the media and, therefore, was public knowledge. As a result of this case, SEBI amended the Regulations to specifically provide that speculative reports in the media (print or electronic) would not be treated as publication of price-sensitive information.

* http://archives.digitaltoday.in/businesstoday/22031998/cf.htm

EVOLUTION OF CAPITAL MARKET IN INDIA

India's financial market began its transformation path in the early 1990s. The Securities and Exchange Board of India (SEBI) was established in 1992 with a mandate to protect investors and usher improvements into the microstructure of capital markets, while the repeal of the Controller of Capital Issues (CCI) in the same year removed the administrative controls over the pricing of new equity issues. India's financial markets also began to embrace technology. Competition in the markets increased with the establishment of the National Stock Exchange (NSE) in 1994, leading to a significant rise in the volume of transactions and to the emergence of new important instruments in financial intermediation.

The first stock exchange set up in India was the Bombay Stock Exchange (BSE), which began formal trading in 1875, making it one of the oldest in Asia. Over the last few years, there has been a rapid change in the Indian securities market, especially in the secondary market. Advanced technology and online-based transactions have modernised the stock exchanges. In terms of the number of companies listed and total market capitalisation, the Indian equity market is considered a large relative to the country's stage of economic development. The debt market, however, was almost non-existent in India though there was a large volume of government bonds which were traded. It has grown over the years but still is not as developed as in West. Banks and financial institutions are the major investors in these bonds for meeting their statutory liquidity requirement. A primary auction market for Government securities had been created and a primary dealer system was introduced in 1995. Mutual funds were opened to the private sector in 1992. In 1987, banks were allowed to enter into this business, but till date Unit Trust of India (UTI) maintains a strong position.

Before 1992, there were many factors which created a hindrance in the expansion of equity market. *Examples:* Capital Issues Control Act used to control fresh capital issues. Trading practices were not transparent, and there was a large amount of insider trading.

Recognising the importance of increasing investor protection, several reforms were introduced to improve the capital market system in India. The Securities and Exchange Board of India (SEBI) was established in 1988 but problems relating to disclosure criteria, lack of broker capital adequacy, and poor regulation of merchant bankers and underwriters still continued.

Therefore, the SEBI Act was enacted in 1992 giving SEBI the statutory status of an apex regulatory body. A series of reforms was introduced to improve investor protection, automation of stock trading, integration of national markets, and efficiency of market operations. India has seen a tremendous change in the secondary market for equity. Its equity market will most likely be comparable with the world's most advanced secondary markets within a year or two. The key ingredients that underlie market quality in India's equity market are:

- Exchanges based on open electronic limit order book,
- Nationwide integrated market with a large number of informed traders and fluency of short or long positions, and
- No counter-party risk.

Before 1995, markets in India used open outcry, a trading process in which traders shouted and hand-signalled from within a pit. One major policy initiated by SEBI in 1993 involved the introduction of "screen-based trading" in all stock exchanges for greater transparency. The first exchange to be based on an open electronic limit order book was the National Stock Exchange (NSE), which started trading debt instruments in June 1994 and equity in November 1994. In March 1995, BSE shifted from an open outcry to a limit order book market.

STRUCTURE AND INSTRUMENTS OF CAPITAL MARKET

Capital market provides long-term finance, i.e. funds for more than one year to a minimum period of ten years. It is used for financing the permanent needs of business—*(i) Investment in fixed assets, and (ii) Permanent component of working capital.* So, capital market is characterised as the provider of long-term financing.

Capital market is classified into "equity market" and "debt market", based on the nature of security.

A. EQUITY MARKET

This is a market for owned instruments, i.e. equity securities of the existing and new corporate firms. These instruments promise returns solely based on performance of the issuing corporation in the form of dividends and appreciation of stock prices. Buying and selling of such instruments take place in this market. Equity market is further classified into two types—New Issues Market (Primary) and the Old (Existing) Issues Market (Secondary Stock Exchange).

In primary market, fresh capital is raised by companies by issuing new shares and units of mutual funds. However, in the secondary market, already existing or old shares are traded. This trading takes place through registered stock exchanges. In India, we have two prominent stock exchanges. They are the BSE (formerly Bombay Stock Exchange) and the NSE (National Stock Exchange). Shares and Depositary Receipts are the two types of earned securities.

1. SHARE

Shares are the most important instruments of raising long-term finance and are issued to the owners of a company. Share is one of the units into which the share capital of a company can be divided. It indicates the interest of a shareholder in the assets and profits of a company.

Shares can be issued in the following forms:

Equity (Ordinary) Shares

Equity shareholders are the real owners of a company. These are those shares which do not carry any special or preferential rights in the payment of annual dividend or repayment of capital.

The rate of dividend on such shares is not fixed. Dividend on equity shares is paid out of the residual profits left after paying interest on debentures and dividend on preference shares. Similarly, equity shareholders are paid at the time of winding up of the company after all debts and preference shareholders have been paid off. Therefore, equity shareholders are the real risk-bearers, but they enjoy full voting rights in the management affairs of the company.

Preference Shares

Preference shares are those shares which carry certain special or preferential rights in the payment of dividend and repayment of capital as compared to equity shareholders.

Dividend is payable at a fixed rate on these shares but preference shares do not carry voting rights. They get preference over equity shares in sharing the income as well as claims on assets. Preference shares have a fixed maturity date. They are a "hybrid security", in the sense that they are a mix of debt and equity. Like equity, they get dividend and like debt, they get a fixed rate of dividend and have fixed maturity.

Types of Preference Shares

Preference shares are of following types:

1. ***Cumulative and Non-cumulative preference shares:*** Cumulative preference shares are those in which the dividend gets accumulated if not paid in a year on account of no profits or insufficient profits, and paid with arrears in the year of profits. In case of non-cumulative preference shares, dividend does not accumulate and therefore, if the company does not have any profits in a year, no dividend will be paid to non-cumulative preference shareholders.

2. ***Redeemable and Non-redeemable preference shares:*** Redeemable preference shares are refundable after the maturity period during the lifetime of the company. Non-redeemable preference shares are those shares which cannot be redeemed during the lifetime of the company.

3. ***Convertible and Non-convertible preference shares:*** In case of convertible preference shares, the shareholders have a right to convert their shares into equity shares, within a specified period of time. The holders of non-convertible preference shares do not have such a right of conversion.

4. ***Participating and Non-participating preference shares:*** Participating preference shareholders have a right to participate in the surplus profits of the company remained after paying dividend to the equity shareholders and preference shareholders at a fixed rate. The preference shares with no such right to participate in surplus profits are known as non-participating preference shares.

2. DEPOSITORY RECEIPTS

They are securities of domestic companies issued in the form of ownership of a foreign land in the foreign currency. Depository receipts are most often issued to represent ownership of a foreign common equity but can also be issued to represent ownership of preferred stock, debt or warrants. They are:

American Depository Receipts (ADRs)

These depository receipts allow non-US companies to raise capital in the US equity market, and allow US investors to invest in international stocks without purchasing ordinary shares. Ordinary shares are shares of a given foreign company trading in the company's domestic market.

Global Depository Receipts (GDRs)

GDRs, essentially identical to ADRs, are securities available in one or more markets outside the company's home country (ADR is actually a type of GDR issued in the US but because ADRs were developed much earlier than GDRs, they kept their denotation). The basic advantage of the GDRs, as compared to the ADRs, is that they allow the issuer to raise capital on two or more markets simultaneously, which increases his/her shareholder base. They gained popularity also due to the flexibility of their structure.

B. DEBT MARKET

This is a market for borrowed instruments of the existing and new corporate firms. The debt market is the market where fixed income securities of various types and features are issued and traded. The debt market in India consists of mainly two categories—the Government Securities or the *G-Sec market*, comprising central government and state government securities, and the *Corporate Bond Market.* Most of these instruments promise to pay either fixed streams of income or a stream of income that is determined according to a specific formula over its entire life and return face-value upon maturity. These fixed income securities are issued by Central and State Governments, Municipal Corporations, government bodies and commercial entities like financial institutions, banks, Public-Sector Units, and Public Ltd. companies. Market transacts in mainly two types of securities—Government Securities and Corporate Bonds.

Capital market risk in the bond market arises due to interest rate changes. There is an inverse relationship existing between the interest rate and the price of the bond. Hence, the bond prices are sensitive to the monetary policy of the country as well as economic changes.

The microstructure of the Indian debt market can be explained, in the form of instruments that are traded, as follows:

1. GOVERNMENT SECURITIES MARKET

This is also known as the *gilt-edged market* and refers to the market for government and semi-government securities backed by the Reserve Bank of India (RBI). Government Securities, or *G-secs*, are not only free from default risk but also provide reasonable returns and, therefore, offer the most suitable investment opportunity from the perspective of safety (Box 6.2).

BOX 6.2: CLEARING CORPORATION OF INDIA LIMITED

Clearing Corporation of India Limited (CCIL) is the clearing agency for G-Sec and it acts as a central counter party for all transactions between two counter-parties.

A Government Security is a debt issued by the government with a promise to repay on maturity. In India, the government issues them to fund their fiscal deficit. These instruments are tradable in the secondary market and are issued for both short-term and long-term. The short-term instruments with a maturity of less than one year are called *Treasury Bills* (T-Bills), discussed in the previous chapter. The long-term instruments with a maturity of more than one year are called *Government Bonds* or *Dated Securities.*

Government securities in the form of T-Bills are a part of money market whereas government securities excluding T-Bills are a part of capital market.

However in India, the Central Government issues T-Bills as well as bonds or dated securities, while the State Government issues only the bonds or dated securities which are called *State Development Loans* (*SDL*).

These securities are issued through auction mechanism conducted by the RBI on the electronic platform called *Negotiated Dealing System* (NDS).

Dated Government Securities

These are long-term instruments which pay a fixed or floating interest rate on the face-value, at fixed time periods, generally half-yearly. The maximum tenure of these securities is 30 years. Following are the types of dated instruments:

Fixed rate bonds: These bonds carry a fixed coupon rate until maturity. The majority of government bonds are issued as fixed rate bonds.

Floating rate bonds: These bonds do not have fixed coupon rate. Their coupon rates are re-set at the pre-announcement intervals (every six months or one year) by adding a spread over a base rate.

Zero coupon bonds: These bonds are issued at a discount to the face-value. They do not have an upfront coupon rate.

Capital indexed bonds: These bonds have the principal linked to an accepted inflation index for protecting the holder against inflation.

Bonds with call or put options: These bonds are issued with a feature of—

(i) Buyback option (call option) for the issuer, or (ii) Sell option (put option) for the investor at par value (equal to face-value). This option can be exercised after the completion of five years from the date of issuance on any coupon date falling thereafter

Special securities: It is a long-term dated security having a coupon rate with a spread of about 20–25 basis points over the yield of the dated securities of comparable maturity. These bonds are issued by the Central Government to the oil marketing fertilizer companies, etc. as compensation in lieu of cash subsidies. These companies further raise cash by selling these securities in the secondary market to banks insurance companies, etc.

STRIPS (Separate Trading of Registered Interest and Principal of Securities) STRIPS are instruments wherein each cash-flow of the fixed coupon security is converted into a separate tradable zero coupon bond. *For example,* if ₹100 of the 7% GS2020 is stripped, each cash-flow of coupon (₹3.5 each half yearly) will become coupon STRIP and the principal payment (₹100 on maturity) will become a principal STRIP. These cash-flows are traded separately as independent securities in the secondary market. STRIPS have zero reinvestment risk.

State Development Loans (SDLs)

These dated securities are issued by the State Government to raise loan from the market. It is done through an auction wherein the interest is paid half yearly and the principal is repaid on maturity.

2. DEBENTURES AND BONDS

Debentures and Bonds are known as *Creditorship Securities* because their holders are the creditors of a company. A *debenture* or bond is a document or certificate issued by a company under its seal as an acknowledgement of its debt. It is also an undertaking to repay the specified sum with interest to its holder.

Interest on debentures is paid at a fixed rate and is payable every year irrespective of profits or not. Debentures carry no voting rights and the interest paid on debentures is tax deductible. Debentures have a maturity period.

Debentures and bonds both are debt instruments and are used interchangeably in India. However, there is a technical difference between the two. A debenture is usually unsecured whereas bond is secured.

Types of Debentures

Following are the various kinds of debentures:

Based on Security

(i) *Secured/Mortgage debentures:* Debentures secured against assets of the company, i.e. if the company is winding up, assets will be sold and debenture holders will be paid back. The charge/mortgage may be fixed or a floating charge. If it is fixed, charge is on a specific asset, say plant, machinery, etc. If it is floating charge, it means it is on general assets of the company.

(ii) *Unsecured/Simple debentures:* Debentures not secured against assets of the company, i.e. if the company is winding up, assets will not be sold in order to pay the debenture holders. In other words, no charge is created on the assets of the company, which means that there is no security of interest and principal payment. The credit-worthiness and soundness of the company serves as a security.

Based on Tenure

(i) *Redeemable debentures:* Debentures which have to be repaid within a certain specified period, for example, 5% 2 years ₹1000 debenture means redeemable period is 2 years and 5% is the interest/coupon payment. After redemption, they can be reissued.

(ii) *Irredeemable/Perpetual debentures:* There is no specified period for redemption. Hence, they are also called *Perpetual Debentures.* Nonetheless, if the company has to wind up, then they have to repay the debenture holders.

Based on Coupon

(i) *Zero coupon debentures:* They do not have a specified interest rate and are issued at a substantial discount. Interest is the difference in the face-value and issue price.

(ii) *Specific coupon rate debentures:* Debentures are normally issued with an interest rate which is nothing but the coupon rate. It can be fixed or floating. Floating is associated with the bank rates.

Based on Convertibility

(i) *Convertible Debentures (fully/partly convertible):* These are debentures which can be converted to either equity shares or preference shares by the company or debenture holders at a specified rate after a certain period. A company can also issue *Partly Convertible Debentures* whereby only a part of the amount can be converted to equity/preference shares.

(ii) *Non-Convertible Debentures (NCDs):* These cannot be converted into equity/ preference shares.

3. PUBLIC DEPOSITS

Public deposits refer to the deposits received by a company from the public as loan or debt. Companies prefer public deposits because these deposits are cheaper than bank loans. The interest on these deposits is more than the interest which is given by banks and post-offices. This is risky investment but an investor can earn higher return on public deposits (Box 6.3).

BOX 6.3: GOVERNMENT REGULATION ON PUBLIC DEPOSITS

Section 58A of the Companies Act 1956 provides the power to Central Government to make rules and regulation for controlling public deposits. Government of India has made Companies (Acceptance of deposits) Rules, 1975*. From time to time, these rules are amended.

* http://www.mca.gov.in/Ministry/pdf/Companies_Act_1956_13jun2011.pdf, http://www.mca.gov.in/Ministry/actsbills/rules/CAoDR1975.pdf.

Types of Public Deposits

Public deposits can be of the following types:

1. ***Non-cumulative schemes:*** As the name suggests, they pay off the interest earned on investment on regular basis (half-yearly basis or annual basis), so the interest will not get acquired on principal to earn higher interest in the years to come.

2. ***Cumulative fixed deposit schemes:*** Here, the interest accumulates with the principal so as to earn higher returns when compared to non-cumulative plan. This scheme pays interest accrued on deposit schemes on maturity of the deposit.

4. INSTITUTIONAL FINANCE

Institutional finance is another important instrument of finance. There are both Central- and State-level financial institutions to provide funds to the business firms. They normally provide long-term and medium-term finance to business houses. Some of the prominent financial institutions are Industrial Finance Corporation of India (IFCI), *now IFCI Ltd.*, Small and Industrial Development Bank of India (SIDBI) and State Financial Corporations (SFCs).

They have been incorporated for a definite purpose. These institutions include the insurance companies, the housing finance companies, mutual funds, merchant banks, credit reporting debt collection companies, etc.

Types of Financial Institutions

Following are the types of financial institutions:

1. ***Development financial institutions:*** They offer a variety of services in addition to providing development funds, *for example,* Industrial Reconstruction Bank of India (IRBI) now Industrial Investment Bank of India, Export-Import Bank of India (EXIM Bank), Small Industries Development Bank of India (SIDBI) and National Bank for Agriculture and Rural Development (NABARD).

2. ***Savings and loan associations:*** These have slightly different ownership arrangements than banks, but they are similar to commercial banks. Savings and loan associations may offer slightly higher rates than commercial banks on deposits and somewhat lower rates than commercial banks on loans.

3. ***Mutual fund companies:*** These companies have broken into the banking arena. With many mutual fund companies, you can now write checks against your mutual fund account, *for example,* Unit Trust of India (UTI).

4. ***Brokerage firms:*** Many brokerage firms now allow you to write checks, issue credit cards and ATM cards, and make loans. Brokerage firms offer these and many other account features that were once reserved for traditional banks.

5. ***Credit unions:*** These are similar to savings and loan associations, but they are not-for-profit organizations and are owned by their members. They can sometimes offer higher rates on savings accounts and lower rates on loans because they are not driven to provide a profit to shareholders.

Table 6.1 differentiates between debt and equity instruments of finance.

TABLE 6.1 Distinction between Equity Shares, Preference Shares and Debentures

S.No.	*Basis*	*Equity Share*	*Preference Share*	*Debentures/Loans*
1.	Type	Ownership	Ownership	Borrowing
2.	Rate of return	Variable	Fixed	Fixed
3.	Repayment	Last	Second	First
4.	Voting right	Yes	No	No
5.	Dilution of control	Yes	No	No
6.	Maturity	Perpetual	Fixed	Fixed
7.	Tax deductible	No	No	Yes

RISKS IN STOCK MARKET

Investor considers the following factors of risk while investing in the capital markets:

1. ***Volatility risk and risk of contagions:*** Capital markets are highly volatile especially in emerging countries. Volatility is added by the factors like lack of legal and judicial infrastructure, immature nature, vulnerability to scandals, and unprecedented inflows and outflows of capital.

2. ***Liquidity risk:*** This risk is predominantly present in the debt market as most of the corporate bonds are illiquid due to absence of developed secondary market in the country.

3. ***Political/Regulatory risk:*** The regulatory risk may affect the investors if the investors' company comes under the obligation of new regulations and laws implemented by the government. Risk is further added due to instability in economy which can be derived from either unstable government, corruption or other problems.

4. ***Currency risk:*** Trade is highly impacted by the fluctuations in the foreign exchange rates. This leads to unexpected losses for investors in the markets.

UNDER-DEVELOPED BOND MARKET IN INDIA

Corporate bond markets are of paramount importance for any economy. For a developed economy like US, debt capital markets, i.e., bonds or fixed income instruments provide about 77% of total financing (against bank/other sources).[1] In India, corporate bond market is not very developed. Though Indian equity market has grown extensively in the last 20 years but the similar rise is not with the bond market. Both, supply side and demand side of bonds do not feel the requirement for the development of bond market. Households looking for fixed income prefer bank deposits. Further, the households see upside in the stock market, but do not see any upside in the bond market. Households feel, if a fixed rate of return is the issue, bank deposits are way superior, as they do not have default risk. Corporates, on the other hand, prefer bank loans to debentures. If they issue debentures, they privately place them with bank and institutions, rather than making a public issue. Thus, both the arms of the market are missing.

Reasons for underdeveloped bond market in India:

1. ***Heavy tilt towards private placement:*** Corporates issuing to more than 50 investors has to go public. So, corporates find it cheaper and easier to privately place debentures with banks and institutions rather than go for a public issue, particularly if the issue size is small. Besides, public issue of debentures requires credit rating as per Securities and Exchange Board of India (SEBI) guidelines, which is both time-consuming and expensive.

Secondly, under private placement, the deals can be tailor-made to suit requirements of both the issuer and the investor. So the advantages of private placement over public issue are lower cost of issue, lesser time frame and minimal regulatory approvals.

1. https://www.go-yubi.com/blog/sebi-circular-bond-markert, November 2, 2022.

2. *Rating problem:* Investors in corporate debt instruments are excessively safety-conscious as can be noted from the fact that there is hardly any demand for paper which is rated below AA or its equivalent by the rating companies. World over, any paper rated BBB (or its equivalent) and above is considered as investment grade, except that the interest rate to be paid on BBB has to be high enough to compensate for the risk attached to it in relation to the highest rated paper. Basically, it is a question of risk-reward matrix with higher risk being compensated by higher return. Globally, there is a considerable demand for debt paper which is rated below AA. In fact, the maturity of the market is often judged by the skill of the investors to factor risk-reward matrix in their investment decision so that they do not miss the high return opportunities that may exist in the case of BBB rated paper. Judged from this matrix, it is clear that Indian debt market is yet to mature. This is indicated by the analysis of the outstanding bond issues with reference to their rating values assigned to them by the recognised rating agencies. Over 90% of the debt paper is AA and above, as demand for other investment grade paper is not large enough. The majority of institutional investors by amount in the corporate debt paper are banks which are all the while in favour of highly rated paper, but extending loans to not so well rated corporate clients. Thus, most of the banks adopt an asymmetric credit evaluation methodology when they are willing to provide loan to a client but unwilling to invest in the debt paper issued by the borrower if the debt paper is not rated very highly by the rating agencies.

3. *Issuance profile:* In the total issuance of corporate bonds, a major part comes from the banks and then the PSUs. The raise from the private sector has been extremely low, its share has been less than or around only 15% which is quite low. So it is not that only investors are hesitant but issuers are also not placing bonds in the market. Municipal bonds are a major category of bonds in most developed markets, including the US. These have, however, not really taken off in India. Therefore, India needs to take measures to improve the issuance of municipal bonds.

4. *Individuals' preference:* Individuals prefer bank deposits, rather than investing in corporate bonds. Investment in corporate bonds is currently not favoured by the retail investors and the global trends are also pointers to the fact that the retail investors in corporate bond are not likely to increase in future. When it comes to investing in fixed income assets, retail investors generally prefer other avenues such as bank deposits, postal savings schemes, mutual funds, etc. The main attraction for the retail investors to invest in equities is the opportunity for capital appreciation. Similar attraction is totally missing in the case of corporate debt.

5. *Fragmentation:* Issuers have been increasingly using the private placement route which leads to creation of multiple numbers of smaller issues as there is no bar on number of issuances a company can make. Therefore, there is no proper consolidation of issues. Such fragmentation of the issues should be stopped to improve liquidity in the market. Corporate entities opt in favour of multiple issues primarily to avoid the hassles involved in going through the public issue route. Under the current regulatory regime, if a bond issue is to be sold to 50 or more investors, the issuer has to follow the public issue route which is cumbersome, costly, and time-consuming. Hence, issuers make several issues of bonds and each such issue is sold to 49 or less number of investors. Some of the issuers have resorted to making several issues of bonds in a single day just to ensure that none of the issues violates the public issue guidelines. Fragmentation of issues is inimical to the creation of liquidity and depth in trading. It also increases costs associated with trading in the secondary markets.

6. ***Stamp duty:*** Stamp duty is different in different states for mortgage and assignment. In the interests of developing the corporate bond market, there is a pressing need for rationalisation of the stamp duty structure across the country. Since stamp duty impacts heavily on the cost of issue of bond paper, it would be desirable to reduce stamp duty levels and also introduce a suitable provision which stipulates the maximum amount of stamp duty that is payable in respect of any single issue.

7. ***Crowding effect:*** Government security market is well developed in comparison to the bond market since the issuance is quite high as compared to the corporate bond issuance. Therefore, it might be possible that the G-Secs, which are issued to the finance fiscal budget, are causing crowding-out effect for corporate bond market.

TYPES OF FINANCIAL MARKETS

Besides money and capital markets, as discussed above and in Chapter 1, financial markets are also classified as following:

A. According to the Issue of Securities

Primary Market

Primary market provides opportunity to issuers of securities—government as well as corporate, to raise resources to meet their requirements of investment and/or discharge some obligations. The issuers create and issue fresh securities in exchange of funds through public issues and/or as private placement. Therefore, it is also called *New Issue Market* (NIM).

When securities are exclusively offered to the existing shareholders, it is called *Right Issue,* and when it is issued to selected, mature and sophisticated institutional investors as opposed to general public, it is called *Private Placement Issue*. Issuers may issue the securities at face-value, or at a discount/premium and these securities may take a variety of forms such as equity, debt or some hybrid instruments. The issuers may issue securities in domestic markets and/or international markets through ADR/GDR/ECB route.[2]

Secondary Market

Secondary market, or *stock market* as it is commonly called is the market where, unlike the primary market, an investor can buy a security directly from another investor in lieu of the issuer. It is also referred as *after market*. The securities are first created and issued in the primary market, and then enter into the secondary market. In the New York Stock Exchange, all the stocks belong to the secondary market.

2. The Policy developments regarding primary market issue are given in the Instructor's manual.

The participants of stock market consist of both—those with surplus funds, and with fewer funds. The persons having surplus money invest in capital market for getting high returns whereas people with fewer funds sell their securities for meeting their cash requirements. This is the essence of capital market.

B. According to the Speculation of Securities

Derivatives Market

India's tryst with derivatives began in 2000 when both the NSE and the BSE commenced trading in equity derivatives. In June 2000, index futures became the first type of derivate instruments to be launched in the Indian markets, followed by index options in June 2001, options in individual stocks in July 2001, and futures in single stock derivatives in November 2001. Since then, equity derivatives have come a long way. New products, an expanding list of eligible investors, rising volumes, and the best risk-management framework for exchange-traded derivatives have been the hallmark of the journey of equity derivatives in India so far.[3]

Derivatives have no independent value. Their value is derived from some other asset, which is called the *underlying asset* and it is a contract between two or more traders. This underlying asset can be a stock, index, or commodities. *For example,* a derivative of Reliance share will derive its value from the share price (current value) of ITC.

They are basically used for speculation, being futuristic in nature but can also be used for hedging as means of protection against future financial losses. One can trade and take a high exposure on a stock or security by paying a small margin. *For example,* if the stocks are priced at ₹20 lacs and you have only ₹1 lac in hand, you can still trade in the derivatives market. Thus, derivatives market offers a huge leverage, which is a big plus for traders who are comfortable with margin trading. But these can be used for hedging (protecting oneself against financial risks).

The common types of derivatives are:

1. ***Forwards:*** A *forward* contract is the customized contract between two parties, where settlement takes place on a specific date in future at today's pre-agreed price. Forwards represent the obligation to make a transaction at a set point in time in the future. Once you enter into a forward-based contract, you are obligated to make the transaction unless both parties agree to cancel or otherwise modify the agreement.

Forward contracts trade over the counter (OTC), thus the terms of the deal can be customized to fit the needs of both the buyer and the seller. They are unique in terms of contract size, expiry date, asset type and quality, and are informal in nature. Forward contracts have the ultimate risk of counter-party risk, i.e. if the counter-party defaults and is unable to pay the cash difference or deliver the asset, it can not be challenged in a court of law.

2. ***Futures:*** A *future* is a contract between two parties to buy or sell an asset in future at a specific price. Future contract is a formal forward contract. They are standard contracts traded in an exchange. Examples include commodities, currencies, and metal.

3. http://www.nseindia.com/content/us/ismr2011ch6.pdf

Futures can be used either for hedging or for speculation. *For example,* an MNC using currency futures for hedging purpose to reduce the risk of currency fluctuation. The futures market is a centralized market place for buyers and sellers to meet and enter into futures contracts.

EXAMPLE 'A' sells the futures contract of Tata Motors stock to 'B'. The price is ₹800, quantity is 200 shares, and the expiry date is after 2 months. If, after 2 months, the price goes up to ₹1,000, then irrespective of the market price of the stock, 'A' would deliver 200 shares of Tata Motors to 'B' at ₹800.

3. *Options:* An *option* gives the contract-holder the right to buy or sell on a specified date in the future but they are under no obligation. The pre-decided price for the exchange of asset here is called the *strike price*. The options are either—American or European. In *American options,* the option can be exercised any time up to the settlement date. In *European options*, the option can be exercised only on the settlement date. Thus, American options are much more flexible. In India, only American options are traded.

There are two types of Options—"Call" and "Put".

(a) *Call:* It gives the buyer the right but not the obligation to buy a certain quantity of the underlying asset, at a given price on or before the specified date in future.

(b) *Put:* It gives the seller the right, but not the obligation to sell a certain quantity of the underlying asset at a given price on or before the specified date.

Major players in the options market are financial institutions, mutual funds, FIIs, brokers and retail players.

4. *Swaps:* *Swaps* are a forward contract between two parties to exchange cash flows in the future according to a predetermined formula. They are generally a private agreement between the parties, *for example,* Interest rate swaps.

Forex Market

The *forex market* or *foreign exchange market* is the market where the participants globally come together to buy, sell, exchange and speculate on currencies. It comprises of banks, financial institutions, central banks, investment management firms, hedge funds, and retail forex brokers and investors.

The foreign exchange market in India is regulated by the Reserve Bank of India through the Exchange Control Department. Till liberalization in 1991, the forex market in India was highly regulated and the government exercised absolute control on the exchange rate, export-import policy, and the FDI (Foreign Direct Investment) policy. The Foreign Exchange Regulation Act (FERA), 1973, strictly controlled all foreign exchange related activities.

Post liberalization, the Government of India liberalized the foreign exchange policy in the form of Foreign Exchange Management Act (FEMA), 1999. FEMA expanded the list of activities in which a person/company can undertake forex transactions. Through FEMA, government liberalized the export-import policy, limits of FDI (Foreign Direct Investment) & FII (Foreign Institutional Investors) investments, cross-border M&A and fund-raising activities.

Features

1. *OTC market:* The forex market is an 'over-the-counter market' (OTC market). This implies that there is no single market or physical stock exchange but an electronic market where trading takes place.

2. *24-hour market:* It is a market that operates 24 hours a day at global level.

3. *Type of markets:* The foreign exchange market can be divided into 'retail market' and 'wholesale market'. In *retail market,* tourists and travelers exchange one currency in the form of currency notes or travelers' checks for meeting their foreign exchange requirements. The *wholesale market* is often called *interbank market.* The participants in this market are commercial banks, investment banks, corporate houses and central banks. The average transaction size is very large (deals may be in millions of US dollars [USD] or other currency) (Box 6.4).

BOX 6.4: SEGMENTS OF FOREX MARKET IN INDIA

In India, the forex market consists of three interdependent segments:

- *RBI and Authorized Dealers (ADs),* This takes place between RBI and authorized dealers, which are usually commercial banks.
- *Inter-authorized Dealers:* This is the major segment of the Indian forex market in which the ADs deal with each other. Trading is regulated by the Foreign Exchange Dealers' Association of India (FEDAI), a self-regulatory association of authorised dealers. The market consists of 108 Authorized Dealers (mostly banks and others include financial institutions and others) as on May, 2016*.
- *Retail Players:* In this segment, ADs deal with their corporate clients and other retail customers.

* http://www.fedai.org.in/MemberBanks.html

4. *Process:* In a forex trade, you buy one currency while simultaneously selling another, i.e. you are exchanging the sold currency for the one you are buying. Currencies are traded in pairs, like the Euro-US Dollar (EUR/USD) or US Dollar/Japanese Yen (USD/JPY).[4]

In India, Clearing Corporation of India Ltd. (CCIL) facilitates settlement of both debt and forex transactions.

Types of Forex Markets

Depending upon the time elapsed between the transaction date and the settlement date, foreign exchange transactions can be categorized into following:

1. *Spot market:* *Spot market* is the market where transactions for the exchange (purchase and sale) of currencies take place two days after the date of the contract. *For instance,* if the contract is made on Wednesday, the delivery should take place on

4. http://www.forex.com/why-trade-forex.html

Friday. The exchange rate for spot delivery is called *spot exchange rate* and is denoted by (S). *For example*, S(₹/USD) = ₹64.33/USD is the relationship between rupees and dollars, which implies that one dollar is equivalent to ₹64.33.

2. *Forward market:* *Forward market* is the place where the transactions for the exchange of currencies take place at a specified future after the spot date. The forward transaction can be for delivery one month or two months or three months, etc. The objective here may be to protect against adverse movements in currencies (*hedging transaction*) or to trade a currency (*speculative transaction*).

3. *Swap market:* It is a combination of a spot and a forward transaction. The term *swap* implies a temporary exchange of one currency for another with an obligation to reverse it at a specific future date. Swaps are two-way deals, one deal involving a buy and the other involving a sell, at different times, but one has to cancel the other.

INITIAL PUBLIC OFFERING (IPO)

Initial Public Offering is the first-time issue of securities by a company in the capital market and raising money thereof. A company gets 'listed' in the stock market through an IPO. Every company to get floated and raise money through IPO has to meet the entry standards as prescribed by the regulators. With IPO, a company does have an easy access to capital but it also results in dilution of control of the company.

Guidelines for Issue of Equity Capital

An unlisted company can make a public issue of equity shares or instrument convertible into equity subject to:

- Net Tangible Assets of at least ₹3 crores in each of the preceding 3 full years of which not more than 50% are held in monetary assets.
- Average Operating Profit of at least ₹15 crores during the preceding three years.
- Net worth of at least ₹1 crore in each of the preceding 3 full years.
- If the company has changed its name within the last one year, at least 50% revenue for the preceding 1 year should be from the activity suggested by the new name.[5]

Pricing of IPOs

After 1992, a 'free pricing of equity' took place under which corporates are free to decide the price of their securities and follow any of the following methods for raising money:

Fixed Price IPO

In case of a *fixed price IPO*, the issue price and the total amount of capital to be raised is fixed and known to the investor prior to the subscription. *For example,* public issue

5. https://www.sebi.gov.in/legal/regulations/nov-2022/securities-and-exchange-board-of-india-issue-of-capital-and-disclosure-requirements-regulations-2018-last-amended-on-november-21-2022-_65522.html

of 100,00,000 equity shares of ₹10 par value at a price of ₹24 (premium of ₹14) each aggregating ₹24 crore.

Book Building IPO

In case of *book building* method, neither the exact issue price nor the total amount of capital to be raised is known in advance. Here, the bids are invited in a price range and based on the investors' response, the final price is decided by the company. *For example,* public issue of 72,243,300 equity shares of ₹10 par value at a price of ₹[*] each aggregating ₹[*] crore. Price Band: ₹100 – ₹110 per share.

Take another example, public issue of 72,243,300 equity shares of ₹10 par value at a price of ₹[*] each aggregating ₹[*] crore. Floor Price: ₹115 per share.

Box 6.5 explains "Greenshoe Option" used in security issues.

BOX 6.5: GREENSHOE OPTION

A good issue is often over-subscribed. When this happens, a company may issue additional shares to the public to absorb the excess amount subscribed by them. Greenshoe option is an option whereby a company can retain a part of the over-subscribed capital by issuing additional shares. The objective behind issuing additional shares may not be to collect additional capital but is to use entire proceeds to stabilize the post listing share price.

CAPITAL MARKET REFORMS

The Indian regulatory framework of securities market has been adequately strengthened through various legislative and administrative measures in the past. The regulatory framework for securities market is consistent with the best international benchmarks like standards prescribed by International Organisation of Securities Commissions (IOSCO).

- Extensive Capital Market Reforms were undertaken during the 1990s, such as Abolition of Controller of Capital Issues took place in 1992 and a statutory market regulator was created in the form of SEBI in 1992.
- National Stock Exchange (NSE) was established in 1994 to diversify the trading operations in India.
- The Depository Act 1996 led to the establishment of the Depositories in India—NSDL (the National Securities Depository Ltd.) and CDSL (the Central Depository Services (I) Ltd.). It resulted in an efficient, low risk and cost infrastructure for paperless handling of securities.
- The intermediaries registered with SEBI, consisted of brokers, sub-brokers, trading and clearing members, portfolio managers, bankers to Issue, merchant bankers, registrars, underwriters and credit rating agencies.
- Dematerialisation started in 1997 and electronic book keeping was provided. Soon, trading in most of the stocks started in the dematerialised form.
- Free pricing of equity and introduction of book building process were done for raising capital. Investors and corporates both had a free choice in equity trading.

- Regarding legal framework for derivatives with the amendment of SCRA in 1999, derivatives trading started in a gradual manner with stock index futures in June 2000. Later, options and single stock futures were introduced in 2000–2001. Now, India's derivatives market turnover is more than the cash market which has made India one of the largest single stock futures markets in the world.
- India's risk management systems have always been very modern and effective. The VaR-based margining system was introduced in mid-2001 and the risk management systems have been really effective.
- India is one of the few countries to have started the screen-based trading of government securities in January 2003.
- RBI had introduced the Real Time Gross Settlement System (RTGS) in 2004 on an experimental basis. RTGS allows delivery of payment within quick span of time, on the lines of international norms recognised by BIS and IOSCO.
- To improve the governance mechanism of stock exchanges, demutualisation and corporatisation of stock exchanges was mandated.

STOCK EXCHANGES IN INDIA

Stock exchanges are marketplace where buyers and sellers come together to trade in a firm's shares and other securities. The buying and selling on an exchange is only open to its affiliates and brokers. In India, stock exchanges can either be a conglomerate/ firm or mutual group. They also assist the issue and release of securities.

As on 15th January 2023, there were 7 stock exchanges in India with due validity[6].

BSE Ltd. (formerly Bombay Stock Exchange)

The oldest stock exchange in Asia (established in 1875) and the first in the country to be granted permanent recognition under the Securities Contract Regulation Act, 1956, BSE has had an interesting rise to prominence around the past 150 years.

While BSE is now synonymous to Dalal Street, it was not always so. The first venues of the earliest stock-broker meetings in the 1850s were in rather natural environs—under banyan trees, in front of the Town Hall where the Horniman Circle is now situated, etc. A decade later, the brokers moved their venue to another set of foliage, this time under banyan trees at the junction of Meadows Street, what is now called Mahatma Gandhi Road. As the number of brokers increased, they had to shift from place to place, but they always overflowed to the streets. At last, in 1874, the brokers found a permanent place, and one that they could, quite literally, call their own. The new place was, aptly, called Dalal Street (Brokers' Street).

In 2002, the name 'The Stock Exchange, Mumbai' was changed to 'Bombay Stock Exchange'. Subsequently on August 19, 2005, the exchange turned into a corporate entity from an Association of Persons (AoP) and renamed as Bombay Stock Exchange Limited.

BSE, which had introduced securities trading in India, replaced its open outcry system of trading in 1995, with the totally automated trading through the BSE Online Trading (BOLT) system. The BOLT network was expanded nationwide in 1997. In 2017, BSE become the 1st listed stock exchange of India.

6. https://www.sebi.gov.in/stock-exchanges.html

Prominent Position

The journey of BSE is as eventful and interesting as the history of India's securities market. In fact, being India's biggest stock exchange in terms of listed companies and market capitalisation, BSE has played a pioneering role in the development of the Indian securities market. It is surely BSE's pride that almost every leading corporate in India has sourced its services in capital raising and is listed with the renowned stock-exchange of India.

Even in terms of an orderly growth, much before the actual legislations were enacted, BSE had formulated a comprehensive set of rules and regulations for the securities market. It had also laid down best practices set up after India gained its independence which are followed by other stock exchanges.

BSE, as a brand, has been and is synonymous with the capital market in India. SENSEX is the benchmark equity index that reflects the health of the Indian economy. BSE is Asia's first and the Fastest Stock Exchange in world with the speed of 6 micro seconds.

National Stock Exchange of India Ltd.

The National Stock Exchange of India Limited (NSE) was set up based on the report of the High Powered Study Group on *Establishment of New Stock Exchanges*. It recommended establishment of a National Stock Exchange by financial institutions to provide access to investors from all across the country on an equal footing. Based on the recommendations, NSE was promoted by leading financial institutions at the behest of the Government of India and was incorporated in November 1992 as a tax-paying company, unlike other stock exchanges in the country.

On its recognition in April 1993 as a stock exchange under the Securities Contracts (Regulation) Act, 1956, NSE commenced operations in the Wholesale Debt Market (WDM) segment in June 1994. The Capital Market (Equities) segment commenced operations in November 1994 and the operations in Derivatives segment commenced in June 2000.

The following years witnessed rapid development of the Indian capital market with introduction of internet trading, Exchange Traded Funds (ETF), stock derivatives and the first volatility index by NSE—IndiaVIX in April 2008.

August 2008 saw the introduction of currency derivatives in India with the launch of Currency Futures in USD-INR pair by NSE. Interest Rate Futures was introduced for the first time in India by NSE on 31st August 2009, exactly one year after the launch of Currency Futures.

With this, both the retail and institutional investors can participate in equities, equity derivatives, currency and interest rate derivatives, giving them a wide range of products to take care of their evolving needs.

Multi Commodity Exchange of India Ltd. (MCX)

MCX is the India's first listed exchange that facilitates online trading, and clearing and settlement of commodity futures transactions. It started its operations in November, 2003.

Other Stock Exchanges of India

The Regional Stock Exchanges in India started spreading their business operations since 1894. The first RSE to start its functioning in India was Ahmedabad Stock Exchange (ASE) followed by Calcutta Stock Exchange (CSE) in 1908.

Note:

1. 28 Regional/Other Stock Exchanges have been granted exit during last 10 years by SEBI, including Ahmedabad Stock Exchange in 2018.
   [*The complete list is available at: https://www.sebi.gov.in/stock-exchanges.html*]

FACTORS FOR INVESTMENT IN CAPITAL MARKETS

An individual investor considers the following factors of risk while investing in capital markets:

Volatility Risk and Risk of Contagions

High volatility is the characteristic of any capital market, especially in emerging markets. They are immature and sometimes, vulnerable to scandal. They often lack legal and judicial infrastructure to enforce the law. Accounting disclosure, trading and settlement practices may at times seem overly arbitrary and unsophisticated. Against this backdrop, many emerging markets had to cope with unprecedented inflows and outflows of capital. The sudden withdrawal of highly speculative, short-term capital has the potential of taking with it much of a market's price support. Such sudden flights of capital triggered by events in one emerging market can spread instantly to other markets through contagion effects even when those markets have quite different conditions.

Liquidity Risk

Many emerging markets are small and illiquid. Volumes of trade are quite low. This kind of thin trading often leads to higher costs because large transactions have a significant impact on the market. Thus, buyers of large blocks of shares may have to pay more to complete the transaction, and sellers may receive a lower price.

Clearance and Settlement Risk

Inadequate settlement procedures still exist in many of the emerging markets. They lead to high 'failure' rates. A fail occurs when a trade fails to settle on the settlement date.

Political Risk

In most of the developing countries, the political systems are less stable as compared to the developed countries. This scenario does not give the political system of a country the opportunity to concentrate more on the capital market happenings and restrict any kind of malfunctions or practices.

Currency Risk

The trade in capital markets is highly impacted by the fluctuations in the foreign exchange rates. The currencies of the developing countries are not stable enough to compete with those of the developed countries. This leads towards unexpected losses for the investors in the markets.

Limited Disclosure and Insufficient Legal Infrastructure

As it is already discussed earlier that disclosure levels will not be upto the required extent in emerging markets, the investors will not have a bright picture of the company in which they are investing, and this may lead to loss.

Regarding the Indian context, it can be said that a proper mechanism has been devised to face and sustain all the above mentioned risks, after facing each of them in a practical way. Thus the growth, which has been found in the Indian capital market, can be described as 'sustainable growth'.

CIRCUIT BREAKERS

Circuit breakers is a very important tool used by the stock exchanges to stop speculative trading. Stock prices can go up or down due to a number of reasons, like corporate results, government policies, industry trends, etc. These price movements are reasonable and logical.

But in some cases, stock prices may go up or down drastically, mostly manipulated by the speculators for their greed or fear. Such movements are harmful for the stock markets. In order to control these heavy price fluctuations, stock exchanges have a system called *circuit breakers*. These are also called *circuit limits or price bands*. They maintain the integrity of the stock market and protect the investors.

Circuit breakers were first introduced in the trading system of Indian stock exchanges in 1992 at BSE. There are separate circuit breakers for the indices and individual stocks. When the volatility of a stock breaks a certain limit as decided by the exchange, trading in that stock is stopped for some time. The limit is fixed by the stock exchange as a percentage of the stock's price. The rules for circuit breaking are decided by SEBI.

The index-based market-wide circuit breaker system applies at 3 stages of the index movement, either way, viz. at 10%, 15% and 20%. So, there are 3 circuit limits for indices—10%, 15% and 20%, as under:

- 10% movement in either direction
- 15% movement in either direction
- 20% movement in either direction

These circuit breakers are applied to Sensex or Nifty whichever is breached first. They result in a trading halt in all equity and equity derivative markets nationwide. The extent of duration of the market halt and pre-open session is given in Table 6.2.

TABLE 6.2 Circuit Breakers' Mechanism

Trigger Limit	*Trigger Time*	*Market Halt Duration*	*Pre-open Call Auction Session Post-Market Halt*
10%	Before 1 pm	45 minutes	15 minutes
	At or after 1 pm upto 2.30 pm	15 minutes	15 minutes
	At or after 2.30 pm	No halt	Not applicable
15%	Before 1 pm	1 hour 45 minutes	15 minutes
	At or after 1 pm before 2 pm	45 minutes	15 minutes
	On or after 2 pm	Remainder of the day	Not applicable
20%	Any time during market hours	Remainder of the day	Not applicable

The exchange computes the index circuit breaker limits for 10%, 15% and 20% levels on a daily basis based on the previous day's closing level of the index rounded off to the nearest tick size[7].

REGULATION OF FINANCIAL MARKETS

The money market in India is primarily governed by Reserve Bank of India, in addition to Securities and Exchange Board of India (SEBI). The capital markets are regulated by SEBI under the provisions of the Securities Contracts (Regulations) Act, 1956 and Securities and Exchange Board of India Act, 1992. SEBI has issued detailed guidelines for capital issues, disclosure by public companies and investor protection.

Nature of Financial Market Regulation

The nature of securities markets is such that they are inherently susceptible to failures due to the existence of information asymmetries and existence of high transaction costs. It needs to be emphasised that when securities markets come into existence, the interest of the member brokers are taken care of through margin requirements, barriers to entry of membership, and listing agreements. However, the investors or clients who buy and sell via their brokers are not able to form an organisation to safeguard their interests due to the cost of creation of such organisations and free rider problems. The distinctive nature of the market can be observed with reference to the commodity, its quality, the system of transactions and the participants in the market, as follows:

(a) The commodity (the security) has a life to perpetuity.

(b) While the outcome of the contract, say the redemption of debt is certain, in the case of the government, it is not always so in the case of a private debt instrument; hence uncertainty comes into focus.

7. http://www.nseindia.com/products/content/equities/equities/circuit_breakers.htm

(c) The quality of private debt instrument is unobservable and hence, it is the trust reposed on the trader or the issuer that is the decisive factor, here the problem of information comes into focus;

(d) In any securities market, in any transaction or deal, there are at least four participants, two clients and two brokers. The brokers negotiate deals with each other on behalf of their clients and thus the problem of transaction cost comes into focus. When there is much scope for failure and opportunism, there appears to be substantial ground for prescribing an institution that oversees the market at different stages to ensure its reliability, efficiency and its existence.

Objectives of Financial Market Regulation

The key objectives of financial regulation can be understood from the following:

Efficient Economic Function

The prime objective of regulation and supervision is to facilitate the efficient and fair performance of economic functions, but a practical regulatory structure must deal with (and will influence) the products and institutions through which those functions are performed. This creates considerable complexities because there is no unique relationship between functions, products, and institutions. Several products might perform the same function, some functions might involve several products, institutions can provide a range of products, etc. These relationships can change over time, in response to technological change and in ways influenced by the existing regulatory structure.

Users' Welfare

One focus of financial regulation is upon the characteristics of financial products, which are explicit or implicit contracts between parties, entered with certain expectations on the basis of information held by those parties. Participants may be unable to obtain information to appropriately evaluate the ability of a counter-party to meet a contractual obligation (such as payment of an insurance benefit), or may be given incorrect information which leads them to form inappropriate expectations of performance (such as of a managed fund). Ultimately, the focus of a regulatory structure must be on the welfare of the end users.

Appropriate Incentive Structure

Also, there should be a good incentive structure for providing information in financial markets, as information is very important to the investor. Investors often find it difficult to evaluate the quality of the security or service offered which calls for an intermediary to disseminate information and services that have to be regulated. Regulations also prevent monopoly of capital markets, which otherwise jeopardize the market mechanism.

Table 6.3 indicates regulatory bodies of financial markets around the world.

TABLE 6.3 Regulatory Bodies of Financial Markets

Country	*Regulatory Body*
India	RBI (Reserve Bank of India), SEBI (Securities and Exchange Board of India)
U.S.A.	FRB (Federal Reserve Board), SEC (Securities and Exchange Commission)
United Kingdom	FCA (Financial Conduct Authority), PRA (Prudential Regulation Authority)

Legislations Governing Securities Market

The main legislations governing the securities market are:

- The SEBI Act, 1992, which established SEBI to protect investors, and develop and regulate securities market
- The Companies Act, 2013 & 1956, which lay down the code of conduct for the corporate sector in relation to issue, allotment and transfer of securities, and disclosures to be made in public issues
- The Securities Contracts (Regulation) Act, 1956, which provides for regulation of transactions in securities through control over stock exchanges
- The Depositories Act, 1996, which provides for electronic maintenance and transfer of ownership of demat securities
- The Prevention of Money Laundering Act, 2002, which prevents money laundering and provides for confiscation of property derived from or involved in money laundering.

These legislations are discussed below.

SEBI Act, 1992

It was passed to establish the Securities and Exchange Board of India (SEBI) to protect the interests of investors in securities and regulate the securities market. SEBI is responsive to the needs of three constituents of the market—the issuers of securities, the investors, and the market intermediaries.

Companies Act, 2013 & 1956

It deals with issue, allotment and transfer of securities and various aspects relating to company management. It provides for standards of disclosure in public issues of capital, particularly in the fields of company management and projects, information about other listed companies under the same management, and management perception of risk factors. Besides, it also regulates underwriting, the use of premium and discounts on issues, rights and bonus issues, payment of interest and dividends, supply of annual report, etc.

Securities Contracts (Regulation) Act, 1956

It provides for direct and indirect control of all the aspects of securities trading and the working of stock exchanges. It gives Central Government regulatory jurisdiction over:

(i) Stock exchanges through a process of recognition and continued supervision.
(ii) Contracts in securities.
(iii) Listing of securities on stock exchanges.

Depositories Act, 1996

The Depositories Act, 1996 provides for the establishment of depositories in securities with the objective of ensuring free transferability of securities with speed, accuracy and security by:

(i) Making securities of public limited companies freely transferable subject to certain exceptions.
(ii) Dematerializing the securities in the depository mode.
(iii) Providing for maintenance of ownership records in a book entry form.

In order to streamline the settlement process, the Act envisages transfer of ownership of securities electronically by book entry without making the securities move from person to person. The Act has made the securities of all public limited companies freely transferable, restricting the company's right to use discretion in affecting the transfer of securities, and the transfer deed and other procedural requirements under the Companies Act have been dispensed with.

Prevention of Money Laundering Act, 2002

The primary objective of the Act is to prevent money-laundering and to provide for confiscation of property derived from or involved in money-laundering. The term *money-laundering* is defined as whoever acquires, owns, possesses or transfers any proceeds of crime, or knowingly enters into any transaction which is related to proceeds of crime either directly or indirectly, or conceals or aids in the concealment of the proceeds or gains of crime within India or outside India commits the offence of money laundering. Besides providing punishment for the offence of money-laundering, the Act also provides other measures for prevention of money laundering. The Act also casts an obligation on the intermediaries, banking companies, etc. to furnish information of such prescribed transactions to the Financial Intelligence Unit India, to appoint a principal officer, to maintain certain records, etc.

DEVELOPMENT OF FINANCIAL REGULATION IN INDIA

The development and regulation of money, foreign exchange and Government securities markets is a function of the RBI that emerges out of its role as a monetary authority as well as a debt manager to the government and its responsibility for the stability of the financial system. In this context, the Reserve Bank has been emphasising a redefinition of its regulatory role vis-á-vis financial markets, particularly in an environment characterised by multiple regulation. The amendments to the Securities Contract (Regulations) Act (SCRA), 1956 which were brought into effect on

March 1, 2000, assume critical significance. They establish the regulatory jurisdiction of the Reserve Bank over transactions in government securities, money market securities, gold related securities, and derivatives based on these securities and ready forward contracts in all debt securities, in conjunction with the RBI's regulation of foreign exchange transactions under the Foreign Exchange Regulation Act, 1973 and later by the Foreign Exchange Management Act, 1999.

The development of financial markets is regarded as a critical pre-requisite for improving the operational effectiveness of the transmission of monetary policy. The development phase is as follows:

First Phase

Accordingly, the first phase of financial sector reforms consisted of easing of various structural rigidities—both price- and quantity-based, in order to increase participation in financial markets, to develop and strengthen inter-linkages between market segments, fostering competition, introduction of more sophisticated financial instruments and innovations in market practices, ensuring adequate liquidity in various segments of the market spectrum, and developing the regulatory, legal, institutional and technological infrastructure for orderly market activity.

Second Phase

In the second phase of reforms, issues relating to the stability of financial markets had received priority in the policy agenda. The liberalisation of financial markets had raised the vulnerability of financial institutions to volatility in financial asset prices and has thereby, increased the potential risks of impairment of their balance sheets, with implications for systemic stability.

The international experience with market failures in 1997–98 and contagion effects had prioritised the regulatory function in the context of the development of financial markets in India. The need for regulation arose for maintaining systemic stability, given the strong complementarity between financial stability and price stability. In the country-specific situation, the challenge is to make micro-regulations consistent with macro-objectives. In this period, policy initiatives had encompassed measures for market discipline, fine-tuning of the market microstructure in order to reflect the evolving sophistication and technological advancement in the functioning of markets, and specific changes in the legal and regulatory framework which would institute healthy market practices and also enable more effective supervision and oversight.

As far as money markets were concerned, a basic objective in these years had been to develop a proper, short-term rupee yield curve with deep liquidity therein. A four-fold strategy was being adopted in this regard:

First, Liquidity Adjustment Facility (LAF) operations are being conducted with a view to keep the short-term interest rates within a corridor.

Secondly, the call money market is being developed into a pure inter-bank market with a phased withdrawal of non-bank participants who only lend in the market.

Thirdly, the traditional sector-specific refinance support is being rationalised and the additional recourse to the standing liquidity facilities of the RBI is being made increasingly market-based.

Finally, the other money market segments, especially the repo market, are being developed with lending as well as borrowing access to the non-banks in these markets.

In respect of Government Securities market, the initiatives over these years have been to develop the market in terms of depth, liquidity, turnover and participants. Given the constraints imposed by conditions in the money and foreign exchange markets and the persistently large government borrowing programme, the RBI has, at times, taken private placements in the primary issues or devolvement at the auctions. It has subsequently undertaken open market operations at ideal points of time to assuage market pressures to contain the monetary impact of the fiscal operations, and to allow for the emergence of a smooth yield curve. The RBI has also adopted a policy of passive consolidation in the number of outstanding loan issuances and facilitated creation of volumes in benchmark securities. Open market operations are undertaken to contain volatility and to provide liquidity to the Government Securities market.

The foreign exchange market in India continues to be relatively thin, localised and expectation-driven with a tendency towards 'herding' and asymmetrical behaviour. The medium-term policy endeavour is to develop the foreign exchange market in terms of depth and liquidity, enable the introduction of new instruments and pricing strategies, and greater integration with other segments of the financial market. In the day-to-day regulation of the foreign exchange market, the policy objective is to manage volatility with no fixed rate target, and allow demand and supply conditions to determine exchange rate movements in a systematic manner. The RBI also enters periodically into foreign exchange transactions with the market to prevent undue fluctuations in the exchange rate.

Third Phase

During 2000–01, the Reserve Bank continued to adopt a strategy of maintaining orderly conditions in the money, government securities and foreign exchange markets with a flexible stance of responding quickly to unforeseen developments in the external environment and reverting to normal conditions as the pressures eased. Liquidity management operations were employed to maintain orderly conditions in the money market. In the Government Securities market, outright sales of securities through Open Market Operating (OMO) was undertaken to minimise the monetary impact of the increase in foreign currency assets on account of India Millennium Deposits (IMDs) and switches/purchases of securities to provide liquidity to the longer end of the market. Long-term securities had devolved heavily on the Primary Dealers (PDs) in the primary auctions in the wake of volatility in the foreign exchange market and monetary tightening in May–August 2000. The strategy regarding management of the exchange rate, continued to maintain orderly conditions in the foreign exchange market, met temporary supply-demand gaps arising due to uncertainties or other reasons, and curbed destabilising and self-fulfilling speculative activities.

Money Markets

A policy priority in the development of the money market has been the positioning of "Liquidity Adjustment Facility" (LAF) as an instrument for modulating liquidity, signalling the monetary stance, and for creating conditions for orderly market activity.

The first stage of the LAF, introduced with effect from June 5, 2000, progressed satisfactorily. The second stage, introduced with effect from May 8, 2001, brought about further refinements in the LAF.

Efforts to develop the call money market into a pure inter-bank market (including PDs) while providing access to other short-term instruments for non-bank participants gathered momentum with the measures announced in the Statement on Monetary and Credit Policy of April 2001. Corporates were allowed to route their call money transactions through PDs upto June 2001. A four-phased exit of non-bank institutions from the call money market commenced from May 5, 2001, wherein as a part of stage I, non-bank institutions were permitted to lend, on an average, upto 85% of their average daily call money lending during a reporting fortnight in 2000–01. This would be followed by reductions in their access to 70% in stage II when the clearing corporation is operationalised. Subsequently, such limits would be reduced to 40% and 10% in stage III and stage IV, respectively, before a complete withdrawal of non-bank participants from the call money market.

In consonance with the phasing out of non-banks from the call money market, other avenues for their short-term investments were made attractive. In 2000–01, the minimum maturity of certificates of Deposit (CD) was reduced to 15 days to bring them at par with other short-term instruments. With a view to provide flexibility and depth to the secondary market, restriction on the transferability period for CDs issued by banks and financial institutions was withdrawn. Similarly, the minimum maturity period for wholesale deposits of ₹15 lacs and above was reduced to 7 days. The repo market was expanded to cover non-bank entities holding both current and SGL accounts with the Reserve Bank. The minimum repo tenor was reduced to 1 day and State Government securities were made eligible for repos.

Guidelines mentioned for Commercial Paper (CP) were modified to provide greater flexibility to issuers, to broaden the investor base and to simplify issuance procedures, including in dematerialised form. The most important measure in this regard was that CP no longer had to be carved out of working capital limit. Banks, FIs, PDs and Satellite Dealers (SDs) were directed to make fresh investments and hold CP in only dematerialised form with effect from June 30, 2001 and convert the outstanding investments in scrip form by October 31, 2001. In this regard, the Fixed Income Money Market and Derivatives Association of India (FIMMDA) has issued a detailed set of standardised market practices and documentations regarding dematerialisation of CP on July 29, 2001.

The main intention of these measures has been to transform call money market into a pure inter-bank market, and evolve call money and repo markets to an integrated set for equilibrating short-term positions of banks as well as non-banks. Furthermore, these measures would enable development of a proper short-term rupee yield curve which, in turn, would influence other financial market segments.

Government Securities Market

The aggregate volume of transactions in Central Government dated securities and Treasury bills (outright as well as repos) during 2000–01 was higher by 30% at ₹6,95,135 crore as compared with ₹5,35,602 crore in 1999–2000, reflecting an increasing depth in the Government securities market. The deepening of the market was attributable to several factors such as generally stable call rates, favourable market expectations especially during the second half of the year, more active trading by the new PDs, mutual funds, some traditional participants like banks and LIC, and active OMO by the Reserve Bank. During 2000–01, the total outright transactions amounted to ₹5,69,174 crore or 82% of the aggregate transactions and the balance of ₹1,25,961 crore or 18% was by way of repos. During 1999–2000, the total outright transactions amounted to ₹4,52,861 crore or 85% of the aggregate transactions and the balance ₹82,741 crore or 15% was by way of repos. During 2000–01, the transactions in State Government securities were lower at ₹2,986 crore as against ₹3,632 crore during 1999–2000.

Foreign Exchange Market

The foreign exchange market has undergone substantial liberalisation, both in terms of freedom for market participants as well as a liberalised exchange and payments system for current and capital transactions. Improvements in the market microstructure are undertaken as a result of continuous monitoring and consultations with market participants. The RBI continued to liberalise foreign exchange market and the payments regime with a view to—(i) pave the way for a smooth transition to the Foreign Exchange Management Act (FEMA), 1999 from the Foreign Exchange Regulation Act (FERA), 1973, (ii) enable a phased movement to capital account convertibility, and (iii) provide a prompt and hassle-free exchange and payments system.

Regulations issued under FEMA would allow units in the Special Economic Zones (SEZs) to credit their entire exchange earnings to Exchange Earners Foreign Currency (EEFC) accounts. Limit for advance remittances towards import without any guarantee was raised to US$ 25,000 (from the existing limit of US$ 15,000). Passport endorsement about the release of foreign exchange for purposes other than private visits was made non-mandatory, while foreign nationals employed in India were permitted to credit 75% of their salary to foreign currency accounts abroad subject to tax deduction on the entire salary.

The progressive liberalisation of capital account transactions continued to receive policy attention. In respect of Indian investment abroad, Indian companies were allowed to acquire foreign companies or make direct investment in joint ventures/wholly-owned subsidiaries abroad:

(i) Upto US$ 50 million (with an additional US$ 25 million in case of Myanmar and SAARC countries other than Nepal, Bhutan and Pakistan), on an annual basis through the automatic route without the earlier three-year profitability condition.

(ii) By utilising the entire proceeds (from the earlier 50%) of their American Depository Receipts (ADR)/Global Depository Receipts (GDR).

The Reserve Bank also introduced a new facility for block allocation of foreign exchange for companies that have exhausted their US$ 50 million limit on fulfilling certain eligibility criteria. The facility of acquiring shares of foreign companies in the same area of core activity upto US$ 100 million or an amount equivalent to ten times of their exports, whichever was higher, after issuance of ADRs/GDRs was extended to all companies irrespective of the sector of activity.

Regarding overseas investment, the ban on such investments by registered partnerships was removed. Partnerships in certain professional services, viz. chartered accountancy, legal services, medical and health care services, information technology and entertainment software services are now allowed to invest abroad in foreign concerns in the same line of activity upto US$ 1 million under the automatic route and beyond US$ 1 million with the approval of the RBI. Partnership firms in other activities would, however, require prior approval of the RBI for their investment proposals. Indian nationals who have the benefit of Employee Stock Ownership Plan (ESOP) in foreign-owned companies are now allowed to invest upto US$ 20,000 per annum (as against the earlier US$ 10,000 in a block of five years).

The guidelines issued by Securities and Exchange Board of India for the regulation of financial markets are available on SEBI's website: http://www.sebi.gov.in/acts/act11.html.[8]

CASE STUDY

Facebook IPO

The IPO of Facebook for a price of $38 per share in May, 2012 was one of the most hyped and sought-after IPOs at that time. From the opening trading price of $42.05 per share, its share price dipped dramatically to $29.16 on May 29, just 11 days later, and millions of investors suffered losses.

The IPO had its own share of problems right from the first day of trading, i.e., May 18. There were software delays from Nasdaq market makers resulting in a delay of 30 minutes in trading of Facebook shares, which made investors lose more than $100 million from lost orders and unconfirmed sales.

It was found out in a Facebook SEC filing on August 2 that as many as 83 million of its reported 955 million members could be fake or duplicate. This dropped Facebook's stock further by 4.02% that day coming down to $20.04. Its shares hit a new low of $17.58 on September 4, 2012, the lowest point since the company went public.

Mark Zuckerberg tried holding onto his Facebook shares for at least another year, making the company's stock jump up 4.8% on September 5 but that was not enough. A lot had to be done to rebound the stock.

The Fundamentals

- Facebook had reported a strong revenue growth of 32% in its first public earnings report.
- It had a strong balance sheet having secured $10 billion in funding its IPO.
- It was focusing on new ad units around mobile to address its past and current ad monetization problems.
- It was continuing to innovate elsewhere too, including in the mobile products space.

Rules of Investment

Investors should not blindly rely on company's numbers and must try to look beyond. They should be questioning the process of pricing initial public offering of the company

8. These guidelines are also available in the Instructor's manual.

so that they are left with a real liquid stock and not an overpriced slip of paper which could not be sold for even half price.

Follow the fundamentals: Analysts warned early that Facebook was over-valued, based on fundamentals. Individual investors had access to this information all along, but many chose to ignore the basics to buy the latest hot stock.

Do not try to time markets: Research suggests that for every stock and so with Facebook, if you decide to buy Facebook stock, plan to buy and hold it for an extended period.

Diversify: Always make sure your portfolio contains a variety of assets. Social media marketing had been all the rage in 2012, and some have speculated that a new tech bubble was forming. So, people built on only one stock.

(*Source:* https://www.nerdwallet.com/blog/investing/understanding-facebook-ipo-facebooks-stock-price-ipo-buy.)

POINTS TO REMEMBER

- Capital market in India is regulated by the "Securities and Exchange Board of India" (SEBI).
- India's financial market began its transformation path in the early 1990s.
- Equity market is a market for owned instruments.
- Equity shares are those shares which do not carry any special or preferential rights in the payment of annual dividend or repayment of capital.
- Preference shares are shares which carry certain special or preferential rights in the payment of dividend and repayment of capital as compared to equity shareholders.
- Cumulative preference shares enjoy the right to receive the dividend in arrears for the years they did not receive it.
- Redeemable preference shares can be redeemed on or after a period fixed for redemption. Irredeemable preference shares are those which cannot be redeemed during the lifetime of the company.
- Convertible preference shares have a right to convert their holding into ordinary shares. The holders of non-convertible preference shares have no such right of conversion.
- Participating preference shares have a right to participate in the surplus profits of the company. The preference shares which do not have such right to participate are known as non-participating preference shares.
- Depository receipts are shares of domestic companies issued in the form of depository receipts in a foreign land in the foreign currency.
- American Depositary Receipts (ADR) allow non-US companies to raise capital in the US equity market, and allow US investors to invest in international stocks.

- Global Depositary Receipts (GDR) are securities available in one or more markets outside the company's home country.
- Debt market is a market for borrowed instruments of the existing and new corporate firms. The debt market in India consists of mainly two categories—the Government Securities and the corporate bond market.
- Government Securities market refers to the market for government and semi-government securities backed by the Reserve Bank of India (RBI). They are—(a) Dated Government Securities, or (b) State Development Loans (SDLs).
- Debentures and bonds are known as creditorship securities because debenture-holders are the creditors of a company.
- Secured/Mortgage debentures are secured against assets of the company whereas unsecured/simple debentures are unsecured.
- Redeemable debentures are to be repaid within a certain specified period. Irredeemable/Perpetual debentures have no specified period for redemption.
- Zero coupon debentures do not have a specified interest rate, thereby to compensate, they are issued at a substantial discount. Specific coupon rate debentures are normally issued with an interest rate.
- Convertible debentures can be converted to either equity shares or preference shares by the company. Non-convertible debentures can not be converted into equity/preference shares.
- Public deposits refer to the deposits received by a company from the public as loan or debt. They can be—(a) Non-cumulative schemes, or (b) Cumulative fixed deposit schemes.
- Institutional finance is another important instrument of finance. There are both central- and state-level financial institutions to provide funds to the business firms.
- The major reasons for under-developed bond market in India are—(i) Heavy tilt towards private placement, (ii) Rating problem, (iii) Issuance profile, (iv) Individuals' preference, (v) Fragmentation, (vi) Stamp duty, and (vi) Crowding effect.
- Primary market consists of issuers creating and issuing fresh securities in exchange of funds. When securities are exclusively offered to the existing shareholders, it is called 'Right Issue' and when it is issued to selected, mature and sophisticated institutional investors as opposed to general public, it is called 'Private Placement Issue'.
- Secondary market is the market where an investor can buy a security directly from another investor in lieu of the issuer.
- Derivatives market deals with derivatives which have no independent value. Their value is derived from some other asset, which is called the 'Underlying Asset'.
- Forwards are the customized contracts between two parties, where settlement takes place on a specific date in future at today's pre-agreed price.
- Futures are agreements between two parties to buy or sell an asset at a certain time in the future at a certain price.
- Options give the contract holder the right to buy or sell on a specified date in the future—but they are under no obligation. Options are of two types—call and put. 'Call' gives the buyer the right but not the obligation to buy a given quantity of

the underlying asset, at a given price, whereas 'Put' gives the buyer the right, but not the obligation to sell a given quantity of the underlying asset at a given price.

- Swaps are a type of forward contracts. They are private agreements between two parties to exchange cash flows in the future according to a pre-arranged formula.
- Forex market or 'foreign exchange market' is the market where the participants globally come together to buy, sell, exchange and speculate on currencies. It is an OTC market which operates in a 24-hour basis. It consists of both retail and wholesale market.
- In India, the forex market consists of three interdependent segments—(i) RBI and authorized dealers (ADs), (ii) Inter-authorized dealers, and (iii) Retail players.
- Spot market is the market where transactions for the exchange (purchase and sale) of currencies take place two days after the date of the contract.
- Forward market is the place where the transactions for the exchange of currencies take place at a specified future after the spot date.
- Swap market is a combination of a spot and a forward transaction. The term 'swap' implies a temporary exchange of one currency for another with an obligation to reverse it at a specific future date.
- Initial Public Offering (IPO) can be Fixed price mechanism or Book Building IPO. In case of the book building method, neither the exact issue price nor the total amount of capital to be raised is known in advance.
- Capital market reform revolutionalised in 1992, when the SEBI Act was formulated giving SEBI the statutory status of an apex regulatory body. National Stock Exchange (NSE) was established in 1994 to diversify the trading operations in India and dematerialisation started in 1997. Free pricing of equity and introduction of book building process were carried out for raising capital. Screen-based trading of government securities started in January 2003. To improve the governance mechanism of stock exchanges, demutualisation and corporatisation of stock exchanges was done. The Depository Act 1996 led to the establishment of two depositories in India—NSDL (National Securities Depository Ltd.) and CDSL (Central Depository Services (I) Ltd.). The Intermediaries got registered with SEBI.
- Stock exchanges are structured marketplace where affiliates of a union gather to sell firm's shares and other securities.
- BSE is the oldest stock exchange in Asia (established in 1875) and the first in the country to be granted permanent recognition under the Securities Contract Regulation Act, 1956.
- National Stock Exchange was set up to provide access to investors from all over the country on an equal footing. NSE commenced operations in the Wholesale Debt Market (WDM) segment in June 1994.
- Multi-Commodity Exchange of India Ltd. (MCX) is the first listed stock exchange of India dealing into commodities. It started its operations in November, 2003.
- Regional Stock Exchanges (RSE) in India started spreading their business operations from 1894. The first RSE to start its functioning in India was Ahmedabad Stock Exchange (ASE) followed by Calcutta Stock Exchange (CSE) in 1908.

- The factors for investment in capital markets are—volatility risk and risk of contagions, liquidity risk, clearance and settlement risk, political risk, currency risk, and limited disclosure and insufficient legal infrastructure.
- Circuit breakers were first introduced in the trading system of Indian stock exchanges back in 1992 at the BSE. The rules for circuit breaking are decided by the Securities Exchange Board. The index-based market-wide circuit breaker system applies at 3 stages of the index movement, viz. 10%, 15% and 20%.
- The basic objectives of financial regulation are—(i) Efficient economic function, (ii) Users' welfare, and (iii) Appropriate incentive structure.

KEY TERMS

- **Capital market** is the market for long-term funds, i.e. for more than one year.
- **Equity shares** are those shares which do not carry any special or preferential rights in the payment of annual dividend or repayment of capital.
- **Preference shares** are those shares which carry certain special or preferential rights in the payment of dividend and repayment of capital.
- **Depository receipts** are securities of domestic companies issued in the form of ownership in a foreign land in the foreign currency.
- **Debentures** are creditorship securities, repressing the creditors of a company.
- **Primary market** is a place for exchange of newly issued stocks and bonds.
- **Secondary market** is the place for buying and selling (trading) existing instruments.
- **Derivatives** are those instruments whose value is derived from some other asset, which is called the "underlying asset".
- **Book building** is a process of raising money through IPO where bids are invited in a price range and based on the investors' response, the final price is decided by the company.

EXERCISES

Objective Questions

1. Tick the correct answer:

(a) Multi-commodity exchange is a:

(i) Regional stock exchange (ii) National level stock exchange
(iii) International stock exchange (iv) None of the above

(b) Financial markets are regulated by:

(i) SEBI (ii) RBI
(iii) Both (iv) None of the above

(c) Preference share is:
(i) Voting security
(ii) No voting security
(iii) Either (i) or (ii)
(iv) None of the above

(d) Stock market is concerned with:
(i) First time issues
(ii) Second time issues
(iii) Subsequent issues
(iv) Subsequent trading

(e) Magadh Stock Exchange is:
(i) Functional
(ii) Closed forever
(iii) Temporarily suspended
(iv) None of the above

(f) ADRs and GDRs are:
(i) Owned instruments
(ii) Borrowed instruments
(iii) None of the above
(iv) Hybrid instruments

(g) Sensex comprises of:
(i) 30 companies
(ii) 50 companies
(iii) 20 companies
(iv) None of the above

Answers: (a) ii (b) iii (c) ii (d) iv (e) ii (f) i (g) i

2. Fill in the blanks:

(a) Government Securities market is also known as ....
(b) .... is speculative in nature.
(c) SEBI was established in ....
(d) .... is a hybrid security.
(e) .... are tax-deductible instruments.
(f) Derivatives market is based on the principal of ....
(g) .... and .... are the two depositories operating in India.

Answers:

(a) Gilt-edged market
(b) Derivatives market
(c) 1992
(d) Preference share
(e) Debentures and Bonds
(f) Speculation
(g) NSDL, CDSL

3. True or False

(a) India has the third largest investor base in the world after USA and Japan.
(b) Capital market is long-term market in nature.
(c) Primary market is IPO market.
(d) Secondary market and stock market are different.
(e) Zero coupon bonds are discounted instruments.
(f) BSE is the oldest stock exchange in India.
(g) One cannot hold shares in physical form.

Answers: (a) True (b) True (c) True (d) False
(e) True (f) True (g) False

Short Questions

1. What is derivatives market?
2. Explain depositary receipts.
3. What is dematerialisation of shares?
4. Define Forex market.
5. Distinguish between money market and capital market.
6. What is Right issue?
7. What are the key eligibility requirements for public issue?
8. What is book-building?
9. Explain greenshoe option.
10. What is a depository?
11. What are Circuit Breakers?

Critical Thinking Questions

1. "Government Securities are considered to be risk-free instruments". Examine.
2. "Companies can raise funds from international market without getting listed over there in the form of depository receipts". Elaborate.
3. "Debt market is underdeveloped in India while equity market is not". Critically review.
4. "Demutualisation of stock exchanges in India has been a major step in improving the governance system". Discuss.
5. "The real speculation is in the derivatives market". Prove.
6. "Preference share is a hybrid instrument". Explain.
7. "Financial regulation is at a nascent stage in India". Do you agree?
8. "Financial instruments need to be more innovative and interesting for increasing the investors' penetration". Discuss.
9. Critically examine the role of SEBI as a regulatory body in capital market reforms during the last decade.

Descriptive Questions

1. Discuss various types of financial markets.
2. What are the sources of owned funds?
3. Discuss the different types of derivatives with examples.
4. Discuss the book building process with illustrations.
5. What are the different types of debt instruments?

6. What are the major reforms that have taken place in the capital market of India after 1991?
7. What are the major regulatory challenges faced by Indian regulators?
8. Discuss the operational framework of merchant bankers in the Indian primary market.

PROJECT EXERCISE

Comparative Analysis of Financial Markets

Financial markets are the nucleus of the financial system of any country. US capital markets rule the world. Compare its financial markets with India for the regulatory framework, structure and functionaries. Also, discuss the major financial instruments of both the nations and suggest some innovative products for the investors at global level.

REVIEW CASE

Mr. Smith's Wealth Irony

Mr. Smith has always been wary of the stock market. To him, shares were like a ball of fire wherein whosoever enters, gets burnt. One of his friends made huge money in the stock market and this changed his entire perspective about stocks and shares. He borrowed ₹50,000 from a bank against his fixed deposits for investment in stock market. His friend cautioned him that he should not have borrowed for investing in the stock market. He further said that because of the relative nature of the market, it is important to study up a bit before jumping in. At the very least, know the basic indicators, such as profitability of company, its net position, industry performance and the people who are running it.

"Trying to guess what will be the next 'Apple', a revolutionary produce or a rumour of earth-shaking earnings, investing on news is a terrible move for first-time investors. The best-case scenario is that you get lucky, and then keep doing it until your luck fails. The worst-case scenario is that you get stuck jumping in late (or investing on the wrong rumour) time and again before you give up on investing. Rather than following rumours, the ideal first investments are in companies you understand and have a personal experience dealing with. This connection makes it easier to stomach the time and research that investing demands".

But he was so fascinated by the airy profits from the stocks that he did not pay attention to any of his advice. Then, his friend told him to open a demat account for the same. His friend came to his rescue and got him a demat account with one of the registered brokers. He then invested in the shares of the same multinational company in which his friend had invested. He wanted good profits and at the same time income for his retirement. Just a week later, he faced a major dip in his stock prices. He almost fainted and thought of disposing his shares. Smith's friend advised against this and asked him to wait. He also cautioned him that 'one should not put all the eggs into one basket'. A week later, he found that now the stock prices were going high making him feel tempted to sell again and make profits before they fall. His friend again advised him against this. Smith was left puzzled and not able to understand this entire game of waiting.

This entire process of stock market was beyond his skin. He was clueless whether to hold the shares and wait for some more time for the gain or sell them off? If he should wait, then for how long should he? Meanwhile, the company also declared interim dividend which everybody received but Mr. Smith did not make his grief aggravate further. He did not know whom to approach and where to go? Once again, his friend helped him out and asked him to write first to the company and then SEBI, if not responded by the company.

His friend counseled him not to panic. He told him that the basics of investing are quite simple but it has to be supported by patience and one must give enough time to his stocks to grow. He asked Smith to follow the pulse of the market and then decide on the next move.

Based on the above, advise on the following:

(i) Was Mr. Smith right in his investment?
(ii) What could have been a good plan for him?
(iii) What type of investor is Mr. Smith?
(iv) What is a demat account? Is it necessary for every investor?
(v) What is the role of SEBI for investor's grievances?
(vi) What are the factors to be considered before investing in a company?
(vii) What mistakes were committed by Mr. Smith which a retail investor should not?
(viii) What is the company's accountability on non-receiving of dividend by a shareholder?

REFERENCES

Centre for Monitoring Indian Economy (1986). *The Liberalisation Process*, Bombay.

Cobham, David and Subramaniam, Ramesh (1995). 'Corporate Finance in Developing Countries: New Evidence from India', Discussion Paper No. 9512, Centre for Research into Industry, Enterprise, Finance and the Firm, University of St. Andrews, Scotland.

Currie, Carolyn (2003). *Towards a General Theory of Financial Regulation: Predicting, Measuring and Preventing Financial Crisis*, www.business.uts.edu.

David, T. and Lle, Wellyn (2006). 'Institutional Structure of Financial Regulation and Supervision', *The Basic Issues*, www.worldbank.org.

de Serres, Alan, Kobaya Kawa, Shuji, Slok, Torsten, and Vartia, Laura (2006). *Regulation of Financial System & Economic Growth*, Eco/wkp34OECD.

Financial regulations in India need to have uniform standard, January 15, 2010, www.financialexpress.com.

Gupta, L.C. (1998). "What Ails the Indian Capital Market?", *Economic and Political Weekly,* **23** (29–30).

Misra, B.M. (1997). "Fifty Years of the Indian Capital Market: 1947–1997", *Banking and Financial Sector Reforms in India*, Vol. **6**, edited by Kapila, Raj and Uma Kapila.

Reddy, Y.V. (1997). "The Future of India's Debt Market", *Reserve Bank of India Bulletin*, November.

Shah, Ajay and Thomas, Susan (1997). "Securities Markets—Towards Greater Efficiency", *India Development Report*, Edited by K. Parikh, UK, Oxford University Press.

Subramanian, V.V. (1998). "Impact Assessment of Capital Market Reforms", Draft paper submitted to Asian Development Bank.

The Parameter of Financial Regulation (2009). www.imf.org. IMF Staff Paper, March 20.

www.archives.digitaltoday.in

www.bseindia.com

www.fedai.org.in.

www.forex.com.

www.go-yubi.com

www.mca.gov.in

www.mcx-sx.com

www.nseindia.com

www.rbi.org.in

www.sebi.gov.in

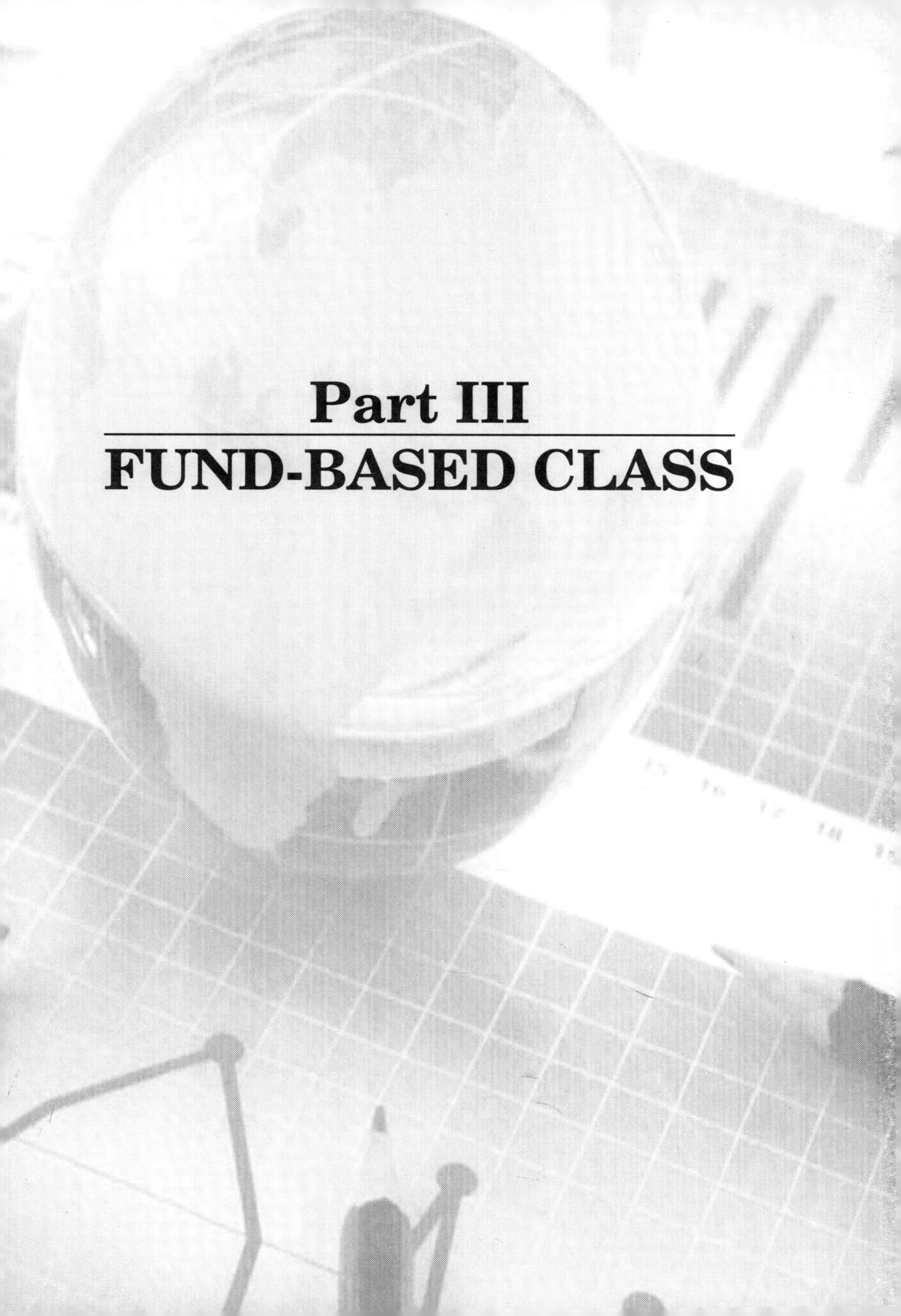

Part III

FUND-BASED CLASS

CHAPTER 7

Insurance

If a child, a spouse, a life partner, or a parent depends on you and your income, you need life insurance.

— **Suze Orman**

LEARNING OBJECTIVES

This chapter discusses the following:

- Concept of insurance
- History of insurance
- Growth of Indian insurance sector
- Principles of insurance
- Structure of insurance sector in India
- Constituents of insurance
- Distribution channels
- Regulatory framework of insurance in India
- Life insurance products in India
- Benefits of life insurance plan
- Premium computation
- General insurance
- Key aspects of insurance
- Comparison of US and Indian insurance industry
- Insurance ombudsman scheme
- Bancassurance
- Financial performance analysis of LIC

INTRODUCTION

Insurance is present in our lives in one form or another. Whether its life insurance, automobile insurance or medical insurance, it provides the necessary risk cover and wealth orientation. Having the right kind of insurance is a critical component of any good financial plan. Insurance allows individuals, businesses and other entities to protect themselves against significant financial losses at a reasonable price. The process of insurance is primarily meant to safeguard the interests of people from uncertainty by providing assurance of payment at a given contingency. However, with the changing times, insurance has also changed considerably. Traditionally, it was considered as a risk management strategy, but in modern times, it is a risk management plus investment strategy. This is why term plans of life insurance face stiff competition by ULIPs. Insurance companies are introducing customised products to tailor the needs of people, either life insurance or general insurance. Since liberalisation, Indian insurance industry has undergone a significant change and with the advent of foreign players, growing competition, and new products, it has really benefited the common man.

THE CONCEPT OF INSURANCE

Insurance is a contractual arrangement wherein one party agrees to compensate another for losses, in return for the payment of a consideration. The party agreeing to pay for the losses is called the *insurer*. The party whose loss is paid by the insurer is called the *insured*. The payment that the insurer receives is called *premium*.

The benefits which the insurance company bestows upon a buyer include indemnification against unexpected losses.

Indemnification *refers to the fact that the maximum financial compensation is limited to the extent of the loss.*

The claim payment from the insurer will help to mitigate the effect of the loss and to restore the revenue earning capacity of the asset.

The existence of a sound insurance market is an essential component of any successful economy. This is the reason why insurance has long been recognised as the key pillar of trade, industry and commerce.

Every Asset Has a Value

Assets such as motorcars, factories or houses, are acquired or built through savings or borrowings with the expectation of deriving benefits from them in the form of convenience and comfort they yield, or the products they manufacture that can be sold for earning revenue. They, therefore, have value. In fact, the assets themselves can be sold at a price.

In the extended sense, these assets could be taken to include human life, our health or even our ability to work and earn. Certainly, unlike physical assets, the value of human life cannot be determined since the pain and suffering that follows the disablement or death of an individual cannot be determined with any degree of precision. However, there could be indirect measures such as the earning potential of the individual in the productive years that were lost due to premature death or disablement.

This has brought in the concept of “Human Life Value” (HLV).

Human Life Value (HLV) *is defined as the present value of all future income that you could expect to earn for your family's benefit, plus other values you expect to* *contribute, less taxes and personal consumption till your planned retirement date. The concept of HLV is, therefore, extended to housewives as well.*

All assets have a certain life, i.e. the period of time during which they perform. Based on the life of an asset, the owner would set aside a certain portion of the earnings from the asset for its replacement at the end of its economic life. *Depreciation provision, set aside every year to purchase a new asset at the end of the useful life of equipment, is an example of this. Another example is the savings we make during our working life to provide for our old age.*

There could be an accident, illness or any other unfortunate event that may reduce the asset's life. This could result in the sudden loss of earnings from the asset. In some cases, the event may result in full loss of the asset, as when a car is stolen or an individual dies. In other cases, it could be a partial loss, requiring expenses to be incurred, as in when the car meets with an accident but is repairable, or when the individual falls sick, requiring hospitalisation. These are unforeseen situations as the timing of the event is uncertain.

Insurance is designed to provide financial compensation in these situations. A motor insurance policy pays the expenses of repair, a sickness insurance policy pays the cost of hospitalisation and a life insurance policy pays the sum insured, including accumulated bonuses, if any, on the death of the policyholder or maturity of the policy. It is, therefore, said that the function of insurance is to protect the economic value of the asset.

Working of an Insurance

In simple terms, insurance is a pooling arrangement wherein contributions are collected from all members who join a pool. The amount so collected is utilised to compensate members who suffer loss. The arrangement works because generally not all members who join the pool suffer losses. In order to ensure equity (fairness), a pool would consist of people who are exposed to similar risks (exposure to loss). *An example* of a pool could be persons in the age group of, say, 35–40, meeting some prescribed set of health standards and financial standing. Other pools could consist of private cars upto, say, 1000 cubic capacity, buildings made of reinforced concrete upto 20 metres in height, goods packed in containers in transit carried by ocean-going vessels, etc. There will, therefore, be several pools.

As insurance evolved over the years, insurance companies have come up to transact insurance business which have developed expertise in assessing the risk (exposure to loss) of an individual, a motorcar, a building or goods in transit. On the basis of this assessment, they decide whether the asset offered for insurance could be covered, and if so, at what premium rate. They also perform a number of other functions including effectively managing the collected funds in the form of the premium payable by policyholders.

Development of Insurance Sector

Insurance penetration and density are two key metrics, often used to assess the level of development of the insurance sector in a country. While "insurance penetration" is measured as the per centage of insurance premium to GDP, "insurance density" is calculated as the ratio of premium to population (per capita premium).

For Indian insurance sector, it is discussed in the structural section.

HISTORY OF INSURANCE

Insurance, both general and life, as a readily recognisable business, first emerged in the UK, at the end of the 16th century. In 1575, during the reign of Queen Elizabeth I, the Chamber of Assurance in the Royal Exchange was opened for the registration of marine parcels. Following this, an Act of Parliament was passed in 1601 to deal with disputes relating to marine insurance. The British introduced marine insurance, in its modern form, in India around 1700. The first company, known as the Sun Insurance Office, was set up in Calcutta in 1710.

It was in the 18th century that societies began to be formed in the UK for issuing life policies. Among such societies, the Amicable Society (1705), the Equitable Assurance Society (1762), and the Westminster Society (1792) were the important ones. The history of general insurance business in India can be traced back to Triton Insurance Company Ltd. (the first general insurance company) which was formed in the year 1850 in Kolkata by the British.

The first Indian life insurance company was set up in India in the year 1818 with the formation of Life Insurance Corporation in Calcutta. The setting up of a large number of other life insurance companies soon followed, as discussed in the next section.

GROWTH OF INSURANCE SECTOR IN INDIA

Insurance industry in India has seen a phenomenal change after the industrial era. Its growth in various phases is discussed below.

Before Independence

As discussed above, the insurance industry originated in India in the year 1818 with the establishment of Life Insurance Corporation in Calcutta. The idea behind starting LIC was to provide insurance coverage for English widows and different premium was charged for the English and for the Indians. In 1870, an English life insurance company, the European and the Albert, was set up. In the same year, Bombay Mutual Life Insurance Society established its insurance business and the same premium was charged for both Indians and English.

In 1912, the insurance sector came under the purview of regulations when the government passed the Life Insurance Companies Act but it was in the year 1938, when the government came up with the first legislation to bring the insurance sector under State control.

Post Independence

In 1956, the Government of India nationalised insurance companies bringing the Indian insurance sector under the purview of the government. The Life Insurance Corporation

(LIC) was formed in September 1956 by the Life Insurance Corporation Act, 1956 (LIC Act) which granted LIC the exclusive privilege to conduct life insurance business in India. The general insurance business was also nationalised from January 1, 1973, through the introduction of the General Insurance Business (Nationalisation) Act, 1972 (GIC Act). Under the provisions of the GIC Act, the shares of the existing Indian general insurance companies and undertakings of other existing insurers were transferred to the General Insurance Corporation (GIC) to secure the development of the general insurance business in India and for the regulation and control of such businesses. The GIC was established by the Central Government in accordance with the provisions of the Companies Act, 1956 in November 1972 and it commenced business on January 1, 1973. Prior to 1973, there were hundred and seven companies, including foreign companies, offering general insurance in India. These companies were amalgamated and grouped into four subsidiary companies of GIC, viz. *the National Insurance Company Ltd., the New India Assurance Company Ltd., the Oriental Insurance Company Ltd., and the United India Assurance Company Ltd.* GIC undertakes mainly re-insurance business, apart from aviation insurance. The bulk of the general insurance business of fire, marine, motor and miscellaneous insurance business is undertaken by the four subsidiaries.

These state-owned insurance companies became inefficient and bureaucratic, had excess manpower and made countless delay in settlement of claims but the nation did not have an alternative. Any effort by the government to privatise the industry met with stiff resistance from the trade unions.

Post Liberalisation

Since 1956, with the nationalisation of insurance industry, the LIC held the monopoly in India's life insurance sector. GIC, with its four subsidiaries, enjoyed the monopoly for general insurance business. From 1991 onwards, the Indian Government introduced various reforms in the financial sector paving the way for the liberalisation of the Indian economy.

Consequently in 1993, the Government of India set up an eight-member committee chaired by Mr. R.N. Malhotra, a former Governor of India's apex bank, the Reserve Bank of India, to review the prevailing structure of regulation, supervision of the insurance sector, and to make recommendations for strengthening and modernising the regulatory system. Under the recommendation of Malhotra Committee, 1994[1], the Insurance Regulatory and Development Authority was set up in 1999 to monitor and control the insurance industry. Some of the initiatives taken by the government after insurance sector reforms are:

- Government should not have more than 50% stake in insurance companies.
- Insurance sector to be opened up for private companies and any number of insurance enterprises can operate.
- Private players with minimum paid up capital of ₹1 billion should be given the opportunity to do business.

1. http://www.business-standard.com/article/specials/malhotra-committee-recommendations-198042201099_1.html

   The Malhotra Committee Report—1994 is given in the Instructor's manual.

- Foreign companies can enter Indian market through joint ventures with Indian companies.

The State-controlled insurance companies like LIC and GIC faced tough competition from private insurance companies post reforms. The monopoly of the national insurance companies, thus, came to an end.

The private insurance companies were able to exploit the short comings in the state-run insurance companies. They launched a variety of new insurance products like health care, pension plans, annuity plans, income protection, market-linked products which were welcomed by the end customers. The business for the private sector boomed in both urban and rural sectors alike.

Milestones in the Indian Life Insurance Business

1. ***1912:*** The Indian Life Assurance Companies Act came into force for regulating the life insurance business.

2. ***1928:*** The Indian Insurance Companies Act was enacted for enabling the government to collect statistical information on both life and non-life insurance businesses.

3. ***1938:*** The earlier legislation consolidated the Insurance Act with the aim of safeguarding the interests of the insuring public.

4. ***1956:*** 245 Indian and foreign insurers and provident societies were taken over by the central government and nationalised. LIC was formed by an Act of Parliament, viz. LIC Act, 1956. It started off with a capital of ₹5 crore and that too from the Government of India.

Milestones in the Indian General Insurance Business

1. ***1907:*** The Indian Mercantile Insurance Ltd. was set up which was the first company of its type to transact all general insurance business.

2. ***1957:*** General Insurance Council, an arm of the Insurance Association of India, framed a code of conduct for guaranteeing fair conduct and sound business patterns.

3. ***1968:*** The Insurance Act improved the regulating investments and set minimal solvency levels. The Tariff Advisory Committee was set up.

4. ***1972:*** The General Insurance Business (Nationalisation) Act, 1972 nationalised the general insurance business in India with effect from 1st January 1973.

107 insurers integrated and were grouped into four companies, viz. the National Insurance Company Ltd., the New India Assurance Company Ltd., the Oriental Insurance Company Ltd. and the United India Insurance Company Ltd. General Insurance Company (GIC) was also incorporated as a company.

The growth of Indian Insurance Sector is depicted in Figure 7.1.

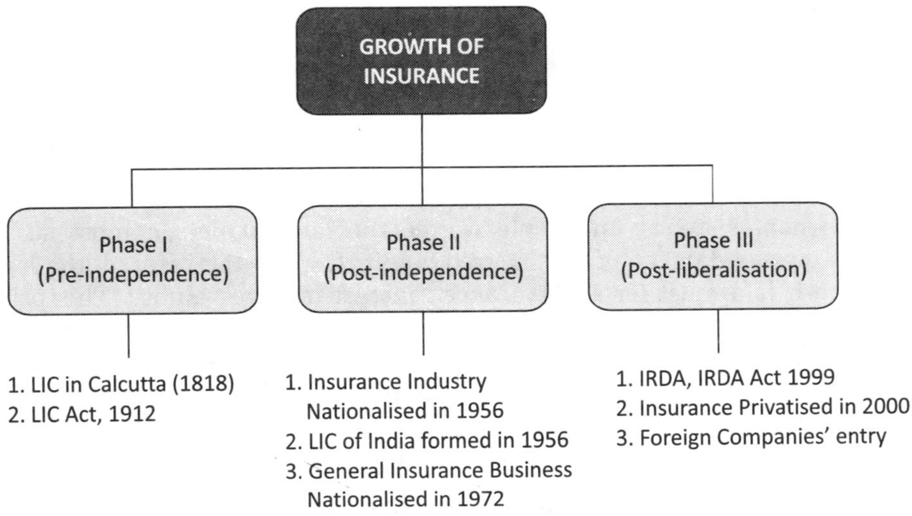

Figure 7.1 Growth of Indian Insurance

PRINCIPLES OF INSURANCE

As noted earlier, the mechanism of insurance involves a contractual agreement in which the insurer agrees to provide financial protection against a 'specified set of risks' for a price called *premium*. It is, hence, essentially an intangible product. The insurance customer cannot see or feel the product he or she is buying. Though the policy document does give the assurance of the coverage, generally no real service is delivered until a claim occurs.

In normal commercial transactions, the legal maxim *Caveat Emptor*, Latin for '*let the buyer beware*', operates. This means that the buyer takes the risk regarding the quality or condition of the property purchased. This, in turn, implies that the buyer has the opportunity to examine the product before purchase but here, the insurance customer has no such opportunity. Therefore, insurance transactions need to be governed by special principles in order to protect the interests of the contracting parties, particularly the customer.

It is in view of this that the contracts are governed by certain special fundamental legal principles. These make insurance contracts unique and distinct from other kinds of commercial contracts. The fundamental principles are:

The principle of utmost good faith: It is the duty of the insured and the insurer to disclose all relevant facts. This is necessary for both life and general insurance. The principle of utmost good faith in Latin, *uberrimae fides*, literally means perfect good faith or abundant good faith. The phrase is used to express that an insurance contract must be made in perfect good faith, concealing nothing. It is the primary principle of insurance. *For example,* while taking a life insurance, if a person has not revealed about his past ailment it will have a substantial effect on the insurance status. In such a case, his claim of payment can be rejected by the insurer on concealment of material facts.

The principle of insurable interest: It states that the person getting insured must have insurable interest in the object of insurance. A person has an insurable interest when he is going to gain from the physical existence of the insured object and will lose from its non-existence. In simple words, the insured person must suffer some financial loss by the damage of the insured object. It gives the insured 'the legal right to insure' and it is a must for an insurance contract to have validity. This principle is also relevant to both life and general insurance. *For example,* the owner of an auto-rickshaw has insurable interest in the auto because he is receiving an income from it but if he sells it, he will not have an insurable interest left in that auto. So, ownership plays a very important role in determining insurable interest. For life insurance, every person has an insurable interest in his own life.

The principle of indemnity: *Indemnity* means a guarantee by the insurer to repair the loss of the insured and improve his condition as it was before the loss. It determines the extent of the insurer's liability in the case of loss. According to the principle of indemnity, an insurance contract is signed only for getting protection against unpredicted financial losses arising due to future uncertainties. Insurance contract is not made for profits. In an insurance contract, the amount of compensation paid is in proportion to the incurred losses and it cannot exceed the amount assured or the actual losses. However, in case of life insurance, the principle of indemnity does not apply because the value of human life cannot be measured in terms of money.

The principle of contribution: It is a corollary to the indemnity principle, exclusively applicable to general insurance. It tells us how the liability is to be met when the insured has taken insurance with more than one insurer on the same subject matter. According to this principle, the insured can claim the compensation only to the extent of the actual loss, either from all insurers or from any one insurer. If one insurer pays full compensation then that insurer can demand proportionate claim from other insurers. *For example,* Amit insures his bike worth ₹40,000 with two insurers—Bajaj Allianz for ₹30,000 and Tata AIG for ₹20,000. If Amit's bike is destroyed, it is worth ₹20,000. He can then claim the full loss either from Bajaj Allianz or Tata AIG, or he can claim ₹12,000 from Bajaj Allianz and ₹8,000 from Tata AIG in the ratio of 60:40 of the insurance taken individually with them.

The principle of subrogation: It is another corollary of the indemnity principle and again exclusively applicable to general insurance. It refers to the rights that an insurer acquires vis-a-vis the insured when the insurer has paid him an indemnity. After paying the insured, the insurer steps into his shoes and acquires all the rights of ownership of the asset. *For example,* Mukesh insures his car for ₹80,000. The car is completely damaged on account of falling off a pole of Department of Telecom. The insurance company shall settle Mukesh's claim for ₹80,000. At the same time, it can file a lawsuit against the Telecom Department for ₹95,000, the market value of the car. If insurance company wins the case and gets ₹95,000, then it will retain ₹80,000 (which it has already paid to Mukesh) plus other expenses such as court fees. The balance amount, if any, will be given to Mukesh, the insured.

The principle of loss minimisation: It states that the insured must take all possible steps to minimise the loss of the insured asset on the happening of an uncertain event, like fire. He should not neglect simply because the property is insured, and should fulfill his responsibility. For example, if Ravi's house is set on fire due to an electric short-circuit. In such a case, he must put in his best efforts to stop the fire by all possible means, like calling the fire department office using buckets of water, etc. If he does not do his duty of stopping the fire, then he is not entitled to claim the payment from the insurance company.

The principle of proximate cause: The rule defines that for insurance, the loss to the asset must have been caused by the event against which the asset has been insured. If the loss is traced to more than one event, some of which are not covered by the insurance contract, then the insured cannot claim the payment. For example, Let us assume that goods are insured against sea hazards during transportation of goods by ship. If goods are destroyed by rats then in this case, the insured will not get his claim payment as rats do not come under the category sea hazards.

STRUCTURE OF INDIAN INSURANCE SECTOR

The Indian insurance sector is headed by the 'Insurance Regulatory Development Authority' (IRDA) and comprises of the following institutions:

1. ***Life insurance sector:*** This is divided into the following categories:
   (a) Public sector companies
   (b) Private sector companies

2. ***Non-Life insurance sector:*** This is further divided into:
   (a) Public sector companies
   (b) Private sector companies

3. ***Health insurance sector:*** This consists of:
   (a) Private sector companies

4. ***Re-insurance sector:*** This consists of:
   (a) Public sector company
   (b) Foreign reinsurer's branches

As on 16th January 2023, there were 55 regulated insurance companies, comprising of 23 life insurance companies, 26 non-life insurance companies, 5 health insurance companies, and 1 reinsurance company in the country.[2]

These are classified in Figure 7.2.

2. http://www.irda.gov.in/ADMINCMS/cms/frmGuidelines_List

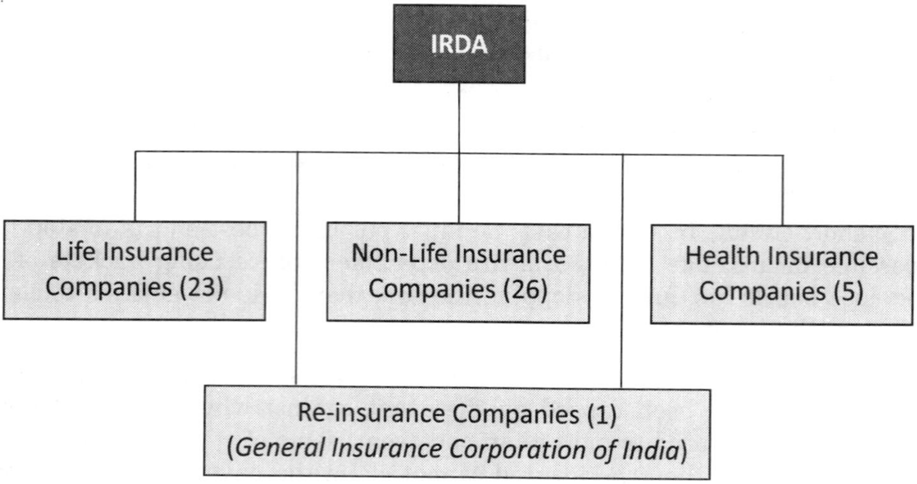

Figure 7.2 Indian Insurance Structure

Notes: 1. The figures in parentheses are given as on 16th January, 2023 (IRDA).
2. Re-insurance companies also include 11 Foreign Reinsurer's Branches in Private sector as on March 31, 2022.

IRDA: The Central Authority

Insurance Regulatory Development Authority was set up as an autonomous body under the IRDA Act, 1999. Its role is to act as a statutory regulator to regulate and promote the insurance industry in India, to protect the interests of the insurance policy holders, and to work for the orderly growth of the industry. It was established on the recommendation of Malhotra Committee, 1994.

The members of the IRDA are appointed by the Central Government from amongst persons of ability, integrity and standing who have knowledge or experience in life insurance, general insurance, actuarial science, finance, economics, law, accountancy, administration, etc. The Authority consists of a chairperson, five whole- time members and four part-time members. Following are the activities of IRDA[3]:

- Framing regulations for the insurance industry in terms of Section 114A of the Insurance Act, 1938.
- Registration of new insurance companies in accordance with regulations from the year 2000 onwards.
- Monitoring insurance sector activities for healthy development of the industry and protection of policyholders' interests.

LIFE INSURANCE COMPANIES

Among the life insurers, Life Insurance Corporation (LIC) is the sole public sector company. Life Insurance Corporation of India is the largest player in the life insurance sector, owned by the Government of India. Remaining 22 are privately-held life

3. http://www.policyholder.gov.in/Who_We_Are

insurance companies. The prominent ones are Aviva Life Insurance, Bajaj Allianz Life Insurance, Aditya Birla Sun Life Insurance, HDFC Life Insurance, ICICI Prudential Life Insurance, and others. The "life insurance" business in India from 2019–20 to 2021–22 is shown in Table 7.1.

Life insurance penetration in India increased from 2.82 per cent in 2019–20 to 3.2 per cent in 2021–22. Life insurance density in India increased from USD 58 in 2019–20 to USD 69 in 2021–22. The number of new life insurance policies issued increased from 288.47 lakh to 291.13 lakh during the years. Total premium saw a jump from ₹5,72,910.19 crore to ₹6,92,614.14 crore during the period.

General Insurance Companies

Out of 31 general insurance companies, 5 private sector insurers are registered to underwrite policies exclusively in health insurance segments. They are Aditya Birla Health Ltd., Manipal Cigna Health Ltd., Niva Bupa Health Ltd., Care Health Ltd., and Star Health & Allied Ltd.

Other general insurers or non-life insurance players include public sector such as National Insurance Co. Ltd., and private players, like Bajaj Allianz General Insurance, ICICI Lombard General Insurance, Tata AIG General Insurance, Reliance General Insurance, etc.

There are two specialised insurers in the category belonging to the public sector, namely, Agriculture Insurance Company of India Ltd. for crop insurance and ECGC Ltd. for credit insurance. The "non-life insurance" business in India from 2019–20 to 2021–22 is shown in Table 7.1.

Non-Life insurance penetration in India increased from 0.94 per cent in 2019–20 to 1.0 per cent in 2021–22. Non-Life insurance density in India increased from USD 19 in 2019–20 to USD 22 in 2021–22. The number of new life insurance policies issued increased from 2415.09 lakh to 2656.70 lakh during the years. Total premium saw a jump from ₹1,92,192.59 crore to ₹2,24,002.82 crore during the period.

BOX 7.1: INDIAN INSURANCE – THE GLOBAL PICTURE

India ranks tenth in global insurance business with a market share of 1.85 per cent in 2021. Total insurance premium in India increased by 13.46 per cent in 2021, whereas global total insurance premium increased by 9.04 per cent during the year.

In life insurance business, India is ranked ninth in the world in 2021. India's share in global life insurance market was 3.23 per cent during 2021.

In non-life insurance business, India is ranked fourteenth in the world in 2021. India's share *in global non-life* insurance market was 0.78 per cent.*

*https://irdai.gov.in/annual-reports

Re-insurance Company

In addition to these, there is a sole national re-insurer, namely, General Insurance Corporation of India. Unlike an insurance company, a reinsurance company does not accept business from the end customer, but acts as the insurer for insurance companies, thus helping to pool the risks that are reinsured with it by all the companies.

TABLE 7.1 Insurance Sector in India

(Amount in ₹ crore)

S. No.	Particular	2019–20			2020–21			2021–22		
		Life	*Non-Life*	*Total*	*Life*	*Non-Life*	*Total*	*Life*	*Non-Life*	*Total*
1	Number of insurance companies	24	33	57	24	32	56	24	31	55
2	Number of offices	11,310	11,394	22,704	11,060	11,248	22,308	11,060	10,775	21,835
3	Insurance penetration (%)	2.82	0.94	3.76	3.2	1.0	4.2	3.2	1.0	4.2
4	Insurance density ($)	58	19	78	59	19	78	69	22	91
5	Number of new policies issued (lakh)	288.47	2415.09	2,703.56	281.27	2467.33	2,748.60	291.13	2,656.70	2,947.83
6	Total Premium	5,72,910.19	1,92,192.59	7,65,102.78	6,28,731.04	2,02,082.30	8,30,813.34	6,92,614.14	2,24,002.82	9,16,616.96
	i. Within India	5,72,531.93	1,88,916.62	7,61,448.55	6,28,330.70	1,98,714.72	8,27,045.42	6,92,194.44	2,20,700.21	9,12,894.65
	ii. Outside India	378.26	3,275.97	3,654.23	400.34	3,367.58	3,767.92	419.70	3,302.61	3,722.31
7	Growth in Premium (%)	12.75	11.43	12.41	9.74	5.15	8.59	10.16	10.85	10.33
8	Premium of PSUs	3,79,389.60	76539.05	4,55,928.65	4,03,286.55	75,211.29	4,78,497.84	4,28,024.97	78,335.45	5,06,360.42
9	Market share of PSUs (%)	66.22	39.82	59.59	64.14	37.22	57.59	61.80	34.97	55.24
10	Assets Under Management	38,90,274.09	3,62,655.67	42,52,929.76	44,79,973.46	4,33,301.36	49,13,274.82	49,52,187.17	4,84,540.21	54,36,727.39
11	Paid-up Capital	28,087.96	21,360.73	49,448.69	28,346.37	32,842.24	61,188.61	35,546.75	37,855.09	73,401.83
12	Other Forms of Capital	230.00	4,875.00	5,105.00	2,210.00	4,875.00	7,085.00	4,194.00	5,151.00	9,345.00
13	Commission expenses	31,192.52	13,893.13	45,085.65	32,994.08	15,409.50	48,403.58	35,887.31	16,931.10	52,818.41
14	Operating expenses	60,121.00	35,844.93	95,965.93	61,422.29	38,281.44	99,703.73	71,435.02	41,455.29	1,12,890.31
15	Claims	3,51,466.70	1,08,390.26	4,59,856.49	3,98,772.47	1,11,549.83	5,10,322.30	5,02,096.92	1,40,565.96	6,42,662.88
16	Income from investments	2,33,743.74	28,605.52	2,62,349.26	4,66,030.35	29,743.55	4,95,773.90	4,16,711.62	32,546.49	4,49,258.11
17	Profit after tax	7,728.30	–1,494.38	6,233.92	8,660.63	3,852.53	12,513.16	7,751.49	–2,856.93	4,894.56
18	Dividend paid	3,890.03	1,306.21	4,949.04	615.35	1,001.06	1,616.41	381.53	1,010.05	1,391.58

Source: Annual Report 2021–22, IRDAI, https://irdai.gov.in/annual-reports

Notes:
1. Non-life includes data of General & Stand-alone health insurers.
2. For life insurers claim indicates benefit paid and for non-life insurers, claims indicate net incurred claims.
3. AUM of non-life insurers include AUM of reinsurers including FRBs.
4. PSUs indicates LIC and 4 PSGICs.

CONSTITUENTS OF INSURANCE BUSINESS

Following are the key performers of insurance industry which form the constitution of insurance industry:

Actuary

An *actuary* is a person who has passed specialised examinations conducted by the Actuarial Society of India or the Institute of Actuaries, London. Actuaries are technical experts who have received special training in the mathematics of insurance. Their job is to ensure that the insurance products provided by the company are mathematically sound. Actuaries undertake various activities like calculation of mortality rates, estimating expenses to be incurred by the insurance company in administrating various policies, and determining the rate of return that will be earned by the company on its investments. Based on the above, they decide on the premiums to be charged on various policies. So, a good actuary has to be a good economist, a good statistician as well as a good security analyst. Every insurance company requires good actuaries to continuously study its operations and advise the management on the appropriateness of their policies.

Underwriter

An *underwriter* scrutinises, analyses and takes the decisions on the proposals received for insurance. While analysing the risks arising from the insurance applications, the underwriters ensure that the company issues the maximum possible policies while keeping the risk of loss within acceptable limits. Any application that poses reasonable risks are accepted and those posing lower or higher than average risks are accepted at lower or higher rates of premium than normal. Any application posing unreasonable risks is declined. The job of accepting or declining the proposals of insurance received by company and deciding on the premium at which to accept the proposals is done by the underwriting department.

Policy Owner Services

The employees in this area are the ones who issue the actual policy documents. They also ensure customer satisfaction by attending to various requirements arising during the period of a contract like nominations, assignments, alterations, etc. These employees are basically responsible for maintenance of policy records, processing customer requests and informing policy owners about any material changes that affect their policies.

Claim Administration

The employees in this area are responsible for the actual settlement of claims. They analyse the claims received against various policies. After thoroughly studying the claims, they decide whether it is valid. They calculate the benefit amounts for settlement of all valid claims and any claims that are found invalid are rejected.

Marketing

The marketing department studies consumer behaviour, needs and wants. On the basis of these studies, they give suggestions for new products which can satisfy those needs. The marketing executives also develop marketing plans, design promotional material for different products, market the products to the customers, and provide them services. The marketing department's role starts even before the inception of a product and carries on well after the product has been sold to the customer.

Investment

The employees in this area manage the company's assets and investments. They study the financial markets in order to give recommendations on the best avenues of investments so that the company can maximise its returns.

Accounting

As in any other organisation, the accountants in an insurance company keep records of the income and expenses. They keep a track of the income from premiums and investments and also the expenses for running the office, agents' commission, claim payments, and the like. They prepare the reports and statements which show the financial position of the company. The policyholders, shareholders, and insurance regulators can get to know the financial status of the insurance company from these reports.

Information Systems

The employees looking after this area provide their services to all the departments of an insurance company. They design and maintain computer systems so that any required information can be easily retrieved at any time. They also develop and test new systems and procedures for the company, install them and ensure that they operate efficiently and effectively.

Legal and Compliance

The employees in this department play an important role in ensuring that the company is complying with all the regulations and laws in the country. They develop the policy forms, contracts for agents, etc. in line with the existing rules and regulations apart from advising the staff and management on any legal issues. In case there is any dispute arising out of a claim, the attorneys from the legal department defend the company's position.

DISTRIBUTION CHANNELS

These are routes by which the product prepared by the producer reaches the ultimate consumer. Thus, the distance between the producer and the consumer is bridged by the "distribution channel". In the case of insurance companies, the distribution system is a network of individuals and organisations that are involved in making the insurance products available to the customers. They form a link between the insurance company and the buyers of insurance products.

Therefore, distribution channels bridge the gap between the players in the background (discussed above) and players in the forefront which are discussed below.

Agents

An *insurance agent* is an agent licensed under Section 42 of the Insurance Act, 1938[4]. He/she receives payment by way of commission for procuring insurance business. He/she is also responsible for business relating to the continuance, renewal or revival of insurance policies. An agent could also be a corporate agent, i.e. a company or a firm. The primary function of an agent is to procure business for the insurance company.

However, the agent can only procure business for the particular insurance company which he/she represents, and for no other company.

Once the insurance contract has been put into force, the agent has to ensure continuance of the policy through regular payment of renewal premiums. In case of a claim, the agent should help the insured in proper settlement of claims.

Insurance Brokers

An individual or firm, whose full-time occupation is the placement of insurance business with insurance companies, is known as an *insurance broker*. The broker receives brokerage as a per centage of the premium from the insurer.

The main difference between an agent and a broker is that there are no restrictions on the procurement of business by a broker for various different insurance companies, while the agent can only procure business for that particular company which he represents. Insurance brokers also give advice to the insured without charging them.

Insurance Consultants

Usually, *insurance consultants* are specialists who give advice to consumers who wish to buy insurance products. However, unlike the brokers, they get paid by the insured for this advice.

Insurance Surveyors and Loss Assessors

An *insurance surveyor* is a technical expert who inspects the damage or loss of an insurance company. A surveyor and loss assessor is required to spend a major part of his time in investigating and managing the losses arising from any contingency and prepare reports. He has the duty and responsibility to ensure that he discloses whether he has any interest in the subject matter in question or whether it pertains to any of his relatives, business partners or through material shareholding; or maintaining confidentiality and neutrality without jeopardising the liability of the insurer and claim of the insured; or conducting inspection and re-inspection of the property in question suffering a loss; or recommending applicability of depreciation, or the per centage and quantum of depreciation, etc.

4. The Insurance Act, 1938, https://irdai.gov.in/acts

Third Party Administrators

Under the provisions of the IRDA (Third Party Administrators Health Services) Regulations, 2001[5], (TPA Regulations), the *Third Party Administrator* (TPA) means one who has obtained a license from the Authority, and is engaged for a fee or remuneration, as specified in the agreement with the insurance company, for the provision of health services. An insurance company may engage more than one TPA and similarly, one TPA may serve more than one insurance company.

Banking Outlets

These days, there has been a trend of using outlets of banks for distribution of insurance products. The 'bancassurance' is one of the most prevalent banking outlet services in present times. The existence of convenient and easily-accessible banking outlets is a significant part of expanding financial inclusion.

REGULATIONS AND LEGISLATION APPLICABLE TO INSURANCE

Insurance in India had a very chequered history until the nationalisation of the industry. Hundreds of private insurance companies practised the business and many of them were unviable. While the legislation on insurance was quite comprehensive, there was little regulatory oversight. Fraudulent practices were also found to prevail in several cases. Over the years, since nationalisation, legislation was tightened and made more meaningful. Besides, in opening up the business to private sector again, a comprehensive regulatory authority has been set up to watch over the development and practice of insurance in India.

An important segment of the law has been created to inhibit 'insurance fraud'—which could be perpetrated either by the insurer or the insured. In India, the most experience of consumer protection in insurance had been very good because the State enterprise, viz. Life Insurance Corporation of India (LIC) which was the only insurer. However, with new private insurers in competition, the need to legislate protection has become more significant.

Besides the insurance related laws, direct tax laws in India have played an important role in the development and adoption of life insurance in India and more recently, there are consumer rights that have become significant in financial sector.

History of Insurance Regulation in India

The Indian Life Assurance Companies Act, 1912 was the first statutory measure to regulate the business of insurance. Later, the Indian Insurance Companies Act was enacted in 1928 to enable the government to collect statistical information about life and non-life insurance business transacted in India.

The Insurance Act, 1938

In 1938, with a view to protect the interest of the insuring public, earlier legislation was consolidated and amended by the Insurance Act, 1938 with comprehensive provisions

5. http://www.irda.gov.in/ADMINCMS/cms/frmGeneral

for detailed and effective control over activities of insurers. For the administration of the above, an insurance wing was established and attached first to the Ministry of Commerce and then to the Ministry of Finance. The actuarial and operational matters were looked after by the Controller of Insurance. This Act was amended in 1950, making far-reaching changes such as:

- Requirement of equity capital for companies carrying on life insurance business
- Ceiling on shareholding in such companies
- Stricter controls on investments of life insurance companies
- Submission of periodical returns relating to investments and such other information to the Controller as called for
- Appointment of administrators for mismanaged companies
- Ceiling on expenses of management and agency commission
- Incorporation of the Insurance Association of India and formation of councils and committees thereof.

LIC Act, 1956

In 1956, the management of the life insurance business of all the insurers and provident societies, then operating in India, was taken over by the Central Government and were nationalised. LIC was formed in September, 1956 with a capital contribution of ₹5 crore from the Government of India. The LIC Act, 1956 was passed by the Parliament. The objectives of LIC were to:

- Conduct business with utmost economy, in a spirit of trusteeship
- Charge premium not higher than warranted by strict actuarial considerations
- Invest the funds for obtaining maximum yield for the policy-holders consistent with safety of the capital.

This Act laid the basis for creating LIC of India out of the several insurance companies which existed prior to nationalisation. LIC of India was vested with the exclusive privilege to transact life insurance business in India. This has been done as a result of amendments made in 1999.

Section 38[6] of this Act provides that LIC cannot be terminated by any law relating to the winding up of companies or corporations, unless the Central Government orders and directs it to be so.

Insurance Regulatory and Development Authority Act, 1999

After liberation of the financial sector in 1991, the Government of India constituted the Malhotra Committee[7] for suggesting reforms in the insurance sector. This committee recommended the opening up of the insurance sector and suggested the setting up of a statutory body called Insurance Regulatory and Development Authority. In 1996, Interim IRA was formed and in 1999, the IRDA Bill was passed. IRA was renamed as Insurance Regulatory and Development Authority (IRDA) to reflect on the development of the insurance sector. The IRDA[8] replaces the Controller under Insurance Act, 1938.

6. http://www.licindia.in/licact.pdf
7. http://www.business-standard.com/ op. cit.
8. http://www.irda.gov.in/ADMINCMS/cms/frmGeneral_Layout

Section 2(f) defines an *intermediary* to include insurance brokers, reinsurance brokers, insurance consultants, surveyors and loss assessors.

IRDA Act provides for the establishment of an authority to protect the interests of holders of insurance policies, to regulate, to promote and ensure orderly growth of the insurance industry and for matters connected or incidental thereto. The insurance authority called "IRDA" has been established under this Act.

The authority consists of a chairperson, not more than five whole-time members and not more than four part-time members.

The members would be appointed by the Central Government for a tenure of 5 years. The attempt is to make sure that every aspect of the practice of insurance is represented by expertise of the members.

Besides the formal forum of the members, the IRDA also encourages a process of dialogue between the practitioners and the Authority through a council of the heads of the insurance companies.

The important functions of IRDA are to:

- Exercise all powers and functions of the controller of insurance.
- Protect the interests of the policyholders.
- Issue, renew, modify, withdraw or suspend certificate of registration.
- Specify requisite qualifications and training for insurance intermediaries and agents.
- Promote and regulate professional organisations connected with insurance.
- Conduct inspections, investigations, and the like.
- Prescribe the method of insurance accounting.
- Regulate investment of funds and margins of solvency.
- Adjudicate upon disputes.
- Conduct inspection and audit of insurers, intermediaries and other organisations concerned with insurance.

LIFE INSURANCE PRODUCTS IN INDIA

Life insurance products have to suit the requirements of customers. The three major concerns of any person could be—premature death, or living for too long, or living with disability.

Besides, there are other concerns like taking care of children and their future, and creating wealth. Life insurance products are generally designed to address such needs. Therefore, life insurance products fundamentally provide for risk cover, investment, and health cover.

The five main types of insurance policies are:

(i) Term insurance
(ii) Whole-life insurance
(iii) Endowment
(iv) Annuities
(v) Unit-linked policies

Term Insurance

Term insurance pays death benefit to the legal heirs if the person insured dies during the term of the policy. Such a policy provides cover for a specified period only and may be described as temporary insurance. *New Jeevan Amar* and *Saral Jeevan Beema* are two most popular conventional term assurance plans of LIC.

Term insurance plans offer pure risk cover without any element of saving, hence, they are the cheapest. The sum assured is payable only if the insured dies during the selected period. In case the insured does not die during the tenure of insurance, nothing is payable. Term insurance plans could be of the following different types:

1. *Level term insurance:* Under this plan, there is a uniform premium and benefit throughout the term of the policy. In the event of death anytime during the term, the same sum assured is payable. If the term is for over a year, the renewal premium is the same each year.

This policy plan is the most popular term insurance plan mainly because of its simplicity. It is an answer to a temporary need for a period of time, *for example,* a lump sum amount which is due at a certain point of time.

2. *Decreasing term insurance:* Under this plan, the premium is constant throughout the term, but the benefit decreases over a period of time. Hence, the amount payable on death depends on the timing of the death, even though the premium being paid is constant. This plan is suitable for cases where there is a temporary need which is reducing. For example, a mortgage loan has to be repaid, which reduces on a monthly or annual basis.

3. *Increasing term insurance:* Under this plan, the premium as well as the benefit amount increases periodically, as agreed upon. The increase could be at a fixed per centage or in line with an agreed index. This plan is helpful in keeping the benefits in line with the time value of money, so that inflation does not erode the value of the benefits received.

4. *Renewable term insurance:* Though the term 'insurance' is used for a fixed period, a renewable term policy gives the right to renew the policy.

Convertible policies are useful for people who have low income today and hence, cannot afford to pay high premium in the initial years.

Whole Life Insurance

Whole life insurance guarantees a death benefit cover throughout the course of life, provided the required premiums are paid.

The advantage of whole life insurance is that the policy, if kept current, covers you over your entire life, unlike term insurance that covers you only for a certain term of years. Whole life insurance policies payout on the death of the assured, whenever it occurs. Premiums may need to be paid throughout the life of the assured, or a lesser limited period.

Endowment Insurance

Pure endowment is a plan where the benefit is payable to the insured only on survival of the specified term. Combining the features of term assurance and pure endowment are endowment policies which payout either on the death of the assured (whenever it occurs) or after a fixed number of years. Hence, the claim under an endowment policy may arise either by death or by maturity.

Annuities (Pension Plans)

Annuities are of two types:

1. *Immediate annuity:* Immediate Annuity begins at once or immediately on expiry of the designated period and is purchased with a single premium called *purchase price*. This type of annuity is typically purchased when a person reaches retirement age and has a lump sum to invest. If the person buying the annuity dies during the term, his/her legal heirs or nominees get the remaining instalments of the annuity.

For example, *Jeevan Akshay–VII* of LIC.

2. *Deferred annuity:* Under a deferred annuity plan, the annuity payments to the annuitant commence at some specified time or specified age of the annuitant. This type of annuity can be funded either by a single payment or a series of regular payments.

The annuity payment starts after the lapse of a selected period called the *deferment period*.

For example, *New Jeevan Shanti* of LIC.

Unit-linked Policies

A *unit-linked policy* is a life insurance policy in which the benefits depend on the performance of a portfolio of shares.

Each premium paid by the insured person is split. One part is used to provide life insurance cover, while the balance is used to buy units in a unit of mutual fund after deduction of costs, expenses, and the like. In this way, a small investor can benefit from investment in a managed fund without making a large financial commitment. The unit-linked policies can increase or decrease in value as they are linked to the value of the shares.

For example, *Nivesh Plus* and *New Endowment Plus* of LIC.

Besides these, there are other types of insurance policies as well. They are:

Moneyback Plans or Cashback Plans

These are plans where some per cent of the sum assured is returned to the insured person at regular intervals as survival benefit. At the end of the term, the balance amount is paid as maturity value.

Children Policies

Such policies are taken for the benefit of the children. This enables parents to get funds when the child reaches various stages in life, such as at 18 years of age for higher education, or at 21 for marriage.

For Examples, *Jeevan Tarun, Kanyadaan Plan* of LIC are for children.

BENEFITS OF LIFE INSURANCE PLAN

Following are the key advantages of taking a life insurance plan:

1. *Source of income:* In case of the death of the policyholder, the dependents can support themselves with the income from his life insurance cover. Therefore, with life insurance, one can ensure a source of income for his family in his absence. This is one of the most important reasons for taking a life insurance policy.

2. *Protection of assets:* With a good insurance cover, the family does not have to sell assets for income after the demise of the head of the family.

3. *Financial planning:* Life insurance policies are also taken for sound financial planning depending on one's requirements and risk appetite. For cautious investors, traditional policies like moneyback and endowment plans are available to provide income at regular intervals of time. The bold investors can invest in ULIPs (Unit Linked Insurance Plans) for market return.

4. *Tax savings:* Another key reason for buying life insurance policy is to reduce tax liability. Total deduction for payment of life insurance premium u/s 80C (along with deduction u/s 80CCC & 80CCD) allowed is up to ₹1,50,000 each financial year. Not only the amount of premium paid on life insurance policies is exempted from income tax but also the amount on maturity is tax exempted under Section 10(10D) of the Income Tax Act, 1961, with certain exceptions.

Box 7.2 shows some do's and don'ts of investing in a life insurance.

BOX 7.2: DO'S AND DON'TS FOR LIFE INSURANCE

Do's

- Buy an insurance policy as per your actual requirements.
- Do proper homework before buying a policy—consider the policy options available, and policy details like if it is a Single Premium or Regular Premium Policy, etc.
- Read out the form carefully before filling.
- Keep a copy of the complete proposal form signed by you for records.

Don'ts

- Do not leave any column blank in the proposal form.
- Do not let anyone else fill the form for you.
- Do not hide or falsify any facts.
- Do not rely on the agent blindly.

COMPUTATION OF PREMIUM

Normally, the insurance companies publish tables of premium rates. These tables give us the tabular premium which is arrived at as follows:

- The *Risk Premium* is calculate first. This is the amount required to meet the risk of death for a given age for a period of one year.
- The *Net Premium* is then calculated, taking into account the interest component.
- When we consider the provisions for administrative expenses, unexpected contingencies, and fluctuations, we get the *Office Premium.*
- Modifications are made considering various factors which might affect the premium computation. This gives us the *Tabular Premium.*

The calculation of premiums to be charged on different insurance policies becomes a complex one due to various factors. *For example,* if it is expected that out of 1000 people of a specified age group, one is likely to die within one year. Then, the mortality rate at that age would be 1/1000, that is 0.1%. The risk premium chargeable for persons at that age would be ₹1 for every ₹1000 of the sum assured. If the person belonging to the above group also suffers from some health problems, then the premium amount chargeable will be more than ₹1 for every ₹1000 of sum assured.

Other complications include the fact that a person becomes more risky as his age increases, that is, the risk factor keeps increasing along with increase in age. However, the premium to be charged in each period has to be kept constant. As a result, a higher premium is charged in the initial years.

Therefore, the risk premium charged should be after taking into account the factors like health, habits and age of the insured. This amount is decided upon by the actuary.

Premium amounts also get affected if the payment is made in a monthly, quarterly, half-yearly or yearly manner. Where the premiums are payable on half-yearly or yearly mode, there is saving in administrative costs as compared to the quarterly or monthly mode. Moreover, in the yearly mode, the insurer can utilise this amount throughout the year and earn interest on it. Usually, the practice is to allow rebates on half-yearly and yearly mode of payments. For monthly mode of payments, by the same logic, extra loading is to be charged to cover up the additional administrative expenses involved.

The actuary decides on the end premium to be charged to the customer, after considering the following four factors:

1. *Mortality:* Mortality is the probability of the insured dying in any given year. The actuary uses mortality tables and interprets the data to project the future most accurately for the type of contract being proposed. The risk premium is calculated taking the mortality rates into consideration.

2. *Investment:* As all premiums received by the insurer are invested and the insurer expects to earn interest on the investments, the actuary makes assumptions about the future rate of interest and allows for it in the premium charged.

3. *Expenses:* Life insurance offices have various operating expenses including agent training, commission, staff salaries, office stationery, etc. All these have to be recovered out of the premiums collected. Hence, every premium has to carry a proportion of these costs. These expenses are allowed with a loading that is applied on the premium rate.

4. *Contingency:* There are some assumptions made in the fixing of premiums, *for example,* assumptions on mortality rates based on the mortality tables. A contingency margin is added on to the premium so that the company can continue to meet its obligations towards policyholders even if the actual experience turns out to be worse than the assumptions used in pricing.

The combination of the mortality factor and the interest gives us the *Net Premium.* Loading for expenses and adding contingency to get the overall premium rate to be charged is known as the *Gross Premium.*

Premium Calculation

The insurer grants life insurance to the life insured on the basis of the information supplied through documents like the proposal form, medical reports, etc. Based on this information, the insurer underwrites the life of the insured at an appropriate rate of premium. The premium charged has to be appropriate to the risk involved.

Before the actual calculation of premiums, one needs to understand the various factors which affect the calculation of the amount to be paid as premium. They are:

1. *Type of Policy*

Different types of policies have different benefits and different circumstances under which the benefits become payable. The expected cost of these benefits, based on the risk of claims, helps determine the amount of premium. For example, a term assurance has lower premiums than an equivalent endowment policy. This is because a term assurance policy results in a claim only in the case of death, whereas an endowment will always lead to a claim.

2. *Age*

As discussed earlier, age has a bearing on the risk of death which increases with age. Therefore, the premium rate usually rise with age. There are three different ways of calculating age. We will consider the following example to understand the concept:

Mr. Sharma is a proposer for life insurance on 13 July 2012. His date of birth is 3 September 1980.

Date of proposal	13.07.2012
Date of birth	03.09.1980
Difference	10.10.31

His age nearer to birthday is 32 years.
His age on last birthday is the number of completed years of age, that is, 31 years.
His age on next birthday is 32 years.

An insurer may follow any of the above three methods for calculation of age for the purpose of premium calculation. He will be following the method of taking the age nearer to the birth date for the purpose of premium calculation.

3. *Term of the Policy*

For savings plans like endowments, the longer the term, the lesser the tabular premium, other things (age, sum assured, etc.) being equal.

For pure protection plans like term insurance, the longer the term, the higher the tabular premium, other things (age, sum assured, etc.) being equal.

4. *Additional Benefits*

If the client selects additional benefits, such as double accident benefit or extended permanent disability benefit along with the basic plan, there will be an additional charge.

5. *State of Health, Occupation and Hazard*

The rates as per the rate book are applicable to standard lives or average persons. If the state of health of the insured is classified as non-standard, an additional premium rate may be charged. Similarly, if either the occupation, or recreational activities of the life insured is hazardous, or exposes him/her to any additional risk, an extra premium would be charged.

6. *Sum Assured*

Higher the sum assured, higher is the premium charged.

GENERAL INSURANCE

As different from the practice of life insurance, the concept of general insurance (also called *non-life insurance*) represents the core of the evolution of the worldwide practice of insurance. It is in the sea-going vessels of the early centuries that the concept of insurance took shape. The risk to shipping-based commerce came in many forms—sea storms, pirates, wars, etc. that led to the formation of companies which pooled mutual risk through a mutually contributed fund.

General insurance evolves with the evolution of business and lifestyle of human beings. With its seeds in the sea-faring mariners and ships, today, general insurance covers everything from space expeditions to the voice of famous singers.

More than life insurance, general insurance forms the lifeline of several commerce and trade activities. Following are the essentials of a general insurance contract:

- When the insured pays premium and the insurer accepts the risk, the contract of insurance is concluded. The policy then issued is the 'evidence' of such a contract.
- The contract is complete when the proposer makes an offer and the insurer accepts it. The insurance cover note is treated as an acceptance of the offer.
- The consideration for an insurer, in a general insurance contract, is the premium paid by the insured, and the consideration for the insured is the indemnity promise made by the insurer.
- The purpose of insurance is not against public policy.
- People entering in the contract must be authorised and competent to enter into such contracts.

Conventionally, the concept of general insurance covers the following categories:

1. Health Insurance

Health insurance or medical insurance is a form of insurance under which the expenses incurred on medical treatment and hospitalisation are covered. It covers the policyholder and his family against any financial burden arising from medical emergencies. *For example,* in case of sudden hospitalisation, health insurance takes care of the expenses such as medicines, hospital room, medical tests, etc.

Key Features and Benefits of a Health Insurance Policy

Besides the basic benefit of health insurance of covering the unexpected medical expenses (called *mediclaim*), following are some other features and benefits of health insurance policies:

(i) ***Family Floater Policy:*** This refers to the option of covering multiple members of the family under the same plan with a slightly higher premium instead of taking an individual health insurance policy. *For example,* the policy is taken for a cover of ₹5 lacs and one member in the family is hospitalised uses around ₹3 lacs for his treatment. Then, the remaining ₹2 lacs can still be availed by others. Hence, the total burden on the family is reduced.

(ii) ***Cashless facility:*** The insured can get admitted to a hospital and be treated without worrying about the medical expenses. Hospitals have a tie-up with insurance companies and therefore, accept the insured's medical identity card (issued by the insurance company) for providing cashless facility to them.

(iii) ***Ambulance charges:*** In most of the cases, the ambulance charges are covered in the policy and the policyholder usually doesn't have to bear its burden.

(iv) ***Free health check up:*** Some health insurance policies have a free health check-up facility for the insured as well.

(v) ***No-claim bonus:*** Some health insurance policies provide a no-claim bonus. If there has been no claim in the previous year, i.e. if the person insured has not availed any hospitalisation benefit, then a bonus is declared, either in the form of reduced premium or by way of increasing the sum assured.

(vi) ***Tax benefits:*** Under Section 80D of the Income Tax Act, income tax benefit is provided to the insured for the premium amount up to ₹25,000 for citizens in a financial year and ₹50,000 for senior citizens respectively.

2. Motor Insurance

It is a protection to the vehicle owner against damages to his/her vehicle, and any 'Third Party Liability' against the owner of the vehicle. Third Party Insurance is a statutory requirement. The owner of the vehicle is legally liable for any injury or damage to third party life or property caused due to the use of the vehicle in a public place. Driving a motor vehicle without insurance in a public place is a punishable offence under the Motor Vehicles Act, 1988.

3. Property Insurance

It includes insurance of buildings, machinery, stocks, etc. against fire and related hazards like burglary and the like. It can be further divided into three categories:

(a) *Fire Insurance*

This branch covers the insurance of property against the risk of fire, riots, flood, earthquake, etc. It also extended itself to loss of profit due to the damage caused by any of these perils.

(b) *Marine Insurance*

This covers two main types of risks, that is, risk to loss or damage to cargo (known as *cargo insurance*) carried by sea, rail, air, road, etc.

(c) *Accident Insurance*

This covers all types of risks that were not covered in any of the above two categories. Besides, burglary, motor, personal accident, sickness, fidelity, etc. are also included.

Thus, accident insurance is a very vast category of general insurance and the type of cover that you need depends upon the type of property you wish to cover.

4. Travel Insurance

It offers insurance protection during travelling. Travel insurance protects you and/or family against travel related accidents, unexpected medical expenditure during travel, losses such as baggage loss, loss of passport, etc., and interruption or delays in flights or delayed arrival of baggage, etc.

Box 7.3 discusses the important groups under which general insurance is categorised.

BOX 7.3: GROUPS OF GENERAL INSURANCE

Today, the concept of general insurance offers highly evolved and sophisticated forms of business and personal risk mitigation. Considering various types of general insurances above, the main groups under which general insurance is categorised is as follows:

1. **Insurance of persons:** This group covers personal accident, disability and health-related risks.
2. **Insurance of property:** This group represents the bulk of general insurance practise. It covers buildings, motor vehicles, aircraft, machinery, factories, ships, livestock, homes, furniture, fixtures, cash, securities, etc.
3. **Insurance of interest:** This mainly covers the fidelity guarantee insurance.
4. **Insurance of liability:** Public liability, product liability and professional indemnities fall in this group.
5. **Special risks:** These include risks that cannot be covered by the general principles of any of the above policies. *Examples* of this could be employment insurance that provides an individual with compensation on account of being laid off or unemployed, or insurance against loss of skills of musicians and other art performers use such policies to insure against financial losses just in case they lose their skill for any reason, space expeditions, exploration of the poles and jungles, etc.

KEY ASPECTS OF INSURANCE

Free-look Period

It is a return option given to the person buying the policy. If a person buys a new insurance policy and receives the policy document and finds that the terms and conditions are not as per his requirements, then he can return the policy to the company during a stipulated period of 15 days. This time period is called *free-look period.*

This provision has been built by IRDA as a consumer-friendly measure to take care of this problem. So, if you have bought a policy and realise you don't want it, you can return and get a refund.

There are conditions for the above:

- This applies only to life insurance policies and to health insurance policy that are for a term of at least 3 years.
- The option should be exercised within 15 days of receiving the policy document.
- The company should be communicated in writing.
- The premium refund will be adjusted for proportionate risk premium for the period on cover, expenses incurred by the insurer on medical examination, and stamp duty charges.

Surrender Value

Surrender value is the cash value of the policy which is payable immediately on cancellation of the entire contract.

A policy acquires surrender value if the premiums are paid at least for 3 consecutive years.

Permanent Disability Benefit

This benefit provides that in the event of the assured becoming totally and permanently disabled before the age of 70 years, the premium on the contract will be waived for sum assured up to a pre-determined amount.

Claim Concession

Another privilege granted to the life assured is that where premiums for at least 3 full years have been paid, and if subsequent premium is not paid, in case of death of the assured within 6 months from the due date of first unpaid premium, the full sum assured is payable after deducting the unpaid premiums with interest. This benefit is known as *claim concession.*

Riders

In addition to the above, the life assured can avail some more benefits on payment of small amounts as extra premium. These benefits are applicable on occurrence of some specified event and are called *riders.* Some examples of such riders are *Waiver of Premium Rider, Accidental Death Rider, and Critical Illness Rider.*

Options

Options are defined as benefits gritted to the life assured in order to ease the handling of the life insurance contract during the complete tenure. These options can be modified at any time during the tenure of the policy. Some of the options available are:

- Every policyholder is given the option to choose the premium payment mode, which can be annual, half-yearly, quarterly or monthly.
- Convertible term assurance plan gives the life assured the option to convert the policy at the end of the specified term either into a limited payment life policy or endowment assurance policy without undergoing medical examination.
- The life assured can exercise the option of receipt of payment of the claim proceeds by way of yearly, half-yearly, quarterly or monthly instalments spread over a period of years. These types of options are known as *settlement options*.

Guarantees

Certain guaranteed additions are provided to the policyholders under particular conditions. *For example,* under certain plans, the sum assured gets enhanced at specified guaranteed rates at the end of each year. The 'guaranteed additions' are payable with the sum assured.

Premium

Premium is the price paid by the insured for purchasing the insurance policy, i.e. the plan and term of assurance for the sum assured chosen by him/her.

The premium has to be paid by the insured person at the commencement of the policy and at regular intervals as specified in the contract.

US AND INDIAN INSURANCE INDUSTRY: A COMPARISON

The Indian industry does not function the way US insurance industry operates. The basic reason can be attributed to the difference in the regulatory structure in the respective countries. The areas of distinction in the insurance industry of both the nations are discussed in Table 7.2.

TABLE 7.2 Distinction between US and Indian Insurance Industry

S.No.	*Basis*	*USA*	*INDIA*
1.	Regulatory framework	The insurance regulatory framework is state-based for most parts. The insurer needs to get licensed directly by the state in which it seeks to operate.	The Indian insurance regulatory system is centrally controlled by IRDA. An insurer licensed by IRDA can operate in all states and union territories of India.
2.	Reinsurance governance	The US regulatory system does not seek to regulate the reinsurance process. Further, there is no state-owned national reinsurer.	IRDA governs the reinsurance parameters for the non-life insurance companies in India. All non-life insurers must cede 30% of the sum assured for each policy for different classes of insurance written in India to Indian reinsurer.

(Contd.)

S.No.	Basis	USA	INDIA
3.	Investment regulations	The US has no specific restriction pertaining to foreign investment. The US regulatory system does not mandate a minimum investment in US treasury instruments.	The Indian regulation does not permit investment of admitted assets outside India. It also mandates that at least 50% of the insurer's assets be invested in government securities.
4.	Mandatory servicing of rural and social sector	The US regulatory system does not mandate any obligation to the service of the rural and social sector.	The Indian insurance regulator man- dates a minimum rural and social commitment by the insurer willing to operate in the Indian market.
5.	Distribution	Distribution channels such as Independent Financial Advisors (IFAs), brokers, bancassurance and electronic channels are more preferred rather than direct selling.	Insurers follow a push strategy to market their offerings. The focus is more on direct selling agents rather than other distribution channels such as Independent Financial Advisors (IFAs), brokers, bancassurance and electronic channels.
6.	Penetration	Being a matured market for insurance, penetration in the US is quite high.	The penetration of life insurance and "general insurance" in particular in India remains low on account of low consumer preference, largely untapped rural markets and constrained distribution channels.
7.	Future outlook	The outlook is negative for US insurance sector. The negative outlook reflects the ongoing concern regarding the industry's expanding equity market, exposure driven by growth in variable annuities, and market performance guarantees which can add significant volatility to financial performance and capital in a period of unstable market conditions.	The increasing literacy rate, especially in rural India, has spread awareness about the need for insurance. Projected per capita GDP is expected to increase, reflecting higher disposable income.

INSURANCE OMBUDSMAN SCHEME

Initially, the Insurance Ombudsman Scheme was created under 'Institution of Insurance Ombudsman', set up in 1999. Presently, there is "Office of Insurance Ombudsman", constituted under the Insurance Ombudsman Rules, 2017.[9] It is an alternate Grievance

9. https://www.cioins.co.in

Redressal platform and has been set up with an aim to resolve grievances of aggrieved policyholders against Insurance Companies and its Intermediaries or Insurance Brokers in a speedy and cost-effective manner.

The Offices of Insurance Ombudsman are under the administrative control of "Council for Insurance Ombudsmen" (CIO), consisting of nine members including the Chairperson.

There are 17 Insurance Ombudsman Centres in different locations in the Country and one can approach the ombudsman with complaint either online or through written communication through e-mail or letter for any policy taken by him,

(i) within one year from
   (a) date of rejection of the complaint by the Insurance Company/Insurance Broker; OR
   (b) expiry of one month of filing the complaint if the Insurer fails to reply.

(ii) The quantum of loss payable under the insurance policy is not above ₹30 Lakhs.

The complaint to the ombudsman can be regarding any of the following:

(i) Any partial or total repudiation of claims by an insurer.
(ii) Delay in settlement of claims.
(iii) Any dispute about premium paid or payable in terms of the policy.
(iv) Non-issue of any insurance document after paying your premium.

If a complaint is settled through mediation, the Ombudsman shall make a recommendation which it thinks fair in the circumstances of the case, within 1 month of the date of receipt of mutual written consent for such mediation and the copies of the recommendation shall be sent to the complainant and the insurer [or insurance broker, as the case may be] concerned. Where the complaint is not settled by way of mediation, the Insurance Ombudsman shall pass an award within a period of 3 months of the receipt of all requirements from the complainant. Such decision shall be binding on the Insurance Companies and its Intermediaries or Insurance Brokers as the case may be.

BANCASSURANCE

Insurance, at one point of time, was taken as risk cover instrument, by a group of people who were futuristic in nature. Today, the scenario has completely changed—everybody likes to secure his/her future and earn reasonable return on these amounts. Also, it is the era of diversification and tie-ups wherein institutions enter into unrelated areas as a part of business growth and join hands with allied institutions for business operations. These changes in the financial horizon have given rise to bancassurance in India. Banks which were meant for deposits, loans and transactions are allowed to provide insurance policies to people. This feature of bank is called *bancassurance*.

An example of bancassurance is ICICI Lombard General Insurance Company Ltd. has tied-up with Yes Bank to sell its insurance products. Other examples of bancassurance companies are SBI Life Insurance Company–SBI, Axis Bank–MetLife India.

Bancassurance in India

With the increasing number of middle-class families in the country, RBI recognised the need of an effective method to make insurance policies reach people of all economic classes. Implementation of bancassurance in India is one such development that took place in this direction. PSU General Insurers tied-up with leading PSU and private banks from 2002 onwards. Individual agent-oriented products evolved into bancassurance-friendly adaptations and aligned with the bankers' customer needs. By 2005, the bancassurance channel had been established as a mainstay in marketing/ sales, and growth path of the insurers.

The bancassurance in India had shown a tremendous growth during 2010–2011, as given in Table 7.3. In 2021, the India bancassurance market reached a value of US$ 85.3 billion in 2021[10].

TABLE 7.3 Bancassurance Growth in India—2010 and 2011

Type of Channel	*Corporate Agents–Banks*	*Corporate Agents–Banks*	*Growth (%)*
	2010–11 (₹ *in crores*)	2009–10 (₹ *in crores*)	
Fire	494	443	12
Marine (cargo)	10	6	77
Marine (full)	2	4	–37
Engineering	32	24	29
Motor (own damage)	746	447	67
Motor third party	225	181	24
Liability insurance	8	6	32
Personal accident	145	144	1
Medical insurance	217	166	30
Overseas medical insurance	3	6	–51
Miscellaneous	372	336	11
TOTAL	**2254**	**1763**	**27.85**

Source: https://www.coi.org.in/documents/10156/24a3a797-84a2-49a5-b586-ead077aff410

Regulations under RBI and IRDA

The Reserve Bank of India and the Insurance Development and Regulatory Authority have a set of guidelines for companies which come together to form bancassurance. For licensing of bancassurance agents, IRDA came out with an exposure draft, 'Licensing of Bancassurance Agents Regulations', 2011[11]. India is divided into various zones and every bank has to choose insurers within the zones. With this, the customer also gets a wider range of insurance products offered by different insurers.

10. https://www.imarcgroup.com/bancassurance-market-india
11. http://www.irda.gov.in/ADMINCMS

Benefits of Bancassurance

- Regular customers of banks can purchase insurance policies, and thereby help in increasing the bank network.
- People can be benefitted through widely spread banking networks for buying insurance products.
- With more number of insurance providers, there will be a better competitive environment for the buyers. They can expect better premium rates and services from bancassurance.
- It will provide a 'one-stop shop' for customers.

Bancassurance: Caselets

Banks of India have taken lot of new initiatives for the benefit of their valued customers. With an objective to offer the customers of the bank a 'one-stop shop' having an array of varied financial products under one roof and for the fulfilment of their diverse needs, banks have entered into tie-ups with renowned insurance companies.

Table 7.4 shows a list of leading banks with their insurance partners.

TABLE 7.4 Banks-Insurance Partners

Product	*Bank*	*Insurance Company*
Life insurance	State Bank of India	SBI Life Insurance Company Ltd.
Life insurance	United Bank of India	HDFC Life Insurance Company
General insurance	Union Bank of India	Bajaj Allianz General Insurance Co. Ltd.

ANALYSIS OF FINANCIAL PERFORMANCE OF LIFE INSURANCE CORPORATION OF INDIA

In this section, we shall analyse the financial performance of Life Insurance Corporation of India to understand the financial indicators and focus areas of an insurance company. Life Insurance Corporation of India is the leading life insurer of the nation. It is the largest state-owned life insurance company in India, and also the country's largest investor. It funds a significant portion of the Indian government's expenses. Established on 1st September 1956 with the merger of 243 insurance companies and provident societies, its objective was to spread life insurance much more widely to everyone. The analysis of financial performance of LIC of India will make the readers aware about the financial challenges and issues faced by an insurance sector company. LIC is primarily governed by Life Insurance Corporation Act, 1956, in addition to Insurance Regulatory and Development Act (IRD Act), 1999 and Insurance Act, 1938.

Financial accounts of an insurance company involve a lot of complexities which are unique in nature. The major reasons for this are:

- Ascertainment of liability in respect of insurance policies issued by the company.
- The concept of Policyholders' Fund and Shareholders' Fund.
- The unit linked business and related investment valuations involved in the same.

Tables 7.5(a-c) present the financial statements of LIC.

TABLE 7.5(a) Balance Sheet of LIC as on 31st March 2022

(₹ in lakhs)

Particulars	31–03–2022	31–03–2021
SOURCES OF FUNDS	₹	₹
SHAREHOLDERS' FUNDS		
Share Capital	632499.77	10000.00
Reserves and Surplus	404304.56	622499.77
Credit/(Debit) fair value change account	4109.56	3569.45
	1040913.89	**636069.22**
BORROWINGS	—	—
POLICYHOLDERS' FUNDS		
Credit/(Debit) fair value change account	40023933.61	27287079.07
Policy liabilities	371003945.52	340375097.09
FUNDS FOR DISCONTINUED POLICIES		
Discontinued on account of non-payment of premium	6633.53	3366.00
Others	1601.02	1699.73
Insurance reserves	1285462.99	1293403.13
Provision for linked liabilities	2388583.06	3293196.17
FUNDS FOR FUTURE APPROPRIATIONS	183443.31	333.99
TOTAL	**415934516.93**	**372890244.40**
APPLICATION OF FUNDS		
INVESTMENTS	—	—
Shareholders'	641213.63	71356.67
Policyholders'	389569349.57	348765485.70
Assets held to Cover Linked Liabilities	2393863.99	3294950.15
Loans	10987563.57	10778333.76
Fixed Assets	355202.31	345338.62
Current Assets		
Cash and Bank Balances	3743214.07	3029325.45
Advances and other Assets	15368569.78	14890777.50
(A)	**19111783.85**	**17920102.95**
CURRENT LIABILITIES	5630154.39	6791017.85
PROVISIONS	1494305.60	1494305.60
(B)	**7124459.99**	**8285323.45**
NET CURRENT ASSETS (C) = (A – B)	11987323.86	9634779.50
MISCELLANEOUS EXPENDITURE	—	—
DEBIT BALANCE IN PROFIT & LOSS ACCOUNT (Shareholders' Account)	—	—
TOTAL	**415934516.93**	**372890244.40**

Analysis

Other than the usual items, the items in the balance sheet of a life insurance company include:

- Shareholders' Funds
- Policyholders' Funds

1. *Shareholders' Funds*

Shareholders' Funds include share capital, reserves and surplus, and fair value change account. There is an increase in funds on account of majorly both share capital and reserves and surplus by ₹404,844.7 lakhs in 2022. It is a good sign in terms of internal corpus of a company.

2. *Policyholders' Funds*

Policyholders' funds consist of fair value change relating to policy fund investments, policy liabilities, insurance reserves, provision for linked liabilities, funds for future appropriations, etc.

The balance in the funds for future appropriations are those funds whose allocation has not been determined on the date of balance sheet, neither to participating policyholders nor to shareholders.

The *policyholders' liabilities* have also increased during the year and they are determined by LIC's Appointed Actuary pursuant to his annual investigation of the Corporation's life insurance business.

3. *Investments of a Life Insurance Company*

The insurance company has to follow the provisions set out in Section 27 of the Insurance Act, 1938, read with Rule 3 of the IRDA (Investment) Regulations, 2000.[12]

Accordingly, the controlled fund of the company has to be invested in the specified securities. The assets relating to Pension business, Annuity business and Linked Life Insurance business shall not form a part of the controlled fund.

The funds relating to Unit-Linked Insurance business are to be invested as per the pattern of investment offered to and approved by the policyholders.

There is an increase in policyholders' investment of ₹4,08,03,863.9 lakhs. It is an indication of sound investment planning by the company. Listed equity securities that are traded in active markets are measured at fair value on the balance sheet date and the change in the carrying amount of equity securities is taken to Fair Value Change Account.

Mutual fund investments are valued on fair value as at 31st March as per IRDA directive.

4. *Provisions and Contingent Liabilities*

A provision is made based on a reliable estimate when it is probable that an outflow of resources embodying economic benefits will be required to settle an obligation.

12. http://irda.gov.in/ADMINCMS/cms/frmGeneral_Layout.aspx.

Contingent liabilities (other than policies), if material, are disclosed by way of notes.

TABLE 7.5(b) Profit and Loss Account of LIC for the year ending on 31st March 2022

(₹ in lakhs)

Particulars	31–02–2022	31–03–2021
Amounts transferred from/to the Policyholders Account	387541.84	288901.01
Income from Investments		
(a) Interest, Dividend and Rent	16095.80	1777.65
(b) Profit on sale/redemption of Investments	4166.57	612.15
(c) (Loss on sale/redemption of Investments)	(139.51)	(91.00)
Other income	—	—
TOTAL (A)	**407664.70**	**291199.81**
Expense other than those directly related to the insurance business	50.33	46.40
Contribution to Policyholders' Account	942.45	475.97
Provisions (other than taxation)	—	—
(a) For diminution in the value of investments	—	—
(b) Provision for doubtful debts	—	—
(c) Others	—	—
TOTAL (B)	**992.78**	**522.37**
Profit/(Loss) before tax	406671.92	290677.44
Provision for taxation	2359.81	620.76
Profit/Loss after tax	404312.11	290056.68
APPROPRIATIONS		
(a) Balance at the beginning of the year	—	—
(b) Dividends paid during the year (5% Valuation surplus paid to Central Government)	—	—
(c) Proposed final dividend		
(d) Dividend distribution on tax	—	—
(e) Transfer to reserve/other accounts	2878.81	290056.68
Profit carried forward to the Balance Sheet	401433.30	—

Analysis

The Profit and Loss account represents all income and expenses relating to Shareholders' Account (in respect of total business).

1. *Income*

The income comprises mainly of investment or income created out of Shareholders' Fund.

There is an increase in total income of ₹1,16,464.89 lakhs during the year 2021–2022. It can be owed to comparatively high growth rate of the company. Given the negligible expenses and high margins, the entire income is attributable as profit.

The net surplus to income ratio is on an increasing trend, showing the brand value of the company in the life insurance sector.

2. *Expenses*

The major components of expenses are:

- Depreciation relating to assets held by shareholders' fund, investment expenses, Directors' Fees, etc.
- Transfer of funds to Policyholders' Fund and preliminary expenses written off.
- The profit or loss as per the account is carried to the balance sheet as usual.

The composition of expenses as a per centage of total income is minor, a positive indicator for the profit margin of company.

TABLE 7.5(c) Cash Flow Statement of LIC for the year ending 31st March 2022

(₹ in lakhs)

Particulars	31–03–2022	31–03–2021
Cash Flows from the operating activities		
1. Premium received from policyholders	42699536.44	40753470.81
2. Other receipts	77947.91	59950.49
3. Payments to the re-insurers	30150.18	(4904.62)
4. Payments of claims/benefits	(35652202.16)	(28529648.07)
5. Payments of commission and brokerage	(2317058.08)	(2184439.10)
6. Payments of other operating expenses	(4228257.71)	(2872522.32)
7. Deposits, advances and staff loans	75988.10	(470441.84)
8. Income taxes paid	(726453.34)	(943002.75)
9. Service tax/GST paid	(273200.22)	(236155.65)
10. Cash flows before extraordinary items	(313548.87)	5572306.96
11. Cash flows from extraordinary items	0.00	0.00
Net cash flow from operating activities:	**(313548.87)**	**5572306.96**
Cash Flows from Investing activities		
12. Purchase of fixed assets	(71532.70)	(107409.61)
13. Proceeds from sale of fixed assets	25820.20	28523.64
14. Purchase of investments	(42739879.65)	(50798824.90)
15. Loans disbursed	(79334.59)	(891919.63)
16. Sale of investments	18960902.69	23137157.11
17. Rents/Interests/Dividends received	24952616.58	23213886.14
Net cash flow from investing activities:	**1048592.53**	**(5418587.24)**

(Contd.)

Particulars	31–03–2022	31–03–2021
Cash Flows from Financing activities		
Proceeds from borrowing	0.00	0.00
Repayment of borrowings	0.00	0.00
Interest/dividends paid	0.00	0.00
Net cash flow from financing activities:	**0.00**	**0.00**
Effect of foreign exchange rates	(10940.47)	17305.64
Net Increase in cash and cash equivalents	724103.18	171025.36
Cash and cash equivalents at the beginning of the year	3033396.06	2862370.70
Cash and cash equivalents at the end of the year	3757499.24	3033396.06

Analysis

The cash flow statement of the insurance company is worked out as per the "Direct Method" according to the IRDA requirement. The statement depicts the inflows and outflows of the company from various business related and other activities.

Given the nature of business, most of the transactions are in cash. On the basis of the cash flow statement, LIC is a cash-rich company. The cash inflow from operating activities is negative this year of 2022 and inadequate enough to support the operating expenses as well as investments made. This is not a good sign during the year. Despite this, the company has been able to have a positive cash in hand from other sources.

Payments of claims/benefits have been paid higher bonus of ₹71,22,554.09 lakhs in the year 2022. It eventually increases the confidence of policyholders and enhances the public image of LIC as a key player in life insurance industry.

CASE STUDY

Sonia's Life Insurance

Sonia was a 40 year-old woman working as a manager in a multi-national company. Two years ago, she and her husband had divorced which left her with the sole responsibility of taking care of her 15 year-old son, Amit.

As a single parent, Sonia was aware of her financial vulnerability. So, on the suggestion of a close friend, she consulted a financial adviser.

The adviser discussed various options with her and devised a plan to financially protect Sonia and her son, if something ever happened to her. Amit had been a good student and done well at school. Sonia wanted to ensure that he should be able to study in one of the leading universities of the state, for his master's degree.

She took a life insurance policy for ₹70 lacs with rider of income protection in case of illness.

Less than a year later, Sonia went home from work early one afternoon with a headache. Later in the evening, she lost consciousness and was rushed to the hospital. She had suffered a cardiac arrest, and died that evening without regaining consciousness.

Under her life policy, Sonia had nominated Amit as her sole beneficiary. He received ₹70 lacs from the policy.

Amit is now working hard for his master's, planning to become a cardiologist.

POINTS TO REMEMBER

- Insurance is a contractual arrangement whereby one party agrees to compensate another for losses in return for the payment of a consideration. The party agreeing to pay for the losses is called the insurer. The party whose loss is paid by the insurer is called the insured. The payment that the insurer receives is called premium.
- Indemnification refers to the fact that the maximum financial compensation is limited to the extent of the loss.
- Human Life Value (HLV) is defined as the present value of all future income that you could expect to earn for your family's benefit, plus other value you expect to contribute, less taxes and personal consumption, till your planned retirement date.
- Insurance, both general and life, as a readily recognisable business, first emerged in the UK at the end of the 16th century. In India, it was introduced as marine insurance in around 1700.
- Insurance industry in India has seen a phenomenal change after the industrial era. Its growth saga is explained as:

  Pre Independence: The insurance industry originated in India in the year 1818 with the formation of Life Insurance Corporation in Calcutta. In 1912, the insurance sector came under the purview of regulations when the government passed the Life Insurance Companies Act but it was in the year 1938 when the government came up with the first legislation to bring the insurance sector under state control.

  Post Independence: In 1956, the Government of India nationalised insurance companies bringing Indian Insurance sector under the purview of the government. The Life Insurance Corporation (LIC) was formed in September 1956. The general insurance business was also nationalised with effect from January 1, 1973.

  Post Liberalisation: Since 1956, the LIC held the monopoly in India's life insurance sector. GIC, with its four subsidiaries enjoyed the monopoly for general insurance business. From 1991 onwards, the Indian Government liberalised the financial sector of the Indian economy. Under the recommendation of the Malhotra Committee, 1994, the Insurance Regulatory and Development Authority was set up in 1999 to monitor and control the insurance industry.
- The 'Principle of Utmost Good Faith' states that it is the duty of the insured and the insurer to disclose all relevant facts. This concerns both life and general insurance.
- The 'Principle of Insurable Interest' states that the person getting insured must have insurable interest in the object of insurance.

- The 'Principle of Indemnity' implies a guarantee by the insurer to repair the loss of the insured and put him/her in the same condition as before the loss.
- The 'Principle of Contribution' tells us how the liability is to be met when the insured has taken insurance with more than one Insurer on the same subject matter.
- The 'Principle of Subrogation' refers to the rights that an insurer acquires vis-a-vis the insured when the insurer has paid him an indemnity.
- The 'Principle of Loss Minimisation' states that the insured must take all the possible steps to minimise the loss of the insured asset on the happening of an uncertain event, like fire.
- The 'Principle of Proximate Cause' defines that for insurance, the loss to the asset must have been caused by the event against which the asset has been insured.
- The Indian insurance sector is headed by Insurance Regulatory Development Authority (IRDA) and comprises of—(a) Life insurance sector, (b) General insurance sector, comprising of Non-Life insurance and Health insurance companies, and (c) Re-insurance sector.
- Insurance Regulatory Development Authority was set up as an autonomous body under the IRDA Act, 1999 to be acting as a statutory regulator to regulate and promote the insurance industry in India and to protect the interests of insurance policy holders and to work for the orderly growth of the industry.
- Among the life insurers, Life Insurance Corporation (LIC) is the sole public sector company. Remaining are privately-held life insurance companies.
- Among the general insurers, there are non-life and insurers registered to underwrite policies exclusively in health, personal accident and travel insurance segments.
- In addition to the above, there is a sole national re-insurer, namely, General Insurance Corporation of India. Unlike an insurance company, a reinsurance company does not accept business from the end customer, but acts as the insurer for insurance companies, thus helping to pool the risks that are reinsured with it by all the companies.
- Actuary is a technical expert who has received specialist training in the mathematics of insurance.
- Underwriter scrutinises, analyses, and takes the decisions on the proposals received for insurance.
- Policy Owner Services are meant towards issuing the actual policy documents.
- Claim Administration is responsible for the actual settlement of claims.
- Marketing department gives suggestions for new products.
- Investment area manages the company's assets and investments.
- Accounting area keeps records of the income and expenses.
- Information Systems design and maintain computer systems.
- Legal and Compliance department play an important role in ensuring that the company is complying with all the regulations and laws in the country.
- Agents are licensed under Section 42 of the Insurance Act, 1938. He/she receives payment by way of commission for procuring insurance business.
- Insurance Brokers may be an individual or firm, whose full-time occupation is the placement of insurance business with insurance companies.
- Insurance Consultants are specialists who give advice to consumers who wish to buy insurance products.

- Insurance Surveyors and Loss Assessors are technical experts who inspect the damage or loss of an insurance company.
- Third Party Administrators are those who have obtained a license from the Authority, and are engaged for a fee or remuneration with the insurance company for the provision of health services.
- Banking Outlets are outlets of banks for distribution of insurance products. The bancassurance is one of the most prevalent banking outlet services in the present times.
- The Indian Life Assurance Companies Act, 1912 was the first statutory measure to regulate the business of insurance. Later, the Indian Insurance Companies Act was enacted in 1928 to enable the government to collect statistical information about life and non-life insurance business transacted in India.
- These legislations are applicable to insurance—The Insurance Act, 1938, LIC Act, 1956, and Insurance Regulatory and Development Authority Act, 1999.
- Term insurance offers pure risk cover without any element of saving.
- Whole-life insurance guarantees a death benefit cover throughout the course of life, provided the required premiums are paid.
- Endowment insurance payout either on the death of the assured, whenever it occurs or after a fixed number of years.
- Annuities are of two types—(a) Immediate annuity, which begins at once or immediately on expiry of the designated period, (b) Deferred annuity, where the annuity payments to the annuitant commence at some specified time or specified age of the annuitant.
- Unit-linked policy is a life insurance policy in which the benefits depend on the performance of a portfolio of shares.
- Moneyback plans return a certain per cent of the sum assured to the insured person periodically as survival benefit. At the end of the term, the balance amount is paid as maturity value.
- Children policies are taken on the life of the children for the benefit of the child.
- Health insurance is also known as medical insurance. It is a form of insurance which covers the expenses incurred on medical treatment and hospitalisation.
- Motor insurance is a protection to the vehicle owner against—damages to his/her vehicle, and any Third Party Liability against the owner of the vehicle. Third Party Insurance is a statutory requirement.
- Property insurance includes insurance of buildings, machinery, stocks, etc. against fire and related hazards like burglary and other. It can be further divided into three categories—(a) Fire insurance, (b) Marine insurance, and (c) Accident insurance.
- Travel insurance offers insurance protection during travelling.
- Free-look Period is a return option of 15 days which is given to the person buying the policy.
- Surrender Value is the cash value of the policy which is payable immediately on cancellation of the entire contract.
- Permanent disability benefit provides that in the event of the assured becoming totally and permanently disabled before the age of 70, the premium on the contract will be waived.
- Claim concession is that where at least premiums for 3 full years have been paid,

and if subsequent premium is not paid, in case of death of the assured within 6 months from the due date, the full sum assured is payable.

- Riders are additional benefits which can be availed on payment of small amounts as extra premium.
- Options are the benefits gritted to the life assured in order to ease the handling of the Life Insurance contract during the complete tenure.
- Guarantees are provided to the policyholders under certain conditions.
- Premium is the price paid by the insured for purchasing the insurance policy.
- Insurance Ombudsman scheme was initially created under Institution of Insurance Ombudsman which was established in 1999. Presently, there is "Office of Insurance Ombudsman", constituted under the Insurance Ombudsman Rules, 2017. It was set up by the Government of India as a part of providing a forum to aggrieved policyholders, to settle their complaints against the insurance companies off the court system, in a cost-effective, efficient and impartial way.
- Bancassurance is a tie-up between banks and insurance companies, wherein banks which were meant for deposits, loans and transactions are allowed to provide insurance policies to people.

KEY TERMS

- **Insurance** is a contractual arrangement where in the insurer agrees to compensate the insured for losses at a premium.
- **Indemnification** refers to the fact that the maximum financial compensation is limited to the extent of the loss.
- **Human life value** is defined as the present value of all future income that one expects to earn deducting the taxes and personal consumption.
- **Re-insurance** is the insurance of insurance companies.
- **Actuary** is a technical expert who has received specialist training in the mathematics of insurance.
- **Underwriter** is one who scrutinises, analyses and takes the decisions on the proposals received for insurance.
- **Third-party administrator** is a person who has obtained a license from the Authority, and is engaged for a fee or remuneration, as specified in the agreement with the insurance company, for the provision of health services.
- **Term insurance** is a plan which offers pure risk cover without any element of saving.
- **Whole life insurance** is the insurance which guarantees a death benefit cover throughout the course of life.
- **Endowment insurance** is one which pays the claim either by death or by maturity, whichever occurs earlier.
- **Unit-linked policy** is a life insurance policy in which the benefits depend on the performance of a portfolio of shares.
- **Free-look period** is a return option of 15 days given to the person buying the policy.

- **Surrender value** is the cash value of the policy which is payable immediately on cancellation of the entire contract.
- **Riders** are the additional benefits which can be availed by the insured in life insurance on payment of extra premium.
- **Bancassurance** is a tie-up between banks and insurance companies to use the banking outlets for selling insurance products.

EXERCISES

Objective Questions

1. Tick the correct answer:

(a) Indemnification implies that the compensation would be:
 (i) Less than the actual loss (ii) Only the actual loss
 (iii) Higher than the actual loss (iv) None of the above

(b) LIC is formed under:
 (i) LIC Act, 1956 (ii) LIC Act, 1947
 (iii) LIC Act, 1912 (iv) LIC Act, 1818

(c) General Insurance Corporation is:
 (i) Life insurance company (ii) General insurance company
 (iii) Re-insurance company (iv) None of the above

(d) Product designing in insurance is done by:
 (i) Actuary (ii) Underwriter
 (iii) Agent (iv) Broker

(e) ULIPS are:
 (i) Market based (ii) Company based
 (iii) Target based (iv) None of the above

(f) Free-look period is a period of:
 (i) 10 days (ii) 15 days
 (iii) 25 days (iv) 5 days

(g) Bancassurance is a tie-up between:
 (i) Bank and the insurance company
 (ii) Bank and the insurance agent
 (iii) Bank and the insurance broker
 (iv) None of the above

Answers: (a) ii (b) i (c) iii (d) i (e) i (f) ii (g) i

2. Fill in the blanks:

(a) Insurance is a contractual arrangement between .... and ....
(b) Indemnity principle is not applicable to ....
(c) IRDA was set up in ....
(d) .... is a Pension Plan.
(e) An insurance policy acquires surrender value after ....

(f) .... is neither a life insurance nor a general insurance.
(g) .... are pure risk plans.

Answers:

(a) Insurer, insured
(b) Life insurance
(c) 1999
(d) Annuity insurance
(e) 3 years
(f) Re-insurance
(g) Term insurance

3. True or False:

(a) Principle of insurance interest is applicable to both life and general insurance.
(b) Whole life insurance is a risk cover plan.
(c) Riders are additional benefits free of charge.
(d) US insurance industry is state-based, whereas Indian insurance industry is centralised.
(e) SEBI regulates insurance industry in India.
(f) Claim settlement is done by an actuary.
(g) Insurance companies are intermediary institutions.

Answers: (a) True (b) True (c) False (d) True
(e) False (f) False (g) True

Short Questions

1. What is Indemnification?
2. Explain the concept of Human Life Value.
3. What is re-insurance?
4. What is the role of third party administrator?
5. Distinguish between Term Insurance and Whole Life Insurance.
6. State two differences between US insurance industry and Indian insurance industry.
7. Write down the main features of IRDA Act.

Critical Thinking Questions

1. "Insurance is an eye wash". Examine the statement highlighting some practical cases.
2. "Principle of Causa-proxima means to reduce the frauds in insurance". Explain.
3. "Insurance ombudsman scheme is a protection to the common man against the frauds of insurance companies". Discuss.
4. "Bancassurane is a milestone in the financial sector in regard to widening of horizon". Elaborate.

5. "ULIPs have changed the definition of insurance". Discuss.
6. "The real sufferers of the insurance sector are policyholders". Argue.
7. "LIC is still the leading player in life insurance segment in India". Critically examine.
8. "Insurance industry is one of the strong pillars of the financial system of any economy". Do you agree? Give reasons in support of your answer.
9. "Health insurance is the last priority of a common man". Examine the possible reasons behind the scenario and suggest improvements to make the scene better.

Descriptive Questions

1. Describe the key players of insurance industry.
2. Discuss the regulatory framework of insurance sector in India.
3. What are the different principles of insurance?
4. Explain the various types of insurance plans in India.
5. Throw light on the evolution of Indian insurance industry.
6. What are the different ways of classifying insurance sector?
7. What are the major changes that took place in the insurance sector in India post-liberalisation?
8. Evaluate the strengths and weaknesses of Indian insurance industry vis-a-vis US insurance industry.

PROJECT EXERCISE

Refining the Global Insurance Industry?

Insurance industry has undergone a phenomenal change in the last two decades worldwide and India is no exception to it. Compare and contrast an Indian and a US insurance company on the basis of their products, business, customer segmentation, polices and other related features. Conduct their SWOT analysis and recommend suitable strategies for the future viability of their business in particular, and the industry in general, at global level.

REVIEW CASE

The Insurance Plight

Anil was very happy. He got his first pay cheque today and was gearing up to treat his friends. His father asks him about his financing planning for future and advises him that he must start saving for future, in particular, he must buy an insurance for old age. To this, Anil replied that there was plenty of time to think about old age, and he wants to enjoy this phase first. His father reminds him of an old saying, "Soon you start working, and you must plan out for future".

He calls upon an insurance agent of A&Z Life Insurance Company of which one of his friends had also bought a policy. The agent comes to his place with all the documents and gives an in-depth explanation about the premium and the benefits of the policy. Anil was impressed with the agent's behaviour and his politeness. On getting convinced, Anil bought the policy and paid him the annual premium amount of ₹50,000. He was happy that he had made his first saving. In the evening, he proudly shows the policy to his father seeing which he asks for the complete Policy Document. Anil shows complete ignorance and replied that this one page document is only what he got from the agent for policy. His father tells him that this is the Cover Note containing only the main information about insured, premium and tenure. All related information is there in the Policy Document which he should have asked from the agent for future. He further brings to his notice that the policy is a pension plan for a limited period. It will start after 60 years of age and last upto 75 years of age only, whereas the premium would be paid for the next 40 years. Therefore, it was a costly policy in terms of benefits.

Anil gets a shock of his life; he calls the agent to cancel the policy to which the agent expressed his helplessness and tells him that the policy once issued cannot be cancelled. His father consoles him and says that he can still cancel it as there is free-look period for every policy. Anil's friend who had also undergone a similar situation points out that this is case of fraud and says that some agents may promise the moon to sell the policy. He cites his own example where he was mislead by a soft-spoken Life Insurance Agent of a company few months back. He was told that a premium of ₹3,000 had to be paid for 15 years. In case of unfortunate death, his family will get ₹1 lac. If not, then he can claim the maturity benefit of ₹1 lac at the end of 15 years. He will start getting money back after 2 years. After diligently paying premium for 2 years, to his shock he found that there is no money back incentive in the policy and if he wants to add that he has to increase his premium by another ₹500.

If it can happen to a literate person, then it is surely an issue for illiterate persons. His friend assures him not to worry and agrees with his father on the issue. He asks him to first approach the company and if unheard, then he can go to the Insurance Ombudsman. So now, Anil has one relief at least that he has someone to approach for his grievance. If the company does not listen to the individual complaint and it does not get solved by IRDA's Integrated Grievance Management System (IGMS), then the consumer still can go to the Insurance Ombudsman, consumer court or civil court. The advantages of ombudsman are at no cost to the insured. While the Insurance Ombudsman is a good option, there is often a delay in getting a hearing. It can range from six months to one year after making a complaint. In some places, the ombudsman's post is vacant for several months. This increases the backlog of complaints.

Issues for Discussion

(i) What is a free-look period?

(ii) What is the relevance of Policy Document in an Insurance Policy?

(iii) Can the agent refuse Anil for cancellation of the policy?

(iv) What are the means of grievance redressal available to Anil as an insured?

(v) Discuss the role of Insurance ombudsman in the present case and related issues.

(vi) How effective really the insurance ombudsman is for grievance redressal? Are their decisions binding on the company?

REFERENCES

Barth, M.M. and Eckles, D.L. (2009), "An empirical evaluation of the effect of growth on short-term changes in loss ratios", *Journal of Risk and Insurance.*

Bradford Network (1999), "Maintaining Interests: How Mortgage Lenders can help Home Owners maintain their Homes". York: Joseph Rowntree Trust.

Donaldson, Gordon (1961), "Corporate Debt Capacity", Boston, Division of Research, Harvard Business School.

Eckles, David L. and Halek, M. (2009), "Effects of Analysts' Ratings on Insurer Stock Returns: Evidence of Asymmetric Responses", *Journal of Risk and Insurance.*

Santerre, R.E. and Hilliard, J.I. (2009), "Health Insurance Research in the JRI and the Health Economy", *Risk Management and Insurance Review*, **12**: 67–79.

www.brandsitestatic.hdfclife.com

www.business-standard.com

www.cioins.co.in

www.coi.org.in

www.imarcgroup.com

www.irda.gov.in

www.irdaindia.org

www.licindia.in

www.policyholder.gov.in

www.sbilife.co.in

www.unitedbankofindia.com

CHAPTER 8

Mutual Funds

And I think the more money you put in people's hands, the more they will spend. And if they don't spend it, they invest it. And investing it is another way of creating jobs. It puts money into mutual funds or other kinds of banks that can go out and make loans, and we need to do that.

— Michael Bloomberg

LEARNING OBJECTIVES

This chapter discusses the following:

- Concept of mutual funds
- Evolution of mutual funds
- Types of mutual funds
- Importance of mutual funds
- Mutual fund regulation in India
- Structure of mutual funds
- Concept of Net Asset Value (NAV)
- Performance measures of mutual fund
- Mutual funds plans and indicators: SIP, SWP, STP, Dividend Sweep, Triggers and Expense ratio
- Emerging challenges of mutual funds

INTRODUCTION

There has been a phenomenal expansion in the geographical coverage and spread of our financial system during the last few decades. Consistent with this evolution of the financial sector, the mutual fund industry in India has also come to occupy an important place.

Mutual funds are an indirect form of investing in securities which reduce the investor's risk attached to the fluctuations of the securities market. They also provide a large number of services that are not available to the investors who invest in securities directly. A mutual fund is therefore, as much a financial product as a financial service. Of course, the services rendered by a mutual fund are not free. The unit holders have to pay for the recurring transactions, annual fees, exit loads, etc., irrespective of whether the fund generates returns or not.

The investors investing in mutual funds range from retail investors to large entities including banks, insurance companies and financial institutions that regularly invest in mutual funds.

MUTUAL FUNDS

A *mutual fund* is a common pool of funds which is mobilised from a large number of investors, and invested on their behalf in securities in the market. The returns from such investments, both in terms of dividends and capital appreciation, and net of operational expenses, accrue to the investors.

A mutual fund, unlike share, is risk diversified, professionally managed, and a cost-efficient investment in the stock market. One can invest as little as ₹100 per month in a mutual fund of his choice from the available bouquet of mutual funds.

Working of a Mutual Fund

It is well known that, 'One should not put all his eggs in a single basket'. A mutual fund diversifies the investment into various sectors instead of one single sector or company. Thus, investors get the benefit of diversification by professionals.

Table 8.1 presents the risk-return trade-off of mutual funds vis-à-vis other financial products.

TABLE 8.1 Risk Return Grid of Investment Products

Risk/Return	*Focus*	*Suitable Products*	*Benefits Offered by MFs*
Low	Debt	Bank/Company FD, Debt-based funds	Liquidity, better post-tax returns
Medium	Partially debt, Partially equity	Balanced funds	Liquidity, better post-tax returns, diversification
High	Equity	Equity funds	Growth, wealth, liquidity, dividends

The investors subscribe to units of a mutual fund just as shareholders subscribe to shares of a company. Mutual funds, like companies, do not guarantee any dividend. The decision of mutual fund managers to declare dividends or not, depends upon factors like profitability of the fund, market conditions, and others.

Each unit of a mutual fund represents a unit holder's ownership in the fund's portfolio holdings. The investors of mutual funds are known as *unit holders*. The companies that operate the mutual funds are known as *Asset Management Companies* (AMCs) or *Investment Managers*. An AMC may float more than one fund (also called *schemes*), with different objectives and investment mandates. The terms mutual fund or scheme are often used interchangeably. The mutual fund process is depicted in Figure 8.1.

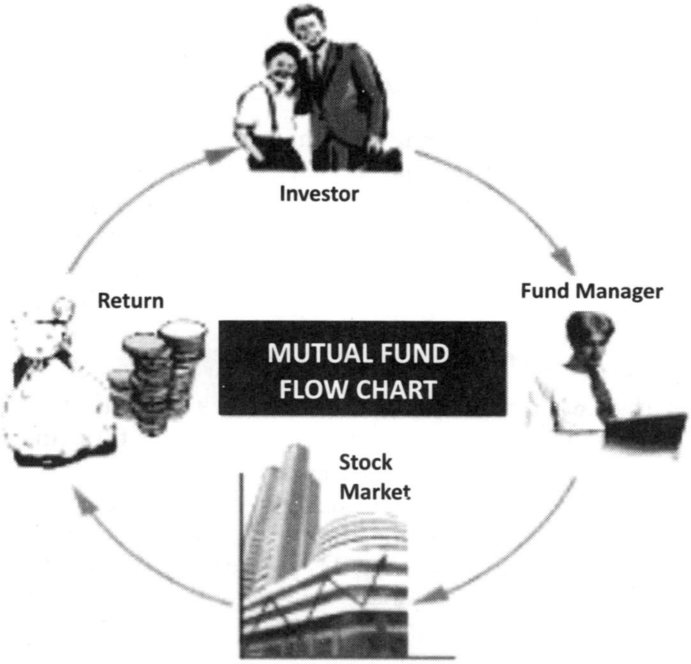

Figure 8.1 Mutual Fund Flow

EVOLUTION OF MUTUAL FUNDS

Mutual funds were introduced in Belgium in 1822 and soon spread to Great Britain and France. They became popular in the United States in 1920s. It was after World War II that they witnessed tremendous growth, especially in the 1980s and 1990s.

In India, the concept of mutual funds started in 1964 with the setting of Unit Trust of India (UTI). UTI was set up with the twin objective of mobilising household savings and investing the funds in the capital market for industrial growth. After two decades of monopoly of UTI, some other public sector organisations like SBI (1987), Canara Bank (1987), LIC (1989), Indian Bank (1989), Punjab National Bank (1989) Bank of India (1990), GIC (1990) were allowed to set up mutual funds. Today, there is a good mix of private and public sector players in mutual funds in India.

Growth of Mutual Funds Industry in India

The growth of mutual fund industry in India can be divided into the following phases:

Phase I: Establishment and Growth of Unit Trust of India (1964–1987)

The Unit Trust of India (UTI), since its inception in 1964, enjoyed complete monopoly for two decades. It was set up and regulated by the Reserve Bank of India until it was de-linked in 1978 when the entire control was shifted to Industrial Development Bank of India (IDBI). UTI launched its first scheme in 1964, named as Unit Scheme 1964 (US-64) which saw a phenomenal response from the investors. At the end of 1988, UTI had ₹6,700 crores of assets under management.[1]

Phase II: Entry of Public Sector Players (1987–1993)

The public sector units started entering into the Indian mutual fund industry in 1987. In November 1987, State Bank of India launched SBI Mutual Fund, the first non-UTI mutual fund in India, later followed by Canbank Mutual Fund, LIC Mutual Fund, etc. At the end of 1993, the mutual fund industry had assets worth ₹47,004 crores[2] under management. However, UTI continued to be the leader with about 80% of the market share.

Phase III: Entry of Private Sector Players (1993–2003)

The Indian securities market gained greater importance with the establishment of SEBI in April 1992 to protect the interests of the investors and to promote the development of, and to regulate, the securities market.

In 1993, the first set of "SEBI Mutual Fund Regulations" came into existence for all mutual funds, except UTI. The erstwhile Kothari Pioneer (now merged with Franklin Templeton MF) was the first private sector MF registered in July 1993. With the entry of private sector funds in 1993, a new era began in the Indian MF industry, giving the Indian investors a wider choice of MF products. The initial SEBI MF Regulations were revised and replaced in 1996 with a comprehensive set of regulations, viz., SEBI (Mutual Funds) Regulations, 1996 which is currently applicable.

The number of MFs increased over the years, with many foreign sponsors setting up mutual funds in India. Also the MF industry witnessed several mergers and acquisitions during this phase. As at the end of January 2003, there were 33 MFs with total AUM of ₹1,21,805 crores, out of which UTI alone had AUM of ₹44,541 crores.[3]

Phase IV: Growth and Consolidation (February 2003–April 2014)

In February 2003, the UTI Act was repealed and UTI was bifurcated into two separate entities—the Specified Undertaking of the UTI (SUUTI), and UTI Mutual Fund which functions under the SEBI MF Regulations. With the bifurcation of the erstwhile UTI and several mergers taking place among different private sector funds, the MF industry entered its fourth phase of consolidation.

Following the global melt-down in the year 2009, securities markets all over the world had tanked and so was the case in India. Most investors who had entered the capital market during the peak, had lost money and their faith in MF products was shaken greatly. The abolition of Entry Load by SEBI, coupled with the after-effects of

1. https://www.amfiindia.com/investor-corner/knowledge-center/history-of-MF-india.html
2. https://www.amfiindia.com.ibid.
3. https://www.amfiindia.com.ibid.

the global financial crisis, deepened the adverse impact on the Indian MF Industry, which struggled to recover and remodel itself for over two years, in an attempt to maintain its economic viability.

Phase V: Current Phase (Since May 2014)

The progressive measures taken by SEBI to "re-energize" the Indian Mutual Fund industry and increase MFs' penetration succeeded in reversing the negative trend that had set in after the global melt-down.

Since May 2014, the Industry has witnessed steady inflows and increase in the AUM as well as the number of investor folios (accounts).

- The overall size of the Indian MF Industry has grown from ₹7.60 trillion as on 31st December 2012 to ₹39.89 trillion as on 31st December 2022, more than 5 fold increase in a span of 10 years.
- The no. of investor folios has gone up from 6.65 crore folios as on 31st December 2017 to 14.11 crore as on 31st December 2022, more than 2 fold increase in a span of 5 years.

MF Distributors have been providing the much needed last mile connect with investors, particularly in smaller towns and this is not limited to just enabling investors to invest in appropriate schemes, but also in helping investors stay on course through bouts of market volatility and thus experience the benefit of investing in mutual funds. MF distributors have also had a major role in popularising Systematic Investment Plans (SIP) over the years. In April 2016, the no. of SIP accounts has crossed 1 crore mark and as on 31st December 2022 the total no. of SIP Accounts are 6.12 crore.[4] As on 22nd January 2023, there were 42 Asset Management Companies.[5]

The assets' growth of the industry during 2021–22 is depicted in Figure 8.2.

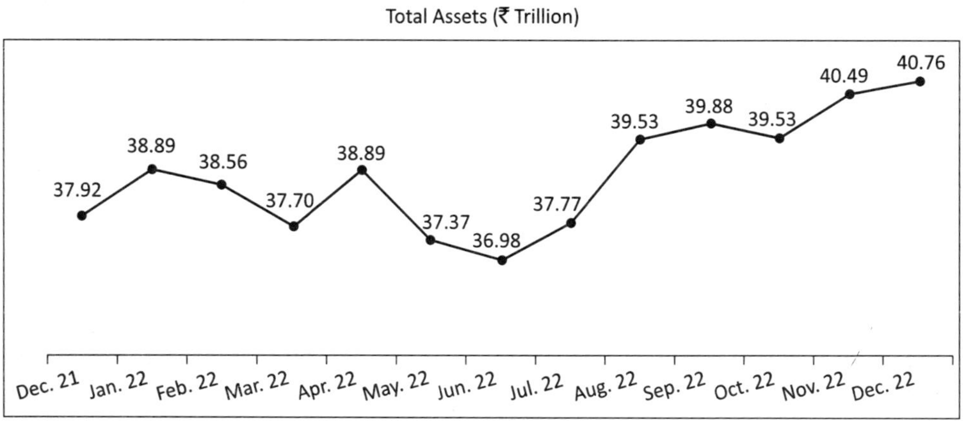

Figure 8.2 Growth of Assets of Mutual Funds Industry in India

Note: Assets managed by the Indian mutual fund industry has increased from ₹37.92 trillion in December 2021 to ₹40.76 trillion in December 2022. That represents 7.50% increase in assets over December 2021.[6]

4. https://www.amfiindia.com. op. cit.
5. https://www.amfiindia.com/know-about-amfi.
6. https://www.amfiindia.com/Themes/Theme1/downloads/home/Industry-Trends.pdf

CATEGORIES OF MUTUAL FUNDS

Mutual funds may be classified in many ways. Following are the different types of mutual funds:

A. Based on Structure

Based on their structure, mutual funds can be categorised as close or open ended.

Open-ended Funds

Open-ended funds are irredeemable, having no finite life. They are open for investment and redemption throughout the year, but, these are not listed in a stock exchange. It is the AMC of the fund that offers to sell and buy the units from the investors at the *Net Asset Value* (NAV). New investors can also buy units of a mutual fund directly from the AMC and not from the secondary market.

In an open-ended scheme, the fund size constantly increases or decreases on a daily basis depending on whether redemption by existing unit holders is less than subscriptions from new investors or vice versa. *Examples:* SBI Small Cap Fund and Aditya Birla Sun Life Banking & Financial Services Fund.

Close-ended Funds

On the other hand, close-ended funds have a fixed maturity date. They have a pre-determined life, at the end of which the capital is returned to the investors. Close-ended funds are mandatorily listed in the stock exchanges. After subscription to the units in the initial funds offer, these cannot be sold back to the AMC until the end of the fund's life. However, if one wishes to redeem (sell) the holdings or buy into such a fund before the maturity date, one may do so in the stock exchange where the units are listed. ICICI Prudential Growth Fund—Series 1 and Series 2 are examples of well-known close-ended mutual funds.

In an open-ended scheme, the number of outstanding units varies on a daily basis, while in a close-ended scheme, the outstanding units, at any point in time, remain constant.

Interval Funds

Interval schemes allow purchase and redemption during specified transaction periods (intervals). The transaction period has to be for a minimum of 2 days and there should be at least a 15-day gap between two transaction periods. The units of interval schemes are also mandatorily listed on the stock exchanges.

B. Based on Asset Class/Investment Objective

Mutual funds based on the asset class of investment may be equity funds, debt funds, money market funds, gilt funds, and so forth. They describe different investment objectives of the investors.

Equity funds are invested in equity or equity related instruments. Equity funds may be categorised based on the valuation parameters adopted in stock selection, such as—*Growth funds* which identify momentum stocks that are expected to perform better than the market and—*Value funds* which identify stocks that are currently undervalued but are expected to perform well over time as the value is unlocked. Under equity category, *large, mid and small cap stocks* are further defined.

Debt funds or Income funds are invested in fixed income securities. It invests in bonds and other debt securities respectively. The stress here is more on paying out a steady dividend or income stream.

Money market funds invest in short-term money market instruments like certificates of deposit, commercial paper, call money market, etc., and ***gilt funds*** invest in gilt, or bullion, or related securities.

Hybrid funds or balanced funds invests in more or less equal mix of equity and debt securities. Sundaram Equity Hybrid Fund and HDFC Balanced Advantage Fund are examples of balanced funds.

C. Based on Industry

Industry specific or *sectoral funds* focus upon specific industries or sectors. The sector could be, *for instance,* information technology, pharmaceuticals, banking, construction, small and medium enterprises, or even geographic sectors such as emerging markets as of Asia Pacific, India, China, etc. *For example,* a FMCG fund limits its investments to securities issued by companies engaged in the business of fast-moving consumer goods and other similar businesses. An MNC fund invests in multinational or transnational companies. Often the name of a sectoral fund fairly describes the investment objective of the fund.

A *real estate fund* predominantly invests in securities issued by the real estate companies and in the absence of these securities, they invest in real estate properties.

D. Based on Indices

These are the *index funds* that invest in companies belonging to specific indices such as Sensex or Nifty. *For example,* a mutual fund that invests only in 50 securities underlying the Nifty will track only Nifty.

An index fund that tracks a specific index not only invests in the securities that comprise the index, but does this in the same proportion as they are represented in the index. *For example,* a mutual fund tracking the Sensex will invest in the stocks of 30 companies that make up the Sensex index, in the same proportion as the weights assigned to these companies in the index.

E. Based on Solution Orientation

The schemes or funds may also be characterised by their solution package. *For example,* a fund may be called a *Children's Fund* or *Young Citizens' Fund.*

Children's Funds

A children's fund provides parents or relatives an opportunity to invest with a specific purpose of generating savings to meet the anticipated expenses of their children in the future.

Young Citizen's Fund

Young citizen's fund may be directed at young professionals.

F. Other Schemes

Besides above, there are other schemes like *Tax Saving Schemes* and *Special Schemes.*

Tax Saving Funds or *ELSS* are those funds in which investment gives you the benefit of tax rebate of ₹1,50,000 under Section 80C and there is a lock-in period of three years. Here, at least 80% is invested in stocks in accordance with Equity Linked Saving Scheme, 2005, notified by Ministry of Finance. Axis Long Term Equity Fund is an example of this category.

Special Schemes are also very popular like ULIPs or funds based on the size of the companies. In addition to the above, there are "Exchange Traded Funds" (ETFs) and "Gold Exchange Traded Funds" as well. An ETF is a marketable security that tracks an index, a commodity, bonds, or a basket of assets like an index fund, and is listed on stock exchanges. Gold ETFs are ETFs with gold as the underlying asset.

The categories of mutual funds are depicted in the Figure 8.3.

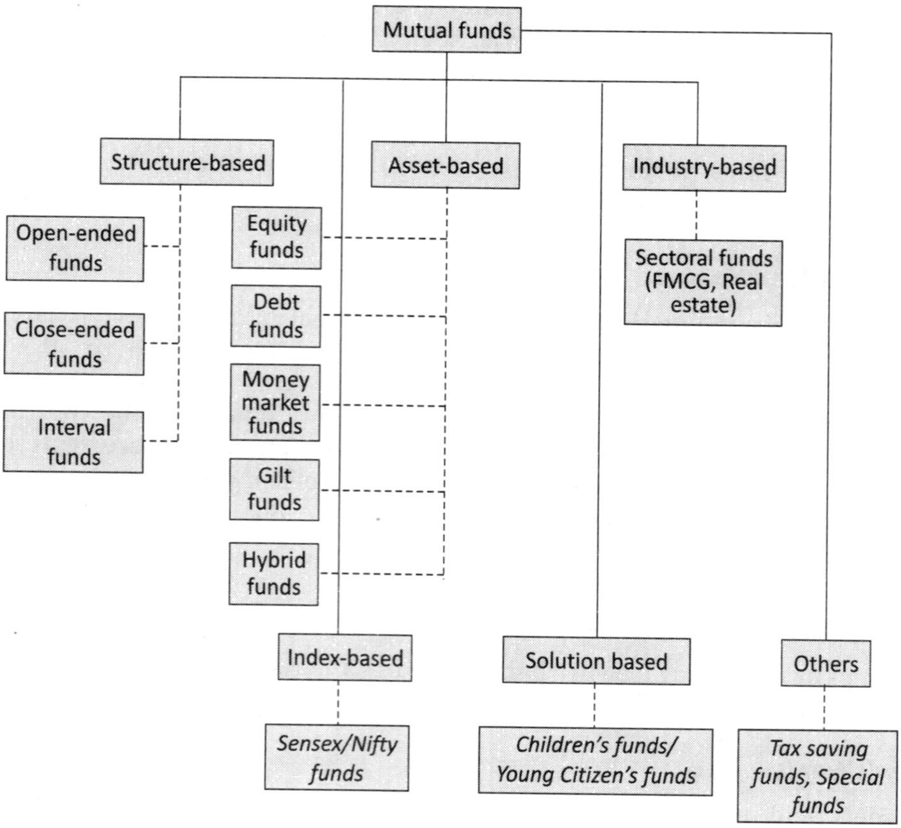

Figure 8.3 Categorisation of Mutual Funds

Box 8.1 discusses the "Fund of funds" and Table 8.2 lists asset and category-wise folios.

BOX 8.1: FUND OF FUNDS

A **Fund of funds** (FoF) is the laziest of all the funds. In other words, these mutual funds invest in other mutual fund schemes (generally those offered by the same AMC) rather than independently in securities such as bonds and shares.

Like any regular mutual fund, an FoF can be an equity fund, debt fund, or any combination thereof.

TABLE 8.2 Asset under Management and Folios—Category-wise-Aggregate, as on September 30, 2022

Types of Schemes	*Investor Classification*	*AUM (₹ Cr)*	*% to Total*	*No. of Folios*	*% to Total*
Liquid Fund/Money Market Fund/ Floater Fund	Corporates	526403.58	80.57	77399	2.56
	Banks/FIs	19470.88	2.98	1159	0.04
	FIIs	22.47	0	13	0
	High Net worth Individuals*	97863.66	14.98	608538	20.12
	Retail	9593.18	1.47	2336752	77.28
	Total	**653353.77**	**100.00**	**3023861**	**100.00**
Gilt Fund/Gilt Fund with 10 year constant duration	Corporates	9341.89	54.32	3026	1.41
	Banks/FIs	169.97	0.99	61	0.03
	FIIs	4.6	0.03	1	0
	High Net worth Individuals*	6422.24	37.34	32515	15.12
	Retail	1260.39	7.33	179454	83.44
	Total	**17199.1**	**100.00**	**215057**	**100.00**
Remaining Income/ Debt Oriented Schemes	Corporates	326373.32	55.35	94412	2.31
	Banks/FIs	18997.52	3.22	1480	0.04
	FIIs	988.44	0.17	47	0
	High Net worth Individuals*	221531.91	37.57	1283413	31.4
	Retail	21737.56	3.69	2707884	66.25
	Total	**589628.75**	**100.00**	**4087236**	**100.00**

(Contd.)

Types of Schemes	*Investor Classification*	*AUM (₹ Cr)*	*% to Total*	*No. of Folios*	*% to Total*
Growth/Equity Oriented Schemes	Corporates	132442.17	9.01	577218	0.62
	Banks/FIs	675.65	0.05	1027	0
	FIIs	2933.77	0.2	95	0
	High Net worth Individuals*	548360.06	37.28	6085271	6.56
	Retail	786331.02	53.46	86137160	92.82
	Total	**1470742.66**	**100.00**	**92800771**	**100.00**
Hybrid Schemes	Corporates	58937.96	12.23	103242	0.87
	Banks/FIs	263.03	0.05	222	0
	FIIs	349.53	0.07	33	0
	High Net worth Individuals*	324056.37	67.27	2694140	22.6
	Retail	98141.27	20.37	9121777	76.53
	Total	**481748.17**	**100.00**	**11919414**	**100.00**
Solution Oriented Schemes	Corporates	67.62	0.22	250	0
	Banks/FIs	0.01	0	1	0
	FIIs	0	0	0	0
	High Net worth Individuals*	9161.83	29.53	98116	1.74
	Retail	21793.63	70.25	5527485	98.25
	Total	**31023.1**	**100.00**	**5625852**	**100.00**
Index Funds	Corporates	53122.25	50.6	18126	0.62
	Banks/FIs	615.83	0.59	89	0
	FIIs	2.61	0	2	0
	High Net worth Individuals*	36962.63	35.2	209029	7.19
	Retail	14290.63	13.61	2681651	92.19
	Total	**104993.95**	**100.00**	**2908897**	**100.00**
Gold ETF	Corporates	10418.13	52.45	8987	0.19
	Banks/FIs	1.28	0.01	6	0
	FIIs	0	0	0	0
	High Net worth Individuals*	7086.75	35.68	42263	0.91

Types of Schemes	*Investor Classification*	*AUM (₹ Cr)*	*% to Total*	*No. of Folios*	*% to Total*
	Retail	2355.17	11.86	4593825	98.9
	Total	**19861.33**	**100.00**	**4645081**	**100.00**
ETFs (other than Gold)	Corporates	415087.08	91.26	49295	0.42
	Banks/FIs	2098.43	0.46	25	0
	FIIs	104.42	0.02	11	0
	High Net worth Individuals*	29354.41	6.45	138937	1.2
	Retail	8210.48	1.81	11416856	98.38
	Total	**454854.81**	**100.00**	**11605124**	**100.00**
Fund of Funds investing Overseas	Corporates	3245.15	17.13	10259	0.82
	Banks/FIs	2.61	0.01	9	0
	FIIs	0.69	0	8	0
	High Net worth Individuals*	10946.29	57.78	143401	11.42
	Retail	4750.24	25.07	1102358	87.76
	Total	**18944.99**	**100.00**	**1256035**	**100.00**
	Grand Total	**3842350.63**		**138087328**	

*Defined as individuals investing ₹2 lakhs and above.

Source: https://www.amfiindia.com/research-information/aum-data/age-wise-folio-data

IMPORTANCE OF MUTUAL FUNDS

Mutual funds have been of great help, especially to small investors who lack professional advice, market information, etc. (Box 8.2). They offer following advantages:

1. *Diversification:* Mutual funds diversify the investment portfolio of an investor and reduce the losses from market risk of a single investment. They provide the investors with an opportunity to invest in many markets and sectors. This is the key benefit of diversification.

2. *Professional management:* Mutual funds are managed by professionals who have a better knowledge of market conditions. They maximise gains by proper selection and timing of investment based on extensive research.

3. *Variety:* One can choose his/her type of fund from a broad category of stock, bond, and money market funds.

4. *Low costs:* Mutual funds charge a nominal fee for their services, based on the total value of your account. For most investors, mutual funds provide professional management and diversification at a fraction of the cost, making such investments cost-efficient.

5. *Liquidity:* A typical Indian investor looks for three parameters in his investment—Yield, Liquidity and Security. Mutual funds are considered to be safer investments with assured returns and are liquid investments that can be sold anytime. Mutual funds are required by law to buy or redeem shares every working day. Therefore, all these benefits are available in a mutual fund.

6. *Convenience:* One can purchase or sell fund units directly from a fund, or through a broker, or in person, or online.

7. *Investor's confidence:* In case of issue of shares, an ordinary investor is not assured of the allotment when he applies for them. But, mutual funds come with a definite allotment of shares and hence, mutual funds have the investor's confidence.

8. *Suitable to small investors:* Mutual funds are best suited for small investors, enabling them to have a profitable investment with small amount.

9. *Reinvestment:* Another important feature is that the dividends and capital gains are reinvested automatically in mutual funds. The automatic reinvestment feature of a mutual fund makes it more attractive for small investors.

10. *Tax relief:* The mutual funds provide also a tax advantage to investors. The schemes of mutual funds provide tax relief under various sections of the Income-tax Act, 1961.

11. *Foreign capital:* Mutual funds attract foreign capital in the country and secure profitable investment avenues abroad for domestic savings through the opening of off-shore funds in various foreign investors.

BOX 8.2: BENEFITS OF MUTUAL FUNDS

- Risk diversification
- Professional management and analysis
- Yield (Dividends, Capital appreciation)
- Liquidity and security
- Choice of schemes
- Low investment and low costs of operations
- Transparency
- Convenient administration (Record Keeping)
- Well regulated by SEBI
- Tax benefits under IT Act, 1961
- Bonus issues

REGULATIONS OF MUTUAL FUNDS IN INDIA

Mutual funds in India are governed by the SEBI (Mutual Funds) Regulations, 1996, as amended from time to time. SEBI is the regulatory body for the mutual funds industry, and it requires that all mutual funds should be established as trusts under the Indian Trusts Act. The minimum net worth of an AMC must be ₹50 crore to act as a manager in any other fund. Mutual funds can be penalised for defaults including non-registration and failure to observe rules set by their AMCs.

Mutual funds dealing exclusively with money market instruments have to be registered with RBI. All other schemes floated by mutual funds are required to be registered with SEBI. In 1995, the RBI permitted private sector institutions to set up Money Market Mutual Funds (MMMFs). They can invest in treasury bills, call and notice money, commercial paper, commercial bills accepted/co-accepted by banks, certificates of deposit and dated government securities having unexpired maturity upto one year. The mutual funds are now regulated by Association of Mutual Funds Industry in India (AMFI) which is a self-regulatory organisation.

All mutual funds, whether promoted by public sector or private sector entities including those promoted by foreign entities, are governed by the same set of regulations. There is no distinction in regulatory requirements for these mutual funds and all are subject to monitoring and inspections by SEBI.

Registering of a Mutual Fund in India

An applicant proposing to sponsor a mutual fund in India must submit an application in Form A along with a fee of ₹5 lacs to SEBI.[7]

The application of the sponsor is examined on various conditions, like—(i) track record in the financial services business for at least 5 years, (ii) possessing positive net worth for the last five years, and (iii) having net profit in three out of the last five years.

Once the sponsor fulfills the above grounds, the remaining formalities for setting up a mutual fund need to be done. These include executing the trust deed and investment management agreement, setting up a trustee company/board of trustees comprising two-thirds independent trustees, incorporating the Asset Management Company (AMC), contributing to at least 40% of the net worth of the AMC and appointing a custodian. Upon satisfying these conditions, the registration certificate is issued, subject to the payment of registration fees of ₹25 lacs (Box 8.3).

Table 8.3 lists various mutual funds companies in India.

BOX 8.3: REGULATORY STRUCTURE OF MUTUAL FUNDS (MFS) IN INDIA

- Mutual funds are governed by SEBI (Mutual Fund) Regulations 1996.
- SEBI is the regulatory body for the functioning of MFs.
- All MFs should be established as trusts.
- AMC registered as companies are registered under Companies Act, 1956/2013.
- As per SEBI (Mutual Funds) (Amendment) Regulations, 2014, the minimum net worth of an AMC or its affiliate must be ₹50 crores to act as a manager in any other fund.
- Bank operated MFs are also supervised by RBI.
- MFs dealing exclusively with money market instruments have to be registered with RBI.
- Mutual funds are regulated by AMFI.

7. https://www.sebi.gov.in/legal/regulations/jan-2022/securities-and-exchange-board-of-india-mutual-funds-regulations-1996-last-amended-on-january-25-2022-_55732.html

TABLE 8.3 List of Asset Management Companies in India (As on 22nd January 2023)

A. Bank Sponsored
1. Joint Ventures—Predominantly Indian
• Baroda BNP Paribas Asset Management India Private Limited
• Canara Robeco Asset Management Company Limited
• SBI Funds Management Private Limited
• Union Asset Management Company Private Limited
2. Others
• Bank of India Investment Managers Private Limited
• IDBI Asset Management Limited
• UTI Asset Management Company Limited
B. Institutions
1. Indian
• IIFCL Asset Management Company Limited
• LIC Mutual Fund Asset Management Limited
C. Private Sector
1. Indian
• DSP Investment Managers Private Limited
• Edelweiss Asset Management Limited
• IDFC AMC Limited
• IIFL Asset Management Limited (formerly known as India Infoline Asset Management Company Limited)
• IL & FS Infra Asset Management Limited
• Indiabulls Asset Management Company Limited
• ITI Asset Management Limited
• JM Financial Asset Management Limited
• Kotak Mahindra Asset Management Company Limited
• Motilal Oswal Asset Management Company Limited
• Navi AMC Limited
• NJ Asset Management Private Limited
• PPFAS Asset Management Private Limited
• Quant Money Managers Limited
• Quantum Asset Management Company Private Limited
• Samco Asset Management Private Limited
• Shriram Asset Management Company Limited
• Sundaram Asset Management Company Limited
• Tata Asset Management Limited
• Taurus Asset Management Company Limited
• Trust Asset Management Private Limited
• WhiteOak Capital Asset Management Limited

(Contd.)

2. **Foreign**
   - Franklin Templeton Asset Management (India) Private Limited
   - HSBC Asset Management (India) Private Ltd.
   - Invesco Asset Management (India) Private Limited
   - Mirae Asset Investment Managers (India) Pvt. Ltd
   - Nippon Life India Asset Management Limited
   - PGIM India Asset Management Private Limited
3. **Joint Ventures—Predominantly Indian**
   - Aditya Birla Sun Life AMC Limited
   - Axis Asset Management Co. Ltd.
   - HDFC Asset Management Company Limited
   - ICICI Prudential Asset Management Company Limited
   - Mahindra Manulife Investment Management Pvt. Ltd.

Source: https://www.amfiindia.com/amfi-members-details.

STRUCTURAL ARRANGEMENT OF MUTUAL FUNDS

1. Top Management of the AMC

The *trustees* appoint the top management of the AMC such as Chief Investment Officer or Chief Executive Officer as well as fund manager(s) for various schemes. The trust company also appoints an *auditor* to audit the books of accounts of all the schemes.

Once the organisation structure is at place, an AMC floats various schemes, each tailored to the requirements of different sections of the public. An AMC may appoint separate fund managers for each scheme under its umbrella or may assign two or three schemes to a specific fund manager.

One of the important aspects of this multi-tiered organisation structure of the mutual fund business is to clearly segregate the involvement of "sponsors". The 'trust company' and the 'board of trustees' act on behalf of the investors and stand in between the promoters of the mutual fund business and the money invested by millions of unit-holders.

2. Record-keeper and Issuer

A *custodian* holds the securities of various schemes of the fund in their custody. Before dematerialisation of shares was introduced, share transfers were done in physical form and so in case of mutual funds, the role of custodian was important. He/she is entitled to receive, transfer and hold the physical certificates on behalf of an AMC. However, after demat of securities, the term 'custodian' was changed with 'depository'. A *depository* maintains an online record of ownership of securities bought and sold by a mutual fund in dematerialised form, just as a bank records the balance in one's account. The *registrar* is appointed in order to accept and process the unit-holders' applications, and inform the AMC regarding the amount received for subscription, redemption, etc.

Transfer agents are responsible for issuing and redeeming units of the scheme and provide other related services such as preparation of transfer documents and updating investor records. They are the channel through which fresh units are issued to new buyers or units are sent back to the AMC for redemption.

Example

Let us consider the mutual funds floated by Kotak Mahindra. Kotak Mahindra Bank Limited (KMBL), as the *sponsor*, establish a "TRUST", wherein Kotak Mahindra Trustee Company Limited (KMTCL) is set up as the *trustee company*. KMBL also float Kotak Mahindra Asset Management Company Limited (KMAMC) as the *AMC/ Investment Manager*. KMAMC offers many different kinds of schemes such as Kotak Global India, Kotak Savings Plan, Kotak MNC, Kotak Tech to Unit-holders, etc.

Computer Age Management Services Private Limited is the *registrar*, Deutsche Bank and ABN AMRO are the *custodians* and Price Waterhouse is the *auditor*.

This is depicted in Figure 8.4.

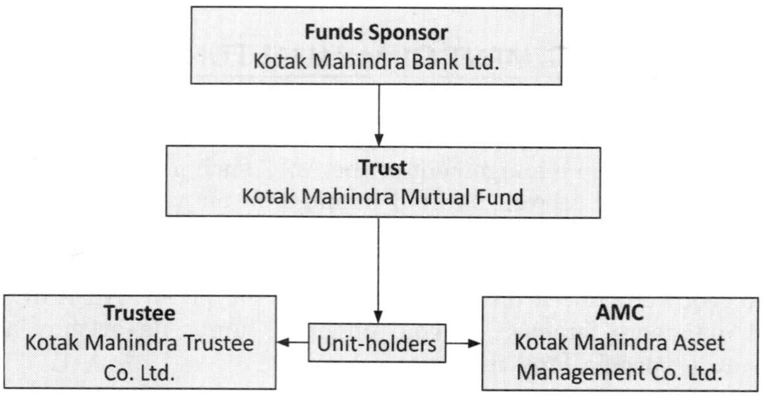

Figure 8.4 Organisational Structure of Mutual Funds

NET ASSET VALUE (NAV) OF A MUTUAL FUND

Net Asset Value (NAV) of a mutual fund is the price at which units of mutual fund are bought and sold. The NAV of a fund at any point in time is the sum total of the market value of the assets (securities) that comprise of its portfolio minus net of any liabilities at that time, divided by the number of outstanding units of the scheme. In other words, the NAV of a fund is the amount that all the unit-holders will receive after paying all its liabilities (Box 8.4).

$$\text{NAV} = \frac{\text{Market value of total assets} - \text{Market value of liabilities}}{\text{Number of units}}$$

Simply put, the NAV of a mutual fund is the market value of one unit (share) of the fund. It is similar to the 'Book value of a share'. Hence, it is the amount a unit-holder would receive if the mutual fund were wound up. *For example,* if the market value of securities of a mutual fund scheme is ₹20 million, net of all its liabilities on a given day and the mutual fund has 1 million units outstanding on that day, the NAV per unit will be ₹20.

As the market price of the underlying securities change daily, so does the NAV of a scheme, although the change is much less than that of a single security.

Unlike stocks, where the price is driven by the stock market and changes from minute-to-minute, NAVs of mutual fund schemes are declared at the end of each trading day after markets are closed. Further, Units of mutual fund schemes under all scheme (except Liquid & Overnight funds) are allotted only at prospective NAV, i.e., the NAV that would be declared at the end of the day, based on the closing market value of the securities held in the respective schemes. A mutual fund may accept applications even after the cut-off time, but you will get the NAV of the next business day. Further, the cut-off time rules apply for redemptions too.

AMCs are required to calculate the NAV of all open-ended schemes on a daily basis and at the least on a weekly basis for close-ended ones, and publish these in a minimum of two national newspapers. The NAVs are also available on the websites of the respective AMCs as well as on the website of AMFI.

BOX 8.4: FORMULA OF NAV

The specific formula for computing NAV is as follows:

A. Total Assets of the scheme = (Market Value of Investments + Receivables + Other Accrued Income + Other Assets)

Less

B. Liabilities = (Accrued Expenses + Other Payables + Other Liabilities)

Divided by

C. No. of units outstanding on the NAV computation date

As shown in Box 8.4, all the items in 1 are the total assets of the mutual fund, while all the items in 2 are the liabilities.

The *market value of investments* of the fund is affected by the individual market prices of the invested securities. *Receivables* arise when certain sale proceeds of the scheme are yet to be received. *Other accrued income and assets* may typically be the various dividends or interest accrued from the fund's investments, but not yet received.

Similarly, *accrued expenses* may represent various loads, issuing expenses or other accrued expenses payable to the AMC from the scheme. *Payables and other liabilities* are what the scheme has yet to pay the unit-holders for their redemptions. They could also be the dividends of the units themselves that are payable to the unit-holders.

The net amount of the two sets of items (A and B) represents the Net Asset Value (or net market value or net realisable value) of the fund for the unit-holders as a whole. When divided by the number of units outstanding on the NAV computation date, it yields the NAV per unit.

EXAMPLE 8.1: Funcorp mutual fund held ₹1,55,00,000 worth of securities, ₹40,00,000 of cash, and ₹5,00,000 of liabilities on the close of trading yesterday. The units outstanding were 10,00,000. What is the yesterday's NAV?

Solution: NAV = (₹1,55,00,000 + 40,00,000 – 5,00,000)/10,00,000

= ₹19

EXAMPLE 8.2: Total assets (underlying securities) are ₹70 crores. Cash and equivalents are ₹10 crores. Liabilities are ₹4 crores. Units outstanding are 2 crores. What is the NAV?

Solution: Value = ₹80 crores (70 + 10) – ₹4 crores

= ₹76 crores

NAV = ₹38 per unit (₹76 crores/2 crores)

Incidentally, the NAV of a close-ended fund is different, and is generally less than its market price. There are several reasons behind this. The most significant of them is while the NAV is computed at the end of the day, it is effectively reported only the next day, by which time the market value of the underlying securities may have risen (though this may not always be the case). When the market price of a fund is greater than the NAV, it is said to trade at a premium, and when it is lower than the NAV, it is said to trade at a discount. It is noteworthy that this does not apply to open-ended funds, as they are not quoted in the stock exchanges and hence, have no market value—they have only NAVs.

PERFORMANCE MEASURES OF MUTUAL FUNDS

Mutual fund industry today, with 42 players and more than five hundred schemes, is one of the most preferred investment avenues in India. However, with hundreds of schemes to choose from, the retail investor faces problems in selecting funds. There are factors *such as, investment strategy and management approach,* but they are qualitative.

Therefore, the funds' record becomes an important indicator. Though past performance alone cannot indicate future performance, it is the only reliable quantitative way to analyse the performance of a fund in present. This is the reason why there is a need to correctly assess the past performance of different mutual funds.

In assessing the performance of mutual funds, 'returns' are considered as the most important factor but 'risk' taken by the fund manager should also be included because different funds will have different levels of risk attached to them.

Risk associated with a fund is defined as the variability or fluctuations in the returns generated by it.

The higher the fluctuations in the returns of a fund during a given period, higher will be the risk associated with it. This risk can be categorised into two types:

(i) **Market risk or Systematic risk:** Which arises due to general market fluctuations, and

(ii) **Specific risk or Unsystematic risk:** Which is specific to the securities present in the portfolio of the fund.

The *Total Risk* of a given fund is the sum of these two and is measured in terms of standard deviation of returns of the fund. Systematic risk, on the other hand, is measured by *Beta*, which represents fluctuations in the NAV of the fund vis-à-vis market. Higher the volatility of the NAV of a mutual fund to the changes in the market, higher will be its beta. Beta is calculated by relating the returns on a mutual fund with the returns in the market.

Beta more than 1 is a risky beta while beta less than 1 is conservative beta.

Unsystematic risk can be diversified through investments in a number of instruments, but systematic risk cannot be diversified and is considered to be uncontrollable. By using the 'risk return relationship', the competitive strength of the mutual funds is analysed in relation to one another in a better way.

In order to determine the risk-adjusted returns of investment portfolios and to evaluate a portfolio within a particular risk class, there are several performance indices available which have been developed over the years. The most important and widely used measures of performance are:

- The Treynor Measure
- The Sharpe Measure
- Jenson Model
- Fama Model

1. The Treynor Measure

This performance measure was developed by Jack Treynor, and it evaluates funds on the basis of Treynor's Index. This index is a ratio of return generated by the fund over and above risk-free rate of return during a given period and systematic risk associated with it.

'Risk free return' is generally taken as the return on government securities due to zero credit risk. Systematic risk, as mentioned above, is measured by Beta.

Symbolically, it can be represented as:

$$\text{Treynor's Index } (T_i) = (R_i - R_f)/B_i$$

where, R_i represents return on fund, R_f is risk-free rate of return, and B_i is beta of the fund.

All risk-averse investors would like to maximise this value. A high and positive Treynor's Index shows a superior risk-adjusted performance of a fund; a low and negative Treynor's Index indicates unfavourable performance. Higher the ratio, better is the performance of the portfolio.

EXAMPLE 8.3: A fund portfolio has a three-year average return of 15% the three-year average of a risk-free investment (of government's treasury bonds) is 5% and the portfolio has a beta of 1.5. Calculate the Treynor Ratio.

Solution: The portfolio's Treynor ratio is 0.067 (0.15 – 0.05/1.5).

2. The Sharpe Measure

The Sharpe index is similar to the Treynor measure, except that the risk measure is the standard deviation of the portfolio instead of only the systematic risk, i.e. 'Beta'.

According to Sharpe, it is the total risk of the fund that the investors are concerned about.

Here, the performance of a fund is evaluated on the basis of Sharpe Ratio, which is a ratio of returns generated by the fund over and above risk-free rate of return and the total risk associated with it. A comparison of Sharpe and Treynor Ratio are given in Box 8.5.

Symbolically, it can be expressed as:

$$\text{Sharpe Index } (S_i) = (R_i - R_f)/s_i$$

where, R_i represents return on fund, R_f is risk-free rate of return and s_i is the standard deviation of the fund.

While a high and positive Sharpe Ratio shows a superior risk-adjusted performance of a fund, a low and negative Sharpe Ratio is an indication of poor performance.

EXAMPLE 8.4: There are two portfolios A and B with a return of 12% and 14% and their standard deviations are 0.7 and 1.2, respectively. Risk free rate is 9%. Compute the return of both the portfolios as per Sharpe.

Solution: $$Ta = \frac{0.12 - 0.09}{0.7} = 0.043$$

$$\text{Risk adjusted rate of return of Portfolio A} = 0.043 + 0.09 = 0.133 = 13.3\%$$

$$Tb = \frac{0.14 - 0.09}{1.2} = 0.042$$

$$\text{Risk adjusted rate of return of Portfolio B} = 0.042 + 0.09 = 0.132 = 13.2\%$$

BOX 8.5: COMPARISON OF TREYNOR AND SHARPE RATIOS

Treynor and Sharpe measures are similar in form, as they both of them divide the risk premium by a numerical risk measure.

'Total risk' is appropriate when we evaluate the risk return relationship for well-diversified portfolios, but, 'systematic risk' is relevant when we evaluate less than fully diversified portfolios or individual stocks.

The rankings based on total risk (Sharpe measure) and systematic risk (Treynor measure) should be identical for a well-diversified portfolio, as the total risk is reduced to systematic risk. Therefore, a poorly diversified fund that ranks higher on Treynor measure, compared with another fund that is highly diversified, will rank lower on Sharpe measure.

Unlike the Treynor measure, the Sharpe ratio evaluates the portfolio on the basis of both—rate of return and diversification (since it considers total portfolio risk as measured by standard deviation in its denominator). Therefore, Sharpe ratio is more appropriate for well diversified portfolios, because it more accurately takes into account the risks of the portfolio.

3. Jenson Model

Jenson's model is also based on *Capital Asset Pricing Model* (CAPM) like previous measures, but it proposes another risk adjusted performance measure. This measure was developed by Michael Jenson and is sometimes referred to as the *Differential Return Method*.

This measure compares the returns generated by the fund versus the expected returns out of the fund, given the level of its systematic risk. The surplus between the two returns is called ***Alpha****, which measures the performance of a fund compared with the actual returns over the period.*

So, Alpha (the net return) at a given level of risk (B_i) can thus be calculated as:

Return of portfolio – Required return/Expected return*

*Required return (R_i) is calculated as:

$$R_i = R_f + B_i(R_m - R_f)$$

where, R_i represents return on fund, R_m is average market return during the given period, R_f is risk-free rate of return, and B_i is beta of the fund.

The Jenson ratio measures how much return is generated above average returns, and adjusted for market risk. Higher alpha represents superior performance of the fund and vice versa. One limitation of this model like Treynor index is that it considers only systematic risk instead of the entire risk associated with the fund, and therefore, an ordinary investor might not be able to mitigate unsystematic risk due to limited knowledge.

Let us extend the example of Sharpe model for Jenson application.

EXAMPLE 8.5: There are two portfolios A and B with a realized return of last year of 12% and 11% and their Betas are 0.7 and 1.2, respectively. Market return is 12% and Beta is 1. Risk-free rate is 9%. What is the return as per Jenson model?

Solution:

The return expected = Risk free return + Beta portfolio × (Return of market – Risk free return)

Using Portfolio A, the expected return = 0.09 + 0.7 (0.12 – 0.09)
= 0.09 + 0.02 = 0.11

Alpha = Return of portfolio – Expected return = 0.12 – 0.11
= 0.01 = 1%

Using Portfolio B, the expected return = 0.09 + 1.2 (0.12 – 0.09)
= 0.09 + 0.04 = 0.13

Alpha = Return of portfolio – Expected return = 0.11 – 0.13
= –0.02 = –2%

Alpha of B is negative, signifying high level of risk in the portfolio. This factor is ignored in Sharpe model.

4. Fama Model

The Eugene Fama model is an extension of the Jenson model.

Fama model also measures the performance of a fund in terms of excessive returns over the required return at a given level of total risk but it calculates the required rate of return in a different way.

The difference between the actual return and required return is known as **net** selectivity.

The "net selectivity" represents the stock selection skill of the fund manager, as it is the excess return over and above the return required to compensate for the total risk taken by the fund manager, the higher value of which indicates that fund manager has earned returns well above the return commensurate with the level of risk taken by him.

Therefore, the net selectivity (net return) is calculated as:

Return of portfolio – Required return or Expected return*

*Required return (R_i) is calculated as:

$$R_i = R_f + S_i/S_m \times (R_m - R_f)$$

where, R_f is risk-free rate of return, (S_i/S_m) is the standard deviation of the fund/standard deviation of market, and R_m is average market return during the given period.

EXAMPLE 8.6: There are two portfolios X and Y. Market return is 17% and risk-free rate is 8% (from PPF). The standard deviations of X and Y are 10 and 6, respectively. The standard deviation of market is 9. Returns of X and Y are 20% and 16%, respectively. Calculate the net selectivity of fund using Fama model.

Solution:

Required rate of return of fund X = 8% + [(10/9) × (17% – 8%)] = 18%

Required rate of return of fund Y = 8% + [(6/9) × (17% – 8%)] = 14%

Net selectivity of fund X = Actual mean return by fund X – Required return by fund X

= 20% – 18% = 2%

Net selectivity of fund Y = Actual mean return by fund Y – Required return by fund Y

= 16% – 14% = 2%

In this case, fund X and Y are equally attractive.

Among the above performance measures, two models namely, Treynor measure and Jenson model use systematic risk, assuming that the unsystematic risk is diversifiable. These models are suitable for large investors like institutional investors with high risk taking capacities and huge funds. They can invest in a number of options across sectors to dilute some risks.

However, Sharpe measure and Fama model that consider the entire risk associated with the fund are suitable for small investors, as the ordinary investor lacks the necessary skill and resources to diversify the risk associated with securities.

SIP, SWP, STP, DIVIDEND SWEEP, TRIGGERS AND EXPENSE RATIO

In order to make their schemes attractive to investors, AMCs offer various investments and redemption plans to the investors. Most of these abbreviations pertain to such plans offered by mutual funds.

Systematic Investment Plan (SIP)

This enables an investor to regularly invest in a fund in the same way as one invests in a recurring deposit scheme of a bank. In a SIP, investors buy units of the fund by contributing a fixed (and often small) amount of money at regular intervals and do not have to worry about market timing. SIP is governed by the principle of "Rupee Cost Averaging" (RCA).

So, in SIP one puts in a small amount every month that is invested in a mutual fund.

Example: A decides to invest INR 1,000 per month for a year. When the market price of shares fall, he benefits by purchasing more units; and is protected by purchasing less when the price rises as explained in Table 8.4.

TABLE 8.4 SIP Computation

Date	*NAV*	*Approx number of units you will get at 1000*
1 January	10	100
1 February	10.5	95.24
1 March	11	90.91
1 April	9.5	105.26
1 May	9	111.11
1 June	11.5	86.96
1 July	11	90.91
1 August	10.5	95.24
1 September	10	100
1 October	9.5	105.26
1 November	10	100
1 December	9.5	105.26
		1186.15

Within one year, A has 1,186 units by investing just INR 1,000 every month at an average cost of 12,000/1186.15 = 10.1170.

This is as against 12,000/10 = 1,000 units or 12,000/11.5 = 1043.5 units or 12,000/9 = 1,333.3 units if he had invested lump sum on 1 January, 1 June or 1 May, respectively.

Wait the NAV rise in this time period

Systematic Withdrawal Plan (SWP)

Under SWP, investors are permitted to withdraw a part of their investment from the fund on a periodic basis. Similar to SIP, in a SWP too, investors do not have to be concerned about the timing of selling their units. The AMC automatically liquidates a portion of units at regular intervals and sends a cheque to the investor. An investor could get regular dividends by opting for the dividend option of a mutual fund but these dividends could be volatile. SWP, on the other hand, provides greater regularity of income at the option of the investor. Normally, AMCs offer two kinds of SWPs to the unit holders—they may withdraw a fixed amount by redeeming some units periodically, or they may opt to redeem units equivalent to the appreciation in their investment value at periodic intervals, thus keeping the initial investment or the original capital intact.

Systematic Transfer Plan (STP)

This plan gives investors the option to transfer fixed amounts from one scheme of the AMC, to another on a periodic basis. Thus, if one believes that another fund is likely to perform better under the STP in the future, one may opt to transfer a part of the portfolio from one scheme to another seamlessly.

Dividend Sweep

This is yet another method of investing in mutual funds with a seamless transfer facility, albeit with a small difference. Unlike an STP, dividend sweep allows one to invest the dividend component of one scheme into another scheme with the same AMC.

Triggers

These help an investor change the investment composition depending on the occurrence of certain events. The investor specifies the triggers and the action to be taken if the trigger event occurs. For example, in an *appreciation trigger*, the AMC may be called upon to automatically book profits when the NAV appreciates to a certain level. Similarly, in a *stop-loss trigger*, if the NAV touches a certain low, the AMC may be obliged to redeem the units on behalf of the investor, thus containing the maximum loss. Triggers help particularly big investor, to instruct the AMC as to what they should do in case of certain events. Triggers can also relate to index levels, interest rate levels, and the like.

The exit loads applicable to these options and plans, the periodicity of SIP, SWP, and STP, the amount invested or redeemed, the allowed triggers, etc. are clearly mentioned in the offer document of funds.

Expense Ratio

Under SEBI (Mutual Funds) Regulations, 1996, Mutual Funds are permitted to charge certain operating expenses for managing a mutual fund scheme—*such as sales and marketing/advertising expenses, administrative expenses, transaction costs, investment management fees, registrar fees, custodian fees, audit fees*—as a percentage of the fund's daily net assets. All such costs for running and managing a mutual fund scheme are collectively referred to as 'Total Expense Ratio' (TER).

The TER is calculated as a percentage of the Scheme's average Net Asset Value (NAV). The daily NAV of a mutual fund is disclosed after deducting the expenses. The regulatory limits of TER that can be incurred/charged to the fund by a Mutual Fund AMC have been specified under Regulation 52 of SEBI Mutual Fund Regulations. **TER has a direct bearing on a scheme's NAV—the lower the expense ratio of a scheme, the higher the NAV.** Thus, TER is an important parameter while selecting a mutual fund scheme.

EMERGING CHALLENGES OF MUTUAL FUNDS

There are many challenges related to mutual funds, which are of prime concern to the people who regularly invest in them.

1. Fluctuating Returns

In spite of being a diversified investment, mutual funds investment is not always a guarantee for return. If the market prices of major shares and bonds fall, then the value of mutual fund shares will also go down, irrespective of how diversified the mutual fund portfolio is.

2. Burden of Expenses

Most of the mutual funds charge shareholder fees and fund operating fees from the investors. In the year in which the mutual fund fails to make profit and the investors get no return, these fees add to the losses. Though there are mutual funds which do not have transaction fee, but there are also mutual funds which charge annual expense ratio on the entire investment. *For example,* if a fund has an expense ratio of 1% and you have ₹10,000 in investment, the annual expense is ₹100. The amount is small. However, if you have ₹5,00,000, the annual expense is ₹5,000—that's a good sum.

This disadvantage however, does not include pitfalls of up-front load and back-end load. *Entry load/Upfront load* is the amount of money some mutual funds would charge for buying their units. Initially it was used but now, it is removed. There shall be no entry load for all mutual fund schemes. *Exit load/Back-end load*, or **redemption fee**, is the amount of money some mutual funds charge for selling your shares. Exit load charged to the investor is a maximum of 7% of the redemption proceeds. Generally, mutual fund schemes charge one to two percent as exit load, however some long term schemes such as retirement schemes have exit load of around five percent.[8] For example, if you are selling ₹10,000 out of a fund that charges 1% back-end load, you will walk away with only ₹9,900.

3. Inefficient Investment

Mutual funds manager cannot hoard cash. When investors buy shares of a mutual fund, the fund manager in return, must buy shares of stocks that fall within the guidelines

8. https://www.sebi.gov.in/sebi_data/meetingfiles/dec-2020/1608703407883_1.pdf

specified by the prospectus. *For example,* if it is a 'small value fund', the manager cannot buy a 'Large Growth' stock even if it represents a better buying opportunity. Moreover, if there are not enough good investment opportunities available, the fund manager may buy stocks that are not profitable.

4. Forced Selling

A fund manager is forced to sell stocks when investors sell shares of mutual fund and the fund does not have enough cash reserve to meet the demand. In this process, he may end up selling stocks when the market is low.

5. Over Diversification

In order to diversify the investment, the mutual fund companies, many a times, get involved in *over diversification*. The risk of holding a single financial security is removed by diversification but in case of over diversification, investors diversify so much that most of the time they end up investing in funds that are highly related. Thus, the benefit of risk diversification is defeated.

6. Taxes

Though mutual funds provide tax advantage to their investors, but there are mutual funds wherein the investors are bound to pay taxes on these incomes, even if they reinvest the income. *Securities Transaction Tax (STT)* is anyways there on specified funds.

CASE STUDY

Active vs. Passive Issue

In every walk of life, people like to win and so is the case in investing. In investing, investors like to earn higher returns to the maximum extent. Thus, most mutual fund investors are not satisfied with the performance of a decent passive benchmark such as the S&P 500 Index. Instead, they look out for an actively managed fund that they believe will beat the benchmark.

Gerstein Fisher, a leading US investment management and advisory firm examined this universal active vs. passive question of mutual funds' investment on the basis of key parameters and came out with some interesting discoveries:

1. ***The funds:*** They used Morningstar's fund database and examined the performance of more than 2,000 active US equity funds during the 15-year period from July 1, 1998 to June 28, 2013.

Result: They found that only 25.6% of the active funds outperformed their benchmarks (nearly 75% trailed the benchmark or had an insufficient track record to compare). Further, they discovered that 69% of all domestic equity funds were either outperformed after expenses by their benchmarks over the prior five years or had been liquidated during the period from January 1, 2008 to December 31, 2012[9].

Therefore, funds most actively managed faced a hard time beating passively managed index funds after fees (higher costs for actively managed funds, such as annual expense ratios and transaction costs). Gerstein Fisher concluded that investors were better off buying the market than trying to beat it.

2. *Costs do matter:* As indicated above, the costs of fund matters but they are not the only factor in choosing a fund nor should they be the most important factor.

Gerstein Fisher went back and compared cost and performance for equity funds from July 1, 1998 to June 28, 2013 (Table 8.5). He found that the best performing quintile of funds was the second most expensive quintile (i.e. the 21–40% highest-cost ones).

Result: It was more or less consistent as above. The cheapest quintile of funds was not the best performing, but the most expensive funds were the worst performing. For example, the second cheapest quintile of funds was twice as likely to outperform as the most expensive funds (30% vs. 15.7%). Clearly, high costs were a big hurdle for active fund managers to clear.

TABLE 8.5 Probability of Returns by Decile, January 1, 1998 to June 28, 2013

Quintiles (1 = Cheapest)	1 *Year* (%)	3 *Years* (%)	5 *Years* (%)	10 *Years* (%)	15 *Years* (%)	*Asset Weighted Returns* (15 *Y*)	*Equal Weighted Returns* (15 *Y*)
1	86.21	5.06	10.57	32.64	29.43	6.97	5.89
2	82.35	4.47	10.12	31.53	30.12	6.56	6.07
3	76.10	4.39	12.06	29.17	28.29	7.20	6.42
4	76.66	7.86	14.99	27.52	24.32	8.11	6.67
5	68.22	8.18	9.11	21.26	15.65	6.09	5.77

Source: Morningstar, Gerstein Fisher Research.

3. *The tax factor:* They found that investment loss to taxes was often ignored as the fund industry tends to report and advertise their returns on a pre-tax basis. The loss to taxes during the same 15-year period (starting in 1998) ranged from 70 to 120 basis points per year for active funds.

4. *The behavioural cost:* They had a surprising revelation. The greatest cost of all—larger than fund fees, tax, or anything else was the loss due to investor behaviour, i.e. poor timing decisions by the investors. This was defined as the difference between mutual fund returns and investor returns.

* S&P Indices Versus Active Funds Scorecard.

Conclusion

The investors wasted their energy looking out for low-cost funds and choosing between an active and passive fund strategy in building a portfolio. The larger issue of all was the investor behaviour. The question of active vs. passive fund depended on the investment strategy of the investor and his/her discipline of sticking to it.

(*Source:* http://www.forbes.com/sites/greggfisher/2013/08/28/in-mutual-funds-is-active-vs-passive-the-right-question)

SOLVED PROBLEMS

PROBLEM 8.1: Mid-invest is one of the leading financial companies in India. Table 8.6 shows the balance sheet of the company as on 31st March 2010.

TABLE 8.6 Balance Sheet as at 31st March 2010

Liabilities	*₹ in mn.*	*Assets*	*₹ in mn.*
Capital (4 mn. units @ ₹ 10)	40	Equity shares	70
Reserves and surplus	70	Bonds	40
Current liabilities and provisions	40	Short-term investments	20
		Other current assets	20
	150		150

From the above information, calculate the following:

(i) Net assets of the fund
(ii) NAV of the unit of fund

Solution:

(i) Net assets of the fund = Investments + Current assets – Current liabilities
= ₹ 150 – 40 = ₹ 110 mn.

(ii) NAV of the unit of fund = Investors fund/units
= ₹ 110/4 = ₹ 27.5

PROBLEM 8.2: The 10-year annual return for the S&P 500 (market portfolio) is 10% with a beta of 1, while the average annual return on T-Bills is 6%. There are three distinct portfolio managers with the 10-year results shown in Table 8.7 as follows:

TABLE 8.7 Average Annual Return and Beta of Managers

Managers	*Average Annual Return*	*Beta*
Manager X	10%	0.90
Manager Y	14%	1.03
Manager Z	15%	1.20

Evaluate them with the help of Treynor value for each.

Solution:

T ratio (market) = (0.10 – 0.06)/1 = 0.04
T ratio (manager X) = (0.10 – 0.06)/0.90 = 0.044
T ratio (manager Y) = (0.14 – 0.06)/1.03 = 0.078
T ratio (manager Z) = (0.15 – 0.06)/1.20 = 0.075

In this case, all three managers performed better than the aggregate market. On evaluating the portfolio manager (or portfolio) on performance of return alone, Manager Z yields the best results.

However, on considering the risks that each manager took to attain their respective returns, Manager Y demonstrated the better outcome. The higher the Treynor measure, the better the portfolio.

PROBLEM 8.3: Using the above problem and assuming that the S&P 500 had a standard deviation of 18% over a 10-year period, determine the Sharpe ratios for the following portfolio managers (Table 8.8) and find out the best portfolio. Does it affect the above result?

TABLE 8.8 Portfolio Standard Deviation of Managers

Manager	*Annual Return*	*Portfolio Standard Deviation*
Manager X	10%	0.11
Manager Y	14%	0.20
Manager Z	15%	0.27

Solution:

S ratio (market) = (0.10 – 0.06)/0.18 = 0.222
S ratio (manager X) = (0.10 – 0.06)/0.11 = 0.364
S ratio (manager Y) = (0.14 – 0.06)/0.20 = 0.4
S ratio (manager Z) = (0.15 – 0.06)/0.27 = 0.333

Once again, we find that the best portfolio is not necessarily the one with the highest return. Instead, it is the one with the most superior risk-adjusted return, or in this case the fund headed by manager Y.

PROBLEM 8.4: The risk-free rate of return is 5% and a market return is 11%, what is the alpha for the funds given in Table 8.9.

TABLE 8.9 Average Annual Return and Beta of Managers

Manager	*Average Annual Return*	*Beta*
Manager A	11%	0.90
Manager B	15%	1.10
Manager C	15%	1.20

Solution: First, we calculate the portfolio's expected return:

ER(A) = 0.05 + 0.90 (0.11 – 0.05) = 0.104 or 10.4% return
ER(B) = 0.05 + 1.10 (0.11 – 0.05) = 0.116 or 11.6% return
ER(C) = 0.05 + 1.20 (0.11 – 0.05) = 0.122 or 12.2% return

Then, we calculate the portfolio's alpha by subtracting the expected return of the portfolio from the actual return:

Alpha A = 11% – 10.4% = 0.6%
Alpha B = 15% – 11.6% = 3.4%
Alpha C = 15% – 12.2% = 2.8%

Manager B did the best because although manager C had the same annual return, though it was expected that manager B would yield a lower return since the portfolio's beta was significantly lower than that of portfolio C.

PROBLEM 8.5: The treasury bills' rate of return is 5% and a market return is 13%. Standard deviations of A and B are .12 and .31, respectively.

(a) What is the alpha for the portfolios given in Table 8.10? What is your recommendation?

TABLE 8.10 Average Annual Return and Beta of Portfolio

Portfolio	*Average Annual Return*	*Beta*
A	12%	0.70
B	16%	1.40

(b) If you will hold only one of the two portfolios, then which measure is the appropriate criterion? Which portfolio would be preferred here?

Solution:

(a) The alphas for the two portfolios are:

$$\alpha_A = 12\% - [5\% + 0.7 \times (13\% - 5\%)] = 1.4\%$$

$$\alpha_B = 16\% - [5\% + 1.4 \times (13\% - 5\%)] = -0.2\%$$

Ideally, you would want to take a long position in Portfolio A and a short position in Portfolio B.

(b) If you will hold only one of the two portfolios, then the Sharpe measure is the appropriate criterion:

$$S_A = \frac{.12-.05}{.12} = 0.583$$

$$S_B = \frac{.16-.05}{.31} = 0.355$$

Using the Sharpe criterion, Portfolio A is the preferred portfolio

PROBLEM 8.6: Table 8.11 shows the data in rupee terms:

TABLE 8.11 Risk and Return of MFs

MF market (growth funds)	*Return (mean)*	*Risk (SD)*
India	1.26% per month	4.43
Singapore	1.23% per month	5.55

The correlation coefficient between the two markets is 0.58. Suppose that you invest equally, i.e. 50% each, in the two markets. Determine the expected return of the resulting portfolio.

Solution: The expected return of the equally weighted portfolio is:

$$E(Rp) = (0.5)(1.26\%) + (0.5)(1.23\%) = 1.25\%$$

POINTS TO REMEMBER

- A mutual fund is a common pool of funds mobilised from a large number of investors, and invested on their behalf in several securities in the market.
- The investors of mutual funds are known as unit-holders. The companies that operate the mutual funds are known as Asset Management Companies (AMCs) or Investment Managers.
- Mutual fund was first introduced in Belgium in 1822, and became popular in the United States in the 1920s. They experienced phenomenal growth after World War II, especially in the 1980s and 1990s.
- In 1964, the concept of mutual fund took shape in India when Unit Trust of India (UTI) was set up.
- After two decades of UTI monopoly, some other public sector organisations like SBI (1987), LIC (1989), Punjab National Bank (1989) and GIC (1990), etc. were permitted to set up mutual funds.
- The growth of mutual fund industry in India can be divided into following phases:

  Phase I. Establishment and Growth of Unit Trust of India (1964–1987): Unit Trust of India enjoyed complete monopoly when it was established in the year 1964 by the Reserve Bank of India and it continued to operate under the regulatory control of the RBI until it was de-linked in 1978 and the entire control was transferred to Industrial Development Bank of India (IDBI).
  Phase II. Entry of Public Sector Funds (1987–1993): The Indian mutual fund industry witnessed a number of public sector players entering the market in the year 1987. In November 1987, SBI Mutual Fund from the State Bank of India became the first non-UTI mutual fund in India later followed by others.
  Phase III. Entry of Private Sector Funds (1993–2003): The private sector funds started coming into the mutual fund industry in 1993.

Phase IV. Growth and Consolidation (2003–2014): In February 2003, the UTI Act was repealed and UTI was bifurcated into two separate entities—the Specified Undertaking of the UTI (SUUTI), and UTI Mutual Fund which functions under the SEBI MF Regulations. With the bifurcation of the erstwhile UTI and several mergers taking place among different private sector funds, the MF industry entered its fourth phase of consolidation.

Phase V. Current Phase (2014 onwards): The progressive measures taken by SEBI to "re-energize" the Indian Mutual Fund industry and increase MFs' penetration succeeded in reversing the negative trend that had set in after the global melt-down.

- Based on their structure, mutual funds can be classified as open- or close-ended. Open-ended funds are irredeemable, having no finite life. It is the AMC of the fund that offers to sell and buy the units from the investors at what is called the '*Net Asset Value (NAV)*'. Close-ended funds on the other hand are redeemable funds having a pre-specified life. These are listed in the stock exchanges.
- Based on Asset Class, mutual funds may be equity funds, debt funds, money market funds, gilt funds and hybrid funds. Equity funds are primary instruments; debt funds are in fixed income securities; money market funds invest in short-term money market instruments; and gilt funds invest in gilt or bullion or related securities. Hybrid or Balanced funds describe the equal mix of asset classes in the investments.
- Industry-specific or sectoral funds focus upon specific industries or sectors. For example, the sector of focus could be information technology, pharmaceuticals, banking, small and medium enterprises, or even geographic sectors such as emerging markets as of Asia Pacific, India, China and so forth.
- Based on Indices, there are index funds that invest in companies belonging to specific indices such as Sensex or Nifty.
- Schemes or funds may also be characterised by their investment solution. For example, a fund may be called a *Children's Fund* or *Young Citizens' Fund.*
- Other schemes like Tax Saving Schemes and Special Schemes of ULIPs are also available.
- A Fund of Funds (FoF) is a mutual fund that invests in other mutual fund schemes rather than independently in securities such as bonds and shares.
- Mutual funds are popular due to the benefits of diversification, professional management, variety, low costs, liquidity, convenience, investor's confidence, reinvestment, tax relief and foreign capital.
- Mutual funds in India are governed by the SEBI (Mutual Funds) Regulations 1996. SEBI regulates the functioning of mutual funds, and it requires that all mutual funds should be established as trusts under the Indian Trusts Act. The minimum net worth of an AMC or its affiliate must be ₹50 crore to act as a manager in any other fund. The mutual funds are now regulated by Association of Mutual Funds Industry in India (AMFI) which is a self-regulatory organisation (SRO).
- An applicant proposing to sponsor a mutual fund in India must submit an application in Form A along with a fee of ₹5 lacs.

- A custodian holds the securities of various schemes of the fund in their custody. However, following demat of securities, the term custodian has given way to the 'depository'. A depository maintains an online record of ownership of securities bought and sold by a mutual fund in dematerialised form.
- The registrar accepts and processes the unit holders' applications.
- Transfer agents are responsible for issuing and redeeming units of the scheme.
- Net Asset Value (NAV) of a mutual fund unit is defined as Market value of total assets—Market value of total liabilities, divided by the outstanding units. Incidentally, the NAV of a close-ended fund is different, and is generally less than its market price.
- The Treynor Measure evaluates funds on the basis of Treynor's Index. It can be represented as: Treynor's Index $(T_i) = (R_i - R_f)/B_i$.
- The Sharpe Measure states that it is the total risk of the fund that the investors are concerned about. It can be written as: Sharpe Index $(S_i) = (R_i - R_f)/s_i$.
- Jenson Model involves evaluation of the returns that the fund has generated versus the returns actually expected out of the fund, given the level of its systematic risk. The surplus between the two returns is called *Alpha*, wherein the expected return is calculated as: $R_i = R_f + B_i\,(R_m - R_f)$.
- The Fama Model is an extension of the Jenson model. Here, the required return can be calculated as: $R_i = R_f + S_i/S_m * (R_m - R_f)$.
- Systematic Investment Plans (SIPs) enable an investor to regularly invest in a fund in the same way as one invests in a recurring deposit scheme of a bank.
- Systematic Withdrawal Plan (SWP) allows investors to withdraw a part of their investment from the fund on a periodic basis.
- Systematic Transfer Plan (STP) gives investors the option to transfer fixed amounts from one scheme of the AMC to another, on a periodic basis.
- Dividend Sweep is yet another method of investing in mutual funds with a seamless transfer facility, although with a small difference.
- Triggers help an investor change the investment composition depending upon the occurrence of certain events.
- All such costs for running and managing a mutual fund scheme are collectively referred to as 'Total Expense Ratio' (TER).
- There are many challenges facing the mutual funds which are of prime concern like the issue of fluctuating returns, burden of expenses, inefficient investment, forced selling, over diversification, and taxes.

KEY TERMS

- **Mutual fund** is a common pool of funds mobilised from a large number of investors, and invested on their behalf in several securities in the market.
- **Asset Management Companies (AMCs)** are the companies that operate mutual funds.

- **Open-ended funds** are irredeemable, having no finite life.
- **Close-ended funds** are redeemable funds having a pre-specified life, at the end of which the capital is returned to the investors
- **Fund of Funds** (FoF) are mutual funds that invest in other mutual fund schemes (generally those offered by the same AMC).
- **Depository** maintains an online record of ownership of securities bought and sold by a mutual fund in dematerialised form.
- **Net Asset Value (NAV)** of a fund is the sum total of the market value of the assets (securities) net of any liabilities at that time.
- **Systematic Investment Plans (SIPs)** are regular investment plans for enabling compulsory investment for small investors.
- **Systematic Withdrawal Plan (SWP)** are periodic withdrawal plans for investors.
- **Systematic Transfer Plan (STP)** are transfer plans for investors to transfer fixed amounts from one scheme of the AMC to another.
- **Dividend sweep** is a reinvestment of dividend of one scheme into another scheme with the same AMC.
- **Triggers** are changing propositions of the investment composition as per the events.

EXERCISES

Numerical Problems

1. The balance sheet of A&Z Investment company as on 31st March 2011 is given in Table 8.12.

TABLE 8.12 Balance Sheet as on 31st March 2011

Liabilities	*₹ in mn.*	*Assets*	*₹ in mn.*
Capital (5 mn. units @ ₹ 10)	50	Equity shares	80
Reserves and surplus	100	Debentures	50
Current liabilities and provisions	20	Short-term securities	20
		Certificate of deposits	10
		Other current assets	10
	170		170

From the above information, calculate NAV of the fund.

2. The annualised return of Company A and Company B of US from 2008–2012 is given in Table 8.13.

TABLE 8.13 Annual Return of Two Companies of USA

	Annual Return (%)					*Average Return (%)*
	YTD	2011	2010	2009	2008	
Company A	18.0	28.2	0.2	7.2	–16.5	7.4
Company B	10.9	12.7	92.9	47.3	–62.3	20.3

The short-term G-Sec rate is 0.7%. The betas of both these companies are 0.71 and 2.36, respectively. Using Treynor ratio, find out which company generates a higher return and comment.

3. Following is the annual return of your five years old portfolio.

   2005 : 12%
   2006 : –3%
   2007 : 9%
   2008 : –8%
   2009 : 6%

   The rate of return on a five-year government bond is 3%. Calculate the Sharpe ratio from the above, if the average standard deviation is 0.18.

4. The risk-free rate of return is 2% and a market return is 8%. Calculate the Jenson's alpha for the funds given in Table 8.14 and comment.

TABLE 8.14 Average Annual Return of Funds

Funds	*Average Annual Return*	*Beta*
Fund 1	12%	1.4
Fund 2	12%	1.0
Fund 3	12%	0.8

5. Suppose you have a choice between investing in two managers—

   Manager A: Alpha = 2%, Beta = 0.9 and

   Manager B: Alpha = 3%, Beta = 1.6.

   Which one would you prefer, based on Treynor ratio?

Answers: 1. ₹30 2. Company A = 0.094; Company B = 0.083
3. 0.011 4. Fund 1 = 1.16%; Fund 2 = 4%; Fund 3 = 5.2%
5. Manager A: 0.0222; Manager B: 0.0187.

Objective Questions

1. Tick the correct answer:

(a) A mutual fund holder is:
(i) Shareholder (ii) Unit-holder
(iii) Deposit holder (iv) Fund holder

(b) In India, the concept of mutual fund started with:
(i) Unit Trust of India
(ii) State Bank of India
(iii) Life Insurance Corporation of India
(iv) None of the above

(c) The first mutual funds regulations were introduced in India in:
(i) 1991 (ii) 1992
(iii) 1993 (iv) 1996

(d) Growth fund is primarily:
(i) Equity fund (ii) Debt fund
(iii) Fixed fund (iv) None of the above

(e) Mutual funds are:
(i) Less risky than shares (ii) More risky than shares
(iii) Equally risky to shares (iv) None of the above

Answers: (a) ii (b) i (c) iii (d) i (e) i

2. Fill in the blanks:

(a) Any time entry and any time exit mutual fund is ....
(b) The main characteristic of Income fund is ....
(c) .... are tax saving funds.
(d) Mutual funds are formed as ....
(e) .... is a measure of volatility of the stock.
(f) Commission payable on selling of mutual funds is called ....
(g) .... invests in real estate properties.

Answers:

(a) Open-ended fund
(b) Debt orientation
(c) ELSS
(d) Trust
(e) Beta
(f) Exit load
(g) Real estate fund

3. True or False:

(a) The mutual funds industry in India now functions under the SEBI (Mutual Fund) Regulations 1996.
(b) Close-ended funds are for perpetuity.
(c) NAV is applicable in open-ended mutual funds.
(d) Liquid funds are the least risky.
(e) SEBI regulates the mutual fund industry in India.
(f) SIP is meant for large investors.
(g) Balanced fund is also called hybrid fund.

(h) A gilt fund basically invests in government securities.
(i) Dividend sweep is a reinvestment plan.
(j) Sharpe ratio is more appropriate for well diversified portfolios than Treynor.

Answers: (a) True (b) False (c) True (d) True (e) True
(f) False (g) True (h) True (i) True (j) True

Short Questions

1. State the structural framework of UTI.
2. What is an Asset Management Company?
3. What is a Net Asset Value?
4. State two mutual funds based on structure.
5. Define 'Fund of Funds'.
6. Define a depository.
7. Explain an index fund.
8. List the differences between Sharpe and Treynor measure.

Critical Thinking Questions

1. "Mutual funds are a risk diversification instrument". Explain.
2. "An investor can choose and invest in a mutual fund of his choice". Elaborate.
3. "Mutual funds have assumed importance on account of inherent merits attached to them". Discuss.
4. "Indian mutual funds industry has been going through a bad phase of late". Discuss.
5. "Mutual funds have not performed as per the expectations". Throw light on the statement.
6. "Mutual funds are a pool of money". Explain.
7. "Mutual funds bring professional management with them". Discuss.

Descriptive Questions

1. Discuss the growth of mutual funds in India.
2. Compare and contrast mutual funds with other financial instruments in the market.
3. Discuss the different types of mutual funds.
4. Describe the regulatory framework of mutual funds in India.
5. Explain the structural arrangement of mutual funds.
6. What are the different performance measures of mutual funds?
7. What are the emerging issues and challenges faced by mutual funds in India?
8. How are mutual funds priced? Discuss in detail.
9. Discuss the registration process of mutual funds in India.

PROJECT EXERCISE

A Tailor-Made Mutual Fund

Select one public sector mutual fund, one private sector fund and one foreign mutual fund in India based on their performance in terms of returns during the last three years. Find out the reasons for their performance and predict their future using performance indices. Based on them, formulate the best possible mutual fund incorporating the features of the above funds and suggestive indicators on your side to recommend a first time small investor in mutual funds.

REVIEW CASE

Fund Acquisition—A Boon or Bane?

Finances Ltd. has finally sold its mutual fund business to A&B Mutual Fund. There is a huge dissatisfaction among the existing investors of Finances Ltd. regarding their future returns. Also, new investors are apprehensive about investment in Finances Equity Fund and Finances India Hybrid Fund, which are some of the good performing funds. SEBI considering the market trend, came out with the notification that, "it is true that Finances Ltd. is selling its Indian mutual fund business to A&B Mutual Fund, but a noteworthy point is that the deal is yet to get regulatory approval. As far as the performance of Finances Equity Fund (FEF) and Finances India Hybrid Fund (FIHF) is concerned, one should decide on its own". Meanwhile, the company also came out with its report card (Table 8.15).

TABLE 8.15 Finances Ltd.'s Report Card

Scheme Name	6 *Month* (%)	1 *Year* (%)	3 *Year* (%)	5 *Year* (%)	*Std. Dev* (%)
Finances Equity	–0.4	–8.6	22.2	8.6	6.23
Finances India Hybrid	–1.2	–9.2	22.2	–	6.31
Category average of equity funds	1.6	–8.7	19.0	5.0	6.86
Category average of hybrid funds	1.6	–10.0	17.6	5.5	6.71
BSE-200	0.4	–12.3	16.3	4.5	7.53

(NAV data as on April 5, 2010. Standard Deviation and Sharpe ratio is calculated over a 3-year period. Risk-free rate is assumed to be 6%).

As a part of the deal, it was expected that the marketing and sales team of Finances Mutual Fund may be absorbed by A&B MF but equity fund management team will be replaced by A&B MF. The equity fund management team is also engaged in research and fund management of Asia-Pacific region for its parent company, and it is a well experienced fund management team.

While this deal gave A&B an opportunity to become the 10th largest fund house with a market share of around 5%, only time will tell if this acquisition can bring turn-around in its performance. It would be a challenge for A&B MF to retain investors who are focused more towards investing in good funds managed by distinguished fund management. Also, L&T MF will have to add new fund managers to its role and will have to efficiently manage the increased operations.

Issues for Discussion

(i) Comment on the financial report of Finances Ltd. using various mutual funds performance indices.

(ii) Is this deal beneficial for investors of Finances Ltd.?

(iii) What are the regulatory implications of this sale?

(iv) What factors should new investors look into before investing in Finances Ltd.?

(v) "Replacing equity fund management team might not be a good idea for investors". Critique.

(vi) How beneficial would the deal be for A&B investors?

(vii) Discuss the SWOT of A&B post acquisition.

REFERENCES

Bhatt, M. Narayana (1993), "Setting Standards for Investor Services", *Economic Times*, December 27.

Chandra, Prasanna (2008), *The Investment Game,* Tata McGraw-Hill, New Delhi.

Dave, S.A. (1992), "Mutual Funds: Growth and Development", *The Journal of the Indian Institute of Bankers*, Jan–March.

De, Mainak (1991), "Mutual Funds and Institutions—Playing to a different tune", *Economic Times*, June 15.

Evans, Richard B. (2003), "Does Alpha Really Matter? Evidence from Mutual Fund Incubation, Termination and Manager Change", November, Finance Department, Wharton School of Business.

www.amfiindia.com

www.forbes.com

www.kotakmutual.com

www.sebi.gov.in

CHAPTER 9

Plastic Money

You don't realize how much you use your credit card not even to buy things. It's a card you get so you can navigate society.

— Adam Carolla

LEARNING OBJECTIVES

This chapter discusses the following:

- Concept of plastic money
- Growth of plastic money in India
- Importance of plastic money
- Types of plastic cards
- Debit card industry
- Credit card industry
- Benefits and pitfalls of credit cards
- Prevention of fraud of credit cards
- Terminology used in plastic money
- RBI's regulation of conduct of plastic card business
- Challenges faced by the plastic money industry

INTRODUCTION

There is no doubt that more and more middle-class people worldwide are letting plastic money rule their day to day lives and Indians are no exception to it. A thriving economy, substantial increase in disposable incomes, consequent rise in consumer expenditure, growing affluence levels, and consumer sophistication have all led to a robust growth in credit cards, and each of the financial players have posted an enviable annual growth rate of more than 100% over the last few years. Today, even if debit cards are overtaking credit cards in popularity, the scorching pace of growth continues unabated.

PLASTIC MONEY: THE CONCEPT

Plastic money is an alternative to cash or the 'standard money'. "It represents currency and near currency, and is used to refer to the debit cards or the credit cards that we use to make purchases in our everyday life". Furthermore, these debit and credit cards use plastic in their manufacturing and that is where the name 'plastic money' has originated from. It is much more convenient to carry around as you do not have to carry a huge sum of money with you. It is also much safer to carry it along or to travel with it because even if it is stolen, one can consult the bank whose service one is using and get it blocked. This saves your money from getting stolen or even lost. Developing countries like India are encouraging the use of this plastic money more than cash due to these reasons.

Plastic money, also known as *plastic cards*, acts as a vital tool for everyday transaction by people today. The various plastic cards include Debit card, Credit card, Smart card, Charge card, etc. There has been a growth in electronic payment due to the shift in technology, growing access to internet among the customers, and convenient modes of delivery and payment.

GROWTH OF PLASTIC MONEY IN INDIA

There has been an explosive growth in plastic money volumes in India during the past few years, resulting into increasing profitability and quality of plastic money services. Today, the Indian card market is at par with the best in the world. There are hundreds of millions of debit cards and credit cards in circulation today; they have almost become a way of life. Initially positioned as a status symbol, these plastic cards have caught on in a big way amongst the educated population of the country.

Plastic money has changed the spending pattern of Indians in a big way. Name any purchase, plastic cards are there at every Indian's disposal. Clothes, dining, jewellery and travelling are the top four purchases that Indians make through plastic cards. Fuel also accounts for a considerable portion of debit card or credit card purchases. The number of debit and credit cards in circulation crossed the 1-billion mark in the country at the end of the September quarter of 2022. There were 1.01 billion credit and debit cards in circulation. The number of outstanding credit cards climbed by 19 per cent from 65 million in September 2021 to 77.7 million in September 2022, while outstanding debit cards increased by 2 per cent from 920.3 million to 938.53 million during the same time. As of September 2022, the top credit card-issuing banks were HDFC Bank, State Bank of India, ICICI Bank, Axis Bank, and Kotak Bank, while the top debit card issuing banks were State Bank of India, Bank of Baroda, Union Bank, Canara Bank, and HDFC Bank.[1]

1. https://www.deccanchronicle.com/business/in-other-news/061222/count-of-debit-and-credit-cards-in-circulation-in-india-crosses-1b-mar.html, December 6, 2022.

Credit card transaction volume was 725 million and value was ₹3.5 trillion in Q3 2022. In the third quarter of 2022, the volume of debit card transactions was 907 million with avlaue of ₹1.88 trillion.[2]

During last two decades, the banking environment has changed progressively. After financial sector reforms during 90s, the banking industry in India has witnessed remarkable changes due to IT applications. The information technology has replaced the brick of traditional banking with the wide range of e-banking products and services like ATM (Automated Teller Machine), Internet Banking, EFTs and most importantly plastic cards like Debit Cards, Credit Cards, etc. There is an increasing number of commercial banks, particularly in the public sector, aggressively launching these new debit and credit cards with value added features to meet the ever-changing requirements of the customers. Given the rising growth in e-payments, Visa International commissioned the National Council of Applied Economic Research (NCAER) which conducted a study on e-payment systems in India. They found out that 'Switching from cash to e-payment puts more money in the bank'. The study estimated that it cost a bank:

- ₹10 to process a cash withdrawal for a walk-in customer,
- ₹4 at an ATM, and
- ₹1 when a debit card is used at a merchant establishment.[3]

IMPORTANCE OF PLASTIC MONEY

Following are the reasons of preference for plastic money which explain its importance:

1. *Effective utilisation:* Plastic cards can be used online with a separate security number to prevent any misuse. This has resulted in increased usage by the individuals and it is more effective to carry out various transactions than with real money.

2. *Increasing reach:* Indian Railways, which runs one of the largest travel booking sites in Asia, offers home-delivery of train tickets if booked online using debit or credit cards. Therefore, plastic cards are now increasingly being used for various other purposes like paying school fees, hospitalisation, and medical expenses, etc.

3. *Utmost safety:* Safety standards followed by the Indian financial institutions to prevent misuse match the highest standards in the world. *For example,* any transaction above a particular sum is automatically referred to the issuing bank which calls up the cardholder within seconds on the mobile phone to confirm the purchase.

4. *Feature-oriented:* Product features are one of the best in the world. Almost all credit cards come with standard features such as free accident insurance, medical insurance at a heavy discount, and much more. The cardholder has the option of converting a big purchase made on credit card into a loan at a lower rate of interest spread over a long period. Banks now offer details of expenses incurred on credit cards under different heads—such as food, clothes and jewellery—to enable easier tracking by the customer.

---

2. https://www.deccanchronicle.com.op. cit.
3. http://indianexpress.com/article/business/banking-and-finance/10-15-pct-cards-used-only-for-online-transactions-rbi-report/April 23, 2014.

Figure 9.1 shows different types of plastic cards available in India.

Figure 9.1 Plastic Money

TYPES OF PLASTIC CARDS

Basically, debit cards and credit cards are the two types of plastic cards which represent monetary transactions. Apart from these are the Charge cards, in-store cards, Smart Cards, Add-on Cards and Petro cards.

Debit Card

Debit cards are substitutes for cash or cheque payments, much the same way that credit cards are. However, the bank issues debit card only if the person has an account in the bank. When a debit card is used to make a payment, the total amount charged is instantly deducted reduced from your bank balance.

A debit card is only accepted at outlets with electronic swipe machines that can check and deduct amounts from your bank balance online.

Following is the *mechanism* of a debit card:

- The debit card scheme requires the customer to open an account with the bank.
- The purchase amount is automatically deducted or debited from the account of the cardholder electronically and appears in the monthly account statement.

Credit Card

A *credit card* is the plastic money that is used to pay for products and services at over 20 million locations around the world. All you need to do is produce the card and sign a charge slip to pay for your purchases. The institution which issues the card makes the payment to the outlet on your behalf; you will pay this 'loan' back to the institution at a later date.

When you use a credit card you are not declared a defaulter even if you miss your due date. A 2.5–3% late payment fees (this differs from one bank to another) is levied in your next billing statement.

Following is the *modus-operandi* of credit cards:

- The cardholder can purchase without paying cash immediately.
- Generally, a limit is set to the amount of money a cardholder can spend.
- Once that limit is reached, he has to clear the earlier amount to get it going.
- The cardholder is issued a monthly statement of his transactions and he has to pay a percentage of outstanding, along with interest (30–36% per annum).

Charge Card

A *charge card* carries all the features of credit cards but after using the charge card, the entire payment of the bills has to be made by the due date. If you fail to do so, you are likely to be considered a defaulter and will have to pay up a steep late payment charge.

AMEX (American Express) and Diners Club cards are well-known branded charge cards. They have their own merchant establishments and tie-ups, and do not depend on the network of MasterCard or Visa. These cards are typically meant for the high income group categories and companies. Charge cards are not acceptable at many outlets but a wide variety of special privileges are enjoyed by the AMEX and Diners Club cardholders.

In-Store Card

It in-store card is issued by retailers or companies and it has currency only at the issuer's outlet for purchasing products of the issuer's company. The payment can be on a monthly or extended credit basis but for the latter, interest is charged.

Smart Card

A *smart card* contains an electronic chip which is used to store cash. This is most useful to pay for small purchases, for example in fairs, coffee shops, and the like. When a transaction is made using the card, the value is debited and the balance comes down automatically. Once the monetary value comes down to nil, the balance is to be restored all over again for the card to become operational. It is generally used for making purchases without necessarily requiring the authorisation of personal identification number (PIN) as in a debit card. No identification, signature or payment authorisation is required for using this card. This product is mostly available in developed countries like US.

Add-on Cards

Add-on cards are a privilege offered to the spouse, parents, children or other family members of the original cardholder. Normally, an issuing bank permits two add-on cards per credit card. All expenses incurred on an add-on card are billed to the primary cardholder.

Petro Cards

Some petroleum companies allow customers to pay for the fuel through electronic medium. It offers a scheme of gifting points to the customers when they pay for fuel using the *petro card*. It is a convenient, secured and speedy mode of transaction. IOC-Citibank and HPCL-ICICI bank are the co-branded petro cards available in the market.

DEBIT CARD INDUSTRY

Debit cards, also known as *check cards*, look like credit cards or ATM cards (Automated Teller Machine card). When a debit card is used at a merchant establishment, the merchant swipes card through an electronic point of sale (POS) terminal which is directly linked up with the debit card issuing bank and the cardholder's account immediately gets debited.

Debit cards are different from credit cards. Credit card is a way to 'pay later', whereas debit card is a way to 'pay now'. When we use a debit card, our money is quickly deducted from the bank account. Debit cards are accepted at many locations including grocery stores, retail stores, gasoline stations, and restaurants. It is an alternative to carrying a cheque book or cash. With debit card, we use our own money and not the issuer's money. In India, almost all the banks issue debit card to its account holders.

Features of a Debit Card

- Obtaining a debit card is often easier than obtaining a credit card.
- Using a debit card instead of writing cheques saves you from showing identification or giving out personal information at the time of transaction.
- A debit card frees you from carrying cash or a cheque book.
- With the help of a debit card, you no longer have to stock up on traveller's cheques or cash when you travel.
- Debit cards may be more readily accepted by merchants than cheques, especially in other states or countries wherever your card brand is accepted.
- The debit card is a quick, 'pay now' product, giving you no grace period.
- Using a debit card may mean you have less protection than with a credit card purchase for items which are never delivered, are defective, or were misrepresented.
- Returning goods or cancelling services purchased with a debit card is treated as if the purchases were made with cash or a cheque.

Tips for Responsible Use of Debit Card

- If your card is lost or stolen, report the loss to your bank immediately.
- If you suspect your card is being fraudulently used, report it to your bank immediately.

- Hold on to your receipts from your debit card transactions. A thief may get your name and debit card number from a receipt and order goods by mail or over the telephone. Your card does not have to be missing in order for it to be misused.
- If you have a Personal Identification Number (PIN), memorize it. Do not keep the PIN number with your card. Also, do not choose a PIN number that a smart thief could figure out, such as your phone number or birthday.
- Never give your PIN number to anyone. Always keep your PIN to yourself.
- Always be aware of how much money is available in your account. Do not forget that your debit card may allow you to access money that you have set aside to cover a cheque which has not been cleared by your bank yet.
- Keep your receipts in one place—for easy retrieval and better oversight of your bank account.

Debit Card Service Rewards

As consumers move in greater numbers from credit cards to debit cards—drawn by convenience and lack of interest fees—banks, in their interest, are beginning to offer more and more debit card services. Aside from the money they generate from one's debit card use, strengthening relationships with consumers through enticing debit card services can lead to opportunities to cross-sell other resources like savings accounts and certificates of deposit.

Credit card companies generally make more money off card transactions than banks do off debit card use, which means that debit card services have been less rewarding than those offered by credit cards. One tactic that banks are now taking even to the playing field is offering debit services for an annual fee, which allows them to offer rewards that match those offered by credit card companies. If you use your cards frequently, an annual fee of ₹100 to ₹200 can be well worth the rewards you will gain. Banks are focusing a lot of debit card services on partnerships with retailers, both online and at in-store locations, offering discounts or rewards much more generous than their regular rewards. In these arrangements, the retailer usually covers the costs, and so the rewards can be as much as 20–25%. What the retailer gains is the opportunity to track your buying patterns, so that they can offer you the targeted rewards. If you are comfortable trading this information for the discounts that result, this kind of service can be worth your while.

Some banks are beginning to offer cashback debit card services, i.e., you get a set number of points each month just for having a checking account. Some community banks and credit unions provide percentage earnings on your checking account depending on how many times you use your card per month.

With so many companies now competing for the customer's loyalty, it is worth doing some research into the variety of card services available before making the final choice.

THE CREDIT CARD INDUSTRY

Credit cards in India are gaining ground. Banks in India are encouraging people to use credit cards. In India, these cards became popular with the coming of foreign banks in the country. The concept of credit card was used in 1950 with the launch of charge cards in USA by Diners Club and American Express. Credit cards, however, became more popular with the use of magnetic strip in 1970. The first card was issued in India by Visa in 1981. The country's first Gold Card was also issued by Visa in 1986. The first international credit card was issued to a restricted number of customers by Andhra Bank in 1987 through the Visa program, after getting special permission from the Reserve Bank of India.

Major Banks Issuing Credit Cards in India

- State Bank of India
- Bank of Baroda
- Union Bank of India
- ICICI Bank
- HDFC Bank
- IDBI Bank
- Standard Chartered
- HSBC
- Citibank

Global Players in the Credit Card Market

MasterCard

MasterCard is a product of MasterCard International and along with VISA, is distributed by financial institutions around the world. Cardholders borrow money against a line of credit and pay it back with interest if the balance is carried over from month to month. Its products are issued by around 23,000 financial institutions in 220 countries and territories.

VISA Card

VISA Card, a product of VISA USA, along with MasterCard is distributed by financial institutions globally. A VISA cardholder borrows money against a credit line and repays the money with interest if the balance is carried over month to month in a revolving line of credit. Nearly 600 million cards carry one of the VISA brands and more than 14 million locations accept VISA cards.

American Express

The world's favourite card is American Express Credit Card. More than 57 million cards are in circulation; the demand has been growing and it is still growing further. American Express cards are very popular in the US, Canada, Europe and Asia, and are widely used in the retail and everyday expenses segment.

Diners Club International

It is the world's leading charge card providers. Diners Club cardholders reside all over the world and the Diners Card is an all-time favourite for corporates. There are more than 8 million Diners Club cardholders. They are affluent and frequent travellers in premier businesses and institutions including Fortune 500 companies and leading global corporations.

Different Variants of Credit Cards

A credit card may be of the following types:

1. ***Standard Card:*** It is a basic card.

2. ***Classic Card:*** It is the 'brand name' for the standard card issued by VISA.

3. ***Gold Card:*** It offers a higher credit than a standard card. Required income eligibility is also higher in this case. Moreover, the issuing company provides extra incentives to cardholders.

4. ***Platinum Card:*** It has a higher limit and additional perks than a gold card.

5. ***Titanium Card:*** It has an even higher credit than a platinum card.

Given below are some of the varieties of credit cards used in India:

- Canara Bank: Cancard
- BoB: Exclusive & Premium
- ANZ: Silver & Gold
- Citibank: Silver & Gold
- Citibank WWF Card
- Citibank Visa Card for Women
- Citibank Silver International Credit Card
- Citibank Gold International Credit Card
- Citibank Citi Diners Club Card
- HSBC: Classic & Gold
- ICICI Sterling Silver Credit Card
- ICICI Solid Gold Credit Card
- ICICI True Blue Credit Card
- SBI Card
- Stanchart—Classic & Gold

BENEFITS OF CREDIT CARDS

The issuers of credit cards have begun offering much more than just credit to the cardholders. The benefits offered include:

1. ***Personal accident insurance:*** Some issuers provide a free insurance cover to the cardholders against loss of life due to accidents.

2. ***Temporary increase in credit lines:*** Cardholders with a good credit recording can seek a temporary increase in their credit limits. For example, a Citi cardholder can increase his credit limit by 25% for 3 months.

3. ***Add-on facility:*** The spouse, or the parents, or children (over 18 years) of the cardholder are entitled to add-on cards on payment of an extra fee. In recent times, add-on facility is being given free of cost for the initial subscription year as an incentive. Otherwise, an annual fee is payable for the purpose of issuing and servicing an add-on credit card.

4. ***Rewards points:*** Most credit cards accumulate points on purchase which can be redeemed against gifts/discount coupons of shops/hotels/restaurants.

5. ***Affinity cards:*** These cards are issued by sponsor banks especially for a particular section of people who take pride in the vocation or alma mater making them periodically donate some amount to improve the cause they love.

6. ***International cards:*** Standard Chartered is known for issuing globally accepted cards in India, the payment for which is done in rupees. Now, every credit card, issued by all the banks in India is internationally accepted.

DRAWBACKS OF CREDIT CARDS

Credit cards should be used only as a standby, when there is an emergency. Financial security for the future is of utmost importance. Although majority of the adults realise that they should plan for their future, many people do not know how. There are some common mistakes people make that have serious consequences in the long run. There are "four most common mistakes" that people commit and become 'addicted' to using credit cards.

The *first mistake* people make is that they fail to pay themselves first. As soon as you get your pay cheque a minimum of 10% should be put into savings. Regardless of the debt that you are financing, that 10% savings is crucial to yourself one day being solvent and on your way to a very healthy financial future.

The *next common mistake* people make is carrying a credit card balance. Credit card debt typically comes with high interest and can quickly spiral out of control. It is essential to pay off all your debt starting with the highest interest bearing debt. In order to do this quickly, you must pay down more than the minimum payment every month. Put as much money as possible into eliminating that debt and you will save yourself thousands of dollars in interest payments over the years.

The *third most common mistake* people make is not having an emergency fund. An emergency fund is the money that should be put away equivalent to at least three to six months worth of your cost of living. It is essential to be prepared for the loss of a job, medical expenses or major repairs to either a car or your home.

The *fourth most common mistake* that people make is living beyond their means. Today, people want to gratify all their desires immediately. Unfortunately, for most of the people this is not possible and hence, they end up paying for vacations, cars and other big ticket items with credit. Except for a house and possibly a car, there is nothing else that should ever be bought on credit.

Table 9.1 presents a comparative picture of the debit card and credit card.

TABLE 9.1 Comparative Picture of Debit and Credit Card

Factors	*Debit Card*	*Credit Card*
Nature	It is a 'pay now product'	It is a 'pay later product'
Mode of operation	Money is automatically deducted from the account	Money has to be paid afterwards.
Requirement of a bank a/c for cardholder	Compulsory	Optional
Type of financing	Owned money	Consumer loan
Basis of alternative	Alternative to a cheque or cash	No such alternative
Membership fees	₹ 50–250 (might vary)	₹ 250–2000 (might vary)
Annual charges	₹ 50–300 (might vary)	₹ 200–2000 (might vary)
Default chances for bankers	Zero	Substantial
Recovery cost of bankers	Zero	Substantial
Cost incurred by the customer	Zero	2–3% per month interest is charged if not paid on time. This might vary with the bank.

PREVENTION OF FRAUDS/MISUSE OF CREDIT CARDS

When you possess a credit card, it is important that you keep them safe.

Ways to Prevent Credit Card Frauds

In today's capitalist-driven society, credit cards are a way of life. Using credit cards wisely can even benefit a person by helping them build a good credit rating which is essential when applying for loans, renting vehicles or staying in a hotel. Credit card fraud is a problem that is now flourishing due to sophisticated scams and credit card theft. Most credit card frauds involve lost or stolen credit cards. There are ways to prevent credit card fraud and are must always be cautious to take steps to ensure the security of your cards. Following are a few ways to guard against credit card fraud:

- Do not carry more than two credit cards with you at all times.
- Always keep copies of your credit cards' toll free numbers with you.
- Do not leave your purse or wallet unattended in public.
- Make sure that you get your credit card back after buying something.
- Do not keep your cards in an obvious place in your home.
- As soon as you receive your card, make sure to sign it in ink.

- Never let anyone borrow your card.
- If you do not receive new or reissued cards by the due date, call the credit card company and report it immediately.
- If possible, make sure that only you and your postal carrier have access to your mail box.
- Shred all credit card receipts and pre-approved credit card offers before throwing them away and keep your billing statements in a secure place.
- Cut the credit card into several pieces once you close your account.
- When making online purchases, make sure that it is a secure website.
- Under no circumstances should one ever give his/her credit card number to anyone over the phone.

By following these simple strategies, one can enjoy the benefits of credit cards to the fullest.

Selecting a Credit Card

Looking for a credit card is always an exciting task as the lure of credit is powerful. However, when planning to buy a credit card, it is necessary to keep a few things in mind. Since good credit is almost a basic need for survival in our economy, it is good to shop around before signing up with the first credit card company you come across. Credit cards are big business and there is a lot of competition to choose from, so choose wisely.

It is always best to look for a credit card with a trusted financial institution; this way you are assured of stability and are at a very low risk of frauds and misuse.

The next thing to look for in a credit card is low interest rate. Currently, there are many low interest credit cards in the market. However, most credit card companies will not offer these low interest cards immediately, instead they will only offer these to clients who ask for them. Look for companies who have great introductory offers such as no interest on transfer balances for six months as incentives to lure clients away from their competition.

Another thing to look for in a credit card is the fees charged. There is no reason to pay user fees on a credit card that already charges interest—this is relevant especially if you do not plan on carrying a balance. Some privileged credit cards charge an annual fee for added benefits such as increased air miles or a larger insurance coverage, but in general, credit cards should not charge annual fees.

Today, many cards offer their clients perks and benefits. Air miles, points towards merchandise, hotels, gas, car rentals, etc. Opt for a credit card that is best suited towards your lifestyle and interests. Some credit cards even offer to personalise your card by embossing it with a design of your choice. With so much selection among credit cards, there is no reason to be stuck with a high interest card that gives nothing in return.

Do's and Don'ts of Credit Cards

Here are some usage tips for credit cardholders.

Do's

- Sign on the signature panel on the reverse of the card with a non-erasable ball-point pen (preferably in black ink). This will ensure that the benefits of membership are wholly and solely yours.
- Draw a line through blank spaces on charge or debit slips above the total so the amount cannot be changed.
- Save your receipts to check against your monthly statements.
- Cut up old cards—cut through the account number before disposing them off.
- Open monthly statements promptly and compare them with your receipts. Report mistakes or discrepancies to the special address listed on your statement for inquiries as soon as possible.
- Keep a record of your account numbers, expiration dates, and the telephone numbers of each card issuer in a safe place separate from your cards so that you can report a loss quickly.
- Carry only those cards that you anticipate you will need.

Don'ts

- Bending the card.
- Exposure to electronic devices and gadgets.
- Direct exposure to sunlight.
- Be cautious about disclosing your account number over the phone to strangers.
- Never put your account number on the outside of an envelope or on a postcard.
- Do not sign a blank charge or debit slip.

Reasons for Credit Card being Rejected at Retail Outlet

- One may have exceeded the borrowing limit or defaulted (constantly) on minimum payment due.
- The card has crossed its expiration date.
- Non-receipt of dues of one-card blocks future transactions on any other card(s) held of the same card-issuing bank.
- The magnetic stripe on the reverse of the card is damaged, i.e. it has been scratched or exposed to continuous heat/direct sunlight or magnetic field—like card kept near a TV set/other electronic appliances.
- Systems or technology failures have, in rare instances, also led to non-acceptance of cards when swiped through an electronic terminal.

TERMINOLOGY USED IN PLASTIC MONEY

Certain terms connoted to plastic money and its usage are given below:

Card Issuers

Card issuers are the banks issuing plastic cards to the consumers. Banks charge about 2–2.5% commission from Member Establishments (MEs) selling goods and services through credit cards. For the customers, banks offer a credit period of 30–45 days but charge around 3% on all outstanding amount on expiry of the credit period.

Cardholders

Cardholders include both salaried individuals and business organisations. The eligibility criteria for an individual to acquire plastic money are predicated on the basis of annual incomes.

Member Establishment (MEs)

Member Establishments (MEs) are organisations enlisted by the plastic money issuer who accept valid credit cards towards payment for the goods sold or services rendered by them in lieu of cash. MEs include retail outlets, departmental stores, restaurants, hotels, hospitals, travel agencies, garages, petrol pumps, co-operative societies, etc. While enlisting MEs, factors like their reputation, integrity, standing and popularity are taken into consideration. Based on the type of business, location, turnover, etc., the floor limit for MEs is fixed. However, MEs like Indian Airlines or Indian Railways do not pay discount to the issuer and in such cases, the issuer card collects a transaction fee for the cardholder.

Member Affiliates (MAs)

Sometimes, the issuer may enter into a tie-up for issuance of credit card. In such cases, the organisations which have tie-ups also issue credit cards of the issuer to their clients. These organisations are called *Member Affiliates*. Credit cards issued by MAs are similar to those issued by the issuer, except that they contain the name and logo of the MA on the face of the card, besides the issuer's name and logo. This agreement enlarges the scope and operations of the plastic money.

Charge Slip

A *charge slip* is a voucher (debit) which is an evidence of the cardholder using the card and consents for the indebtedness of the amount mentioned therein. It is prepared in triplicate by the member establishment and signed by the customer/cardholder in token of acknowledgement of receipt of goods and/or services in the amount of total shown thereon and agrees to perform the obligations set forth in the cardholder's agreement with the issuer.

RBI'S REGULATION OF CONDUCT OF PLASTIC CARD BUSINESS

RBI came out with Master Direction for "Credit Card and Debit Card Issuance and Conduct" in 2022 in the public interest. These are discussed below in brief.[4]

4. *Master Direction—Credit Card and Debit Card—Issuance and Conduct Directions, 2022*, https://rbi.org.in/Scripts/BS_ViewMasDirections.aspx?id=12300, April 21, 2022.

A. CONDUCT OF CREDIT CARD BUSINESS

Eligibility

(a) Scheduled Commercial Banks (SCBs) other than Regional Rural Banks (RRBs) with net worth of ₹100 crore and above are permitted to undertake credit card business either independently or in tie-up arrangement with other card issuing banks/NBFCs with the approval of their Boards. SCBs (excluding Small Finance Banks and Regional Rural Banks) desirous of setting up separate subsidiaries for undertaking credit card business shall require prior approval of the Reserve Bank.

(b) RRBs are permitted to issue credit cards in collaboration with their sponsor bank or other banks.

(c) Financially sound and well managed Scheduled Urban Cooperative Banks (UCBs) with minimum net worth of ₹100 crore which are CBS enabled may issue Credit Cards subject to the given conditions in addition to the other general conditions applicable to credit cards.

(d) Non-Banking Financial Companies registered with the Reserve Bank shall not undertake credit card business without prior approval of the Reserve Bank. Any company including a non-deposit taking company intending to engage in this activity shall require a Certificate of Registration, apart from specific permission to enter into this business, the pre-requisite for which is a minimum net owned fund of ₹100 crore and subject to such terms and conditions as the Reserve Bank may specify in this regard from time to time. Without obtaining prior approval from the Reserve Bank, NBFCs shall not issue debit cards, credit cards, charge cards, or similar products virtually or physically.

Governance Framework

(a) Each card-issuer shall have a well-documented Board approved policy for the issuance and conduct of credit cards. The Board approved policy shall be in consonance with various instructions on the subject issued by the Reserve Bank from time to time, as well as the directions contained in this Master Direction. The Board approved policy shall be available on the website of the card-issuer.

(b) Card-issuers shall put in place a mechanism for review of their credit card operations on half-yearly basis by the Audit Committee of the Board of Directors. The review shall include, inter-alia, customer service, frauds, complaints and grievance redressal, card usage analysis including cards not used for long durations and the inherent risks therein.

B. ISSUE OF DEBIT CARD BY BANKS

(a) Banks shall formulate a comprehensive debit cards issuance policy with the approval of their Boards and issue debit cards to their customers in accordance with this policy. Prior approval of the Reserve Bank is not necessary for banks desirous of issuing debit cards to their customers.

(b) Debit cards shall only be issued to customers having Savings Bank/Current Accounts.

(c) No bank shall issue debit cards to cash credit/loan account holders. However, it will not preclude the banks from linking the overdraft facility provided along with Pradhan Mantri Jan Dhan Yojana accounts with a debit card.

(d) Banks shall not force a customer to avail debit card facility and shall not link issuance of debit card to availment of any other facility from the bank.

CHALLENGES FACED BY THE PLASTIC MONEY INDUSTRY

There are a number of issues and challenges faced by the plastic money industry. Let us analyse them.

1. Plastic Money Problems Create Pressures

Credit label debt service is what each debt-struck credit label hilt is seeking for. Credit label debt service is not only about shortening or expelling credit label debt, it is, in addition, about removing the stress.

There have been no products in the market which can give much happiness as credit label debt service. So, if we have been refraining from purchases, we should not, all of a sudden, begin purchasing all those prime products which we had been avoiding. The endorsement for post credit label debt service duration has been more than achieving credit label debt relief. Here are five useful tips regarding this:

1. Plan your losses regulating a monthly budget.
2. Do not buy anything which you do not need.
3. Do not go for too many credit cards (just a single or dual should be sufficient).
4. Always have full payments of your credit label, and do it prior the due date.
5. Never make use of more than 60–70% of the credit limit accessible to you.

2. Is Plastic Money for Real?

Plastic money entered the Indian market promising a cashless society, but if we evaluate it after a decade, certain deviations are easily seen—like the change in focus from cashless society to plastic money as a debt instrument. As a new product, people used to flash colourful cards. However, the present plastic money definitely lacks sufficient infrastructure, as pointed out in the following:

Fundamental Flaws

Plastic money was designed to help society overcome the hassles of carrying excessive cash but it has been misdirected by the multinational banks at middle-class segment (around 200 million people) in India.

Almost every bank in India has introduced credit cards and every card issuer is claiming superiority over the other. Extravagant use of cards has resulted in increasing suicides worldwide. Being a revolving credit, it may lead everyone to a debt trap.

Ill-informed Sales Team

Almost every bank is selling cards through their Direct Sales Associates (DSA). DSAs work on the basis of commissions. Generally, the sales team comprises of non-finance background graduates and undergraduates with hardly a week's training, and having very little knowledge about charges and interest rates. They target people with poor financial awareness to make good business. This is an unhealthy trend and creates growing problems for the customers.

Ineffective Automated Teller Machines (ATMs)

These machines are the backbone of plastic money but have their own limitations too. The user's transaction requests can be repeatedly denied due to failure of network, or non-availability of cash, or non-availability of specific currency. Also, there have been instances when machines go wrong, thereby debiting excess or lesser amount from a customer's account or crediting lesser or more amount than requested by a customer.

3. High Interest Rates

Despite slashing of interest rates, the interest rate charged to the cardholder on the outstanding amounts beyond the due date more or less remains the same. Most card issuers highlight the monthly rate of interest charged by them. It might sound low at 3%, but when you look at the effective annual interest rate, it turns out to be as high as 40%.

4. Poor Domestic Outlet Penetration

There are more than six million cards are in the market with an average growth of 30%, but the domestic penetration of online transaction machines is very poor. Only shops catering to the higher class segment of customers have transaction machines. Still, for essential items such as vegetables, milk, etc., the payment is accepted only in cash. Banks are also not really catering to these areas as most of them are servicing only the metros.

CASE STUDY

True Story of a Victim

About two years ago, Arbind Koul, a PSU executive working in Delhi, was approached by one of the marketing executives of Standard Chartered Bank who convinced him to apply for a credit card of their bank.

After some time, Arbind received a copy of the 'Credit Card Statement' in his name with an amount of ₹33,315 being debited to his account in respect of three commercial transactions taken place on 19th September, 1999. This statement also carried the number of the credit card that had never been delivered to him. The matter was checked up with 'BankCard Customer Service Center' of the bank at New Delhi office whereby it was confirmed that the card was not delivered to him and it had been fraudulently used during the delivery stage, probably by the courier agency.

Meanwhile, the said customer service center advised him to send an affidavit to this effect which he submitted on 24th December, 1999 in the performa sent to him.

The said affidavit was addressed to the bank's Bangalore branch as well as New Delhi office, as advised by the bank cell. However, since then, the banks' executives had visited Arbind's residence from time to time. Every time, he was assured that the matter would be closed and that no one in future would visit him but, this was not the end. He was served a notice by the bank through their legal consultants vide letter dated 3rd March, 2000 advising him to clear his outstanding and also to contact the bank manager, who was looking after the case. However, on approaching the bank, he was once again assured that no such thing would occur in future and that the case stood closed.

But, the case remained open even after that as the bank employees continued to visit him. After some time, he was again contacted by the bank's legal consultants who wanted to inquire about the case. After these experiences, Arbind said that he was too scared to even glance at credit cards. Of late, Arbind was planning to fight a legal battle against the bank.

It can be easily concluded that plastic money has its own set of shortcomings but, it is of immense use in an emergency; one is free from the hassle of carrying cash, and the like. These shortcomings, however, need immediate attention.

Source: http://www.financialexpress.com/story.php?id=50720.

POINTS TO REMEMBER

- Plastic money is an alternative to cash or the 'standard money'. It is used to refer to debit cards or credit cards that we use to make purchases in our everyday life.
- The growth in the use of plastic money, mainly debit and credit cards during the last couple of years in India, has been phenomenal. Clothes, dining, jewellery and travelling are the top four purchases that Indians make through plastic cards.
- Plastic money is preferred on account of—(i) effective utilisation, (ii) increasing reach, (iii) safety, and (iv) feature orientation.
- Debit cards are substitutes for cash or cheque payments, and when a debit card is used to make a payment, the total amount charged is instantly deducted from the bank balance.
- A credit card is the plastic money that is used to pay for products and services at a later date.
- A charge card is similar to a credit card except the entire payment of the bills has to be made by the due date. AMEX (American Express) and Diners Club cards are well-known branded charge cards.
- A smart card contains an electronic chip which is used to store cash. This is most useful to pay for small purchases, for example, in fairs, coffee shops, etc.
- Global players in credit card market are MasterCard, VISA Card, American Express and Diners Club International.
- The most common mistakes that people make in using credit cards are—(i) failing

to pay themselves first, (ii) carrying a credit card balance, (iii) not having an emergency fund, and (iv) living beyond their means.

- Card issuers are the banks issuing plastic cards to the consumers.
- Cardholders include both salaried individuals and business organisations.
- Member Establishments (MEs) are organisations enlisted by the plastic money issuer who accept valid credit cards towards payment for the goods sold or services rendered by them in lieu of cash.
- Member Affiliates (MAs) are the organisations having tie-ups with the main issuer and issue credit cards of the issuer to their clients.
- RBI came out with Master Direction for "Credit Card and Debit Card Issuance and Conduct" in 2022 in the public interest.
- The plastic money industry creates pressures and debate about its real need for a common man.

KEY TERMS

- **Plastic money** is an alternative to the cash or the 'standard money' and refers to the credit cards or the debit cards that we use to make purchases in our everyday life.
- **Debit card** is the plastic money that is used to pay instantly for the purchases from your bank account.
- **Credit card** is the plastic money that is used to pay for products and services at a later date.
- **Charge card** is similar to credit card except that the entire payment has to be made by the due date.
- **Member Establishments (MEs)** are organisations accepting valid credit cards towards payment for the goods sold or services rendered by them in lieu of cash.
- **Member Affiliates (MAs)** are the organisations having tie-ups with the main issuer and issue credit cards of the issuer to their clients.

EXERCISES

Objective Questions

1. **Tick the correct answer:**

   (a) The main function of plastic money is to:

   (i) Provide funds (ii) Replace funds
   (iii) Facilitate purchases (iv) All of the above

   (b) ATM stands for:

   (i) Automated Teller Machine (ii) Any Time Money
   (iii) Anti-theft Machine (iv) None of the above

(c) In-Store card has a:
  (i) Limited applicability (ii) Unlimited applicability
  (iii) Unlimited appeal (iv) None of the above

(d) A smart card is used to:
  (i) Save codes (ii) Store cash
  (iii) Keep identity (iv) None of the above

(e) Add-on cards are:
  (i) Additional (ii) Exclusive
  (iii) Specific (iv) None of the above

Answers: (a) iv (b) i (c) i (d) ii (e) i

2. Fill in the blanks:

(a) Plastic money is an alternative to the ....
(b) .... offers home-delivery of train tickets if booked online using debit or credit cards.
(c) The use of .... is subject to the bank balance.
(d) .... always has a limit of spending.
(e) .... is a basic card.
(f) .... are cost-free for customers.
(g) .... is an organisation which accepts valid credit cards towards payment for the goods sold or services.

Answers:

(a) Cash
(b) Indian railways
(c) Debit card
(d) Credit card
(e) Standard card
(F) Debit cards
(g) Member Establishment

3. True or False:

(a) Plastic money is a substitute for plastic goods.
(b) Debit and credit cards are called plastic money because they have plastic used in their making.
(c) Credit card means 'pay later'.
(d) Debit card means 'pay now'.
(e) Charge card and credit card are similar.
(f) Titanium card is the card with highest credit.
(g) It is compulsory to have a bank account for credit card.
(h) Default chances for bank in case of dent card are zero.
(i) Member Affiliate is a tie-up body with Member Establishment

Answers: (a) False (b) True (c) True (d) True (e) False
(f) True (g) False (h) True (i) True

Short Questions

1. Define plastic money.
2. State two types of plastic cards.
3. Distinguish between debit card and credit card.
4. What are the different variants of a credit card?
5. List key requirements before choosing a credit card.

Critical Thinking Questions

1. "Plastic money is an alternative to cash or the 'standard money'". Discuss.
2. "Charge card is a clone card of credit card". Explain.
3. "Indian credit cards industry has undergone a phenomenal change during the last two decades". Justify.
4. "Credit cards are encouraged but with caution". Elaborate with suitable illustrations.
5. "Plastic money has changed the definition of cash". Discuss.
6. "Credit cards have led to disguised sending by a common man". Critique.
7. "Debit card is real money but credit card is shadow money". Explain.
8. "Cards services industry is considered to be existing in vacuum". Do you agree?

Descriptive Questions

1. Discuss the growth of plastic money services in India.
2. What are the advantages of using plastic cards?
3. Discuss the different types of plastic cards with examples.
4. What are the various financial services which are operating in India?
5. Explain the various benefits offered with credit cards.
6. What are the common pitfalls people commit while using credit cards?
7. How can credit card fraud be prevented?
8. List some do's and don'ts of credit cards.
9. Discuss the tips for responsible use of debit cards.
10. What are the major issues and challenges faced by the plastic money industry?

PROJECT EXERCISE

Evaluation of Fast-changing Indian Plastic Card Industry

Every day, there is a new plastic card in the market which lures the customer with its add-on features. Review the plastic cards industry in India regarding the past set of cards floating and the new cards emerged out during the last three years. Compare and contrast them with respect to their features and suitability for a common Indian. Find out the growth trends of plastic money in India in the coming times.

REVIEW CASE

Mindcard Application

Ravi was an IT professional who was retrenched at the age of 52 after working with the same company for 30 years. His wife was a home-maker and they had two children. The elder was at university, and the younger was in class 8th at secondary school.

He intended to get another job following a four-week family break but it was not an easy task. He was also overlooked for the few positions available in favour of younger candidates. He had a large mortgage and all his past savings had finished. He had even used all of his PF amount. He was now facing a tough time to make both ends meet.

He and his wife both had credit cards which they did not use for very long. They had heard a lot of fancy stories about its usage, like "vendors no longer need to ask if you can spare any kronor. They take credit cards". In the most cashless society on the planet, sellers often accept these portable cards for payments from customers. Therefore, due to shortage of cash fund, both husband and wife started using their credit cards for most of their purchases. Their previous "good credit rating" from the past provided them with access to new lines of credit with very few questions asked.

They forgot that though credit cards have advantages, they can also be dangerous. One has to make sure that he/she is aware of the dangers in order to use them properly and not get into trouble. The biggest danger of credit card debt is that the interest rates charged on these cards is extremely high. It can always create problems for you because the amount that you owe grows fast. Another great danger of credit card debt is that it can completely destroy your credit quickly. Miss a few payments and the damage is done. One danger of credit card debt is that people are not able to save any money. There are a lot of people who are unable to save for retirement because of the money that they owe to the credit card companies. Perhaps, the biggest danger of credit card debt is simply the fact that it allows you to spend money that you cannot afford. Of course, it will all blow up in your face eventually since you do have to be able to pay the money back.

Ravi and his wife also had a similar experience. Their credit card debts and associated interest began to build up to a massive level. Looking at his monthly statement, he found out that he has been falsely charged for one of the purchases, and for another transaction, the amount was invariantly higher, but his situation kept him quiet about what was happening. He planned to settle it out by paying the growing debts once he finds a new job.

Meanwhile, he contacted a financial counsellor who prepared a current financial statement that revealed he had purchased some shares in the past. The financial counsellor encouraged him to sell the shares and pay the proceeds off the credit card debt. He also helped him to work out a plan to reduce his credit card debt by paying the card with the highest interest rate first, and cutting up all but one credit card that was only to be used in case of emergencies.

After several months, Ravi managed to get a job, though a low paid one compared to what he had been used to but the income was enough for him to cover day-to-day expenses and to work out payment plans with his creditors. He promised himself to use credit card more judiciously in a planned manner for future.

Issues for Discussion

1. Discuss the suitability of credit card as a means of finance in the present context.
2. What is the process of credit rating used by credit card companies?
3. Is the credit limit always fixed? Can credit limit be changed according to the requirements?
4. What is the status of a defaulter in case of credit card?
5. What is the remedial action for the cardholder in case of any discrepancy in his balances by the company?
6. What is 'restructuring of debt' as highlighted in the above case?
7. Discuss means of finance other than credit card for transactional purposes.

REFERENCES

Davies Glyn (2002), *A History of Money from Ancient Times to the Present Day*, University of Wales Press, Cardiff, UK.

Jaffery, S.A. (1990), "The Feasibility of Plastic Money in Pakistan", *Economic Review*, **21**, No. 3.

Newlyn, W.T. (1962), *Theory of Money*, Clarendon Press, Oxford.

Rowlingson, K. and Kempson, E. (1994), *Paying with Plastic: A Study of Credit Card Debt*, Policy Studies Institute, London.

www.bettermoneyskills.com

www.cashzilla.co.uk

https://www.deccanchronicle.com

www.financialexpress.com

www.indianexpress.com

www.rbidocs.rbi.org.in

www.rbi.org.in

www.thehindubusinessline.com

CHAPTER 10

Home Loans

The 2009 stimulus law got the ball rolling, allowing the agency to reduce and eliminate fees and raise loan guarantees to 90% of the total. I knew that we had the opportunity to use S.B.A. products to fill that gap in a rapid manner, as we ended up doing in the Recovery Act.

— **Karen Mills**

LEARNING OBJECTIVES

This chapter discusses the following:

- Concept of home loan
- Evolution of home loan
- Costs of home loan
- Types of home loans
- Innovative home loans
- Reforms in Indian housing loan sector

INTRODUCTION

The retail banking has been one of the most profit-oriented areas for the Indian banks. In the retail banking, housing sector has been the most promising segment, expected to grow about 30% for the next five years. In financial year 2022, banks in India advanced around two trillion Indian rupees in housing loans. This reflected increasing homebuyer sentiment, as a higher number of Indians were investing in buying residential property.[1] With the government keen on infrastructure development and announcing various tax sops, housing loan segment is a tempted area for many

1. https://www.statista.com/statistics/1201678/india-housing-loans-before-and-during-covid-19-pandemic/266

banks to enter. Housing sector is present as both organised and unorganised segments, with the unorganised segment accounting for over 75% of the housing units constructed.

During the past couple of years, the housing sector has grown phenomenally, due to the support from growing housing finance industry. India's housing finance industry mainly comprises of Banks and Housing Finance Companies (HFCs), and to a certain limited extent, smaller institutions in the form of community organisations, self-help groups, etc. The National Housing Bank (NHB) is the principal agency for promoting, regulating and providing financial and other support to HFCs at local and regional levels, while banks and NBFCs are managed and regulated by the RBI. As per NHB, on 27th May, 2022, 73 HFCs with asset size of ₹100 crore and above were there in India.[2]

HOME LOAN

Home loan is a 'secured loan' offered against the security of a house/property by the bank. In other words, housing loan is a loan taken by a borrower from the bank against the property intended to be bought by him. This provides the bank with a conditional ownership over the property, i.e. if the borrower fails to pay back the loan, the bank can recover its lent money by selling the property.

Key Features

1. *Purpose:* For purchase of house from the builder/resale and construction/extension of existing house.

2. *Loan amount:* One can avail home loans up to 80–90% of the home value, depending on his eligibility, income and repayment capacity.

3. *Type:* Home loan is a secured loan wherein collateral is required.

4. *Loan tenure:* The maximum loan tenure is normally 20 years.

Let us calculate the home loan eligibility amount with the help of an example:

At an interest rate of 9.75% per annum, the monthly instalment of ₹1 lac amount, 20-year loan is ₹949.

Banks then calculate your loan eligibility using a simple formula:

$$\text{Home loan eligibility in lacs} = \frac{\text{Amount determined by the bank as available for loan repayment}}{\text{Loan instalment per lac for the selected tenure}}$$

Suppose amount available for loan = 50% of monthly disposable income (₹50,000)

= ₹25,000

Then, Loan Eligibility = (25,000/949) × 1,00,000 = ₹ 26,34,352 lacs

2. https://nhb.org.in/wp-content/uploads/2022/11/Asset-Size-as-on-March-31-2022-English.pdf

HOUSING FINANCE EVOLUTION

Historically, the housing finance industry was dominated by HFCs. Housing Development Finance Corporation (HDFC) was the first housing finance company to setup operations in India in 1977. NHB came into existence with the passing of National Housing Bank Act, 1987, as a subsidiary of the Reserve Bank of India (RBI) to regulate housing finance companies and provide them with refinancing to supplement their fund requirements.

Public sector banks were allowed to provide housing loans directly to retail clients only in 1988. Therefore, towards the end of the 1990s, the scheduled commercial banks became very active in lending to the housing sector on account of lower interest rates, rising disposable incomes, stable property prices and fiscal incentives by the government. While banks depend primarily on their deposits for funding their housing loan portfolios, HFCs primarily depend on funding sources such as loans from banks and financial institutions, financing from NHB, borrowing through bonds and debentures, commercial paper, subordinate debt and fixed deposits from public, besides their own capital. Increased competition in the housing finance industry has also led to the introduction of new mortgage products in the market such as variable interest rate loans, loan for repairs and renovation, and customised products with features like ballooning EMI, as per the need and eligibility of the borrowers concerned.

Table 10.1 shows the comparative picture of home loan interest rates of leading Indian banks.

TABLE 10.1 Home Loan Interest Rates Comparative Picture in India as on 1st February, 2023

Bank Name	*Floating Interest rate*	*Per lac EMI*	*Benchmark Rates on*	*Processing Fee*	*Prepayment Charges*
SBI	8.60%–9.40%	₹812–₹867	7.70%	50% off till 31.09.2022	Nil
ICICI Bank	8.75%–9.80%	₹822–₹895	7.90%	3000 + Tax	N.A
HDFC Ltd.	8.65%–9.35%	₹815–₹863	16.95%	3000 + Tax (Salaried), 5000 + Tax (S. Employed)	Nil
LIC Housing	8.65%–10.25%	₹815–₹926	15.80%	Below 1 Cr: Upto ₹10,000 + AT Above 1 Cr: ₹20,000 + AT	Nil
Bank of Baroda	8.45%–9.80%	₹802–₹895	8.15%– 9.15%	0.25% of loan amount Min. ₹1000 and Max. ₹20,000	N.A
Piramal Housing Finance	9.50%	₹874	N.A	0.10%–0.25% (GST)	N.A
AXIS Bank	8.60%–9.05%	₹812–₹843	8.05%	Up to 1% of the Loan amount subject to minimum of ₹10,000	Nil

(Contd.)

Bank Name	*Floating Interest rate*	*Per lac EMI*	*Benchmark Rates on*	*Processing Fee*	*Prepayment Charges*
IDBI	8.00%–11.15%	₹772–₹991	7.85%	NIL	Nil
Union Bank of India	7.90%–9.60%	₹765–₹881	7.70%	0.50% of loan amount subject to a maximum of 15,000 + GST	Nil
Bank of India	7.80%–9.65%	₹759–₹884	7.60%	0.25% of loan amount Min. ₹1,000 and Max. ₹20,000	Nil
Bank of Maharastra	7.80%–9.70%	₹759–₹888	7.50%	As per applicable	Nil
L&T Housing Finance	8.35%	₹795		0.25% plus taxes (for salaried and for self employed)	Nil
Tata Capital Housing Finance Ltd.	7.75%			Up to 0.5% of loan amount + GST	N.A
HSBC Bank	7.44%–7.55%	₹735–₹742	7.80%	N.A	Nil
Allahabad Bank	7.40%–8.15%	₹732–₹782	8.45%	N.A	Nil
Central Bank of India	6.85%–7.30%	₹697–₹726	7.50%	0.50% of the Loan Amount subject to maximum ₹20,000	N.A
UCO Bank	7.15%–7.25%	₹716–₹723	7.55%	0.5% of the loan amount, minimum ₹1500 and maximum ₹15,000	N.A
Canara Bank	8.60%–10.80%	₹812–₹966	7.65%	0.50% of loan amount + GST	
Kotak Bank	8.30%–8.90%	₹792–₹832	8.10%	Upto 1.25% of Loan amount	Nil
First Blue Home Finance	10.25% (for Salaried/ SEP), 10.75% (for Self Employed)	₹926 (for Salaried/ SEP), ₹962 (for Self Employed)		Salaried: Up to 30 lacs: 7300 30–75 lacs: 11,800 75 lacs and above: 15,000 + service tax (12.36%)	Nil
Syndicate Bank	7.30%–9.25%	₹726–₹856	8.65%	N.A	N.A
Citibank	8.50% onwards	₹805 onwards	6.50%	₹5000 (Application fee)	Nil

(Contd.)

Bank Name	*Floating Interest rate*	*Per lac EMI*	*Benchmark Rates on*	*Processing Fee*	*Prepayment Charges*
Punjab National Bank	8.40%–9.55%	₹798–₹877	7.65%	0.50% of loan + GST	Nil
Indian Bank	8.40%–8.50%	₹798–₹805	8.20%–8.55%	0.230% on loan amount + GST or Max. ₹20,470	Nil
Oriental Bank of Commerce	7.00%–7.60%	₹707–₹746	8.65%	0.50% of the loan amount, subject to maximum of ₹20,000 plus GST	Nil
Federal Bank	9.05%–9.20%	₹843–₹853	8.50%	Up to ₹7500 + GST	N.A
PNB Home Loan	7.90%–8.55%	₹765–₹809		0.50% or 10,000 + GST, whichever is higher.	Nil
Andhra Bank	8.40%–8.60%	₹862–₹874	8.40%	0.50% of the loan amount or maximum of ₹10,000 + service tax	N.A
Andhra Bank	8.40%–8.60%	₹799–₹812	8.40%	0.50% of the loan amount or maximum of ₹10,000 + service tax	N.A
GIC Housing Finance	8.20%		15.00%	₹2500 + GST	N.A
India Infoline Housing Finance Ltd.	9.00%	₹839		Up to 1% of loan amount + GST	N.A
Karnataka Bank	8.24%–10.31%	₹788–₹931	8.30%	N.A	N.A
Reliance Home Finance Private Ltd.	9.75%–13.00%	₹891–₹1128	18.40% PLR	Up to 2% + GST	N.A
Repco Home Finance Ltd.	7.70%–10.40%	₹752–₹937	8.75%	1% of loan amount + GST	N.A

Source: https://www.deal4loans.com/home-loans-interest-rates.php
Note: The above figures are for loan amount up to ₹20 lacs with tenure of 25 years.

BOX 10.1: MARGINAL COST OF FUNDS BASED LENDING RATE (MCLR)

Marginal Cost of Funds based Lending Rate (MCLR) is a new methodology introduced by RBI for setting lending rates by commercial banks. It has modified the existing base-rate system from April 2016 onwards. MCLR will be the internal benchmark of lending rates and based upon this, the interest rate for different types of customers will be fixed as per their degree of risk.

The MCLR should be revised monthly by considering some new factors including the repo rate and other borrowing rates. Now, banks have to set five benchmark rates for different tenures or time periods ranging from overnight (one day) rates to one year.

BASIC COSTS OF A HOME LOAN

One should have a good understanding of the various costs and savings out of a home loan in order to determine its total cost. The cost of the loan not only includes the interest to be paid but it also covers several other costs which can be summed up as follows:

(i) *Processing fee*

The processing fee is payable at that time when you apply for the home loan. As this fee in not refundable at all, it is charged to cover the administration costs incurred by the bank for inspecting your loan taking eligibility. The banks charge from a few thousand rupees to a percentage of the applied loan amount.

(ii) *Administration fee*

This is the next added fee charged. When the loan amount is sanctioned to you, at the same time the administration fee is charged. It is charged at the time when the process goes to the loan disbursement. It ranges from 0.25%–1% of the total sanctioned loan amount.

(iii) *Legal cost*

These are the costs which are incurred by the bank related to the legal expenses and are passed to you as the legal costs. This is because during the processing of a home loan application, the banks go through a legal evaluation of the property.

Key Points to be Considered while Applying for Home Loan

- Firstly, the person applying for the home loan should have at least 20%–40% of the price of the home loan to be paid as the down payment. For the remaining payment, the bank would sanction the loan depending upon the loan eligibility of the applicant.
- Each bank would have different criteria for checking the eligibility of the applicant and this eligibility criterion is kept transparent to the customers.
- The EMI of the loan depends upon the applicant's paying capacity and preference, and hence the tenure as well.
- There are two types of interest rate loans—*fixed interest rate* and *fluctuating interest rate*. One can choose as per his/her preference. It also depends upon the base rates

charged by the banks. In case of fixed interest rates, the banks do offer an option of change after a particular time period. So, a good knowledge about the loan before taking it is very important.

TYPES OF HOME LOANS

The various types of home loans, their nature and characteristics are discussed below:

I. Home Purchase Loan

Home Purchase Loans are the basic home loans taken for purchasing a new home.

Interest Rate

Interest rates continue to be calculated in different ways. The methods that are widely used are:

1. ***Fixed interest rate:*** The interest rate in these loans remains constant throughout the tenure of the loan. These loans are normally priced higher than variable rate loans for a similar tenure. Of late, some banks have also started offering a resettable fixed rate loan under which the rate remains fixed for a particular period (say, three years) and is reset every three years. The interest rate on these resettable fixed rate loans is generally higher than other fixed rate loans.

2. ***Variable interest rate:*** Variable interest rate loans are also called *adjustable rate home loans*. Here, the interest rate is linked to a benchmark rate which can be prime lending rate or the inflation rate, depending upon the bank's policy, and is called *Retail Prime Lending Rate* (RPLR) or *Base Prime Lending Rate* (BPLR). Typically, the interest rate on customer loans is lower than the benchmark rate.

Basis of Calculation

Following bases are used to calculate interest rates:

1. ***Annual reducing basis:*** Here, an *Equated Annual Instalment* (EAI) is calculated first and then divided by twelve to find out the monthly EMI. The EAI is calculated assuming that it is payable at the end of the year even though in practice, the instalments are paid on a monthly basis. So, the actual cost to the borrower is higher than the stated cost. It is basically an inflated way of calculating interest and therefore, has been scrapped in almost every large bank. However, some small banks still use this, particularly for short duration loans such as home improvement loans.

2. ***Monthly reducing basis:*** This is the most commonly used form of calculating interest rates. It results in good savings as compared to annual basis. Here, the interest rate is calculated on every month basis.

II. Home Improvement Loan

Home improvement loans are given by several banks and housing finance companies for any renovation or repair that adds to the value of the home, and improves its utility, durability and comfort. Unlike home purchase loans, these loans are mainly unsecured. Unsecured home improvement loans bear a high interest rate as compared to the ordinary home loans. However, the loan sanction process is easy and fast. Almost every bank in India provides home improvement loans.

The process goes, as given below:

- Once you decide on the extent of work, you get an estimate on a written statement from the contractor or architect. The bank issues the amount to you or in some cases directly to the contractor. Some banks conduct a verification text to check if the money is being put to right use.
- The repayment period, interest rates and specific conditions differ greatly depending on the bank or institution and the provisions of the scheme you want to avail. Many banks offer the same rates as applicable for their home loan schemes.
- Home improvement schemes are also open to NRIs, and some institutions like HDFC and SBI have exclusive schemes that offer attractive terms and special rates to them.
- An old customer is sometimes given 100% cost of improvement, whereas the new customers are generally sanctioned 85% of the cost of improvement. The maximum loan amount differs from bank to bank. It also depends on the amount of loan taken and the repayment capacity of the customer.
- Tax deduction is available for home improvement loan. However, Principal payment on such a loan is not eligible for deductions. Under Section 24 of Income Tax Act 1961, the interest paid on the home improvement loan is tax deductible upto ₹30,000 per annum. If you are already servicing a home loan and availing the tax benefit for the interest paid on the loan, then the combined overall limit for the tax deduction for interest paid on both the home loan and home improvement loan is ₹200,000. In case the interest paid on home loan is ₹170,000 or below, then you will be able to get the maximum benefit of ₹30,000 on the home improvement loan, provided you have paid so much interest during the year.[3] (Box 10.2).

III. Home Construction Loan

A construction loan is similar to a line of credit. Under this loan scheme, the borrower is approved to spend up to a certain amount of money to build their new home. Construction loans require interest-only payments during construction and become due upon completion, which means that when the house has received its certificate of occupancy, the balance due is then rolled over or 'converted' into a typical 30-year mortgage.

The main purpose of the loan is if the borrower wants to self construct the house on a plot of land that he owns. Construction home loans are categorised as the *story loans* as the lenders need to understand the story behind requirement for the loan prior financing the borrower. Availing a home construction loan is therefore, easy and generally requires the interest-only payments during the construction of the home. The home construction loan becomes due with the end of the construction and with the issuance of the certificate of occupancy.

3. https://cleartax.in/s/deductions-under-section24-income-from-house-property.

Flexibility complements the structure of the construction home loan and the interest rate for this loan is usually a variable one. Another important feature of the home construction loans is that it can be converted into a mortgage loan after the completion of the project, and also provides the advantage of experiencing one application and one closing to enjoy the affordable financial deal.

They can be classified into two categories:

1. *Construction only Loans*

Construction loans are short-termed and are converted or replaced by a standard mortgage once the construction is finished. Some borrowers get a 'construction-only' loan in which only the building of the home is financed. They then have the choice to go for another lender and/or a lower rate once the home is occupied.

2. *Construction to Permanent Loans*

The construction loan is converted into a standard loan by the same lender, once the borrower has a certificate of occupancy. This saves time and money since the borrower only has to fill out one mortgage application and close once. The type of mortgage the construction loan is converted into is decided at close.

IV. Home Extension Loan

As the name suggests, this type of home loan is basically taken when an individual plans to extend his existing home. It is basically for adding more space to your existing home. With the increase in size of the family, the extension of house becomes extremely important. Some instances where one needs home extension loan:

- To construct an additional floor or additional room for kids.
- To construct garage in the building.

The tenure of home extension loan generally varies from 1 to 20 years which does not extend beyond the retirement age of 60. As per Section 24 of the Income Tax Act, the interest paid on the loan can be claimed as a deduction from your Gross Taxable Income to a maximum of ₹1,50,000.

BOX 10.2: TAX TREATMENT ON HOME LOANS

Home loan results in tax savings. Under the Indian Income Tax Act, 1961, the total deduction of ₹3.5 lacs is allowed on home loan.

The 'principal amount' in the repayment of a home loan can be added to the 80C limit of ₹1.5 lacs for tax savings.

The 'interest' component of home loans is allowed as deduction under Section 24(b) for upto ₹2 lacs in case of a self-occupied house interest deduction disclosure is as follows:

1. Interest payable on loans borrowed for the purpose of acquisition, construction and renovation.
2. Interest payable on fresh loan taken for repaying the original loan raised for house property.

3. Interest relating to the year of completion of construction.
4. Interest payable on borrowed capital for the period prior to the previous year in which property has been acquired or constructed can be claimed as deduction.

Tax benefits on home loan for payment of interest on home loan can be claimed as deduction under Section 24 as well as under Section 80EE. Additional deduction of ₹50,000 under Section 80EE has been allowed to first-time home buyers and is valid for loans sanctioned till 31st March 2017 only.

To promote the housing sector, Budget 2019 has introduced an additional deduction under Section 80EEA for first time homebuyers for **a maximum of up to ₹1,50,000**. The loan must have been sanctioned between 1 April 2019 to 31 March 2022.

Source: https://cleartax.in/s/home-loan-tax-benefit

V. Land Purchase Loan

Banks provide loan to purchase land for residential purpose. It is available for both salaried and self-employed people and also for the NRIs but not available for the purchase of agricultural land. A land loan is exclusively for purchase of plot for residential purpose. Some banks only finance land that is within municipal limits. Further, certain banks also add restrictive clauses such as buyer needs to start the construction in six months to 2 years. This is to make sure that people do not take loan for speculative investments.

1. *Down Payment*

Usually, people who seek for such a loan have to make a high down payment. Loan-to-value ratio is often as high as 60% to 80% and the buyer has to arrange 20% of the cost of property.

2. *Term*

It is offered for maximum of 15 years, after taking into consideration the retirement age of a borrower.

3. *Tax Implication*

The rate of interest in case of land loan is almost same as home loan but unlike home loan, one does not get tax break on land loan. A person might be able to take tax benefit if he applies for home loan after he applied for land loan because in that case, loan would be considered as summation of both land loan and home loan.

The tax deductions will be applicable only in the year in which the construction is completed under Section 80C as discussed in the Box 10.2.

VI. Home Conversion Loan

Another kind of home loan which is becoming very popular these days is *Home Conversion Loan*. This kind of a loan is a subtle variant of a regular home loan. It is availed by a customer who wants to buy a new home and has already taken a loan on the property where he is currently living. In home conversion loan, the customer does not have to worry about the pre-payment of his existing loan and applying for a new loan. In such an arrangement, the existing loan is transferred into a new loan with additional amount needed to buy the new home being added to the existing loan. This kind of a loan is provided by banks to customers who wish to change their home and move to a better one. These loans make housing decisions of people a little easier as houses become more affordable. The interest rates charged by banks are same as what they charge for basic home loans.

For example, suppose, Mr. Mohit has a home loan of ₹10 lacs on his current home. He wants to buy a new home for which he would need additional funds worth ₹1 lac. In this situation, he can go for a Home conversion loan where his existing loan of ₹10 lacs will be converted into a loan of ₹11 lacs. In this situation he will not have to go through the hassle of repaying existing loan and applying for a new loan. This kind of a loan saves a lot of time, effort and costs in terms of file charges, etc.

By providing this kind of a loan, banks get the following benefits:

- They are able to retain their customers.
- Their interest earning asset increases as the amount of loan increases.
- Quality of collateral improves as the new home will have better value than the older one.

VII. Bridge Loans

Bridge loan is a variant of home conversion loan but are short-term in nature as compared to home conversion loans. They are offered by various banks and HFCs to people who wish to purchase a new house while wishing to sell the house they presently live in. Customers can avail bridge loans and use them to purchase the new home until they find a buyer for their old home.

However, these loans have a limitation over normal home loans regarding interest rates charged by banks. Most banks and financial institutions charge a high rate of interest on bridge loans than they charge for other home loans, which can be fixed or floating.

Some institutions also put in a condition for the borrowers to dispose off their old home. Usually, they are given a time limit of 6 to 12 to 24 months before which they have to sell their house and repay the loan. If they are unable to do so, it can revert into a mortgage loan which may have a high rate of interest. The institution may require its customers to pledge their new property papers to them as collateral (Box 10.3).

From customers' point of view, bridge loan facilitates quick investment once they opt for it. He/she can then make the payment for his current mortgage and the remaining funds can be utilised towards making advance payment for the purchase of a new house. Once the old house is sold, the borrower will use the funds to reimburse the bridge loan.

A bridge loan is normally used for commercial real estate purchases to quickly close on a property, release a real estate from foreclosure or just take an opportunity of a short-term loan for securing a long-term financing goal.

BOX 10.3: DOCUMENTS REQUIRED FOR HOME LOANS/LAND LOANS

For salaried customers:

- Application form with photograph
- Identification and residence proof
- Latest salary slips
- Form 16
- Last 6 months bank's statement
- Processing fee cheque

For businessman/self employed professionals:

- Application form with photograph
- Educational qualification
- Identity and residence proof
- Proof of business existence with business profile and last three years income tax return
- Last 3 years income statement and balance sheet
- Last 3 month's personal and business bank statements
- Processing fee cheque

INNOVATIVE HOME LOANS

In the last couple of years, banks have come out with various innovative home loans to attract the borrowers in the market. These are discussed below:

1. Flexi Home Loan

SBI Flexipay Home loan provides an eligibility for a higher loan amount exclusively for the salaried borrowers. It offers customer the option to pay only interest during the moratorium (pre-EMI) period, and thereafter, pay moderated EMIs. The EMIs will be stepped-up during the subsequent years.

This variant of SBI home loan is very useful for young earners. The SBI Flexipay home loan has the potential to lure a large section of home loan buyer towards SBI.

2. Home Saver Loans

Home Saver is a new concept in home loan that aims at saving the borrower's interest, thereby letting him pay off his loan faster.

The Standard Chartered bank offers a special home loan called *Home Saver*. In this loan, interest offset is calculated on daily balances. The borrower can transfer his existing home loan to the bank and ease his EMIs with simplified balance transfer solutions at reduced rates with top-up facility. He can deposit and withdraw his money whenever he needs it.

3. Home Loan with Add-ons

Some banks provide home loans with various add-on benefits, which have become a key factor in the competitive era of home loans. The banks have also tied up with various property insurance companies in order to make their home loan competitive.

The ABN-AMRO bank which had entered the home loan segment in October 2003, launched its product 'All Smiles Home Loans' with the lowest interest rate of 6% in the first year and 6.5% in the second year, and from the third year it would be floating rate of interest prevailing in the market.

REFORMS IN HOUSING LOAN SECTOR IN INDIA

Various reforms have taken place in the Indian housing loan sector in the recent times, making it attractive for a common man. These are discussed below:

1. Waving off of Pre-payment Penalty on Home Loans

The quantum of pre-payment penalty on floating rate home loans usually varied from 1% to a high of 6%. The Reserve Bank of India (RBI) asked the banks to waive the pre-payment charges in floating rate loans.[4] Now, the pre-payment charges of home loans are waived off.

2. RBI Streamlines the Loan-to-Value Ratio

For all new house loans issued up until March 31, 2022, the RBI streamlined the risk weights and tied them to loan-to-value (LTV) ratios. This linkage of the risk weight of mortgages to LTV for all new housing loans has proven to be a smart move.

3. Banks' House Loan Book

Home loans, being secured loans have historically had the lowest delinquencies. It results in banks providing the greatest rates to create a house loan book during times of crisis, rather than focusing on unsecured lending books such as personal loans and credit cards. From the perspective of the banks, home loans are a safer proposition.

4. Loan Moratorium

A loan moratorium was implemented to give a temporary reprieve from repayments to borrowers who had been hurt by the outbreak. Restructuring, partial pre-payments and switching to fixed rate loans are other options for relieving borrowers of the stress of hefty EMIs.

5. Digital Banking

Banks quickly took advantage of the growing demand from millennials for home loans by setting up online channels to speed up loan distribution. Many banks and financial

4. http://www.business-standard.com/article/finance/home-loans-pre-payment-penalty-scrapped-111102600351.html; http://rbi.org.in/Scripts/NotificationUser.aspx?Mode=0&Id=7258.

institutions have introduced digital initiatives to help customers get loans more quickly and go forward with their plans to buy a home.

6. Government Initiatives

Working with state governments, the Union government has taken a number of steps to promote industry growth. Real estate firms may make use of the Smart City Project, which aims to build 100 smart cities.[5]

The outlay for Prime Minister Awas Yojana (PMAY) got enhanced by 66 per cent as compared to 2022–23 to over ₹79,000 crores in the Union Budget 2023–24.[6]

CASE STUDY

Privileged Home Loan

Mukesh and Seema purchased their home 4 years ago. They were also paying off a car loan and a personal loan they took for the family holiday last year. Now, they were finding it difficult to manage their repayments (Table 10.2).

TABLE 10.2 Loan Accounts of Mukesh and Seema

Loan Account	*Balance*	*Minimum Monthly Repayment*
Home loan	25,00,000	25,000
Car loan	4,00,000	3,500
Personal loan	2,00,000	3,000
Total	**31,00,000**	**31,500**

Mukesh and Seema's minimum monthly repayments on their loan accounts totalled ₹31,500 per month.

As per their present financial circumstances, it was unlikely that they would be able to pay all the instalments in time. They approached a new financial company, People Financial Corporation, for a new home loan.

Their new home loan for ₹31 lacs allowed them to consolidate all their debts. They had to make one repayment per month now rather than multiple repayments. The loan was offered at 9.25% per annum.

Mukesh and Seema's minimum monthly repayment with their new home loan was reduced from ₹31,500 per month to ₹23,896 per month, thus saving them ₹7,604 per month.

5. *The Housing Finance Industry in India—The Road Ahead,* July 2022, https://www.assocham.org/uploads/files/Study_Housing%20Finance%202022.pdf
6. https://timesofindia.indiatimes.com/business/budget/budget-2023-24-sitharamans-big-announcement-allocation-for-pm-awas-yojana-raised-by-66-per-cent/articleshow/97527123.cms, February 1, 2023.

POINTS TO REMEMBER

- In India, housing sector is present as both organised and unorganised segments, with the unorganised segment accounting for over 75% of the housing units constructed.
- India's housing finance industry mainly comprises of banks and Housing Finance Companies (HFCs), and to a limited extent, smaller institutions in the form of community organisations, self-help groups, etc. The National Housing Bank (NHB) is the principal agency for promoting, regulating, and providing financial and other support to HFCs at local and regional levels, while banks and NBFCs are managed and regulated by the RBI.
- Home loan is a secured loan offered against the security of a house/property which is funded by the bank's loan; the property could be a personal property or a commercial one.
- Historically, the housing finance industry was dominated by HFCs. Housing Development Finance Corporation (HDFC) was the first housing finance company to setup operations in India in 1977. NHB came into existence, with the passing of the National Housing Bank Act, 1987, as a subsidiary of the Reserve Bank of India (RBI) to regulate housing finance companies and provide them with refinancing to supplement their fund requirements. Public sector banks were allowed to provide housing loans directly to retail clients only in 1988. Therefore, towards the end of the 1990s, scheduled commercial banks became very active in lending to the housing sector.
- The cost of the loan not only includes the interest to be paid but it also covers several other costs, like processing fee, administration fee and legal cost.
- Home Purchase Loans are the basic home loans taken for purchasing a new home. Interest rate can be fixed or variable here. The bases of calculation are annual reducing basis or monthly reducing basis. Monthly reducing is the most commonly used form of calculating interest rates.
- Home improvement loans are given by several banks and housing finance companies for any renovation or repair that adds to the value of your home, and improves its utility, durability and comfort. These loans are mainly unsecured unlike home purchase loans.
- A home construction loan is similar to a line of credit. Under this loan scheme, the borrower is approved to spend upto a certain amount of money to build their new home. Construction loans require interest-only payments during construction and become due upon completion which means that when the house has received its certificate of occupancy. The balance due is then rolled over or 'converted' into a typical 30-year mortgage.
- Home extension loan is basically taken when an individual plans to extend his existing home. It is taken for adding more space to your existing home.

- Home loan results in tax savings. Under the Indian Income Tax Act, 1961, now total deduction of ₹3.5 lacs is allowed on home loan. The 'principal' amount in the repayment of a home loan can be added to the 80C limit of ₹1.5 lacs for tax savings. The 'interest' component of home loans is allowed as deduction under Section 24(b) for upto ₹2 lacs in case of a self-occupied house.
- Land purchase loan is taken to purchase land for residential purpose. It is available for both salaried and self-employed people and also for the NRIs but is not available for the purchase of agricultural land. The rate of interest in case of land loan is almost same as home loan, but unlike home loan, one does not get tax break on land loan.
- Home conversion loan is a subtle variant of a regular home loan. It is availed by a customer who wants to buy a new home and has already taken a loan on the property where he is presently living. In home conversion loan, the customer does not have to worry about the pre-payment of his existing loan and applying for a new one.
- Bridge loan is a variant of home conversion loan. These loans are short-term in nature as compared to home conversion loans. Bridge loans are offered by various banks and HFCs to people who wish to purchase a new house while wishing to sell the house they presently live in.
- In the last couple of years, banks have come out with a lot of innovative home loans to attract the borrowers in the market such as flexi-home loan, home saver loans and home loans with add-ons.
- Various reforms have taken place in the Indian housing loan sector in the recent times, making it attractive for a common man.

KEY TERMS

- **Home loan** is a loan taken by a borrower from the bank issued against the property security intended to be bought on the part by the borrower, giving the banker a conditional ownership over the property.
- **Home improvement loan** is given for any renovation or repair that adds to the value of your home, and improves its utility, durability and comfort.
- **Home extension loan** is taken when an individual plans to extend his existing home. It is basically for adding more space to your current home.
- **Home conversion loan** is availed by a customer who wants to buy a new home and has already taken a loan on the property where he is presently living.
- **Bridge loan** is for those people who wish to purchase a new house while wishing to sell the house they currently reside in.
- **Home saver loan** is designed to save you interest, thereby letting you pay off your loan faster.

EXERCISES

Objective Questionss

1. Tick the correct answer:

(a) HFC in housing sector stands for:
   (i) Housing Finance Company (ii) Housing Film Company
   (iii) Hut Finance Company (iv) All of the above

(b) The administration fee is charged when the loan:
   (i) Is sanctioned (ii) Is applied for
   (iii) Is repaid (iv) None of the above

(c) EMI refers to:
   (i) Easy Monthly Instalments (ii) Equated Monthly Instalments
   (iii) Equal Money Instalments (iv) None of the above

(d) Home improvement loan is given:
   (i) To improve the utility of the house
   (ii) For renovation in the house
   (iii) Either (i) or (ii)
   (iv) None of the above

(e) The interest component of home loans is allowed as deduction under Section 24(b) upto:
   (i) ₹1.5 lacs (ii) ₹1 lac
   (iii) ₹2.5 lacs (iv) None of the above

***Answers*:** (a) i (b) i (c) ii (d) iii (e) i

2. Fill in the blanks:

(a) .... is the principal agency for promoting, regulating and providing financial and other support to HFCs at local and regional levels in India.

(b) The .... is payable at that time when you apply for the home loan.

(c) .... is basically an inflated way of calculating interest and therefore, has been scrapped almost every large bank.

(d) .... is basically taken to extend the existing home.

(e) .... allows tax benefits to the borrower.

(f) .... saves you interest, thereby letting you pay off your loan faster.

***Answers*:**

(a) National Housing Bank (NHB)

(b) Processing fee

(c) Annual reducing basis of interest

(d) Home extension loan

(e) Home loans

(f) Home saver loan

3. True or False:

(a) Housing sector is a part of retail banking.

(b) The unorganised segment of housing sector accounts for more than 50% of the housing units constructed.

(c) Home loan is unsecured in nature.

(d) The cost of the loan not only includes the interest to be paid but it also covers several other costs.

(e) The interest paid on the home improvement loan is tax deductible up to ₹30,000 per annum.

(f) An assessee will be able to take additional interest deduction of ₹50,000 on House Property Loan under Section 80EE.

(g) Land purchase loan does not get tax benefit to the borrower.

(h) Bridge loans are long-term in nature like home loans.

Answers: (a) True (b) True (c) False (d) True (e) True
(f) True (g) True (h) False

Short Questions

1. Define home loan.
2. What are the basic costs of home loan?
3. Elaborate the key points to be kept in mind at the time of home loans?
4. State the different types of home construction loan.
5. Define a Bridge loan.

Critical Thinking Questions

1. "Banks vary the home loan rates as per their own risk appetite and customer policy". Explain.
2. "Different banks with different interest rate structures on home loans have widened the housing finance market". Justify.
3. "Home loans have realised the dream of a common man of having his own house". Elaborate.
4. "Home improvement loan is hugely relied for short-term housing needs". Discuss.
5. "Home conversion and extension loans came with limited use". Explain.
6. "With the changing times, housing finance industry has also changed and come out with various innovative home loan concepts". Throw some light on this.

Descriptive Questions

1. Discuss the growth of housing finance in India.
2. What is the regulatory framework of housing finance in India?

3. Explain the concept and process of home purchase loan in detail.
4. What are the various types of home loan offered in India?
5. Explain the tax relief in case of home loans.
6. What is the documentation process in case of home loans?
7. Discuss the major issues and challenges faced by the Indian housing finance industry.

PROJECT EXERCISE

Evaluation of Indian Housing Finance Industry

Select top ten leading banks and financial institutions in India offering home loans in all segments. Compare their products, structure and process, and recommend the one which is most profitable for the borrower. Also, evaluate their financial viability in the context of present economic scenario and suggest some innovative home loan concepts, keeping in view the common household sector.

REVIEW CASE

Pre-payment Investment or Not?

Mr. Wise received ₹2 lacs from the sale of his family shop. He has a housing loan of ₹5 lacs for which he is paying an EMI of ₹15,000 at the rate of interest 11% compounded annually. The tenure of the loan is eight years and he has completed 2 years. He does not have a very handsome salary, and is facing problems in meeting his day-to-day expenses. Therefore, he is thinking about repaying a part of the loan with this amount, whereas his wife is of the view that they must invest a part of it for their children's education in Child Saving Plan of ABC Finance with a return of ₹4 lacs after 5 years.

Since he does not wish to act in haste, he approaches one of his friends who also advises him against his decision. He further says that had it been a car loan or a personal loan, he should have paid it immediately because the interest is very high and the value of a loan investment will only depreciate.

The decision for him now becomes more difficult. So, he seeks advice from his boss who also happens to be a financial man. [Bosses are known for only directing, not advising, but Mr. Wise is lucky enough to get his valuable advice free of cost]. He tells him that the common refrain is that if there is any surplus money, it should not be used to prepay the loan but before taking any decision he must evaluate all the alternatives.

Much of the confusion gets cleared if you see debt prepayment as just another investment. If you prepay ₹1 lac of a personal loan which was charging you an interest rate of 11%, you save ₹11,000 in interest per annum and since money saved is money earned, this ₹1 lac will effectively earn you ₹11,000 in a year. That is a good return and should be the first option for anybody with surplus cash. Evaluate your debts on the basis of the interest you are paying and start with repaying the costliest ones first.

The credit card balance and personal loans should be the first in your cross-hairs. It does not make sense to keep money in a fixed deposit that fetches only 9% which is taxable but you may have a situation where the loan is cheaper than what your investments can earn, that is, when you should stop prepaying the loan and start investing. Follow the simple rule that the return from the investments should be more than the interest on the loans.

So, he finally analyses his position himself and finds out that at an interest of 11%, he ends up paying around ₹1,10,000 annually only on the interest amount which works out to ₹8,80,000 in 8 years, raising the cost of the house by over 50%. If he uses this money to repay the loan, the number of instalments he has to pay will be reduced, which implies that the total amount to be repaid will be reduced since the duration of the loan will also come down.

Issues for Discussion

(i) Should Mr. Wise prepay the loan?

(ii) Calculate the reduction in the duration of the loan if he uses the entire money towards prepaying the loan.

(iii) Would he be able to earn substantially with the investment as advised by his wife and pay off a bigger chunk of her debt?

(iv) How do you compare the benefits from the investments as advised by his wife and prepayment of loans?

(v) What is the greatest advantage of pre-payment of a loan?

(vi) Discuss the tax implications in the above case in all scenarios.

REFERENCES

www.assocham.org

www.business-standard.com

www.cleartax.in

www.deal4loans.com

www.financialexpress.com

www.guide2homeloan.com

www.homeloans.sbi

www.indiabudget.nic.in

www.indianexpress.com

www.indiaincometax.co.in
www.nhb.org.in
www.rbidocs.rbi.org.in
www.sc.com
www.sebi.gov.in
www.statista.com
www.timesofindia.indiatimes.co

CHAPTER 11

Leasing and Hire Purchase

Nobody wants the expenditure of a lease on a factory which lasts 21 years. You can't plan 21 years ahead.

— James Dyson

LEARNING OBJECTIVES

This chapter discusses the following:

- Concept of leasing
- Types of leasing
- Advantages and disadvantages of leasing
- Growth of leasing in India
- Structure of Indian leasing industry
- Leasing regulation in India
- Financial evaluation of leasing
- Concept, evolution and regulation of hire purchase in India
- Rights and obligations under hire purchase

INTRODUCTION

The acquisition of assets, particularly expensive capital equipment, is a major commitment for business organisations. The funding of the acquisition requires careful planning. Instead of paying for the asset outright using cash, it can often make sense for businesses to look for alternate ways of spreading the cost of acquiring an asset over its useful life, matching with the revenue generated by business. The most common sources of medium-term finance for investment in capital assets are 'Leasing' and 'Hire purchase'.

Leasing and *Hire purchase (HP)* are financial facilities which allow a business to use an asset over a fixed period, in return for regular payments. The business house decides the equipment it requires and the finance company buys it on behalf of the business.

The various types of business assets which are commonly acquired through financing route using lease or hire purchase include:

- Plant and machinery
- Office equipment
- Business cars and commercial vehicles
- Agricultural equipment
- Hotel equipment
- Medical equipment

LEASING

A *lease transaction* is a commercial arrangement, wherein an equipment owner or manufacturer passes on the right to use the equipment in return for a rental to the user. In other words, lease is a contract between the owner of an asset (the *lessor*) and its user (the *lessee*) for the right to use the asset during a specified period in return for a mutually agreed periodic payment (the *lease rentals*). Ind AS17 defines lease as "an agreement wherein the lessor conveys to the lessee, in return for a payment or series of payments, the right to use an asset for an agreed period of time"[1].

The fundamental characteristic of a lease is that ownership doesn't pass to the business customer in general cases. Instead, the leasing company claims the capital allowances and passes some of the benefit on to the business customer, by way of reduced rental charges. The business customer can generally deduct the full cost of lease rentals from taxable income, as a trading expense.

Essential Elements

The essential elements of a lease are as follows:

1. *Parties:* The parties to a lease are the 'lessor' and the 'lessee'. The lessor is also called the *landlord* and the lessee the *tenant*.

2. *Subject matter of lease:* The subject matter of lease is the movable/immovable property. The word 'immovable property' may not be only house, or land but also benefits that arise out of land, right to collect the fruit of a plantation, right to extract coal or minerals, rights of fisheries or market dues. The contract for right to grazing is not lease. A mining lease is a lease and not a sale of minerals.

1. https://www.mca.gov.in/Ministry/pdf/Ind_AS17.pdf

3. *Duration of lease:* The right to enjoy the property must be transferred for a certain time, express or implied or in perpetuity. In India, the lease may be in perpetuity. The lease should commence either in the present or on some date in future. Though the lease can commence from a past day but for the purpose of computation of lease period, the interest of the lessee begins from the date of execution. No interest passes to the lessee before execution.

4. *Consideration:* The consideration for lease is either premium or rent, which is the price paid or promised in consideration of the property.

5. *Sub-lease:* A lessee can transfer the whole or any part of his interest in the property by sub-lease. However, this right is subject to the main contract and he can be restrained by the contract from transferring his lease by sub-letting. The lessee can create sub-leases for different parts of the leased premises. The sub-lessee gets the rights, subject to the covenants, terms and conditions in the lease deed.

Let us understand lease with the help of an *example (buying a vehicle)*. You borrow money from a bank for leasing the car, pay the dealer, and then make monthly payments on the loan until it is paid off. With paying off the loan, you gain the ownership rights of the vehicle. You can use the vehicle and do whatever you want with it. Leasing is simple is it not? You pay the leasing company a monthly payment that is lower than when buying. Then, after enjoying the vehicle trouble-free for two or three years, you simply bring it back to the dealer and lease another new one, or walk away. No botheration, no repairs, no pain of selling your old car. Therefore, you enjoy the following advantages:

- There is often no down-payment required when leasing, or very low.
- You can drive a higher-priced, better-equipped vehicle which you might not be able to buy.
- You are always driving a new model vehicle that is usually covered by the manufacturer's warranty.

Undoubtedly, leasing has multiple benefits to offer but there are disadvantages to leasing also:

- It might become a habit. Once you become used to leasing, monthly payments go on forever.
- You have a limited number of miles in your contract and will have to pay extra if you exceed.
- You must maintain the vehicle in good condition. If you do not, you will have to pay penalties for excess wear and tear.
- If you need to get out of a lease before it expires, you may have to pay a huge early-termination fee and penalties—all at once.
- Leasing is not a substitute for buying. It is mostly a limited usage facility.
- At the end of the lease, you have no equity in the vehicle.
- You can not customise the vehicle in any permanent way.

Therefore, leasing can be a complicated and expensive process that can easily leave you paying more than you should. One should not mistake leasing as an easier or less expensive facility than buying.

TYPES OF LEASING

IAS 17 *Leases* prescribe the accounting policies and disclosures applicable to leases, both for lessees and lessors. Leases are classified as either 'finance lease' (which substantially transfer all the risks and rewards incidental to ownership of an asset. Title may or may not be eventually transferred and 'operating lease' is other than a finance lease[2] (which result in expense recognition by the lessee, with the asset remaining recognised by the lessor). These types and other variants are discussed below and briefed in Box 11.1:

1. Financial Lease

Long-term, non-cancellable lease contracts are known as *financial leases.* In a financial lease agreement, the lessee is given an option to buy the leased property from the lessor at a nominal cost at the end of the lease period. So, the essential point of financial lease agreement is that it contains a condition wherein the lessor agrees to transfer the title for the asset at the end of the lease period at a nominal cost.

*The finance lease or **full payout lease** is closest to the hire purchase alternative. The leasing company recovers the full cost of the equipment plus charges, over the period of the lease.*

Under this arrangement,

- *the lessor recovers 90% of the fair value of the asset as lease rentals,*
- *the lease period is minimum 75% of the economic life of the asset,*
- *the lease agreement is irrevocable,*
- *all risks and benefits arising from the use of the property are transferred to the lessee who bears the cost of maintenance, insurance and repairs, and*
- *only title deeds remain with the lessor.*

*Therefore, a lease is classified as a **finance lease** if it substantially transfers all the risks and rewards incidental to ownership[3]. A financial lease is loan look-alike and these leases are given for high-cost and high technology equipments.*

Although the business customer does not own the equipment, he has most of the 'risks and rewards' associated with ownership. He is responsible for maintaining and insuring the asset and must show the leased asset on his balance sheet as a capital item.

When the lease period ends, the leasing company usually agrees to a secondary lease period at significantly reduced payments. Alternatively, if the business wishes to stop using the equipment, it may be sold second-hand to an unrelated third party. The business arranges the sale on behalf of the leasing company and obtains the bulk of the sale proceeds.

For example, an office is on lease for five years and its expected life is six years, with price ₹2,75,000. The rent decided for the first three years is ₹4,000 per month and for remaining two years is ₹5,000 per month. There is also a clause to pass through any increase in property tax which may occur. At the end of the lease, the title of the office passes on to the lessee and this makes it a financial lease. Also, the lease

2. https://www.mca.gov.in.op. cit.
3. https://www.mca.gov.in.op. cit.

period is 5 years which is more than 75% of six years, the economic life of the office. It also satisfies the condition of rental recovery as the lessor recovers ₹2,64,000 which is more than 90% of the value of the office of ₹2,75,000.

(a) *Sale and Leaseback*

This is a sub-part of finance lease. Under this, the owner of an asset sells the asset to a party (the buyer), who in turn leases back the same asset to the owner in consideration of lease rentals. However, under this arrangement, the assets are not physically exchanged but it all happens in records only and is nothing but a paper transaction. Sale and leaseback transaction is suitable for those assets which are not subjected to depreciation but appreciation, such as land. The advantage of this method is that the lessee can satisfy himself completely regarding the quality of the asset and after possession of the asset, convert the sale into a lease arrangement (Figure 11.1).

Figure 11.1 Structure of a Sale and Leaseback

(b) *Leveraged Leasing*

Under *leveraged leasing* arrangement, a third party is involved besides lessor and lessee. The lessor borrows a part of the purchase cost (say 80%) of the asset from the third party (the lender) and the asset so purchased is held as security against the loan. The lender is paid-off from the lease rentals directly by the lessee and the surplus, after meeting the claims of the lender, goes to the lessor. The lessor (owner of the asset) is entitled to depreciation allowance associated with the asset (Figure 11.2).

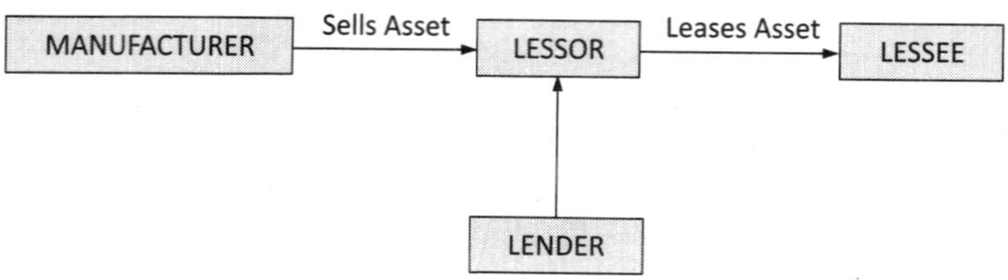

Figure 11.2 Structure of a Leveraged Lease

2. Operating Lease

A lease is classified as an *operating lease* if it does not substantially transfer all the risks and rewards incidental to ownership[4]. If a business needs a piece of equipment

4. https://www.mca.gov.in.op. cit.

for a shorter time, then operating lease may be the answer. This lease agreement gives only a limited right to the lessee to use the asset. The lessor himself is responsible for the repairs and maintenance of the asset. Also, unlike financial lease, the lessee is not given any option to buy the asset at the end of the term of lease.

Generally, the operating lease is for a short period and is revocable at a short notice. The leasing company will lease the equipment, expecting to sell it second-hand at the end of the lease, or to lease it again to someone else. It will, therefore, not need to recover the full cost of the equipment through the lease rentals.

This type of leasing is common for equipment where there is a well-established second-hand market (for example, cars and construction equipment). The lease period will usually be for two to three years, although it may be much longer but is always less than the working life of the machine.

Assets financed under operating leases are not shown as assets on the balance sheet. Instead, the entire operating lease cost is treated as a cost in the profit and loss account.

For example, the new photocopy machine costs ₹2,000. Mr. Amit (the lessor) is willing to lease it to you for 3 years at a price of ₹95 per month, paid at the beginning of each month. This is inclusive of ₹10 as the cost of maintenance. If you borrow money for three years to buy, you will have to pay an interest of 8.5%. If you buy the machine, the normal depreciation period will be 5 years as per the useful life of the machine. The lessor has not given an option to buy the machine at the end of the lease though the machine is estimated to have ₹350 as its fair market value at that time. In this case, there is no ownership transfer as a part of the lease agreement and therefore, it is a case of operating lease.

(a) *Contract Hire*

Contract hire is a form of operating lease and is often used for vehicles. The leasing company undertakes some responsibility for the management and maintenance of the vehicles. Services can include regular maintenance and repair costs, replacement of tyres and batteries, providing replacement vehicles, roadside assistance and recovery services, and payment of the vehicle licences.

3. Other Leasing Agreements

(a) *Direct Leasing*

Under *direct leasing,* a firm acquires the right to use an asset from the manufacturer directly. The manufacturer himself retains the ownership of the asset. The major types of direct lessors include manufacturers, finance companies, independent lease companies, special purpose leasing companies, etc.

(b) *Skip Lease*

Skip lease is used in case of seasonal businesses like agricultural companies and recreational service firms, and other firms which require flexible payment schedule due to their seasonal business conditions. Under this, the firm specifies the months when it would not be possible for them to make payments. Thus, it offers a very flexible payment schedule.

(c) *Master Lease*

Master lease is used when the business is expected to have more leasing requirements with the expanding business over time. Under this, a master lease governs the basic terms and conditions for all the leasing arrangements made by the business with the company. However, separate lease schedules are created to accommodate the additional equipment leased according to the specifications of the business. It thus, makes the job of acquiring additional equipment more convenient.

(d) *Municipal Lease*

Municipal lease is designed specifically for local and state government organisations that want to acquire equipment. The tax structure and details vary considerably under this lease arrangement as compared with other standard business leases.

BOX 11.1: SNAPSHOT OF LEASING AGREEMENTS

This section describes the *suitability* of different leases and their modus-operandi.

1. Finance Lease or Capital Lease

Best For: If you wish to own the equipment after the end of lease agreement.

How It Works: The full purchase price plus interest, is spread over the length of the lease agreement.

Benefits: At the end of the lease, you own the equipment for a minimal payment, a small percentage of the original purchase price.

Sale Leaseback

Best For: Customers who have purchased their equipment but now plan to go for leasing. Sale leaseback also allows companies to raise cash for other investments or cash flow purposes.

How It Works: The business that has already purchased equipment sells it to a leasing company which then takes ownership of the equipment and leases it back to the business.

Benefits: The sale-leaseback allows you to put money back into your business or into investments.

Leverage Lease/60 or 90 Days Deferred Lease

Best For: Businesses that need equipment for operation or development that will not immediately generate revenue.

How It Works: A 60 or 90 days deferred lease can be structured as a finance lease or a true lease. With this form of lease, there is usually no advance payment required, and the first payment is not due for 60 or 90 days after the lease begins.

Benefits: The equipment can be acquired with very little money up front and no payments for 2–3 months.

2. Operating or True Lease

Best For: Equipments with high rate of depreciation or obsolescence, such as a computer.

How It Works: The leasing company retains ownership of the equipment during the lease and customers show these payments as an operating expense.

Benefits: Lower payments and typically the most tax-friendly form of leasing, it offers three choices at the end of the lease:

- Return the equipment to the leasing company,
- Purchase the equipment at its fair market value or option amount,
- Extend the lease term.

Skip Lease

Best For: Seasonal businesses, agricultural companies, and organisations which require a more flexible payment schedule.

How It Works: One can specify the months when he/she prefers not to make payments.

Benefits: Flexible, as it can be adjusted to irregular cash flow.

Master Lease

Best For: Increasing leasing requirements over time.

How It Works: Separate lease schedules are created to accommodate the addition of equipment over a period of time.

Benefits: Acquiring additional equipment is more convenient.

Municipal Lease

Best For: Local and state government organisations that wish to acquire equipment.

How It Works: The tax structures and details of municipal leases are different from standard business leases.

Benefits: Municipal leases are designed specifically for local and state government organisations.

Step Up Lease

Best For: Businesses whose financed equipment generates more profitability over a period of time.

How It Works: Payments increase according to a regular schedule over the life of the lease.

Benefits: Payments can be structured to match current cash flow.

ADVANTAGES OF LEASING

The benefits attached to leasing are discussed as follows:

A. To the Lessor

1. *Complete security:* The lessor's interest is fully secured as he is the permanent owner of the leased asset. He can take repossession of the asset if the lessee defaults. It is more advantageous than mortgaging the assets for debt financing.

2. *Tax benefit:* The greatest advantage for the lessor is the tax relief by way of depreciation. By leasing out the asset with high depreciation rates, he can always reduce his tax liability to a greater extent.

3. *Higher profitability:* The leasing business is highly profitable since the rate of return is more than what the lessor pays on his borrowings. Therefore, leasing always leads to higher profits for the lessor.

4. *High growth potential:* The leasing industry has a high growth potential on account of its evergreen requirement. Lease financing enables the lessees to acquire equipment and machinery even during a period of depression, since they do not need to have huge capital to buy them.

B. To the Lessee

1. *Financing benefits/Saving of capital:* The company does not have to incur huge capital expenditure and is required to make only periodical rental payments. So, the money used for buying the equipment can be used for other productive purposes which results in immediate capital saving. Many business leases come with 100% financing, leading to saving of money at the inception of the lease and enhanced revenues that the company earns because of the lease.

2. *Flexibility:* The lease agreement can be customised as per the requirement with respect to lease period and lease rentals. The lease can be drawn for either just a few months or the entire expected life of the asset.

3. *Cash flow management:* In leasing, the amount of rental is known beforehand, so the lessee can plan its cash flows properly. Lease payments are usually lower than loan payments, and enable higher cash reserves for expansion and growth.

4. *Better liquidity:* Sale and leaseback provide an arrangement wherein the liquidity position of the company is improved and the company has enough funds for working capital management.

5. *Lower-cost financing:* Leasing is less costlier than purchasing. Also, it is faster and more accommodating in respect of terms of financing. So, it is a better option for new firms or firms with limited means of finance.

6. *Tax benefit:* The company can utilise tax benefits associated with leasing. Lease payments can reduce taxable income in a much more effective way like in the case of operating leases where the entire lease payment can be expensed.

7. *Off-balance-sheet financing:* Operating leases provide off-the-books (or balance sheet) financing. The company's obligation to pay the lease, which is a liability, does not reflect on the balance sheet. This enhances the solvency of a company.

8. *Covenant free:* The financial institution while lending money usually puts several restrictions on the borrowers regarding management structure, debt-equity norms, declaration of dividends, etc. Such restrictions are absent in the case of lease financing.

DISADVANTAGES OF LEASING

Leasing is not free from limitations. The major disadvantages of leasing are as follows:

1. ***Deprived ownership:*** In a leasing arrangement, the lessee does not get the ownership of the asset and only has the right to use. Also, the lessee cannot pledge the asset for securing loan from financial institutions.

2. ***Higher cost:*** The total cost of leasing over the life of the asset is generally higher than purchasing the asset. The rental payments include not only the acquisition and financing costs, but also the cost towards lessor's retained risk of continuing ownership.

3. ***Limited access:*** In case the lessee makes a default in rental payment, the lessor is entitled to take over the asset and the lessee has no right to prevent him from doing so.

4. ***Unnecessary binding:*** Once you sign a lease agreement, you are generally committed to making payments for the entire lease period even if you stop using the property. Most equipment leases are either non-cancellable or impose a stiff penalty for early termination.

5. ***Maintenance and upkeep:*** Though a lessee does not have to pay for mechanical problems that occur with the asset, he has to maintain it in a good condition.

6. ***Unsuitable for new businesses:*** The lease rentals become payable soon after the acquisition of assets and no grace period is permissible, like in the case of term loans from financial institutions. The lease finance may, therefore, not be suitable for the new businesses and projects as it would result in cash outflows even before the project comes into operation.

GROWTH OF LEASING IN INDIA

In India, leasing has grown by leaps and bounds and hardly 1% of its industrial investment is estimated to be covered by the lease finance, as against 40% in USA, 30% in UK and 10% in Japan. Of late, the leasing prospects in India are rising due to growing investment needs of the business houses and scarce funds with public financial institutions. Leasing in the sphere of land and building has been in existence in India for a long time, while equipment leasing has become common in the recent times.

The growth of leasing in India can be discussed under three phases:

I. First Phase

Leasing activity was initiated in India in 1973 with the setting of the 'First Leasing Company of India Ltd.' by Farouk Irani and A.C. Muthia. This company enjoyed the monopoly for many years until the 20th Century Finance Corporation was set up in around 1980.

By 1981, many companies involved with the hire-purchase of commercial vehicles had started looking for a tax break. Leasing was the ideal choice for them. Companies like Shetty Investment and Finance, Jaybharat Credit and Investment, Motor and General Finance, and Sundaram Finance joined the leasing business.

II. Second Phase

The next stage of growth of leasing industry in India started in late 1982, with the entry of numerous financial institutions and commercial banks. ICICI entered the industry in 1983 and gave the required boost to the leasing industry in India. International Finance Corporation announced its decision to open four leasing joint ventures in India. Soon after, leasing became the new 'gold mine'. The Finance Ministry announced strict measures for enlistment of investment companies on stock-exchanges, which led to many investment companies turning overnight into leasing companies.

As per RBI's records of 31st March, 1986, there were 339 equipment leasing companies in India whose assets leased totalled ₹2,395.5 million. One can notice the surge in number—from merely 2 in 1980 to 339 in 6 years[5].

Another significant phase in the development of Indian leasing was the 'Dahotre Committee's recommendations[6] based on which the RBI formed guidelines on commercial bank funding to leasing companies.

III. Third Phase

The post-liberalisation era has witnessed a steady increase in foreign investment into Indian leasing. Starting with GE Capital's entry, an increasing number of foreign-owned financial firms and banks are currently engaged in leasing in India.

Since 1994, banks have been allowed to offer leasing facilities. There had not been barriers until 1996, but from 1997 onwards, RBI made compulsory for NBFCs to have prior registration.

STRUCTURE OF INDIAN LEASING INDUSTRY

Presently, there are over 400 private and public limited leasing companies in the country which are involved in diverse leasing activities.

1. Private Sector Leasing

The private sector plays a significant role in providing lease facilities to different industries, and helps in raising funds from various unexplored sources. The following are the important constituents of the private sector leasing industry:

(i) *Pure Leasing Companies*

These companies exclusively conduct the leasing business and operate on an independent level. *For examples,* First Leasing Company of India Ltd., and The Twentieth Century Finance Corporation Ltd.

(ii) *Hire Purchase and Finance Companies*

These companies were primarily engaged in hire purchase and finance business prior

5. http://www.karvy.com/market/docs/SpecialReports/karvysSpecialReports_20120307192217.pdf.
6. http://www.karvy.com.ibid.

to 1980, which later on diversified into leasing activities and turned into leasing companies. *Examples* include Sundaram Finance Ltd., Mercantile Commercial and Credit Corporation Ltd., and Motor and General Finance Ltd.

(iii) *Manufacturing Companies*

These companies consist of two categories: (i) Subsidiaries of manufacturing companies, known as *vendor leasing companies*; and (ii) In-house leasing known as *captive leasing companies*.

Vendor leasing companies are basically present to boost and promote the sales of their parent companies' products through leasing. A few *examples* of subsidiaries of manufacturing companies are Ashok Leyland Finance Ltd. of Ashok Leyland Ltd., Bajaj Auto Finance of Bajaj Auto Ltd. Besides, a few leasing companies are subsidiaries of finance and leasing companies like Cholamandlam Finance Ltd. is a subsidiary of Cholamandlam Investment and Finance Ltd.

The latter category meets the group companies' fund requirements and avoids income-tax by the group companies. Because of these advantages, big industrial houses have set up in-house and vendor subsidiary companies. *For example,* Swadeshi Leasing Ltd. was floated by the Hindustan Motors Ltd., the Classic Leasing by ITC Ltd., and Nagarjuna Finance Ltd. by the Empire Industries.

2. Public Sector Leasing

The public sector leasing organisations are divided into—(a) Leasing divisions of financial institutions; (b) Subsidiaries of nationalised commercial banks; and (c) Other public sector leasing organisations.

(i) *Financial Institutions*

Financial institutions are a very important constituent of the public sector leasing industry in India. They were set up to provide long-term finance to the private sector firms. Recently, they have moved to leasing business such as IFCI, ICICI, IRBI, National Small Industries Corporations (NSIC), etc.

(ii) *Subsidiaries of Commercial Banks*

This is the growing segment of the public sector leasing industry. Till 1991, there were around ten bank subsidiaries active in leasing but in February 1994, the RBI allowed banks to directly enter into leasing.

Consequent upon the amendment of Section 19(1) of the Banking Regulation Act 1949[7]*, banks can set up subsidiaries for undertaking leasing activities. Hence, banks are setting up subsidiaries with not less than 51% of shareholding, for transacting equipment leasing business or to invest in shares within the limits specified in Section 19(2) of the Act. The aggregate investment of a bank in a subsidiary and/or not in shares of the leasing companies should not exceed 10% of the paid-up capital and reserves of the bank.*

7. http://www.rbi.org.in/scripts/BS_ViewMasCirculardetails.

The leading players in this segment are SBI Capital Markets Ltd. (SBI Cap) and Canbank Financial Services Ltd. (Canbank), wholly-owned subsidiaries of the State Bank of India and Canara Bank, respectively. Other banks which have joined this business are BOB Fiscal Services Ltd. (a subsidiary of the Bank of Baroda) and PNB Capital Services Ltd. (a subsidiary of the Punjab National Bank).

(iii) *Other Public Sector Organisations*

A few State-level industrial development organisations such as the State Industrial Investment Corporation of Maharashtra (SICOM) and the Gujarat Industrial and Investment Corporation (GIIC) have floated their own subsidiary leasing companies.

Public sector manufacturing companies like Electronics Corporation of India Ltd. (ECIL), CMC Computers Ltd. and Bharat Electronics Ltd. (BEL) have also started leasing to sell their equipment.

The above structural framework of leasing industry in India is depicted in Figure 11.3.

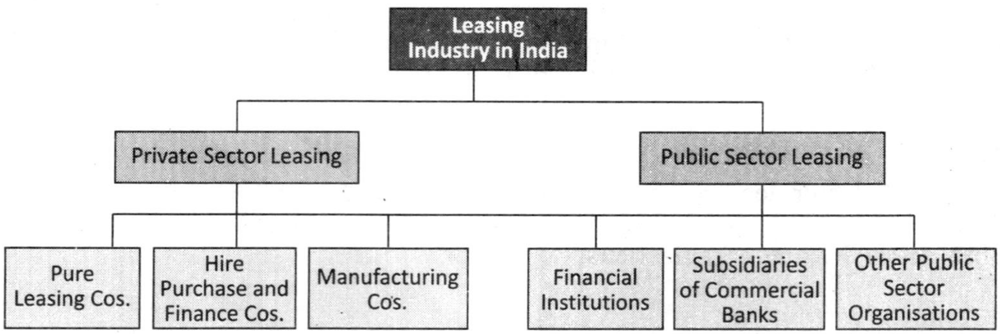

Figure 11.3 Indian Leasing Industry

REGULATORY FRAMEWORK OF LEASING IN INDIA

The regulations which have been laid down for leasing in India and the procedural requirements are discussed below:

Laws and Acts Governing Leasing in India

Leasing involves compliance of relevant provisions of various Acts and Legislations which are enumerated as follows:

- Indian Contract Act, 1872
- Transfer of Property Act, 1882
- Sale of Goods Act, 1930
- Indian Easement Act, 1882
- Companies Act, 1956
- Partnership Act, 1932
- Income Tax Act, 1961
- Urban Land (Ceiling and Regulation) Act, 1976
- Limitation Act, 1930

- Indian Stamp Act, 1899
- Arbitration Act, 1940
- Sales Tax Laws

Documents Required for Leasing

Leasing requires a series of documentation which comprise of both commercial as well as legal documents. *Commercial documents* include purchase order, invoice, acknowledgement of delivery, insurance cover, import license, guarantees and the like. *Legal documents* include lease agreement, letter of guarantee and indemnity, service agreement for leased asset, and lease deed (for real estate).

Contents of Lease Agreement

A lease agreement is entered between a *lessor* and a *lessee*. The agreement contains the terms and conditions subject to which the property has been leased out by the lessor to the lessee. Before entering into a lease agreement, a lessee should ensure that the lessor has proper title to the property. The lessor should either be the owner of the property or an authorised power of attorney holder.

The lessee may verify the society's share certificate in order to ensure that the lessor has title to the property. The agreement should be signed by the lessor himself or his duly authorised power of attorney. A lease agreement should be drafted out carefully.

The following clauses are found in most of the lease agreements:

(a) *Party to the Lease*

The first part of a lease agreement will almost always state the two parties that are involved in the binding agreement. Normally, these two parties are referred to as the *Landlord* and the *Tenant*.

(b) *Property*

Of course, the lease agreement must specifically state the location of the property that is being provided by the landlord and leased to the tenant. This section also includes a provision about furniture and appliances that are being included in the lease agreement.

(c) *Term*

The term of the lease agreement refers to the period for which the property will be occupied and paid for by the tenant. Typically, this will include wording that states the term starts on January 1, 2XXX and ends on December 31, 2XXX. Commonly, this section of the lease agreement includes a lease option to extend the period of occupancy. *For example,* the tenant's lease option might allow him/her to extend the lease for another six months.

(d) *Rent*

The lease agreement would be severely lacking if it did not include terms for the monthly payment as well as the date on which the payment is due.

(e) *Utilities/Services*

The lease agreement should outline who pays for what. Some landlords will pay for everything, while others will make the tenant foot the actual costs for utilities and services.

(f) *Deposit*

Most landlords will require a deposit equalling one month's rent upon signing the lease agreement. This provides the landlord some insurance should the tenant try to skip out on his last month's rent or damage the property. However, if the tenant leaves the apartment in good condition and his account is paid in full, then he should receive most, if not all, of his deposit back in the form of a cheque via mail a few weeks after moving out.

The rest of the lease agreement will vary from here on depending on what other terms and provisions the landlord chooses to include in the lease agreement. If the tenant lease includes additional lease options, they may be included at the end of the lease agreement as well.

FINANCIAL EVALUATION OF LEASING

Lease financing is financially evaluated from the point of view of both lessor and lessee.

Following are the steps in financial evaluation of a financial lease:

(a) Evaluation of client with respect to his financial strength and creditworthiness,
(b) Evaluation of security/collateral security offered, and
(c) Financial evaluation of the proposal.

A lease can be evaluated either as an investment decision or as a financing mean. The lessee has to decide whether to go for a lease arrangement or whether to buy the equipment. Thus, lease evaluation for him is 'debt financing' versus 'lease financing'.

From the lessor's perspective, the decision is whether to accept a lease proposal or to go for the other alternative. The deciding factor in both the cases is "net advantage".

Methods of Evaluation of Lease

There are three methods of evaluating a leasing proposal—(i) Present Value method, (ii) Internal Rate of Return method, and (iii) the Bower Herringer Williamson method. These are explained below:

1. *Present Value Method*

Here, the present value of the annual lease payments tax adjusted is compared with the annual loan repayments adjusted for tax shield on depreciation and interest, and the alternative which has the lesser cash outflow is selected.

So, the lease-versus-buying decision involves use of capital budgeting technique of 'NPV'. *[NPV here stands for Net Present Value of Leasing NPV (L) or Net Advantage of Leasing (NAL)].*

Decision Rule: If NPV(L)/NAL is positive, the leasing alternative to be used, otherwise borrowing alternative would be preferable.

Calculation of NPV(L)/NAL

Cost of an Asset

Less: PV of Lease Rentals (LR) (Discounted at Kd)
Add: PV of tax shield on LR (Discounted at Ke)
Less: PV of interest on debt tax shield (Discounted at Ke)
Less: PV of tax shield on depreciation (Discounted at Ke)
Less: PV of salvage value (Discounted at Ke)

Note: The discount rate used is the marginal cost of capital (Ke) for all cash flows other than lease payments and the pretax cost of long-term debt for lease payment (Kd).

The value of the interest tax shield is included as forgone cash flow in the computation of NPV(L)/NAL (Box 11.2).

BOX 11.2: LEASE RENT DETERMINATION

A lease payment has three components—depreciation fee, finance fee, and sales tax.

Lease Rent = Depreciation Fee + Finance Fee + Sales Tax

(i) Depreciation Fee

Depreciation fee is the payment being made to the leasing company for the loss in value of the asset. It is spread over the lease term (number of months) to calculate the monthly lease payment. This is paid as the leasing company incurs the cost, though the equipment is at the disposal of the lessee for the entire lease period and will only obtain the residual value at the time of resale.

Depreciation Fee = (Net Capital Cost – Residual)/Term

where,

Net Capital Cost is Gross Capital Cost (selling price negotiated with the dealer) plus any add-on dealer fees and taxes that will not be paid up-front in cash, minus any Capital Cost Reductions (down payment, trade-in, or rebates). It does not include any lease charges that are paid in cash, when the lease agreement is signed.

Residual is lease-end resale or residual value.

Term is the length of lease (in months).

(ii) Finance Fee

The finance fee is the payment to the leasing company for the use of their money. It is similar to interest on a loan and is paid on the average amount financed.

Finance Fee = (Net Capital Cost + Residual) x Money Factor

(iii) Sales Tax

Sales tax is the statutory tax levied on the value of sales.

EXAMPLE

Amit has decided on 3 years (36 months term) lease of a car that has a sticker price of ₹24,600 (MSRP*). He negotiated the price down to ₹23,000 and decides not to make a down payment, but to have a trade-in worth ₹5000. Annual interest rate is 9.0% and the residual value is 60%. Calculate the monthly lease payment.

Solution:

Net Capital Cost = ₹23,000 – ₹5000 = ₹18,000.

The dealer informs him that the money factor is 0.00375.
The residual percentage is 60% of MSRP.
Therefore, residual amount = 0.60 x ₹24,600 = ₹14,760.

Now, calculating the monthly lease payment to be made by him:
Depreciation Fee = (₹18,000 – ₹14,760)/36 = ₹90
Finance Fee = (₹18,000 + ₹14,760) x 0.00375 = ₹122.85
Monthly Lease Payment = ₹90.00 + ₹122.85
= ₹212.85
Therefore, Monthly Lease Payment to be made by him is ₹212.85 (excluding Sales Tax).

*MSRP stands for 'Manufacturer's suggested retail price'.

ILLUSTRATION 11.1: A leasing company expects a minimum yield of 10% on its investment in the leasing business. It proposes to lease a machine costing ₹5,00,000 for 10 years @ ₹72,000. Should the lessee buy the machine or lease it? Calculate the net cash outflows of lease rentals to lessee and its PV. The borrowing rate is 15%. The corporate tax rate is 35% and the depreciation is charged on S-L-M basis.

Solution: The discount rate, after tax is 15(1 – .35) = 9.75%.

Table 11.1 shows the cash outflows under leasing; Table 11.2 gives a schedule of debt repayments and Table 11.3 shows cash outflows under debt financing.

TABLE 11.1 Schedule of Cash Outflows under 'Leasing'

End of Year	*Lease Payment* ₹ (1)	*Tax Shield Cash Outflows* ₹ (2) = [(1) *t]	*Net Cash Outflows* ₹ (3) = (1) – (2)	*Present Value of Net Cash Outflows at* 9.75% (₹)
0				(2,90,680)
1	72,000	25,200	46,800	
2	72,000	25,200	46,800	
3	72,000	25,200	46,800	
4	72,000	25,200	46,800	
5	72,000	25,200	46,800	
6	72,000	25,200	46,800	
7	72,000	25,200	46,800	
8	72,000	25,200	46,800	
9	72,000	25,200	46,800	
10	72,000	25,200	46,800	

TABLE 11.2 Schedule of Debt Repayments (for a Loan of ₹5 lacs)

End of Year	*Annual Instalment* (₹)	*Annual Interest @15%* (₹)	*Principal Amount Owing at the End of Year* (₹)	*Principal Balance* (₹)
0				5,00,000
1	99,626	75,000	24,626	4,75,374
2	99,626	71,306	28,320	4,47,054
3	99,626	67,058	32,568	4,14,486
4	99,626	62,173	37,453	3,77,033
5	99,626	56,555	43,071	3,33,962
6	99,626	50,094	49,532	2,84,430
7	99,626	42,665	56,962	2,27,469
8	99,626	34,120	65,506	1,61,963
9	99,626	24,294	75,332	86,631
10	99,626	12,995	86,631	0
	5,97,756	**3,82,186**	**2,15,570**	

Note: In case of buying the asset, the firm will have to borrow ₹5,00,000 at 15% p.a. interest. It is assumed that this loan will be repaid with interest in the same period as the term of the lease. This assumption places the loan on an equivalent basis with the lease.

TABLE 11.3 Schedule of Cash Outflows under 'Debt Financing'

End of Year	*Annual Loan Instalment*	*Interest @15%*	*Depreciation* (SLM = C/N)	*Tax Shield*	*Net Cash Outflows*	*Present Value of Net Cash Outflows at* 9.75%
	(1)	(2)	(3)	(4) [(2)+(3) × t]	(5) (1)–(4)	(6)
	₹	₹	₹	₹	₹	₹
0						(3,91,305)
1	99,626	75,000	50,000	43,750	55,876	
2	99,626	71,306	50,000	42,457	57,169	
3	99,626	67,058	50,000	40,970	58,656	
4	99,626	62,173	50,000	39,261	60,365	
5	99,626	56,555	50,000	37,294	62,332	
6	99,626	50,094	50,000	35,033	64,593	
7	99,626	42,665	50,000	32,433	67,193	
8	99,626	34,120	50,000	29,442	70,184	
9	99,626	24,294	50,000	26,003	73,623	
10	99,626	12,995	50,000	22,048	77,578	
(t = tax rate)						

The present value of cash outflows under lease financing is ₹2,90,680 while that of debt financing (i.e. owning this asset) is ₹3,91,305. Thus, leasing is advantageous vis-à-vis ownership in this case. It has been assumed that the lessor does not pass on the tax benefits of additional depreciation to the lessee.

2. *Internal Rate of Return Method*

Under this method, after tax 'cost of capital' of lease is calculated, it is compared with that of the other available sources of finance such as a fresh issue of equity capital, retained earnings or debt. *In simple words, it helps to find out the rate at which the lease rentals, net of tax shield on depreciation are equal to the cost of leasing.* Using the above example, the calculation of this rate, i.e. cost of leasing, is shown in Table 11.4.

Using the above example, when we compute the rate of discount that equates the negative cash flows with the positive cash flows, we get 4.9%. This is explained below as well. After comparing this with the after-tax cost of debt finance, i.e. 9.75%, it can be inferred that the cost of lease is lower than after-tax cost of debt finance. Thus, the former is preferred.

TABLE 11.4 Computation of Cash Flows for Internal Rate of Return

End of Year	*Cost of Asset*	*Lease Rental*	*Depreciation* (SLM = C/N)	*Additional Tax Shield on Lease Rental*	*Net Cash Outflows*
(1)	(2)	(3)	(4)	(5) (3) – (4) * t	(6) (3) – (5)
	₹	₹	₹	₹	₹
0	5,00,000				5,00,000
1		72,000	50,000	7,700	(64,300)
2		72,000	50,000	7,700	(64,300)
3		72,000	50,000	7,700	(64,300)
4		72,000	50,000	7,700	(64,300)
5		72,000	50,000	7,700	(64,300)
6		72,000	50,000	7,700	(64,300)
7		72,000	50,000	7,700	(64,300)
8		72,000	50,000	7,700	(64,300)
9		72,000	50,000	7,700	(64,300)
10		72,000	50,000	7,700	(64,300)

Let us discount cash flows at 5%, then the NPV is:

₹5,00,000 + (₹64,300) × PVIFA (4%, 10)

= ₹5,00,000 + (₹64,300) × 8.111

= ₹5,00,000 + (₹5,21,537)

= – ₹21,537

Since the value is negative, now we shall discount at a higher rate, at 5%. At 5%, the value is positive.

$$= ₹\ 5,00,000 + (₹\ 64,300) \times 7.722$$

$$= ₹\ 5,00,000 + (₹\ 4,96,525) = ₹\ 3,475$$

Using interpolation formula:

$$= 4\% + \frac{-21,537}{-21,537\ -\ 3,475}\ (5\% - 4\%)$$

$$= 4\% + \frac{21,537}{25,012}(5\% - 4\%)$$

$$= 4\% + 0.86\% = 4.86\%$$

$$= 4.9\% \text{ (after rounding off)}$$

IRR method is preferred to the other methods for the simple reason that there is no need to assume any cost of capital for discounting purposes in the IRR method, unlike the present value method.

3. *Bower-Herringer-Williamson Method*

This method divides the financial and tax aspects of lease financing. If the operating advantage of a lease is more than its financial disadvantage or vice-versa, lease is preferred. This is also used as "equivalent loan" method. Its process is discussed in brief as follows:

1. Compare the present value of debt with the discounted value of lease payments (gross), the rate of discount being the gross cost of debt capital. The net present value is the financial advantage (or disadvantage).
2. Calculate the comparative tax benefit during the period and discount it at an appropriate cost of capital. The present value is the operating advantage (or disadvantage) of leasing.
3. If the net result is an advantage, choose leasing.

For the above given example:

	₹
Present value of loan payments	5,00,000
Present value of lease payments discounted at 15%	3,61,368
i.e., ₹ 72,000 × 5.019	
Financial advantage	1,38,632

The present value of comparative tax-benefits, i.e. the operating advantage (disadvantage) is calculated in Table 11.5.

TABLE 11.5 Computation of Present Value of Incremental Tax Benefits for Operating Result

End of Year	Tax Shield, on Leasing (₹ 72,000*t)	Tax Shield, on Borrowings (Refer Table 11.3)	Incremental Saving in Tax due to Leasing	Present Value Factor at 15%	Present Value at 15%
(1)	(2)	(3)	(4) = (2)–(3)	(5)	(6) = (4)×(5)
	₹	₹	₹	₹	₹
1	25,200	43,750	(18,550)	0.87	(16,139)
2	25,200	42,457	(17,257)	0.76	(13,115)
3	25,200	40,970	(15,770)	0.66	(10,408)
4	25,200	39,261	(14,061)	0.57	(8,015)
5	25,200	37,294	(12,094)	0.50	(6,047)
6	25,200	35,033	(9,833)	0.43	(4,228)
7	25,200	32,433	(7,233)	0.38	(2,749)
8	25,200	29,442	(4,242)	0.33	(1,400)
9	25,200	26,003	(803)	0.28	(225)
10	25,200	22,048	3,152	0.25	788
			Operating disadvantage		(61,537)

Note: The rate of 15% is the appropriate cost of capital.

Since the financial advantage is more than the operating disadvantage in lease, it is advantageous to go for leasing.

HIRE PURCHASE

Hire purchase is a type of instalment credit under which the hire purchaser called the *hirer*, takes the goods on hire at a stated rental, with an option to purchase. Under this transaction, the hirer acquires the property (goods) immediately on signing the hire purchase agreement but its ownership or title is transferred only when the last instalment is paid.

Evolution of Hire Purchase

The concept of HP in India is believed to be introduced by the British. Commercial Credit Corporation was the first HP company to be set up in Madras (now Chennai). Then there were companies like Motor and General Finance, and Instalment Supply Company, which were set up in 1920s and 1930s in North India.

HP developed in two forms—consumer durables and automobiles. *Consumer durables HP* was promoted by the dealers in the respective equipment. Therefore, Singer Sewing Machine Company, or Murphy Radio dealers would provide instalment facilities on HP basis to the customers of their products.

The *automobiles HP* developed rapidly in the form of *HP of commercial vehicles.* The dealers in commercial vehicles as well as pure financing companies flourished this segment on account of good value of assets and easy repossession.

Regulation of Hire Purchase in India

The hire purchase system is regulated by the Hire Purchase Act, 1972[8]. This Act defines a *hire purchase* as "an agreement under which goods are let on hire and under which the hirer has an option to purchase them in accordance with the terms of the agreement and includes an agreement under which:

(i) Possession of goods is delivered by the owner thereof to a person on condition that such persons pays the agreed amount in periodical instalments, and
(ii) The property in the goods is to pass to such person on the payment of the last of such instalments, and
(iii) Such person has a right to terminate the agreement at any time before the property so passes.

Therefore, as per this definition, an option is given to a buyer either to purchase the property after payment of all the instalments or not to take the ownership. In case, the latter option is chosen by the buyer, the property comes back to the seller.

For example, one machine costs around ₹10 crores. The customer may not be in a position to pay ₹10 crores immediately. Therefore, the seller and buyer enters into agreement by which the buyer will pay ₹1 crore per year and will get immediate possession of a machine. After 10 years of paying all the instalments, seller will transfer the title of the machine to the buyer.

The buyer gets the benefit of immediate possession by which his utility for machine is satisfied. Companies selling goods on hire purchase usually charge higher amount than the price of product, for a deferred payment; let us call it interest on deferred payment. Therefore, the company also receives the amount more than the normal price of the product.

To conclude, Hire Purchase (HP) is an agreement wherein, after making all the payments, the customer becomes the owner of the equipment. For tax purposes, from the beginning of the agreement, the business customer is treated as the owner of the equipment and so he can claim capital allowances as tax incentives. The business customer is responsible for maintenance of the equipment.

Hire purchase is advantageous to customers because it spreads the cost of expensive items over the time period (Box 11.3).

BOX 11.3: HIRE PURCHASE VS. OTHERS

Hire purchase should be distinguished from 'instalment sale' wherein property passes to the purchaser with the payment of the first instalment. But in case of HP, ownership remains with the seller until the last instalment is paid, and the buyer gets ownership after paying the last instalment.

Hire purchase differs from a 'mortgage' and similar forms of lien-secured credit in the sense that in HP, the so-called buyer who has the use of the goods is not the legal owner during the term of the contract. If the buyer defaults in paying the instalments, the owner may repossess the goods.

8. http://clap.nls.ac.in/legis/legis28.pdf.

Features

- Hire Purchase is an agreement to hire an asset over a predefined period with an option to purchase it at the end of the agreement.
- After all the payments have been made, the business customer becomes the owner of the equipment.
- Under hire purchase system, the buyer takes possession of goods immediately and agrees to pay the total hire purchase price in instalments.
- In case the buyer defaults in making payments of any instalments, the seller has the right to repose the goods.
- Normally, a deposit is requested, i.e. 10%.
- Funding period is usually between 2–10 years.

Advantages of Hire Purchase for Company

- Higher rate of interest can be charged and as the calculation is on the original advance, higher income would be realised.
- As the company is the owner, attachment of the vehicle and subsequent sale even by private auction would keep the NPAs low.
- As the borrowers would end up losing the instalments paid as well as the vehicle, defaults would be lower.
- The banks can effectively recycle the funds recovered.

Standard Provisions

A valid HP agreement must be in written form, and signed by both the parties. They must clearly set out the following information in a print which can be read by everyone as follows:

- A clear description of the goods
- The cash price of the goods
- The HP price, i.e. the total sum that must be paid to hire and then purchase the goods
- The deposit
- The monthly instalments to be paid
- A comprehensive statement of the parties' right, including the right to cancel the agreement during a 'cooling-off' period
- The right of the hirer to terminate the contract when he decides to do so.

RIGHTS AND OBLIGATIONS UNDER HIRE PURCHASE

Following is the discussion about the rights/warranties and obligations of different parties under hire purchase agreement.

Implied Warranties and Conditions to Protect the Hirer

The extent to which buyers are protected varies from jurisdiction to jurisdiction but the following are usually present:

- The hirer will be allowed to enjoy the possession of the goods, i.e. no one will interfere with the hirer's possession during the term of this contract;
- The owner will be able to pass title to, or ownership of the goods, when the contract requires it;
- The goods are of merchantable quality and fit for their purpose;
- Where the goods are let by reference to a description or to a sample, the goods actually supplied must correspond with the description and the sample.

The Hirer's Rights

The hirer usually has the following rights:

- To buy the goods at any time by giving notice to the owner and paying the balance of the HP price minus a rebate as applicable;
- To return the goods to the owner if he is not satisfied—this is subject to the payment of a penalty to reflect the owner's loss of profit;
- To assign both the benefit and the burden of the contract to a third person with the consent of the owner.
- Where the owner wrongfully repossesses the goods, either to recover the goods plus damages or to claim damages for the value of the goods lost.

The Hirer's Obligations

The hirer usually has the following obligations:

- Pay the hire instalments,
- Take reasonable care of the goods (if the hirer damages the goods by using them in a non-standard way, he or she must continue to pay the instalments and, if appropriate, compensate the owner for any loss in asset value),
- Inform the owner where the goods will be kept.

The Owner's Rights

The owner usually has the right to terminate the agreement where the hirer defaults in paying the instalments or breaches any of the other terms in the agreement. This entitles the owner to:

- Forfeit the deposit;
- Retain the instalments already paid and recover the balance due;
- Repossess the goods by application to a Court; and
- Claim damages for any loss suffered.

DISTINCTION BETWEEN LEASING AND HIRE PURCHASE

Leasing and HP can be differentiated as in Table 11.6.

TABLE 11.6 Distinction between Leasing and Hire Purchase

Basis	*Lease Financing*	*Hire Purchase*
Nature	A lease transaction is a commercial arrangement, wherein an equipment owner or manufacturer passes on to the equipment user the right to use the equipment in return for a rental.	The hire purchaser takes the goods on hire for a rental, which is inclusive of the repayment of principal as well as interest, with an option to purchase.
Option to user	No option is provided to the lessee (user) to purchase the goods.	Option is provided to the hirer (user).
Ownership	It is transferred to the purchaser on payment of the first instalment.	It is passed to the hirer only if he exercises the option to purchase and after payment of the last instalment.
Type of expenditure	Lease rentals paid by the lessee are treated as revenue expenditure of the lessee.	Only interest element included in the HP instalments is treated as revenue expenditure.
Tax benefits	Lessor is allowed claim of depreciation. Lessee is allowed claim of interest on borrowed funds used for rentals/maintenance.	Hirer is allowed depreciation claim and finance charge.
Elements	Lease rentals comprise of 2 elements—finance charge, and capital recovery.	HP instalments comprise of 3 elements—trading profit, finance charge, and recovery of cost of goods/assets.

CASE STUDY

R. Kempraj vs M/s. Barton Son & Co.

(29 August, 1969, Supreme Court of India)

Act

Transfer of Property Act, 4 of 1882, s. 14-Lease of premises with option to lessee to renew it every ten years-Covenant whether offends rule against perpetuity.

Headnote

The respondent by a deed executed in 1951 took on lease certain premises in Bangalore from the appellant. It was stipulated in the deed that the lease would be for a period of 10 years in the first instance with an option to the lessee to renew the same every ten years so long as desired. In 1961 when the first period of ten years was about to expire, the respondent asked for a renewal of the lease. On the appellant's refusal to do so, the respondent filed a suit for specific performance. The suit was decreed by the trial court, the first appellate court and the High Court. Appeal in this court was filed by special leave. The contention of the appellant was that the lease in question, being in the first instance for ten years only, was not a lease in perpetuity as contemplated by s. 105 of the Transfer of Property Act; however, the clauses relating to renewal which were covenants that ran with the land, offended the rule against perpetuity in σ. 14 of the Act.

Held

The appeal must be dismissed.

(a) Section 14 of the Act is applicable only where there is transfer of property. Even if creation of a lease hold interest is a transfer of a right in property and would fall within the expression 'transfer of property', the transfer was for a period of ten years only by means of the indenture in the present case. The stipulation relating to renewal could not be regarded as transferring property or any rights therein. [143 B]

(b) The option of renewal given to the lessee did not contain a covenant which created an interest in the property of the nature that would fall within the ambit of s. 14. [143 F] Ganesh Sonar v. Purnendu Narayan Singha & Ors. (1962) Pat. 201, applied; Woodall v. Clifton, [1905]2 Ch. 257, referred to.

(c) In English law, the court would give effect to a covenant for perpetual renewal so long as the intention is clear and it will not be open to objection on the ground of perpetuity. In India the equitable rule that the burden of a covenant runs with the land is to be found in s. 40 of the Transfer of Property Act but that section itself expresses that the right of the covenanted is not an interest in the land bound by neither the covenant nor an easement. It is not an interest because the Act does not recognise equitable estate. [143 G; 144 F]

Thus, even on the footing that the clauses relating to renewal in the lease, in the present case, contained covenants running with the land, the 141 rule against perpetuity contained in s. 14 of the Act would not be applicable as no interest in property had been created of the nature contemplated in the provision. [144 G] Muller v. Trafford, [1901]1 Ch. 54; Weg Motors Ltd. v. Hales & Ors. [1961] 3 A.E.L.R. 181, 188, and London & South Western Rly. v. Goreto, (1882) 20 Ch. D. 56.2, 580, referred to.

Judgement

Civil Appellate Jurisdiction: Civil Appeal No. 1655 of 1968.

Appeal by special leave from the judgment and order dated December 20, 1967 of the Mysore High Court in Regular Second Appeal No. 811 of 1965.

The judgment of the Court was delivered by J. Grover. This is an appeal by special leave from a judgment of the Mysore High Court in which the question involved is whether an option given to a lessee to get the lease, which is initially for a period of 10 years, renewed after every 10 years, is hit by the rule of perpetuity and is void.

The respondent entered into a deed of lease on October 26, 1951 with the appellan in respect of premises Nos. 8 and 9, Mahatma Gandhi Road, (South Parade), Civi Station, Bangalore. It was stipulated that the lease would be for a period of 10 year in the first instance with effect from November 1, 1961 "with an option to the lessee t renew the same as long as desired as provided". Clauses 9 and 10 which are materia may be reproduced:

"*Clause 9:* The lessee shall have the right to renew the lease of the schedule premises at the end of the present period of ten years herein, secured on the sam rental of ₹450 per month, for a similar period and for further similar periods thereafte on the same terms and conditions as are set forth herein; and the lessee shall b permitted and shall have the right to remain in occupation of the premises on th same terms and conditions for any further periods of ten years as long as they desir to do so.

Clause 10: The lessor shall not raise any objection whatsoever to the lesse exercising his option to renew the lease for any further periods of ten years on the sam terms and conditions as long as they desire to be in 142 occupation, provided that th lessee shall not have the right to transfer the lease or alienate any right thereunder"

It appears that before the expiry of the period of ten years from the date o the commencement of the lease, the lessee wrote to the lessor informing him of th intention to exercise the option given to him under the deed of lease to get the sam renewed on the same terms and conditions as before, for a period of ten years fron November 1, 1961. The lessor did not comply with the request. After serving a notice the lessee filed a suit for specific performance of the covenant in the lease for renewal It was prayed that the lessor be directed to execute a registered deed to lease ir favour of the lessee and if he failed to do so the court should execute a deed in hi favour. The lessor pleaded, inter alia, that the condition relating to renewal had hi the rule against perpetuity. Certain other pleas were taken with which we are no concerned with. The trial court decreed the suit. The first appellate court and th High Court affirmed the decree. The rule against perpetuity is embodied in s. 14 o the Transfer of Property Act, hereinafter called the 'Act'. According to this rule, n transfer of property can operate to create an interest which is to take effect after th lifetime of one or more persons living at the date of such transfer and the minority o some person who shall be in existence at the expiration of that period and to whom if he attains full age, the interest created is to belong. It is well known that the rul against perpetuity is rounded on the principle that the liberty of alienation "shall no be exercised to its own destruction and that all contrivances shall be void which tend to create a perpetuity or place property forever out of the reach of the exercise of th power of alienation". The words "transfer of property" have been defined by s. 5 of th Act to mean an act by which a living person conveys property in present or in futur to one or more other living persons etc. The words "living persons" include a Company or association or body of individuals. Section 105 of the Act defines "lease". A *lease* o immovable property is a transfer of a right to enjoy such property made for a certain time, expressed or implied or in perpetuity in consideration of a price paid or promised or of money, a share of crops, service or any other thing of value. A lease of land is not a mere contract but it is a transfer of an interest in land and creates a right in rem. Owing to the provisions of Section 105, a lease in perpetuity can be created but even then, an interest still remains in the lessor which is called a *reversion*.

It is not disputed on behalf of the appellant that a lease in perpetuity could have been created but the lease in the present case was not of that kind and was for a period of ten years only in the first instance. It is said that the mischief is created by the clauses relating to renewal which are covenants that run with the land. It is pointed out that on a correct construction of the renewal clauses, the rule of perpetuity contained in section 14 would be immediately attracted. We are unable to agree. Section 14 is applicable only where there is transfer of property. Even if creation of a lease-hold interest is a transfer of a right in property and would fall within the expression "transfer of property", the transfer was for a period of ten years only by means of the indenture Exh. P-I. The stipulation relating to the renewal could not be regarded as transferring property or any rights therein. In Ganesh Sonar v. Purnendu Narayan Singha & Ors.(1) in the case of lease of land, an option had been given to the lessor to determine the lease and take possession of the lease-hold land under specified conditions. The question was whether such a covenant would fall within the rule laid down in the English case Woodall v. Clifton(2), in which it was held that a provision in a lease giving an option to the lessor to purchase the piece of land at a certain rate was invalid as infringing the rule against perpetuity. The Patna High Court distinguished the English decision quite rightly on the ground that after the counting into force of the Act, a contract for the sale of immovable property did not itself create an interest in such property as was the case under the English law. According to the Patna decision, the option given by the lessee to the lessor to resume the lease-hold land was merely a personal covenant and was not a covenant which created an interest in land and therefore, the rule against perpetuity contained in Section 14 of the Act was not applicable. The same principle would govern the present case. The clauses containing the option to get the lease renewed on the expiry of each term of ten years can, by no means, be regarded as creating an interest in property of the nature that would fall within the ambit of Section 14. Even under the English law, the court would give effect to a covenant for perpetual renewal so long as the invention is clear and it will not be open to objection on the ground of perpetuity (see Halsbury's Laws of England, 3rd Edn. Vol. 23, p 627). In Muller v. Traf Jword(3), it was held that the covenant in a lease for renewal was not strictly a covenant for renewal. But J. Farwell, proceeded to observe that a covenant to renew had been held for at least two centuries to be a covenant running with the land. If so, then no question of perpetuity would arise. It appears that in England, whatever might have been the reason, the objection of perpetuity had never been taken to cases (1) (1962) Patna 201. (2) (1905) 2. Ch. 257. (3)(1901) 1 Ch. 54. of covenants for renewal. The following observations of J. Farwell, which were quoted with approval by Lord Evershed, M.R. in Weg Motors Ltd. v. Hales & Others(1) are noteworthy:

"But now I will assume that this is a covenant for renewal running with the land; it is then, in my opinion, free from any taint of perpetuity because it is annexed to the land. See Rogers v. Hosegood, (1900)2 Ch. 388".

The equitable rule that the burden of a covenant runs with the land is to be found in Section 40 of the Act. This section reads:

"*Section 40:* Where for the more beneficial enjoyment of his own immoveable property, a third person has, independently of any interest in the immoveable property of another or of any easement thereon, a right to restrain the enjoyment in a particular manner of the latter property, or where a third person is entitled to the benefit of an obligation arising out of contract, and annexed to the ownership of immoveable property but not amounting to an interest therein or easement thereon, such right or obligation may be enforced against a transferee with notice thereof or a gratuitous transferee of the property affected thereby but not against a transferee for consideration and without notice of the right or obligation nor against such property in his hands".

As pointed out in Mulla's Transfer of Property Act, 5th Edn. at page 194, Section 40 expressly says that the right of the covenantee is not an interest in the land bound by the covenant nor an easement. It is not an interest because the Act does not recognise equitable estates and it cannot be said as Sir George Jessal said in London & South Western Rly. v. Gomm(2)—that if a covenant "binds the land it creates an equitable interest in the land". The expression "covenant runs with the land" has been taken from the English law of real property. It is an exception to the general rule that all covenants are personal. Even on the footing that the clauses relating to renewal in the lease, in the present case, contain covenants running with the land, the rule against perpetuity contained in Section 14 of the Act would not be applicable as no interest in property has been created of the nature contemplated by that provision. For the above reasons, the appeal fails and it is dismissed with costs.

G.C. Appeal dismissed.

Source: http://indiankanoon.org/doc/706590.

SOLVED PROBLEMS

PROBLEM 11.1: Aman & Co. agrees to enter into a new lease arrangement with Sumit (the lessor). The lessor agrees to pay the lessee's moving costs as an incentive to the lessee for entering into the new lease. The lessee's moving costs are ₹2,000. The new lease has a term of 20 years, at a fixed rate of ₹3,000 per year. Account for this.

Solution: The lessor recognises moving costs of ₹2,000 as an expense in Year 1.

Net consideration of ₹58,000 consists of ₹3,000 for each of the 20 years in the lease term, less ₹2,000 incentive for relocation costs.

Both the lessor and lessee would recognise the net rental consideration of ₹58,000 over the 20-year lease term using a single amortisation method.

PROBLEM 11.2: Mohit agrees to enter into a new lease arrangement with Anil (the lessor). The lessor agrees to a rent-free period for the first two years as incentive to the lessee for entering into the new lease. The new lease has a term of 10 years, at a fixed rate of ₹2,000 per year. What is its accounting treatment?

Solution: Net consideration of ₹16,000 consists of 2,000 for each of 8 years in the lease term. Both the lessor and lessee would recognise the net consideration of ₹16,000 over the 10-year lease term using a single amortisation method.

PROBLEM 11.3: The pre-tax cost of capital of the ABC Leasing Ltd. (ABCL) is 20%. Its expected pre-tax return on investment is 25%. Assume a non-cancellable lease period of five years. Determine the lease rental per ₹1,000 so as to give ABCL its expected return.

Solution: While computing the pre-tax return, the lease may be viewed as a loan-bearing interest equal to the expected rate of return by the lessor payable in equal instalments corresponding to the lease period.

Or, it may be treated as a series of future cash inflows discounted by the expected rate of return, their present value equals the investment in the lease transactions (Table 11.7).

TABLE 11.7 Computation of Lease Rental

Year	*Lease Rental*	*Present Value Factor @ 25%*	*Present Value of Rental* [(2) × (3)]
(1)	(2)	(3)	(4)
1	L	0.80	0.80 L
2	L	0.64	0.64 L
3	L	0.51	0.51 L
4	L	0.41	0.41 L
5	L	0.33	0.33 L
Total			**2.69 L**

Thus, L 2.69 = ₹1,000

L = ₹371.75

The pre-tax return of 0.25 for ABCL has two components—pre-tax cost of capital, 0.20, and a net profit of 0.05.

PROBLEM 11.4: ABC Co. is planning to install a machine with a life of 3 years. Its cost is ₹150 lacs and scrap value ₹15 lacs. The company has following options:

1. To take a loan @ 18% and buy that machine, the loan being repayable in 3 equal yearly instalments at the end of the year.
2. Take it on lease @ 450/1000 payable annually for 3 years.

Depreciation is 30% (WDV). Tax rate is 35%. Determine which option is better.

Solution:

Pre-tax rate is 18%.

Post tax rate is 18% (1 – 0.35) = 11.7%.

(a) P.V. of lease rentals

Lease rental for ₹150 lacs = ₹150 lacs × 450/1000 = ₹67.50 lacs p.a.

P.V. of LR = PVIFA (11.7%, 3) × ₹67.50 lacs

= 2.402 × ₹67.50 lacs

= ₹162.14 lacs

(b) P.V. of tax shield

Taxes to be paid are = Tax Rate × Amount

= 0.35 × ₹67.50 lacs

= ₹23.63 lacs per year

Present value of tax shield is PVIFA (11.7%, 3) × 23.63

i.e., 2.402 × ₹23.63 = ₹56.76 lacs

(c) The loan amount is repayable together with the interest at the rate of 18% on loan amount in 3 equal instalments at the end of each year.

The PVIFA at the rate of 18% for 3 years is 2.174, the amount payable will be:

$$\text{Annual payment} = \frac{₹\ 150}{2.174}$$

= ₹ 68.99 lacs

(d) P.V. of Depreciation

Depreciation for 1st year is 30% of ₹ 150 lacs = ₹ 45 lacs.

Depreciation for 2nd year is 30% of ₹ 105 lacs = ₹ 31.5 lacs

Depreciation for 3rd year is 30% of ₹ 73.5 lacs = ₹ 22.05 lacs

Depreciation tax shield = ₹ 45 lacs × 0.35 = ₹ 15.75 lacs

= ₹ 31.5 lacs × 0.35 = ₹ 11.025 lacs

= ₹ 22.05 lacs × 0.35 = ₹ 7.72 lacs

P.V. of Depreciation tax shield = 15.75 × PVIF (11.7%, 1) + 11.025 × PVIF (11.7%, 2) + 7.72 × PVIF (11.7%, 3)

= ₹ 27.98 lacs

(e) P.V. of interest tax shield in case of debt

If purchaser takes a loan instead of a lease, then the P.V. of tax shield will be as shown in Table 11.8.

TABLE 11.8

₹ lacs

End of the Year	*Instalment* (1)	*Interest @ 18%* (2)	*Principal* (3) (1) – (2)	*Loan Outstanding at the End of the Year* (4)
0				150
1	68.99	27.00	41.99	108.01
2	68.99	19.44	49.55	58.46
3	68.99	10.53	58.46	0
			150.00	

Interest tax shield:

Interest × Tax rate = Interest tax shield

₹ 27 lacs × 0.35 = ₹ 9.45 lacs

₹ 19.44 lacs × 0.35 = ₹ 6.80 lacs

₹ 10.53 lacs × 0.35 = ₹ 3.69 lacs

P.V. of tax shield:

₹ 9.45 lacs × PVIF (11.7%, 1) + ₹ 6.80 lacs × PVIF (11.7%, 2) + ₹ 3.69 lacs PVIF (11.7%, 3)

= ₹ 16.49 lacs

(f) P.V. of Salvage:
Salvage value is 15 lacs after 3 years.
So, P.V. of salvage in 3rd year is 15 × PVIF (11.7%, 3) = 10.68 lacs

Analysis:

NPV(L)/NAL = 150 − 67.5 × PVIFA(18%, 3) + 56.76 − 27.98 − 16.49 − 10.68
= 150 − 67.5 × 2.174 + 56.76 − 27.98 − 16.49 − 10.68
= 150 − 146.75 + 56.76 − 27.98 − 16.49 − 10.68
= 4.86

Since NPV of leasing is positive, hence, it is advisable to opt for leasing.

PROBLEM 11.5: The following details relate to an investment proposal of the Indian Corporation Ltd. (ICL):

- Investment outlay, ₹200 lacs
- Useful life, 3 years
- Depreciation on straight line basis
- Net salvage value after 3 years, ₹40 lacs

To finance the investment, the ICL has two options to choose from:

Option 1: Borrow and buy the equipment. The cost of capital of the ICL is 10%; marginal rate of tax is 35%; cost of debt is 18% per annum.

Option 2: Lease the equipment from the Leasing India Ltd. on a three year full-payout basis @ ₹525/₹1,000 payable annually.

Which option should the ICL choose and why? Show the loan amortisation.

Solution: Table 11.9 shows the decision analysis and Table 11.10 shows the debt amortisation schedule.

TABLE 11.9 Decision Analysis

	(₹ lacs)
1. Investment outlay	200.00
2. *Less:* Present value of lease rentals (Note 1)	228.3
3. *Add:* Present value of tax shield on lease rentals (Note 2)	91.4
4. *Less:* Present value of tax shield on depreciation (Note 3)	119.63
5. *Less*: Present value of interest shield on debt (Note 4)	39.45
6. *Less:* Present value of net salvage value (Note 5)	30.04
NAL/NPV (L)	**(126.02)**

Since the NAL is negative, lease is not economically viable. The ICL should select the option to borrow and buy.

Working Notes:

1. Present value of lease rentals:

   = ₹(200 lacs × 0.525) × PVIFA (18, 3)

   = ₹105 lacs × 2.174 = ₹228.3 lacs

2. Present value of tax shield on lease rentals:

   = ₹(200 lacs × 0.525 × 0.35) × PVIFA (10, 3)

   = ₹36.75 lacs × 2.487 = ₹91.4 lacs

3. Present value of tax shield on depreciation:

   = [66.6 × PVIFA (10, 1) + 66.6 x PVIFA (10, 2) + 66.6 × PVIFA (10, 3)] × 0.35

   = [66.6 × 0.909) + (66.6 × 1.736) + (66.6 × 2.487)] × 0.35

   = ₹119.63 lacs

4. Present value of interest tax shield on displaced debt, as given in Table 11.10:

   = [36 × PVIFA (10, 1) + 25.92 (10, 2) + 14.03 × PVIFA (10, 3)] × 0.35

   = [(36 × 0.909) + (25.92 × 1.736) + (14.03 × 2.487) × 0.35

   = ₹39.45 lacs

5. Present value of net salvage value:

   = 40 × PVIF (10, 3)

   = 40 × 0.751 = ₹30.04 lacs

TABLE 11.10 Debt Amortisation Schedule

(₹ lacs)

Year	*Instalment*	*Interest (@ 18%)*	*Capital Content Amount*	*Loan Outstanding at the End*
0				200
1	91.98	36.00	55.98	144.01
2	91.98	25.92	66.06	77.95
3	91.98	14.03	77.95	0

POINTS TO REMEMBER

- A lease transaction is a commercial arrangement wherein an equipment owner or manufacturer (the lessor) passes on to the equipment user (the lessee) the right to use the equipment in return for a rental.
- In financial lease agreement, the lessee is given an option to buy the leased property from the lessor at a nominal cost at the end of the lease period.
- In Sale and Leaseback, the owner of an asset sells the asset to a party, who in turn leases back the same asset to the owner in consideration of lease rentals.
- Under leveraged leasing arrangement, a third party is involved, besides the lessor and lessee. The lessor borrows a part of the purchase cost of the asset from the third party (the lender) and the asset so purchased is held as security against the loan. The lender is paid off from the lease rentals directly by the lessee and the surplus, after meeting the claims of the lender, goes to the lessor.
- A lease is classified as an operating lease if it does not transfer substantially all the risks and rewards incidental to ownership.
- Contract hire is a form of operating lease and it is often used for vehicles. The leasing company undertakes some responsibility for the management and maintenance of the vehicles.
- Under direct leasing, a firm acquires the right to use an asset from the manufacturer directly.
- Skip Lease is used in case of seasonal businesses like agricultural companies, recreational service firms, and other firms which require flexible payment schedule due to their seasonal business conditions.
- Master Lease is used when the business is expected to have more leasing requirements with the expanding business, over time.
- Municipal Lease is designed specifically for local and state government organisations that want to acquire equipment.
- The benefits attached to leasing for the lessor are: (i) complete security, (ii) tax benefit, (iii) higher profitability, and (iv) high growth potential. The lessee enjoys

these benefits: (i) financing benefit, (ii) flexibility, (iii) cash flow management, (iv) better liquidity, (v) lower-cost financing, (vi) tax benefit, (vii) off-balance sheet financing, and (viii) covenant free.

- The major disadvantages of leasing are: (i) deprived ownership, (ii) higher cost, (iii) limited access, (iv) unnecessary binding, (v) maintenance and upkeep, and (vi) unsuitable for new businesses.
- Leasing in India was initiated in India in 1973 with the setting of the first leasing company of India, First Leasing Company of India Ltd. By 1981, many companies joined the business like Shetty Investment and Finance, Jaybharat Credit and Investment, Motor and General Finance, and Sundaram Finance. This was the first phase of leasing in India. Second phase started in late 1982, when numerous financial institutions and commercial banks either started leasing or announced plans to do so. ICICI, prominent among financial institutions, entered the industry in 1983. Another significant phase was the Dahotre Committee's recommendations based on which the RBI formed guidelines on commercial bank funding to leasing companies. The post-liberalisation era was the third phase which saw GE Capital's entry and an increasing number of foreign-owned financial firms and banks in leasing in India.
- The Indian leasing industry is structured into private sector and public sector. In private sector, there are pure leasing companies like First Leasing Company of India Ltd.; Hire Purchase and finance companies like Sundaram Finance Ltd. and manufacturing companies. The last category of companies consist of two categories: (i) subsidiaries of manufacturing companies known as vendor leasing companies; and (ii) in-house leasing (captive leasing) companies. The former companies basically boost and promote the sales of their parent companies' products through leasing, like Ashok Leyland Finance Ltd. of Ashok Leyland Ltd., Bajaj Auto Finance of Bajaj Auto Ltd. The latter category meets the group companies' fund requirements and avoids the income-tax by the group companies, like Swadeshi Leasing Ltd. which was floated by the Hindustan Motors Ltd. and the Classic Leasing by ITC Ltd.
- The public sector leasing organisation is divided into (a) leasing divisions of financial institutions, such as IFCI, ICII and IRBI, and (b) subsidiaries of nationalised commercial banks, such as SBI Capital Markets Ltd. and Canbank Financial Services Ltd. which are wholly-owned subsidiaries of the State Bank of India, and Canara Bank, respectively and (c) other public sector leasing organisations, such as the State Industrial Investment Corporation of Maharashtra (SICOM) and the Gujarat Industrial and Investment Corporation (GIIC) have floated their own subsidiary leasing companies.
- Lease must have contents like details about the party to the lease, property, term, rent, services and amount of deposit.
- Lease financing is financially evaluated both from the point of view of lessor and lessee. There are three methods of evaluating a leasing proposal—(i) Present Value method, (ii) Internal Rate of Return method, and (iii) the Bower Herringer Williamson method.
- In present value method, NPV is the deciding factor between lease-versus-buying decision. Internal rate of return method helps to find out the rate at which the

lease rentals, net of tax shield on depreciation are equal to the cost of leasing. Bower-Herringer-Williamson Method divides the financial and tax aspects of lease financing. This is also used as equivalent loan method.

- Hire purchase is a type of instalment credit under which the hire purchaser, called the hirer, agrees to take the goods on hire at a stated rental, with an option to purchase, wherein the ownership is transferred only when the last instalment is paid.
- The first HP company is believed to be Commercial Credit Corporation, based in Madras. Then, there were companies like Motor and General Finance, and Instalment Supply Company, which were set up in 1920s and 1930s in North India. Development of HP took two forms: consumer durables and automobiles. Consumer durables HP was promoted by the dealers in the respective equipment. Thus, Singer Sewing Machine company, or Murphy Radio dealers would provide instalment facilities on HP basis to the customers of their products. HP of commercial vehicles developed very fast.

KEY TERMS

- **Leasing** is an agreement wherein the lessor gives the right to the lessee in return for payment(s) to use an asset for an agreed period of time.
- **Financial lease** is a long-term, non-cancellable lease contract.
- **Operating lease** is one which does not transfer all the risks and rewards incidental to ownership.
- **Hire purchase** is a credit arrangement under which the hire purchaser, called the hirer, takes the goods on hire at a stated rental, with an option to purchase.

EXERCISES

Problems

1. Greatways Ltd. is in the business of manufacturing copper utensils. They plan to diversify and add a new product line. They can either buy the required machinery or get it on lease.

   The machine can be purchased for ₹15,00,000. It is expected to have a useful life of 5 years. The purchase can be financed by 20% loan repayable in 5 equal annual instalments becoming due at the end of each year. Alternatively, the machine can be taken on year-end lease rentals of ₹4,50,000 for 5 years.

   Advise the company on which option should it choose with following assumptions:

   (i) Tax rate is 35% and cost of capital is 13 per cent.

   (ii) Lease rents are to be paid at the end of the year.

2. On August 1, 2013, Idea Ventures (lessee) and Hi-tech Computer Industries (lessor) sign a lease with the following terms:

1. Term: 5 years	2. Annual payments of ₹39,000
3. Implicit interest rate: 10%	4. Lessor retains ownership of asset at end of lease
5. Fair value of asset: ₹1,68,834	6. Cost of asset: ₹1,30,000
7. Incremental borrowing rate: 12%	8. Estimated useful life of asset: 7 years
9. Lessor and lessee both use straight-line depreciation method for fixed assets.	10. No collection or cost uncertainties for lessor
11. Estimated fair value of asset at end of lease: ₹10,000	

a. Classify and explain this lease from the perspective of the lessee.
b. Classify and explain this lease from the perspective of the lessor.

3. AB Finance Ltd. is considering to enter into the computer leasing business. Advanced technology computers can be purchased for ₹2,00,000 each and, in turn, be leased out at ₹50,000 per year for 8 years with the initial payment occurring at the end of the first year.

   Ignore taxes and depreciation.

   Estimate the annual before-tax expense and internal rate of return (IRR) for the company.

4. Bright Leasing Ltd. (BLL) has structured a leveraged lease with an investment cost of ₹50 crores. The investment is to be financed by equity from it and loan from a local bank in the ratio of 1:4. The interest on loan is 20 per cent per annum to be repaid in five equated annual instalments.

   The required rate of return (gross yield) of the BLL is 24 per cent.

   Calculate: (a) the equated annual instalment. (b) the annual lease rental.

5. On 1st April, 2014, North India Refineries Ltd. purchased a machine on the hire purchase system, the total amount payable being ₹2,50,000. Payment was to be made ₹50,000 cash down and the balance in four annual instalments of ₹50,000 each. Interest charged was at the rate of 15 per cent.

   At what value should the machine be capitalised?

Answers: 1. PV of cash outflows under leasing: ₹10,28,723
Loan instalment under buying: ₹5,01,505 p.a.
Advise is to go for leasing.
2. (a) Operating lease
(b) Sale type lease
3. 18 per cent
4. (a) ₹13.4 crores
(b) ₹17.04 crores
5. ₹1,92,750

Objective Questions

1. Tick the correct answer:

(a) The essential elements of a lease are:
  (i) Parties (ii) Subject matter
  (iii) Duration and consideration (iv) All of the above

(b) Sale and lease back is:
  (i) A type of finance lease (ii) A type of operating lease
  (iii) Specific lease (iv) None of the above

(c) Financial evaluation of a leasing proposal is done by:
  (i) Present value method
  (ii) Internal rate of return method
  (iii) Bower Herringer Williamson method
  (iv) All of the above

(d) In hire purchase, the ownership is transferred on the payment of:
  (i) First instalment (ii) Last instalment
  (iii) 50% of instalments (iv) None of the above

(e) Lease rentals paid by the lessee are treated as:
  (i) Revenue expenditure (ii) Capital expenditure
  (iii) Deferred revenue expenditure (iv) None of the above

(f) Interest element included in the HP instalments is treated as:
  (i) Revenue expenditure (ii) Capital expenditure
  (iii) Miscellaneous expenditure (iv) None of the above

Answers: (a) iv (b) i (c) iv (d) ii (e) i (f) i

2. Fill in the blanks:

(a) A lease agreement is between the .... and ....
(b) .... is non-cancellable.
(c) The lessee pays a .... to the lessor for the use of an asset for a specified period.
(d) .... is an alternative to long-term financing.
(e) .... is a short-term lease.
(f) Under ...., a third party is involved besides the lessor and lessee.
(g) Municipal lease is best for ....
(h) The first leasing company set up in India was ....
(i) Banks have been allowed to offer leasing facilities since ....

Answers:

(a) Lessor, lessee
(b) Capital lease
(c) Lease rental
(d) Financial lease
(e) Operating lease
(f) Leveraged leasing
(g) Local and state government organisations
(h) First Leasing Company of India Ltd.
(i) 1994

3. True or False:

(a) A lessee should classify a lease transaction as a capital lease if it is non-cancellable.
(b) The present value of minimum lease payments between the lessor and lessee is always the same.
(c) The lease can be for perpetuity.
(d) In case of operating lease, all the risks are borne by the lessee.
(e) Operating lease is a substitute for long-term financing.
(f) If the NPV of lease is positive, leasing is financially advantageous.
(g) The consideration for lease is either premium or rent, which is the price paid or promised in consideration of the property.
(h) Under direct leasing, a firm acquires the right to use an asset from the manufacturer directly.
(i) Skip lease is flexible in nature.
(j) Operating lease provides off-balance sheet financing.
(k) The Bower Herringer Williamson method is also used as equivalent loan method.

Answers: (a) True (b) False (c) True (d) False (e) False
(f) True (g) True (h) True (i) True (j) True (k) True

Short Questions

1. Explain the term Leasing. State two types of lease.
2. Distinguish between financial lease and operating lease.
3. Define leveraged lease. As a lessee, will you prefer this, and why?
4. Distinguish between sale and leaseback lease and leveraged lease. As a lessee, which one will you prefer and why?
5. What is hire purchase financing? How does it differ from lease financing?
6. State any two criteria for capital lease.
7. What is net advantage in leasing?
8. What are the elements of a lease transaction?

Critical Thinking Questions

1. "Financial lease is a substitute for long-term financing". Explain.
2. "Operating lease is tailor-made for working capital needs". Justify.
3. "Leasing has assumed different forms with changing times". Elaborate with suitable illustrations.
4. "Government organisations are also not untouched by the leasing magnet". Discuss.
5. "The structure of Indian leasing industry is a varied mix of participation from all corners". Highlight.
6. "IRR method is preferred to other methods for financial evaluation of a lease proposal". Explain.

7. "Hire purchase system is more volatile than lease financing for the borrower". Argue.
8. "Like other businesses, leasing business also got affected by the global turmoil". Do you agree?
9. "Financial lease is considered to be riskier and costlier than any other lease". Critique.
10. The 2008 annual report of the A&B Corporation reported minimum lease payments receivable of ₹30,00,000 and a net investment in direct financing leases of ₹25,00,000. Explain the reasons for the difference between these two amounts.

Descriptive Questions

1. Discuss various types of lease agreements with the help of illustrations.
2. What are the advantages and disadvantages of leasing?
3. Discuss the cash flow consequences of lease financing with the help of an illustration.
4. What are the different financial methods of evaluating lease?
5. Among pre-tax and after-tax borrowing rate, which rate is an appropriate discounting rate for evaluating the lease alternative? Explain the implications, taking an example.
6. How is interest determined in a capital lease transaction? How does the approach compare to other forms of debt (say, bonds payable or notes payable)?
7. What type of businesses go for financial lease and why?
8. Discuss the growth and prospects of leasing industry in India.
9. Discuss the hirer's rights and obligations under hire purchase system.
10. Illustrate the hire purchase mechanism.

PROJECT EXERCISE

Studying the Leasing of Industry Mix

It is very common to lease fixed assets like land and machines in business organisations, either manufacturing or service industry. Aviation industry is prominent for high leasing arrangements of aircrafts and Boeing planes. Apply your critical-thinking ability to the knowledge you have gained and review one manufacturing company and one service company for their leasing arrangements. Take one leasing company as well as a specific example. Refer to their recent financial statements and related disclosure notes. Discuss their leasing modalities in terms of type of assets, life and the nature of lease. Analyse their comparative cost-benefit analysis for the operational effectiveness of the leasing industry as a whole.

REVIEW CASE

Smart Lease Act

Mr. Smart shifted with his family from Kolkata to Delhi due to job reasons. Accommodation became the biggest problem. He did not have enough money to buy a house so he kept on searching for a house on rent. Finally, he found one and took the flat on lease from Mr. James for 5 years who was a real estate developer and renter. The year was 1956. The lessee had an option in the deed to renew it every five years so long as desired. Mr. James had bought the house for ₹50 lacs and has an expected useful life of 40 years. Its normal sales price was ₹65 lacs. The present value of the minimum monthly rental payments for both the lessor and lessee was ₹8,000. The first payment was made at the inception of the lease. Thereafter, payments were to be made at the beginning of each month. James & Co. depreciates assets by the straight-line method. Their implicit rate of return was 16%, which was less than incremental borrowing rate.

After many years, Mr. Smart still could not buy his own house. So, in 1961 he asked for a renewal of the lease but Mr. James refused. To this, he even proposed to increase the rental but Mr. James was not willing and he filed a suit in the court. Mr. James's contention was that the lease was for five years only and not in perpetuity as contemplated by Section 105 of the Transfer of Property Act, 1882. Therefore, Mr. Smart did not have a legal right for renewal of lease and his appeal must be dismissed. He further added that only Section 14 of the Act was applicable where there was transfer of property. Moreover, this transfer was for a period of five years only. So, the stipulation relating to renewal could not be regarded as transferring property or any rights therein. Mr. Smart only had an option of renewal which could not create an interest in the property of the nature. Mr. James further added that this type of continuity by Mr. Smart might pose a threat to his ownership of the house because in specific cases in US and other parts, a rent-stabilised lease had been treated as an asset in a personal bankruptcy, just like a car or a piece of land, and used to pay off creditors. Hence, it would be easier for the tenant to enjoy the ownership of the rented house, especially at a time when housing affordability and income inequality have been the driving factors in the increasing cost of living.

Mr. Smart also put forward in his petition that at this home, he and his family had celebrated birthdays and holidays, and therefore, had an emotional attachment with the house. Besides the above clause and emotional factor, he also expressed the practical difficulties in getting a house on rent in metro which is a real problem for outsiders. So, he requested that his case should be given a due consideration on all these factors.

Issues for Discussion

(i) What type of lease is referred to in the above case?

(ii) What are the rights of lesser and lessee, respectively?

(iii) Can the option of renewal to the lessee create an interest in the property?

(iv) Can the lease be for perpetuity?

(v) What should be the judgment of the Court?

(vi) Calculate the amount Mr. James should record as a leased asset and lease liability for this lease.

(vii) Prepare an amortisation schedule that describes the pattern of interest expense for James & Co. over the lease term.

(*Hint*: Refer to the R. Kempraj v. M/s. Barton Son & Co. case).

REFERENCES

Agrawal, N.K. and Joshi, P.L. (1983), "Accounting for Leases", *The Chartered Accountant,* August, pp. 92–97:237.

Ghosh, T.P. (1987), "Leasing: A Financing Decision", *The Chartered Accountant*, June 1987, pp. 996–967.

Mukhopadhyay, D. (1995), "Lease Financing: An Overview", *The Management Accountant*, May, pp. 354–356.

Pandey, I.M. (2005), *Financial Management*, 9th ed., Vikas Publishing House Pvt. Ltd., New Delhi.

www.clap.nls.ac.in

www.icai.org

www.indiankanoon.org

www.karvy.com

www.mca.gov.in

www.rbi.org.in

CHAPTER

12

Factoring and Forfaiting

Factoring is an easier way to get additional funding for business compared to the traditional financing methods which require lots of paperwork and long waiting periods.

— Matt Shupe

LEARNING OBJECTIVES

This chapter discusses the following:

- Concept of factoring
- Factoring mechanism
- Pros and cons of factoring
- Exemplary cases of factoring
- Distinction between factoring and other credit services
- Types of factoring services
- Overview of factoring in India
- Regulatory framework of factoring
- Factoring products of corporate houses
- Futuristic outlook of factoring
- Forfaiting and its fundamental aspects
- Flow chart of forfaiting
- Advantages of forfaiting

INTRODUCTION

The companies extending liberal credit to their customers from 30–60 days and more get into a cash bind as they have to meet their short-term requirements of working capital. This problem gets worse with the growing sales. Factoring provides immediate cash to meet these requirements of paying for labour or materials, against invoice as collateral for a short-term loan. If your business is growing and you are unable to qualify for additional financing from a bank because your business is either too new or you have had credit problems in the past, factoring can help your business grow by providing the necessary cash to support your additional working capital requirements. This way, it helps the business by bridging the gap between sales and realisation of sales into cash.

Various industries can utilise commercial invoices for factoring. According to the Commercial Finance Association, accounts receivable based financing exceeds $60 billion per year in the United States alone[1]. The global factoring services market size is expected to reach USD 7,005.90 billion by 2030, registering a CAGR of 8.8% from 2022 to 2030.[2]

The origin of factoring goes back to the 19th century when in countries like U.S.A., U.K., and France, specialised financial institutions were established to assist the firms in meeting their working capital requirements by purchasing the receivables. The word 'factor' is derived from the Latin word *facere*, which means to make or do or to get things done. In other words, factor is an agent who does things for his principal, i.e., the client, for a consideration called *commission*. Hence, traditionally, factor was considered as commission agent.

FACTORING: THE CONCEPT

"Factoring is the financing of receivables". It is a method of financing wherein a firm sells its trade debts at a discount to a financial institution factor in order to raise finance for working capital requirements. The factor may or may not accept the incumbent credit risk. It is an ongoing arrangement between a financial institution *(the factor)* and a firm *(the client)* wherein the factor purchases the client's accounts receivables, provides the capital tied up in accounts receivables, and supports the financial requirement of suppliers.

In a *narrow sense,* factoring means cash facility on receivables. In *broader sense,* factoring implies managing the credit and other operations of the client for a certain fee. The factor finances, collects and manages sales ledger administration. The buyer and the seller usually have a long-term relationship. In the process, cash flow is accelerated, purchasing power increases, production moves up, and credit-rating gets improved.

Factoring: 'Instant Cash'

Factoring is a collection service designed to improve the cash flow, turning your credit sales invoices into ready cash. Through factoring, factors agree to:

1. https://www.cfa.com/eweb/upload/CFA_Member_ABLFactoring_2011_Reports.pdf
2. https://www.businesswire.com/news/home/20220803005527/en/Global-Factoring-Services-Market-Report-2022-Increasing-Open-Trade-Accounts-and-Cross-Border-Businesses-An-Expanding-Manufacturing-Industry-in-Asia-Driving-Growth---ResearchAndMarkets.com

- Factor your invoices on a continuing basis
- Pre-pay upto 80% of the value of the invoices immediately
- Perform the accounting function of sales ledger maintenance and the collection function of realising invoices factored.

So, the firms require this facility because of the gap that exists between their operating cash outflow (cash paid) and cash inflow as shown in Figure 12.1.

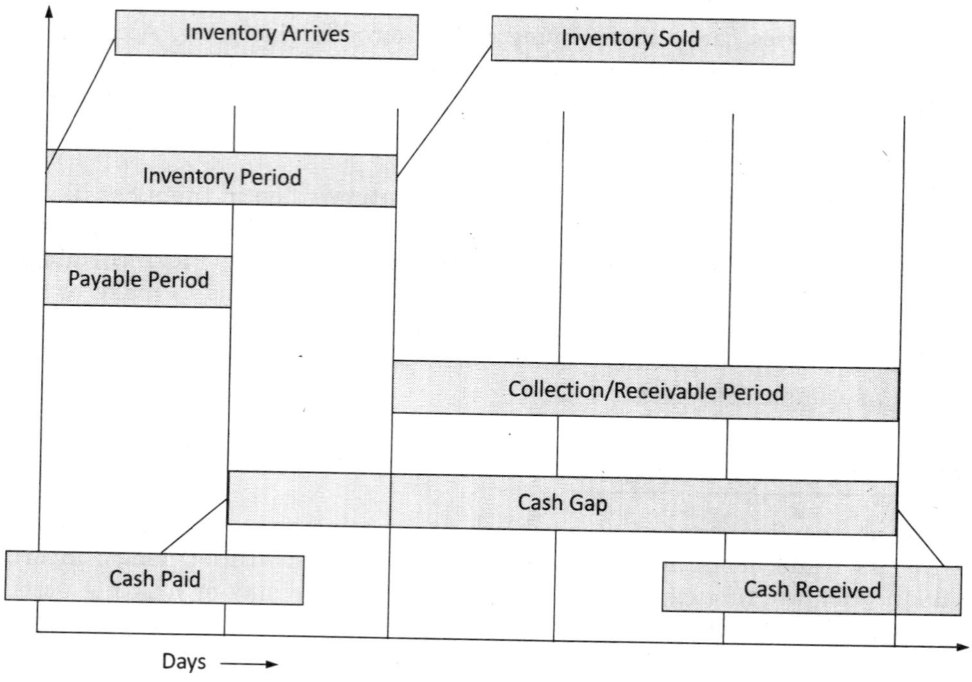

Figure 12.1 Operating Cycle Cash Gap

Characteristics of Factoring

1. Generally, the period for factoring varies from 90–150 days.
2. Factoring receivables is an ideal financial solution for new and emerging firms without enough collaterals and/or guarantees for loan. This is because credit-worthiness is evaluated based on the financial strength of the customer (debtor). Hence, these companies can leverage on the financial strength of their customers.
3. Credit-rating is not mandatory for factoring though the factoring companies usually carry out credit risk analysis before entering into the agreement.
4. Cost of factoring includes 'finance cost' and 'operating cost'. Factoring cost vary according to the transaction size, and financial strength of the customer, from 1.5–5% per month depending upon the financial strength of the client's customer.
5. Factoring is considered to be a costly source of finance as compared to other sources of short-term borrowings.
6. There is penalty levied on the delayed payments beyond the approved credit period, of around 1–2% per month over and above the normal cost.
7. Indian firms offer factoring for invoices as low as ₹1,000.

Parties to Factoring

The three parties directly involved in the factoring process are: (i) the one who sells the receivable, (ii) the debtor, and (iii) the factor.

The *seller* is the one who sells one or more of its invoices (*the receivables*) at a discount to the third party, the specialised financial organisation *(the factor)*, to get cash.

The *debtor* or *receivable* here refers to the customer whose receivable is sold off. Usually, the account debtor is notified of the sale of the receivable, and the factor bills the debtor and makes all collections. The receivable is essentially a financial asset associated with the debtor's liability to pay money owed to the seller (usually for work performed or goods sold).

The *factor* means a bank or financial institution which buys the receivable and provides the necessary financing to the seller.

Costs of Factoring

The cost of factoring services primarily comprises of two components: (a) *discount charge;* and (b) *administrative fee.* The factor provides various services at some cost (in the form of a commission) charged on the value of debt purchased. It is collected in advance.

The cost of factoring services primarily constitutes of the following two components:

(i) *Discount Charge*

This is levied towards providing instant credit to the client by way pre-payment and the risk borne. The commission charged is usually 2–4% of the face value of the receivables factored, the rate depending upon whether it is with or without recourse. The factor also charges interest on advances drawn by the firm against uncollected and non-due receivables.

(ii) *Administrative Charges*

This is charged towards providing various services to the clients—(a) sales ledger administration, (b) credit control including processing, operational overheads and collection of debts, (c) providing protection against bad debts. This charge is usually some per cent of the projected sales turnover of the client for the next twelve months. It varies between 1–2.5% of the projected turnover. The quantum of charge depends upon the following factors:

(i) Type of industry
(ii) Financial strength of the client as well as of the debtors
(iii) Volume of sales
(iv) Average invoice value
(v) Terms of trade
(vi) Type(s) of service(s) offered
(vii) Security to the factor

Factoring commission *represents the compensation to the factor for the credit risk borne and/or the administrative services provided. The total commission* *charged depends upon the various forms of service and whether it is with or without recourse.*

There are three principal parts to the factoring transaction: (i) the **advance money** *(a percentage of the invoice face value that is paid to the seller upon submission), (ii) the* **reserve** *(the balance amount of the total invoice amount held until the payment by the account debtor is made), and (iii) the* **fee**, *the cost associated with the transaction which is deducted from the reserve prior to it being paid back to the seller.*

Sometimes, the factor charges the seller a service charge as well as interest based on how long the factor must wait to receive payments from the debtor. The factor also estimates the amount that may not be collected due to non-payment, and makes accommodation for this when determining the amount that will be given to the seller. The factor's overall profit is the difference between the price paid for the invoice and the money received from the debtor, less the amount lost due to non-payment.

Following is an example to understand the viability of factoring decision.

ILLUSTRATION: New Age Enterprises has credit sales of ₹20 lacs. Its average collection period is 60 days. Their bad debts ratio is 2% of credit sales. Being a new firm, the firm spends almost ₹1 lac on the management of its credit sales. Therefore, the firm is planning to explore the factoring option @ 2% commission. They will be paid 85% of the amount. Is it economical for the firm to consider it?

Solution: Let us first calculate the average age of receivables.

The credit sales are ₹20 lacs and the collection period is 60 days. Therefore, the 'Average level of receivables' with 365 days in a year is:

$$= \frac{20{,}00{,}000}{365} \times 60 = ₹\ 3{,}28{,}767$$

The amount paid by the factor will be the average level of receivables less factoring commission and reserve. Factoring commission is 2% of average receivables, i.e. 60 days and reserve is 15%.

So, factoring commission is = 0.02 × 3,28,767 = ₹ 6,575

and Reserve is = 0.15 × 3,28,767 = ₹ 49,315

Thus, the total amount paid by the factor is:

3,28,767 – 6,575 – 49,315 = ₹ 2,72,877

Cost of factoring to the firm:

Factoring commission: 6,575 × 365/60 = ₹ 39,998

Saving to the firm:

Cost of credit management	=	₹1,00,000
Cost of bad-debt: 0.02 × 20,00,000	=	₹40,000
		1,40,000

Net saving to the firm = ₹1,40,000 – 39,998 = ₹1,00,002

So, it is economical for the firm to go for factoring.

FACTORING MECHANISM

Factoring is an arrangement or a contract between the factor and the supplier and is governed by the 'law of contract'.

The sale of the receivables essentially transfers ownership of the receivables to the factor, signifying that the factor has got all the rights and risks associated with the receivables. Accordingly, the factor gets the right to receive payments from the debtor for the invoice amount and must bear the loss if the debtor does not pay the invoice amount.

The terms of the factoring contract are mutually settled in writing. The major steps in the process of factoring are:

(i) Assignment of debt in favour of factoring agency by handing them over the copies of invoices.

(ii) Defining terms and conditions whether the factor will have no recourse to seller on non-payment from buyer or will he have recourse.

(iii) Working out the cost of factoring services.

(iv) Drafting an agreement.

(v) Fixing percentage of the amount of invoice value to be received from the factor by seller.

(vi) Determining the schedule of payment.
- The factor makes payment up to 80% of the value of the assigned invoice.
- The seller will receive balance payment from the factor after the deduction of factor's service charges when the buyer makes payment for the invoice to the factor.

(vii) Accounting procedure at bank
- All bills discounted or purchased should be entered in the bills discounted or purchased register in serial order and the serial number is changed annually. Particulars of documents and the like, due date and other relevant details are to be recorded legibly (Figure 12.2).

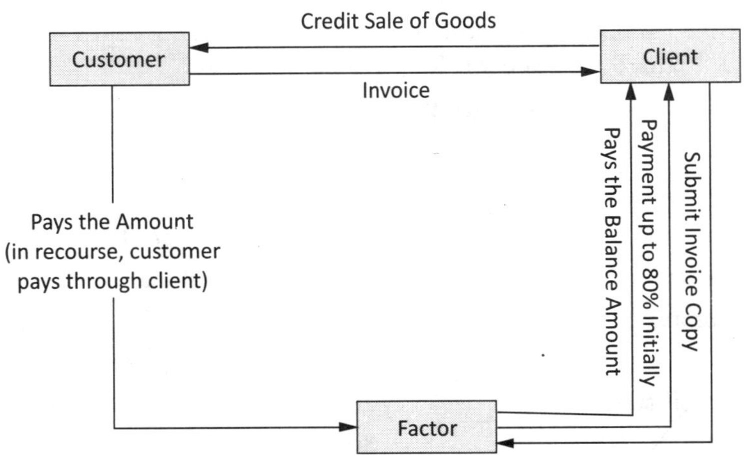

Figure 12.2 The Process of Factoring

FACTORING: PROS AND CONS

A. Advantages of Factoring

The advantages which arise from factoring are listed below:

1. ***Increased cash:*** Factoring provides more cash than traditional bank credit and supports the client with the necessary working capital.

2. ***No arbitrary line of credit:*** Business firms use factoring based on their sales activity so financial credibility is automatically set up to finance the growth.

3. ***Cash flow is more predictable:*** In addition to speeding up client's cash flow, factoring also makes it easier to manage and predict cash based on invoicing.

4. ***Maximise profitability:*** Factoring helps to reduce supplier credit costs. A company can pay suppliers more quickly with funds received through factoring, reducing or even eliminating the costs of supplier credit. Factoring funds can be used to purchase supplies on discount terms (volume or cash purchases), thereby reducing the costs of raw materials.

5. ***Flexible financing:*** Factor when you want, as much as you want, and for as long as you want. There is no minimum factoring level or commitment to factor for the future.

6. ***Improved credit evaluation:*** Factoring can be an essential tool for building credibility by facilitating timely payments to suppliers and reduction of debt to creditors.

7. ***Maintenance of the receivables account:*** The factoring company manages the trade debts of the client, keeping the sales accounts' ledgers and sending out the invoices.

8. ***Off-balance sheet financing:*** The most important advantage of factoring is that it can be used to 'restructure the balance sheet', i.e. to make the balance sheet look good, especially for long-term borrowing purpose. This is explained in the following example.

ILLUSTRATION: Following is the balance sheet of Moving and Co. Ltd. as on 31st December, 2010, highlighting the working capital position.

Balance Sheet: Post-Factoring Scenario

(₹ in lacs)

Current Liabilities		*Amount*	*Current Assets*	*Amount*
Bank borrowings:			Stock-in-trade	70
Overdraft facility	30		Receivables	50
Cash credit against receivables	50	80	Cash and Bank	20
Creditors		30	Other current assets	10
Other current liabilities		10		
Net Working Capital (NWC)		30		
Total current liabilities + NWC		**150**	**Total current assets**	**150**

Current ratio = 1.25:1

The firm is planning to factor 80% receivables on non-recourse basis to primarily restructure the balance sheet for a term loan. The cost is 4% up front. Examine the impact.

Solution: Factoring of receivables is 80% non-recourse @ 4% up front. So, advance amount is ₹38 lacs.

Balance Sheet: Post-Factoring Scenario

(₹ in lacs)

Current Liabilities		*Amount*	*Current Assets*	*Amount*
Bank borrowings:			Stock-in-trade	70
Overdraft facility	—		Receivables	12
Cash credit against receivables	42	42	Cash and Bank	20
Creditors		30	Other current assets	10
Other current liabilities		10		
Net Working Capital (NWC)		30		
Total current liabilities + NWC		**112**	**Total current assets**	**112**

Current ratio = 1.37:1

Effects

1. Here, bank borrowings are reduced by ₹38 lacs. ₹30 lacs has been used to clear off overdraft as it is a rotating facility and can be used again at any time. Rest ₹8 lacs has been used to pay cash credit.
2. This has maintained the working capital at the same level of ₹30 lacs and at the same time resulted in an Improvement in current ratio.

Notes:

1. Non-recourse factoring, as in the above example, appears nowhere in financial statements.
2. Recourse finance appears as a contingent liability.

Box 12.1 summarises the possible reasons why business enterprises avail the services of factoring.

BOX 12.1: FACTORING BENEFITS

Fundamental:

- Purchase of receivables of a firm/Financing of trade debts

Others:

- Maintenance of sales accounts and credit management
- Credit collection and protection against default and bad-debt losses
- Payment for payroll and operational expenses
- Financial assistance, including loans and advance payments
- Credit investigation
- Information and counselling
- Off-balance sheet financing

Benefits of Factoring in Specific Cases

There are certain cases where factoring is very much beneficial on account of its services.

(i) *For Payroll Financing to Staffing Companies*

One of the fastest growing industries in most of the countries (including US) is labour outsourcing in the staffing industry. Often, staffing firms find themselves tight on the cash front for meeting payroll expenses at short intervals when the client does not pay them for the service for 30–45 days. *Payroll factoring* can meet this cash flow gap by providing the staffing agency necessary cash due on billed revenue upon being confirmed by the client.

Another staffing financing issue is that staffing companies typically have limited collateral for loan due to the nature of the business. Banks often cannot provide any credit facility due to volatility of profitability. The payroll factoring often does not require additional collateral other than the accounts receivable of the staffing company. This allows the staffing agency to utilise the credit-worthiness of their customers.

So, at marginal commission of 1–3% of the amount of the bill of the client, the staffing companies find this a very reasonable source of funding to grow their business in size and scale of operations.

(ii) *For Small-scale Business*

Unfortunately for small business owners, banks are generally reluctant to give a loan or credit facility. Factoring companies and other non-bank sources continue to act as best alternatives to the entire bank loan transactions and often provide more working capital in the long run. Though the cost of funding is higher, it is beneficial in totality with all the benefits of 'receivables financing'.

Factoring companies typically can advance 80–90% of the accounts receivable in good standing. The cost for these cash advances can range from 0.5–5% of the total invoice value depending on how much factoring is done by the customer and the credit quality of the customers.

B. Disadvantages of Factoring

There are certain disadvantages of factoring which are as discussed below:

1. *Cost Factor*

The upfront cash price of the invoices is usually 70–90% of the face value, depending on the credit history of the customers and the nature of the business. The initial amount is treated as a cash advance and the seller receives an additional portion of the face value on the collection of invoices. The longer the invoice period, the rate is higher. The seller's final cost might exceed the amount paid as an interest rate on a short-term commercial loan for an equal amount. Factoring companies usually keep their fee between 1% and 3% of a receivable.

2. *Potential Threat to Customer Relationship*

The factoring company, being in-charge of the invoice collecting, might employ methods for collecting money which might not go well with the customers. This might affect the personal relationship with their customers.

3. *Distortion of Company Image*

When a company employs the services of a factor, it might be considered a sign that the respective company is in financial difficulties. It might lead to distortion of image of the company in the market.

4. *Covenants*

Factoring may impose restrictions on the way you conduct business. For non-recourse factoring, the factoring company could ask you not to do business with a particular customer because of its poor credit history or rating. Also, the factor will apply credit limits to individual customers.

EXEMPLARY CASES OF FACTORING

Here are some examples of how factoring helps a business firm:

1. Complete Factoring

Rally Ltd. has to collect ₹5,000 by the debtor company which is expected to pay in a couple of months. The firm sells its invoice to a factoring company which gives ₹4,800 immediately. Rally Ltd. uses that cash for immediate working capital requirement.

2. Partial Factoring of Account Receivables

A'N'Z Company is one of the leading manufacturers of royal watches. They currently have outstanding invoices totalling ₹50,000. The majority of this money is due in net 45 days. In one week's time, the company needs to purchase a large quantity of glass that will cost ₹12,000. However, if they pay the full amount at the time of purchase, they will receive a 10% discount. Currently, they have ₹6,000 available to purchase raw materials. This makes the company consider 'factoring a portion of their account receivables'. They could factor ₹5,000 worth of invoices and pay a fee of 3%. The total fee would then equal ₹150 and the additional money will be used to purchase the glass. The 10% discount would result in a saving of ₹1,200. By factoring a portion of their account receivables, the company will be able to save a net total of ₹1050 (1200–150).

3. Avoiding Hassle of Collecting Bad Debt

Aggarwal & Company has a due worth ₹40,000 to be collected but is not able to collect it from the debtor company. They sell their invoice to a factoring company for ₹35,000, under a 'non-recourse factoring agreement'. Now, it is the responsibility of the factoring company to recover the money.

4. Overall Management and Smoothing Cash Flow

Jack and Mack Brothers issue invoices of approximately ₹40,000 each month and have a number of clients who take between 2 to 4 months to pay. In this situation, the irregularity of payment makes it difficult for the company to manage its cash flow.

Therefore, they contract out the collection of all their invoices to a factoring company which is very efficient in collection of debts, and pays Jack and Mack immediately for the invoices, as they are raised, every month. They not only collect the debt but also manage their sales ledger, which cuts down on their administration costs.

5. Borrowing Money, Secured by Debt

Amit Company has no assets for security, and issues invoices of approximately ₹5 lacs each month and their clients pay in approximately two months. The company has an outstanding book debt of ₹10 lacs and requires a loan of ₹7 lacs for expansion. Their bank lends them the money, secured against outstanding invoices that the business holds.

Every time, factoring account receivables might not be a good choice but at times, it is a great mechanism for a company to enjoy significant savings as in the above case. The key is to carefully analyse the 'net benefit' before making a final decision.

FACTORING VS. OTHER CREDIT SERVICES

Here, we compare factoring with other credit services.

Factoring vs. Invoice Discounting

Factoring is often confused with *invoice discounting*. Factoring is the sale of receivables whereas invoice discounting is borrowing where the receivable is used as collateral. *Bills discounting* is a financing provision against bills. Factoring is a broader term including financing provision, and rendering of other services like maintenance of sales ledger, advisory services, etc.

Bill discounting is always with recourse, i.e. in case of default, the client will have to make the payment. Factoring may be with or without recourse.

Bill finance is always 'in balance sheet' financing, i.e. both the amounts of receivables and bank credit are reflected in the balance sheet of the clients as current assets and current liabilities on account of recourse nature. The factoring service is 'off balance sheet' financing (Table 12.1).

Factoring vs. Bank Loan

Factoring is a financial transaction wherein a business sells its accounts receivable (i.e. invoices) to a third party (factor) at a discount and uses that money for financing its business. 'Factoring' differs from a 'bank loan' in three main ways. First, factoring is not a loan—it is the purchase of a financial asset (receivable). Second, in factoring, the emphasis is on the value of the receivables (essentially a financial asset), not the firm's credit-worthiness. Third, a bank loan involves two parties whereas factoring involves three. Table 12.2 distinguishes between them.

TABLE 12.1 Distinction between Factoring and Bills Discounting

Basis	*Factoring*	*Bills Discounting*
Services provided	Includes debt collection and sales ledger management	Includes only financing service
Scope	Broader term	Narrower term
Volume	Factoring facility covers the whole turnover	It is individual transaction oriented
Basis of analysis	Based on current and projected sales volume	Based on historical basis
Transaction handling	Instant cash against invoices in respect of sales, on delivery of goods	Each bill is individually accepted by the buyer; this is a time consuming process
Grace period	Grace period is more liberal	Grace period is strict

TABLE 12.2 Distinction between Factoring and Bank Loan

Basis	*Factoring*	*Bank Loan*
Nature	Cash flow based	Balance sheet–current asset based
Performance prospects	Sales linked growth	Historic performance
Periodicity	More regular and quick response result	Enhancement of limits in annual reviews
Basis of judgment	Quality of debtors	Collateral oriented

Factoring vs. Forfaiting

It is different from forfaiting in the sense that forfaiting is a transaction-based operation while factoring is a firm-based operation, i.e. in factoring, a firm usually sells all its receivables while in forfaiting, the firm sells one of its transactions.

Forfaiting is a service to help the seller sell his goods on credit and yet receive the cash well before the due date. In other words, it is trade finance extended by a forfaiter to an exporter/seller for an export/sale transaction involving deferred payment terms over a long period at a rate of discount. Forfaiting is generally extended for export of capital goods, commodities and services where the importer insists on supplies on credit terms.

The total cost of forfaiting comprises of a commission and an interest if the firm draws an advance against receivables. Alternatively, it is also possible that the exporter may leave his funds after collection with the forfaiter to receive an interest from him.

In factoring, only 75–80% of the accounts receivable is financed and the balance is retained by the factor and paid after maturity; while in forfaiting, 100% of the receivables are discounted. In factoring, financing is with or without recourse while forfaiting is always without recourse. Most importantly, factoring is a short-term arrangement whereas forfaiting generally lasts for years.

TYPES OF FACTORING

Factoring can be classified as follows:

- Disclosed
- Undisclosed
- Recourse
- Non-recourse
- Other factoring

A single factoring company may not offer all these services.

1. Disclosed Factoring (Notified Factoring)

In *disclosed factoring*, client's customers are notified of the factoring agreement. Disclosed type can either be recourse or non-recourse.

2. Undisclosed Factoring (Non-notified or Confidential Factoring)

In *undisclosed factoring*, client's customers are not notified of the factoring arrangement. Sales ledger administration and collection of debts are undertaken by the client himself. The client has to pay the amount to the factor irrespective of whether the customer has paid or not. In disclosed type, factor may or may not be responsible for the collection of debts depending on whether it is recourse or non-recourse.

3. Recourse Factoring

In *recourse factoring,* client undertakes to collect the debts from the customer. If the customer does not pay the amount on maturity, factor will recover the amount from the client. This is the most common type of factoring. Here, the balance amount is paid to the client when the customer pays the factor. Recourse factoring is offered at a lower interest rate since the risk by the factor is low. Thus, recourse factoring is cheaper than non-recourse factoring. Let us cite an example to understand this.

The factoring agreement requires payment to be made in two months. It also states that 80% of each invoice will be advanced. On 30 June an invoice for ₹20,000 is issued and the factor advances ₹16,000. After two months, you have to ask for the payment from the customer. The factor will not have a claim against your customer and it will be up to you to take measures to recover the outstanding debt. On 30 August, regardless of whether you have received payment from the customer or not, ₹20,000 must be repaid to the factor with the necessary fee and interest.

4. Non-recourse Factoring

In non-recourse factoring, the factor undertakes to collect the debts from the customer. The balance amount is paid to the client at the end of the credit period or when the customer pays the factor, whichever comes first. The company (seller) does not have to refund the advance to the factor but has to pay interest to the factor for the period specified by the factoring agreement.

The factor takes over all the seller's rights to pursue the customer for payment, including the right to take legal action. The advantage of non-recourse factoring is that it eliminates the need for credit and collection departments in the organisation.

5. Other Factorings

Apart from the services discussed, there are some other factoring services which may include:

(i) *Bank Participation Factoring*

In *bank participation factoring*, the client company creates a floating charge on the factoring reserves in favour of banks and borrow against these reserves. For instance, if factor reserve is 20%, the client can borrow to the extent of 80% of this reserve from the bank, thereby reducing its investments on receivables.

(ii) *International Factoring*

This deals with export sales. The factoring service may include completing the legal and procedural formalities pertaining to export.

FACTORING IN INDIA

The 80's in India witnessed a virtual deregulation of capital market and so a number of innovative financial instruments and schemes were born. The working group (1987) on the money market, observed[3]:

"Despite various measures taken over the years to enable the small-scale sector to recover its dues from the medium and large industries (and in particular the public sector), the small-scale units face a liquidity problem because of their inability to collect the dues. Banks should move to bill financing, particularly the CAS borrowers".

These efforts to popularise a bill market in India did not have the desired results; an alternative had to be found. Thus, factoring as a remedy became an accomplishment. A committee was constituted under the chairmanship of Kalyana Sundaram (1988) by RBI to examine the feasibility of factoring services in India, their constitution, organisational setup and scope of activities. The group recommended setting up of specified agencies or subsidiaries for providing factoring services in India. The study group under the leadership of Mr. C.S. Kalyana Sundaram estimated the value of outstanding open account credit sales available for financing during 1989–90 at ₹12,000 crores in respect of SSI, and ₹4500 crores for medium and large-scale sectors. Assuming that only 50% of the above business will be available for factoring, the aggregate potential demand for factoring was expected to be around ₹4000 crores per annum, mainly emerging from the SSI, and large and medium companies.

Banks did not provide non-banking financial services such as housing finance, leasing and hire-purchase, factoring and forfaiting. Therefore, an amendment was made in the Banking Regulation Act in 1983, wherein banks were permitted to provide the services either through their own departments, or divisions, or through

3. http://www.bankingindiaupdate.com/summary.

their subsidiaries. This is how factoring and forfaiting services originated following the recommendation of the Kalyana Sundaram Committee.

The RBI Guidelines

The Reserve Bank of India (RBI), on the basis of the recommendations of the expert committee headed by C.S. Kalyana Sundaram, issued the following guidelines in 1988 for banking companies to start factoring services:

1. Banks shall not undertake directly the factoring business, while banks may invest in shares of other factoring companies; they shall not act as promoters of such companies. Banks may set up separate subsidiaries or invest in factoring companies jointly with other banks with the approval of Reserve Bank of India.
2. A factoring company may undertake factoring business and other such activities which are incidental and defined.
3. Investment of a bank in the shares of factoring companies inclusive of its subsidiaries carrying factoring business should not, in aggregate, exceed 10% of the paid up capital and reserves of the bank.
4. Banks or their subsidiaries undertaking factoring business should furnish the required information to RBI periodically.

RBI has preferred banks to operate in factoring business through separate subsidiaries and not through their merchant banking divisions because the nature of factoring business is different from merchant banking and it involves handling of voluminous paper work and large amount of money on an on-going basis.

Major Players

The first factoring company was started by State Bank of India (SBI) in 1991, Factors and Commercial Ltd. (SBI FACS), followed by Canara Bank and Punjab National Bank (PNB) setting the subsidiaries for factoring. Following are the major factoring players:

- Canbank Factors Limited
- SBI Factors and Commercial Services Private Limited
- The Hongkong and Shanghai Banking Corporation (HSBC) Limited
- Foremost Factors Limited
- Global Trade Finance Limited
- Export Credit Guarantee Corporation of India Limited
- Citibank NA, India
- Small Industries Development Bank of India (SIDBI)
- Standard Chartered Bank

Legal Aspects

The legal status of a factor is that of an assignee. Once the factor purchases the receivables of a firm and this fact is intimated to the customers, they are under a legal obligation to make all the payments to the factor. The factoring agreement governs the legal relationship between a factor and the firm, whose receivables are factored, specifying the period of validity of the contract and modalities of termination.

REGULATORY FRAMEWORK OF FACTORING

Factoring is a method to improve the liquidity of the businesses especially the micro, small and medium enterprises. In 1993, to address this issue, the Government had enacted the Interest on Delayed Payments to Small Scale and Ancillary Industrial Undertakings Act. It mandated the buyer to pay the seller within the stipulated time, failing which he is supposed to pay the interest on outstanding payment. It was revoked by the introduction of Micro, Small and Medium Enterprises Development Act in 2006. This act also addressed the issue of non-payment and delayed payment to the seller but the liquidity position of MSMEs was not improving through these acts.

In December 2011, the Government finally passed the Factoring Regulations Act, 2011 with the objective to address this issue of delayed payments. It gave RBI the right to regulate and monitor the working of factors in India.

Factoring Regulation Act, 2011

This Act was notified by the Government on January 22, 2012. The salient features are as follows:

1. A company can operate as a Factor after registering itself as a Non-Banking Finance Company Factor with the RBI.
2. The banks or corporations incorporated under any parliamentary Act can also undertake factoring without being required to obtain registration. So, the NBFCs like SIDBI and EXIM bank can also undertake factoring.
3. The Act clearly defines what are the receivables covered under factoring.
4. It provides a wide coverage in comparison to previous laws, thus including MSMEs, large industrial houses and MNCs engaged in manufacturing, trading and service sector under the purview of the law.
5. A Central Registry was established under the SARFAESI Act, 2002. This law mandates the registration and recording of all the transactions carried out by the Factors with this registry which would also be available to public.
6. In case of violations, the Act also provides for the punishments to be imposed.
7. The factors are now allowed to take legal actions against buyers on behalf of sellers in case of default.

The new category NBFC-factor has been created under the Factoring Regulation Act, 2011 and a separate set of directions has been devised to define the clear framework for their working. These directions were declared on July 23, 2012.

Box 12.2 discusses the **RBI regulations issued in January 2022, under the amendments done in Factoring Regulation Act, 2011.**

BOX 12.2: AMENDMENTS (2022) IN FACTORING REGULATION ACT, 2011

Government of India has amended the Factoring Regulation Act, 2011 ("the Act") in January 2022, which widens the scope of companies that can undertake factoring business.

The Act permits Trade Receivables Discounting System (TReDS) to file the particulars of assignment of receivables transactions with the Central Registry on behalf of the Factors for operational efficiency. Further, the Act empowers the Reserve Bank of India to make regulations prescribing the manner of grant of certificate of registration and for prescribing the manner of filing of assignment of receivables transactions by TReDS on behalf of the Factors.

In exercise of the powers conferred under the Act, the Bank has issued the following regulations:

a. Registration of Factors (Reserve Bank) Regulations, 2022
b. Registration of Assignment of Receivables (Reserve Bank) Regulations, 2022

Under the provisions of the regulations mentioned above, all existing non-deposit taking NBFC-Investment and Credit Companies (NBFC-ICCs) with asset size of ₹1,000 crore and above will be permitted to undertake factoring business subject to satisfaction of certain conditions. This will increase the number of NBFCs eligible to undertake factoring business significantly from 7 to 182. Other NBFC-ICCs can also undertake factoring business by registering as NBFC-Factor. Eligible companies may apply to the Reserve Bank for seeking registration under the Act. Further, in respect of trade receivables financed through a Trade Receivables Discounting System (TReDS), the particulars of assignment of receivables shall be filed with the Central Registry on behalf of the Factors by the TReDS concerned within 10 days.

Source: https://www.rbi.org.in/Scripts/BS_PressReleaseDisplay.aspx?prid=53131

"Registration of Factors (Reserve Bank) Regulations", 2022 specifies the criteria for a company intending to become a 'Factor', which is as follows:

Registration: Every company intending to undertake factoring business shall make an application for grant of Certificate of Registration (CoR) as NBFC-factor to the RBI

Net Owned Fund: Every company should have a minimum Net Owned Fund (NOF) of ₹5 crore.

Principal Business: An NBFC-Factor should ensure that its financial assets in the factoring business constitute at least 50% of its total assets and its income derived from factoring business is not less than 50% of its gross income.

PRODUCTS OF FACTORING: CORPORATE CASES

Let us analyse some of the corporates involved in factoring:

1. SBI Global Factors

SBI Global Factors Ltd. (SBIGFL), a subsidiary of the State Bank of India, is one of the leading factoring companies (non-banking financial companies) in India. It was created out of merger of two leading factoring companies, viz. SBI Factors and Commercial Services Pvt. Ltd. and Global Trade Finance Ltd. in 2010. SBIGFL is a member of Factor Chain International (FCI), an umbrella organisation of global factoring companies.

The two major products of SBIGFL are:

(a) *Domestic Factoring*

The seller assigns to the factor the accounts receivables within the country on open account terms and receives the payments against that to the extent of 80–90% from the factor, depending upon the credit terms. Some of its characteristics are:

- The seller's performance obligation should be completed before fund releasing.
- There should be a continuous sales flow on an ongoing basis with the same buyer or group of buyers.
- It is mostly suited for a credit term of 30–90 days.
- The transactions between two parties should be on 'open account' terms.
- Credit sales to a buyer to be assigned to SBIGFL on a continuous basis after the execution of the factoring arrangement.

(b) *Export Factoring*

SBIGFL's export factoring service offers a complete package to help the clients develop their overseas business profitably and with confidence.

Some of the characteristics of export financing are:

- They provide a two-way export factoring system. Under this, the factor handling the collection of export receivables of clients (exporters) is called *Export Factor* (EF), and the factor in buyer's country undertakes collection and credit protection services is called *Import factor*.
- The factor invoices drawn on overseas buyers and make a pre-payment of upto 90% of the invoice amount, immediately.
- Export factor remit 10% remaining balance to exporter's account less any charges.

Besides above, the company also offers products like *Dealer factoring, Vendor factoring and Discounting of bills under Letter of Credit.*

2. HSBC

HSBC is one of the world's largest banking and financial services organisations. The origin of HSBC Ltd., India (HSBC India) date back to 1853, when the Mercantile Bank of India was established in Mumbai. The bank has since, steadily grown in reach and service offerings, keeping pace with the evolving banking and financial needs of its customers. The factoring services provided by HSBC India are discussed below:

(a) *Domestic Factoring*

Through domestic factoring, the bank looks at financing client's receivables. Additionally, they also undertake to finance vendor/supplier payments. Receivables finance is structured on a '*with recourse basis*' (where they set up lines on company) or on a '*without recourse basis*'.

Payments of all service and utility bills, for example courier payments, electricity bills payments, etc. could be done through their vendor finance product. Through this mechanism, the bank will pay out the client's service provider on the due date of the invoice/bill and collect the money from the client after a pre-determined credit period.

(b) *International Factoring*

In *international factoring*, there are usually two factors. The *export factor* looks at financing the exporter and sales administration (presenting invoices at the right time and collecting payments being the key tasks). The *import factor* is interested in evaluating the buyer, collecting the money on time, simultaneously ensuring that he is protected against default. International factoring encompasses all the four services—pre-payments, sales ledger administration, credit protection, and collection of debt.

(c) *Distributor Finance*

The Distributor Finance Programme (DFP) of HSBC sets up a financing and collection arrangement for customer's delivery chain.

The credit-worthiness of distributors is established independently by HSBC and credit limits are set up on each distributor. Their approach is to become customer's business partner providing value-added services over and above the basic funding against customer's receivables from the channel. This allows the customer to focus the efforts of their sales team on actual sales rather than collection.

Their current portfolio carries a healthy mix of corporate clients across various industry sectors, viz. telecommunications, automotive components, FMCG and textiles, to name a few.

3. IFCI Factors

IFCI Factors Limited (erstwhile Foremost Factors Limited) is a subsidiary of IFCI Limited, which is a leading financial institution of India. It pays 80–85% of the invoice instantly. Following are the factoring products and services of IFCI Factors.

(a) *Domestic Factoring*

It is provided for open account credit sales of goods and services made within India. Services offered primarily comprise of funding, sales ledger administration and collections.

(b) *International Factoring*

It is given for open account credit sales of goods and services to overseas buyers. Services offered primarily comprise of funding, credit protection, sales ledger administration and collections.

Table 12.3 describes the factoring specifications followed by IFCI[4].

4. http://www.ifcifactors.com/SME%20Finance.pdf

TABLE 12.3 Eligibility Criteria for a Client (IFCI Factors)

S.No.	*Particulars*	*Standard*
1	Minimum borrower's net worth	₹1.00 crore
2	Maximum TOL/TNW ratio	6:1
3	Current ratio as per industry norm	—
4	Company in existence (minimum)	3 years
5	Operations for past years	Profit making for last 2 years

FACTORING: THE ROAD AHEAD

In India, factoring is on an increasing spree and is being viewed as a sought after source of short-term finance by business houses. Globally, factoring is primarily seen as a financing function—a source of funds to fill the void of bank financing for small-scale industries and others. The Factoring and Commercial Finance Industry had shown significant growth in 2010 and 2011. Factoring can provide companies with more finance than traditional cash flow lending and at the same time, the industry has a proven track record of lower default losses. This makes factoring unique and contributes to its growth and increased acceptance by business communities, bankers and policy-makers.

As mentioned in the introduction, the global factoring services market size is expected to register a CAGR of 8.8% from 2022 to 2030. The market growth can be attributed to the increasing open trade accounts and cross-border businesses. The expansion of the manufacturing industry in Asian countries and the growing need among start-ups and SMEs for an alternate source of finance are further driving the market growth. The manufacturing segment accounted for the largest market share of over 30% in 2022. *Region wise,* Europe accounted for the major market share of over 55% in 2022 owing to the growing focus of transport companies on export business factoring. Emerging start-ups continue to line up for factoring services from countries such as the U.K., Germany, Italy, Romania, and Sweden. The Asia Pacific region is expected to witness considerable growth with a CAGR of 11.5% over the forecast period of 2030 owing to the expansion of the manufacturing sector in economies such as India and other Southeast Asian countries.[5]

There are wide opportunities for growth in the factoring industry worldwide but at the same time there are challenges to deal with. In launching factoring service, the thrust should be on the twin areas of *receivables management*, and *credit appraisal*. Since the small-scale sector lacks these sophisticated skills, factors fill the gap. The financing function and the receivable management should go hand-in-hand, else the purpose of factoring would be defeating.

Factoring generally requires good historical credit information on all buyers, otherwise there is a large credit risk on the part of the factor. This adds to the increasing number of frauds which is already a big problem in this industry, for example, bogus receivables and non-existent customers.

5. https://www.grandviewresearch.com/industry-analysis/factoring-services-market

FORFAITING

In today's competitive world business environment, the exporter is often required to provide credit terms to the buyer but every buyer credits present a dilemma to the exporter owing to the probable risk of default. Apart from the non-payment risk, exporters also face various issues such as liquidity constraint, bank borrowing, foreign exchange exposure, etc.

Forfaiting is a form of trade finance that addresses these concerns. The word 'forfaiting' is derived from a French term *à forfait* that means to surrender ones' rights on something to someone else. *Forfaiting* is a method of trade financing that allows exporters to get cash by selling their medium-term accounts receivables at a discount on a without recourse basis. A *forfaiter* is a dedicated firm or a division in a bank that performs non-recourse export financing by purchasing the medium-term accounts receivables from the exporters.

Similar to factoring, forfaiting almost eliminates the risk of non-payment, once the goods have been delivered to the importer as per the terms of sale. Forfaiting is typically related with exporters who sell capital goods, commodities, or large projects, and offer a credit of 180 days to 7 years.

There are five parties in a transaction of forfaiting. These include:

(i) Exporter
(ii) Importer
(iii) Exporter's bank
(iv) Importer's bank
(v) The forfaiter

Table 12.4 differentiates between factoring and forfaiting.

TABLE 12.4 Distinction between Factoring and Forfaiting

Basis	*Factoring*	*Forfaiting*
Extent of finance	Usually 75–80% of the value of the invoice	100% of invoice value
Credit worthiness	Factor does the credits rating in case of non-recourse factoring transaction	The forfaiting bank relies on the creditability of the availing bank
Services provided	Day-to-day administration of sales and other allied services	No such services are provided
Recourse	With or without recourse	Always without recourse
Sales	By turnover	By bills

History

Forfaiting is a trade finance technique with a vast history. Fundamentally, forfaiting is discounting of bills of exchange, promissory notes on a non-recourse basis—a practice that has its origin in the discounting of merchants acceptance in the city of London hundreds of years ago. Modern forfaiting developed in the late 1950s and 1960s when Western European exporters needed export finance to cover the risk of their sales to the countries of Eastern Europe. Initially, forfaiting was controlled by a very small group of specialist banks and institutions based in Switzerland. Today, the international forfaiting market has reached around 80–90 countries.

Forfaiting Regulations

Forfaiting, as an export finance option, has been approved by RBI via Circular No. 42 in 1992[6]. The forfaiting facility has to be provided by an International forfaiting agency through an authorised dealer. The forfaiting proceeds should be received in India after the shipment as soon as possible but definitely within the 180-days period specified by RBI for all exports. The transaction has to be routed through an authorised dealer who will not only handle documentation but also provide custom certificates for GR form.

Uniform Rules of Forfaiting

ICC (International Chamber of Commerce) introduced Uniform Rules of Forfaiting (URF) to govern the international forfaiting market, to be effective from 1 January, 2013[7]. They specify a set of rules for the sale of instruments used for financing trade, for example, bills of exchange, promissory notes, etc.

IFA (International Forfaiting Association) had been trying to produce a single set of standardised terms and conditions for the two types of forfaiting market—primary and secondary. *Primary forfaiting market* is where transactions are carried out between the exporter and the seller of goods and services whereas secondary market is that market where transactions are made between banks and financial institutions.

The key provision would be examination of the documents for buyers and sellers in both primary and secondary markets. This ensures that the transaction would not be rejected on false grounds. This will also give the buyer assurance of having a suitable set of documents. Secondly, a descending scale of recourse has been implemented with the exporters who will be accountable if the goods they are selling are defective which leads to payment problems for the seller in the secondary market. Further, a balance will be maintained between the non-recourse nature of forfaiting and the need to ensure that parties carry out reasonable responsibilities in the transaction chain. This will speed up the resolution of disputes, avoid lawsuits and encourage new entrants in the market.

FUNDAMENTAL ASPECTS OF FORFAITING

The key aspects of forfaiting are as follows:

1. Repayments

Repayment of forfaiting is mostly done in periodic instalments. When balance due is supported by promissory notes or bills of exchange, a series of drafts are issued, usually

6. http://www.banknetindia.com/banking/forfait.htm
7. http://www.iccwbo.org/News/Articles/2012/ICC-unveils-new-rules-for-forfaiting.

at a 6-month interval. Forfaiting applies to the amount of approx. US$ 1,00,000.00 and above.

2. Currency

The credit is usually denominated in US Dollars, German Marks or Swiss Francs; although this is not a regulatory requirement and any other currency may be used as well. Since the cost of forfaiting is mostly determined by the forfaiter's funding cost, a weak currency would make such a forfaiting transaction too expensive. It is essential that payments are made in strong currency.

The essential elements of forfaiting are given in Box 12.3.

BOX 12.3: FORFAITING FACTORS

Forfaiting is based on three factors:

1. *Discount rate*

The claims are discounted at an all-in discount rate. The rate is usually quoted as margin over LIBOR* (funding cost) and consists of the following:

- Cost of covering commercial, country and interest rate risk
- Cost of funds based on the Euromarket rates (LIBOR)

2. *Grace days*

Grace days are added to each maturity when calculating interest. These will compensate for delays in payment that are common in certain countries.

3. *Commitment fee*

Exporters will often need a commitment from the forfaiter's firm to purchase a claim long before the delivery of goods. A commitment fee will then be charged from the day of commitment until disbursement.

* LIBOR stands for London Interbank offered rate and it serves as the first step to calculate interest.

3. Discounting

The forfaiter or the banker will discount the drafts after the exporter has shipped the goods to the importer and handed the required documents mentioned in the contract to the Forfaiter. The cut rate will be deducted from the face value of the drafts and the rest will be paid out immediately.

4. Instruments Used for Forfaiting

(i) *Promissory Note/Bills of Exchange*

Mostly, forfaiting is done using Bills of Exchange drawn by the beneficiary and accepted by the debtor, or promissory note issued by the importer in favour of the exporter. These are generally guaranteed by a bank.

(ii) *Documentary Credit*

Documentary credit is also known as *Letter of Credit* which is the most common way of payment in international business transactions.

The difference between all three credit services is given in Table 12.5.

TABLE 12.5 Comparative Analysis of Bills Discounting, Factoring and Forfaiting

Basis	*Bills Discounting*	*Factoring*	*Forfaiting*
Scrutiny	Individual sale transaction	Service of sale transaction	Individual sale transaction
Extent of finance	Upto 75–80%	Upto 80%	Upto 100%
Recourse	With recourse	With or without recourse	Without recourse
Sales administration	Not done	Done	Not done
Term	Short term	Short term	Medium term
Charge creation	Hypothecation	Assignment	Assignment

FLOW CHART OF FORFAITING

Figure 12.3 is the flow chart representing forfaiting transaction.

Let us take an *example,* National Exports Ltd., India had a contract in hand to supply readymade garments worth US$ 2 million to a New York based company. In order to win the contract against the competition, the company had to provide the buyer with deferred payments over the next two years following the delivery. The delivery had to happen over a period of six months following the signing of contract.

The deferred payments were to be made via bills of exchange drawn under a letter of credit opened by a second tier invest bank (the buyer's native bank) maturing on each of the deferred payment dates. The Indian supplier did not want to wait for two years for the payment nor could he afford the risk of non-payment by the customer.

The supplier discussed forfaiting as a potential trade financing solution with Export Forfaiting Solutions Ltd. (EFSL), a specialist trade finance unit operating in both the countries. Under forfaiting financing, EFSL would contract to purchase from the supplier the bills of exchange that represented the deferred payments on a non-recourse basis to the supplier. So, EFSL had an undertaking to pay the supplier a pre-agreed amount of US Dollars upon each shipment of the delivery to the customer, against delivery by the supplier to EFSL of the original bills of exchange endorsed in EFSL's favour. Thus, the supplier could be confident of its profit margin and also that its terms of payment would be effectively managed through the forfaiting mechanism. On this basis, the supplier got the required support to sign the contract and immediately commenced the production of the goods.

Figure 12.3 Flow Chart of Forfaiting Transaction

ADVANTAGES OF FORFAITING

Following are the key advantages of forfaiting:

1. Risk Management

Forfaiting covers all the risks attached to international trade as follows:

Country Risk

Forfaiter frees the exporter from any kind of political risk that may arise during the debt period like war, revolution or civil unrest, which could stop payments.

Commercial Risk

It absorbs the commercial risk of the exporter, i.e. incapability or unwillingness of the importer or the guarantor to pay the credit on due date.

Interest Rate Risk

All the forfaiting cost, i.e. discount, commission, and days of grace, are obligatory and remain same for the whole financing period.

2. Instant Cash

Forfaiter provides the exporter with instant cash which improves his liquidity. The credit sales get converted into cash sales.

3. Other Benefits

(i) Forfaiter offers 'without recourse' finance to an exporter and it does not affect the exporter's borrowing limits.

(ii) Forfaiting absolves the exporter from botheration of credit administration and collection issues.

(iii) Forfaiting is specific to a business deal. It does not require a long banking relationship with the forfaiter.

(iv) Exporter also saves the money on insurance cost as forfaiting eliminates the need for export credit insurance.

CASE STUDY

An Anatomy of a Factoring Fraud

This is the story of how three factoring companies were duped by a client and its 'customers', losing several million pounds in the process. As a result, one of the factoring companies had to sell it off and exit.

Lesson: "Sometimes, appearances can be deceptive."

- ***Details about the Factoring Client***

Well spread ledger, increasing turnover and balancing monthly reports to boot. Is he the ideal client? Yes!

- ***Background to the Factoring Fraud***

The fraudster was an importer of shoes from India and Italy. He had been into the business for two years and had an annual turnover of £6 m. For a period of 12 months, the company was financed by a 'full service' factoring facility. The client's customer portfolio consisted of 15 customers, two of whom had existing factoring agreements. No one customer accounted for more than 10% of the overall sales ledger.

- ***What the Client Manager of the Factoring Company Saw***

On books, this was a successful factoring client. There was nothing tangible which pointed to anything suspicious, still the client manager noticed:

- Large volumes of stock flowing to a small customer base.
- The client putting pressure on the invoice financier to increase customer funding limits.
- The rapidly increasing turnover of client.
- Lack of quality financial information.
- The two of the client's customers were newly incorporated companies.
- In addition, collections notes indicated the client was heavily involved in the collection of its assigned debts.

On account of absence of any material evidence and in order to reduce the invoice financier's exposure to risk, the client manager decided to put the client on a three-month notice period.

- ***Revealing the Factoring Fraud***

When the notice was given, initially collection procedures delivered positive results. However, around four to six weeks of the notice period, collections started vanishing. It was then that the client manager decided to visit the client's customers. In fact, it was at this point that the client manager found:

- In some cases, the fraudster's 'customer' was indeed the client's own shoe shop. The fraudster had tactfully instructed to its employees', telling them what to say if the invoice financier phoned!
- Two 'customers' were, in fact, neglected industrial units.
- A couple of the customers had directors with names borrowed from those of the client's own directors.

On notice being given, the fraudster had set up a new company and financed it with another factoring company. It used funds made available from this new facility to cover the 'collections' from the old facility.

- ***Outcome of the Factoring Fraud***

- The client manager appointed receivers.
- The fraudster's directors fled the country.
- A legal fight ensued between the factoring company victims regarding ownership of the stock.
- All 'customers' ceased to trade, whether voluntarily or following legal action by the combined invoice financiers.
- The fraudster's initial invoice financier lost £1 m (including 400 K of legal costs). The two other factoring companies involved lost £2.5 m between them (over three clients). One of the factoring companies ended up selling it off.

- ***Lessons Learnt from the Factoring Fraud***

1. Physical verification is vital to the client's business.
2. It is good to talk. The 'new company' factor did not take a reference or make contact at all with the older invoice financier.
3. Degree of professionalism is required by the factoring company.
4. Prevention is better than the cure. Loss of fee income caused delay in notice being given to the client.

Source: The Business Bureau http://www.business-bureau.com/anatomy-factoring-fraud.

SOLVED PROBLEMS

PROBLEM 12.1: Trust 'N' Win company has sales of ₹18,00,000 and ₹16,20,000 in operating costs. Receivables' collection period is two months and they have an average balance of ₹3,00,000. Receivables are of high quality, being related to government contracts. Factoring charges are 9% and 80% advance is given by the factor. The cost of capital is 10%. The administrative clerk's annual salary is ₹30,000. Calculate the net factoring fee.

Solution: Cost/Benefit Analysis of Factoring ₹3,00,000 receivables six times a year

Annual Benefit/(Cost) (₹)

Factoring Costs (the receivable is paid at the end of 60 days):

Factoring Fee = 9% × ₹ 3,00,000 receivable = ₹ 27,000

Annual Factoring Cost = ₹ 27,000 factoring fee × 6 receivable periods per year

or = 9% × ₹ 18,00,000

= 1,62,000

Annual interest saved by shortening cash gap by 60 days through factoring:

Operating Costs/day = ₹16,20,000/360 = ₹4,500

Reduced Financing Need = 60 days × ₹4,500/day = ₹2,70,000

Reduced Financing Cost = ₹2,70,000 × 10% cost of capital = ₹27,000

Adjustment: Only 80% cash advance from factoring (80% × ₹27,000)

= ₹21,600

Annual savings in accounts receivable clerk's salary: ₹30,000

Net annual cost of factoring = ₹1,10,400 (1,62,000 – 21,600 – 30,000)

Net annual factoring Fee (%) = (₹1,10,400/₹18,00,000) = 6.13%

Note: Receivables are factored six times a year. Around 80% of the cash is advanced immediately. Remaining 20% is advanced when the receivables are collected at the end of sixty days.

PROBLEM 12.2: R&Co.'s average sales are ₹75 lacs. 80% sales are on credit. They take on an average, 60 days to realise and are financed by short-term bank finance. The bad debts ratio is 2% of the sales. The rate of interest on bank finance is 18%.

There is a factoring proposal of In Factors Ltd. (IFL) for receivables management. This would save their administrative overheads by ₹50,000 and result in higher efficiency. Their charges for recourse and non-recourse are 2% and 5% respectively. They would advance 75% and 85% in case of recourse and non-recourse factoring. Compute the cost-benefit analysis of both the factorings and advices which one is preferable for R&Co.?

Solution:

1. Cost of present In-house system	(₹)
(a) Cost of funds in receivables	
= ₹ 60,00,000 × 60/360 × 0.18	= 1,80,000
(0.80 × ₹ 75 lacs = ₹ 60 lacs)	
(b) Bad debt losses	
= ₹ 75 lacs × 0.02	= 1,50,000
(c) Administrative overheads	50,000
Total	**= 3,80,000**

2. Cost of recourse factoring	(₹)
(a) Factoring commission	
= ₹ 75,00,000 × 0.02	1,50,000
3. Cost of non-recourse factoring	
(a) Factoring commission	
= ₹ 75,00,000 × 0.05	3,75,000

Decision Analysis: Recourse Factoring

Benefits (₹ 1,80,000 + 50,000)	2,30,000
Costs (₹ 1,50,000)	1,50,000
Net benefit	**80,000**

Decision Analysis: Non-Recourse Factoring

Benefits (₹ 1,80,000 + 1,50,000 + 50,000)	3,80,000
Costs (₹ 3,75,000)	3,75,000
Net benefit	**5,000**

Therefore, it can be inferred, based on net benefit, that 'recourse factoring' is more beneficial for the company.

PROBLEM 12.3: Under an advance factoring arrangement AB Factors Limited (ABFL) has agreed to advance a sum of ₹14 lacs against the receivables purchased from X Ltd. The factoring agreement provides for an advance payment of 80 per cent of the value of factored receivables and for guaranteed payment after three months from the date of purchasing the receivables.

The advance carries a rate of interest of 16% p.a. compounded quarterly and the factoring commission is 1.5 per cent of the value of factored receivables. Both the interest and commission are collected upfront. Compute the amount actually made available to X Ltd.

Solution:

	(Rs. in lacs)
Value of factored receivable (= 14/0.8)	17.50
Maximum permissible advance	14.00
Less: Commission @ 1.5 per cent (= 17.5 × 0.015)	0.26
	13.74
Less: Discount charge (14 × 0.16 × 90/360)	0.56
Funds made available to X Limited	13.18

PROBLEM 12.4: R&Co., situated in France, wants to buy garments from Company 'B', located in India. Company 'B' signs the deal but finds the payment period of 90 days quite long. It, therefore, approaches forfaiter 'FC' to fulfill its immediate funding requirements. Company 'B' submits all the deal documents to forfaiter 'FC', who analyses the risk involved in the trade and agrees to fund. The invoice amount is ₹1,00,000, and forfaiter 'FC' charges a fee of 3% of the deal amount.

Company 'B' then notifies R&Co. about the forfaiting arrangement and asks for a guarantee from its bank. Once the guarantee is provided, Company 'B' ships garments to R&Co. Calculate the complete payment received by B. Explain the final settlement procedure.

Solution:

Company B receives the complete payment after fee deduction, i.e., (₹1,00,000 minus ₹3,000) from the forfaiter 'FC'. ₹97,000

After 90 days, forfaiter 'FC' approaches R&Co.'s bank with the necessary documentation. R&Co. pays its bank an amount of ₹1,00,000.
Then, the bank pays the same amount, i.e., ₹1,00,000, to the forfaiter.

PROBLEM 12.5: Company 'A' ships garments to Company 'B' and raises an invoice of ₹10 lacs which would be due for payment after three months. Company 'A' requires immediate funds to run the business and therefore approaches the factoring company 'FX' to sell the invoice. Company 'A' sends a copy of the invoice to 'FX', who then asks for the necessary documentation to analyse the trade deal and assess the risk involved.

If all conditions meet, 'FX' might agree to factor the invoice and pay ₹8,00,000 to company 'A'. Once the three-month credit period is over, 'FX' approaches Company B to clear the invoice. What is the amount to be paid by B to FX and finally to A @ 4% factoring fee?

Solution:

Company 'B' pays the entire invoice amount to 'FX', i.e., ₹10,00,000
The balance amount that needs to be paid to Company 'A' is ₹2,00,000
'FX' deducts its factoring fee of 4% from this amount and extends the remaining amount to Company 'A', i.e., ₹1,92,000

POINTS TO REMEMBER

- Factoring is a method of financing wherein a firm sells its trade debts at a discount to a financial institution factor to raise finance for working capital requirement.
- The three parties directly involved in the factoring process are— (i) the one who sells the receivable, (ii) the debtor, and (iii) the factor.
- The cost of factoring services primarily comprises of the following two components—discount charge and advisory fee.
- Factoring is an arrangement or contract between the factor and the supplier and is governed by the 'law of contract'.
- Factoring is a word which is often confused with invoice discounting. Factoring is the sale of receivables whereas invoice discounting is borrowing where the receivable is used as collateral.
- Factoring differs from a bank loan as it is not a loan—it is the purchase of a financial asset (the receivable).
- Factoring is different from the forfaiting in the sense that forfaiting is a transaction-based operation while factoring is a firm-based operation, that is, in factoring, a firm sells all its receivables while in forfaiting, the firm sells one of its transactions.
- In disclosed factoring, client's customers are notified of the factoring agreement. Disclosed type can either be recourse or non-recourse.
- In undisclosed factoring, the client's customers are not notified of the factoring arrangement.
- In recourse factoring, client undertakes to collect the debts from the customer. If the customer does not pay the amount on maturity, factor will recover the amount from the client.
- In non-recourse factoring, factor undertakes to collect the debts from the customer. The balance amount is paid to client at the end of the credit period or when the customer pays the factor, whichever comes first.
- Factoring in India commenced in 1980s with a virtual deregulation of capital market and birth of a number of innovative financial instruments and schemes. A committee was constituted under the chairmanship of Kalyana Sundaram (1988) by RBI to examine the feasibility of factoring services in India, their constitution, organisational setup and scope of activities. The Reserve Bank of India (RBI), on the basis of the recommendations of this committee, issued various guidelines in 1988 for banking companies to start factoring services.
- The first factoring company started by State Bank of India (SBI) in 1991 was known as Factors and Commercial Ltd. (SBI FACS), followed by Canara Bank and Punjab National Bank (PNB), setting the subsidiaries for the purpose.
- In December 2011, the Government finally passed the Factoring Regulations Act, 2011. Its objective was to address the issue of delayed payments and it gives RBI

the right to regulate and monitor the working of factors in India. The new category NBFC-factor has been created under the Factoring Regulation Act, 2011. These directions were declared on July 23, 2012 and put into effect immediately.

- Forfaiting is a method of trade financing that allows exporters to get cash by selling their medium-term accounts receivables at a discount on a 'without recourse' basis.
- There are five parties in a transaction of forfeiting—Exporter, Importer, Exporter's bank, Importer's bank, and the forfaiter.
- Forfaiting as an export finance option has been approved by RBI via Circular No. 42 in 1992. The forfaiting facility has to be provided by an international forfaiting agency through an authorised dealer.
- ICC (International Chamber of Commerce) introduced Uniform Rules of Forfaiting (URF) to govern the international forfaiting market, and were effective from 1 January 2013.

KEY TERMS

- **Factoring** is a method of financing wherein a firm sells its trade debts at a discount to a financial institution factor to raise finance for working capital requirement.
- **Disclosed factoring (Notified factoring)** implies when client's customers are notified of the factoring agreement.
- **Undisclosed factoring (Non-notified or Confidential factoring)** means that client's customers are not notified of the factoring arrangement.
- **Recourse factoring** is one where the client bears the risk of default by the customer.
- **Non-recourse factoring** involves the transfer of all the risks to the factor.
- **Forfaiting** is a method of trade financing that allows exporters to get cash by selling their medium-term accounts receivables at a discount on a 'without recourse' basis.

EXERCISES

Problems

1. Star Ltd. average sales are ₹10 lacs. 80% sales are on credit. They take on an average 30 days to realise and are financed by short-term bank finance. The bad debts ratio is 0% of the sales. The rate of interest on bank finance is 10%.

   There is a factoring proposal of DAC Factors Ltd. for receivables management. This would save their office expenses by ₹1,000 and improve efficiency. Compute the total cost of receivables.

2. Big Brothers company has sales of ₹5,00,000 and ₹2,00,000 as operating costs. Receivables' collection period is three months and their average balance is of ₹50,000. Receivables are of moderate quality. Factoring charges are 8% and 80% advance is given by the factor. Calculate the net factoring charge.
3. Brokers Ltd. advance a sum of ₹5 lacs against the receivables purchased from Amit. The factoring agreement provides for an advance payment of 60 per cent of the value of factored receivables, being of high risk and for guaranteed payment after three months from the date of purchasing the receivables.

   The advance carries a rate of interest of 12% p.a. compounded annually and the factoring commission is 2 per cent of the value of factored receivables. Compute the funds made available to Amit.
4. Ajay airs chips to a US Company and raises an invoice of ₹10 lacs which would be due for payment after two months. He is in need of urgent funds to run the business and therefore approaches the factoring company 'AX' with a copy of the invoice. 'AX' evaluates the risk involved in the transaction and agrees to factor for 75%.

   After two-month credit period, 'AX' approaches US Company to settle the payment. What is the amount to be paid to AX and then to Ajay @ 5% factoring fee?
5. Young Enterprises has credit sales of ₹2 lacs. Its average collection period is 60 days. Being a new firm, it is planning to explore the factoring option @ 2% commission. They will be paid 80% of the amount. What is the total amount paid to them?

Answers:

1. ₹7,666.67
2. ₹16,000
3. ₹4.84
4. ₹1,87,500
5. ₹38,466

Objective Questions

1. Tick the correct answer:

(a) The primary function of factoring is to:
   (i) Provide funds
   (ii) Assist in management of accounts receivables
   (iii) Advise on financial matters
   (iv) All of the above

(b) Factor is:
   (i) The broker bank (ii) Customer
   (iii) The seller (iv) None of the above

(c) In forfaiting, the firm sells:
   (i) All the transactions (ii) Few transactions
   (iii) One of its transactions (iv) None of the above

(d) Recourse factoring implies:
   (i) Partial transfer of loss to factor
   (ii) Complete transfer of loss to factor
   (iii) No transfer of loss to factor
   (iv) None of the above

(e) Factoring is the conversion of:
   (i) Receivables (ii) Inventory
   (iii) Other resources (iv) None of the above

Answers: (a) i (b) i (c) iii (d) iii (e) i

2. Fill in the blanks:

(a) Factoring is the financing of ....
(b) .... is used for off-balance sheet financing.
(c) In ...., 100% of the receivables are discounted.
(d) Without recourse factoring involves complete risk to be borne by the ....
(e) Forfaiting is generally used as .... finance.
(f) Forfaiting is on .... basis.

Answers:

(a) Receivables
(b) Factoring
(c) Forfaiting
(d) Factor
(e) Export
(f) Without recourse

3. True or False:

(a) Factoring implies instant cash.
(b) One gets the full amount in factoring.
(c) Factoring is a short-term financing activity.
(d) Factoring is sale, while invoice discounting is borrowing.
(e) Factoring is similar to a bank loan.
(f) In recourse factoring, commission is higher than non-recourse.
(g) Factoring and forfaiting both are used for short-term financing.
(h) Factoring firms are intermediary institutions.
(i) Factoring may be with or without recourse.

Answers: (a) True (b) False (c) True (d) True (e) False
(f) False (g) False (h) True (i) True

Short Questions

1. What is factoring?
2. State the parties to factoring.
3. Distinguish between factoring and forfaiting.
4. What are the parties to forfaiting?

5. List three functions of a factor.
6. What are the main costs to factoring?

Critical Thinking Questions

1. "Factoring is an outsourcing of management of trade receivables". Elaborate.
2. "A company can increase its efficiency and reduce the total costs by factoring activity". Do you agree?
3. "Factoring is not free from evils". Justify.
4. "Factoring aims at restructuring a balance sheet". Prove.
5. "Forfaiting is an effective tool of risk management in external trade.
6. Discuss your viewpoint about the superiority of factoring over traditional bank finance.
7. "Forfaiting is a trade finance used for international trade". Elaborate with examples.
8. "Over the years, factoring has emerged as one of the bankable credit services for business houses". Comment.
9. "Forfaiting is nothing but factoring in international trade". Do you agree?

Descriptive Questions

1. Why do firms choose factoring? Discuss the benefits attached to factoring.
2. Factoring is often confused with bills discounting and bank loan. Highlight the differences between them.
3. What are the different types of factoring? Explain with examples.
4. Discuss the process of factoring in detail.
5. What are the various issues and challenges faced by the Indian factoring industry?
6. Discuss the general and technical aspects of forfeiting.
7. What are the various advantages of forfaiting?

PROJECT EXERCISE

Financial and Commercial Appraisal of Factoring Companies in India

Pick up top ten factoring companies operating in India. Study the nature of factoring service offered by them in terms of client base and geographical location. Determine their viability index on parameters, like recovery rate, profitability margin, growth pattern, and future outlook. Draft a questionnaire and send it to them. Follow up by telephone and meet them personally, if required. Integrate the information in report and discuss in the class for suggestive inputs.

REVIEW CASE

Ambit Collection Outsourcing—to be or not to be?

Ambit Age Ltd. is a leading paper-bag manufacturing company. As credit is an inevitable part of growing business, it sells goods on credit and manages to generate revenues worth ₹10 lacs with the present credit. The management has identified these customers into three categories, based upon their default rate, i.e. lease, low, and moderate. It is considering whether to sell to customers whom it has classified into the high-risk class because it can generate sales worth ₹5,00,000 more but it will increase their bad debts by another 3%. Also, the ACP of these customers is 60 days. The marginal cost of funds is 15%. Additional 5% collection cost will also have to be incurred. Present variable cost ratio is 70% and fixed cost is ₹10,000.

The company does not want to lose out this customer segment for long-term growth prospects. Therefore, it plans to explore the option of factoring service for collection of receivables @ 5% for non-recourse for high risk customers. The advance amount from the bank in this case would be 90%. Table 12.6 is their data sheet and Table 12.7 shows their present working capital position.

TABLE 12.6 Data Sheet of the Company

Risk Class	*Sales (₹)*	*ACP*	*Bad Debts Ratio*
Least	3 lacs	30 days	0%
Low	4 lacs	45	1%
Moderate	3 lacs	45	2%
High risk (Proposed)	5 lacs	60	5%

TABLE 12.7 Present Working Capital Position of the Company

Balance Sheet (₹ in lakhs)

Current Liabilities		*Current Assets*	
Bank loans	5	Inventory	12
Other current liabilities	10	Trade receivables	5
Net current assets	3	Prepaid expenses	1
Total	**18**		**18**

Issues for Discussion

(i) Advise them whether to extend credit to high-risk class?

(ii) Determine whether the company should adopt factoring for a high-risk customer? If yes, what is the maximum benefit they will get?

(iii) Is non-recourse factoring advantageous for them or should they switch to recourse factoring?

(iv) Are there any net benefits of factoring if the firm also outsources low and moderate customers?

(v) Does factoring have any impact on their balance sheet?

REFERENCES

Bradford Network, (1999), *Maintaining Interests: How mortgage lenders can help Home owners maintain their homes*, New York: Joseph Rowntree Trust.

Chartered Institute of Housing, (1997), "Private Sector Housing: In Need of Urgent Repair", Edinburgh.

Glasgow City Council, (1998), *Owner's Guide to Factoring Services*, Glasgow.

Graham, J.R. (2004), *The economic implications of corporate financial reporting*, Working Paper, Social Science Research Network.

Siegel, J.G., Dauber, N., and Shim, J.K. (2005), *The Vest Pocket CPA*, New York, Wiley, 2005.

RBI guidelines—*C.S. Kalyanasunderam Committee Report*.

www.bankingindiaupdate.com

www.banknetindia.com

www.business-bureau.com

www.businesswire.com

www.cfa.com

www.cashflowuk.com

www.canbankfactors.com

www.fci.nl

www.financialservices.gov.in

www.foremostfactors.net

www.grandviewresearch.com

www.hsbc.co.in

www.iccwbo.org

www.ifgroup.com

www.ifcifactors.com

www.rbi.org.in

www.sbiglobal.in

CHAPTER 13

Securitisation

Securitisation could become a solution for those banks that want to transfer the risks posed by the high-level concentrations of similar assets, while retaining customer relationships.

— **Maria Xuereb**

LEARNING OBJECTIVES

This chapter discusses the following:

- Concept and process of securitisation
- Structure and types of securitisation
- Need for securitisation
- History of securitisation in India
- Regulatory framework of securitisation in India
- Securitisation and the fiasco of 2008
- Nature and scope of asset reconstruction companies
- Issues faced by the Indian securitisation market

INTRODUCTION

The sub-prime mortgage crisis in 2008 once again brought securitisation on a global map but in a bad taste. Securitisation started in 1970s, when home mortgages were pooled by US government-backed agencies. Later on, other income-producing assets also began getting securitised, and today, the market of securitisation is one of the leading markets in the world despite the subprime fiasco.

Securitisation was started by the financial institutions and corporations to find new sources of funding—either by moving assets off their balance sheets or by borrowing against them to refinance their original loans. As mentioned above, initially securitisation was used to finance simple, self-liquidating assets such as mortgages but over the years, besides mortgages, it has extended to corporate loans, project finance, and lease/trade receivables. Now, there are Mortgage-Backed (MBS) and Asset-Backed (ABS) Securitisations prevailing in the market.

SECURITISATION: DEFINITION

Securitisation is "the process in which certain types of assets of homogenous nature are pooled for repackaging into marketable securities (interest-bearing securities) that can be sold to investors". The interest and principal payments from the assets are transferred to the purchasers of the securities.

Basically, it is a tool of financing where a firm transfers ownership of assets to a wholly-owned, limited purpose, Special-Purpose Vehicle (SPV), which in turn finances a portion of the assets with debt that does not recourse to the originating firm. FT[1] defines it as, "pooling of assets, such as mortgages, into securities that are sliced up and sold to different types of investors. Lenders pass on loans quickly, giving them few incentives to ensure they are repaid. Limited information on underlying assets makes them illiquid and hard to value". In general, SPV can be financed in many ways like:

- Issuance of asset-backed securities
- Asset-backed commercial paper
- Loan from a bank, etc.

Some of the assets that can be securitised are loans like car loans, housing loans, etc. Securitisation reduces the borrowing costs of the corporate and in case of banks, it lowers the regulatory minimum capital requirements.

Unlike traditional debt, securitisation does not inflate a company's liabilities. Instead, it produces funds for future investment. Securitisation also helps issuers in customising the risk-return profile of portfolio as per the risk appetite of investors. For example, suppose a leasing company needs cash. Under usual circumstances, the company would either borrow a loan or sell bonds. This also depends on its financial health and credit-rating but if it can find some buyers and sell some of its leases to them, effectively converting a future income stream to cash, this will result into 'securitisation'.

PROCESS OF SECURITISATION

The primary objective of securitisation is to separate the credit risk of originating firm from the credit risk of SPV which is done by legally transferring the assets from the balance sheet of the originating firm to SPV. The process consists of two steps:

***Step 1*:** A company with loans or other income-producing assets, known as the 'originator', decides the assets it wants to remove from its balance sheet and pools them together into reference portfolio. They then sell this asset pool to an 'issuer', such as a Special Purpose Vehicle (SPV).

1. http://lexicon.ft.com/Term?term=securitisation.

***Step 2*:** The issuer finances the pooled assets acquired by issuing securities which are tradable and interest bearing and these are then sold to the capital investors. Fixed and floating rate payments are received by the investors from a trustee account depending on the cash flows generated by the reference portfolio. In general, the originator services the loans in the portfolio. They collect payments from the initial borrowers and pass them directly to the SPV or the trustee after deducting the servicing fee. It is a form of a typical transaction which is generally called *true sales,* that means the originating firm loses direct access to the receivables beyond any residual ownership interest.

Illustrations

1. Fin Bank

Fin Bank operates in the northern part of India. The loans given out by this bank are its assets which represent blocked funds. The customers who have borrowed from the bank are known as *obligors.*

To clear these blocked funds, the assets are transferred by the originator (the person who holds the assets, Fin. Bank in this case) to a Special Purpose Vehicle (SPV). The 'SPV' is a separate entity set up solely for the securitisation process and providing funds to the originator.

The assets which are transferred to the SPV need to be uniform in terms of the underlying asset, maturity and risk profile. It implies that only one type of asset (e.g. home loans) of similar maturity (e.g. 15 to 20 years) will be bundled together for creating the securitised instrument. The SPV acts as an intermediary which divides the assets of the originator into marketable securities.

These securities issued by the SPV to the investors are known as *Pass-Through-Certificates (PTCs).* The cash flows received (which include principal repayment, interest and prepayments received) from the obligors are passed on to the investors of PTCs after deducting the service fees. The difference between rate of interest payable by the obligor and return promised to the investor investing in PTCs is the 'servicing fee' for the SPV.

The securitised assets are removed from the bank's books and the money generated through securitisation can be used for other profitable uses like for giving new loans. For an originator (Fin. Bank in the example), securitisation is an alternative to raising funds from corporate debt or equity for meeting its funding requirements. As the securitised instruments can have a better credit-rating than the company, the originator can get funds from new investors and additional funds from existing investors at a lower cost than debt.

2. Cineplex–Sumit

Sumit wants to open a cineplex and needs funds for the same. To raise funds, he can sell his 'future cash flows' (cash flows arising from sale of movie tickets and food items in future) in the form of securities to raise money. The investors will have a claim over the future cash flows generated from the cineplex.

Sumit will benefit as his funds' requirement can be met from the cash flows generated of the cineplex itself.

This is how securitisation is beneficial.

BOX 13.1: QUALIFIED INSTITUTIONAL BUYERS

In India, only Qualified Institutional Buyers (QIBs), who possess the expertise and the financial power to invest in securities market, are allowed to invest in PTCs.

Financial Institutions (FIs), scheduled commercial banks, mutual funds, insurance companies, provident funds, pension funds, state industrial development corporations, etc. come under the category of a QIB.

STRUCTURE OF SECURITISATION

In the process of securitisation, the originator or holder of assets sells the assets (existing or future) to the SPV created which holds title to assets underlying securities. Then, the SPV, with the help of an investment banker, issues securities (financial instruments) which are distributed to the investors. These securities have ownership interest and are secured by a pool of assets (secured or unsecured). Finally, the SPV pays the originator for the assets with the proceeds from the sale of securities (Figure 13.1).

A. Primary Parties to a Securitisation Deal

1. *The originator:* Originator is the owner of the asset who sets up the basic structure to execute the deal. He is, therefore, the prime mover of the deal. The assets to be scrutinised exist in his books and when these assets are sold, he receives the funds generated from the sale. He transfers both the legal and the beneficial interest in the assets to the Special Purpose Vehicles in case of a true sale.

2. *The SPV:* Special Purpose Vehicle (issuer) is the one who buys the assets to be securitised from the originator. He is the issuer of the debt instruments. The SPV is a low-capitalised entity with narrowly defined purposes and activities and has independent trustees/directors.

SPV holds assets in its books and makes upfront payment to the originator for buying them. Hence, assets are removed from the originator's books.

SPV is the 'bankruptcy remote', which means that if the originator goes into bankruptcy, the assets of the issuer will not be distributed to the creditors of the originator.

3. *The investors:* Investors are those who buy a participating interest in the total pool of receivables. They receive their payment in the form of interest and principal as per the agreed pattern. Investors can be in the form of:

- Mutual funds
- Provident funds
- Pension funds
- Insurance companies, etc.

4. *The obligor(s):* The obligor is the borrower of the original loan or originator's debtor. The amount outstanding from the obligor is the asset that is transferred to the SPV via administrator. In a securitisation transaction, the credit-worthiness of the obligor(s) is of utmost importance.

B. Other Parties in a Securitisation Deal

The other parties involved in a securitisation deal are:

1. ***The rating agency:*** It is the investor who takes the risk of the asset pool and not the obligator, therefore rating by an external rating agency is very crucial. The responsibility of the rating agency is:

- Evaluating the strength of the cash flow.
- Evaluating the quality of instruments and assign a credit rating.
- Evaluating the mechanism designed to ensure full and timely payment.

2. ***Administrator or servicer:*** Administrator is the one who collects the payment due from the obligator(s) and forwards the payment to the SPV. He also follows up with the defaulting borrowers and pursues legal actions against them. He is also known as the *receiving and paying agent* as he receives the instalments and forwards it to the SPV.

3. ***Agent and trustee:*** He is the one who is responsible for overseeing that all the parties to the securitisation deal are performing in line with the securitisation trust agreement. He looks after the interests of the investors and deals with issuer, credit enhancer and servicer on behalf of the security-holders.

4. ***Structurer:*** An investment banker is the structurer responsible for bringing together the partners to a securitisation deal: originator, obligor, the investors and other partners. He is the one who helps in structuring the transactions and also works with the originator. He underwrites or places the securities for a fee.

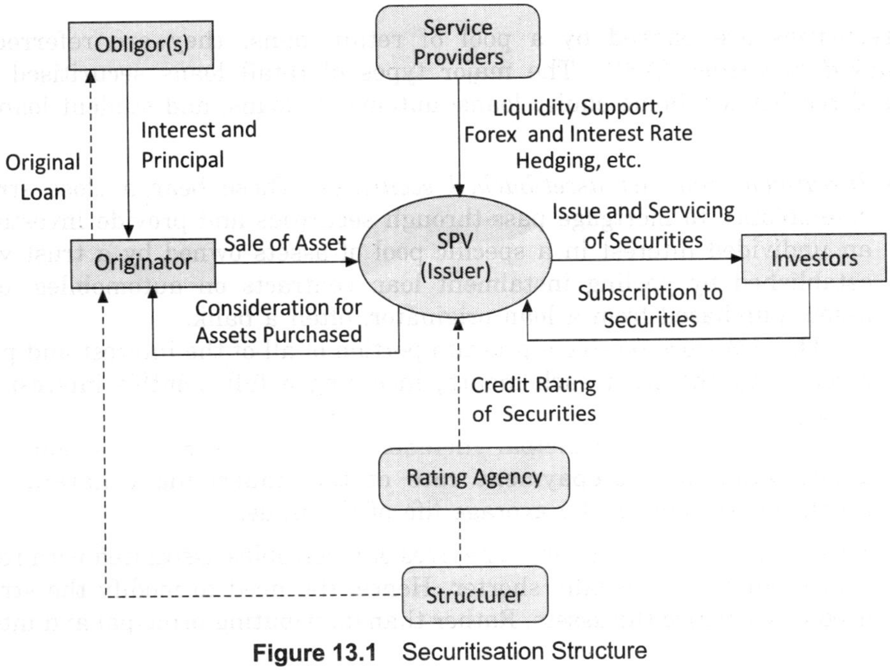

Figure 13.1 Securitisation Structure

5. *The swap counterparty:* He is the one who provides interest rate/currency swap, if needed.

6. *The credit enhancer:* It can be a bank, surety company, or insurer, who provides credit support through a letter of credit, guarantee, or other assurance.

TYPES OF SECURITISATION

There are two kinds of securitisation—(i) mortgage-backed securitisation, and (ii) asset-backed securitisation.

1. Mortgage-backed Securitisation

The securities created by securitisation of a pool of mortgage loans are referred to as *Mortgage-Backed Securities (MBS)*. These are further classified as:

(i) A pool of high-quality residential mortgage loans are called *Residential Mortgage-Backed Securities*, and

(ii) A pool of commercial loans, i.e. mortgage loans for income-producing properties such as apartment buildings, office buildings, and shopping centres, etc. are called *Commercial Mortgage-Backed Securities*.

These products are generally used as funding vehicles for financial entities such as depository institutions (banks and savings and loan associations) and finance companies. For non-financial entities, the account receivables are mostly used for securitisation.

2. Asset-backed Securitisation

When securities are backed by a pool of retail loans, they are referred to as *Asset-Backed Securities (ABS)*. The major types of retail loans securitised include credit card receivables, home equity loans, automobile loans, and student loans. They can be:

(i) *Instalment contract asset-backed securities:* These bear a close structural resemblance to mortgage pass-through securities and provide investors with an undivided interest in a specific pool of assets owned by a trust which is established by pooling instalment loan contracts on automobiles, or other assets purchased from a loan originator, often a bank.

The investors receive a pro-rata portion of all of the interest and principal received by the trust each month, including a full month's interest on any prepayments.

The amount of principal included in each payment depends on the amortisation and prepayment rate of the underlying collateral. Faster prepayments shorten the average life of the issue.

(ii) *Revolving asset transactions:* The lives of receivables associated with revolving loan products are usually shorter. Hence, the need to modify the structures used to securitise the assets. Rather than distributing principal and interest to investors as received, the securities distribute cash flow in stages—a revolving phase, followed by an amortisation phase.

During the revolving period, only interest is paid and principal payments are reinvested in additional receivables as, *for example*, customers use their credit cards or take additional draws on their home equity lines. At the end of the revolving period an amortisation phase begins, and principal payments are made to investors along with interest payments because the principal balances are repaid.

Box 13.2 describes Collateralised Debt Obligations.

BOX 13.2: COLLATERALISED DEBT OBLIGATIONS (CDOs)

A Collateralised Debt Obligation (CDO) is a type of 'asset-backed security' (ABS). It varies in structure and underlying assets but the basic principle is the same.

- These are investment vehicles consisting of sub-classes (called tranches) of bonds, stratified by credit rating.
- CDOs represent different types of debt that are often referred to as 'tranches' or 'slices'. Each slice has a different maturity and risk associated with it. The higher the risk, the more the CDO pays.
- The underlying security of CDO is a large pool of other bonds such as basic corporate, asset-backed securities (ABS), or even tranches of other CDOs.
- The interest and principal payments from this underlying pool get pressed through the CDO tranches to produce stratified returns for their investors.
- CDO only redistributes the total risk associated with the underlying pool of assets to the prior ordered tranches. It neither reduces nor increases the total risk associated with the pool.

NEED FOR SECURITISATION

A. For Originators

Depending on the type of structure, it may help lower borrowing costs, release additional capital for expansion or reinvestment purposes, and improve asset/liability and credit risk management.

1. *Improves Capital Adequacy Ratio*[2]: Securitisation enables the banks and financial institutions to reduce the regulatory capital requirement and improves their CAR. Capital Adequacy Ratio is the measure of a banks' capital sufficiency to their risk portfolio. It is calculated as: Capital/Risk Weighted Assets. As per Basel regulations, the minimum ratio is 8% whereas RBI guidelines recommend it to be higher than 9%. The impact of securitisation on CAR is explained with the help of example given in Table 13.1.

---

2. For CAR and Risk weighted assets, refer 'Chapter 2' on Banking and 'Chapter 3' on Risk Management in Banks.

TABLE 13.1 Balance Sheet of ABC Bank

Liabilities	*Amount* (₹ in mn)	*Assets*	*Amount* (₹ in mn)
Equity	30	Cash and balances with RBI	50
Demand deposits	550	Balances with banks and call money	150
Term deposits	210	Investments in Government bonds	100
Borrowings	10	Mortgage loans	200
		Corporate loans	200
		Fixed assets	100
	800		**800**

(i) *CAR pre-securitisation*

Risk Weighted Assets (RWA)

= 0% × (50, 100) + 20% × (150) + 50% × (200) + 100% × (200, 100)

= 430

Tier I Capital = 40/430

= 9.30%

Tier II Capital = 10/430

= 2.33%

CAR = 9.30% + 2.33% = 11.63%

(ii) *CAR post-securitisation of mortgage loans*

Risk Weighted Assets (RWA)

= 0% × (50, 100) + 20% × (150) + 100% × (200, 100)

= 330

Tier I Capital = 40/330

= 12.12%

Tier II Capital = 10/330

= 3.03%

CAR = 12.12% + 3.03% = 15.15%

It can be seen from the above example that CAR of ABC bank improves from 11.63% to 15.15% after securitisation of mortgage loans.

2. *Off-balance sheet financing:* Securitisation helps enhance returns on capital by converting an 'on-balance-sheet' lending business into an 'off-balance-sheet' fee income stream that is less capital intensive. The receivables are moved "off-balance sheet" and replaced by a cash equivalent (less expenses of securitisation). This improves the originator's balance sheet and results in gain or loss, which itself is usually an intended, beneficial consequence. The originator does not have to wait until it receives payment of the receivables (or in a "future flow" securitisation, until it even generates them) to obtain funds to continue its business and generate new receivables. In many cases, this is essential and a role otherwise filled by more traditional methods of financing including factoring (in some ways, securitisation is a sophisticated form of factoring).

This is more significant when the receivables are relatively long-term such as with real property mortgages, auto loans, student loans, etc. and not as significant with short-term receivables such as trade and credit card receivables.

By securitising some of their assets which qualify as a sale for accounting purposes, these firms will be able to remove assets from their balance sheets while maintaining the 'earning power' of the assets. Therefore, by improving the leverage ratio of a firm, it basically reduces the capital requirement of a company. Securitisation can also generate matched funding for balance sheet assets. Further, it may also enable the disposal of non-core assets through suitable structuring.

The impact of securitisation on the company's balance sheet and debt-equity ratio is evident in Tables 13.2(a, b).

TABLE 13.2(a) Balance Sheet Pre-Securitisation

Liabilities	*Amount* (₹)	*Assets*	*Amount* (₹)
Rec. Loan	60	Receivables	60
Debenture	30	PP&E	40
Equity	10		
	100		**100**

Total Debt-equity Ratio = 9:1.

TABLE 13.2(b) Balance Sheet Post-Securitisation

Liabilities	*Amount* (₹)	*Assets*	*Amount* (₹)
Debenture	30	PP&E	40
Equity	10		
	40		**40**

Total Debt-equity Ratio = 3:1.

As visible, there is reduction in leverage ratio on Account of securitisation.

3. *More capital:* Securitisation provides more capital to the banks. RBI guidelines prescribe minimum capital to be 9% of risk weighted assets. If bank securitises risk weighted assets, then the bank would have more capital at its disposal to do business (Table 13.3a).

Risk assets of the bank here are ₹60 here, so 9% of 60 is ₹5.4 but the bank has maintained ₹6 as capital which is more than ₹5.4.

Now, if the bank securitises ₹20 risk assets out of total ₹60 and converts ther into cash then the bank's capital requirement would reduce to ₹3.6 (9% of ₹40). I means that the bank would have more ₹2.4 of capital to do business, as depicted i Table 13.3(b).

TABLE 13.3(a) Balance Sheet Pre-Securitisation

Liabilities	*Amount* (₹)	*Assets*	*Amount* (₹)
Capital	6	Risk free assets (including cash)	40
Deposits	50	Risk assets	60
Borrowings	30		
Current liabilities and provisions	14		
	100		**100**

TABLE 13.3(b) Balance Sheet Post-Securitisation

Liabilities	*Amount* (₹)	*Assets*	*Amount* (₹)
Equity	6	Risk free assets (including cash)	60
Deposits	50	Risk assets	40
Borrowings	30		
Current liabilities and provisions	14		
	100		**100**

Therefore, there is more percentage of free capital post-securitisation.

4. *Reduction in cost of funds:* A securitisation of high-quality assets may allow a relatively young firm or a firm with a low credit-rating to access capital market funds a lower cost than would otherwise be available. The securities issued in the securitisation are highly rated by the participating rating agencies (because of the isolation of the receivables in a 'bankruptcy-remote' entity), thus reducing the cost of funds to the originator when compared to traditional forms of financing. Additionally, it creates a broad array of attractive investment options available. ABS/MBS usually offers higher yields over securities of comparable credit and maturities. The yield spread typically represents the premium paid to compensate for prepayment risk, amortising cash flows and the uniqueness of the instrument. In some cases, ABS/MBS also provides an opportunity to invest into a pool of otherwise illiquid and inaccessible assets.

Through securitisation, a company rated BB but with AAA worthy cash flow, would be able to borrow at possibly AAA rates. A well-structured securitised asset stands on its own credit-rating and thus, generates genuine incremental funding. This can have tremendous impacts on borrowing costs. The difference between BB debt and AAA debt can be multiple hundreds of basis points.

5. *Higher benefit:* In cases where the receivables bear interest, there is usually a significant spread between the interest paid on the securities and the interest earned on the receivables. Ultimately, the originator receives the benefit of the spread. In addition, the originator usually acts as a servicer and receives a fee for its services.

6. *Better transparency:* Since the originator acts as a servicer and there is normally no need to give notice to the obligors under the receivables, the transaction is transparent to the originator's customers and other persons with whom it does business.

7. *Re-allocation of risks:* The pool of assets representing the obligations of a number of entities is usually more resilient to event risks than the obligations of a single borrower, i.e. the risk that the credit-rating of the security will deteriorate due to circumstances usually beyond the obligor's control is much higher in the latter case. The diversity that the securitisation pool represents makes the securitisation largely immune to event risks. Securitisation transfers much of the credit risk in the portfolio to the ABS/MBS investors and helps to quantify the residual credit risk that the originator is exposed to. This is very useful, as the originator can then take larger exposure to individual obligors as well as provide a higher degree of comfort to his creditors.

8. *Reduces asset-liability mismatch:* Depending on the structure chosen, securitisation can offer perfect matched funding by eliminating funding exposure in terms of both duration and pricing. Essentially, in most banks and finance companies, the liability book or the funding is from borrowings. This often comes at a high cost. Securitisation allows such banks and finance companies to create a self-funded asset book.

9. *Conversion of illiquid assets into liquid securities:* Through securitisation, illiquid assets can be immediately converted into liquid assets, i.e. the assets which are currently not available for spending, once securitised, the cash would be available for immediate spending or investment.

B. For Investors

Securitised assets offer the following to the investors:

1. Attractive yields (compared with other instruments of similar quality).
2. Increasing secondary market liquidity.
3. Higher protection by way of collateral overages and/or guarantees by entities with high and stable credit ratings.
4. Flexibility because their payment streams can be structured to meet the investors' particular requirements.
5. Diversification as the securitised products present fixed-income investors with an alternative to government, corporate or municipal bonds.
6. Most importantly, in structural credit enhancements and diversified asset pools, there is no need for the investors to obtain a detailed understanding of the underlying loans.

C. For Borrowers

Borrowers benefit from the following:

1. Increasing availability of credit on terms that lenders may not have provided had they kept the loans on their balance sheets. For example, due to the existence of a market for mortgage-backed securities, lenders can now extend fixed-rate debt, which many consumers prefer over variable-rate debt, without overexposing themselves to interest rate risk.
2. Credit card lenders can generate large loan pools for a diverse customer base at lower rates than if they had to fund the loans on their balance sheet. Stiff competition among credit originators and strong investor appetite for the securities has significantly expanded the availability of credit and the pool of cardholders over the past decade.

HISTORY OF SECURITISATION IN INDIA

The growth in the Indian securitisation market can be identified to the early 1990s with banks and FIs repackaging their retail assets and residential mortgages. This market developed significantly post 2000. Though there is a large increase in the volumes of issues in the last few years, it is still very less as compared to the international volumes.

Asset Backed Securitisation (ABS) is the largest product class which has grown due to increase in the retail loan portfolio of banks and other FIs with short maturity period. The Mortgage-Backed Securities (MBS) market has been rather slow in taking off despite a growing housing finance market due to the long maturity periods, lack of secondary market liquidity and the risk factor of pre-payment of the underlying loan.

The Indian securitisation market grew by 58% to ₹1.17 lakh crore in the April-December 2022 period as compared to the same period last year. Buoyancy in securitisation can be attributed to the stable macroeconomic scenario and high credit growth for non-bank lenders, ICRA Ratings said. Securitisation volumes have long been dominated by mortgage-backed loans, followed by vehicle loans. The trend reversed in Q3FY23 when vehicle loans, at 33 per cent of the total volumes, inched slightly ahead of mortgage loans, the agency said.[3]

In the early 1990s, securitisation was used more for personal use by the finance companies but in the recent years, loan sales have become common through the direct assignment route. From auto loans in 1990s, the securitisation market has spread into several asset classes—housing loans, corporate loans, commercial mortgage receivables, future flow, etc. Within the auto loan segment, the car loan segment has been more successful than the commercial vehicle loan segment, mainly because of factors like low credit risk, higher volumes and homogenous nature of receivables.

In India, issuers have typically been private sector banks, foreign banks and Non-banking Financial Companies (NBFCs) with their underlying assets portfolio of retail and corporate loans.

---

3. https://www.outlookindia.com/business/securitisation-volumes-likely-to-jump-to-rs-1-70-lakh-crore-in-fy23-icra-news-252945, January 12, 2023.

The key motivation for Indian banks is liquidity. Securitisation is an easy route as compared to raising deposits which are subject to reserve requirements.

Examples in India

Some 'examples of securitisation' in the Indian context are:

- The first securitisation deal in India was between Citibank and GIC Mutual Fund in 1991 for ₹160 mn.
- L&T raised ₹4,090 mn through the securitisation of future lease rentals to raise capital for its power plant in 1999.
- India's first securitisation of personal loan by Citibank in 1999 was for ₹2,841 mn.
- India's first Mortgage-Backed Securities (MBS) issue was worth ₹597 mn. by NHB and HDFC in 2001.
- Securitisation of aircraft receivables by Jet Airways was around ₹16,000 mn. in 2001 through offshore SPV.
- India's first sales tax deferrals securitisation was by Government of Maharashtra in 2001 for ₹1,500 mn.
- India's first deal in the power sector was signed by Karnataka Electricity Board for receivables worth ₹1,940 mn. and it placed them with HUDCO.
- India's first Collateralised Debt Obligation (CDO) deal was signed by ICICI bank in 2002.
- India's first floating rate securitisation issuance was made by Citigroup of ₹2,810 million in 2003. The fixed rate auto loan receivables of Citibank and Citicorp Finance India were included in the securitisation.
- India's first securitisation of sovereign lease receivables was done by Indian Railway Finance Corporation (IRFC) of ₹1,960 mn. in 2005. The receivables consisted of lease amounts payable by the Ministry of Railways to IRFC.
- India's largest securitisation deal was made by ICICI bank for ₹19,299 million in 2007. The underlying asset pool was auto loan receivables[4].

REGULATORY FRAMEWORK OF SECURITISATION IN INDIA

The regulatory framework for the securitisation market in India has eveloved in the phases as discussed below.

I. First Phase

Enactment of the 'Securitisation and Reconstruction of Financial Assets and Enforcement of Security Interests Act, 2002' (SARFAESI Act, 2002) enabled securitisation of the Non-Performing Assets of banks, which could sell off their NPAs to asset reconstruction companies registered with RBI. The SARFAESI Act laid the framework to the constitution of Asset Reconstruction Companies (ARCs) specialising in securitising distressed assets purchased from banks. The issuance of security receipts has since

4. http://www.dnb.co.in/Arcil2008/Securitisation%20in%20India.asp

then grown significantly. The recommendations of the High Level Committee on Corporate Debt and Securitisation (Chairman Dr. R.H. Patil) in 2005 proved to be the turning point towards the development of the corporate debt and securitisation market. Some of the key recommendations of the Committee on securitisation[5] are given below:

- Evolve a consensus on the affordable rates and levels of stamp duty on debt assignment.
- Pass through Certificates (PTCs) and Security Receipts (SRs) across States (Box 13.3).
- An explicit tax Pass-through treatment to securitisation SPVs/Trust SPVs should be provided. Wholesale investors should be permitted to invest in and hold units of a close-ended, passively managed mutual fund whose sole objective is to invest its funds in securitised paper. There should be no withholding tax on interest paid by the borrowers to the securitisation trust and on distributions made by the securitisation trust to its PTCs and/or SR holders. PTCs and other securities issued by securitisation SPVs/Trust SPVs should be notified as "securities" under SCR.
- Large-sized NBFCs and non-NBFCs corporate bodies established in India may be permitted to invest in SRs as Qualified Institutional Buyers (QIBs).
- SEBI as Venture Capital Funds (VCFs) may also be permitted to invest in SRs within the limits that are applied for investment by VCFs into corporate bond.

The Committee also recommended:

- Introduction of credit enhancement mechanism for corporate bonds.
- Creation of specialised debt funds to cater to the needs of the infrastructure sector.
- Fiscal support like tax benefits, bond insurance and credit enhancement, for municipal bonds and infrastructure SPVs.

BOX 13.3: PTCs AND SRs

A Pass Through Certificate (PTC) is a certificate that is given to an investor against certain mortgaged-backed securities that lie with the issuer. The interest that is paid to the issuer on these securities comes to the investor in the form of a fixed income. Investors in such instruments are usually financial institutions like banks, mutual funds and insurance companies.

In a pass through certificate, interest earned on the receivable is directly passed to the holders whereas in a pay through certificate, interest received from the receivables is not passed to the holder of the unit. Instead, the SPV issues new securities to them.

Security Receipt means a receipt or other security, issued by a securitisation company or reconstruction company to any qualified institutional buyer pursuant to a scheme, evidencing the purchase or acquisition by the holder thereof, of an undivided right title or interest in the financial asset involved in securitisation. SRs shall be redeemed only out of realisation from financial assets held under the Trust and they carry no fixed returns. SRs may also be sold in the secondary market.

5. The complete document is given in the Instructor's Manual.

II. Second Phase

In February 2006, the RBI issued guidelines for securitisation of standard assets by banks, FIs and NBFCs. These guidelines provided the regulatory framework for several critical aspects of securitisation and are expected to take forward the establishment of a robust-structured credit market. They clearly defined some of the key aspects such as true sale criteria, capital treatment for credit enhancement, exposure recognition, etc. In view of differing practices by banks and concerns raised regarding accounting, valuation and capital treatment, the guidelines issued by RBI[6] were broadly discussed as follows:

- Detailed guidelines to ensure 'arms-length' relationship between the originator and the SPV.
- Credit enhancements provided by the originator for the first as well as second losses to be deducted from the capital.
- Any profit/premium arising on account of sale is not allowed to be booked upfront and is to be amortised over the life of the securities issued or to be issued by the SPV.
- Provision of liquidity facility to be treated as an off-balance sheet item and attract 100% credit conversion factor as well as 100% risk weight.
- Disclosure by the originator, as notes to accounts, a comparative position for two years of the following items:
  (i) The total number and book value of loan assets securitised;
  (ii) Sale consideration received for the securitised assets and gain/loss on sale on account of securitisation.

III. Third Phase (Present)

Presently, Reserve Bank of India (Securitisation of Standard Assets) Directions, 2021 *(Updated as on December 05, 2022)* regulate the securitisation in India. These directions have replaced the existing instructions on the matter of securitisation of standard assets.

The provisions of these directions shall apply to the following entities (lenders):

(a) Scheduled Commercial Banks (excluding Regional Rural Banks);
(b) All India Term Financial Institutions (NABARD, NHB, EXIM Bank, and SIDBI);
(c) Small Finance Banks and,
(d) All Non-Banking Financial Companies (NBFCs) including Housing Finance Companies (HFCs).

A. *Assets Eligible for Securitisation*

Lenders, including overseas branches of Indian banks, shall not undertake the securitisation activities or assume securitisation exposures as mentioned below:

(a) Re-securitisation exposures;
(b) Structures in which short-term instruments such as commercial paper, which are periodically rolled over, are issued against long-term assets held by a SPE;

6. http://www.rbi.org.in/scripts/NotificationUser.aspx?Id=2723&Mode=0.

(c) Synthetic securitisation; and
(d) Securitisation with the following assets as underlying:
  (i) Revolving credit facilities as underlying;
  (ii) Restructured loans and advances which are in the specified period;
  (iii) Exposures to other lending institutions;
  (iv) Refinance exposures of AIFIs;
  (v) Loans with bullet payments of both principal and interest as underlying; and
  (vi) Loans with residual maturity of less than 365 days.

B. *Minimum Retention Requirement (MRR)*

The MRR is primarily designed to ensure that the originators have a continuing stake in the performance of securitised assets so as to ensure that they carry out proper due diligence of loans to be securitised.

The originators should adhere to the MRR as detailed below while securitising loans leading to issuance of securitisation notes other than residential mortgage backed securities.

The complete directions are available at:

https://www.rbi.org.in/Scripts/BS_ViewMasDirections.aspx?id=12165; https://rbidocs.rbi.org.in/rdocs/notification/PDFs/85MDSTANDARDASSETSBE149B86CD3A4B368A5D24471DAD2300.PDF

SECURITISATION AND THE FINANCIAL CRISIS OF 2008

There is a strong relationship between the 2008 financial crisis and the process of securitisation. The real estate and the housing industry in the US were booming during the 1990s which made mortgage lending a lucrative option for the banks. The market for debt securitisation was huge and considered to be at its best in the financial market. The investment banks such as Goldman Sachs, Lehman Brothers, Citicorp, Merrill Lynch invested heavily. MBS and ABS offer investors various fixed income products with attractive yields.

The US government has long promoted home-ownership, making mortgages available through *Federal Housing Administration* and *Veterans Administration Loans*, as well as by creating Fannie May, Freddie Mac, and related entities. FHA and VA mortgages require lower down payments and offer lower interest rates than conventional mortgages due to a government guarantee on the former. This enables lower income individuals to be able to afford home-ownership. This is how Fannie May and Freddy Mac expanded the depth and breadth of mortgage markets, increasing the reach of home loans to all low income and underserved customers. Both entities buy individual mortgages from mortgage lenders, and then securitise them for sale in the secondary mortgage market. This brought in funding from investors—both US and foreign—who would not buy individual mortgages but will buy mortgage-backed securities. In 2008, agency mortgage-backed securities—in other words, AMBS issued by Fannie May, Freddie Mac, and Ginnie May (FHA loans)—accounted for over 96%

of the U.S. RMBS market. Private-label mortgage-backed securitisation accounted for less than 4% of the market that year[7]. The total US issuance of mortgage-backed securities from 1990 to June 2009 is depicted in Figure 13.2.

By the end of 2008, the US mortgage market had $14.6 trillion outstanding of which $7.6 trillion was mortgage-backed securities including $5 trillion held or guaranteed by Fannie May and Freddie Mac, and $2.6 trillion in held by private entities[8].

As securitisation of mortgages increased, the investment banks urged the mortgage lending industry (Countrywide, Washington Mutual, New Century Financial, Wells Fargo, Household Finance, Quikloans, etc.), to increase their loan volumes. They did this by offering even to the sub-prime borrower and issuing Alt-A (limited documentation) loans. This was primarily because the investment banks were too keen to securitise the loans.

The mortgage and investment banking community continued to believe in securitisation as a way to reduce risk. The share of MBSs backed by sub-prime and Alt-A loans increased dramatically in that period. From 1996 to 2006, the share of sub-prime and Alt-A MBSs rose from 47% to 71% of total private sector MBS issuances[9]. However, the sub-prime lenders defaulted on the payment leading to the failure of the banks as well as the investment banks. Some of them were AIG, Lehman Bros., and Fannie May.

Figure 13.2 shows the total issue of mortgage-backed securities from 1990 to 2009 in US.

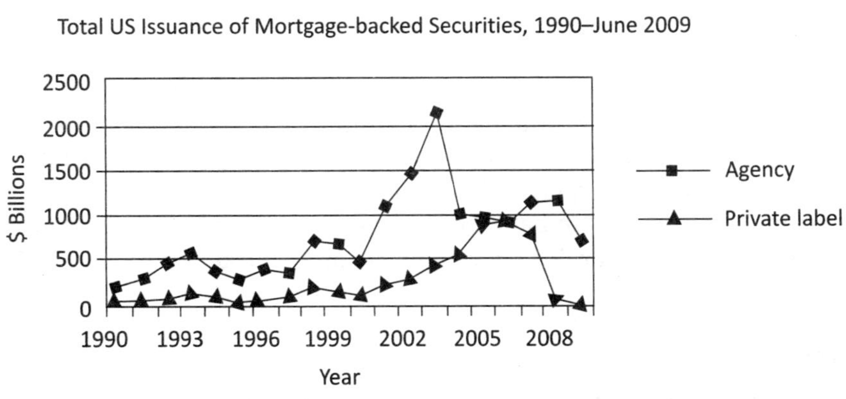

Figure 13.2 Issuance of Mortgage-backed Securities in US

(*Source:* http://www.gpo.gov/fdsys/pkg/CHRG-111shrg56262/pdf/CHRG-111shrg56262.pdf.)

ASSET RECONSTRUCTION COMPANIES

Securitisation by the banks would give rise to bad loans. Asset reconstruction companies emerged as a part of the securitisation process under SARFAESI Act,

7. http://www.gpo.gov/fdsys/pkg/CHRG-111shrg56262/pdf/CHRG-111shrg56262.pdf
8. http://2008financialcrisis.umwblogs.org/analysis/housing-finance-the-securitisation-of-mortgages.
9. http://isites.harvard.edu/fs/docs/icb.topic750202.files/Chicago%20Fed%20on%20securitisation %20in%20mortgage%20lending.pdf.p.2.

2002 for recovering bad debts. Therefore, Asset Reconstructions Companies (ARCs) are created to manage and recover Non-performing Assets in the banking system. They help in clearing the Non-performing Assets from the balance sheet of the bank/FII and facilitate them to focus on normal banking activities.

The phenomenon of ARCs is worldwide due to the global problem of bad loans. They are not merely concerned with realisation of bad loans but they 'reconstruct', i.e. they try and resurrect bad loans into good ones. They may take following measures within the guidelines of Reserve Bank of India:

- Change-in or take-over of the management of the borrower.
- Sale or lease of a part or whole of the business of the borrower.
- Re-scheduling of payment of debts payable by the borrowers.
- Enforcement of security interest in accordance with the provisions of the Act.
- Settlement of dues payable by the borrowers.
- Conversion of any portion of debt into equity of a borrower company.

Need for Asset Reconstruction Companies

(i) *Primary Motive*

- As mentioned above, they are primarily set up to acquire, manage, and recover illiquid or NPAs from the lenders.
- They help in reducing the risk of credit crunch in the financial market and consequent financial degradation.

(ii) *Other Benefits*

- They maximise recovery value while minimising costs and help in restoring the confidence of the depositor and investor by ensuring the lender's financial health.
- They provide industry expertise in loan resolution, besides serving as a catalyst for important legal reforms in bankruptcy procedures and loan collection.
- They play an important role in developing capital markets through secondary asset instruments.

ARC Models

ARCs usually operate through one of the two basic models, namely, (i) a government-based model, centralised approach, or (ii) a bank-based model, which is a decentralised approach. These are described below:

1. *Government-based Model*

Here, an agency is sponsored by the government which acquires and resolves the bad assets. The NPAs are owned by the government and managed by the ARC or partially contracted out to private managers. The ARC can be a SPV which will be entrusted to acquire, manage and recover NPAs. It can also have other operations like deposit insurance or bank recapitalisation. Due to centralisation of NPAs, there is effective asset packaging and marketing, which ensures consistency and transparency within the ARC. In addition, the risk of decrease in sale values of assets by the competing bank-based ARCs is also reduced.

2. *Bank-based Model*

It has two approaches, 'workout units' and 'bad banks'. In *workout units*, NPAs are moved to a separate bank department but remain in the bank's books. On the other hand, the *bad bank* approach includes the transfer of NPAs to a separate affiliated organisation, i.e. ARC, which specialises in the management of bad assets.

ISSUES FACED BY THE INDIAN SECURITISATION MARKET

1. *Regulatory issues:* In India, *stamp duty* is payable on any instrument which aims to transfer rights or receivables. Therefore, the process of transfer of the receivables from the originator to the SPV involves a cash outlay due to stamp duty. This makes the process of securitisation commercially unviable in states with a high stamp duty. Therefore, if the securitised instrument is issued as 'debt' (debenture or bond), it would be subject to stamp duty, and if the instrument is structured as a 'Pass-Through Certificate (PTC)', which is merely a "title to the receivables", then such an instrument would not attract stamp duty. Some states do not distinguish between conveyances of real estate and that of receivables, and levy the same rate of stamp duty. To avoid these problems, SEBI suggested 'the need for rationalisation of stamp duty' to the government with a view to develop the corporate debt and securitisation markets in the country.

2. *Foreclosure laws:* Lack of effective foreclosure laws also restrict the growth of securitisation in India. The existing foreclosure laws are not lender-friendly and increase the risks of MBS by making it difficult to transfer property in cases of default.

3. *Taxation related issues:* There is ambiguity in the tax treatment of mortgage-based securities, SPV trusts, and NPL trusts. Presently, the investors or the buyers (PTC and SR holders) pay tax on the earnings from the SPV trust. As a result, the trustee makes income payouts to the investors without any payment of tax.

4. *Legal issues:* Investments in PTCs are typically held-to-maturity. As there is no trading activity in these instruments, the yield on PTCs and the demand for longer tenures especially from mutual funds is dampened.

A Security Receipt (SR) gives its holder a right of title or interest in the financial assets included in securitisation. This definition holds good for securitisation structures where the securities issued are referred to as 'pass through certificates'. However, the rationale fails in the case of pay-through certificates with different classes of primary and secondary rights to the cash flow. Also, the SARFAESI Act has been structured such that SRs can be issued and held only to Qualified Institutional Buyers (QIBs). There is a need to relook at this and increase the investor base by including NBFCs, non-NBFCs, private equity funds, etc.

CASE STUDY

Trade Receivables Securitisation by LBBW

Landesbank Baden-Wurttemberg (LBBW) is one of Germany's largest international commercial banks, with total assets of around € 374 billion and 13,000 employees.

In 2002, LBBW looked for an effective trade receivables securitisation solution for its Mittelstand (medium-sized enterprise) customers. 'Asset-Backed Securitisation' was mainly confined to the large enterprises and an exception in Europe—to be offered in its traditional form to medium-sized companies. To support its Mittelstand customers with an additional financing channel, LBBW developed a slim-line ABS solution especially for this market, *ABS Kompakt*. Firms were offered a trade receivables securitisation facility from an eligible invoice volume of € 20 million upwards. The service included a complete bouquet from deal structuring through an automated submission and monitoring platform, to correct contract documentation.

According to Sascha Chevalier, Executive Director Securitisations, "to automate, manage, process and report ABS Kompakt, LBBW selected Demica's technology platform Citadel as the optimal solution to run trade receivables securitisation transactions". Since the first transaction in 2002, LBBW had experienced steady growth and structured many transactions for its Mittelstand clients, whose annual turnover ranged from € 100 million to € 1 billion. "Trade receivables securitisation requires a superior management of the asset portfolio. Thus, a robust IT system is an absolute prerequisite for the effective monitoring of receivables. Demica's Citadel plaform enabled them to provide their clients with an automated system, with easy ledger entry that massively reduces the ongoing administrative burden of running such a programme on their clients' side. By having the system under their control, they have an intimate insight into their clients' businesses and can provide a line of finance even to clients whose rating might otherwise cap their access to credit. Real-time delivery and item level reporting of data not only allow them to conduct stringent monitoring and evaluation of receivables of our multiple clients, they also enable them to identify any hidden problem transaction in aggregate reporting. Close, immediate monitoring is the key to operational risk management and mitigation".

(*Source:* http://www.demica.com/case-studies/securitisation-case-study?start=2)

POINTS TO REMEMBER

- Securitisation started in 1970s, when home mortgages were pooled by US government-backed agencies.
- Securitisation is the process in which certain types of assets are pooled so that they can be repackaged into interest-bearing securities. The interest and principal payments from the assets are passed-through to the purchasers of the securities.
- The primary objective of securitisation is to separate the credit risk of the originating firm from the credit risk of SPV, which is done by legally transferring the assets from the balance sheet of the originating firm to SPV.
- Primary parties to a securitisation deal consist of (a) the originator, who is the owner of the asset, (b) the special purpose vehicle (issuer), who buys the assets to be securitised from the originator, (c) the investors who buy a participating interest in the total pool of receivables, and (d) the obligor(s), the borrower of the original loan or originator's debtor.

- Other parties in a securitisation deal are: the rating agency, administrator or servicer, agent and trustee, structurer, the swap counterparty, and the credit enhancer.
- The securities created by securitisation of a pool of mortgage loans are referred to as mortgage-backed securities (MBS). These are further classified as—residential mortgage-backed securities, and commercial mortgage-backed securities.
- When securities are backed by a pool of retail loans, they are referred to as asset-backed securities (ABS). They can be: instalment contract asset-backed securities, or revolving asset transactions.
- For originators, it improves capital adequacy ratio, provides off-balance sheet financing, releases more capital, and reduces the cost of funds. For investors, it offers attractive yields, liquidity, more protection and flexibility. For borrowers, it benefits in the form of increasing availability of credit.
- The growth in the Indian securitisation market can be attributed to the repackaging of retail assets and residential mortgages of banks and FIs. This market has been in existence since the early 1990s, which developed significantly post 2000. Asset-Backed Securitisation (ABS) is the largest product class. The Mortgage-Backed Securities (MBS) market has been rather slow.
- The regulatory framework for the securitisation market in India has eveloved in three phases. In first phase, Enactment of the Securitisation and Reconstruction of Financial Assets and Enforcement of Security Interests Act, 2002 (SARFAESI Act, 2002) enabled securitisation of the non-performing assets of the banks. In second phase, in February 2006, the RBI issued guidelines for securitisation of standard assets by banks, FIs and NBFCs. Presently, Reserve Bank of India (Securitisation of Standard Assets) Directions, 2021 regulate the securitisation in India.
- There is strong relationship between the '2008 financial crisis' and the process of securitisation. The market for debt securitisation in US was massive and the investment banking community (Goldman Sachs, Bear Stearns, Lehman Brothers, Citicorp, Merrill Lynch) was having a good securitisation of mortgages. However, the sub-prime lenders defaulted on the payment leading to the failure of the banks as well as the investment banks.
- Asset Reconstruction Companies are created to manage and recover Non-performing Assets acquired from the banking system.
- ARCs usually operate through one of the two basic models namely, bank-based model, which is a decentralised approach, or a government-based model, which is a centralised approach.
- Issues faced by the Indian securitisation market include regulatory issues, foreclosure laws, taxation and legal issues.

KEY TERMS

- **Securitisation** is the process in which certain types of assets are pooled so that they can be repackaged into interest-bearing securities.

- **Special Purpose Vehicle (SPV)** is a wholly-owned, limited purpose which buys the assets to be securitised from the originator.
- **Qualified Institutional Buyers (QIBs)** are those who possess the expertise and the financial power to invest in securities market.
- **Originator** is the owner of the asset and sets up the basic structure to execute the deal.
- **Obligor** is the borrower of the original loan or Originator's debtor.
- **Mortgage-Backed Securities (MBS)** are those which are created by securitisation of a pool of mortgage loans.
- **Asset-Backed Securities (ABS)** are securities backed by a pool of retail loans.
- **Pass-through Certificate (PTC)** is a certificate that is given to an investor against certain mortgaged-backed securities that lie with the issuer.
- **Security Receipt** is a receipt or other security, issued by a securitisation company or reconstruction company to any qualified institutional buyer pursuant to a scheme, evidencing the purchase or acquisition by the holder thereof.

EXERCISES

Objective Questions

1. **Tick the correct answer:**

(a) Securitisation is the process in which assets are:
  (i) Pooled (ii) Repackaged
  (iii) Sold (iv) All of the above

(b) SPV stands for:
  (i) Special-purpose vehicle (ii) Special periodic vehicle
  (iii) Specific-police vehicle (iv) None of the above

(c) QIBs are those who have:
  (i) Investment expertise in stock market
  (ii) Investment power in stock market
  (iii) Both (i) and (ii)
  (iv) None of the above

(d) The one who collects the payment due from the obligor(s) and forwards the payment to the SPV is:
  (i) Administrator (ii) Outsider
  (iii) Third party (iv) None of the above

(e) The credit enhancer can be a:
  (i) Bank (ii) Surety company
  (iii) Insurer (iv) Either of the above

(f) Securitisation results in:
  (i) Reduced cost of funds (ii) Increased cost of funds
  (iii) No effect on cost of funds (iv) None of the above

Answers: (a) iv (b) i (c) iii (d) i (e) iv (f) i

2. Fill in the blanks:

(a) The sub-prime mortgage crisis happened in ....

(b) .... is a certificate that is given to an investor against certain mortgaged-backed securities that lie with the issuer.

(c) .... is the owner of the asset and sets up the basic structure to execute the deal.

(d) .... buys the assets to be securitised from the originator.

(e) The obligor is the .... of the original loan or originator's debtor.

(f) The securities created by securitisation of a pool of mortgage loans are referred to as ....

(g) The securities backed by a pool of retail loans are referred to as ....

(h) SARFAESI Act of securitisation was passed in ....

(i) .... is a receipt issued by a securitisation company or reconstruction company to any qualified institutional buyer pursuant to a scheme.

Answers:

(a) 2008

(b) Pass-through-certificates (PTCs)

(c) Originator

(d) Special purpose vehicle

(e) Borrower

(f) Mortgage-backed securities (MBS)

(g) Asset-backed securities (ABS)

(h) 2002

(i) Security receipt

3. True or False:

(a) Securitisation is a tool of financing.

(b) SPV finances a portion of the assets with debt that does not recourse to the originating firm.

(c) Like conventional debt, securitisation does inflate a company's liabilities.

(d) In India, only Qualified Institutional Buyers (QIBs) are allowed to invest in PTCs.

(e) Structurer is responsible for bringing together the partners to a securitisation deal.

(f) Securitisation improves capital adequacy ratio of the banks.

(g) Securitisation provides off-balance sheet financing to the originator.

(h) There is a reduction in available capital of the banks due to securitisation.

(i) The fiasco of 2008 in US had securitisation as the key factor responsible for it.

(j) ARCs are created to manage and recover Non-performing Assets acquired from the banking system.

Answers: (a) True (b) True (c) False (d) True (e) True
(f) True (g) True (h) False (i) True (j) True

Short Questions

1. What is securitisation?
2. State the different types of securitisation.
3. Define QIB.
4. State the primary motive of securitisation.
5. Who are the two primary parties in securitisation?
6. Distinguish between mortgage-backed securities and asset-backed securities.
7. What is PTC?
8. What is a security receipt?

Critical Thinking Questions

1. "The structure of securitisation is dependent upon the shoulders of multi-parties". Explain.
2. "Securitisation is a way of off-balance sheet financing to the originator". Elaborate with an illustration.
3. "The banks can not only improve their regulatory capital requirement through securitisation but also release more capital". Do you agree?
4. "The regulatory structure of securitisation in India is still at a developing stage". Discuss.
5. "The structure of global securitisation industry is heavily centred by banks and financial institutions". Highlight.
6. "Mortgage-backed securitisation is less developed than asset-backed securitisation in India". Explain.
7. "Car loan segment has been more successful than the commercial vehicle loan segment for securitisation in India". Argue.
8. "Securitisation business leads to leads global turmoil". Do you agree?

Descriptive Questions

1. Discuss the process of securitisation with examples.
2. What are the types of securitisation? Explain in detail.
3. Discuss the benefits of securitisation to various parties.
4. Throw some light on the evolution of securitisation in India.
5. What are Asset Reconstruction Companies? Why are they needed?
6. What are the different models of ARCs?
7. Discuss the issues faced by the Indian securitisation market.

PROJECT EXERCISE

Regulatory Model of Indian Securitisation

India's regulatory structure of securitisation industry as compared to other parts of the world needs a real push. The SARFAESI Act is only a beginning. Therefore, study the Indian securitisation regulation in detail, compare with the rest of the world, find out the gap areas, suggest measures to improve them and strengthen the system for future viability. But on the same hand, keep in mind what happened in the US in 2008. It means that their system is not equally foolproof. So, your objective should be to take best of all, remove the worst and develop the best possible regulatory model for the Indian economy.

REVIEW CASE

Puzzle Act of Securitisation

Puzzle Bank is always in one or the other trouble. They started with a huge pump show and in that race they released loans to even borrowers with a high default rate. Now, they are facing the problem of managing these non-performing assets. About 60% of their lending portfolio comprises of mortgage loans and remaining comprises of others. Despite all efforts, they are not able to streamline their collection. The mortgage loans carry an effective interest of 16% p.a. and average maturity of five years. Therefore, they are thinking to go the securitisation route to get out of this and make their balance sheet better. They have observed that all their rival banks have been securitising loans for years.

One of their competitor banks has done huge business by securitising loans behind the backs of the customers. It offloaded private debt onto the public very quickly. There were defaults on a loan but on account of securitisation, the debt to the SPV and its investors were covered by an insurance policy, and with insurance pay out, the debt got settled. Securitisation has yielded massive profits for the bank. They also wish to reduce the regulatory capital requirement and improve their CAR. On account of these NPAs, they are struggling on the capital front. Therefore, they need more capital for future growth but without any cost. Presently, the bank is rated BB but they expect better cash flow post securitisation. Hence, they also hope to get better rating of their assets after securitisation.

They are aware that though securitisation has been largely blamed as one of the main contributors to the financial meltdown, it is an important example in place for bailouts. While in some countries it played an important role, in other nations the resort to activities in these markets was insignificant. Indian banking is also not new to the process. It is a fact that apart from the amount of funding available to banks, securitisation activity has a significant and positive impact on credit growth but at the same time, it reduces lenders' incentives to carefully screen and monitor borrowers, thereby affecting loan quality. Now, Puzzle Bank is in a mixed state—whether to go for the same or not? Table 13.4 shows the balance sheet of the bank.

TABLE 13.4 Balance Sheet of Puzzle Bank

Liabilities	*Amount* (₹ in mn)	*Assets*	*Amount* (₹ in mn)
Capital	100	Reserve with RBI	60
Demand deposits	600	Balances with banks and call money	240
Term deposits	220	Investments in government bonds	200
Borrowings	50	Mortgage loans	180
Current liabilities and other provisions	30	Corporate loans	120
		Fixed assets	200
	1000		**1000**

Issues for Discussion

(i) What type of securitisation is referred to in the above case?
(ii) What would be the effect of securitisation on the asset portfolios of the bank?
(iii) What is the capital adequacy ratio of the bank?
(iv) Discuss the impact of securitisation on CAR of the bank.
(v) What is the leverage ratio of the bank?
(vi) What would be the effect on the leverage ratio post-securitisation? Discuss off-balance sheet financing in this context.
(vii) Can they have more funds on account of securitisation?
(viii) Analyse the rating impact on account of securitisation.

REFERENCES

Campolongo, Francesca, et al. (2013), *Quantitative Assessment of Securitisation Deals*, Springer.

Suleman Baig, et al. (2013), *The Mechanics of Securitisation: A Practical Guide to Structuring and Closing Asset-Backed Security Transactions*, John Wiley & Sons.

www.drat.tn.nic.in

www.demica.com

www.dnb.co.in

www.economictimes.indiatimes.com

www.2008financialcrisis.umwblogs.org

www.finmin.nic.in
www.gpo.gov
www.hklaw.com.
www.isites.harvard.edu
www.lexicon.ft.com
www.outlookindia.com
www.rbi.org.in
www.umwblogs.org

CHAPTER 14

Venture Capital

Venture capital is about capturing the value between the startup phase and the public company phase.

— Fred Wilson

LEARNING OBJECTIVES

This chapter discusses the following:

- Nature and history of venture capital
- Significance and related aspects of venture capital funding
- Distinction between conventional and venture capital
- Stages of venture capital financing
- Types of venture capital
- Venture capital process
- Regulation of venture capital firms in India
- Venture capital documents
- Venture capital valuation methods

INTRODUCTION

The success of a project involving high risk largely depends upon capturing the whole, or at least a good part of the market, for that particular product or service. It is this promising prospect of cornering the market and consequently driving away the car home that persuades a venture capitalist to risk his money. Of course, the prospect of such high growth and profits naturally brings with it the risk of losing it all.

What is venture capital and how does it differ from other forms of equity procurement? The answer lies in an understanding of the relationship of risk and return in investing. One of the key principles of investment is 'greater the risk, greater the potential for high rate of return'. This might be called the "no guts, no glory" theory. If you are looking for a very safe and secure investment, there are plenty of options other than venture capital but in that case, the rate of return will be low. These low returns but safe investments are designed for traditional investments. If you are interested in making money on your investment, you must be willing to take risks. This is where 'venture capital' originates.

The advantage of venture capital is that it is often the only way to launch the business. It is pretty much a safe assumption that if people initiating a high risk business were able to secure financing through normal channels at a lower cost and without surrendering any ownership control, they would do so. The disadvantages of using venture capital as opposed to normal debt financing for start up costs include the fact that some ownership rights are given up and the cost of repayment is very high.

NATURE AND CHARACTERISTICS OF VENTURE CAPITAL

Venture Capital (VC) is a financial capital which is provided to early-stage, high-growth potential, start-up companies. It is a form of 'risk capital' which is invested in a business where there is a substantial element of risk relating to the future creation of profits and cash flows. Risk capital is invested as shares (equity) rather than as a loan and the investor requires a higher 'rate of return' to compensate him for his risk. The typical VC investment occurs after the seed funding has been provided as growth funding. The underlying proposition is to generate a return through an eventual realisation event such as an Initial Public Offering (IPO) or a trade sale of the company.

Venture Capital provides long-term, committed share capital to help unquoted companies grow and succeed. Obtaining VC is substantially different from raising debt or a loan from a lender. Lenders have the legal right to interest on a loan and repayment of the capital, irrespective of the success or failure of a business. As a shareholder, the venture capitalist's return is dependent on the growth and profitability of the business. This return is generally earned when the venture capitalist 'exits' by selling its shareholding in the business.

Characteristics

- It provides the spirit of ownership.
- It is based on 'Risk–Reward' sharing.
- There is an active participation of venture capitalist firms in the business and value addition in the form of their expertise.
- It has a long-term perspective.
- It is an investment and not assistance.
- In this type of funding, returns are linked to performance.
- There is an expectation of high returns due to degree of risk involved.

HISTORY OF VENTURE CAPITAL

Venture capital, as a form of financing, had some similarities with a few ancient forms of financing. The true history of venture capital began in the years following World War II.

There was a form of partnership arrangement practiced in medieval Islamic society that bears a striking resemblance to the current system of venture capital investment. Mostly, the history of venture capital could be related with the formation of the American Research and Development Corporation (ARDC) in 1946 which was one of the first publicly-owned venture capital firms launched in 1946 in New England to support the local economy. Besides local companies, ARDC also invested in companies from Midwestern and Western USA and finally from Europe, Canada and even Australia. ARDC's most well-known investment was Digital Equipment Corporation (DEC)—a vendor of computers and software that grew from a $70,000 investment in 1957 to a $355 million return in 1971[1].

ARDC's main competitor was Small Business Administration, which launched Small Business Investment Company Programme (SBIC)[2]. The Small Business Administration became involved with the venture capitalist idea when Congress passed the Small Business Investment Act of 1958. This Act allowed the licensing of Small Business Investment Companies (SBICs). In the years, prior to World War II, it was mostly the rich and the influential family that provided VC for projects that were breaking new technological ground. Since traditional lending institutions tended to shy away from such risky investments, Congress had recognised a need to encourage and enable the flow of investment capital into these areas to help keep the economy growing and the country technologically competitive.

The advent of the Information and Technological Revolution in the later part of the last century led to the sound growth of VC. The emergence of Silicon Valley in California made San Francisco a centre for VC investment. The VC industry has been extremely sensitive to stock markets as these investments are usually in the form of stock ownership. The stock market decline of 1974 was a big setback for venture capital firms.

The internet boom of the late 1990s followed by the NASDAQ and technological burst of the early 2000s was another roller-coaster ride for venture capitalists. However, today the industry is rebounding and moving ahead slowly on those early levels of investment principles. Usually, VC is risky financing but VC investors are always on the lookout of important advances in the business world. Today, alternative fuels and alternative forms of energy seem to be the most sought after areas of investment besides digital world and e-commerce.

Venture Capital in India

The history of venture capital in India goes back to early 1970s when Government of India appointed a committee laid by Late Shri R.S. Bhatt to find out the ways to fill

1. http://pelosophy.com/2013/04/12/american-research-and-development-corporation-the-first-venture-capital-firm.
2. http://pelosophy.com.ibid.

the void in conventional financing in order to fund the start-up companies based on absolutely new innovative technologies. Such companies either did not get any financial support or the funding was inadequate which resulted into their premature washout. The committee recommended starting of VC industry in India. In the mid 80s, all three financial institutions of India, viz. IDBI, ICICI, and IFCI, started investing into the equity of small technological companies.

In November 1988, the Government of India decided to institutionalise the VC industry and announced guidelines in the parliament. The Controller of Capital Issues implemented these guidelines known as *CCI guidelines* for VC. These guidelines were very restrictive and followed a very narrow definition of VC. They required VC to be invested in companies based on innovative technologies started by first generation entrepreneur. This made VC investment highly risky and unattractive. Nonetheless, many private initiatives were taken. At the same time, World Bank selected 6 institutions to start VC investment in India. This included TDICICI (ICICI), GVFL, Canbank Venture Capital Fund, APIDC, RCTC (now known as IFCI Venture Capital Funds Ltd.) and ILF (now known as Pathfinder).

In 1995, the Government of India permitted foreign finance companies to make investments in India and many foreign VC private equity firms entered India. In 1996, government announced guidelines to regulate the VC industry in the form of "SEBI (Venture Capital Fund) Regulations, 1996".

In 1997, IT boom in India made VC industry more significant and prominent as a major source of funding for the rapidly growing IT industry. Indian VC industry which was so far investing in all the sectors, changed their focus to IT and telecom industry. The recession during 1999–2001 took the wind out of the VC industry. Most of the VCs either closed down or wound-up their operations. Almost all of them changed their focus to existing successful firms for their growth and expansion. VC firms also got engaged into funding buyouts, privatisation and restructuring. Currently, firms are taking the risk of investing into the start-up companies more judiciously than ever (Box 14.1).

BOX 14.1: VENTURE CAPITAL—THE RISK ABSORBER

Venture capitalists bear all possible risks associated with a business, which are:

Risks in Start-ups/Early Stage Companies

Concentration risk: Focus on small market (either product or geographic) segment raises vulnerability to sectoral downturn.

Product risk: Products may have little or zero track record and being largely untested in markets, have high obsolescence rates.

Duration risk: Long-gestation period raises the period for which funding is needed.

Size risk: Small deal size, hence not found economical by most investors.

Asset risk: Lack of collateralisable assets due to a high proportion of fixed assets with high obsolescence, and a high proportion of human capital raise the risk.

Entrepreneur risk: It may be hard to evaluate new management and/or new business proposal without track record.

Technology risk: It may be difficult to evaluate new technology and are focused on small set of products.

VENTURE CAPITAL FUNDING

Venture Capital is one of the most appropriate ways of financing start-ups. Therefore, venture capital funding is rightly described as "Business of Businesses".

Advantages of Venture Capital

Venture capital has a number of advantages over other forms of finance, such as:

1. ***Finance:*** The venture capitalist injects long-term equity finance which provides a solid capital base for future growth. He/she may also be capable of providing additional rounds of funding should it be required to finance growth.

2. ***Partnership:*** The venture capitalist is a business partner who shares the risks and rewards. They are rewarded by business success and capital gain.

3. ***Mentoring:*** The venture capitalist is able to provide strategic, operational and financial advice to the company based on past experience with other companies in similar situations.

4. ***Alliances:*** The venture capitalist also has a network of contacts in many areas that can add value to the company such as in recruiting key personnel, providing contacts in international markets, introductions to strategic partners and if needed, co-investments with other venture capital firms when additional rounds of financing are required.

5. ***Exit facility:*** The venture capitalist is experienced in the process of preparing a company for an Initial Public Offering (IPO) and facilitating the trade sales.

6. ***Security free:*** It does not require collateral nor charge interest payments. It is free from hassles of traditional debt funding.

Requirements of Venture Capitalists

- *Core management team:* Venture funds back entrepreneurs and the team.
- *Market size, opportunity and scalability:* Competitive advantage today or potentially, the potential to change the rules of the game, the opportunity and capability to play globally are the likeable factors.
- *Intellectual capital:* Potentially, in the form of brand, intellectual property, methodologies, processes, network, customers, and the like, apart from human capital which determines valuations, are very important parameters.
- *Clean structure:* Most preferred is a single company, no cross-holding, no subsidiary structure. Transparency is expected in a company.
- *Valuations:* Based on this, appropriate stake offered in the company is computed.
- *Returns on investment:* ROI potential is calculated of a business.
- *Coinvestment and future investment potential:* This value addition is analysed in business.
- *Exit opportunity:* It is measured.

Conventional v/s Venture Capital Funding

The distinction between traditional funding and VC funding can be studied in Table 14.1.

TABLE 14.1 Conventional vs. Venture Capital Funding

Basis	*Conventional Funding*	*Venture Capital Funding*
Security	Security backed	Unsecured/need based
Role	Passive role	Active role
Return	Fixed obligation	Performance linked return
Nature	Term loans	Equity/Quasi equity
Risk	Risk averse	High risk appetite
Perspective	Short and medium term perspective	Long term
Type of Business	Conventional business	High growth business

VENTURE CAPITAL FINANCING STAGES

There are many stages in VC financing. These are the typical funding stages that a start-up moves through over the course of its life.

A. Early Stage Financing

1. *Seed or Concept Stage Financing*

The venture is still in the idea formation stage and its product or service is not fully developed. Following are the phases under this stage:

(i) *The condition of the company:* At this phase, talk of a 'company' is still premature. What usually exists is an immature idea and an incomplete management team, and there is no guarantee that the idea is technologically feasible or commercially viable.

(ii) *Sources:* The preliminary financing in the first stage is obtained from individuals who are close to the entrepreneur and know him personally, like family and friends, or private investors who are not organised in investing institutions, or incubators.

(iii) *Use:* The money is needed to support the development of the idea and bring it to the stage in which its feasibility is proven and the business plan is written.

2. *Start-up Financing*

At this stage, there is a company with a basic team of managers and/or entrepreneurs and possibly a basic business plan as well. Early stage venture capitalists—who are as rare as a hen's teeth—may fund this stage, but more likely, it will be sophisticated 'angel investors' (private investors).

At this stage, the money is used for appointing a broader management team and employees, completing the business plan, and developing the product to achieve the desired results.

3. *First-stage Financing*

The venture is launched and achieves initial pick-up. Sales are occurring and a management team is in place along with employees. The funding from this stage is used to fuel sales, reach the break-even point, increase productivity, cut unit costs, and build the corporate infrastructure and distribution system. At this point, the company is two to three years old. It is at this stage that venture capitalists prefer to get involved.

B. Expansion Financing

1. *Second-stage Financing*

Sales at this point are starting to snowball. The company is also rapidly accumulating accounts receivable and inventory. Capital from this stage is used for funding expansion in all forms, from meeting the increasing marketing expenses, and entering new markets to financing rapidly increasing accounts receivable.

Venture capital firms specialising in later stage funding enter the picture at this point.

2. *Third-stage Financing*

At this stage, the future is so bright that the founders 'gotta wear shades', i.e. they can be at ease. Sales are climbing and the customers are happy. The second level of managers is in place.

Money from this financing is used for increasing the plant capacity (or other capacity depending on the nature of the business), marketing, working capital, and product improvement or expansion.

C. Mezzanine or Bridge Financing

At this point, the company is a proven winner and investment bankers have agreed to take it public within 6 months. *Mezzanine* or *bridge financing* is a short-term form of financing used to prepare a company for its IPO. This includes cleaning up the balance sheet to remove debt that may have accumulated, buy out early investors and founders who might not be strong enough to run a public company, and pay for various other costs for the public issue.

The funding may come from a VC firm or bridge financing specialist. They are usually paid back from the proceeds of the IPO.

Initial Public Offering (IPO)

The company finally has the public investing into it and getting the desired level of liquidity. Founders sell off stock and often go back to square one with another start-up.

TYPES OF VENTURE CAPITAL

Types of venture capital depend upon the stage of financing. These distinctions refer to the timing of the investment or its specific purpose within the life of the target company but the need for a high return in exchange for the risk remains constant.

The types of VC can be divided into three main groups. These are *Early Stage, Expansion,* and *Acquisition/Buyout.* Each of the three main groups can be further divided into sub-groups based on the specific timing of the investment or its intended purpose. It should be kept in mind that these distinctions do not alter the basic idea of VC as a private equity being invested in high risk/high return companies that are on the innovative cutting edge.

1. Early Stage Capital

It comprises of three sub-divisions—(i) seed financing, (ii) start-up financing, and (iii) first stage financing. *Seed financing* is in usually smaller amounts, intended to encourage the research and provide capital during the time prior to actual start-up of operations. *Start-up capital* refers to the funds needed to actually launch operations. *First stage capital* refers to funds used to sustain operations following start-up but prior to the actual production of goods.

2. Expansion Capital

This is the next group of investment type which includes: (i) second stage, and (ii) third stage funding. *Second stage* is usually the period after production has commenced, but before profitability has been reached. *Third stage* is the time after profit, or even when the break-even point is reached. This is the time when additional products or even research into expansion ideas can be started.

Bridging capital *is another type and has several meanings but it mostly refers to the capital that 'bridges' a time gap. For example, if some traditional financing is expected or funds are anticipated as a result of a pending IPO, bridging capital is used to carry on active operations until the funding event occurs.*

3. Acquisition/Buyout Capital

It is the final group of capital which is used for the acquisition of assets including other companies that are being adsorbed into the organisation. There is an association with this type of funding and the exit strategy idea of VC. The exit strategy idea is a hedge against possible failure of the high risk investment in the form of a plan to recoup investments by selling off assets.

Once again, the types of VC listed are thus related to the actual timing and purpose of the capital. Capital investment opportunities do not only exist in the early stages of a company's life but are present through all stages of its growth as long as the basic requirements of high return are met. It is always understood that when less expensive and restrictive financing options are available, the company will seek them.

VENTURE CAPITAL INVESTMENT PROCESS

The VC process involves the following steps:

I. Deal Origination

First, the VC investor creates potential deals or investment opportunities for investment which may originate from any of the sources including referral system, open search, and intermediaries. Deals are referred to VCFs by their parent organisations, trade partners, industry associations, or friends. Open search is made through networks, trade fairs, conferences, seminars, foreign visits, etc. Intermediaries are used by venture capitalists for matching VCFs and the potential entrepreneurs.

II. Screening

Then, initial screening of all projects is carried out on the basis of broad parameters. *For example,* the screening criteria can be the area of familiarity to the VCFs in terms of technology, or product, or market scope. Other criteria can be the size of investment, geographical location, etc.

III. Due Diligence

Due diligence refers to the process of evaluating an investment proposal. The venture capitalists evaluate the quality of an entrepreneur and ask for a business plan to make an assessment of the possible risk and return on the venture. Business plan contains detailed information about the proposed venture.

IV. Deal Structuring

Once the VCFs are satisfied with the business plan, they negotiate the terms of the deals, i.e. the amount, form and price of the investment. The agreement also includes details about the venture capitalist's right to control the venture company, buyback arrangements, acquisition, making IPOs, etc. It also specifies the entrepreneur's equity share and the objectives to be achieved.

V. Post-Investment Activities

Once the deal has been structured and the agreement is finalised, the venture capitalist gets into the role of a partner. He also gets involved in shaping the direction of the venture. The degree of the venture capitalist's involvement depends on the agreement and policy terms. If a financial or managerial crisis occurs, the venture capitalist may intervene for the required bail-out.

VI. Exit

Venture capitalists usually like to cash-in their gains in five to ten years after the initial investment. They may exit in one of the following ways:

1. Initial Public Offerings (IPOs).
2. Acquisition by another company.
3. Purchase of the venture capitalist's shares by the promoter, or
4. Purchase of the venture capitalist's share by an outsider.

The VC process is presented in Figure 14.1.

Figure 14.1 VC Process

REGULATION OF VENTURE CAPITAL IN INDIA

This is discussed under three heads—(a) legal provisions, (b) structure, and (c) types of VCFs.

Legal Provisions

Indian VCF are regulated by the "SEBI (Venture Capital Fund) Regulations, 1996". The regulation clearly states that any company or trust proposing to carry on activity of a VCF shall get a grant of certificate from SEBI. *Section 12(1B) of the SEBI Act, 1992* also makes it mandatory for every domestic VCF to obtain a certificate of registration from the SEBI in accordance with the regulations. It states that "No person shall sponsor or cause to be sponsored or carry on or caused to be carried on any venture capital funds or collective investment scheme including mutual funds, unless he obtains a certificate of registration from the Board in accordance with the regulations[3]. Hence, there is

3. http://fiuindia.gov.in/relatedacts-sebi.htm

no way that an Indian Venture Capital Fund can exist outside SEBI Regulations. All Indian VCFs must be registered with SEBI and pay ₹1,00,000 as application fee and ₹10,00,000 as registration fee for grant of certificate[4].

The registration of Foreign Venture Capital Investors is governed by "SEBI (Foreign Venture Capital Investors) Regulations, 2000".[5]

Legal Structure

A Venture Capital Fund (VCF) means a fund created in the form of a trust, or company, including a corporate body, and registered with SEBI which—(i) has a dedicated pool of capital; (ii) is raised in a manner specified in the regulations, and (ii) invests in accordance with the regulations.

A *Venture Capital Undertaking* (VCU) means a domestic company—(i) whose shares are not listed in a recognised stock exchange in India, and (ii) which is engaged in the business of providing services, production or manufacture of article or things or does not include such activities or sectors which are specified in the negative list by the Board (SEBI) with the approval of the Central Government[6] (Box 14.2).

BOX 14.2: COMPENSATION OF VC FIRM

VC firms receive compensation for their investment and management activities in two ways:

First, they receive an annual management fee paid by the fund.

Secondly, the VC firm receives compensation through the allocation of the net income of the fund. The fund's primary source of net income is capital gains from the sale or distribution of stock of the companies in which it invests.

Types of Venture Capital Funds (VCFs)

Generally, VC funds are of two types: (i) venture capital funds set up by "angel investors"/high net worth individual investors, and (ii) VC subsidiaries of corporations and private VC firms.

In India, venture capital funds can be classified on the basis of the type of promoters:

1. *VCFs promoted by the Central Government-controlled development financial institutions* such as TDICI by ICICI, Risk Capital and Technology Finance Corporation Limited (RCTFC) by the Industrial Finance Corporation of India (IFCI) and Risk Capital Fund by IDBI.
2. *VCFs promoted by the State Government-controlled development finance institutions* such as Andhra Pradesh Venture Capital Limited (APVCL) by Andhra Pradesh State Finance Corporation (APSFC) and Gujarat Venture Finance Company Limited (GVFCL) by Gujarat Industrial Investment Corporation (GIIC).
3. *VCFs promoted by Public Sector banks* such as Canfina by Canara Bank and SBI-Cap by State Bank of India.

4. http://www.sebi.gov.in/acts/vcf2amend.html
5. http://www.sebi.gov.in/cms/sebi_data/commondocs/fvci_updated_21December2010.pdf
6. http://www.sebi.gov.in/sebiweb/home/list/1/3/0/0/Regulations.

4. *VCFs promoted by foreign banks or private sector companies and financial institutions* such as Indus Venture Fund, Credit Capital Venture Fund and Grindlay's India Development Fund.

VENTURE CAPITAL FINANCING DOCUMENTS

The model venture capital financing documents consist of the following:

1. Term Sheet

A *term sheet*, or *letter of intent* as it is commonly referred to, is a statement of the proposed terms and conditions of a proposed investment. It basically acts as the template for developing more detailed legal documents at a finalisation stage. For example, it may contain details such as the amount of investment, the percentage stake sought and valuation. Institutional venture capital term sheets are often quite detailed, and are almost exclusively prepared by the investor (called the 'lead')[7].

2. Stock Purchase Agreement

The *stock purchase agreement* sets forth the basic terms of the purchase and sale of the preferred stock to the investors (such as the purchase price, closing date, conditions to closing) and identifies the other financing documents. The main items of negotiation in the 'stock purchase agreement' are the price and number of shares being sold, and the representations and warranties that the company must make to the investors.

3. Certificate of Incorporation

The *certificate of incorporation* is a key document certifying a venture capital portfolio investment. It establishes the rights, preferences, privileges and restrictions of each class and series of the company's stock.

4. Investor Rights Agreement

An *investors' rights agreement* mainly covers matters relating to the rights of information, registration rights, contractual rights and various post-closing covenants of the company.

5. Voting Agreement

This contains voting provisions of Board of Directors with respect to their size, composition, removal, etc.

6. Right of First Refusal and Co-sale Agreement

This sets forth the information about the agreements among the company, the investors and key-holders for right of refusal and co-sale and effects of failure to comply.

---

7. See the model term sheet of 'National Venture Capital Association' in the Instructor's manual. That is the common form followed worldwide.

7. Management Rights Letter

Venture funds often request a *management rights letter* when investing in a company which typically include the ability to attend, advise and consult with the management of the company, attend board meetings and inspect the company's books and records.

8. Indemnification Agreement

Indemnification agreements are often provided to a company's directors and officers to minimise potential personal liability for actions taken in their capacity as directors and officers. In some cases, a director will serve as a nominee of one or a group of investors (e.g. an individual venture capitalist serving as a nominee of a venture capital fund).

For example, it states that "The Company and Indemnitee recognise the increasing difficulty in obtaining liability insurance for directors, officers and key employees".

9. Model Legal Opinion

It refers to the legal opinions in a typical venture-backed preferred stock financing by other law firms on specific circumstances. This is meant only as a starting point for reference purposes.

VENTURE CAPITAL VALUATION METHODS

Venture capital investment process is dependent on valuation of the business-seeking outside investment. The valuation of the company is critical to the investor-entrepreneur relationship and the ultimate success of the company. Valuation methodologies differ by the stage of investment. Following are the commonly used valuation methods:

1. Pre- and Post-Money Valuation

Valuation in the context of a venture capital transaction can be expressed in terms of pre-money valuation or post-money valuation. *Pre-money valuation* refers to the valuation of the company prior to the investment whereas *post-money valuation* refers to the value after an investment has been made.

Generally, a private equity deal focuses on the 'pre-money' valuation of the company. This is the 'estimated value' of the company prior to the purchase. The pre-money valuation of the company, combined with the amount of capital accepted by the company, determines the amount of equity ownership sold in exchange for capital. The resulting valuation after the investment of capital is called *post-money valuation*.

EXAMPLE 14.1: Calculation of pre-money valuation

In a venture capital investment, the investor gives Mr. X (the entrepreneur) ₹2 million for 10% of the company. What is the pre-money valuation in this example?

Solution: You might think the answer for pre-money valuation is ₹20 million but that is actually the post-money valuation.

So, 'post-money valuation' is calculated as:

= Amount of the investment/the percentage share received by the investor
= ₹2 million/10%
= ₹20 million

To get the 'pre-money valuation', first calculate the post-money valuation and then back into the pre-money valuation.

Pre-money valuation is calculated as:

= Post-money valuation – Amount of investment
= ₹20 million – ₹2 million
= ₹18 million

EXAMPLE 14.2: Calculation of post-money valuation

An investor proposes an investment of ₹1 million at ₹2 million pre-valuation. You have 1 million shares outstanding prior to the investment. Calculate the post-money valuation and the ownership stake of the investor.

Solution: To calculate post-money valuation, we need pre-money valuation and the amount of investment.

Pre-money value = ₹2 million and
Investment = Share price × Shares issued

The price per share will be:

$$\text{Share price} = \frac{\text{Pre-money valuation}}{\text{Pre-money shares}} = \frac{₹2 \text{ million}}{₹1 \text{ million}} = ₹2.00$$

$$\text{Share issued} = \frac{\text{Investment}}{\text{Share price}} = \frac{₹1 \text{ million}}{₹2 \text{ million}} = ₹0.5 \text{ million}$$

The total amount invested is:

Investment = Share price × Shares issued
= ₹2 × 0.5 million = ₹1 million

Post-money valuation = Pre-money valuation + Investment
= ₹2 million + ₹1 million
= ₹3 million

The investors will own 33.33% of the company after the transaction:

$$\frac{₹1 \text{ million}}{₹2 \text{ million} + ₹1 \text{ million}} = \frac{1}{3} = 33.33\%$$

2. The VC Method

This is the most common method used in business valuation. It values the business on the basis of net income projected in the last year of the exit. It discounts future earnings to present value, at a required rate of return specified by investors.

It consists of the following steps:

1. Estimate the company's net income at the time of investment, based on the sales and profit margin projections of the business.

2. Determine the Price to Earnings (P/E) ratio based on industry parameters.
3. Calculate the projected terminal value as Net Income × P/E ratio.
4. Discount the terminal value to find the present value of the investment. The discount rate ranges from 35–80% for accounting the future cash flows forecasted on an optimistic side by the entrepreneurs.

EXAMPLE 14.3:

Business Valuation	
Revenue in year 5	₹10 million
PAT in year 5	**20% = ₹2 million**
Industry P/E ratio	10
Company value	**₹20 million (₹2 million × 10)**
Investor Data	
Investment	₹1 million
Exit year	5th year
Required ROI	60%
Required valuation	₹10 million
% business required	**50% = ₹10 million/₹20 million**
Pre-money value	**₹1 million = (₹20 million – ₹10 million)/10**

Solution: The above example shows that the company's value in year five, when sold, will be ₹20 million based on a Price Earnings Ratio of 10. For an investment of ₹1 million, the percentage of the company required to earn ₹10 million would be 50%.

Many investors use EBITDA (Earnings Before Interest, Tax, Depreciation and Amortisation) instead of net earnings to value a company because it removes the effect of leverage and write-offs. When EBITDA is used, the "EBITDA multiple" (the Enterprise Value of the Company/EBITDA, i.e. [equity plus debt]/EBITDA is used in place of Price Earnings Ratio.

3. Net Present Value Method

The Net Present Value Method is the most widely used Discounted Cash Flow (DCF) method in all types of capital investment decisions. NPV of a time series of cash flows is defined as the Present Value (PV) of the cash inflows minus the present value of cash outflows. The discounting rate is the cost of capital.

Mathematically, it is expressed as:

$$\text{NPV} = \left[\frac{C_1}{(1+k)} + \frac{C_2}{(1+k)^2} + \frac{C_3}{(1+k)^3} + \ldots + \frac{C_n}{(1+k)^n}\right] - C_0$$

$$\text{NPV} = \sum_{t=1}^{n} \frac{C_t}{(1+k)^t} - C_0$$

Acceptance Rule

If NPV > 0

EXAMPLE 14.4: The investors are planning to buy the coolant unit of Fresh 'N' Cool Ltd. for ₹3 lacs. The projected life of the unit is 5 years. Following are the cash flows associated with the unit over its life period of 5 years.

Year	*Cash Flows after Tax*
1	₹1,00,000
2	₹1,40,000
3	₹1,40,000
4	₹1,20,000
5	₹90,000

Determine whether the unit should be bought or not by the investors using NPV criterion, if the target return on capital is 30%.

Solution: Net present value = PV of cash inflows – PV of cash outflows

Year	1	2	3	4	5
PV at 30%	.77	.59	.46	.35	.27

Present value of inflows

$$= 1,00,000 \times .77 + 1,40,000 \times .59 + 1,40,000 \times .46 + 1,20,000 \times .35 + 90,000 \times .27$$

$$= 77,000 + 82,600 + 64,400 + 42,000 + 24,300 = ₹2,90,300$$

Hence, NPV = 2,90,300 – 3,00,000 = – ₹9,700

The investors should not go in for the unit as the NPV is negative, in other words, the benefits associated with the business are less than the costs associated with it.

The comparison of all the above three methods is presented in Table 14.2.

TABLE 14.2 Comparison of Various Valuation Methods in Private Equity/Venture Capital Settings

Method	*Strengths*	*Weaknesses*
1. Pre- and Post-valuation	• Simple to understand • Commonly used in industry	• Pre-valuation is the estimated value of the company • Problems with the amount of capital accepted in post-valuation
2. VC method	• Simple to understand • Commonly used in industry • Quick to use • Market-based	• Relies on terminal values derived from other methods • Over-simplified (large discount rate) • Industry figures might not be available, particularly in private companies
3. NPV method	• Theoretically sound • Commonly used	• Cash flows may be difficult to estimate • Reliability of discounting rate is subjected to WACC and assumes a constant • Sensitivity to discount and terminal growth rate assumptions

CASE STUDY

Refocus by Private Equity

Client Situation

A leading private equity firm specialising in investments targeted at small to mid-sized manufacturing and distribution companies was seeking to refocus and reenergize growth in one of its portfolio companies. The portfolio company was into the business of providing capital equipment maintenance and other services to large manufacturing facilities throughout the United States.

Although the portfolio company had an established track record of growth, the company recently missed projections and needed a strategic solution to accelerate profitable growth. Alliance was asked by the lead venture capital investor to assist in this effort.

Alliance Approach

Based on the experience of working with private equity investors and their portfolio companies, Alliance worked closely with the senior management team and brought out a three-phase strategy development process as shown in Figure 14.2.

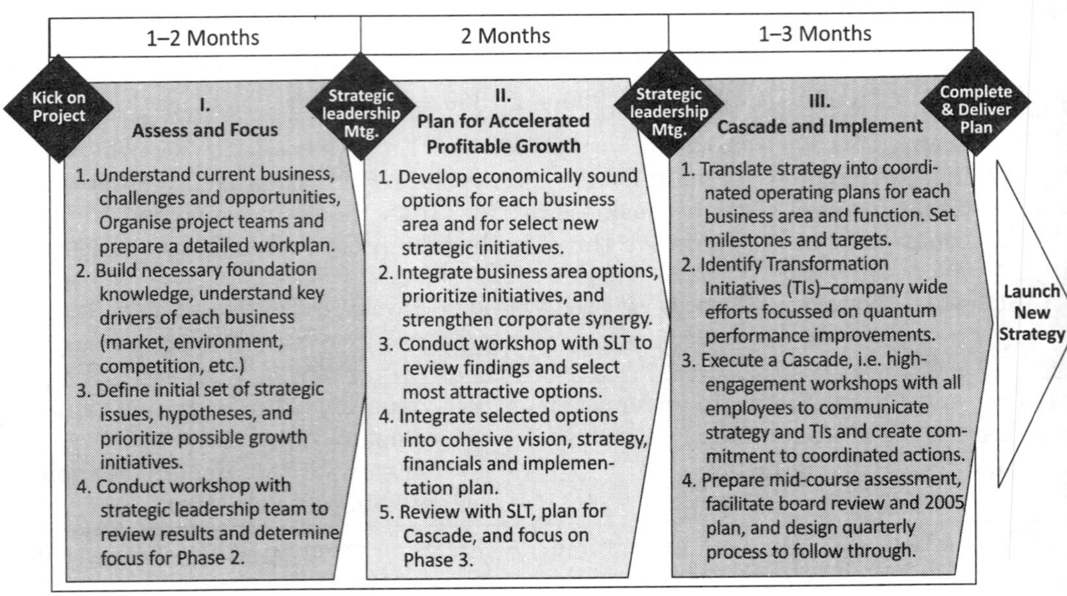

Figure 14.2 Three-phase Strategy Development Process

Results and Impact

As a result of this planning effort, the private equity investor and the portfolio company's management team formulated a common agreement on key strategic initiatives, priorities and resource requirements. The company is currently on-track to achieve its growth and profitability goals.

Source: http://www.alliancecg.com/private_venture_cap_case_study.asp

SOLVED PROBLEMS

PROBLEM 14.1: Start-up Investment's new venture fund offers to invest \$3 million into a food start-up for 40% stake of the company. Determine the pre-money valuation.

Solution: First find out the Post-money valuation = \$3 million/.40 = \$7.5 million

Now, we know the post-money valuation and the investment amount.

Thus, pre-money valuation = \$7.5 million – \$3 million = \$4.5 million

PROBLEM 14.2: Think-tank plans to invest INR5 million into a tech start-up for 10% share of the business. Determine the valuation at pre stage.

Solution: The Post-money valuation = INR5 million/.10 = INR50 million

The post-money valuation and the investment amount is known.

Thus, pre-money valuation = INR50 million – INR5 million = INR45 million

PROBLEM 14.3: Expo Corp., a venture capital firm, offers a start-up company a \$5 million investment at \$6 million pre-money. Determine how much stake the start-up should give up in exchange for \$5 million.

Solution: Post-money valuation = Pre-money + Investment = \$11 million

Now, to find the Venture Capital firm's percentage:

\$11 million = \$5 million/Venture Capital Firm Ownership Percentage (VCFOP)

VCFOP = \$5 million/\$11 million

= 45%

PROBLEM 14.4: Mohit is a partner in a very successful Bangalore-based venture capital firm. He plans to invest ₹5 lacs in a start-up IT consulting business. He has to decide what share of the company he should demand for his investment?

The company's projected net income after tax in the seventh year is ₹20 lacs. The industry P/E of IT sector in BSE is 20. The company's current outstanding shares are 4,00,000. Mohit is looking for a rate of return of 51%, keeping risk in mind.

Solution: Future value of firm:

₹20 lacs × 20 = ₹400 lacs

(Projected profits × P/E of industry)

Future value of investment:

₹5,00,000 × $(1 + 0.51)^7$ = ₹89.4 lacs (Mohit's desirable ROI is 51%)

Required percent ownership:

Future investment/Future value

= ₹89.4 lacs/₹400 lacs = 22%

PROBLEM 14.5: Mr. Ramesh, the CMD and promoter-shareholder of an event management company (Bright Pvt. Ltd.) is planning to sell his stake in the company and settling abroad. He has two options—either to sell to a public-listed company, or to sell it to private company. Both are competitor firms. Therefore, he has asked his CFO to calculate the value of the firm. The CFO compares the company's financials with two leading companies A and B in the same industry.

Following is the data for the last financial year 2010.

(Amounts in ₹ lacs)

	Bright Pvt. Ltd.	*Co. A*	*Co. B*
Balance Sheet			
Assets	160	300	380
Net worth	80	120	175
Long-term debt	5	100	0
Short-term liabilities	75	80	205
Income Statement			
Revenue	350	420	850
EBITDA	45	55	130
Net income	30	20	75
Market Data			
Earnings per share (₹/share)	3.00	0.67	2.14
Price-earnings ratio (times)	NA	21.0	14.5
Shares outstanding (lacs)	10	30	35

From the above information, calculate the valuation price for Bright.

Solution: Table shows the Average of Company A and B.

	Co. A	*Co. B.*	*Average*	*Bright's Value*
P/E ratio	21.0	14.5	17.75	NA
BV of equity	4	5	4.5	8
MV of equity	31.34	6.78	19.06	NA
Total MV of equity (₹ lacs)	940.2	237.3	588.75	—

Total MV of Bright should be fixed around industry average of ₹588.75 lacs. The CFO of the company also felt that overall the book value of Bright is good. Further, Co. A's long-term debt to total assets at 33% was substantially more leveraged than Bright's (3%).

POINTS TO REMEMBER

- Venture Capital (VC) is a financial capital which is provided to early-stage, high-growth potential, start-up companies. It is a form of 'risk capital' invested in a business where there is a substantial element of risk relating to the future creation of profits and cash flows.
- The true history of venture capital began in the years following World War II. It started with the formation of the American Research and Development Corporation (ARDC) in 1946 which was one of the first publicly-owned venture capital firms launched in New England to support the local economy. The dawn of the Information and Technological Revolution in the later part of the last century provided a solid growth medium for VC. The internet boom of the late 1990s followed by the NASDAQ and technological burst of the early 2000s was another roller-coaster ride for venture capitalists.
- History of venture capital in India dates back to early 70s when Government of India appointed a committee laid by Late Shri R.S. Bhatt to find out the ways to meet a void in conventional financing for funding the start-up companies. In the mid 80s all three Indian financial institutions, viz. IDBI, ICICI, IFCI started investing into the equity of small technological companies. In November 1988, the Government of India decided to institutionalise VC Industry and announce guidelines in the Parliament, known as CCI guidelines for VC. At the same time, World Bank selected 6 institutions to start VC investment in India which included TDICICI (ICICI), GVFL, Canbank Venture Capital Fund, APIDC, RCTC (now known as IFCI Venture Capital Funds Ltd.) and ILF (now known as Pathfinder). In 1995, the Government of India permitted foreign finance companies to make investments in India and many foreign VC private equity firms entered India. In 1996, government announced guidelines to regulate the VC industry in the form of SEBI (Venture Capital Fund) Regulations, 1996. In 1997, IT boom in India made VC industry more significant.
- Venture capitalists bear all possible risks associated with a business, viz. concentration risk, product risk, duration risk, size risk, asset risk, entrepreneur risk and technology risk.
- Venture capital provides a number of advantages over other forms of finance, like long-term equity finance, risk cover by partnership, professional expertise, tie-ups or alliances, exit facility and no collaterals.
- Venture capitalists look for core management team, market size, opportunity and scalability, intellectual capital, clean structure, valuations, returns, future investment and exit opportunity.
- The stages in VC financing consist of early stage, expansion stage, and mezzanine stage. Early stage financing includes seed financing, start-up financing, and first-stage financing. Expansion Financing includes second-stage financing and third-stage financing. Mezzanine or bridge financing includes IPO.

- Types of VC can be divided into three main groups—Early Stage, Expansion, and Acquisition/Buyout. Each of the three main groups can be further divided into sub-groups based on the specific timing of the investment or its intended purpose.
- The VC process involves six steps: deal origination, screening, due diligence, deal structuring, post-investment activities, and exit.
- VCF are regulated by the SEBI (Venture Capital Fund) Regulations, 1996. The regulation clearly states that any company or trust proposing to carry on activity of a VCF shall get a grant of certificate from SEBI. The registration of Foreign Venture Capital Investors (FVCI) is governed by SEBI (Foreign Venture Capital Investors) Regulations, 2000.
- The legal structure of a VC fund can be a trust or a company, including a corporate body. A Venture Capital Undertaking (VCU) means a domestic company.
- There are two types of organised or institutional VC funds: venture capital funds set up by angel investors (high net worth individual investors); VC subsidiaries of corporations, and private VC firms/funds. Venture capital subsidiaries are established by major corporations, commercial bank-holding companies and other financial institutions.
- The venture capital financing documents consist of term sheet, stock agreement, certificate of incorporation, investor agreement, voting agreement, right of first refusal and co-sale agreement, management rights letter, indemnification agreement and model legal opinion.
- Pre- and post-money valuation method states that the valuation of the company prior to the investment is pre-valuation and the value after an investment has been made is post-valuation.
- The VC method values the business on the basis of net income projected in the last year of the exit and discounts future earnings to present value, at a required rate of return specified by investors.
- Net Present Value method is the most widely used Discounted Cash Flow (DCF) method in all types of capital investment decisions. NPV of a time series of cash flows is defined as the Present Value (PV) of the cash inflows minus the Present Value (PV) of cash outflows. The discounting rate is the cost of capital.

KEY TERMS

- **Venture Capital (VC)** is a financial capital which is provided to early-stage, high-growth potential, start-up companies.
- **Seed Financing** is the idea formation stage when the product or service is not fully developed.
- **Mezzanine or Bridge Financing** is a short-term form of financing used to prepare a company for its IPO.
- **Venture Capital Fund (VCF)** means a fund created in the form of a trust, or company, including a corporate body, and registered with SEBI.

- **Venture Capital Undertaking (VCU)** means a domestic company—(i) whose shares are not listed on a recognised stock exchange in India, and (ii) which is engaged in the business of providing services, production or manufacture of article or things.
- **Term Sheet**, or letter of intent, is a statement of the proposed terms and conditions of a proposed investment.

EXERCISES

Problems

1. On average, the Light portfolio returns about 27% on average. If the investor expects 10× as her return on investment and her terminal value is $10,000, then what is its post-money valuation?
2. SS company will have revenues of $20 m upon exit. They expect to have post-tax earnings of 15% or $3 m. Using available industry-specific price to earnings (PE) ratios, a 15× PE ratio is available for SS company.

   Calculate the estimated terminal value.
3. In the exercise above, with anticipated ROI of 25× and SS's requirement of $500,000 m, calculate the post and pre-money valuation.
4. Consider an investment in computer equipment business. It calls for an initial cash outlay of $100, and returns $200 over the next five years making for a net gain of $100. Using a 10% discount rate compute the Net Present Value (NPV) of A Limited and advice on its acceptance.

   The cash inflows for various years are given below:

Year 1	$60.00
Year 2	$60.00
Year 3	$40.00
Year 4	$20.00
Year 5	$20.00

5. AB Ventures Limited is studying the possible investment in CD start-up. The following data is available.

Particulars	*AB Ltd.*	*CD Ltd.*
Profits after Tax (PAT)	INR 60,00,000	INR 10,00,000
No. of equity shares	10,00,000	2,00,000
Market value per share	INR 200	INR 160

If the investment is done and the purchase price is based on current market price, what is the new EPS for AB Ltd.?

Answers:

1. \$1,000 2. \$45 m 3. \$1.8 m & \$1.3 m
4. \$60.30 (Accepted) 5. INR 6.03

Objective Questions

1. Tick the correct answer:

(a) .... is a financial capital which is provided to early-stage, high-growth potential, start-up companies.
 (i) Early stage companies (ii) High growth potential companies
 (iii) Start-up companies (iv) All of the above

(b) Venture capital is:
 (i) Risk capital (ii) Non-risk capital
 (iii) Semi-risk capital (iv) None of the above

(c) Venture capital is:
 (i) Form of equity (ii) Form of loan
 (iii) Form of grant (iv) None of the above

(d) First-stage financing means:
 (i) Sales are picking up (ii) Sales are yet to happen
 (iii) Production is picking up (iv) Production is yet to happen

(e) Those who invest money into the venture fund are known as:
 (i) Financial (ii) Limited
 (iii) General (iv) None of the above

Answers: (a) iv (b) i (c) i (d) i (e) ii

2. Fill in the blanks:

(a) Return in venture capital is earned at the time of ....

(b) In 1996, government announced guidelines to regulate the VC industry in the form of ....

(c) .... financing stage is setting the stage for IPO.

(d) .... refers to the activities that are associated with evaluating an investment proposal.

(e) .... is a statement of the proposed terms and conditions of a proposed investment.

(f) The VC method values the business on the basis of net income projected in the ....

(g) .... is the most widely used discounted cash flow (DCF) method in all types of capital investment decisions.

Answers:

(a) Exit

(b) SEBI (Venture Capital Fund) Regulations, 1996

(c) Mezzanine

(d) Due diligence
(e) Term sheet
(f) Last year
(g) NPV method

3. True or False:

(a) In venture capital, ownership rights are given up.
(b) In November 1988, the GOI decided to institutionalise VC Industry and announce guidelines known as CCI guidelines for VC.
(c) Traditional funding is security-backed whereas venture capital is not.
(d) Seed financing is in the later stage.
(e) Start-up financing is at the business plan stage.
(f) IPO implies exit of venture capital.
(g) Registration of Foreign Venture Capital Investors is not mandatory under the FVCI regulations.
(h) Indian Venture Capital Fund can exist outside SEBI Regulations.
(i) The net present value method is the Discounted Cash Flow (DCF) method.

Answers: (a) True (b) True (c) True (d) False (e) True
(f) True (g) True (h) True (i) True

Short Questions

1. State the key characteristics of venture capital.
2. Give three differences between conventional funding and venture funding.
3. List two factors which venture capitalists look for.
4. What are different types of exit in venture capital?
5. What are the types of venture funds?

Critical Thinking Questions

1. Venture capital funding is described as "Business of Businesses". Explain.
2. "Seed financing lays down the foundation for venture investment". Argue.
3. "Mezzanine or financing prepares the company for its IPO". Do you agree?
4. "Due diligence makes or breaks the venture investment". Elaborate.
5. "Venture capital and Private equity are the sides of the same coin". Prove with examples.
6. "Term sheet is the most important financing document in venture capital documentation". Discuss.
7. "The VC method is the most common method used in business valuation". Explain.
8. "The global recession has changed the venture funding outlook in a considerable way". Discuss.

Descriptive Questions

1. Discuss the historical perspective of venture capital.
2. What are the risks associated with start-up companies?
3. Discuss the different financing stages of venture capital.
4. What are the various types of venture capital?
5. Explain the venture capital investment process.
6. What is the regulatory framework of venture capital in India?
7. Discuss the structure of venture capital firms.
8. What are the major issues and challenges faced by the Indian venture industry

PROJECT EXERCISE

Venture Fund Simulation Exercise

Create a Venture Capital Fund which is specifically ear-marked for the developmen of original student inventions. Propose, plan and implement an original produc development enterprise. It should describe the results of your entrepreneurial projec Discuss and compare the results with the existing domain enterprise. Find out the ga areas and suggest areas of improvement for future growth and viability. Also, evaluat the impact of the changing Indian venture capital regulatory and organisationa structure on the project.

REVIEW CASE

Innovative Ventures

Enterprising Brothers want to acquire an old government woolen mill. The governmen is willing to sell the mill for ₹1,500 million. Being an old one, the mill would need a additional investment of ₹250 million for working capital operations. For this, the would need ₹1,800 million to acquire and then expand nationwide, and experimen with developing the company culture to create a quality woolen lifestyle brand. Th company employs around 200 people—20 of whom work in the corporate office—an has plans to open additional shops in various states of India. They have approache Innovative ventures for funding.

Innovative Ventures are a leading player in the venture funding and have com of age and over the last few years, they have generated a wealth of success stories— with their investment and right support. They really spend a large amount of tim identifying and tracking potential projects and their behavioural trends. Investment in the venture business typically have an incubation period of three to five year before realising an 'exit'—through acquisition or IPO. Therefore, similar to US, the have now established 'super angel' funds and with this, they finance highly ambitiou entrepreneurs. They provide all types of funding, right from liquid seed-stage funding to expansion. Innovative Ventures follows an approach that many venture capitalists take to identify intriguing investment opportunities in order to develop an investment thesis from analysis of emerging sectors. An investment thesis helps to focus the investor on the type of company that will take best advantage of market opportunities.

They have significant interest in Consumer Internet, and Software and Mobile sectors. Woolen industry would be a first time project for them. "For us it (the sector) is a little bit different but somehow we like the team and their ability to expand significantly. They've ambitions on the surface but promise better customer service and operational efficiency", said Mr. Smith, the CEO of Innovative Ventures, about Enterprising Brothers.

According to the market valuation, the mill including working capital could be sold for ₹2,200 million after the planning horizon of five years. The corporate planners have estimated the profit from the mill operation as given in Table 14.3.

TABLE 14.3 Profitability Projections

(₹ in million)

Year	1	2	3	4	5
Sales	3,700	4,200	5,000	3,500	3,600
Materials and consumables	180	250	270	200	250
Corporate office costs	200	200	200	200	200
Selling and distribution costs	550	700	920	500	750
Depreciation	300	300	300	300	300
Interest	750	750	750	750	750
Profit (loss) before tax	1,720	2,000	2,560	1,550	1,350
Less: tax @ 35%	602	700	896	543	473
Profit after tax	1,118	1,400	1,664	1,007	877

The depreciation is charged on a straight-line basis. The financing cost would be around 10%. The executives of Innovative venture are not unanimous on accepting the project.

Issues for Discussions

(i) Should the project be accepted and funded by Innovative ventures? Use the most suitable method of evaluation to give your recommendation and explicitly state your assumptions.

(ii) Do you accept the project change if you use other methods of evaluation?

(iii) Why do you think that the method chosen by you is the most suitable method in evaluating the proposed investment?

(iv) What are the other factors, apart from financial appraisal, the Innovative ventures should consider?

REFERENCES

Josephson, Matthew (1972), "The Money Lords: the Great Finance Capitalists, 1925–1950", Weybright and Talley, New York.

Kirsner, Scott (2008), "Venture Capital's Grandfather", *The Boston Globe*, April 6.

Metrick, Andrew (2007), *Venture Capital and the Finance of Innovation,* John Wiley & Sons, New York.

Pollack, Andrew (1989), "Venture Capital Loses Its Vigor", *New York Times*, October 8.

The New Kings of Capitalism (2004), "Survey on the Private Equity industry", *The Economist*, November 25.

www.alliancecg.com

www.fairfaxcountyeda.org

www.fiuindia.gov.in

www.ifciventure.com

www.nvca.org.

www.pelosophy.com

www.sebi.gov.in

www.venturecapitalinvestmentfirms.com

Part IV

FEE-BASED CLASS

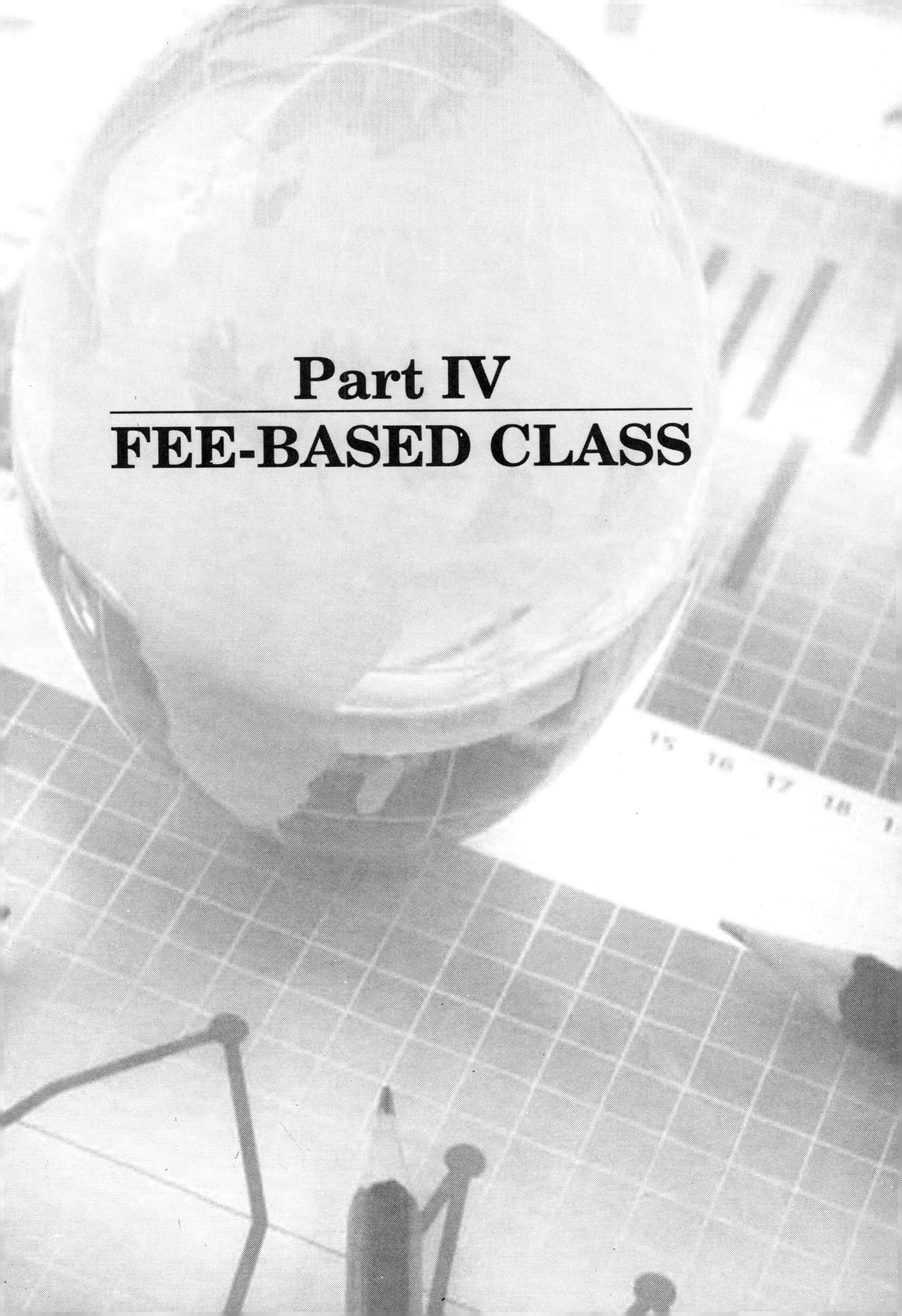

CHAPTER 15

Merchant Banking/Investment Banking and Depositories

merchant who approaches business with the idea of serving the public well has nothing to fear from the mpetition.

— James Cash Penney

LEARNING OBJECTIVES

This chapter discusses the following:

- Overview of merchant banking
- Merchant banking in India
- Functions of merchant banks
- Concept, legal framework and types of underwriting
- Stockbrokers and their types
- Regulation of merchant banking in India
- Merchant banks vs. investment banks
- Regulatory framework of investment banking in India
- Meaning, legalities and functions of depositories in India
- Similarities between banks and depositories
- ASBA concept and rationale

INTRODUCTION

'inancial intermediaries[1] consist of all those, institutions or individuals who help in the ransfer or channeling of funds from those who have surplus funds to those who need

. Refer "Indian Financial Institutions" in 'Chapter 1: Financial System' for further discussion on Intermediaries.

it. They act as a middleman between the surplus parties to the deficit ones. The rol of intermediaries is crucial in making the financial markets vibrant, and to functio smoothly and continuously. These intermediaries provide their professional service to different users and form an integral part of financial system. Merchant banks an depository bodies are important intermediaries in the securities market.

Modern merchant banks are commonly known as "accepting and issuing houses in the UK and "investment banks" in the US. They not only provide banking service to the business but also consultancy on financial, managerial, marketing and lega matters.

The depositories provide their major service of dematerialisation of shares an other services through depository participants, and facilitate the consolidation c accounts of investors.

MERCHANT BANKING: OVERVIEW

In banking domain, a merchant bank is traditionally used for an 'Investment Bank It is also used to describe the private equity activities of banking. Therefore merchar banking and investment banking are used interchangeably at various levels, in differer parts of the world.

Merchant banks evolved from mediaeval merchants who traded in commoditie Historically, the purpose of merchant banks was to facilitate and/or finance th production and trade of commodities. In present times, they provide variety of service such as *issue management, portfolio management, asset management, underwritin loan syndication, and act as consultants, advisors, registrars, share transfer agent trustees, etc.* They act as "financial engineers for a business".

Merchant banking is an important service provided by various financial institution that helps in the growth of the corporate sector and in the overall economic developmer of the country. With a large amount of public funds being invested in equity in th capital markets, merchant banking has emerged as a popular medium of bridging th gap between investors and corporate that are looking for funding to meet their busines needs of expansion, diversification or setting up a new enterprise. A merchant banke is considered to be a specialist in mobilizing funds from private investors, and can hel both large corporations and SMEs in accessing funds and ensuring better utilizatio of financial resources.

As per SEBI (Merchant Bankers) Regulations, 1992[2]*, merchant banker mean "any person who is engaged in the business of issue management either by makin arrangements regarding selling, buying or subscribing to securities or acting as manage consultant, advisor or rendering corporate advisory service in relation to such issu management". In addition, merchant banking services also include advisory services o corporate restructuring, debt or equity restructuring, loan restructuring, etc. Fees ar charged by the merchant banker for rendering these services*[3].

2. http://www.sebi.gov.in/acts/Merchantbankers.pdf
3. Refer "Types of Banking" in 'Chapter 2: Banking: Products, Services and Functioning' als

EXAMPLE: A leading multinational company of India in the steel industry plans to acquire a steel plant in one of the developing nations. The company will solicit the services of a "merchant bank" for advice on the best deal in the acquisition process. Additionally, the merchant bank may also assist in the financing the acquisition, providing underwriting or/and legal services.

MERCHANT BANKING IN INDIA

The Banking Commission Report, 1972 had highlighted the need for setting up merchant banking institutions in India for offering services, like syndication of financing, promotion of project, investment management advisory services to small and medium savers, and to provide various types of funds.

In India, ANZ Grindlays started merchant banking in 1967 which was followed by Citibank in 1970. In 1972, the State Bank of India became the first Indian Commercial Bank to set up a separate Merchant Banking Division. Later, the Industrial Credit and Investment Corporation of India (ICICI) set up its merchant banking division in 1973 followed by a number of other commercial banks, like Canara Bank, Bank of Baroda, Bank of India, Syndicate Bank, Punjab National Bank, Central Bank of India, UCO Bank, etc.

The FERA regulations in 1973, which required a large number of foreign companies to dilute their shareholdings in India, gave a boost to the merchant banking activities in India. Since then, a number of development banks and financial institutions such as IFCI and IDBI have also entered this field.

Today, there is a whole mix of banks, financial institutions and organizations like private brokerage firms and financial consultancy firms in the field of merchant banking in India. But merchant banks in India primarily operate as issue houses than full-fledged merchant banks as in other countries.

Thus, at present merchant banking services in our country are provided by the following types of organisations:

(i) Commercial banks and their subsidiaries.

(ii) All India Financial Institutions and Development Banks such as, ICICI, IFCI.

(iii) Foreign banks, like ANZ Grindlays Bank, Citi Bank, etc.

(iv) State Level Financial Institutions, viz. State Industrial Development Corporations (SIDCs) and State Financial Corporations (SFCs).

(v) Private Financial Consultancy Firms and Brokerage Firms, such as JM Financial Ltd.; DSP Financial Consultants Ltd., etc.

The top merchant banks in India for 2016 as per 'Leaders League Ranking' are given in Table 15.1.

TABLE 15.1 2016 Ranking of the Top Merchant Banks in India—TMT

	Leading	*Excellent*	*Highly recommended*	*Recommended*
1.	Kotak Investment Banking	Avendus Capital	Axis Capital	BMR Advisors—Translink Corporate Finance
2.	Morgan Stanley	Citibank International	Bank of America Merrill Lynch	KPMG
3.		Credit Suisse	Barclays	O3 Capital Advisors Pvt. Ltd.
4.		Goldman Sachs	Deutsche Bank AG	Standard Chartered
5.		ICICI Securities Ltd.	EY Société D'Avocats	
6.		J.P. Morgan	Signal Hill Capital	
7.		Rothschild & CIE		

Source: https://www.leadersleague.com/en/rankings/2016-ranking-of-the-top-merchant-banks-in-india-tmt.

FUNCTIONS OF MERCHANT BANKS

As discussed earlier, merchant banking is a combination of banking and advisory services. A merchant bank is a financial institution which performs the following key activities, as presented in Figure 15.1.

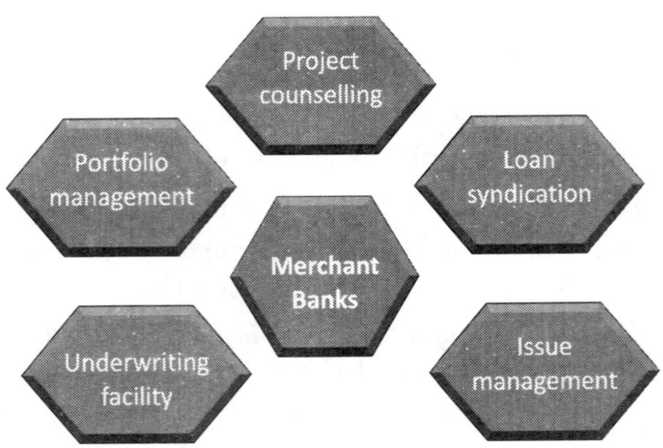

Figure 15.1 Functions of merchant banks

1. **Project counselling:** This involves determining the project feasibility of the client. A series of steps are involved in the process, i.e., *preparing the project report, determining the right financing mix, and assisting in execution of the project.*

2. **Loan syndication:** They organize term loans for the projects on consortium basis via banks or financial institutions. One of the institution acts as "Lead Bank/ Financer" and others fund the remaining part of the loan.
3. **Issue management:** This deals with managing the public issue of corporate securities, viz. equity shares, preference shares, and debentures for the corporate. In this capacity, the merchant bank more often than not, acts as a sponsor of issues.

   For "Initial Public offering (IPO) Process" and "Stock Exchanges" refer 'Chapter 6: Capital Market'.
4. **Underwriting facility:** This is one of the major services of a merchant bank. An underwriting is a guarantee given to the client stating that in case of issue of securities, if the subscription is less than a specified level, they would subscribe the said amount. *[Refer the next section for detailed discussion]*
5. **Portfolio management:** A merchant bank invests in different kinds of investments on behalf of clients; and then manages their portfolio. The portfolio services are provided not only to the corporate but also to the individual investors. Thus, merchant bankers act as "brokers" in the stock exchange. [*Refer next to next section for detailed discussion on stockbrokers*]

UNDERWRITING: CONCEPT AND FRAMEWORK

Underwriting is, 'an agreement, entered into by a company with a financial agency, wherein the agency guarantees to subscribe the unsubscribed amount of the issue of shares or debentures made by the company'.

According to the Securities and Exchange Board of India (Underwriters) (Amendment) Regulations, 2006, "Underwriting means an agreement with or without conditions to subscribe to the securities of a body corporate when the existing shareholders of such body corporate or the public do not subscribe to the securities offered to them". An underwriter means a person who engages in the business of underwriting of an issue of securities of a body corporate.[4]

Legal Framework of Underwriting

1. *Registration as underwriter*

Every person to act as underwriter is required to hold a certificate granted by the Board under these regulations.

2. *Conditions of registration*

Any registration or any renewal is subject to the following conditions, namely:

(a) where the underwriter proposes to change its status or constitution, it shall obtain prior approval of the Board for continuing to act as such after the change;

(b) it shall enter into a valid agreement with the body corporate on whose behalf it is acting as underwriter;

4. https://www.sebi.gov.in/sebi_data/commondocs/uwamend_h.html

(c) it shall pay the fees for registration or renewal;
(d) shall maintain capital adequacy requirements; and [the capital adequacy requirement is the net worth of rupees twenty lakhs5.]
(e) it shall abide by the regulations made under the Act in respect of the activities carried on by it as underwriter.

3. *Period of validity of certificate*

The certificate of registration granted and its renewal granted under, shall be valid for a period of three years from the date of its issue to the applicant.

4. *Fee for registration*

The non-refundable fee payable along with an application for registration or an application for renewal of registration is sum of twenty-five thousand rupees[6].

Types of Underwriting

- *Syndicate Underwriting:* This involves joint underwriting of an issue of securities by two or more underwriters. Such collaboration mostly happens when the total issue is beyond the capacity of one underwriter on account of resource constraint.
- *Sub-Underwriting:* In this case, an underwriter gets a part of the issue further underwritten by another agency mainly to divide the risk involved in underwriting.
- *Firm Underwriting:* It is an underwriting agreement where an underwriter agrees to buy a fixed number of shares or debentures. This is in addition to the shares or debentures he has promised to subscribe under the underwriting agreement. So, the underwriters are liable to take up the agreed number of securities even if the issue is over subscribed.

BOX 15.1: TYPES OF UNDERWRITERS

There are two types of underwriters, as follows:

1. **Institutional underwriters**—IDBI Bank Ltd., IFCI Ltd., SBI Capital Markets Ltd.
2. **Non-Institutional underwriters**—NBFCs

STOCKBROKERS

A stockbroker or brokerage is a licensed and regulated financial firm that facilitates buying and selling of transactions in various financial instruments for clients for commission; the clients could be individuals, firm or/and corporate. According to SEBI (Stockbrokers and Sub-Brokers) Regulations, 1992, "stockbroker" means a member of a stock exchange and "sub-broker" means any person who is not a member of stock

5. https://www.sebi.gov.in/sebi_data/commondocs/uwritereg93_p.pdf
6. https://www.sebi.gov.in/sebi_data/commondocs/uwamend_h.html

exchange and acts on behalf of a stockbroker as an agent or otherwise for assisting the investors in buying, selling or dealing in securities through such stockbrokers.[7]

The registration, code of conduct, and the management of stockbrokers and sub-brokers, is governed by Securities and Exchange Board of India (Stockbrokers and Sub-brokers) Regulations, 1992 and relevant notifications of Government authorities as may be in force from time to time.

The brokerage firms can be classified as follows: *full-service*, *discount* and *direct-access.*

(i) *Full-service brokers*

These are full-fledged brokerage houses with their own stock trading and research departments that provide in-house analyst recommendations to the clients. They usually assign a personal broker to each client. Therefore, they charge higher commission or a percentage of assets.

In addition to the above, they offer the largest assortment of diversified financial services. They have less day trading tools as their focus is more on long-term investors.

(ii) *Discount brokers*

These brokers charge smaller commissions for trades. They tend to have more trading and research tools than the full-service brokers since they cater to active investors and day traders.

(iii) *Direct access brokers*

Online brokers are also known as "direct-access brokers" and they cater to active day trading clients with the smallest commissions often priced on a per-share basis.

It is the duty of the stockbroker to continuously satisfy itself about the genuineness and financial soundness of the client and investment objectives relevant to the services to be provided. The stockbroker shall take steps to make the client aware of the precise nature of the stockbroker's liability for business to be conducted, including any limitations, the liability and the capacity in which the stockbroker acts.

REGULATION OF "MERCHANT BANKING" IN INDIA

SEBI had introduced effective regulatory measures for the purpose of disciplining the functioning of the merchant bankers in India in 1992. The key regulations of SEBI (Merchant Bankers) Regulations, 1992 (as amended as on August 3, 2021) are discussed below[8].

A. Registration of Merchant Bankers

The application for registration as merchant banker shall be made for any one of the following categories of the merchant banker namely:

7. https://www.sebi.gov.in/acts/stockreg1.pdf
8. https://www.sebi.gov.in/legal/regulations/aug-2021/securities-and-exchange-board-of-india-merchant-bankers-regulations-1992-last-amended-on-august-03-2021-_35135.html

(a) *Category I*

(i) to carry on any activity of the issue management, consisting of preparation of prospectus and other information relating to the issue, determining financial structure, tie up of financiers and final allotment and refund of the subscriptions; and

(ii) to act as adviser, consultant, manager, underwriter, portfolio manager;

(b) *Category II*

to act as adviser, consultant, co-manager, underwriter, portfolio manager;

(c) *Category III*

to act as underwriter, adviser, consultant to an issue;

(d) *Category IV*

to act only as adviser or consultant to an issue.

B. Consideration of Application

The Board shall take into account for considering the grant of a certificate, all matters which are relevant to the activities relating to merchant banker and in particular the applicant complies with the following requirements, namely:

(a) the applicant shall be a body corporate other than a non-banking financial company as defined under clause (f) of section 45-I of the Reserve Bank of India Act, 1934 (2 of 1934), as amended from time to time:

[Provided that the merchant banker who has been granted registration by the Reserve Bank of India to act as a primary or satellite dealer may carry on such activity subject to the condition that it shall not accept or hold public deposit;]

(b) the applicant has the necessary infrastructure like adequate office space, equipments, and manpower to effectively discharge his activities;

(c) the applicant has in his employment minimum of two persons who have the experience to conduct the business of merchant banker;

(d) a person directly or indirectly connected with the applicant has not been granted registration by the Board, i.e., any person being an associate, subsidiary or inter-connected or group company of the applicant in case of the applicant being a body corporate;

(e) the applicant fulfils the capital adequacy requirement;

(f) the applicant, his partner, director or principal officer is not involved in any litigation connected with the securities market which has an adverse bearing on the business of the applicant;

(g) the applicant, his director, partner or principal officer has not at any time been convicted for any offence involving moral turpitude or has been found guilty of any economic offence;

(h) the applicant has the professional qualification from an institution recognised by the Government in finance, law or business management;

(i) the applicant is a fit and proper person;
(j) grant of certificate to the applicant is in the interest of investors.

C. Criteria for Fit and Proper Person

The Board will determine whether an applicant or the merchant banker is a fit and proper person according to the criteria specified in Schedule II of the Securities and Exchange Board of India (Intermediaries) Regulations, 2008.

D. Capital Adequacy Requirement

The capital adequacy requirement shall be a net worth of not less than five crore rupees. 'Net worth' means the sum of paid-up capital and free reserves of the applicant at the time of making application.

E. Conditions of Registration

Registration granted shall be subject to the following conditions, namely:

(a) where the merchant banker proposes [change in control], it shall obtain prior approval of the Board for continuing to act as such after the change;
(b) it shall pay the fees for registration, in the manner provided in these regulations;
(c) it shall take adequate steps for redressal of grievances of the investors within one month of the date of the receipt of the complaint and keep the Board informed about the number, nature and other particulars of the complaints received;
(d) it shall maintain capital adequacy requirements;
(e) it shall abide by the regulations made under the Act in respect of the activities carried on by it as merchant banker.
(f) it shall immediately intimate the Board, details of changes that have taken place in the information that was submitted, while seeking registration.
(g) where the merchant banker is acting as an underwriter, it shall enter into a valid agreement with the body corporate on whose behalf it is acting as an underwriter and shall abide by the regulations made under the Act in respect of the activities carried on by it as underwriter.

F. Payment of Fee

Every applicant eligible for grant of a certificate shall pay such fee in such manner and within the period specified in *Schedule II.*

(i) *Every merchant banker shall pay a sum of twenty lakh rupees as registration fee at the time of grant of certificate of registration.*
(ii) *A merchant banker who has been granted a certificate of registration, to keep its registration in force, shall pay a fee of nine lakh rupees every three years from the sixth year, from the date of grant of certificate of registration or from the date of grant of certificate of initial registration.*

A Merchant Banker is required to pay fee as mentioned in following table.

S.No.	*Fees*	*Amount* (₹)
1.	Application Fee	50,000
2.	Initial Registration	20,00,000
3.	Regular/Permanent Registration	9,00,000

BOX 15.2: BANKS AS 'MERCHANT BANKS'

As per *RBI's Master Circular on Para-Banking activities*, banks are allowed to undertake merchant banking activities through a separate subsidiary which would be required to comply with SEBI regulations. Banking Institutions performing merchant banking activities are also required to follow the requirements laid down in the prudential exposure norms prescribed by RBI, as well as the statutory limits contained in Section 19(2) & (3) of the Banking Regulation Act, 1949.

Merchant banking can also be pursued by entities other than banks (however, they should not be NBFCs as defined under the RBI Act), provided they are registered with SEBI. In case a bank pursues merchant banking activities, it would need a banking license from RBI (to carry out banking activities) and a SEBI registration under the SEBI Merchant Bankers Regulations to carry out merchant banking business.

MERCHANT BANKS VS. INVESTMENT BANKS

As discussed earlier, merchant banking and investment banking are used synonymously at various levels. But, there are finer differences among them which are cited in Table 15.2.

Primarily, 'Merchant banking' is related to the process of issue management. 'Investment banking' is an umbrella term with a much broader perspective and refers to all types of capital market activities.

TABLE 15.2 Distinction between Merchant banks and Investment banks

	Merchant banks	*Investment banks*
1. Meaning	They are financial institutions that fulfil the capital requirements of companies in the form of share ownership	They are middleman between the issuer of securities and the investors, and also provides various financial services to the clients
2. Scope	Narrow term	Broader term
3. Activities	International financing activities	Underwriting and issuance of securities
4. M&A activity	Generally, don't assist companies in mergers and acquisitions	Assist companies in mergers and acquisitions
5. Model	Fee based	Fee based and fund based
6. Trade financing	Offered to the clients	Rarely provided
7. Dealing	Deal with small companies	Deals with large companies

REGULATORY FRAMEWORK OF "INVESTMENT BANKING" IN INDIA

Investment banking in India is regulated in various facets under separate legislations or guidelines issued under statute. The regulatory powers are also distributed between different regulators depending upon the constitution and status of 'Investment Bank'.

Pure investment banks *which do not have presence in the lending or banking business are governed primarily by the capital market regulator (SEBI).*

However, ***Universal banks and NBFC investment banks*** *are regulated primarily by the RBI for their core business of banking or lending. Their investment banking segment is also regulated by SEBI.*

An overview of the regulatory framework is cited below:

1. **Constitution:** At the *constitutional level,* all investment banking companies incorporated under the Companies Act, 1956 or under Companies Act, 2013 are governed by the provisions of that Act.
2. **Statue:** Investment banks, such as IDBI that are incorporated under a *separate statute* are regulated by their respective statute.
3. **Regulator:** Universal Banks and Non-Banking Financial Companies are regulated by the *Reserve Bank of India* under the RBI Act, 1934 and the Banking Regulation Act which put restrictions on the investment banking exposures to be taken by banks.
4. **Function:** *At functional level*, different aspects of investment banking are regulated under the Securities and Exchange Board of India Act, 1992.
5. **Law:** Investment banks that are set up in India with foreign direct investment either as joint ventures with Indian partners or as fully owned subsidiaries of the foreign entities are governed with respect to foreign investment by the *Foreign Exchange Management Act, 1999.*

Besides above specific regulations relating to investment banking, investment banks are also governed by other laws applicable to all other businesses such as— tax laws, contract laws, state laws, and the other laws that are applicable in India.

DEPOSITORIES: NATURE AND SCOPE

A depository is an organisation which holds securities, such as stocks and bonds of an investor in electronic form through a registered depository participant.

The "depository" means a company formed and registered under the Companies Act, 1956 (1 of 1956) and which has been granted a certificate of registration under sub-section (1A) of section 12 of the Securities and Exchange Board of India Act, 1992 (15 of 1992)[9];

In India, there are two depositories, namely National Securities Depository Limited (NSDL) and Central Depository Services (India) Limited (CDSL) that are registered with SEBI. They both have their offices in Mumbai. NSDL, the first and largest depository in India, set up in August 1996. CDSL received the certificate of commencement of business in February, 1999.

9. https://www.sebi.gov.in/acts/act03a.pdf

The securities in depository accounts are similar to funds in bank accounts, presented in Table 15.3.

TABLE 15.3 Banks and Depositories

	Banks	*Depositories*
1. Instrument	Holds funds in an account	Holds securities in an account
2. Transfer	Transfers funds as instructed by the account holder	Transfers securities as instructed by the beneficiary owner (BO) account holder
3. Facilitation	Facilitates transfer without handling money	Facilitates transfer of ownership handling securities
4. Custodian	Safekeeping of money	Safekeeping of securities

Depository Participant

A depository participant (DP) is an agent of the depository through which it interfaces with the investor and provides depository services.

As per SEBI rules, banks, financial institutions and the trading members registered with SEBI are eligible to act as depository participants.

Legal Requirement for Depositories

Following are the legal requirements for depositories under the Securities and Exchange Board of India (Depositories and Participants) Regulations, 2018 [Last amended on February 23, 2022].

(i) *Certificate of commencement of business by depositories*

No depository shall act as a depository unless it obtains a certificate of commencement of business from the Board.

The Board shall not grant it certificate unless it is satisfied that the depository has adequate systems and safeguards to prevent manipulation of records and transactions.

(ii) *Agreement between depository and participant*

A depository shall enter into an agreement with one or more participants as its agent.

(iii) *Services of depository*

Any person, through a participant, may enter into an agreement, in such form as may be specified by the bye-laws, with any depository for availing its services[10].

(iv) *Minimum net worth required for a depository*

The minimum net worth stipulated by SEBI for a depository is ₹100 crore[11].

10. https://www.sebi.gov.in/acts/act03a.pdf
11. https://www.sebi.gov.in/legal/regulations/feb-2022/securities-and-exchange-board-of-india-depositories-and-participants-regulations-2018-last-amended-on-february-23-2022-_56449.html

BOX 15.3: ASBA

ASBA (Application Supported by Blocked Amount) was introduced by SEBI in 2010. "It is an application mechanism containing an authorisation to block application money in a bank account when subscribing to an issue."

ASBA, does not require investors to furnish demand drafts or cheques when applying for IPO. Under this option, investors can apply through banks, which will block only the amount for the subscription until the allotment process. If the application of an investor is selected for allotment, his application money will be debited from the bank account. If shares are not allotted to the applicant, the funds will be released without any delay. It has been made mandatory for all IPOs from 1st January 2016.

There are two benefits to this ASBA system: (a) the problems associated with refunds are avoided, and (b) the ASBA funds continue to earn interest even during the application process.

Main Functions of Depositories

The depository bodies provide their services through depository participants (brokers). The key services are as follows:

- Opening a demat account for the investors;
  [Dematerialisation of shares means converting physical securities into electronic form]
- Maintaining record of securities held by the beneficial owners in the electronic form;
- Settlement of trades by delivery or receipt of securities from / in BO accounts;
- Receiving noncash corporate benefits such as allotment of bonus and rights shares or any other noncash corporate benefits given by the issuers in electronic form on behalf of its demat account holders;
- Pledging of dematerialized securities and facilitating loans against shares.

CASE STUDY

Atherstone's Half Role Play

Atherstone Capital Markets Limited, Mumbai based investment banking and advisory services company, was imposed a fine of ₹12 lakh by the capital market regulator Securities and Exchange Board of India. It was for mis-statement and non-disclosures of material developments in the IPO papers of 'Onelife Capital Advisors and violating 'Issue of Capital & Disclosure' (ICDR) regulations as well as code of conduct for merchant bankers. In December 2011, the regulator had barred Atherstone from taking up any new assignment as merchant banker till further directions. These directions were confirmed in January 2013 and continued to be in force till July 2016[12].

Onelife Capital Advisors came out with its initial public offer (IPO) in September 2011 to raise ₹36.85 crore. There were non-disclosures or mis-statements in the red herring prospectus (RHP) filed by Atherstone. Further, certain material developments

12. http://www.newindianexpress.com/business/2018/mar/16/sebi-slaps-rs-12-lakh-fine-on-merchant-banker-in-onelife-capital-ipo-case-1788032.html

that took place after the filing of RHP were neither updated in the prospectus nor informed to the investors through advertisements[13].

SEBI found that Atherstone had failed to conduct its duties as merchant banker in the above case. This was a blow to the trust and confidence of investors.

POINTS TO REMEMBER

- Financial intermediaries provide their professional services to different users and form an integral part of financial system. Merchant banks and depository bodies are important intermediaries in the securities market.
- Merchant banks, in modern sense, are commonly known as "accepting and issuing houses" in the UK and "investment banks" in the US. They not only provide banking services to the business but also consultancy on financial, managerial, marketing and legal matters.
- As per SEBI (Merchant Bankers) Regulations, 1992 merchant banker means "any person who is engaged in the business of issue management either by making arrangements regarding selling, buying or subscribing to securities or acting as manager, consultant, advisor or rendering corporate advisory service in relation to such issue management". In addition, merchant banking services also include advisory services on corporate restructuring, debt or equity restructuring, loan restructuring, etc.
- In India, ANZ Grindlays started merchant banking in 1967 which was followed by Citibank in 1970. In 1972, SBI became the first Indian Commercial Bank to set up a separate Merchant Banking Division. Later, ICICI set up its merchant banking division in 1973 followed by a number of other commercial banks, like Canara Bank, Bank of Baroda, etc. The FERA regulations in 1973, gave a boost to the merchant banking activities in India.
- A merchant bank performs the following key activities, *(i) project counselling, (ii) loan syndication, (iii) issue management, (iv) underwriting facility, and (v) portfolio management.*
- Underwriting is, 'an agreement, entered into by a company with a financial agency, wherein the agency guarantees to subscribe the unsubscribed amount of the issue of shares or debentures made by the company'. Every person to act as underwriter is required to hold a certificate granted by the Board. The certificate of registration and its renewal shall be valid for a period of three years. The non-refundable fee payable along with an application for registration or an application for renewal of registration is sum of twenty five thousand rupees.
- The common types of **underwriting** are: *(i) syndicate underwriting* which involves joint underwriting of an issue of securities by two or more underwriters, *(ii) sub-underwriting,* wherein an underwriter gets a part of the issue further underwritten

13. http://www.newindianexpress.com/op. cit.

by another agency, and *(iii) firm underwriting* in which an underwriter agrees to buy a fixed number of shares or debentures in addition to promised securities.

- A stockbroker or brokerage is a licensed and regulated financial firm that facilitates buying and selling of transactions in various financial instruments for clients for commission. The registration, code of conduct, and the management of stockbrokers and sub-brokers, is primarily governed by Securities and Exchange Board of India (Stockbrokers and Sub-brokers) Regulations, 1992. The brokerage firms can be classified as follows: full-service, discount and direct-access.
- The regulation of merchant banking in India is governed by of SEBI (Merchant Bankers) Regulations, 1992 (as amended as on August 3, 2021). The **registration of merchant bankers** require that the applicant shall be a body corporate other than a non-banking financial company, the applicant fulfils the capital adequacy requirement; and the applicant is a fit and proper person. The capital adequacy requirement shall be a net worth of not less than five crore rupees.
- Banks are allowed to undertake merchant banking activities through a separate subsidiary, complying with SEBI regulations. Banking institutions performing merchant banking activities are also required to follow the requirements laid down in the prudential exposure norms prescribed by RBI, as well as the statutory limits of the Banking Regulation Act, 1949.
- Merchant banking and investment banking are used synonymously at various levels. But, there are finer differences among them, like merchant banks fulfil the capital requirements of companies, while investment banks act as intermediary between issuer of securities and investors. Merchant banks mainly deals in international financing, while investment banks deal in underwriting and securities' issue. Merchant banks follow fee based model, whereas investment banks follow both fee-based and fund based model. Merchant banks deal with small companies as compared to investment banks which deal with large companies.
- Investment banking in India is regulated in various facets under separate legislations or guidelines issued under statute. At the *constitutional level,* all investment banking companies incorporated under the Companies Act, 1956 or under Companies Act, 2013 are governed by the provisions of that Act. Investment banks, such as IDBI that are incorporated under a *separate statute* are regulated by their respective statute. Universal banks and Non-banking financial companies are regulated by the *Reserve Bank of India* under the RBI Act, 1934 and the Banking Regulation Act. *At functional level*, different aspects of investment banking are regulated under the SEBI Act, 1992. Investment banks that are set up in India with foreign direct investment by the *Foreign Exchange Management Act, 1999.* Besides these specific regulations, investment banks are also governed by other laws applicable to all other businesses such as—tax laws, contract laws, state laws, and the other laws that are applicable in India.
- A depository is an organization which holds securities, such as stocks and bonds) of an investor in electronic form through a registered depository participant. In India, there are two depositories, namely National Securities Depository Limited (NSDL) and Central Depository Services (India) Limited (CDSL) that are registered

with SEBI. They both have their offices in Mumbai. The securities in depository accounts are similar to funds in bank accounts. A depository participant (DP) is an agent of the depository through which it interfaces with the investor and provides depository services.

- The legal requirements for depositories are covered under the Securities and Exchange Board of India (Depositories and Participants) Regulations, 2018. They mainly include: *(i) certificate of commencement of business by depositories, (ii) agreement between depository and participant, (iii) services of depository, and (iv) minimum net worth for a depository of ₹100 crore.*
- ASBA (Application Supported by Blocked Amount) was introduced by SEBI in 2010. "It is an application mechanism containing an authorisation to block application money in a bank account when subscribing to an issue."
- The depository bodies provide their services through depository participants (brokers), like (i) opening a demat account; (ii) maintaining record of securities, (iii) settlement of trades, (iv) receiving noncash corporate benefits, and (v) pledging of dematerialized securities and facilitating loans against shares.

KEY TERMS

- **Merchant Banking** is a service provided in relation to the issue management or acting as manager, consultant, advisor or rendering corporate advisory service in relation to such issue management.
- **Investment Banking** has a much broader perspective and refers to all types of capital market activities.
- **Project Counselling** involves determining the project feasibility of the client.
- **Loan Syndication** implies organize term loans for the projects on consortium basis.
- **Issue Management** means managing the public issue of corporate securities.
- **Underwriting** is a guarantee given to the client to subscribe the unsubscribed amount in case of issue of securities.
- **Portfolio Management** refers to the process of investment in different kinds of instruments on behalf of clients.
- **Stockbroker** is a member of stock exchange that facilitates buying and selling of transactions in various financial instruments for clients for commission.
- **Sub-broker** is any person who is not a member of stock exchange and acts on behalf of a stockbroker as an agent.
- **Net Worth** means the sum of paid-up capital and free reserves of the enterprise.

EXERCISES

Objective Questions

1. Tick the correct answer:

(a) Universal banks and NBFC investment banks are regulated by:
   (i) SEBI (ii) RBI
   (iii) RBI & SEBI (iv) None of the above

(b) In loan syndication, there is:
   (i) one bank (ii) group of banks
   (iii) international bank only (iv) None of the above

(c) Guarantee to subscribe the unsubscribed amount in case of issue of securities:
   (i) underwriting (ii) overwriting
   (iii) surety (iv) assurance

(d) The capital adequacy requirement for the registration of merchant banker under SEBI is:
   (i) net worth of ₹5 crore (ii) net worth of ₹10 crore
   (iii) net worth of ₹1 crore (iv) net worth of ₹50 crore

Answers: (a) iii (b) ii (c) i (d) i

2. Fill in the blanks:

(a) Investment banks with foreign direct investment are governed by ....

(b) .... was the first Indian commercial bank to set up a separate merchant banking division.

(c) The initial registration fee for merchant banker as per SEBI Regulations is ....

(d) There are .... categories under which registration of merchant bankers can be done as per SEBI Regulations.

(e) .... involves joint underwriting of an issue of securities by two or more underwriters.

Answers:

(a) Foreign Exchange Management Act, 1999
(b) State Bank of India
(c) ₹20 lacs
(d) four
(e) syndicate underwriting

3. True or False:

(a) Pure investment banks do not have presence in the lending or banking business.

(b) In India, ANZ Grindlays started merchant banking in 1967.

(c) State Industrial Development Corporations and State Financial Corporations are state level merchant banks.

(d) For the registration of merchant banker under SEBI Regulations, 1992 the applicant does not need to be fit and proper person.

(e) Merchant banking and investment banking are functionally similar.
(f) Sub-broker is a member of stock-exchange.

Answers: (a) True (b) True (c) True (d) False (e) False (f) False

Short Questions

1. Distinguish between merchant banks and investment banks.
2. What is underwriting?
3. Explain the concept of loan syndication.
4. State two similarities between banks and depositories.
5. What is ASBA?

Critical Thinking Questions

1. "Merchant banking helps in the growth of the corporate sector and in the overall economic development of the country." Elaborate.
2. In banking domain, a merchant bank is traditionally used for an 'Investment Bank'. Examine.
3. "Merchant banking is a contribution of the west." Critique.
4. "Merchant banking is not confined to commercial banks in present times." Discuss and cite the different types of players operating in the merchant banking industry in India.

Descriptive Questions

1. Discuss various functions performed by merchant banks.
2. What are the different types of underwriting?
3. What activities are undertaken by investment banks?
4. Outline the evolution of merchant banking in India.
5. Explain the key provisions of merchant banking regulation in India.
6. What are the salient features of investment banking regulatory framework in India?
7. Discuss the main functions of depositors in India.
8. Explain the categories of stockbrokers.

PROJECT EXERCISE

Merchant Banking Strategic Appraisal

Pick up one merchant bank from each category, like one from commercial banking segment, one from development banking segment and so on. Do their SWOT analysis and discuss the challenges faced by them, and devise suitable strategies for the improvement of merchant banking industry in India.

REVIEW CASE

Shareholders' Value Creation of AFS

Asian Bank of India (ABI) is a leading commercial bank in India, operating over forty years. Its merchant banking division is five years old. It was converted into a separate company as Asian Financial Services Ltd. (AFS) and came out with its IPO two years ago. Within a short span of time, it has strongly positioned to offer perfect financial solutions to business groups. It specializes in the arrangement of various forms of foreign currency credits for corporate. The company also provides services in the area of capital market, fund management, factoring, and brokerage services.

AFS has more than 50 offices in nearly 35 other countries, including multiple locations in the US, the UK, and Canada. Its income comes from following sources:

(i) merchant banking and advisory fees, (ii) income from securities, (iii) factoring and commissioning income, and (iv) other income.

Its expenditure falls under following heads: (i) employee costs, (ii) depreciation and amortization, (iii) provisioning and non-operating expenses, (iv) interest expense, and (v) other expenses.

The profit after tax of AFS for 2018 is ₹240.00 crore as compared to the profit of ₹265 crore for 2017.

The other financial figures are as given below:

	2018	*2017*
Equity Share Capital	48	48
Reserves and Surplus	860	822
Earnings per share (₹)	58.24	45.71
Return on Equity (%)	33	27

Analyze the company's performance on:

(i) Top line vs. bottom line performance.
(ii) Cost management.
(iii) Earnings potential.
(iv) Return generation capacity.
(v) Future growth potential.

REFERENCES

Allen, F. and Faulhaber, G.R. (1989), "Signalling by Underpricing in the IPO Market", *Journal of Financial Economics*, 303–23.

Ritter, J.R. (1991), "The Long Rum Performance of Initial Public Offerings". *Journal of Finance,* 46 (3–28).

www.leadersleague.com

www.newindianexpress.com

www.rbidocs.rbi.org.in

www.rbi.org.in

www.sebi.gov.in

CHAPTER 16

Credit Rating

Today, credit rating agencies rate companies, countries and bonds.

— Mike Fitzpatrick

LEARNING OBJECTIVES

This chapter discusses the following:

- Origin and concept of credit rating
- Importance of credit rating
- Process of credit rating
- Overview of credit rating agencies in India
- Credit rating symbols
- Registration process of credit rating agencies
- Credit rating problems

INTRODUCTION

Credit rating originally refers to the process of providing information to individual and institutional investors whether issuers of debt instruments and fixed-income securities will be able to meet their obligations on due time or not. Over the years, credit rating has not been restricted to rating of debt instruments only, rather it has extended to rating of equity, corporate governance and many more.

Credit Rating Agencies (CRAs) provide investors with objective analysis and independent assessment of companies and countries that issue such securities or instruments. Globalisation of the investment market coupled with diversification in the types and quantities of securities issued, pose a challenge to institutional and individual investors for analysing the risks associated with both foreign and domestic investments. CRAs' role has expanded with financial globalisation and has received an additional boost from Basel II which incorporates the ratings of CRAs into the rules for setting weights for credit risk.

The primary purpose of obtaining a rating is to enhance access to private capital markets and lower the debt issuance and interest costs. Research suggests that credit rating agencies, in their role as information gatherers and processors, can reduce a firm's capital costs by certifying its value in a market, thus solving or reducing the informative asymmetries between purchasers and issuers. For sovereign borrowers, there is evidence of a clear correlation between Bond Spreads and Ratings Grade.

There are other indirect benefits from ratings for low-income countries—*(i) to foster FDI, (ii) to promote more vibrant local capital markets, and (iii) greater public sector financial transparency*. As a result, some sovereigns that do not even intend to issue cross-border debt in the immediate future are seeking credit ratings from CRAs.

ORIGIN OF CREDIT RATING

The origin of credit rating is discussed as follows:

- Credit Rating originated in 1840 following the crisis in 1837.
- The First Mercantile Credit Agency was set up in New York by Lewis Tappan in 1841.
- John Broad Street set up a similar agency in 1849 which published its rating books in 1857.
- The first rating guide was published in 1859.
- The initial rating exercise was started by Henry Poor who published financial statistics of Railroad companies in 1860.
- In 1900, John Moody founded "Moody's Investors Services" and in 1909 published his manual of "Rail Road Services".

The rating activity got a boost post-Great Depression of 1933 when the US Government Controller of Currency directed the banks in USA to purchase bonds rated BBB/BAA and above, and the rest came to be known as *junk bonds*. Presently in the US markets, all commercial bonds are invariably rated. The high levels of default, which occurred after Great Depression in the US capital markets gave the impetus for the growth of credit rating.

The default of commercial papers of $82 million by Penn Central in the 1970s and the consequent panic of the investor in commercial paper resulted in massive defaults and liquidity crisis. US made rating mandatory for institutions such as Government pension funds and insurance companies.

CONCEPT OF CREDIT RATING

Credit Rating is "an assessment of the creditworthiness of individuals and corporations". It is based upon the history of borrowing and repayment as well as the availability of assets and extent of liabilities. Credit rating is thus a symbolic indicator of the current opinion of the relative capability of a corporate entity to service its debt obligations both in terms of interest and principal with specific reference to the instrument being rated.

The "quantitative" risk analysis carried out by credit rating agencies includes comparison of certain financial ratios with chosen benchmarks, and the "qualitative" analysis focuses on the management character, legal, political and economic environment in a jurisdiction.

Credit ratings are of different types, depending upon the requirements of the rater and the rated. Following are the common types of credit rating:

1. ***Bond and debt rating:*** Rating of bonds and debt securities issued by a company and government organisation(s).

2. ***Equity rating:*** Rating of equity of capital market.

3. ***Commercial paper rating:*** It is mandatory on the part of a corporate body to obtain the rating of an approved credit rating agency to issue specified commercial paper(s).

Besides above, a new form of rating known as *corporate governance rating* has emerged in the last decade.

IMPORTANCE OF CREDIT RATING

As discussed earlier, credit rating provides investors and debtors with important information regarding the creditworthiness of an individual, corporation, agency or even a sovereign government. It helps to measure the quantitative and qualitative risks of these entities and allows investors to make wiser decisions by benefiting from the skills of professional risk assessment carried out by these agencies. The significance of credit rating can be attributed to the following factors:

1. Development of Financial Markets

Credit rating helps in providing risk measures for various entities and makes it easier for financial market participants to assess and understand the credit risk of the parties involved in the investing process. Individuals can get a credit score in order to be eligible for easy access to credit cards and other loans. Institutions can borrow money easily from banks, avoiding the hassles of lengthy evaluations from each individual lender separately. Also, corporations and governments can issue debt in the form of corporate bonds and treasuries to attract investors based on the credit ratings.

2. Regulation of Financial Markets

The credit ratings provided by popular rating agencies such as Moody's, Standard & Poor's, and Fitch, have become a benchmark for regulation of financial markets. Legal policies require certain institutions to hold investment-graded bonds. Bonds are classified to be investment-graded based on their ratings by these agencies. Any corporate bond with a rating higher than BBB is considered to be an investment-graded bond.

3. Estimation of Risk Premiums

The credit ratings are used by various banks and financial institutions in determining the risk premium they will charge on loans and corporate bonds. A poor credit rating implies a higher risk premium with an increase in the interest rate charged to corporations and individuals with a poor credit rating. Issuers with a good credit rating are able to raise funds at a lower interest rate.

4. Enhanced Transparency in the Credit Markets

The credit rating provides improved efficiency in the credit markets and allows for more transparency in dealings. The ratings help monitor the credit soundness of various borrowers through a set of well-defined rules.

5. Standardisation of the Evaluation Process

Most credit agencies use their own methodology for determining credit ratings but they are more or less standardised in the rating process. The credit ratings of different borrowers can be easily compared using ratings provided by a credit rating company and the applications can be easily sorted.

THE RATING PROCESS

Rating is an indicator of the capability of the corporate entity for timely servicing of debts and obligations, regarding the instrument rated by the rating agency. It is based on the analysis of the information received from the entity and other reliable sources. Ratings help investors in their investment decision. Credit rating services are generally offered to the following sectors:

- Banking and financial sector
- Manufacturing sector
- Infrastructure sector
- Small and medium sector
- Health care sector
- Maritime sector
- Agricultural sector

Rating process is presented in Figure 16.1 and consists of the following steps:

1. ***Initiation on formal request:*** It is initiated on receipt of a formal request from the prospective issuer.

2. ***Evaluation by rating team:*** A rating team, which usually consists of two-three analysts with the expertise and skills, evaluates the business of the issuer.

3. ***Discussion with the issuer:*** An issuer is provided a list of information requirements and the broad framework for discussion on the basis of the issuer's business. It broadly covers all aspects that may have a bearing on the rating.

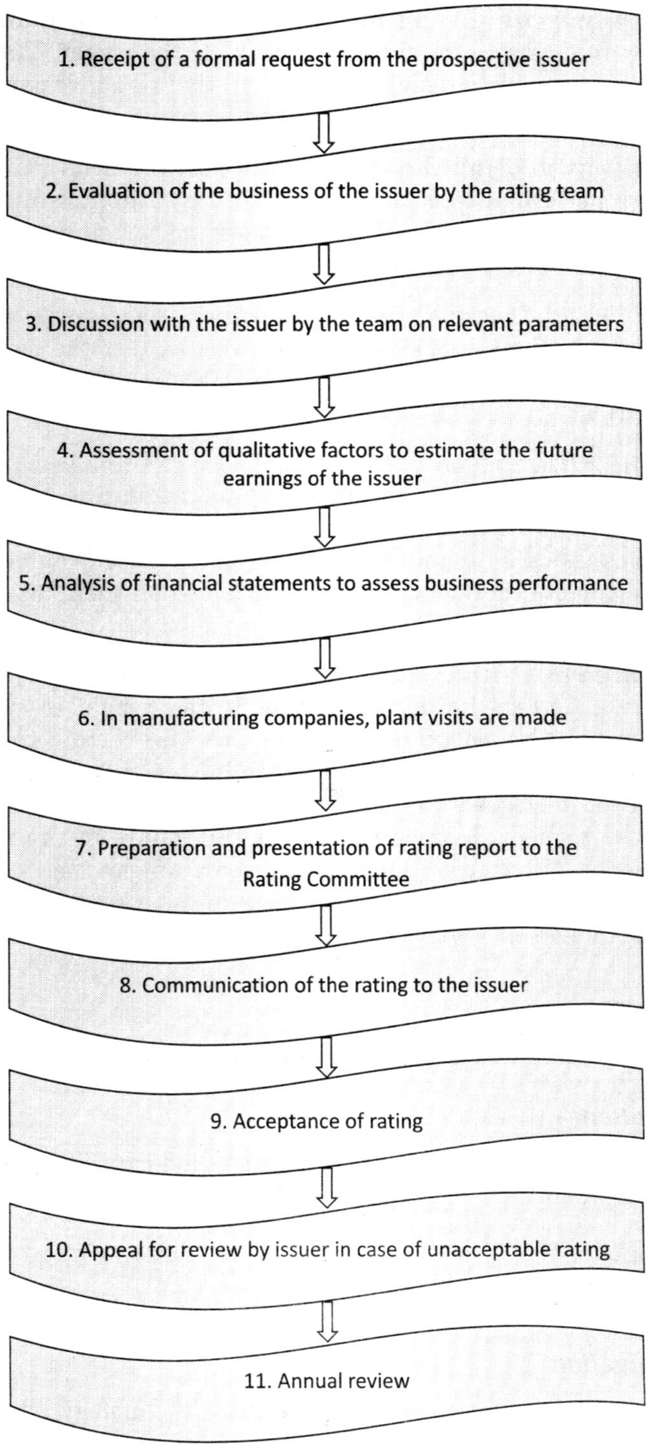

Figure 16.1 Rating Process

Note: Steps 6 and 10 may arise depending upon the sector and acceptance/non-acceptance of rating.

4. *Qualitative assessment:* Rating involves assessment of a number of qualitative factors with a view to estimate the future earnings of the issuer. These factors include industry characteristics, competitive position of the issuer, operational efficiency, management quality, and funding policies of the issuer.

5. *Financial analysis:* A detailed analysis of the past financial statements is made to assess the business performance of the issuer. Future estimates of earnings are made under various scenarios over the tenure of the instrument being rated. The main focus here is to judge the issuers' cash-flows to service obligations.

6. *Plant visits:* In case of *manufacturing companies,* plant visits are made to gain a better understanding of the issuer's production process, test the equipment and main facilities, evaluate the quality of technical personnel, and find out the level, quality and cost of production.

7. *Presentation of rating report:* After completing the analysis, a 'rating report' is prepared by the team, which is then presented to the Rating Committee—the final authority for assigning ratings. This assigned rating, along with the key issues, is communicated to the issuer's top management for acceptance. Non-accepted ratings are not disclosed and complete confidentiality is maintained on them unless such disclosure is required under any law/regulation.

8. *Review and follow-up:* *It is a culmination of steps (8–11) in the chart given below.* If the issuer does not find the rating acceptable, it has a right to appeal for a review. Such reviews are usually taken up if the issuer provides certain fresh inputs. During a review, the issuer's response is presented to the Rating Committee which may revise the initial rating decision based on fresh inputs. As part of a mandatory surveillance process, all accepted ratings are monitored over the tenure of the rated instruments. The ratings are generally reviewed once every year, unless the circumstances of the case require an earlier review. The earlier rating may be retained or revised (that is, upgraded or downgraded) on review.

Rating Parameters

The various rating parameters used for rating a company are discussed as following:

(i) *Industry Evaluation*

Industry profile, competition, growth potential, installed capacity, government policies, technological development, etc.

(ii) *Unit Evaluation*

Position of the unit, product range, market segmentation, future programmes.

(iii) *Technical Evaluation*

Level of technology, modernisation, de-bottlenecking, technology absorption, locational advantages.

(iv) *Financial Evaluation*

Financial statements: Profitability, financial strength, and cash flow analysis, accounting policies, auditors report, ROCE, debt servicing, working capital management.

(v) *Statutory Evaluation*

Compliance, pending disputes and litigations, payment of statutory dues.

(vi) *Management*

Shareholding pattern, composition of board of directors (BOD), MIS, Quality of key employees, recruitment, training, career planning.

CREDIT RATING AGENCIES IN INDIA

The Credit Rating Agencies (CRAs) in India besides credit appraisal, offer varied services *like mutual consulting services, and risk management.* They have special sections to carry on research and development work of the industries. CRAs provide training to the employees and executives of the companies for better management. They also examine the risk involved in a new project, chalk out plans to fight with the problem successfully and thus, ameliorate the percentage of risk to a great extent. For this, these agencies carry on a thorough research into the respective industry and offer services to the financial sector through the application of fund utilisation services (Box 16.1).

BOX 16.1: GROWTH OF CREDIT RATING AGENCIES

1841: Mercantile Credit Agency (USA)
1900: Moody's Investors Services (USA)
1916: Poor Publishing Company (USA)
1922: Standard Statistics Company (USA)
1924: Pitch Publishing Company (USA)
1941: Standard and Poor (USA)
1974: Thomson Bank Watch (USA)
1975: Japanese Bond Rating Institution (JAPAN)
1987: CRISIL by ICICI (INDIA)
1991: ICRA by IFCI (INDIA)
1994: CARE by IDBI (INDIA)

1. CRISIL Limited

As a global entity and India's leading ratings, research, risk and policy advisory company, it delivers ratings and solutions through its subsidiary "CRISIL Ratings". Its majority shareholder, Standard and Poor, is the world's largest provider of independent credit ratings, indices, risk evaluation, investment research and data.

CRISIL was set up in the year 1987 in order to rate the firms, and then it entered into the field of assessment service for the banks. It is headed by Mr. Amish Mehta as the Managing Director and Chief Executive Officer of the company. The company has set up a large number of committees to look after various services offered by the company such as investor grievance committee, investment committee, rating committee, compensation committee and others. The company is a listed company with head office at Mumbai.

2. ICRA Limited

ICRA Limited (formerly Investment Information and Credit Rating Agency of India Limited) was set up in 1991 by leading financial institutions as an independent and professional Investment Information and Credit Rating Agency.

Today, ICRA and its subsidiaries together form the ICRA Group of Companies (Group ICRA). ICRA is a Public Limited Company, listed on the Bombay Stock Exchange and the National Stock Exchange.

Mr. Ramnath Krishnan is the Managing Director & Group CEO of ICRA Ltd. The company offers products like short-term debt schemes, issue-specific long-term rating and offers fund-based as well as non-fund based facilities to its clients.

3. Credit Analysis and Research Limited (CARE)

Credit Analysis & Research Ltd. (CARE Ratings) is a service rating company that offers a wide range of rating and grading services across sectors. CARE has been promoted in 1992 by IDBI jointly with Canara Bank, UTI, private sector banks and insurance companies. The services offered by CARE include credit rating of debt instruments, credit assessment of companies, advisory services, credit reports and performance ratings. CARE is recognised by Securities and Exchange Board of India (SEBI), Government of India (GoI), and Reserve Bank of India (RBI).

4. ONICRA Credit Rating Agency of India Ltd.

ONICRA is a rating organisation that provides assessment, rating and grading models for the telecom, banking, insurance, financial, health, education and automobile sectors.

5. India Ratings and Research Private Limited

India Ratings & Research (Ind-Ra) provides credit ratings and research services for India-based credits. Ind-Ra is a part of the Fitch Group, which in turn is a jointly-owned subsidiary of Fimalac, S.A. and Hearst Corporation. Ind-Ra currently covers corporate issuers and financial institutions with head office in Mumbai. It is recognised by the Securities and Exchange Board of India, the Reserve Bank of India and National Housing Bank.

6. Brickwork India

Brickwork India was founded by Vivek Kulkarni. The company has hundreds of clients—both small and large companies from all over the world. In addition to 200 full–time remote executive assistants, analysts and managers, the company has a large panel of consultants who work on the more challenging industry—specific projects. In early 2008, Brickwork got a license from SEBI as a credit rating agency under the new company, Brickwork Ratings.

CREDIT RATING SYMBOLS

The credit rating agencies of India provide credit ratings to the companies that are involved in offering debt obligations like bonds, debentures, etc. to the investors.

These products are traded on the secondary securities market and are provided by several companies as well as the national government. The credit rating agencies of India provide a clear picture of the creditworthiness of a particular financial institution. The creditworthiness of a particular financial institution describes the financial ability of that company of paying back a loan and providing good interest rates for those loans.

These ratings are provided after considering the financial history of the companies. On the other hand, the value of assets of the companies and present financial liabilities are also considered for the purpose. These ratings provided by the credit rating agencies of India are very helpful for investors because they can get a clear idea of the expected returns and risk factor involved in the process. At present, these credit ratings are used for several other purposes like determining the insurance premiums, etc.

The credit rating agencies of India assign the following ratings to the companies:

1. AAA: These ratings provided by the credit rating firms denote highest safety. This means that the investment done in the company or in the government bonds are safe and at the same time high interest rates are guaranteed.

2. AA: Investment in the companies with AA ratings is also very secured. The AA ratings represent a high degree of safety.

3. A: Companies provided with 'A' rating by the CRAs of India can provide adequate safety to the investments but there are some risks involved in the process.

4. BBB: This rating is not negative, but investment in these companies includes some risk factors. According to the credit rating agencies of India, these companies can provide moderate safety to the investment.

5. BB: A company with such rating is eligible for providing sub-moderate safety to the investment.

Credit ratings such as 'B', 'C' and 'D' are somehow negative because these ratings denote inadequate safety, substantial risk and default, respectively. Therefore, investing in these companies can be risky.

Each agency has its own rating symbol. The rating symbols of famous rating agencies in India are described in Tables 16.1–16.6. *Part A discusses "debt rating", Part B deals with "equity rating" and Part C discusses "corporate governance" rating.*

A. Debt Rating

TABLE 16.1 CRISIL Rating Scale

I. *Long-Term Instruments Rating Scale*

CRISIL AAA (Highest safety)	• 'Highest degree of safety' regarding timely servicing of financial obligations • Lowest credit risk of instruments
CRISIL AA (High safety)	• 'High degree of safety' regarding timely servicing of financial obligations • Very low credit risk of instruments
CRISIL A (Adequate safety)	• 'Adequate degree of safety' regarding timely servicing of financial obligations • Low credit risk of instruments
CRISIL BBB (Moderate safety)	• 'Moderate degree of safety' regarding timely servicing of financial obligations • Moderate credit risk of instruments
CRISIL BB (Moderate risk)	• 'Moderate risk of default' regarding timely servicing of financial obligations
CRISIL B (High risk)	• 'High risk of default' regarding timely servicing of financial obligations
CRISIL C (Very high risk)	• 'Very high risk of default' regarding timely servicing of financial obligations
CRISIL D (Default)	• These instruments are in default or expected to be in default soon

Note: CRISIL may apply '+' (plus) or '–' (minus) signs for ratings from 'CRISIL AA' to 'CRISIL C' to reflect comparative standing within the category.

II. *Short-Term Instruments Rating Scale*

CRISIL A1	• 'Very strong degree of safety' regarding timely servicing of financial obligations • Lowest credit risk of instruments
CRISIL A2	• 'Strong degree of safety' regarding timely servicing of financial obligations • Low credit risk of instruments
CRISIL A3	• 'Moderate degree of safety' regarding timely servicing of financial obligations • Higher credit risk of instruments
CRISIL A4	• 'Minimal degree of safety' regarding timely servicing of financial obligations • High credit risk of instruments and they are susceptible to default
CRISIL D	• These instruments are in default or expected to be in default on maturity

Source: http://www.crisil.com/ratings/credit-rating-scale.html
Note: CRISIL may apply '+' (plus) sign for ratings from 'CRISIL A1' to 'CRISIL A4' to reflect comparative standing within the category.

Table 16.2 given below shows ICRA rating.

TABLE 16.2 ICRA Rating Scale

I. *Long-Term Bonds, NCDs, and other debt instruments (excluding Public Deposits)*

ICRA AAA	• 'Highest degree of safety' regarding timely servicing of financial obligations • Lowest credit risk of instruments
ICRA AA	• 'High degree of safety' regarding timely servicing of financial obligations • Very low credit risk of instruments
ICRA A	• 'Adequate degree of safety' regarding timely servicing of financial obligations • Low credit risk of instruments
ICRA BBB	• 'Moderate degree of safety' regarding timely servicing of financial obligations • Moderate credit risk of instruments
ICRA BB	• 'Moderate risk of default' regarding timely servicing of financial obligations
ICRA B	• 'High risk of default' regarding timely servicing of financial obligations
ICRA C	• 'Very high risk of default' regarding timely servicing of financial obligations
ICRA D	• These instruments are in default or expected to be in default soon

Source: http://www.icra.in/Content.aspx

Note: For long-term ratings, modifiers '+' (plus) or '–' (minus) can be used with the rating symbols for the categories AA to C. The modifiers reflect the comparative standing within the category.

Table 16.3 shows the rating symbols of CARE.

TABLE 16.3 CARE Rating Scale

I. *Long-Term and Medium-Term Instruments (FD/SO/CPS/RPS)*

CARE AAA	• 'Highest degree of safety' regarding timely servicing of financial obligations • Lowest credit risk of instruments
CARE AA	• 'High degree of safety' regarding timely servicing of financial obligations • Very low credit risk of instruments
CARE A	• 'Adequate degree of safety' regarding timely servicing of financial obligations • Low credit risk of instruments
CARE BBB	• 'Moderate degree of safety' regarding timely servicing of financial obligations • Moderate credit risk of instruments
CARE BB	• 'Moderate risk of default' regarding timely servicing of financial obligations
CARE B	• 'High risk of default' regarding timely servicing of financial obligations
CARE C	• 'Very high risk of default' regarding timely servicing of financial obligations
CARE D	• These instruments are in default or expected to be in default soon

Source: http://www.careratings.com/market-segments/corporates-debt-rating.aspx

B. Equity Rating

Equity rating is not regulatory as specified debt rating and is done at the issuer's want. Table 16.4 shows commonly used equity rating scales. The grading is classified into six broad categories in the descending order of earnings prospects: *excellent, very good, good, moderate, weak and poor.* Each grading has three sub-categories correlated with the degree of risk.

TABLE 16.4 Common Equity Rating Grades

Excellent earnings prospects	ER1A Low risk
	ER1B Moderate risk
	ER1C High risk
Very good earnings prospects	ER2A Low risk
	ER2B Moderate risk
	ER2C High risk
Good earnings prospects	ER3A Low risk
	ER3B Moderate risk
	ER3C High risk
Moderate earnings prospects	ER4A Low risk
	ER4B Moderate risk
	ER4C High risk
Weak earnings prospects	ER5A Low risk
	ER5B Moderate risk
	ER5C High risk
Poor earnings prospects	ER6A Low risk
	ER6B Moderate risk
	ER6C High risk

C. Corporate Governance Rating

Corporate governance rating has become popular in the last two decades because of growing awareness about corporate transparency. It is also not a legal requirement for the companies in India. It can be *Confidential*—company may accept and disclose only to select entities, or *Public*—disclosed only on acceptance. Here, the focus is on Board and its processes.

Table 16.5 shows ICRA's stakeholder value and governance rating.

TABLE 16.5 ICRA's Corporate Governance Rating

CGR1	'Highest assurance' on the quality of corporate governance
CGR2	'High level of assurance' on the quality of corporate governance
CGR3	'Adequate level of assurance' on the quality of corporate governance
CGR4	'Moderate level of assurance' on the quality of corporate governance
CGR5	'Inadequate level of assurance' on the quality of corporate governance
CGR6	'Low level of assurance' on the quality of corporate governance

Source: http://www.icra.in/Content.aspx

Note: A sign of '+' may be suffixed to any of the rating symbols other than CGR1, to indicate a relatively higher standing within the category represented by the particular symbol.

Table 16.6 shows CRISIL's CG rating.

TABLE 16.6 CRISIL's Governance and Value Creation Rating

CRISIL GVC Level-1	'Highest' corporate governance and value creation for all stakeholders
CRISIL GVC Level-2	'Very High' corporate governance and value creation for all stakeholders
CRISIL GVC Level-3	'High' corporate governance and value creation for all stakeholders
CRISIL GVC Level-4	'Above Average' corporate governance and value creation for all stakeholders
CRISIL GVC Level-5	'Average' corporate governance and value creation for all stakeholders
CRISIL GVC Level-6	'Below Average' corporate governance and value creation for all stakeholders
CRISIL GVC Level-7	'Low' corporate governance and value creation for all stakeholders
CRISIL GVC Level-8	'Lowest' corporate governance and value creation for all stakeholders

Source: http://www.crisil.com/ratings/other-rating-scales.html

REGISTRATION OF CREDIT RATING AGENCIES

The "Securities and Exchange Board of India (Credit Rating Agencies) Regulations, 1999" **[Last amended on January 24, 2022]** offers various guidelines with regard to the registration and functioning of the credit rating agencies in India. The registration procedure includes application for the establishment of a credit rating agency, determining the eligibility criteria and providing all the details required. They have to undergo strict examination procedure for the details furnished by them. The credit rating agencies are provided with compliance officers and they are required to show their accounting records.

Application for Grant of Certificate

Following are the provisions for registration of credit rating agencies under Securities and Exchange Board of India (Credit Rating Agencies) Regulations, 1999[1]:

1. Any person proposing to commence any activity as a credit rating agency on or after the date of commencement of these regulations shall make an application to the Board for the grant of a certificate of registration for the purpose.
2. An application for the grant of a certificate under sub-regulation (1) or sub-regulation (2) shall be made to the Board in Form A of the First Schedule and shall be accompanied by a non-refundable application fee, as specified in Form A of the second Schedule, to be paid in the manner specified in Part B thereof.

Promoter of Credit Rating Agency

The Board shall not consider an application under regulation (3) unless the applicant is promoted by a person belonging to any of the following categories, namely:

(a) A public financial institution, as defined in Section 2(72) of the Companies Act, 2013 (18 of 2013).
(b) A scheduled commercial bank included for the time being in the Second Schedule to the Reserve Bank of India Act, 1934 (2 of 1934).
(c) A foreign bank operating in India with the approval of the Reserve Bank of India.
(d) A foreign credit rating agency incorporated in a Financial Action Task Force (FATF) member jurisdiction and recognised under their law, having a minimum of five years' experience in rating securities.
(e) Any company or a corporate body, having continuous net worth of minimum rupees one hundred crores as per its audited annual accounts for the previous five years prior to filing of the application with the Board for the grant of certificate under these regulations.

Eligibility Criteria

The Board shall not consider an application for the grant of a certificate under regulation 3 unless the applicant satisfies the following conditions, namely:

(a) The applicant is set up and registered as a company under the Companies Act, 2013.
(b) The applicant has, in its Memorandum of Association, specified rating activity as one of its main objects.
(c) The applicant has a minimum net worth of rupees twenty five crore.
(d) The applicant has adequate infrastructure, to enable it to provide rating services in accordance with the provisions of the Act and these regulations.
(e) The applicant and the promoters of the applicant, referred to in regulation 4, have

1. https://www.sebi.gov.in/legal/regulations/jan-2022/securities-and-exchange-board-of-india-credit-rating-agencies-regulations-1999-last-amended-on-january-24-2022-_55541.html

professional competence, financial soundness and general reputation of fairness and integrity in business transactions, to the satisfaction of the Board.

(f) Neither the applicant, nor its promoter, nor any director of the applicant or its promoter, is involved in any legal proceeding connected with the securities market, which may have an adverse impact on the interests of the investors.

(g) Neither the applicant, nor its promoters, nor any director of its promoter, has at any time in the past been convicted of any offence involving moral turpitude or any economic offence.

(h) The applicant has, in its employment, persons having adequate professional and other relevant experience to the satisfaction of the Board.

(i) Neither the applicant, nor any person directly or indirectly connected with the applicant has in the past been:
- Refused by the Board a certificate under these regulations, or
- Subjected to any proceedings for a contravention of the Act or of any rules or regulations made under the Act.

Explanation: For the purpose of this clause, the expression "directly or indirectly connected person" means any person who is an associate, subsidiary, inter-connected or group company of the applicant or a company under the same management as the applicant.

(j) The applicant, in all other respects, is a fit and proper person for the grant of a certificate.

(k) Grant of certificate to the applicant is in the interest of investors and the securities market.

The credit rating system in India, as discussed above, is depicted in Figure 16.2.

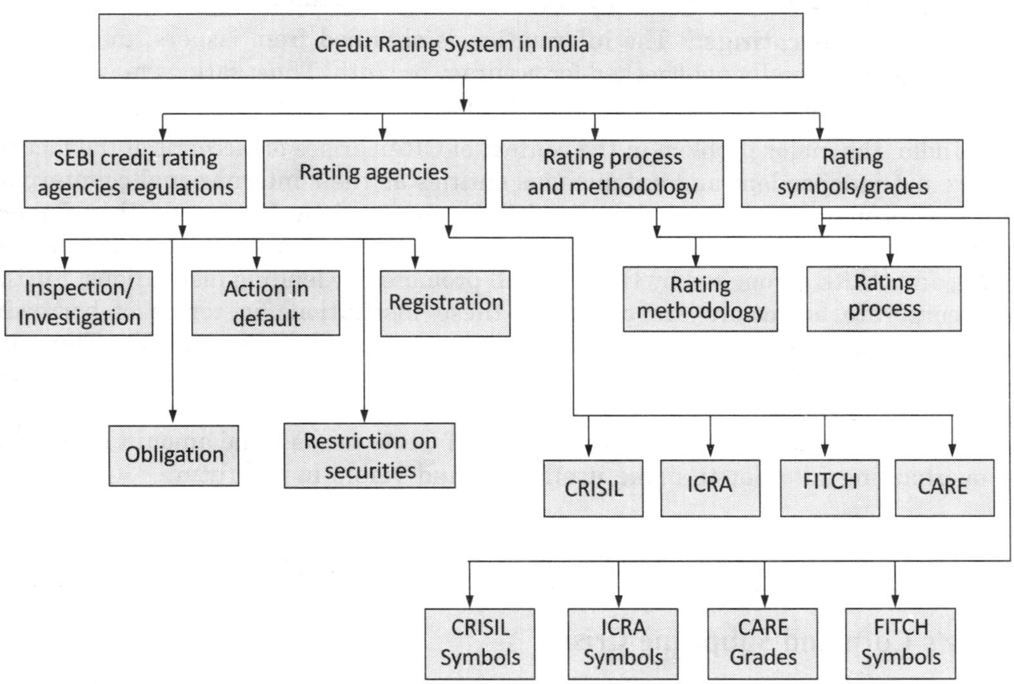

Figure 16.2 Credit Rating System in India

PRACTICAL PROBLEMS WITH CREDIT RATING

Credit rating is full of issues and challenges. The problems associated with this process are discussed as follows:

- **Inadequate skills:** All the branches of the rating agency may not possess skills in rating.
- **Inexperienced staff:** Inexperienced, unskilled or overloaded staff may not do justice to their job and the results may not be perfect.
- **Past data:** Rating is based on the past and present performances of the company but it does affect the future outcome of the company.
- **Rating is not permanent:** The rating is not permanent but subject to change and moreover, it is not a guarantee for the investors.
- **Possibility of inflated ratings:** Rating agencies receive a sizable fee from the companies for ratings, therefore the possibility of inflated ratings cannot be ruled out.
- **Lack of accountability:** There is often a possibility of biased ratings and misrepresentation due to lack of accountability in the process and the close nexus between the agency and the issuer.
- **Concealment of information:** Rating is based on the information provided by the company and therefore, there is always a risk of concealment of information on part of the company.
- **Differences in risk:** Small differences in degrees of risk are usually not indicated by CRAs. Thus, issues with the same rating may actually be of differing quality.
- **Change in ratings:** The information is obtained from issuers, underwriters, etc. and is usually not checked for accuracy or truth. Thus, ratings may change on account of non-availability of or inadequate information.

In India, the major problem in the context of CRAs arises on account of the fact that they are not independent and autonomous entities as their international counterparts. The three primary CRAs in India, viz. ICRA (promoted by IFCI and other financial institutions and banks), CRISIL (promoted by ICICI, Asian Development bank and others), and CARE (promoted by IDBI) are all promoted by lending institutions. Further, many corporate borrowers are clients of these institutions in terms of borrowing. Institutions like ICICI, IDBI also have stakes in such client companies. Thus, it is very important for these agencies to distance themselves from their promoters if they want to gain credibility.

It is therefore, needless to say, the system of CRAs needs some amount of relooking and overhauling in order to make it effective and viable in the future.

CASE STUDY

Moody's Corp and Subprime Crisis

Like other rating agencies, Moody's Corporation also facilitated a financial structure that was banking upon illusory assets and ineffective regulation but holding them or other agencies primarily responsible for the 2008 global financial crisis would not be a realistic approach. Therefore, the basic question arises—Is what is legal necessarily ethical? In case of Moody's Corporation, there was no violation of any regulation or law that the enterprise was bound to abide by. Nonetheless, was there not a moral and professional obligation on the part of the company to follow?

Following is the discussion and analysis about these issues:

1. *Did Moody's do Anything Wrong?*

Legally, as mentioned above, Moody's has committed no crime and it stands true, yet one cannot overlook its stance on ratings on residential mortgage-backed securities. The Chairman and Chief Executive Officer of Moody's, Raymond McDaniel, testified before the Financial Crisis Inquiry Commission, while Moody's did observe a trend in the declining quality of mortgage-backed securities as early as 2003. But it is neither the role of Moody's nor any other credit rating agency to serve as the 'gate-keeper' of the securities market. Moreover, their ratings are merely opinions, not definitive advice or recommendation on the stability of a particular financial instrument.

2. *How did Moody's Actions Affect the Stakeholders?*

The immediate beneficiaries of Moody's ratings were the securities issuers, those institutions which provided these securities made huge profits from their continued distribution throughout the market, and Moody's received a good amount of fees to rate said instruments.

An employee of Moody's indirectly described the competitive pressures which led to the lapses in the ratings systems:

He described RMBS (residential mortgage-backed securities) as the "worst team to work on at Moody's. It's difficult to maintain market share in a market that has become commoditised and where Moody's downgrade analysis means higher costs for issuers".

The losers were the investors who had great confidence in the quality of Moody's credit ratings and bought these securities with full confidence that these ratings were analytically sound and unbiased in any way. These investors were the most severely affected by the eventual downturn of the market.

3. *Did Moody's have a Conflict of Interest?*

In the current credit ratings agency business model, the conflict of interest is unavoidable though Moody's CEO Raymond McDaniel stated, that conflict of interest will arise whether rating agencies utilise an issuer or investor-pays system. Each party has an interest in influencing the determinations of the credit ratings agencies—from issuers to institutional investors. Additionally, the distinctions between issuers and investors does not have real meaning as parties in the present-day global financial system actively participate in both roles.

4. *What is the Responsibility of Moody's and Its Executives for the Financial Crisis?*

One cannot quantify the exact contribution of Moody's to the crisis, yet the conduct of this corporation as well as other credit ratings agencies was questionable in the structured finance market. They may legally deny their role in the crisis but it is true that these agencies ultimately failed in their responsibility to provide their customers with accurate information. They committed injustice by continuously providing such information despite internal misgivings.

5. *What Steps can be taken to Prevent a Recurrence of an Event like this?*

The industry transparency and regulation both governmental and self-imposed, are the areas that must be addressed if the mortgage crisis is to be prevented from re-emerging. The Financial Crisis Inquiry Commission's investigations had revealed to the general public the existence of a little understood *shadow banking system*. This refers to the operations of financial entities that are legal, yet so under-regulated that they escape the scrutiny and criticism to which their commercial banking counterparts are subject to. The combination of this practically unmonitored and unregulated banking sector with a mortgage-lending environment that was delving deeply into what would come to be known as the *subprime market*, representing those borrowers with poor credit histories and unsatisfactory debt to income ratios, were the primary components in the creation of the financial crisis.

The Dodd-Frank Wall Street Reform and Consumer Protection Act of 2010 directly addresses the vulnerabilities of the financial services industry and strengthens the regulatory authority, specifically in the areas which were responsible for the near collapse of the financial system. This disruption of the financial system simply reinforces profitability as the guiding principle of the corporations even at the expense of responsible and ethical corporate citizenship.

Source: The Crisis of Conscience, February 3, 2012, http://thecrisisofconscience.blogspot.in/2012/02/case-study-of-moodys-corp-and-subprime.html

POINTS TO REMEMBER

- Credit rating is an assessment of the creditworthiness of individuals and corporations. It is based upon the history of borrowing and repayment as well as the availability of assets and extent of liabilities.
- Over the years, credit rating has not been restricted to rating of debt instruments only, rather it has extended to rating of equity, corporate governance etc.
- CRAs' role has expanded with financial globalisation and has received an additional boost from Basel II which incorporates the ratings of CRAs into the rules for setting weights for credit risk.
- The primary purpose of obtaining a rating is to enhance access to private capital markets and lower debt issuance and interest costs.
- There are other indirect benefits from ratings for low-income countries—*(i) to foster FDI; (ii) to promote more vibrant local capital markets; and (iii) greater public sector financial transparency.*
- Rating process is initiated on receipt of a formal request (or mandate) from the prospective issuer. A rating team evaluates the business of the issuer and the issuer

is provided a list of information requirements along with the broad framework for discussions. Rating involves assessment of a number of qualitative factors with a view to estimate the future earnings of the issuer. A detailed analysis of the past financial statements is made to assess performance under 'real world' business dynamics. In the case of manufacturing companies, plant visits are also made. After completing the analysis, a Rating Report is prepared, which is then presented to the Rating Committee. If the issuer does not find the rating acceptable, it has a right to appeal for a review. The ratings are generally reviewed once every year.

- Rating parameters used for rating include industry evaluation, unit evaluation, technical evaluation, financial evaluation, statutory evaluation and management.
- The credit rating agencies in India offer varied services like mutual consulting services which comprise of operation upgradation, and risk management. They have special sections to carry on research and development work of the industries. Some popular rating agencies are CRISIL, ICRA, CARE, ONICRA, India Ratings (Fitch Group) and Brickwork India.
- Credit rating provides investors and debtors with important information regarding the creditworthiness of an individual, corporation, agency or even a sovereign government. It provides benefits like development and regulation of financial markets, risk estimation, transparency, and standardised evaluation.
- The credit rating agencies of India assign the following ratings to the companies: AAA denote highest safety; AA represents a high degree of safety; A provides adequate safety to the investments; BBB includes some risk factors; and BB provides sub-moderate safety to the investment.
- The Securities and Exchange Board of India (Credit Rating Agencies) Regulations, 1999 offer various guidelines with regard to the registration and functioning of the credit rating agencies in India. The registration procedure includes application for the establishment of a credit rating agency, matching the eligibility criteria and providing all the details required. They have to undergo a strict examination procedure with regard to the details furnished by them.
- Credit rating process has its own set of problems like—(i) inadequate skills by branches of rating agencies, (ii) inexperienced, unskilled or overloaded staff, (iii) past data, (iv) rating is not permanent, (v) possibility of inflated ratings, (vi) lack of accountability, (vii) risk of concealment of information, (viii) small differences in degrees of risk, and (ix) change in ratings.

KEY TERMS

- **Credit rating** is an assessment of the creditworthiness of individuals and corporations.
- **Rating process** is a symbolic indicator of rating agency's current opinion on the relative capability of the corporate entity concerning timely service debts and obligations, with reference to the instrument rated.

- **Debt rating** is rating of fixed income instruments.
- **Equity rating** is rating of variable income securities.
- **Corporate governance** rating is the rating of fairness and transparency of the company.

EXERCISES

Objective Questions

1. Tick the correct answer:

(a) Credit rating' is common for issuance of the following instruments:
  (i) Convertible and redeemable bonds
  (ii) Commercial paper
  (iii) Fixed deposits of NBFCs and limited companies
  (iv) All of the above

(b) 'AAA' in credit rating denotes:
  (i) Highest safety (ii) High safety
  (iii) Very high safety (iv) None of the above

(c) 'A' in credit rating signifies:
  (i) High safety (ii) Highest safety
  (iii) Adequate safety (iv) None of the above

(d) 'BBB' in credit rating signifies:
  (i) High safety (ii) Lowest safety
  (iii) Moderate safety (iv) None of the above

(e) 'D' grade is:
  (i) Positive (ii) Negative
  (iii) Neutral (iv) None of the above

Answers: (a) iv (b) i (c) iii (d) iii (e) ii

2. Fill in the blanks:

(a) CRAs' role has received an additional boost from ....
(b) Corporate governance rating is ....
(c) In case of .... , plant visit is made for credit rating.
(d) .... is a subsidiary of Standard and Poor.
(e) GVC rating of CRISIL stands for ....
(f) .... offers various guidelines with regard to the registration and functioning of the credit rating agencies in India.

Answers:

(a) Basel II
(b) Voluntary
(c) Manufacturing companies
(d) CRISIL
(e) Governance and Value Creation
(f) The Securities and Exchange Board of India (Credit Rating Agencies) Regulations, 1999

3. True or False:

(a) Credit rating is an assessment of the creditworthiness of individuals and corporations.

(b) Credit rating is a symbolic indicator of the opinion of the relative capability of a corporate entity.

(c) Credit rating has not been restricted to rating of debt only, rather it has been extended to rating of equity, corporate governance, etc.

(d) The issuer has an exit option in case of unacceptable rating.

(e) SEBI regulates credit rating agencies in India.

(f) Equity rating is compulsory in India.

(g) Treasury bills' rating is mandatory.

(h) Private limited companies are outside the rating umbrella.

Answers: (a) True (b) True (c) True (d) True (e) True
(f) False (g) False (h) True

Short Questions

1. State three benefits of credit rating.
2. Define credit rating.
3. What is debt rating?
4. What is equity grading of ICRA?
5. List the key rating parameters.

Critical Thinking Questions

1. "Over the years, the process of credit rating has undergone a significant change in terms of its nature and scope". Explain.
2. "Credit rating not only develops the financial markets but also regulates them". Discuss.
3. "Credit rating is one of the most important fee-based financial services across the globe". Elaborate.
4. "Grading of instruments based on their rating has changed the definition of sound company in the present times". Discuss.
5. "The real beneficiaries of the credit rating are common public". Justify.
6. "Rating is as reliable as you want it to be". Do you agree?
7. "The rating agencies need to be regulated in all regards of rating". Discuss.
8. "Credit rating process is considered to be subjective in nature". Prove.

Descriptive Questions

1. Throw some light on the importance of credit rating.
2. Discuss the process of credit rating in detail.
3. What are the various instruments which are rated by the rating agencies in India?
4. Explain the registration process of the credit rating agencies in India.
5. What are the different ways of classifying financial markets?

6. What are the key innovations that have redefined the financial system in India?
7. What are the major issues and challenges faced by the Indian financial services industry?

PROJECT EXERCISE

Rating Analysis

Make sector-wise groups and each group should not have more than 5–6 students. Every group is required to pick up two comparative companies in a particular sector and rate them based on the parameters as defined in the text. Find out their standing for debt, equity and corporate governance. Compare your rating with the rating companies and study the gap areas for future reference. Also, discuss the regulatory provisions for credit rating industry in India in the said context.

REVIEW CASE

Sound or Unsound!

New Age is a leading cloth manufacturing company. Its credit policy is to sell goods on credit with a credit term of 30 days. It manages to generate revenues worth ₹1 million with the present credit. The management knows that if it loses its credit policy by 10 more days, it can generate sales worth ₹0.5 million which will give it a strong foothold in the market and help to expand in future. For this, they are planning to raise a loan of ₹0.2 million from the bank for working capital and therefore, thinking of getting a credit rating for the said purpose.

In today's global marketplace, business moves at a fast pace and therefore, decisions must be made spontaneously. Competitors do not rest, and if you hesitate to act quickly, the result can be disastrous. They know that companies that seek credit from banks, or give credit to accounts, are part of the vast global network of commercial borrowers and lenders. Every day, among the millions of businesses that operate in every corner of the world, billions of dollars in cash are loaned, and goods and services worth billions are provided on credit. To create a mark and have a better credibility, companies must have a credit rating signifying the creditworthiness of the business enterprise.

Credit rating agency gains access to your professional and objective source of business and its credit information. This information is critical to good decisions, especially in financing. When your company applies for a loan or for credit, your good business credit rating serves as assurance to your creditors that you are a good credit risk. Banks check your credit rating before approving you for loans, including a mortgage or working capital loan. A variety of businesses check your credit rating before doing business with you. Your credit report affects many parts of your business, so it is important that the information included is accurate and positive. Your credit rating is the sole source of information for your financial soundness—high credit rating shows that you have positive information on your financial part while low credit rating indicates the presence of negative information.

Maintaining a good credit rating is important and your company can achieve this in three ways:

- Being fiscally sound and paying all debts on time
- Reporting all favourable data and changes to a credit reporting agency
- Requesting your company's credit reports, and examining them objectively.

New Age's Income and Expenditure Forecasts for next three years, (2014–16) is given in Table 16.7.

TABLE 16.7 New Age's Income and Expenditure Forecasts (2014–16)

Year	*Credit sales* ₹	*Credit purchases* ₹	*Manufacturing expenses* ₹	*Office expenses* ₹	*Selling expenses* ₹
2013	9,00,000	3,60,000	90,000	40,000	20,000
2014	11,00,000	4,50,000	80,000	30,000	10,500
2015	12,00,000	3,50,000	1,00,000	40,500	20,500
2016	12,50,000	3,00,000	85,000	30,500	20,000

Cash balance on 1st January, 2014 is ₹80,000. The company has a policy to maintain a minimum cash balance of ₹1,00,000. Cash sales for 2014, 2015 and 2016 are ₹2,50,000, 2,50,000 and 2,60,000, respectively. Period of credit allowed by suppliers is 2 months.

Issues for Discussion

(i) What other information will the rating agency need for debt rating in the present case?

(ii) What is your comment on the rating of New Age?

(iii) How credible are these credit ratings?

(iv) Discuss the effective criteria to rate debts in the market.

(v) Is credit rating really relevant at a regulatory level?

REFERENCES

Acharya, V.V. and Richardson, M., Eds. (2009), *Restoring Financial Stability: How to Repair a Failed System*, Hoboken, N.J.: Wiley Finance.

Becker, B. and Milbourn, T. (2008), "Reputation and Competition: Evidence from the Credit Rating Industry', *Working Paper* 09–051, Harvard Business School, Cambridge, MA.

IOSCO (International Organization of Securities Commissions) (2008), "The Role of Credit Rating Agencies in Structured Finance Markets", *Technical Committee Final Report*.

Joint Forum (2009), *Stocktaking on the Use of Credit Ratings,* Basel: Bank for International Settlements.

Veron, N. (2009), "Rating Agencies: An Information Privilege Whose Time Has Passed", *Bruegel Policy Contribution 2009/01*, Briefing Paper for the European Parliament's ECON Committee.

www.brickworkindia.com

www.careratings.com

www.crisil.com

www.thecrisisofconscience.blogspot.in

www.duffandphelps.com

www.icra.in

www.indiaratings.co.in

www.sebi.gov.in

CHAPTER

17

Corporate Restructuring

How do you make money? Spinoffs, split-ups, liquidations, mergers and acquisitions.

— **Mario Gabelli**

LEARNING OBJECTIVES

This chapter discusses the following:

- Concept and scope of corporate restructuring
- Forms of corporate restructuring
- Types of mergers
- Motives of mergers and acquisitions
- Process of mergers and acquisitions
- Valuation methods of mergers and acquisitions
- Regulatory framework of M&A in India

INTRODUCTION

Growth is vital for every business organisation. It may be attained either internally or externally. *Internal growth* is achieved through capital investment process whereas *external growth* is accomplished through various business combinations, viz. mergers, amalgamations and acquisitions. These business combinations are an important feature of corporate structural changes and have played an important role in the external growth of a number of leading companies over the world. Therefore, corporate restructuring is mainly done in response to changes in the external and internal environment to create maximum value for the stakeholders.

Restructuring a corporate entity is often seen as a necessity for the future growth of the company at times when the present structure does not efficiently manage the resources and yield desired results for the company. *For example,* a corporate restructuring may call for spinning off some departments into SBUs for more effective management as well as taking advantage of tax benefits but corporate restructuring—financial or operational—does not always happen for growth motives and result in the necessary reforms by the management. The promoter shareholders and the management may have their own interest prevailing for an extended time period during which minority shareholders suffer an erosion of value. A number of East Asian corporations, struggling with debt, nearly collapsed during the financial crisis of 1997. However, many have managed to avoid both repayment and restructuring, and remain overly-indebted and invested in unprofitable businesses[1].

CORPORATE RESTRUCTURING: CONCEPT AND SCOPE

Corporate restructuring is "the process of redesigning one or more aspects of a company". The process of reorganising a company can take place due to a number of factors such as competitive positioning, survival threats in an adverse economic climate, or diversification. Corporate restructuring entails a fundamental change in a company's business or financial structure, designed to increase the company's value to shareholders. It is often divided into two parts—financial restructuring, and operational restructuring.

Financial restructuring implies change in the capital structure of the firm, like increasing debt component in the capital mix to reduce the overall cost of capital of the firm. If the firm is sick or plunging towards bankruptcy, this financial restructuring results in complete reorganisation.

Operational restructuring is the process of increasing the economic viability of the underlying business model. *Examples include* mergers, the sale of divisions or discontinuance of product line, or cost-reduction.

In most of the cases, particularly turn-arounds and bankruptcy situations, both financial and operational restructuring must occur simultaneously to save the business.

Different Dimensions

Corporate restructuring has different layers attached to its dimension and it can be defined in number of ways. These are discussed below:

- Any change in the business portfolio through an inorganic route;
- Any non-ordinary change in the capital structure of a company;
- Any change in the ownership of or control over the management of the company, or a combination thereof.

(i) *Change in the Business Portfolio through an Inorganic Route*

- Tata Motors' acquisition of Jaguar Land Rover from Ford, through Jaguar Land Rover Limited is categorised as 'corporate restructuring'.

1. http://people.stern.nyu.edu/igiddy/restructuring.htm

Tata Motors launched Indigo and Indica which lead to an expansion of its business portfolio. However, these products were launched from Tata Motor's own manufacturing capacity through an organic route. Hence, it is not 'corporate restructuring'.

(ii) *Non-ordinary Change in the Capital Structure of a Company*

- An initial public issue, or a follow-on public issue, or buy-back of equity shares, would permanently reduce the capital structure of a company and would thus amount to 'corporate restructuring'.

If the debt is repaid as a planned activity to reduce liabilities, then such changes in the capital structure do not amount to 'capital restructuring'.

Borrowing of a significant amount of term loan again does not qualify to be 'corporate restructuring'.

(iii) *Any Change in the Ownership of a Company or Control over its Management*

- Merger of two or more companies belonging to different promoters.
- Demerger of a company into two or more with control to other.
- Acquisition of a company.
- Sell-off of a company or its substantial assets.
- Delisting of a company.

FORMS OF CORPORATE RESTRUCTURING

As discussed above, the major forms of corporate restructuring can be classified into *financial* and *operational restructuring*. A brief overview of each form of restructuring is given in Figure 17.1.

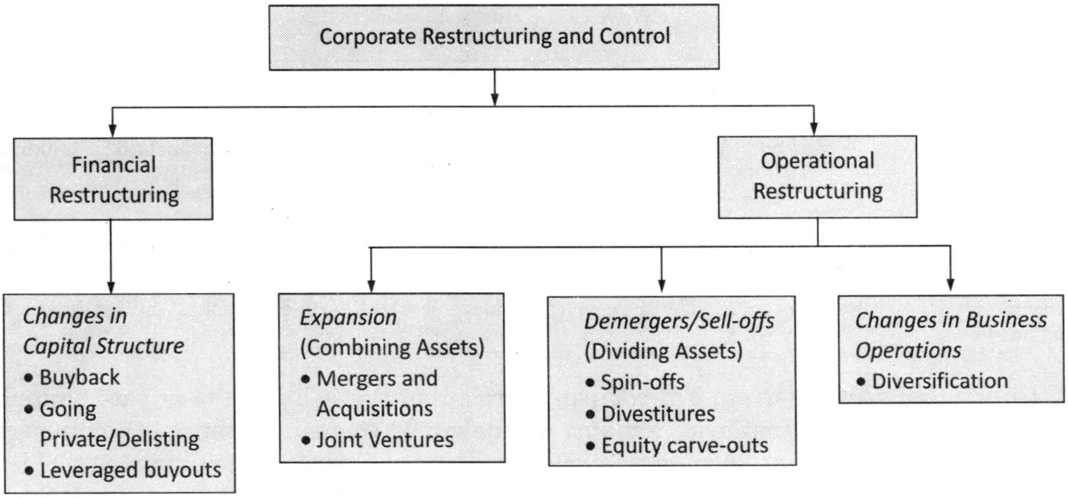

Figure 17.1 Forms of Corporate Restructuring

A. Financial Restructuring

In this restructuring, the capital structure as well as ownership structure of the firm gets affected. It takes place in the following ways:

1. *Buy-back of equity shares:* A firm buybacks its common shares through an open-offer. This is done by the promoters mainly to increase the controlling stake in the company.

Table 17.1 shows a list of NASDAQ companies that had initiated or extended 'share buy-back programmes' that could shrink the number of shares outstanding by more than 10%.

TABLE 17.1 List of NASDAQ companies for Buy-back (as on 2nd August, 2013)

Company	*Recent Price*	*52-Week High/Low*	*Market Cap.*	*Buy-back*	*% of Market Cap.*	*Projected 2014 EPs*	*2014 P/E*	*Dividend Yield*
CBS Corp. (CBS)	$52.40	$53.84/$31.84	$32.16B	$6B	19%	$3.40	15.4	0.9%
Halliburton (HAL)	$45.54	$46.66/$29.83	$42.13B	$5B	12%	$4.07	11.2	1.1%
Time Warner Cable (TWC)	$115.72	$119.46/$83.83	$33.67B	$4B	12%	$7.67	15.1	2.2%
Juniper Networks (JNPR)	$21.51	$22.98/$15.62	$10.82B	$2B	18%	$1.33	16.2	N/A
Maxim Integrated Produces (WXIM)	$28.31	$33.67/$25.54	$8.21B	$1B	12%	$2.03	13.9	3.7%
Lincoln Electric Holdings (LECO)	$58.65	$63.29/$37.63	$4.87B	$870M	18%	$3.87	15.2	1.3%
PulteGroup (PHM)	$16.50	$24.47/$10.82	$6.36B	$352M	6%	$1.49	11.1	1.2%
Intuitive Surgical (ISRG)	$388.97	$586/$387	$15.45B	$1.5B	10%	$17.60	22.1	N/A
Iconix Brands Group (ICON)	$32.71	$32.95/$16.99	$1.87B	$300M	16%	$2.46	13.3	N/A
Platinum Underwriters Holdings (PTP)	$57.80	$59.79/$37.66	$1.69B	$250M	15%	$3.96	14.6	0.6%
Forrester Research (FORR)	$35.24	$39.77/$24.88	$723M	$80M	11%	$1.08	32.6	1.7%

Source: http://www.nasdaq.com/article/these-companies-are-scrambling-to-buy-back-20-billion-in-stock-cm264136.

2. *Going Private/Delisting:* The company turns from public limited to private limited, i.e., it gets delisted and no more remains a widely-held company. Now it is not subject to compulsory obligations such as financial reporting to investors, holding shareholder meetings, etc. In December 2013, Michael Dell—CEO of Dell Computers, announced to take Dell Private[2].

2. *As quoted on 9th December, 2013,* http://www.forbes.com/sites/nathanvardi/2013/09/12/michael-dell-we-are-going-back-to-our-roots-taking-dell-private.

3. *Leveraged Buyouts (LBOs):* It is the acquisition of another company using a significant amount of borrowed money (bonds or loans). These loans are often secured against the assets of the company. In an LBO, there is usually a ratio of 90% debt to 10% equity. Some of the famous LBO deals include $8 billion Tata bid for Corus, 271 million pounds for UK brand Tetley by Tatas, and Suzlon Energy's acquisition of Belgium's EVE Holding for $565 million[3].

B. Operational Restructuring

It is the process of increasing the efficiency of undertaking through various forms.

1. *Expansion:* It includes activities that help firms to expand and grow through external means, i.e., by acquiring other businesses. Mergers and Acquisitions (M&As) and joint ventures are different forms by which a firm can expand externally.

(i) *Merger:* It is a combination of two or more firms into one, where the assets and liabilities of all the firms are vested into one surviving firm. This surviving firm can be one of the existing firms or it can be a new entity.

- When all the firms are merged into the surviving firms, it is called as merger through *absorption*. *For example,* absorption of Tata Fertilisers Ltd. (TFL) by Tata Chemicals Ltd. (TCL). TCL, an acquiring company (a buyer), survived after merger while TFL, an acquired company (a seller), ceased to exist. TFL transferred its assets, liabilities and shares to TCL[4].
- When all the firms are combined to form a new entity, it is a case of merger through 'consolidation' or an 'amalgamation'. *For example,* merger of Hindustan Computers Ltd., Hindustan Instruments Ltd., Indian Software Company Ltd. and Indian Reprographics Ltd. into an entirely new company called HCL Ltd[5].

(ii) *Acquisition:* It basically means buying of assets (a plant or a division) of a company, acquiring a brand of a company or acquiring ownership or controlling rights in a company through share purchase. The last one more prevails in regard to business combinations.

Despite major geopolitical and financial headwinds, Asia-Pacific (APAC) M&A activity in H1 2022 had been robust. With 648 deals of a total value of US$403b, M&A in H1 2022 may have seen a drop compared to this time last year (down 14% by value and 16% by volume), but activity is significantly up compared to H1 2020 (up 85% by value and 29% by volume). Elevated deal volumes and values and an increased focus within the APAC region suggested that APAC companies were leveraging M&A as a vehicle to transform their businesses. Following China (US$144b), which traditionally tops the table of the most active M&A market in APAC, Australia had an extremely active start to the year with the combined value of its outbound, inbound and domestic deals jumping to US$48b, an increase of 123% compared to the average of the last deal cycle (2015–19). Looking at sector performance, cross-sector deals comprised of 68% of total deal volume and 55% of the total deal value for APAC in H1 2022. Technology

3. http://articles.economictimes.indiatimes.com/2006-10-19/news/27441254_1_lbo-spv-tata-bid.
4. http://business.gov.in/growing_business/mergers_acq.php
5. http://business.gov.in/.ibid.

was the most sought-after sector, with technology-targeted deals accounting for 21% of cross-sector deals. The Power and utilities sector also saw increased deal activity from other sectors (US$30b, up 122% against 2021 and 204% against the average of the last deal cycle (2015–19)), driven by increased investment in renewable energy companies.[6]

Box 17.1 differentiates between Acquisitions and Takeovers.

BOX 17.1: ACQUISITIONS VS. TAKEOVERS

Though acquisition and takeover have a similar connotation in corporate restructuring, acquisitions basically are willingly done, whereas takeovers are done hostile. A 'forced' acquisition is called a takeover.

(iii) *Joint venture:* A *joint venture* is when two or more firms come together for a common business. Here, an independent legal entity is formed with participation from each of the organisations for a limited time period. The participation can be in the form of funds, expertise, manpower, etc.

2. *Demergers/Sell-offs:* It involves reducing assets. Major types of sell-offs are:

(i) *Spin-offs:* When a parent company forms a new legal entity out of its existing business, it is a spin-off. The existing shareholders are given the shares of the new entity on a pro-rata basis and they continue to hold the same proportion of ownership in the new entity. *For example,* a diversified company may have a fast-growing software business that is largely ignored or not valued by the market because it is a small part of a large company. Thus, the spin-off of such a business into a separate company could enhance the total value of the parent company, since it would be ultimately valued as a part of the current total company, like Wipro Ltd. made its IT division into a separate company. However, a spin-off does not involve any cash transactions and only shares are transferred.

There are two variants of spin-offs—*split-off* and *split-up*.

In the *first case,* some existing shareholders receive stock in the new company in exchange for the parent company stock.

In the *second case,* the entire firm is broken into a series of spin-offs so that the parent company no longer exists and the new company survives. Reliance Industries Ltd. demerger in 2005–06 is a prominent example of split-up wherein the parent company was divided into two group companies, one owned by Mukesh Ambani and another owned by Anil Ambani.

(ii) *Divestiture:* A *divestiture* involves a sale of a part (like plant or a unit) or assets of a firm to an outside party to get rid of unproductive, unprofitable or non-performing assets and use the cash received for business expansion.

(iii) *Equity carve-outs:* It is a variation of divestiture and also known as an *IPO carve-out* or a *subsidiary IPO*. Here, the parent company sells its portion to the public or outsider in an initial public offering. The carve-out creates a new legal entity whose ownership remains with the parent company.

---

6. https://www.ey.com/en_gl/news/2022/08/asia-pacific-m-and-a-activity-remains-robust-in-2022-as-companies-look-to-accelerate-their-transformation.

3. ***Change in business:*** This form of restructuring takes place as a part of normal growth plans of a company in the form of diversification, wherein new product lines are added to the main business. Almost every company has added new business lines to its main business for the company's growth.

TYPES OF MERGERS

Mergers are of the following types:

1. Horizontal Merger

This is a combination or joining of two or more firms in the same area of business. For example, two manufacturers of toothpaste may merge with each other. The merger of Reliance Communications Ltd. with Aircel is an *example* of horizontal merger.

2. Vertical Merger

This is a combination of two or more firms involved in different stages of the production or distribution. *For example,* a laptop manufacturing company joins with a laptop marketing company. Pepsi's merger with restaurant chains that it supplies with beverages is a vertical merger.

3. Conglomerate Merger

This is a combination of two or more firms which are engaged in unrelated lines of business activity. Merging of different businesses like manufacturing of cement products and electronics products is such a case. *For example,* L&T and Voltas Ltd.

4. Congeneric Merger

This is achieved by acquiring a firm that is in the same general industry but neither in the same line of business nor a supplier or customer. *For example,* the merger of a machine tool manufacturer with the manufacturer of industrial pump systems. Citigroup's acquisition of Travellers Insurance is an example of congeneric merger. They both were in the financial services industry but had different product lines.

MOTIVES OF MERGERS AND ACQUISITIONS

Mergers and acquisitions take place for many strategic business reasons but the overriding goal of any merger and acquisition is the maximisation of the owners' wealth. In general, mergers and acquisitions are intended to the following:

1. ***Higher growth:*** This is one of the most common motives for mergers. It may be cheaper and less risky for the acquiring company to merge with another company in a similar line of business than to expand operations internally as it is much faster to grow by acquisition. This is particularly relevant when its internal growth is constrained due to shortage of resources.

Therefore, a company can acquire more resources and production facilitie through mergers and acquisitions. Companies can easily combine to leverage costl manufacturing operations (as in the acquisition of Volvo by Ford). This becomes all th more important for entering in new products/markets. Acquiring an existing compan or companies with requisite infrastructure and skills help the company to grow quickly

2. *Increased profitability:* Mergers and acquisitions enhance the profitability of th business because a combination of two or more companies always results in highe profits due to better economies of scale, synergy benefits and efficient utilisation c resources (Box 17.2).

BOX 17.2: "SYNERGY" BENEFITS

One of the most important motive for mergers and acquisitions is to have synergic benefits. Synergy occurs when the whole is greater than sum of its parts. Mathematically, it can be represented as "1 + 1 = 3" or as "2 + 2 = 5".

In the context of mergers, 'synergy' means the performance of firms after a merger (in certain areas and overall) will be better than the sum of their performances before the merger. *For example,* a larger merged company may be able to order larger quantities and obtain greater discounts from the suppliers.

There can be two types of synergy. The first type of synergy results in *'economies of scale'*, which refers to decreased costs. Another type of synergy results in increased revenues such as *'cross-selling'*.

Economies of scale imply that the total cost of production of services or products is lowered as the volume increases; the company therefore, maximizes total profits.

Cross-selling means selling each other's products to different customers. If some of the products and services of merged companies differ, then cross-selling those products and services to the other firm's customer base can be a cost-effective way to increase sales. This will also increase customer loyalty due to higher customer satisfaction.

3. *Diversification:* Diversification is an external growth strategy and is also motive for a merger. It means growth through the combination of firms in unrelate business line. *For example,* if an organisation operates in a volatile industry, it ma decide to undertake a merger to hedge itself against fluctuations in its own market. I results in reduction of total risks through reduction in operations' cycle. The combine firm always has better management control which strengthens the firm's capacity t withstand unforeseen economic factors more confidently.

4. *Competitive strength:* Companies may decide to merge to have a bette distribution or marketing network. There is an increased firm's competitive strengt on account of mergers and acquisitions as it increases the company's market powe A merger can increase the market share and thereby, the profitability of the merge firm which results in an enhanced bargaining power of the firm.

5. *Survival:* No company would like to willingly give up its identity to anothe company but sometimes it is the only option left in order for the company to surviv A number of companies used mergers and acquisitions to grow and survive durin the global financial crisis from 2008 to 2012. During the financial crisis, many banks merged in order to reduce their loaded debt.

6. *Tax benefits:* Tax benefits can also be the underlying motive for a merger in certain situations. For example, when a firm with accumulated losses and unabsorbed depreciation merges with a profit-making firm, tax benefits are utilised better because its accumulated losses/unabsorbed depreciation can be set off against the profits of the profit-making firm.

PROCESS OF MERGERS AND ACQUISITIONS

The process of merger and acquisition is the most challenging and most critical in corporate restructuring as one wrong decision move can land you into a loss. Therefore, due diligence is must in the process. Following stages are involved in evaluating the decision for mergers and acquisitions:

Stage I: Pre-planning

This is the foundation stage of mergers and acquisitions which involves evaluating one's own position. It consists of following steps:

1. *Planning:* It includes the analysis of industry-specific and firm-specific information. The acquiring firm should conduct a SWOT analysis and review its objective of acquisition accordingly. It must have industry data on market growth, nature of competition, availability of capital and labour, regulations, etc. This will help the company in developing the appropriate product-market strategies and also in identifying the viable business units.

2. *Search and Screening:* Search focuses on how and where to look for suitable companies for acquisition. Screening is the process of short-listing the suitable one from available lot and obtaining detailed information about each of them.

Stage II: Target Specific Evaluation

Here, the target company (company to be acquired) is valued on various parameters. It comprises of following steps:

1. *Business valuation:* Business valuation or assessment includes evaluation of both present and future market value of the target company. A thorough research is done on the history of the company with regard to organisational structure, market share, distribution channel, corporate culture, specific business strengths, and credibility in the market. The basic objective is to find out whether the proposed company is right or not for a successful merger.

2. *Financial evaluation:* Though, in a way, it is a part of business evaluation only but it is done separately because this is the most important pillar of the deal. This is the evaluation of the proposed company on financial parameters such as earnings and cash flows, risk, the maximum price payable to the target company and the best way to finance the merger. In a competitive market situation, the current market value is the correct and fair value of the share of the target firm. The target firm may, in fact, expect the offer price to be more than the current market value of its share since it may expect that merger benefits will accrue to the acquiring firm.

Stage III: Executing the Deal

This is the stage where necessary steps are taken to finalise the deal.

1. ***Proposal phase:*** Proposal phase is a phase in which the company sends a proposal for a merger or an acquisition with complete details of the deal including the strategies, amount, and the commitments. Most of the time, this proposal is sent through a non-binding offer document.

2. ***Planning exit:*** When any company decides to sell its operations, it has to undergo the stage of exit planning. The company has to take firm decision as to when and how to make the exit in an organised and profitable manner. In the process, the management has to evaluate all financial and other business issues like taking a decision of full sale or partial sale, etc.

3. ***Structuring business deal:*** After finalising the merger and the exit plans, the new entity or the take-over company has to devise suitable marketing and other strategies to enhance the business and its credibility. The key focus is on structuring the deal.

4. ***Implementation of deal:*** The structured deal is implemented here. It includes the entire process of preparing the document, signing the agreement, and negotiating the deal. It also defines the parameters of the future relationship between the two.

Stage IV: Post-deal Integration and Synergy

This is the post-effect stage of the deal.

1. ***Stage of integration:*** After signing the deal, this stage includes both the companies coming together with their own parameters and combines their operations or activities for future business.

2. ***Operating the venture:*** After entering into the venture, it is equally important to operate the venture. This operation involves meeting the said and pre-defined expectations of all the companies involved in the process. It basically includes all the essential measures and activities carried out to make the business prosper.

The stage-wise representation of M&A is depicted in Figure 17.2.

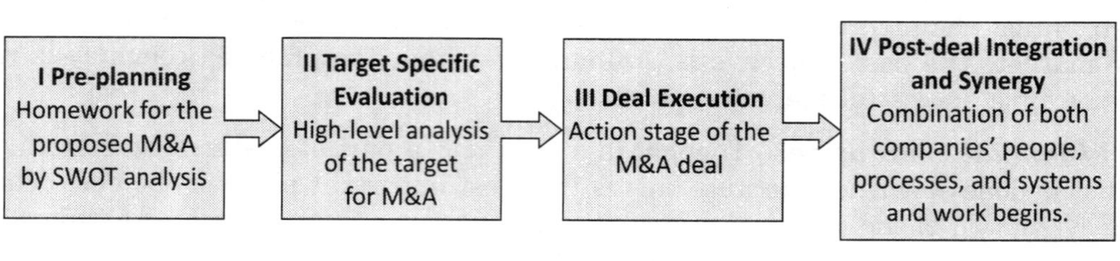

Figure 17.2 Process Chart of M&A

MERGERS AND ACQUISITIONS VALUATION METHODS

Before we decide on the valuation computation, we must know what are we trying to value? The reason is that the valuation of a going concern is different from the valuation of a company expected to be liquidated.

Discounted-Cash-Flow (DCF) method is the most commonly used valuation method in M&A. Besides DCF approach, other methods of valuation used are *market multiples of peer firms, book value, market value, and comparable multiples.* These methods are discussed below and presented in Figure 17.3.

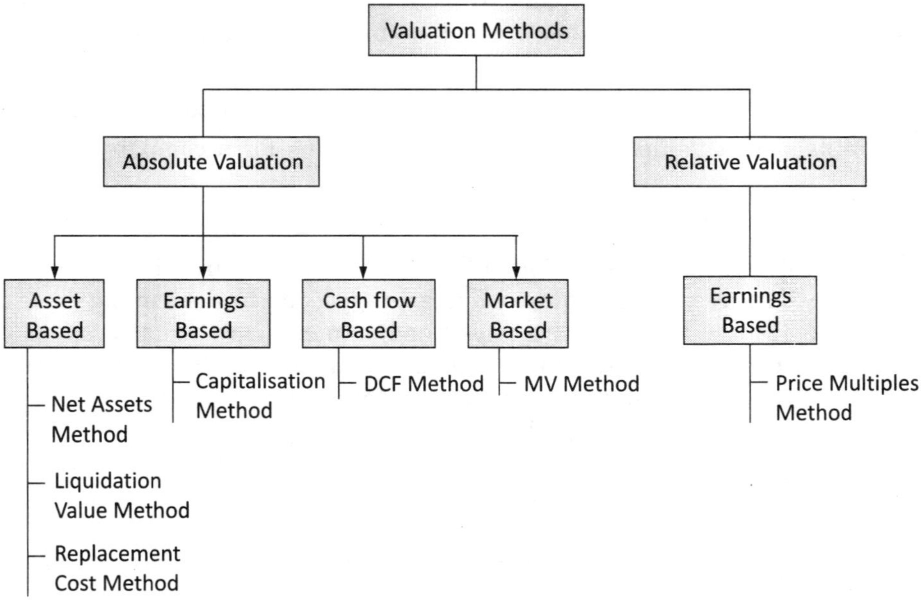

Figure 17.3 M&A Valuation Methods

1. Net Assets Method

In case of privately held companies, market information is not available. Therefore, net assets method is used in these acquisitions. The comparative analysis is done of the target company is carried out with regard to its total assets size and its outstanding liabilities to have the net purchase price.

ILLUSTRATION E'n'T has agreed to acquire 100% ownership (equity) of FinCorp. for ₹100 million. FinCorp. is a private limited company has ₹25 million of outstanding liabilities. What is the purchase price as per net assets method?

Solution:

Amount paid to acquire FinCorp. = ₹100 million
Outstanding liabilities = 25 million
Total purchase price = ₹125 million

Note: E'n'T has acquired FinCorp. based on the assumption that FinCorp.'s business will generate a Net Value of ₹125 million.

2. Liquidation Value Method

This is used in case of bankruptcy or sick companies. The liquidation value is the amount of proceeds that could be realised by a stockholder if a company ceased operations, if all assets were sold at prevailing market prices, and if all liabilities and tax obligations were satisfied.

3. Replacement–Cost Value Method

Replacement value is the cost that would be incurred if one tries to replicate all of the assets and liabilities of a company by building them or purchasing them on the market. Replacement cost estimates are not highly reliable and are often drawn by simplistic rules of thumb.

Liquidation value ⟶ Minimum value for a company

Replacement value ⟶ Maximum value for a company

4. Capitalisation Method

This method involves the 'capitalisation of historical earnings'. In this method, the past earnings of the business to be acquired are averaged out to determine the expected earnings in the future. Within the analysis, adjustments are usually made for the owner's compensation as per the management salaries (for the buyer's anticipated salary if the buyer is going to be an owner-operator/manager, or for a manager if the business is going to be operated in his absence).

A reasonable 'Return on Investment' (ROI) on the selling company's book value of assets is calculated and subtracted from the adjusted earnings. The remaining earnings are called *excess earnings* and represent the earning power of the assets. These 'excess earnings' are capitalised at an appropriate rate, related to the risk of owning the business.

ILLUSTRATION A private equity firm is interested in acquiring Ram & Co. Ltd. but being a public unlisted company, its market figures are not available. Therefore, they wish to arrive at its value for the acquisition using capitalisation method, assuming its own salary benefits as ₹50,000.

Ram & Co.'s past three years income are ₹18,000, 22,000 and 26,000 respectively. The owners of the company are drawing a salary of ₹70,000. The net book value of assets of the company is ₹60,000 (furniture and fixtures, plant and equipment). Expected ROI is 6% and the capitalisation rate is 20%.

Calculate the capitalised value of the business.

Solution:

Net Income	=	₹22,000 (average, last 3 years)
Add: Seller's Salary	=	70,0000
Less: Buyer's Anticipated Salary	=	50,000
Adjusted Earnings	=	42,000
Net Book Value of Assets	=	60,000

Fair Return on Assets	=	3,600 (ROI of 6%)
Excess Earnings	=	38,400 (42,000 – 3,600)
Capitalisation of Excess Earnings	=	₹192,000 (38,400/.20) (20% Cap. Rate)
Add: Book Value of Assets	=	60,000
Value of Business	=	2,52,000

5. Discounted-Cash-Flow Method

The Discounted-Cash-Flow method in an M&A deal attempts to determine the value of the company (or 'enterprise value') by computing the present value of cash flows over the life of the company. It involves discounting the future expected cash flows over a forecast period and comparing it with the investment price to arrive at the decision. Basically, NPV approach is used here, as followed in capital budgeting decision.

If the Net Present Value of the investment is positive, we add value through a merger and acquisition, and vice-versa.

ILLUSTRATION Masters Corporation is considering acquiring Alta Company for ₹1,00,000 in cash. Alta's cost of capital is 16%. Based on market analysis, a targeted cost of capital for Alta is 12%. Masters Corporation has estimated that Alta can generate ₹8,000 of free cash flows over the next 12 years.

Using Net Present Value, advise should Masters Corp. acquire Alta?

Solution:

Initial Cash Outlay	=	₹1,00,000
FCF of ₹8,000 × 6.19*	=	49,520
Net Present Value	=	₹ –50,480

*Present value factor of annuity at 12%, 12 years.

Based on NPV, Masters Corp. should not acquire Alta since there is a negative NPV for this investment (Box 17.3).

BOX 17.3: FREE CASH FLOW

One of the most reliable cash flows for valuations is Free Cash Flow (FCF). FCF accounts for future investments that must be made to sustain cash flow. FCF is considered to be more reliable than EBITDA and other earnings-based income streams. The basic formula for calculating Free Cash Flow (FCF) is:

FCF = EBIT (1 – t) + Depreciation – Capital Expenditures ± Net Working Capital

6. Market Value Method

This method is used in case of publicly held companies. The belief behind using MV method is that market value reflects all public information about the company and its industry. Merger negotiations rarely settle at a price below the market price of the target. On average, mergers and tender offers command a 30%–50% premium over the price.

Here, first the value (the equity) of the firm (E) is found out as:

Stock price × Outstanding shares

Then the market value of debt (D) is found out as:

The price per bond × Number of bonds outstanding

Finally, the value of the enterprise (V) is calculated as sum of E + D.

ILLUSTRATION A&Z Ltd. is a public listed company has 25,00,000 shares outstanding.

Its market price per share is ₹50.00 and the fair market value of its debt is ₹20 million. Calculate the market value of the firm for the proposed acquisition by New Age Ltd.

Solution:

Market value of stock (25,00,000 × ₹50.00) = ₹125 million

Market value of debt = ₹20 million

Total value = ₹145 million

7. Price Multiples

Price multiples are a relative valuation method because they are used as an industry analysis, i.e., peer group comparison.

The *Price-to-Earnings (P/E) ratio*, which is equal to a company's market price per share divided by its Earnings Per Share (EPS), is the most widely used earnings multiple. It provides an indication of how much investors are willing to pay for a company's earnings. *For example,* a company whose P/E ratio is 18 is said to be selling for 18 times earnings, i.e., investors are willing to pay ₹18 for each ₹1 of current or future earnings. Companies with high earnings growth prospects usually have high P/E ratios.

Another price multiple is the *price-to-book (P/Book) ratio.* It indicates the relative premium that investors are willing to pay over the book value of their equity investment in a company. The company's book value is highly dependent upon the management's accounting decisions, therefore, the P/B ratio is used selectively and not often considered as a viable valuation method for most companies, except for financial institutions and insurance companies. Box 17.4 explains the "exchange ratio".

BOX 17.4: EXCHANGE RATIO/SWAP RATIO

It is very important to find out the exchange ratio for paying in case of a merger or acquisition.

Suppose, Company A buys Company B. Company A's stock sells for ₹75 per share while B's stock sells for ₹40. As per the merger terms, A offers ₹35 per share.

The exchange ratio is 0.467 (₹35/₹75).

This shows that Company A exchanges 0.467 shares of its stock for one share of Company B.

REGULATORY FRAMEWORK OF MERGERS & ACQUISITIONS IN INDIA

Mergers and acquisitions are regulated under various laws in India. The basic objective of these laws is to make the process transparent and protect the interest of shareholders. The various regulations are discussed below:

I. The Companies Act, 2013 and 1956

The Acts lay down the following legal procedure for mergers or acquisitions:

- *Permission for merger:* Two or more companies can amalgamate only when the amalgamation is permitted under their Memorandum of Association. Also, the acquiring company should have the permission in its Object clause to carry on the business of the acquired company. If these provisions are not there in the Memorandum of Association, it is necessary to seek the permission of the shareholders, board of directors and the Company Law Board before initiating the merger.
- *Information to the stock exchange:* The acquiring and the acquired companies should inform the stock exchanges (where they are listed) about the merger.
- *Draft approval by board of directors:* The board of directors of the individual companies should approve the draft proposal for amalgamation and authorise the managements of the companies to go ahead with the proposal.
- *Application in the High Court:* An application for approving the draft amalgamation proposal duly approved by the board of directors of the individual companies should be made to the High Court.
- *Shareholders' and creditors' meetings:* The individual companies should hold separate meetings of their shareholders and creditors for approving the amalgamation scheme. At least, 75% of shareholders and creditors in separate meeting, voting in person or by proxy, must approve to the scheme.
- *Sanction by the High Court:* After the approval of the shareholders and creditors on the petitions of the companies, the High Court will pass an order, sanctioning the amalgamation scheme after it is satisfied that the scheme is fair and reasonable. The date of the court's hearing will be published in two newspapers, and also, the regional director of the Company Law Board will be intimated.
- *Filing of the Court order:* After the Court order, its certified true copies will be filed with the Registrar of Companies.
- *Transfer of assets and liabilities:* The assets and liabilities of the acquired company will be transferred to the acquiring company in accordance with the approved scheme, with effect from the specified date.
- *Payment by cash or securities:* As per the proposal, the acquiring company will exchange shares and debentures and/or cash for the shares and debentures of the acquired company. These securities will be listed on the stock exchange[7].

7. http://business.gov.in/op. cit.

II. The Competition Act, 2002

The Act regulates the various forms of business combinations through Competition Commission of India. Under the Act, no person or enterprise shall enter into a combination, in the form of an acquisition, merger or amalgamation, which causes or is likely to cause an appreciable adverse effect on competition in the relevant market and such a combination shall be void.

Enterprises intending to enter into a combination may give notice to the Commission but this notification is voluntary. The Commission while regulating a 'combination' shall consider the following factors:

- Actual and potential competition through imports
- Extent of entry barriers into the market
- Level of combination in the market
- Degree of countervailing power in the market
- Possibility of the combination to significantly and substantially increase prices or profits
- Extent of effective competition likely to sustain in a market
- Availability of substitutes before and after the combination
- Market share of the parties to the combination individually and as a combination
- Possibility of the combination to remove the vigorous and effective competitor or competition in the market
- Nature and extent of vertical integration in the market
- Nature and extent of innovation
- Whether the benefits of the combinations outweigh the adverse impact of the combination.

Thus, the Competition Act does not seek to eliminate combinations and only aims to eliminate their harmful effects[8].

Box 17.5 explains the MRTP Act of 1969 and 1991.

BOX 17.5: MRTP ACT 1969 & 1991

Presently in India, the mergers are controlled under the Competition Act of 2002 (Act). Before this Act, it had been regulated by the MRTP Act of 1969 but only till 1991, as in 1991 the MRTP Act was amended and the merger control provisions were repealed from the MRTP Act.

The MRTP Act, 1969 created the greatest hindrance in the way of corporate mergers in India. Till the enactment of the MRTP (Amendment) Act, 1991, Sections 23 and 24 of the Act had remained operative requiring the corporate undertakings to be subjected to MRTP Act and seek Government approval before contemplating mergers.

In 1999, the Government of India set up a 'High Level Committee on Competition Law and Policy' under the chairmanship of SVS Raghavan to recommend on the need for an effective competition law regime as the earlier law, i.e., the MRTP Act, 1969 was insufficient to promote effective competition in the market. In 2000, the Committee submitted its report and thus, the Competition Act, 2002 was accordingly enacted.

Source: http://www.cci.gov.in/images/media/ResearchReports/Acquisition%20of%20Minority%20Shareholding%20and%20Merger%20Control%20in%20India.pdf

8. http://business.gov.in/op. cit.

III. Other Acts

The other Regulatory Acts relating to M&A are FEMA, 1999 and the Income Tax Act, 1961. Besides, the Securities and Exchange Board of India (SEBI) has issued guidelines to regulate mergers and acquisitions.

1. Foreign Exchange Management Act, 1999

The foreign exchange laws relating to issuance and allotment of shares to foreign entities are contained in the Foreign Exchange Management (Transfer or Issue of Security by a person residing out of India) Regulation, 2000 issued by RBI vide GSR no. 406(E) dated 3rd May, 2000. These regulations provide general guidelines on issuance of shares or securities by an Indian entity to a person residing outside India or recording in its books any transfer of security from or to such person. RBI has issued detailed guidelines on foreign investment in India vide "Foreign Direct Investment Scheme" contained in Schedule 1 of said regulation[9].

2. The Indian Income Tax Act (ITA), 1961

'Merger' has not been defined under the IT Act but has been covered under the term 'amalgamation' as defined in Section 2(1B) of the Act. It defines an 'amalgamation' as the merger of one or more companies with another company, or the merger of two or more companies to form one company. The ITA also requires that the following conditions must be met by virtue of the merger, for such merger to qualify as an 'amalgamation' under the ITA:

- All the property of the amalgamating company(ies) becomes the property of the amalgamated company
- All the liabilities of the amalgamating company(ies) become the liabilities of the amalgamated company, and
- Shareholders holding not less than 75% of the value of the shares of the amalgamating company become shareholders of the amalgamated company

The IT Act contemplates and recognises the following types of mergers and acquisitions activities:

- Amalgamation (i.e., a merger which satisfies the conditions mentioned below)
- Slump sale/Asset sale
- Transfer of shares, and
- Demerger or spin-off[10].

Following is the "tax treatment" under the Act:

- ***Capital gains tax:*** Under the IT Act, gains arising out of the transfer of capital assets including shares are taxed. However, if the resultant company in the scheme of amalgamation or demerger is an Indian company, then the company is exempted from paying capital gains tax on the transfer of capital assets.

---

9. http://www.legalserviceindia.com/article/l463-Laws-Regulating-Mergers-&-Acquisition-In-India.html
10. http://www.nishithdesai.com/fileadmin/user_upload/pdfs/Research%20Papers/Mergers%20%26%20Acquisitions%20in%20India.pdf.

- ***Tax on transfer of share:*** Transfer of shares may attract securities transaction tax and stamp duty. However, when the shares are in dematerialised form, then no stamp duty is attracted.
- ***Tax on transfer of assets/business:*** Transfer of property also attracts tax which is generally levied by the states.
  - *Immovable property:* Transfer of immovable property attracts stamp duty and registration fee on the instrument of transfer.
  - *Movable property:* The transfer of movable property attracts VAT, which is determined by the State, and also stamp duty on the instrument of transfer.
- ***Transfer of tax liabilities:***
  - *Income tax:* The predecessor is liable for all income tax payable till the effective date of restructuring. After the date of restructuring, the liability falls on the successor.
  - *Central excise act*: Under the Central Excise Act, when a registered person transfers his business to another person, the successor should take a fresh registration and the predecessor should apply for deregistration. In case the predecessor has CENVAT credit, the same could be transferred.
  - *Service tax:* Regarding service tax, the successor is required to obtain fresh registration and the predecessor is required to surrender his registration certificate in case it ceases to provide taxable services. The provisions regarding transferring the CENVAT credit are similar to the Central Excise provisions.
  - *Value added tax:* Usually, statutes governing levy of VAT specify for an intimation of change of ownership and name to the relevant authority but these statutes do not provide any specific guidelines with regard to the transfer of tax credit. The obligation of the predecessor and the successor is joint and several[11].

Thus, in case of "foreign investment" in India, the foreign investing entity before investing generally makes a comparison between certain tax havens like Mauritius, Singapore, Cyprus to see which country will be better to route the investment into India such that maximum tax benefits can be obtained.

It is seen that most investments in India are normally routed through Mauritius and it is still most preferred. The choice of the jurisdiction also depends on the nature of the instrument to be issued to the foreign investor. For example, in the case of an interest bearing compulsorily convertible debenture, Cyprus is preferred over Singapore and Mauritius. The reason being that withholding tax on interest paid on compulsorily convertible debenture is 10% in Cyprus as compared to 15% in Singapore and around 40% in Mauritius. Therefore, Mauritius may be a preferred route for equity investment but in case of an interest bearing compulsorily convertible debenture, Cyprus scores over Mauritius[12].

3. SEBI Takeover Code 1997, 2011 [Last Amended on December 06, 2021]

The Securities and Exchange Board of India (SEBI) is the nodal authority regulating entities that are listed on stock exchanges in India. The Securities and Exchange Board

11. http://www.indialawjournal.com/volume1/issue_1/m_a_regulations.html.
12. http://www.ficci.com/spdocument/20280/Knowledge-paper-FINAL.pdf

of India (Substantial Acquisition of Shares and Takeovers) Regulations, 1997 has been repealed by the Securities and Exchange Board of India (Substantial Acquisition of Shares and Takeovers) Regulations, 2011 (the Takeover Code) with effect from October 23, 2011. The Takeover Code restricts and regulates the acquisition of shares, voting rights and control in listed companies. Acquisition of shares or voting rights of a listed company, entitling the acquirer to exercise 25% or more of the voting rights in the target company. However, this obligation is subject to the exemptions provided under the Takeover Code[13].

CASE STUDY

The Rover Acquisition by BMW AG

The Rover Company was one of the leading British car manufacturing companies set up in 1878 as Starley & Sutton Co. which originally produced bicycles and motorbikes. It produced its first car in 1904 under its now famous marque of the Viking Longship. In 1968, it became a part of the British Leyland Motor Corporation. The group was sold to British Aerospace in 1988 and in 1994, BMW of Germany acquired it for £800 million. It invested about £2 billion in the company but got no synergies, so it sold the company in 2000 to Phoenix Consortium.

BMW AG is a German automobile, engine and motorcycle manufacturing company. It started as an aircraft engine company in the early 1900s. In 1923, it began manufacturing its first motorcycle and in 1928, it began car production.

Part I Acquisition

BMW had acquired the Rover Company with a number of motives. The main motive was growth. BMW wanted to increase their market share with Rover as it was highly cost efficient due to the usage of Japanese production methods. They also had the front-wheel driving and the 4 × 4 technology that BMW wanted to acquire.

Another major factor in the acquisition was the low level of cost in the British manufacturing sector compared to the costs in Germany. These costs, which were 60% lesser in Britain, could substantially reduce BMW costs. Further, Rover also had brands such as Mini and MG Rover, through which BMW wanted to exploit new markets and segments.

Part II Analysis

The motive for acquiring Rover by BMW was definitely strategic and synergies based. However, the acquisition was unsuccessful because they did not plan the entire process well. According to Palmer (2003), the strategic plan got stuck with the senior management due to lack of communication and coordination. BMW's integration plan suggested a three-phase process in which the initial two years were 'wasted' in just providing financial help without any integration of the two companies and in 1999 only, the two companies were fully integrated.

13. https://www.sebi.gov.in/legal/regulations/dec-2021/securities-and-exchange-board-of-india-substantial-acquisition-of-shares-and-takeovers-regulations-2011-last-amended-on-december-06-2021-_40714.html

Another important problem for this deal was the linguistic differences between the two companies. Although BMW's top management could do business in English, the engineers and the middle managers were unable to do so. This created a serious communication problem which eventually delayed the integration process. There were also substantial differences between the business culture of BMW and Rover. Batcheler (2001) pointed out that the German direct approach was in contrast to the more relaxed approach followed by the British.

Sirower (1997) suggested that it is incorrect to analyse the soundness of an acquisition based on the cost of developing the business from scratch. The acquisition of Rover had the same problem as BMW's decision was partly based on the substantial cost difference between developing the technologies in-house and buying it from Rover. When BMW could not achieve the synergies despite spending £2 billion, they sold it to Phoenix Consortium.

Source: http://dhardhar.wordpress.com/2013/09/16/two-case-studies-in-mergers-and- acquisitions-why-some-succeed-while-others-fail.

SOLVED PROBLEMS

PROBLEM 17.1 AB plans to acquire 100% stake in CD Pvt. Ltd. for ₹50 million. CD is an unlisted company with ₹10 million of debt obligations. Calculate the purchase price as per net assets method?

Solution:

Amount paid to acquire CD = ₹50 million
Outstanding debt = 10 million
Total purchase price = ₹60 million

Note: AB acquires CD, assuming that it will generate a Net Value of ₹60 million.

PROBLEM 17.2 Following table shows the balance sheet of Company A and Company B as on 31st December, 2010.

Balance Sheet of Company A and B

	Company A (₹)	*Company B* (₹)
Liabilities		
Common equity	250	80
Long-term debt	100	100
Current liabilities and provisions	50	30
Deferred tax	100	40
Total	**500**	**250**
Assets		
PP&E	200	100
Current assets	200	100
Goodwill	100	50
Total	**500**	**250**

Both A and B decide to combine their operations for better growth prospects. Find out the value of the merged entity.

Solution: Combined value of liabilities of Company A and B.

Combine Value

	Company A + B (₹)
Liabilities	
Common equity	330
Long-term debt	200
Current liabilities and provisions	80
Deferred tax	140
Total	**750**
Assets	
PP&E	300
Current assets	300
Goodwill	150
Total	**750**

Note: In the above case, 'Pooling of Interest method' has been used. In this method, balance sheets of the merging entities are added together, line by line, eliminating any inter-company investments which are treated as treasury stocks, to find out the value of the merged entity. This can also be done through *Income Statement treatment.*

PROBLEM 17.3 Company X is contemplating purchasing Company Y for ₹90,000. The current cost of capital of Company X is 12% and Y's estimated overall cost of capital after the acquisition is 10%. Projected cash inflows from year 1 through 8 are ₹13,000 (assume no residual value.) Calculate the net present value and advise on the acquisition.

Solution: The net present value is given in the following table:

Year	*Present Value*
0 (– ₹90,000 × 1)	(₹90,000)
1–8 (₹13,000 × 5.335)	+ 69,355*
Net present value	(₹20,645)

*Using 10% as the discount rate for present value of an annuity of ₹1.

The acquisition is not feasible since there is a negative net present value.

PROBLEM 17.4 Company J wants to buy Company K by issuing its shares. Relevant information is given below:

	Company J	*Company K*
Net income (₹)	40,000	16,000
Outstanding shares	20,000	8,000

The exchange ratio is 2 to 1. Calculate the EPS of the combined entity.

Solution: EPS of combined equity = Combined net income/Total shares

$$\frac{56{,}000}{20{,}000 + (8{,}000 \times 2)} = \frac{56{,}000}{36{,}000 \text{ shares}} = 1.55$$

EPS of J (₹) = 1.55

EPS of K (₹) = 1.55 × 2 = 3.10

PROBLEM 17.5 New Investments is planning to acquire a set-top box manufacturing company for ₹4 million. The estimated profitability and cash flows of the company for the next five years are arrived at after careful study of the market. Expected sales are 18,000 units.

Other details:

Unit selling price is ₹800
Variable cost per unit is ₹500
Fixed cost is ₹40,000
Depreciation is ₹8,000 (SLM)
Tax rate @ 35%

The cost of capital (equity) of the firm is 10%. Compute NPV of the project and recommend New Investments whether to purchase the firm or not?

Solution: To arrive at NPV, we need cash flows and to have cash flows in the present case, first net profit of the firm to be acquired needs to be computed. Then cash flows are arrived at and discounted at 10% to find out NPV. This is explained in table below.

NPV Calculation of the Firm to be Acquired P

	1	2	3	4	5
Annual demand of television	18,000	18,000	18,000	18,000	18,000
Unit selling price	800	800	800	800	800
Revenue	1,44,00,000	1,44,00,000	1,44,00,000	1,44,00,000	1,44,00,000
Variable cost per unit	500	500	500	500	500
Variable cost	90,00,000	90,00,000	90,00,000	90,00,000	90,00,000
Fixed cost	40,000	40,000	40,000	40,000	40,000
Less: Depreciation*	8,000	8,000	8,000	8,000	8,000

PBT	53,52,000	53,52,000	53,52,000	53,52,000	53,52,000
Less: Tax	18,73,200	18,73,200	18,73,200	18,73,200	18,73,200
PAT	34,78,800	34,78,800	34,78,800	34,78,800	34,78,800
Add: Depreciation	8,000	8,000	8,000	8,000	8,000
Cash flow	34,86,800	34,86,800	34,86,800	34,86,800	34,86,800
Present value of cash flow	1,32,17,715				

NPV (38,67,82,285)

Since, NPV is negative, it is not recommended to acquire the firm.

POINTS TO REMEMBER

- Internal growth is achieved through capital investment process and external growth is accomplished through various business combinations, viz. mergers, amalgamations and acquisitions. These business combinations are an important feature of corporate structural changes.
- Corporate restructuring is the process of redesigning one or more aspects of a company. It entails a fundamental change in a company's business or financial structure, designed to increase the company's value to shareholders. It is often divided into two parts: (i) financial restructuring, and (ii) operational restructuring.
- Financial restructuring implies change in the capital structure of the firm, like increasing debt component in the capital mix to reduce the overall cost of capital of the firm.
- Operational restructuring is the process of increasing the economic viability of the underlying business model. *Examples* include mergers, the sale of divisions or discontinuance of product line, or cost-reduction.
- Financial Restructuring takes place in these ways—(a) Buy-back, (b) Going private, (c) LBOs.
- Operational restructuring happens through various forms of expansion, demerger and change in business. Expansion can take place in the form of merger, acquisition, and joint venture. Demerger can be a spin off, a divestiture or carve-out.
- Merger is a combination of two or more firms into one, where the assets and liabilities of all the firms are vested into one surviving firm. The surviving firm can be one of the existing firms or it can be a new entity.
- Acquisition means buying of assets (a plant or a division) of a company, acquiring a brand of a company or acquiring ownership or controlling rights in a company through share purchase.
- A joint venture is when two or more firms come together for a common business in the form of funds, expertise, manpower, etc.

- Spin-off is when a parent company forms a new legal entity out of its existing business. The existing shareholders are given the shares of the new entity on a pro-rata basis and they continue to hold the same proportion of ownership in the new entity.
- A divestiture is a sale of a part (like plant or a unit) or assets of a firm to an outside party to get rid of unproductive, unprofitable or non-performing assets and use the cash received for business expansion.
- Equity Carve-out is the process of a parent company selling its portion to the public or outsider in an initial public offering. The carve-out creates a new legal entity whose ownership remains with the parent company.
- Mergers are of four types. *Horizontal Merger* is a combination or joining of two or more firms in the same area of business. *Vertical Merger* is a combination of two or more firms involved in different stages of the production or distribution. *Conglomerate Merger* is a combination of two or more firms which are engaged in unrelated lines of business activity. Merging of different businesses like manufacturing of cement products and electronics products is such a case. Congeneric Merger is achieved by acquiring a firm that is in the same general industry but neither in the same line of business nor a supplier or customer.
- Mergers and acquisitions are intended to have higher growth, increased profitability, diversification, competitive strength, survival, tax benefits and, most importantly synergistic benefits.
- Merger and acquisition process is the most challenging and most critical in corporate restructuring and involves *four stages*. Pre-planning is the foundation stage of mergers and acquisitions which involves evaluating one's own position. Target specific evaluation is the stage of evaluating the target company. Deal execution stage is to finalise the deal. Post-deal integration and synergy is the post-effect stage of the deal.
- Net assets method of valuation is used in case of privately held companies. A comparative analysis of the target company is carried out with regard to its total assets size and outstanding liabilities to have the net purchase price.
- Liquidation value method is used in case of bankrupt or sick companies. The liquidation value is the amount of proceeds that could be realised by a stockholder if a company ceased its operations.
- Replacement-Cost value method measures cost that would be incurred if one tries to replicate all the assets and liabilities of a company by building them or purchasing them on the market.
- Capitalisation method involves the capitalisation of historical earnings. In this method, the past earnings of the business to be acquired are averaged out to determine the expected earnings in the future.
- Discounted-Cash-Flow method in an M&A deal determines the value of the company (enterprise value) by computing the present value of cash flows over the life of the company. Basically, NPV approach is used here, as followed in capital budgeting decision.

- Market Value method is used in case of publicly held companies. The belief behind using MV is that market value reflects all public information about the company and its industry.
- Price Multiples are a relative valuation method because they are used as an industry analysis, i.e., peer group comparison. The multiples used here are P/E ratio and P/B ratio.
- Mergers and acquisitions are regulated under various laws in India, like the Companies Act (1956), the Competition Act (2002), FEMA (1999), IT Act (1961), and SEBI Takeover Code 1997, 2011.

KEY TERMS

- **Corporate restructuring** is the process of redesigning one or more aspects of a company. It entails a fundamental change in a company's business or financial structure.
- **Financial restructuring** implies change in the capital structure of the firm, like increasing debt component in the capital mix to reduce the overall cost of capital of the firm.
- **Operational restructuring** is the process of increasing the economic viability of the underlying business model.
- **Merger** is a combination of two or more firms into one, where the assets and liabilities of all the firms are vested into one surviving firm.
- **Absorption** is a merger where all other firms are absorbed into the surviving firm.
- **Consolidation** or an **Amalgamation** is a merger where all the firms are combined to form a new entity.
- **Acquisition** means buying assets of a company, acquiring a brand of a company or acquiring ownership or controlling rights in a company through share purchase.
- **Joint venture** is when two or more firms come together for a common business.
- **Spin-off** is when a parent company forms a new legal entity out of its existing business.
- **Split-off** is a case where some existing shareholders receive stock in the new company in exchange for parent company stock.
- **Split-up** is the case where the entire firm is broken into a series of spin-offs so that the parent company no longer exists and the new company survives.
- **Divestiture** involves a sale of a part or assets of a firm to an outside party to get rid of unproductive, unprofitable or non-performing assets and use the cash received for business expansion.
- **Equity Carve-outs** involve the parent company selling its portion to the public or outsider in an initial public offering.
- **Horizontal merger** is a combination or joining of two or more firms in the same area of business.

- **Vertical merger** is a combination of two or more firms involved in different stages of the production or distribution.
- **Conglomerate merger** is a combination of two or more firms which are engaged in unrelated lines of business activity.
- **Congeneric merger** is achieved by acquiring a firm that is in the same general industry but neither in the same line of business nor a supplier or customer.

EXERCISES

Problems

1. Simmy Company has plans to acquire Bolt Company by exchanging stock. Simmy will issue 1.5 shares of its stock for each share of Bolt. Financial information for the two companies is as follows:

	Simmy	*Bolt*
Net profit	₹4,00,000	₹1,00,000
Number of shares	2,00,000	15,000
Earnings per share	₹2.00	4.00
Market price per share	₹40.00	48.00

Simmy expects P/E Ratio for the combined company to be 15.

What will be the combined EPS and the expected price to be paid per share for acquiring Bolt Company?

2. Simon Company has decided to sell its business for a sales price of $ 50,000. Following is its balance sheet as on 31st March, 2014.

Balance Sheet as at 31st March, 2014

Cash	$3,000
Accounts receivable	7,000
Inventory	12,000
Property, plant and equipment I	1,50,000
Property, plant and equipment II	30,000
Total assets	**2,02,000**
Liabilities	80,000
Equity	1,22,000
Total liabilities and equity	**$2,02,000**

Maria Company is interested in purchasing Property, Plant and Equipment I. The estimated free cash flows from these acquired equipments will be $ 26,000 per annum over the next 8 years. The remaining assets can be sold by Maria Company for $ 35,000. The cost of capital is 10%.

Advise, should Maria Company acquire Simon Company?

3. Following are the financials of two firms A and B:

	Firm A	*Firm B*
PAT (₹)	5,00,000	2,50,000
Number of shares (N)	1,00,000	50,000
Earnings per share (₹)	5	5
Market price per share (₹)	50	20
P/E ratio (Times)	10	4
Total market value of the firm (₹) [Market price × Number of shares]	50,00,000	10,00,000

Firm A is planning to acquire Firm B. The exchange ratio of shares decided between A and B is 1.5:1. Determine the total market value of Firm A after acquisition.

4. A leading bank is on the look-out for the acquisition of a local bank in its region. Following are the financials of local bank for past 5 years:

Year	*EPS* (₹Per Share)	*DPS* (₹Per Share)
1	1.76	0.66
2	1.93	0.72
3	2.11	0.79
4	2.32	0.87
5	2.54	0.95

The stock of the local bank is currently trading at ₹25.61. Expected growth of the local bank is 5%. The payout ratio of the local bank is 66.67%. The cost of equity is 8.82% in stable growth and 9.02% in high growth. The risk-free rate is 5%.

Should the leading bank acquire the local bank at the current market price?

5. Agarwal & Co.'s balance sheet shows a net current asset value of ₹80,000, and a net long-term asset value of ₹2,00,000. Return on Current assets is 7.5% and Return on Long-term assets is 9.4%. Their historical annual earnings is ₹1,50,000. The capitalisation rate is 20%.

What will be the minimum or base price for their business to be sold off?

Answers: 1. ₹33.75
2. NPV of $ 46,710
3. ₹75,07,500
4. PV of Terminal price is ₹–29
5. ₹9,06,000

Objective Questions

1. **Tick the correct answer:**

(a) The growth achieved through capital investment process is:

(i) Internal growth (ii) External growth
(iii) Market growth (iv) All of the above

(b) The growth accomplished through various business combinations is:
   (i) Internal growth (ii) External growth
   (iii) Competitive growth (iv) None of the above

(c) Corporate restructuring is:
   (i) Change in business portfolio (ii) Change in capital structure
   (iii) Change in ownership (iv) All of the above

(d) A combination of two or more firms into one is:
   (i) Takeover (ii) Acquisition
   (iii) Joint venture (iv) None of the above

(e) Sale of a part or assets of a firm, to an outside party, which are unproductive is:
   (i) Divestiture (ii) Demerger
   (iii) Merger (iv) None of the above

(f) Merger of two or more firms engaged in unrelated lines of business activity is:
   (i) Vertical (ii) Horizontal
   (iii) Conglomerate (iv) None of the above

Answers: (a) i (b) ii (c) iv (d) iv (e) i (f) iii

2. Fill in the blanks:

(a) .... is the process of redesigning one or more aspects of a company.

(b) .... restructuring results in change in the capital structure of the firm.

(c) .... restructuring leads to increased economic viability of the underlying business model.

(d) .... merger is a combination of two or more firms in the same area of business.

(e) Financial evaluation of the target company is done in the .... stage.

(f) .... method of valuation is cash flow based.

Answers:

(a) Corporate restructuring
(b) Financial
(c) Operational
(d) Horizontal
(e) Second
(f) DCF

3. True or False:

(a) Restructuring a corporate entity is often seen as a necessity for the future growth of the company.

(b) Buy-back is an operational restructuring

(c) LBO route is financial restructuring.

(d) In case of JV, an independent legal entity is formed.

(e) Split-off and split-up are variants of spin-off.

(f) The most important motive for mergers and acquisitions is synergy.

(g) Capitalisation method considers past earnings of the target firm.

(h) Price multiples are a relative valuation method.

Answers: (a) True (b) False (c) True (d) True (e) True
(f) True (g) True (h) True

Short Questions

1. Distinguish between financial and operational restructuring.
2. What is the difference between acquisition and takeover?
3. What are the two variants of spin-off?
4. What is call option and put option?
5. Define a financial asset.

Critical Thinking Questions

1. "Corporate restructuring is not confined to mere one dimension, rather it has various dimensions to it". Discuss.
2. "Financial restructuring is affecting the sources side of the balance sheet". Justify.
3. "Operational restructuring is real strategy to increase the shareholders' value". Elaborate with suitable illustrations.
4. "The most important motive for mergers and acquisitions is to have synergy benefits". Discuss.
5. "The real stakeholders of corporate restructuring are internal people". Prove.
6. "Discounted-cash-flow method is the most commonly used valuation method in M&A". Explain.
7. "Price multiple is a relative valuation method which presents fair industry picture". Discuss.

Descriptive Questions

1. Explain the conceptual framework of corporate restructuring in detail.
2. What are the different forms of corporate restructuring?
3. Discuss the different types of mergers.
4. What are the various motives of mergers and acquisitions?
5. Explain the process of mergers and acquisitions.
6. What are the different valuation methods used in M&A?
7. What are the innovative sources of funds that have emerged in M&A?
8. What are the major issues and challenges faced by Indian regulators for M&A?

PROJECT EXERCISE

Restructuring Deal Analysis

Identify a company in the news that is undergoing corporate restructuring. Find out the nature of restructuring, whether the restructuring is financial or operational? Study their process of valuation in detail. Discuss the legal implication of the deal. Also, analyse the proposed post-restructuring effects by the company, i.e. will the company be able to produce fundamental improvements afterwards? Evaluate the risk component as well regarding the problems and challenges faced by the company in handling the entire process of restructuring.

REVIEW CASE

Fitment of M&A Valuation

A company 'A' Ltd. is into the business of leather goods. They now wish to expand in US and have two options in front of them—(i) set up their own business there, or (ii) buy Company B which is already an existing brand of the leather industry in the US. Buying an existing business represents less of a risk than starting a new business from scratch, especially in a foreign land. The opportunity of buying an existing business may be less risky in some aspects. One must perform with due diligence to ensure that you are fully aware of the terms of the purchase so that you make the right decision.

The target investment price for acquiring Company B is pitched at ₹4 million. Its stream of expected earnings before depreciation, interest and taxes (EBDIT) and cash flows for next five years is given below:

Year	*EBDIT*	*Cash Flows after Tax*
1	₹2 million	₹1.5 million
2	3 million	2 million
3	3 million	2 million
4	4 million	3 million
5	5 million	4 million

Following is the balance sheet of Company B as on 31st December, 2011.

Balance Sheet of Company B

	Company B (₹)
Liabilities	
Equity	150
Long-term Debt	—
Current Liabilities and Provisions	30
Deferred Tax	20
Total	**200**
Assets	
PP&E	120
Current Assets	60
Intangible Assets	20
Total	**200**

Company B is a Public Limited company. Its average P/E ratio for the last 3 years is 15 as compared to the industry average P/E of 14.5. Yearly interest is zero and tax rate is 35%. Depreciation is charged on a straight-line basis and the cost of funds is 22%.

A merger and acquisitions is like a marriage; the two partners must be compatible. Each side should add value so that together the two are much stronger, but unfortunately, many fail to work. So, before you buy a business determine its worth. This is a crucial business activity. If you purchase a business that is overvalued, you paid more money than the business was worth. If you purchase a business that is undervalued, you may have saved money upfront but that business might be weak. Value is important; you want to look at assets, accounts receivable, sales and balance sheets. The valuation of the business should also be agreed upon by the seller and the potential buyer, else further negotiations are pointless. Business valuation is a very important aspect of this process.

Therefore, Company A wants to know the real business value and the real value of the business depends upon the income that the business generates. Business purchase should be based on the return on investment, not on the stated price. The buyer should always remember that the seller's own statements are likely to be overly optimistic and even overstated. The buyer must be wary of the business that looks too good to be true. For how long should these statements be projected? One year? Three? The best ways to decide is in terms of the expected return on investment. If it is estimated that the business should return 20% on the investment, then the investment capital should be returned in five years. On this basis, the projected statements should cover five years. Overpaying for the acquisition is a common mistake because of application of a wrong valuation model.

Company A wishes to apply the correct valuation model for acquiring Company B but they are confused which to follow among net assets, EBITDA or DCF method or Relative valuation of P/E?

Issues for Discussion

(i) Should the firm acquire Company B?

(ii) Which method of valuation should they follow to evaluate Company B's viability?

(iii) Does valuation method affect the decision of acquisition?

(iv) What are the risks associated with post-merger integration?

(v) What are the key factors for consideration in business acquisition?

REFERENCES

Ansoff, H.L., et al. (1971), *Acquisitive Behaviour of U.S. Manufacturing Firms*, 1946–65, Vanderbitt University Press.

Damodaran, Aswath (2005), *Corporate Finance*, John Wiley & Sons, 2nd ed., New York.

Rappaport, A. (1979), "Strategic Analysis for More Profitable Acquisitions", *Harvard Business Review,* July–August, pp. 99–110.

www.articles.economictimes.indiatimes.com
www.business.gov.in
www.cci.gov.in
www.deloitte.com
www.dhardhar.wordpress.com
www.ey.com
www.ficci.com
www.forbes.com
www.indialawjournal.com
www.legalserviceindia.com
www.nasdaq.com
www.people.stern.nyu.edu
www.sebi.gov.in

CHAPTER

18

Barter Exchange

All government, indeed every human benefit and enjoyment, every virtue, and every prudent act, is founded on compromise and barter.

— Edmund Burke

LEARNING OBJECTIVES

This chapter discusses the following:

- Concept and types of barter
- Commercial barter practice
- Economics of barter
- Barter exchange and its features
- Types of barter exchanges
- Process of barter exchange
- Bartering in India

INTRODUCTION

Exchanging one of your books with a friend in return for one of his book is 'barter'. Barter exchange was the only basis of trade in early civilisations because at that time there was no currency prevalent. Therefore, barter system is not new to the world. It has been there since ages, rather since the trade started happening. With the introduction of currency as a medium of exchange, the barter system lost its recognition but it is still in practice in various forms of business and trades worldwide.

One of the first evidences of bartering can be found in 6000 BC. The barter system traded all sorts of goods and services such as weaponry, food, or tea. One problem that was discovered with the barter system in areas such as Mesopotamia was that there was no way to assign a specific value to the traded goods and services. One of the most popular things traded in the barter system was salt because it was considered valuable. Bartering grew and flourished as people began to travel more during the Middle Ages. The Europeans introduced new things into the barter system market that Americans did not have access to and also did not have the money to afford. During the Great Depression, the barter system began to grow even more rapidly than ever. The Great Depression is one of the most significant time periods throughout the history of bartering. Money was scarce and people had a difficult time getting what they needed. It allowed people to get food or clothing when they needed to and they were allowed to create accounts with businesses[1].

Today, bartering has evolved into a highly sophisticated online trade and that popularity continues to increase. Business houses, individuals can trade excess goods or services or even free time for barter dollars and save those dollars for rough time periods.

BARTER: NATURE AND OVERVIEW

Barter is "a method of exchange wherein goods or services are directly exchanged for other goods or services without using a medium of exchange, such as money". It is usually bilateral but may be multilateral, and usually exists parallel to monetary systems in most developed countries.

Advantages of Barter

Bartering has come out as a valuable new addition, particularly to the small business owners for several reasons. Major advantages of barter exchange include the following:

(i) *Conservation of Cash*

One of the main advantages of barter trading is that it gives people the opportunity to conserve cash. A business may already have access to products or services. They can use these products and services in exchange for the products and services that they would usually pay for. This would have more stable cash flows for a company both in the short and long term.

(ii) *Use of Idle Resources*

Making use of idle resources is a huge advantage of barter trading. *For example,* assume you own a publishing company. Your employees have work for only 7 hours a day but you pay them for 8 hours a day. With one extra hour of theirs, you could barter their services for other products and services. The time which was essentially being wasted, is now converted into useful products and services that save your business money.

1. http://www.barternewyork.net/history-of-bartering.html

(iii) *Networking*

Business-to-business networking is one of the main advantages of bartering. By introducing your business there, facilitating deals and engaging with potential clients even without cash basis, you are building awareness of your business and brand. This exposure earns you revenue in the future.

(iv) *Better Employee Compensation*

Small business enterprises often face shortage of cash for paying bonuses or perks to their employees but barter exchange is a potential avenue for companies to reward their workforce in some way. *For example,* some companies have established a system within barter networks so that employees can choose rewards from the offerings of other exchange members (within certain financial limits).

(v) *Higher Productivity*

Barter helps companies to use inventory, equipment and employees more efficiently, generating an increasing revenue that would not have been possible otherwise. Essentially, a company's less productive assets are exchanged for more valuable goods or services through the help of a barter exchange.

(vi) *Less Wastage*

Barter reduces non-performing assets of a business. Businesses with obsolete inventory frequently find that bartering the assets yields a much better value than liquidating it as junk. The company can sell the inventory to a barter member for trade credits close to the carrying cost or book value, and then use those credits to other business expenses such as marketing, entertainment, travel or raw materials.

(vii) *Increased Cash Sales and Profits*

Barter facilitates new cash sales. If you perform a good job for a client you serviced through a barter exchange, he will undoubtedly refer their cash-paying friends, clients, family and associates to you. Therefore, increased sales mean increased profits.

Risks and Limitations of a Barter Economy

Undoubtedly, bartering offers a lot of advantages both to the seller and buyer but it also has limitations. They are:

1. ***Presence of common needs:*** For barter to occur between two people, both need to have what the other wants.

2. ***Absence of common measure of value:*** In a monetary economy, money plays the role of a measure of value of all goods, so their values can be measured against each other; this role may be absent in a barter economy.

3. ***Indivisibility of certain goods:*** If a person wants to buy a certain amount of another's goods but for payment has only one indivisible unit of another good which is worth more than what the person wants to obtain, a barter transaction cannot occur.

4. *Lack of standards for deferred payment:* This is related to the absence of a common measure of value, although if the debt is denominated in units of the good, that will eventually be used in payment.

5. *Difficulty in storing wealth:* If a society relies exclusively on perishable goods, storing wealth for the future may be impractical. However, some barter economies rely on durable goods, like pigs or cattle for this purpose.

COMMERCIAL BARTER

Commercial bartering is a payment technique that facilitates merging two transactions between two companies (parties). Each of them sells a product to the other. There are two sales, and therefore two risks. The smaller sale is subtracted from the bigger sale in order to barter for import or export transactions. The commercial barter can also be referred to as "compensation trade".

The Need for Commercial Barter

1. *Imbalance in trade*: The exchange of a diversified range of products and services having different value units is difficult. Moreover, the services, because of intangible nature, are difficult to measure in monetary terms. These products or services may be produced or generated in various areas with different mediums of exchange. All this leads to an imbalance in trade, and a commercial barter effectively overcomes all these problems.

2. *Problem of fraud*: The system of exchange at a global level brings along an element of risk, like whether the parties involved are genuine and honest to each other, etc. Hence, there arises a need for a written contract underlining the terms of the barter contract. A commercial barter exchange checks the credentials of the barter partners involved and makes sure the trade is conducted in the appropriate legal manner.

Taxation Standards of Bartering

Barter should be viewed as 'cash income'. There are no inherent tax advantages or disadvantages just because you use a barter trade exchange. Barter is a marketing tool, not a tax tool. As with cash income, barter purchases which are business-related, are deductible and conversely, barter purchases which are made for personal use are not deductible. Naturally, your barter income (sales) and business deductions (purchases) should be accounted for within your tax return. All city and State taxes are always payable in cash to the seller.

Traditional vs. Commercial Barter

Table 18.1 lists the difference between traditional barter and commercial barter.

TABLE 18.1 Distinction between Traditional and Commercial Barter

Basis	*Traditional Barter*	*Commercial Barter*
1. Parties involved	One-to-one transaction	Multi-party transaction
2. Mode of payment	'Non-cash'. Both parties are obliged to sell and buy from each other.	'Trade credit'. The members buy and sell to each other in the internal currency of trade credit.
3. Third party involvement	No third party is involved to facilitate trade.	Trading exchange acts as a third party and provides the trading platform.
4. Trading partners	Difficult to find trade partner with matching requirements.	No such need here.

ECONOMICS OF BARTER

Let us understand how the barter system works economically for the parties under trade with the help of following *example.*

Situation: There is a computer manufacturer, Company AB which wants to trade computers for advertising space. The company becomes a member of A2Barter (the barter exchange). The details of his offer are given below:

- Cost price per computer: INR 10,000
- Selling price per computer: INR 15,000
- Number of computers: 20

AB thus agrees to sell computers worth ₹3 lacs (20 computers) and take advertising space worth ₹3 lacs. Company AB would of course, be required to pay A2Barter the fees @ 10% (in cheque) on the purchase value at the time of purchase (Table 18.2).

TABLE 18.2 Working of the Deal(s)

Cash Transaction/Normal Transaction	*Barter Transaction*
Sale of 20 computers: Assuming normal trade/customer discount of 20% on MRP	Sale of 20 computers at MRP (no trade margin or customer discounts)
Sale = 20 × ₹12,000 (net of discount) = ₹2,40,000	**Sale** = 20 × ₹15,000 (earns barter credits) = ₹3,00,000
Less: Expenses = 20 × ₹10,000 = ₹2,00,000	***Less:*** Expenses = 20 × ₹10,000 = ₹2,00,000
Profit **= ₹40,000**	**Profit** **= ₹1,00,000**
	AB has higher profit and also earns barter credits worth ₹3 lacs (sale value) and purchases media space in lieu of the value earned.
	Purchases ad space in newspapers on barter for ₹3,00,000.
	Pays 10% fee on ₹3,00,000 to A2Barter = ₹30,000 (in cheque)

Evaluation of the economics of the above Transaction: The higher purchase rates on barter get covered by the higher margins earned on barter sales. Prices on barter are normally quoted at MRP's or are higher than the rock-bottom rates quoted for cash deals but there are negotiated rates on barter deals as well, especially where the difference between the MRP and normal cash rates is significant (e.g., Hotel rooms during a lean period, etc.).

Therefore, while purchasing, Company AB would take into account:

- A comparison of the purchase price of the ad space on barter with the regular/lowest rates for the media space when purchases normally for cash—assume a market discount of 10%
- Factor in the 10% fee paid to A2Barter upon purchases (which also adds to the cost)—10%
- While selling Company AB would take into account the profit margin earned on barter sales—33.33% (1,00,000/3,00,000)

Thus, it earns a net margin of 33.33% less 20% (10% + 10%) = 13.33% in the barter deal.

Note: As long as the margins earned on sale are higher than the extra cost of purchases on barter, it makes economic sense to transact on barter. The added benefit to AB to be taken into account is also the fact that through barter, it has been able to purchase ad space cash free—without affecting its cash reserves.

BARTER EXCHANGE

A *barter exchange* or *trade exchange* is a commercial organisation that provides a trading platform and book-keeping system for its members or clients. The member companies buy and sell products and services to each other using an internal currency known as *barter* or *trade credits (dollars).*

Barter exchanges are usually local or regional, and they have websites which list products or services for sale. If you buy products or services from exchange members, your trade account is debited; if you sell products or services to other members, your account is credited. At the end of each year, the barter service provides a record of your statement. Barter exchanges charge an initial membership fee, a transaction percentage, and a monthly maintenance fee.

The Swiss WIR Bank was the first barter system and one of the largest still existing barters at present, established in 1934. The direct cause for establishing the WIR was the shortage of conventional currency after the stock market crash of 1929[2].

Key Features

Barter exchange has the following key features:

1. ***Online trading platform:*** Internet provides the medium of trading for the barter exchange industry. These commercial trade exchanges are different from the traditional exchanges in the sense they do not have a physical office.

2. http://qoin.org/barter-exchanges.

. ***Fee-based:*** A barter exchange functions primarily as the organiser of a marketplace here members buy and sell products and services among themselves. The modern kchange facilitates the entire process for a fee.

. ***Trade credits:*** Barter exchanges have their own unit of currency for exchange ie barter or trade credits, usually dollars which are valued in US currency. Barter kchanges act as the book-keeper for keeping track of trade dollars that participants cumulate. Earning trade or barter dollars through a barter exchange is considered ıxable income, just as if your product or service was sold for cash.

. ***Third-party record keeper:*** The exchange maintains the listings of goods and ervices available on trade, and makes sure that all trade accounts are up-to-date.

. ***Clearing house:*** Through the system of authorisations, before finalising a ansaction, the exchange virtually ensures that the seller is assured of payment for ie products that he sells.

. ***Banking services:*** The exchange also extends various types of loans to its members help them tide over periods of scarcity of funds.

. ***Product portfolio:*** Following products and services are often traded via barter kchanges:

- Media space
- Printing services
- Advertising
- Website design
- Vacations and hotels
- Legal services
- Housekeeping services
- Medical services
- Restaurants/dinners

TYPES OF BARTER EXCHANGES

rimarily, barter exchanges of commercial nature, are of two types—*retail barter,* nd *corporate barter,* as evident in Figure 18.1. These barters and their systems are iscussed below:

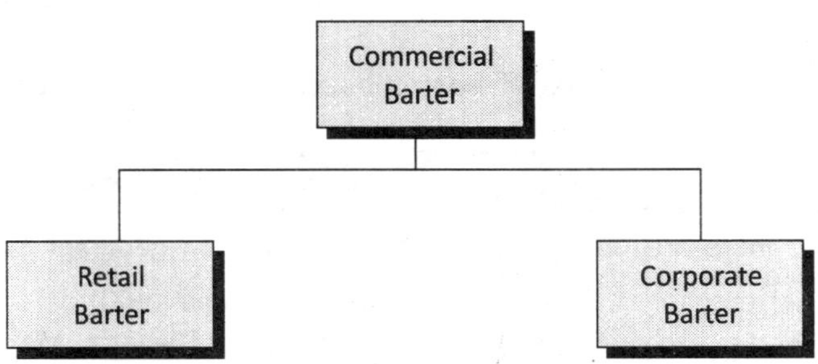

Figure 18.1 Types of Barter

1. Retail Barter

A *Retail Barter Exchange* is a company that acts as a third-party record keeper facilitate transactions among members of the exchange using a non-cash curren called *trade credit*.

Small and medium-sized businesses are the members of the retail barter exchang The feature of this barter exchange is that it has a large number of members a relies on low value transactions.

Retail barter exchanges typically employ trade brokers, who communicate inform tion between members to facilitate trades. For example, a broker will put a memb who is looking to purchase auto repair in touch with a member who they know provid auto repair.

2. Corporate Barter

A *Corporate Barter* Company takes a principle position in goods or services purchasing these assets with trade credits and/or cash-equivalent credit (not dolla pounds/marks, etc). Corporate barter is typically used to move excess capacity a under-performing assets. This focuses on large transactions which are different fr a traditional, retail-oriented barter exchange. The transactions are of high value su as exchange of big service contracts.

It differs from commercial barter because the Corporate Barter Company actua owns the asset(s) after they purchase it with trade credits. Table 18.3 lists t differences between retail barter and commercial barter.

TABLE 18.3 Difference between Retail and Corporate Barter

	Retail Barter	*Corporate Barter*
Members	Majorly individuals	Corporate houses
Role of exchange	Clearing house	Purchaser/intermediary
Sources of revenue	Commission as fee	Profit on negotiated deals an commission
Purpose	Generally, to conserve cash and help people who are not cash rich	Using unproductive assets an excess capacity to gain
Value of transactions	Can range from \$1–\$200	Can involve millions of dolla

Box 18.1 gives detail on types of barter based on geography of operation.

BOX 18.1: OTHER BARTER EXCHANGES

Besides the above, there are other types of barter based on geography of operation:

- Domestic barter exchanges, such as India Barter Exchange (IBX)
- Cross-border barter exchanges, such as BarterTrust.com (Canada, Mexico, and the Unite States) and IMS Inc.

WORKING OF A BARTER EXCHANGE

The process of barter is explained in Figure 18.2 and consists of the following steps:

1. ***Identification of prospects:*** First, key business houses are identified as potential members who would like to be a part of the commercial barter exchange and facilitate their business operations.

2. ***Invitation to enrol:*** These potential members are briefed about the various benefits they will derive from the barter facility and once they are convinced, they are invited to be a member of the system. It can be the other way round also, i.e. business houses approach these exchanges for the membership. Different members with different offerings and requirements are enrolled onto these exchanges.

3. ***Membership fee:*** When these potential members officially join, they are charged a membership fee, a one-time sign-up fee, plus an annual membership fee. In addition, they are charged a commission, often 10–15%, on the gross value of each transaction. Membership fees are generally payable in official currency but commissions may be payable in trade credits.

4. ***Fixing the limit of transaction:*** There is a contract between the trade exchange and its members which specifies the respective responsibilities of each party. As a part of the agreement, trade dollars are issued by a trade exchange by making loans to its members. Each member will have a particular 'line of credit' (in trade dollars) which defines the maximum debit balance a member is allowed to carry. This limit is fixed based on the track record, capacity and requirement of the member.

5. ***Opening of trade account:*** A barter exchange opens a trade account of each member which carries his balance based upon his transactions. This account is used to make debits or credits to various barter transactions done through the exchange. This process is very similar to the way in which banks create an account.

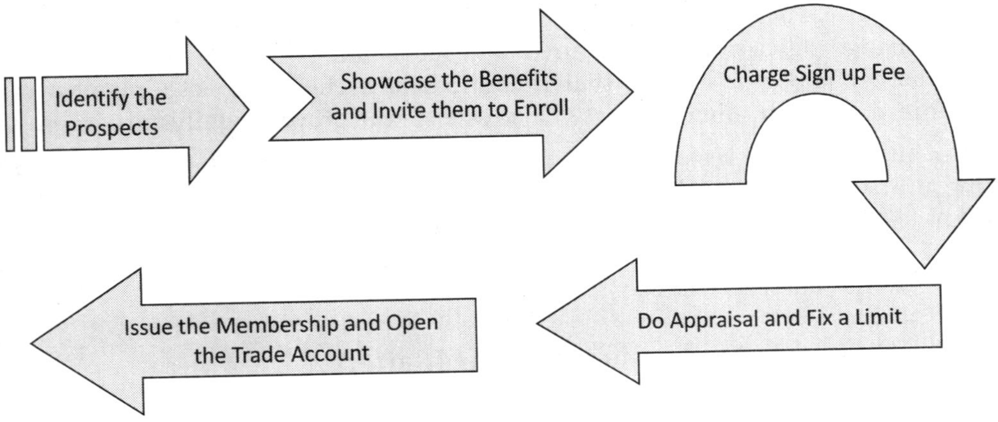

Figure 18.2 Barter Process

Box 18.2 discuss the sources of revenue for exchange.

BOX 18.2: SOURCES OF REVENUE FOR EXCHANGES

Commercial exchanges make money by charging a commission on each transaction, either all on the buy side, or all on the sell side, or a combination of both. Transaction fees typically run between 8–15%. The exchange plays an important role because they provide the record-keeping, brokering expertise and monthly statements to each member.

Usual sources of revenue are:

- One time sign-up fee;
- Management or administration fee for the particular account;
- Commission charged on each transaction;
- Advertising fee based on portal or newsletter.

INDIAN SCENARIO OF BARTER

In India, barter has existed since ages but in a traditional way. As commercial barter, it started gaining momentum following the credit crunch of global recession. In recession-ridden America during the early 1970s, companies facing an acute cash crunch, excess inventory and manufacturing capacity went for the corporate barter business to come out of the red. Many companies in India are doing the same today. Corporate barter means buying media space and time on radio, television, print and outdoor in exchange for manufacturing products. However, barter is still a fraction of Indian trade. As compared to 30% of world barter business, Indian barter is a around 10–12%.

There are various shortcomings that Indian barter suffers from:

- It offers a limited range of products or services. This considerably reduces the utility of these exchanges for the participants which implies, they have limited options to trade for.
- The infrastructure is not developed in terms of technology and to support barter exchange, efficient infrastructure is indispensable.
- Another major problem is that Indian barter exchange is not a member of any international trading network. This restricts the growth significantly.

The current global recession has fuelled barter trade and the trend in India is picking up as well. A lot of business owners are looking for different ways on how they can save cash, as well as continue to market to new customers. Businesses are becoming more receptive to the idea of barter. The slowing economy has certainly helped grow the barter exchange.

Example: Corporate Trading in India–Net4Barter

Net4Barter is a corporate trading company providing barter solutions to businesses across industries. Net4Barter's trade network of more than 500 companies across India helps clients purchase cash-free by paying in kind, liquidate excess stocks and capacities, and grow with incremental sales.

Net4Barter operates as a trade exchange, facilitating trading transactions, developing the member network, marketing products and services across members, maintaining records and accounts and most importantly, underwriting transactions.

Net4Barter's revenue stream consists of 'transaction fees' charged to clients. Whenever they make a purchase (and not upon selling), a fee of 10% of the transaction value is charged. Net4Barter's clientage includes blue-chip names such as 'Business India', 'Business World', 'Godrej', 'Grand Hyatt', 'Hindustan Times', 'Hotel Radisson', etc.

Success Stories of Barter in India

1. *Timex Inventory Episode*

Timex faced a massive inventory problem on a particular model of its watches. Stuck with ₹20 lacs worth of unsold stock, the company was unsure if it could spend on its badly-needed media plan. Net4Barter firm picked up ₹15 lacs worth of Timex watches at their full MRP value and in return, gave Timex the opportunity to execute a new media plan, that too without having to spend any hard cash.

2. *Archies Media Case*

The Archies story is also interesting. Though Archies was doing well, its proprietor, Mr. Moolchandani, was in a dilemma. He needed massive media spend to keep customers acquainted with his ever-changing list of gift items, personal accessories, cards and utility products. At the time when his products got backfired, he was stuck with inventory as well as massive media bills. Net4Barter helped him on both fronts. The company no longer pays for media campaigns, and their unused capacities are also picked up in the bartering process.

3. *Revenue and Visibility Boost for OCM*

OCM Woollen Mills, popularly known as OCM, is a unit of Birla VXL India Limited and is involved with the manufacturing of all-wool worsted and wool-blended worsted suiting. OCM decided to be a member of Net4Barter for incremental sales of its products and barter the same against promotional expenses of its planned winter campaign in leading dailies all across the country. They successfully marketed OCM suiting as an ideal gift and promotional product for the various schemes of media companies and corporates. In a span of two months, OCM was able to open new markets for its products and liquidate suiting worth ₹75 lacs. It gave OCM the necessary boost in revenue and visibility.

4. *Expansion Fuel of Luxor*

Luxor Writing Instruments, a leader in producing writing instruments has mega brands such as Parker, Luxor, etc. They were facing tough market conditions and cut-throat competition, so they wanted to plan out their expansion through sales promotions schemes. Net4Barter successfully managed to influx Luxor with promotional products worth ₹80 lacs like cameras, music systems, microwaves, CTV's, ACs for its dealer and distribution schemes. This product contribution tremendously helped Luxor in curtailing their cash outlays.

5. *Profits Out of Under-utilised Resources for Radisson*

Radisson Hotels & Resorts is a global leader in the hotel industry. Rooms are the most perishable commodities for hospitality industry. Radisson bartered rooms for automation equipment, flooring, gifts for customers and furnishing facilities. Net4barter helped turn their under-utilised capacities into profit and expand their market share.

6. *Dainik Jagran's Increased Sales*

Dainik Jagran decided to spread its circulation and readership to other states but they were in a state of confusion. Their marketing plan involved giving away various appliances, cell phones, leather planners, etc. This required an investment of ₹25 lacs which was a risk. Net4barter procured appliances for Jagran in exchange of advertising space in their paper. Jagran saved cash worth ₹20 lacs and accomplished its objective to become a leading North Indian daily. Therefore, Dainik Jagran bartered advertisement space for appliances.

Source: http://www.net4barter.com/Success.aspx

CASE STUDY

GBC Barter Nectar

A store dealing in sport's goods was on the verge of closure. Instead of selling its goods to a wholesale liquidator for cents on the dollar, the retailer traded its goods on GBC to a chain of fitness clubs, clearing its remaining inventory at full price.

It enabled him to buy what he needed with trade dollars that cost much less than an actual dollar. Had the retailer traded to the liquidator, he would have received 20 cents on the dollar for the sports goods. Now, the same goods were bartered for full retail price. A liquidator offer of $2,000 in goods (20 cents on the dollar) was worth $10,000 trade dollars!

The retailer then had $10,000 dollars to use for barter purchases. He used these earnings to trade with a moving company to relocate to another area, and he had money to hire a web designer to create a retail website, a radio station to advertise the new location and a sign firm to show off his store to its best advantage!

With bartering, he had all the advantage to move his products and at full price. He could now improve the business' profitability and cash flow.

Who does not want to save cash? Who does not want to purchase goods and services for 30 cents or less on the dollar? If the outlay is your cost of goods or unused time and labour, but you are trading for full retail price, you are getting a tremendous bargain. Therefore, bartering can convert your net losses into purchase power.

Source: http://www.globalbartercorp.com/case_studies/how_barter_works_retail_ store_owner.php

POINTS TO REMEMBER

- One of the first evidences of bartering can be found in 6000 BC. During the Great Depression, the barter system began to grow even more rapidly than it had been. Today, it has evolved into a highly sophisticated trade.
- Barter is a method of exchange wherein goods or services are directly exchanged for other goods or services without using a medium of exchange such as money.
- Barter offers advantages like conservation of cash, use of idle resources, networking, better employee compensation, higher productivity, less wastage, and increased cash sales and profits.
- Bartering also has limitations such as need for presence of double coincidence of wants, absence of common measure of value, indivisibility of certain goods, lack of standards for deferred payments and difficulty in storing wealth.
- Traditional barter is one-to-one transaction and non-cash whereas commercial barter is multi-party with trade credit as the currency.
- A barter exchange or trade exchange is a commercial organisation that provides a trading platform and book-keeping system for its members or clients. The Swiss WIR Bank was the first barter system and one of the largest still existing barters at present, established in 1934.
- A Retail Barter Exchange is a company that acts as a third-party record keeper to facilitate transactions among members of the exchange using a non-cash currency called trade credit.
- A Corporate Barter Company takes a principle position in goods or services by purchasing these assets with trade credits and/or cash-equivalent credit (not trade dollars/pounds/marks, etc).
- The process of barter consists of the following steps: *(i) identification of prospects, (ii) invitation to enroll, (iii) membership fee, (iv) fixing of limit, and (v) opening the account.*
- In India, barter has existed since ages but in a traditional way. As commercial barter, it started gaining momentum following the credit crunch of global recession. Corporate barter is buying media space and time on radio, television, print and outdoor in exchange for manufacturing products.

KEY TERMS

- **Barter** is a method of exchange wherein goods or services are directly exchanged for other goods or services without using a medium such as money.
- **Traditional barter** is a one-to-one transaction and non-cash.
- **Commercial barter** is a multi-party with trade credit as the currency.

- **Barter exchange** or trade exchange is a commercial organisation that provides a trading platform and bookkeeping system for its members or clients.
- **Retail barter exchange** is a company that acts as a third-party record keeper to facilitate transactions among members of the exchange using a non-cash currency called trade credit.
- **Corporate barter company** takes a principle position in goods or services by purchasing these assets with trade credits and/or cash-equivalent credit.

EXERCISES

Objective Questions

1. **Tick the correct answer:**

(a) Exchanging one of your DVDs with a friend in return for one of his book is:
  (i) Charter (ii) Barter
  (iii) Cheater (iv) None of the above

(b) One-to-one transaction is:
  (i) Traditional barter (ii) Commercial barter
  (iii) Both (i) and (ii) (iv) None of the above

(c) A barter exchange or trade exchange is:
  (i) Charity organisation (ii) Commercial organisation
  (iii) Voluntary organisation (iv) None of the above

(d) The currency in barter exchange is:
  (i) Trade credit (ii) Cash
  (iii) Metal (iv) None of the above

(e) A Corporate Barter Company takes a:
  (i) Principal position (ii) Secondary position
  (iii) Present position (iv) None of the above

(f) A Retail Barter acts as a:
  (i) Clearing house (ii) Issue house
  (iii) Purchase house (iv) None of the above

Answers: (a) ii (b) i (c) ii (d) i (e) i (f) i

2. **Fill in the blanks:**

(a) One of the first evidences of bartering can be dated back to ....
(b) .... results in conservation of cash.
(c) .... is multi-party trade.
(d) .... barter exchange has mainly small and medium businesses as members.
(e) .... barter has corporates as members.

Answers:

(a) 6000 BC
(b) Barter
(c) Commercial barter

(d) Retail
(e) Corporate

3. True or False:

(a) The Great Depression is one of the most significant time periods throughout the history of bartering.
(b) Barter is a method of exchange involving money.
(c) There are no inherent tax advantages in a barter trade exchange.
(d) In commercial barter, third party involvement is present.
(e) A Retail Barter Exchange acts as a third party record keeper.
(f) Corporate barter is used to move excess capacity and under-performing assets.

Answers: (a) True (b) False (c) False (d) True (e) True (f) True

Short Questions

1. Define bartering.
2. State the key reasons for barter.
3. Distinguish between traditional and commercial barter.
4. What is retail barter and corporate barter?
5. Define financial asset.
6. What are the sources of revenue of barter exchange?

Critical Thinking Questions

1. "Barter is basically a method of conservation of cash". Explain.
2. "The business houses which are strapped of cash should go for bartering". Justify.
3. "Barter is misinterpreted as tax relief tool". Elaborate with an illustration.
4. "Barter is a marketing tool, not a tax tool". Explain.
5. "Barter system has made the business more flexible". Discuss.
6. "Barter is not full of advantages". Prove.
7. "The global recession of late has contributed to the growth of barter". Discuss.
8. "In India bartering is still at a crawling stage". Do you agree?

Descriptive Questions

1. What are the advantages of barter?
2. Explain the economics of barter in detail.
3. What are the key aspects of barter exchange?
4. Discuss the different types of barter exchanges.
5. Explain the barter exchange process.
6. Discuss some success stories of bartering in India.
7. What strategies need to be adopted to develop the Indian barter industry?

PROJECT EXERCISE

A Social Bartering Activity

Tell the students to bring in items, those they would like to exchange with each other. The exchange has to be for real. They will not get back the item once exchanged. Make sure that everyone has brought an item that is between ₹50–100 to have a fair exchange. On the day of exchange, give them the time limit of 30 minutes to do the exchange and act as a facilitator. Students have to demonstrate the process of 'bartering' by exchanging with each other an item that is more valuable to them and learn the technicalities to convert into a commercial trade.

After the completion of the process, ask everyone to discuss on grounds like:

(i) How many students traded their item?
(ii) How many did not trade at all? Why?
(iii) Was there anyone who traded more than once to get the item of their choice?
(iv) Lastly, ask one key learning from everyone.

REVIEW CASE

T&T Barter Teaching

T&T School is all for 'teaching passion'. It is always on the lookout for people for whom 'love is teaching and teaching is love'. They inspire their teachers to be as creative and descriptive as possible with their teaching methods for a better learning by the students. Discussion, hands-on exercise, experimental format—it is up to the individual teacher how he/she would like to go ahead. They do not require any formal teaching experience and also no money is exchanged.

Teaching at T&T School: T&T School is an alternative learning project where students exchange barter items for a teacher-facilitated class. After one submits his class idea, i.e. when he would like to teach, and what he wants in exchange for teaching, the school organisers review the submission and post it on the website, if found suitable, for students to sign up. Once, you complete your class, you receive your barter items.

The class: The class can be on any topic and can be structured in any way you like. The focal point is that you and the students both should enjoy the class and there should be some value addition for them.

The barter items: In your proposal, you have to submit a list of barter items. The list should be as comprehensive as you can think of. Be specific regarding your wish but do consider the accessibility factor of the items.

Activities

(i) Students sit at their desks. Discuss the topic with the students. Direct the attention of the students to the topic.
(ii) Explain that the students will have a set amount of time (10 mins.) to discuss after your lecture and come out with their own thoughts.
(iii) Ask them to present then.
(iv) Following the class, you may have students discuss the process of bartering—its strengths and weaknesses.

Assessment: Observe the students while they present. Using post-it notes, write a brief comment on each student during their presentation. Are they participating? Are they presenting in the right direction? Did they gain something out of it?

Issues for Discussion

(i) What type of barter is mentioned in the case?
(ii) Does the school profitably employ any idle resources as associated with bartering?
(iii) How does it help the school to grow?
(iv) Is it economically viable? How can this be turned into a real commercial trade?
(v) What are the tax implications of this type of barter?

REFERENCES

Langrick, Roger (1994), "Barter Systems: A Business Guide for Trade Exchanges: A New Way to Offset Start-Up Expenses, Reduce Inventories, Conserve Cash Flow, and Open New M. *Longmeadow Pr*, 1st ed. (October).

www.barternewyork.net

www.globalbartercorp.com

www.hudsonbarterexchange.com

www.net4barter.com

www.qoin.org

Part V

CUSTOMER CENTRICITY

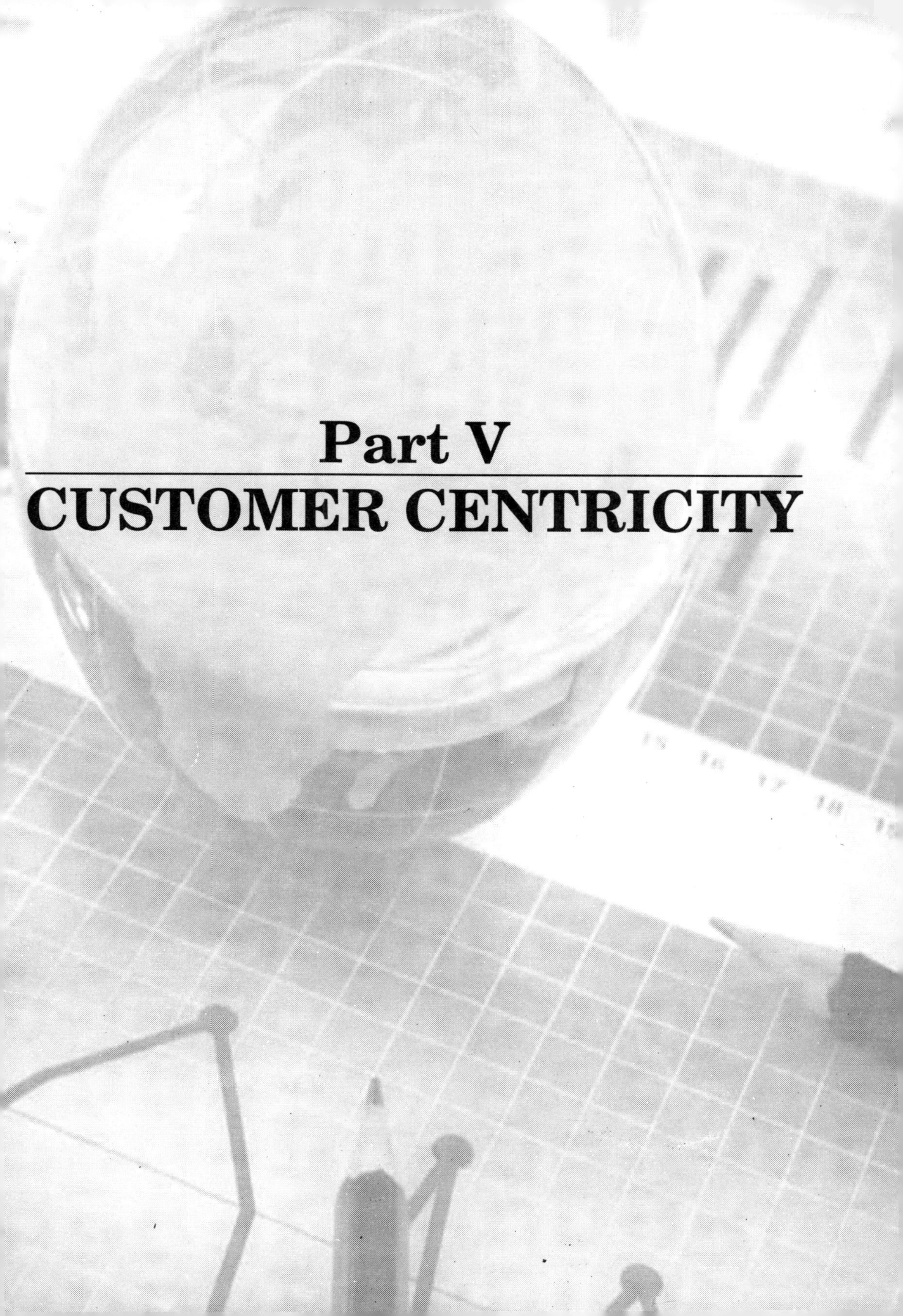

CHAPTER

19

Marketing of Financial Services

If you want to rear financial blessings, you have to sow financially.

— Joel Osteen

LEARNING OBJECTIVES

This chapter discusses the following:

- Overview of marketing of financial services
- Challenges in financial services marketing
- Marketing of banking
- Marketing of insurance
- Marketing of plastic money
- Emerging trends in financial services marketing

INTRODUCTION

According to Martin Lewis of *moneysavingexpert.com*, "loyalty doesn't pay". However, customer inertia, about switching current accounts, implies that even if customers do not 'like' or feel loyal to their financial services provider, they are unlikely to switch to a competitor. But that might be about to change with the 'perfect storm' conditions of Virgin Money taking over Northern Rock[1]. Therefore, the impact that the nature of marketing has on the understanding about financial services by the society has seen a new perspective emerging on these services, i.e., 'marketing of financial services'.

Marketing of financial services is far more complex as it involves selling a financial product than selling a normal consumer durable product. The financial product features are difficult to show in a television advertisement. Further, financial services are relatively uninteresting in nature, and do not attract the consumer's attention at the first place. The environment in which financial services are marketed is also becoming more competitive, making the task of financial services marketing increasingly challenging and difficult.

Every month, new players enter into the market and experiment by bringing out new products and services. India is a nation with 1.3 billion people and every institution is trying to capitalise this growing consumer base. The Indian consumers are open to new things as most of the Indian population is young and hence receptive to changes.

MARKETING OF FINANCIAL SERVICES: AN OVERVIEW

The marketing of financial services is a unique and highly specialised branch of marketing where one has to think of specialised strategies in order to promote and sell financial products. Undoubtedly, it is challenging but the consumers often exhibit much predictable behaviour in their dealings with financial services providers. The inevitability of this behaviour and the abundance of data on existing and potential customers enable to develop and execute a unique and a much more scientific approach for the marketing of financial services, than in other areas.

A. Financial Services Marketing vs. Other Marketing(s)

The key aspects of financial services marketing which differentiate it from other marketing practices, relating to the product, pricing, place and promotion are discussed below:

1. *Product Quality*

A unique aspect of financial services marketing is the illusive notion of 'product quality'. In the traditional context of marketing manufactured goods, quality is objectively measurable. However, in the context of financial services, the parameter of quality is highly subjective. *For example,* it is difficult to judge the objective quality of willingness of an insurance company to pay out customer claims, unless one experiences it. The reason is that the majority of policyholders do not utilise their policy benefits since the events being insured typically have low probabilities of occurrence. As a result, most policyholders never undergo the process of filing a claim and for those that do, the outcome of their experience may not really be recorded anywhere for others to examine and learn from. Thus, a quality assessment in such a context is not objective and is largely based on subjective factors.

---

1. http://news.opinium.co.uk/sites/news.opinium.co.uk/files/Financial%20Services%20Marketing%20in%202012%20-%20an%20Opinium%20report.pdf

Similarly, in the context of stock trading services, customers may not necessarily be able to find out whether the broker is providing them with the most appropriate advice, until those securities are sold off. In all these financial services, quality assessment is highly subjective.

2. *Price Complexity*

The prices of financial services are intrinsically complex. *For example,* the lease price of a machine might consist of cash down payment and monthly payments, rather than the single offer price used when purchasing the machine in cash. This not only makes the task of understanding the various prices available in the marketplace difficult for the consumer but also creates problems for the marketers to come out with the competitive pricing. "Pricing too low or too high can have detrimental effects on profitability of financial services organisations".

3. *Market Differentiation*

Another unique aspect of financial services marketing is that consumers' needs for financial services vary significantly from one customer to the other. As a result, the types of services that a financial services organisation introduces may be best suited to one marketplace, i.e., for specific groups of consumers but not for other groups. Therefore, it is important to have an accurate understanding of consumer segments that are most relevant to a given financial service, especially in the light of availability of voluminous amount of customer data. *For example,* most of the financial companies now a days tie up with online database companies for understanding each person's credit behaviour and financial needs.

4. *Promotional Factor*

Advertising is a fundamental part of most of the successful marketing strategies in both financial and non-financial services. It is the primary mechanism by which marketers create awareness among consumers about their products and services. However, it has a special role in the marketing of financial services since financial services are generally intangible. Thus, the responsibility of informing the consumers about the beneficial aspects of a financial service lies on the shoulders of the advertiser.

The financial services advertisers have to educate consumers on the unique and beneficial features of their services. Advertising in financial services can be formally defined as marketing communications carried out through the mass media or through direct marketing means to induce the customers to purchase these financial products. Electronic media such as television and radio, as well as print media such as newspapers and magazines, are often used as a part of mass media, whereas direct advertising methods such as direct mail and direct e-mail are used as direct marketing tools to elicit consumer responses.

3. Approaches in Marketing of Financial Services

Companies adopt either the *customer-centric approach* or *product-centric approach* in marketing processes and those offering specialised services often follow the former, while the companies catering to masses follow the latter. Majorly, the trends given below reinforce the need for companies to undergo transformation from product to customer-centricity in today's market:

- Increasing pressure on improving productivity
- Increasing market diversity
- Cut-throat competition
- Consumer awareness
- Advances in technology

Financial institutions are just as exposed to these pressures as other companies and therefore, the need for them to renovate their marketing at the tip of iceberg is more crucial. Table 19.1 provides a comparison between customer-centric and product centric approaches.

TABLE 19.1 Comparison of Customer-centric and Product-centric Approaches in Financial Services

Basis	*Customer-centric Approach*	*Product-centric Approach*
1. Key focus	Customer satisfaction	Product profitability
2. Business orientation	Relationship-oriented	Sale-oriented
3. Perspective	Long-term	Short-term
4. Product positioning	Tailor-made product as per individual customer needs	Bulk products for masses
5. Selling approach	How many customers can we win?	How many products can we sell to the customers?

CHALLENGES IN FINANCIAL SERVICES MARKETING

Several factors make the marketing process in financial services unique and challenging. Therefore, it is necessary to appreciate them in order to capitalise on the unique rol that successful marketing can play in financial services. These factors are listed below

1. *Vague product/service attributes:* One of the challenges in marketing financia services is that consumers may not be fully aware of the various dimensions of financial service. *For example,* while buying automobile insurance, consumers ma focus on the low premiums and ignore the terms of the contract which decide thei claim settlement. Consumers' limited knowledge and education about the choices i the marketplace can result in inefficient and uncompetitive market conditions.

2. *Lack of measurement of benefits:* One of the other challenges facing financia services marketing is that the benefits to be derived from a financial service cannot b measured. *For example,* it is difficult to measure the claims settlement behaviour of a insurance company and ultimately, it affects the customers. Therefore, the marketer financial services needs to create an understanding and appreciation for the underlyin qualities of a financial offer.

3. *Lack of visual appeal:* One of the unique challenges in marketing financial product is that it is not always possible to communicate them properly to consumers, lik consumer goods, due to visual appeal. *For example,* an automobile manufacturer may feature pictures of a car in a magazine advertisement or in a television advertisement.

Visualisation of these products increases the reception by the consumer. In contrast, advertising an insurance policy or an investment product is far more difficult.

4. *Regulations:* The practice of financial services marketing is further complicated by the massive number of regulations that restrict the contents of financial services advertisements, and the number of regulatory agencies that closely monitor and influence the content. It is right also because regulations in financial services are there to ensure that marketers do not present consumers with misleading information but this restricts the marketing of financial products.

5. *Variable Prices:* Another challenge in the marketing of financial services is that price does not often remain constant and varies as per the individual's circumstances. *For example,* the processing charges of loans by a bank vary from one consumer to the next depending on his income level. This complicates the process of pricing in financial services.

MARKETING OF BANKING

With the privatisation of banks and entry of foreign banks, Indian banking industry has seen a decline in customer loyalty by as much as 40%. This has put tremendous pressure on the public sector banks and forced them to serve their customers well. The banking industry in India has evolved over the years with the help of technology, resulting into multi-channels of banking. The rise in number of ATMs and growth of internet penetration in the country has completely changed the way banks serve their customers. The introduction of 5G services and mobile banking has led to more and more people using these alternate means of banking and this ultimately results in more 'financial inclusion'. The competition has also forced the industry to come out with innovative products such as reverse mortgage, flexi deposits, etc. to serve their customers.

Various facets of bank marketing are discussed below.

• Internet Banking

Internet banking has changed the way people bank. It has reduced the need for people to visit banks physically. Online banking allows people to transfer funds between accounts, inter-bank transfer and avail the issue of demand drafts and cheques. This has increased customer convenience and has reduced the hassles of daily banking. Other most significant use of internet banking is that one can use it to pay their bills online. Besides bill payments, the customers can also book railway tickets online.

• Funds Transfer

Facilities such as Real Time Gross Settlement System (RTGS) and National Electronic Fund Transfer System (NEFT), and Immediate Payment Service (IMPS) enable the customers to transfer money from their accounts in secure and efficient manner. In

RTGS, settlement is done on real-time basis and is available for transactions worth more than ₹2 lacs. This is particularly good for people who constantly transfer large amounts. NEFT is also helpful for walk-in customers who want to transfer money to the beneficiary's account but do not have their own account with the bank. IMPS is a revoluation which acts as an instant payment inter-bank electronic funds transfer system in India, through mobile phones.

- **Plastic Cards**

With growth in internet penetration, more and more people are shopping online as it gives them access to a wide variety of products. This has led to the increased use of plastic money such as credit cards and debit cards. Banks have come out with their own plastic cards for the customers.

- **ATM**

ATMs provide people with 24 hour access to cash and ability to transact anywhere anytime. This has proved to be a boon for people who travel constantly. Of late, some ATMs have also started providing facility of recharging pre-paid mobile phones.

- **Mobile Banking**

Growth of smartphones and increasing use of internet on these phones, has resulted in the mobile banking service of India gaining momentum. It could also prove to be a platform for financial inclusion as mobile penetration in India is increasing day by day. In order to make it more accessible, the government has already approved the concept of 'no frill accounts' in which a customer does not have to maintain minimum balance in their account. The service is known as Interbank Mobile Payment Service (IMPS).

- **New Innovations**

Apart from the hybrid accounts which comprise of the facilities of savings and current account, some banks have also started the facility of saving accounts with 'auto-sweep' facility. When money in the account goes above a certain value, it is converted into fixed deposit and when the money goes below a certain value, the fixed deposit is broken and the balance is automatically credited into the savings account of the customer. This facility provides better yield to the customers.

MARKETING OF INSURANCE

Insurance is a form of risk-management which spreads the risk (accident, theft, natural disaster, illness, etc.) of many people in exchange for small payments from each individual known as an insurance premium. Premiums are often annual or monthly but depending on the type of insurance they can be at other intervals. Figure 19.1 shows various insurance companies of India.

The key facets of insurance marketing are explained below.

• Bouquet of Insurance Plans

Companies, of late, have come out with a lot of innovative insurance products both life and general, as a marketing strategy. Even company like LIC had to come out with Unit Linked Insurance Plan (ULIP) as a part of competitive measure against the private sector.

In life insurance, there are policies like term insurance, whole life, endowment, money back, annuities and pension, and the most favoured by the youth, ULIP. Similarly in general insurance, there are multiple options available from the insurance companies.

Figure 19.1 Major Insurance Companies

• Competitive Analysis

Every company, in order to better sell their policies, often shows comparative chart with the rival company. In this race, they highlight their better features and cover up the weaker areas. Table 19.2 shows the comparison between ULIPs of some leading insurance companies of India.

TABLE 19.2 Kotak Mahindra with LIC (Life Insurance)

Company	LIC	Kotak Mahindra
Policy Name	LIC Nivesh Plus	Kotak e-Invest Plan
Website	http://www.licindia.in	https://www.kotaklife.com
Type of insurance	Unit Linked Plan	Unit Linked Endowment Plan
Type of policy (individual, group)	Individual	Individual
Frequency of premium payment (monthly, quarterly, semi-annual, annual)	Single Premium	Yearly, Half-yearly, Quarterly, Monthly
Entry Age	Minimum: 90 days	Minimum: 3 years
	Maximum: 70 years	Maximum: 60 years
Premium amount	Minimum: ₹1,00,000 single	Minimum: ₹750 monthly
Death Benefit	Yes • On death before & after the Date of Commencement of Risk	Yes • Starting from end of 6 Policy year, maturity or death whichever is earlier
Survival/Maturity Benefit	On Life Assured surviving the date of maturity, an amount equal to Unit Fund Value shall be payable.	From end of 6 Policy year, maturity or death whichever is earlier
Additional Riders Available	Yes • Accidental Death Benefit Ride	Yes • Accidental Death Benefit Rider • Kotak Permanent Disability Benefit Rider
Potential problems or disadvantages of this coverage	Less Number of Riders Available	Benefits from end of 6th year
	Comparatively Expensive	

MARKETING OF PLASTIC MONEY

Plastic money is not just a trend rather it has become a necessity and a part of life of many people around the world. Though there are people who prefer carrying cash wherever they go, the risk associated with the cash is of being getting stolen. Various type of plastic money is there in the form of credit card, debit card, charge card, in-store card, smart card, etc.

Since these cards are mainly used by the privileged class, their marketing also has to be very special and focused. India is one of the fastest growing economies in the world, with about 65% of India's population below the age of 35 years. The youth in India is more and more demanding, the income levels are rising and so is the middle income group, which has led to change in the lifestyles of Indians. The number of credit cards issued in India has increased exponentially in the recent years. According to the sources, only 20% of the affluent class people in India have a credit card which is very less as compared to the developed nations. This shows the tremendous opportunity of growth in the Indian market for plastic money.

• Key Marketing Factors for Plastic Money

Plastic card companies devise their marketing around following key areas:

- *Credit limit:* The amount of transactions that the card-holder can do without repaying by the due date.
- *Credit time offered:* The repayment period within which the card-holder has to pay for his transactions.
- *Rate of interest:* The interest which is charged upon the payment due on the card.
- *Eligibility criteria:* These are decided differently by various financial institutions, some take age as the eligibility criteria; some look in for a good job of the card-holder.
- *Acceptance of the card:* They have acceptability at various points.

• Marketing Offers/Schemes

Plastic money is marketed using various schemes like:

1. *Cashback:* It is like getting paid to spend. *For example,* you made a purchase of ₹10,000 using your credit card. The statement reflects a credit of ₹500 in your account next month. Your bank has paid you back 5% against the ₹10,000 you spent. Cashback is the most important tool used by financial institutions to promote plastic money. The cashback offers influence customer behaviour and tempts them to shop more. The percentage of cashback varies from bank to bank and is also governed by various policies of the banks which are often overlooked by the consumers.

Catch in cashback offers:

- The details of cashback are printed in very small letters on the agreement we sign;
- Cashback may not be actual cashback but may be in the form of gift points;
- Some banks do not include retail stores such as Easy Day or Reliance as grocery stores and do not include them in cashback offers.

Examples

- *Indian Oil Citibank Titanium Credit Card:* Offers cashback of `200. But the condition says that the cashback is valid only on the first `1000 sent and it should be within 1st month when the card is issued.
- *Kotak Mahindra Bank:* Waives off a railway booking surcharge of 1.8% on the transaction amount but the condition says that a maximum of ₹500 surcharge will be waved off in a year.

- *HSBC:* Gives a 10% cashback on all dining and movies. The terms and conditions say: "The cashback will be provided only on the first five dining and movie transactions and upto a maximum of ₹600 in a billing cycle. No cashback would be available on a single dining or movie transaction whose value exceeds ₹4,000".
- *HDFC:* HDFC Visa Value cashback credit card, for instance, lets you avail cash-back only when your outstanding balance is ₹10,000 or above. High interest is charged upon outstanding balance in turn.

2. *Reward points:* They let you earn flights, holidays, CDs, Dining, Shopping, Movies, gift vouchers or more by getting points. Working of reward points needs to be understood properly because this is the trap area for the customers. These points ultimately lead to more shopping from the same outlet.

3. *Travel miles:* These benefits are provided on frequent flying from the same airline.

- Many cards provide frequent flyer advantage.
- Miles in the form of points get accumulated every time you fly.
- Later, you can redeem these points to fly for free up to the free miles accumulated.

Examples

- JetPrivilege HDFC Bank World
  - (i) 1 Base-fare waived Jet Airways ticket and upto 10,000 JP Miles.
  - (ii) 3x JP Miles for ticket booking on www.jetairways.com and www.jetkonnect.com.
- Citibank PremierMiles Card
  - (i) Earn 10 Miles for every ₹100 spent on airlines.
  - (ii) Earn 4 Miles for all non-airlines spend.
  - (iii) Redeem your miles instantly on www.PremierMiles.co.in for air tickets, hotels and car rentals.
  - (iv) Enjoy the privilege of transferring your miles to the Frequent Flyer Programme of any of our partner airlines.
  - (v) Get 10,000* Miles on your first spend.

TRENDS IN FINANCIAL SERVICES MARKETING

During the last few years, various new trends have emerged in financial services marketing. They are discussed as follows:

1. *Increasing customer engagement:* There is an increasing customer engagement in the financial services sector now. This challenges the level of engagement in the marketing world. This customer engagement is not just engagement with the service provider but also how customers engage among themselves 'about the provider'. Therefore, the challenge is to establish and maintain an engaging relationship with them.

2. *Problems in marketing analytics:* Marketing analytics fuel the growth of financial services industry but the data available is mostly in the form of unformatted data. Finding out the skilled people who can analyze this data is a difficult task. Most financial institutions have to rely on external partners for these insights, and compete with other companies for these resources.

3. ***Role of social media:*** There is no field today which is untouched by the social media. Realising the importance of social media for its outreach, banks and other financial institutions have also started using in their database and incorporating them in their customer and prospect segmentation.

4. ***Mobile marketing:*** Mobile marketing, particularly mobile banking, has gained a much stronger foothold in the recent times. With smartphones and other platforms (iPhone, Android phones, iPad, etc.), banking has really touched upon to more customers now.

5. ***IT touching:*** Due to security and privacy concerns, multi-channel marketing has been slower in most financial service firms. It can be attributed more to the recent online and IT financial scams. But financial institutions still have a headstart in this regard in the form of existing networks of ATMs and online banking, for making it easy for the customers.

POINTS TO REMEMBER

- Marketing of financial services is one of the unique branches of marketing where one has to think of specialised strategies to promote and sell financial products. Selling a financial product is far more complex than selling a normal consumer-durable product because the features of a financial product cannot be really shown in a television advertisement. Financial services are also relatively uninteresting in nature, not attracting the consumer attention at the first place.
- A unique aspect of financial services marketing is the illusive notion of 'product quality'. In the traditional context of marketing manufactured goods, quality is objectively measurable. However, in the context of financial services, the parameter of quality is highly subjective.
- The prices of financial services are intrinsically complex. Pricing too low or too high can have detrimental effects on the profitability of financial services organisations.
- Another unique aspect of financial services marketing is that consumers' needs for financial services vary significantly from one customer to the other. As a result, the types of services that a financial services organisation introduces may be best suited to one marketplace, i.e. for specific groups of consumers but not for other groups. Therefore, it is important to have an accurate understanding of consumer segments.
- Advertising is a fundamental part of most of the successful marketing strategies in both financial and non-financial services. However, it has a special role in the marketing of financial services since financial services are generally intangible. Advertising in financial services can be formally defined as marketing

communications carried out through the mass media or through direct marketing means which induce the customers to purchase these financial products.

- Companies adopt either the customer-centric approach or product-centric approach in marketing processes. Customer approach is long-term with prime focus on relationship building, while product approach is short-term in nature.
- Several factors make the marketing process in financial services unique and challenging—(a) vague service attributes, (b) lack of measurement of benefits, (c) lack of visual appeal, (d) regulations, and (e) variable pricing.
- The banking industry in India has evolved over the years with the help of technology, which has emanated other multi-channels of banking. The rise in number of ATMs and growth of internet penetration in the country has completely changed the way banks service their customers. The introduction of 4G services and mobile banking has lead to more and more people using these alternate means of banking, ultimately resulting in more financial inclusion. The competition has also forced the industry to come out with innovative products such as reverse mortgage, Islamic banking, etc. to serve their customers.
- Insurance companies, of late, have come out with a lot of innovative insurance products both life and general, as a marketing strategy. Even, company like LIC had to come out with ULIP as a part of competitive measure against the private sector. Every company, in order to better sell their policies, often shows comparative chart with the rival company. In this race, they highlight their better features and cover up the weaker areas.
- Plastic money is not just a trend, rather it has become a necessity and part of life of many people around the world. Since these cards are mainly used by the privileged class, their marketing also has to be very special and focused. India is one of the fastest growing economies in the world, with about 65% of India's population below the age of 35 years. The number of credit cards issued in India has increased exponentially in the recent years.
- During the last few years, various new trends have emerged in financial services marketing such as increasing customer engagement, problems in marketing analytics, role of social media, mobile marketing and right touching.

KEY TERMS

- **Marketing of financial services** is a unique branch of marketing which involves specialised strategies to promote and sell financial products.
- **Customer-centric approach** is long-term in nature which focuses on customer satisfaction as 'Customer is the King'.
- **Product-centric approach** is short-term in nature with product profitability as the key focus.

EXERCISES

Objective Questions

1. Tick the correct answer:

(a) Marketing of financial services is complex because:
- (i) Financial services are intangible
- (ii) Financial services are uninteresting
- (iii) Financial services are not measurable
- (iv) All of the above

(b) In the context of financial services, the parameter of quality is:
- (i) Objective
- (ii) Subjective
- (iii) Massive
- (iv) None of the above

(c) Market differentiation implies:
- (i) Different customers
- (ii) Different customers with same needs
- (iii) Different customers with different needs
- (iv) None of the above

(d) Customer-centric approach focuses on:
- (i) Relationship
- (ii) Sales
- (iii) Profits
- (iv) None of the above

Answers: (a) iv (b) ii (c) iii (d) i

2. Fill in the blanks:

(a) Marketing of .... services is a unique branch of marketing.

(b) Advertising is a marketing communication carried out through the .... or direct marketing.

(c) Companies adopt either the customer-centric approach or .... approach in marketing processes.

(d) Cash back is marketing offer of ....

Answers:

(a) Financial services

(b) Mass media

(c) Product centric

(d) Plastic money

3. True or False:

(a) A unique aspect of financial services marketing is the illusive notion of 'product quality'.

(b) In the traditional marketing of manufactured goods, quality is objectively measurable.

(c) Price complexity is an irrelevant factor in financial services marketing.

(d) Product-centric approach is long-term in nature.
(e) Vague service attributes is a major challenge in marketing of financial services.
(f) Pricing of financial services varies as per the individual's circumstances.

Answers: (a) True (b) True (c) False (d) False (e) True (f) True

Short Questions

1. Distinguish between product-centric and customer-centric marketing approach.
2. What are the key factors in marketing of plastic money?

Critical Thinking Questions

1. "Financial services marketing is completely different from traditional marketing". Explain.
2. "Financial services marketing is not free from challenges". Justify.
3. "Marketing of financial services is not confined to only one medium". Elaborate with suitable illustrations.
4. "Social media has brought a new revolution in the financial services marketing". Discuss.
5. "Marketing of banking has really helped banking evolved of late". Prove.
6. "Every company, in order to better sell their financial services highlights their better features and covers up the weaker areas". Illustrate.

Descriptive Questions

1. Describe the pillars of marketing of financial services.
2. What are the approaches followed in marketing of financial services?
3. What are the various marketing offers made in plastic money?
4. Explain the emerging trends in financial services marketing.
5. Throw some light on the marketing scenario of financial services in India.
6. What are some limitations that apply to the marketing of financial services?

PROJECT EXERCISE

Analysing the Ethical Code of Marketing in Financial Services

Turn to the 'best-buy stocks" recommendations of a financial advisory firm in a leading newspaper. Select one of the stocks and trade in the same accordingly. After the due period, compare and find out whether you have the gain as advised or not? Draw up a table of comparative stocks and analyze their performance. Also, try to explore and find out about the investors who might be facing the same issue. Was the recommendation y the financial company correct? Can this marketing strategy of the financial company e considered ethical?

REVIEW CASE

he Right 'Marketing Strategy'

Iillennium Funds Company is planning to launch a new investment product offering a eturn of 9% on 2 years deposit. The financial planner has forecasted a revenue of ₹18 iillion from the same in the very first year, but, at the end of the year, the results 'ere not as expected. They decided to cut down on the processing fees from ₹5,000 to 1,000 and resorted to aggressive advertisement campaign. Still, the picture was more r less same at the end of the second year. Therefore, they went for the market analysis. 'hey found out some shocking revelations. Their competitor company was offering the ame product at a lower return of 8.5% and was also charging the processing fees of 5,000. Despite this, its revenue still got doubled in these years. The target market of oth the companies was same and their working model was also very similar.

The Millennium Co. was in utter confusion that despite a reduction in processing harges and offering a higher rate on interest, they were not able to attract customers, 'hereas their rival company was winning over them even with lower interest and igher processing charges. When they had launched the scheme, they were confident bout its success because they were offering the highest rate of return in the market. 'he MD of the company called on the meeting of his functional heads to solve out the roblem. One suggested on cutting down the cost, particularly the running cost part. nother recommended for increasing the return further. Another came out with the lea of making the processing charges to be zero but the MD knew that the problem s somewhere else.

Then, expertise of a well-known consulting company was sought. They were told hat this was not surprising. Financial service providers often fail to build and execute ynamic content marketing programmes. Instead, they frequently rely on tried-and-rue but far less creative, tactics. To be clear, the problem is not the product or ervice, or the lack of effort, and it is certainly not a lack of high-quality content. nstead, it is the way the industry seemingly operates under the misconception that ts of less relevance to the potential customers. Another problem is the clear point f view. This is, in a large part, why so much financial content rides the fence, and vhy so many companies are just beginning to dip their toes into social media. They uggested forging ahead and taking a more innovative approach to content with the elp of scenario analysis.

Other relevant details are given below:

- Minimum deposit amount: ₹20,000
- Variable cost per plan: ₹10,500
- Fixed cost: ₹5,000

Issues for Discussion

(i) What is the major problem in the present case? Is it anything to do with th scenario under which the company performs or markets?

(ii) What major steps should the company take to improve its revenue stream?

(iii) How is the rival company able to double its revenue with lower rate of interes and higher processing charges?

(iv) Do the customers not consider these financial factors while choosing a investment product? Are they guided by some other factors?

(v) Can the above failure of the company be attributed to the marketing strategy

(vi) Does cost structure of the company have any role to play in this failure?

REFERENCES

Cheverton, P., Hughes, T., Foss, B. and Stone, M. (2005), *Key Account Management i Financial Services*, London and Philadelphia, Kogan Page.

www.hdfcbank.com

www.ibef.org

www.irda.gov.in

www.kotaklife.com

www.licindia.in

www.news.opinium.co.uk

www.online.citibank.co.in

APPENDICES

TIME VALUE OF MONEY TABLES

APPENDIX 1

Future Value Interest Factor of a Lumpsum of ₹1 per Period at i% for n Periods, FVIF (i,n)

Period	1%	2%	3%	4%	5%	6%	7%	8%	9%	10%	11%	12%	13%	14%	15%	16%	17%	18%	19%	20%
1	1.010	1.020	1.030	1.040	1.050	1.060	1.070	1.080	1.090	1.100	1.110	1.120	1.130	1.140	1.150	1.160	1.170	1.180	1.190	1.200
2	1.020	1.040	1.061	1.082	1.103	1.124	1.145	1.166	1.188	1.210	1.232	1.254	1.277	1.300	1.323	1.346	1.369	1.392	1.416	1.440
3	1.030	1.061	1.093	1.125	1.158	1.191	1.225	1.260	1.295	1.331	1.368	1.405	1.443	1.482	1.521	1.561	1.602	1.643	1.685	1.728
4	1.041	1.082	1.126	1.170	1.216	1.262	1.311	1.360	1.412	1.464	1.518	1.574	1.630	1.689	1.749	1.811	1.874	1.939	2.005	2.074
5	1.051	1.104	1.159	1.217	1.276	1.338	1.403	1.469	1.539	1.611	1.685	1.762	1.842	1.925	2.011	2.100	2.192	2.288	2.386	2.488
6	1.062	1.126	1.194	1.265	1.340	1.419	1.501	1.587	1.677	1.772	1.870	1.974	2.082	2.195	2.313	2.436	2.565	2.700	2.840	2.986
7	1.072	1.149	1.230	1.316	1.407	1.504	1.606	1.714	1.828	1.949	2.076	2.211	2.353	2.502	2.660	2.826	3.001	3.185	3.379	3.583
8	1.083	1.172	1.267	1.369	1.477	1.594	1.718	1.851	1.993	2.144	2.305	2.476	2.658	2.853	3.059	3.278	3.511	3.759	4.021	4.300
9	1.094	1.195	1.305	1.423	1.551	1.689	1.838	1.999	2.172	2.358	2.558	2.773	3.004	3.252	3.518	3.803	4.108	4.435	4.785	5.160
10	1.105	1.219	1.344	1.480	1.629	1.791	1.967	2.159	2.367	2.594	2.839	3.106	3.395	3.707	4.046	4.411	4.807	5.234	5.695	6.192
11	1.116	1.243	1.384	1.539	1.710	1.898	2.105	2.332	2.580	2.853	3.152	3.479	3.836	4.226	4.652	5.117	5.624	6.176	6.777	7.430
12	1.127	1.268	1.426	1.601	1.796	2.012	2.252	2.518	2.813	3.138	3.498	3.896	4.335	4.818	5.350	5.936	6.580	7.288	8.064	8.916
13	1.138	1.294	1.469	1.665	1.886	2.133	2.410	2.720	3.066	3.452	3.883	4.363	4.898	5.492	6.153	6.886	7.699	8.599	9.596	10.699
14	1.149	1.319	1.513	1.732	1.980	2.261	2.579	2.937	3.342	3.797	4.310	4.887	5.535	6.261	7.076	7.988	9.007	10.147	11.420	12.839
15	1.161	1.346	1.558	1.801	2.079	2.397	2.759	3.172	3.642	4.177	4.785	5.474	6.254	7.138	8.137	9.266	10.539	11.974	13.590	15.407
16	1.173	1.373	1.605	1.873	2.183	2.540	2.952	3.426	3.970	4.595	5.311	6.130	7.067	8.137	9.358	10.748	12.330	14.129	16.172	18.488
17	1.184	1.400	1.653	1.948	2.292	2.693	3.159	3.700	4.328	5.054	5.895	6.866	7.986	9.276	10.761	12.468	14.426	16.672	19.244	22.186
18	1.196	1.428	1.702	2.026	2.407	2.854	3.380	3.996	4.717	5.560	6.544	7.690	9.024	10.575	12.375	14.463	16.879	19.673	22.901	26.623
19	1.208	1.457	1.754	2.107	2.527	3.026	3.617	4.316	5.142	6.116	7.263	8.613	10.197	12.056	14.232	16.777	19.748	23.214	27.252	31.948
20	1.220	1.486	1.806	2.191	2.653	3.207	3.870	4.661	5.604	6.727	8.062	9.646	11.523	13.743	16.367	19.461	23.106	27.393	32.429	38.338
25	1.282	1.641	2.094	2.666	3.386	4.292	5.427	6.848	8.623	10.835	13.585	17.000	21.231	26.462	32.919	40.874	50.658	62.669	77.388	95.396
30	1.348	1.811	2.427	3.243	4.322	5.743	7.612	10.063	13.268	17.449	22.892	29.960	39.116	50.950	66.212	85.850	111.065	143.371	184.675	237.376
35	1.417	2.000	2.814	3.946	5.516	7.686	10.677	14.785	20.414	28.102	38.575	52.800	72.069	98.100	133.176	180.314	243.503	327.997	440.701	590.668
40	1.489	2.208	3.262	4.801	7.040	10.286	14.974	21.725	31.409	45.259	65.001	93.051	132.782	188.884	267.864	378.721	533.869	750.378	1,051.668	1,469.772
50	1.645	2.692	4.384	7.107	11.467	18.420	29.457	46.902	74.358	117.391	184.565	289.002	450.736	700.233	1,083.657	1,670.704	2,566.215	3,927.357	5,988.914	9,100.438

APPENDIX 2

Future Value Interest Factor of an Annuity of ₹1 per Period at i% for n Periods, FVIFA (i,n)

Period	1%	2%	3%	4%	5%	6%	7%	8%	9%	10%	11%	12%	13%	14%	15%	16%	17%	18%	19%	20%
1	1.000	1.000	1.000	1.000	1.000	1.000	1.000	1.000	1.000	1.000	1.000	1.000	1.000	1.000	1.000	1.000	1.000	1.000	1.000	1.000
2	2.010	2.020	2.030	2.040	2.050	2.060	2.070	2.080	2.090	2.100	2.110	2.120	2.130	2.140	2.150	2.160	2.170	2.180	2.190	2.200
3	3.030	3.060	3.091	3.122	3.153	3.184	3.215	3.246	3.278	3.310	3.342	3.374	3.407	3.440	3.473	3.506	3.539	3.572	3.606	3.640
4	4.060	4.122	4.184	4.246	4.310	4.375	4.440	4.506	4.573	4.641	4.710	4.779	4.850	4.921	4.993	5.066	5.141	5.215	5.291	5.368
5	5.101	5.204	5.309	5.416	5.526	5.637	5.751	5.867	5.985	6.105	6.228	6.353	6.480	6.610	6.742	6.877	7.014	7.154	7.297	7.442
6	6.152	6.308	6.468	6.633	6.802	6.975	7.153	7.336	7.523	7.716	7.913	8.115	8.323	8.536	8.754	8.977	9.207	9.442	9.683	9.930
7	7.214	7.434	7.662	7.898	8.142	8.394	8.654	8.923	9.200	9.487	9.783	10.089	10.405	10.730	11.067	11.414	11.772	12.142	12.523	12.916
8	8.286	8.583	8.892	9.214	9.549	9.897	10.260	10.637	11.028	11.436	11.859	12.300	12.757	13.233	13.727	14.240	14.773	15.327	15.902	16.499
9	9.369	9.755	10.159	10.583	11.027	11.491	11.978	12.488	13.021	13.579	14.164	14.776	15.416	16.085	16.786	17.519	18.285	19.086	19.923	20.799
10	10.462	10.950	11.464	12.006	12.578	13.181	13.816	14.487	15.193	15.937	16.722	17.549	18.420	19.337	20.304	21.321	22.393	23.521	24.709	25.959
11	11.567	12.169	12.808	13.486	14.207	14.972	15.784	16.645	17.560	18.531	19.561	20.655	21.814	23.045	24.349	25.733	27.200	28.755	30.404	32.150
12	12.683	13.412	14.192	15.026	15.917	16.870	17.888	18.977	20.141	21.384	22.713	24.133	25.650	27.271	29.002	30.850	32.824	34.931	37.180	39.581
13	13.809	14.680	15.618	16.627	17.713	18.882	20.141	21.495	22.953	24.523	26.212	28.029	29.985	32.089	34.352	36.786	39.404	42.219	45.244	48.497
14	14.947	15.974	17.086	18.292	19.599	21.015	22.550	24.215	26.019	27.975	30.095	32.393	34.883	37.581	40.505	43.672	47.103	50.818	54.841	59.196
15	16.097	17.293	18.599	20.024	21.579	23.276	25.129	27.152	29.361	31.772	34.405	37.280	40.417	43.842	47.580	51.660	56.110	60.965	66.261	72.035
16	17.258	18.639	20.157	21.825	23.657	25.673	27.888	30.324	33.003	35.950	39.190	42.753	46.672	50.980	55.717	60.925	66.649	72.939	79.850	87.442
17	18.430	20.012	21.762	23.698	25.840	28.213	30.840	33.750	36.974	40.545	44.501	48.884	53.739	59.118	65.075	71.673	78.979	87.068	96.022	105.93
18	19.615	21.412	23.414	25.645	28.132	30.906	33.999	37.450	41.301	45.599	50.396	55.750	61.725	68.394	75.836	84.141	93.406	103.74	115.27	128.12
19	20.811	22.841	25.117	27.671	30.539	33.760	37.379	41.446	46.018	51.159	56.939	63.440	70.749	78.969	88.212	98.603	110.28	123.41	138.17	154.74
20	22.019	24.297	26.870	29.778	33.066	36.786	40.995	45.762	51.160	57.275	64.203	72.052	80.947	91.025	102.44	115.38	130.03	146.63	165.42	186.69
25	28.243	32.030	36.459	41.646	47.727	54.865	63.249	73.106	84.701	98.347	114.41	133.33	155.62	181.87	212.79	249.21	292.10	342.60	402.04	471.98
30	34.785	40.568	47.575	56.085	66.439	79.058	94.461	113.28	136.31	164.49	199.02	241.33	293.20	356.79	434.75	530.31	647.44	790.95	966.71	1,181.9
35	41.660	49.994	60.462	73.652	90.320	111.43	138.24	172.32	215.71	271.02	341.59	431.66	546.68	693.57	881.17	1,120.7	1,426.5	1,816.7	2,314.2	2,948.3
40	48.886	60.402	75.401	95.026	120.80	154.76	199.64	259.06	337.88	442.59	581.83	767.09	1,013.7	1,342.0	1,779.1	2,360.8	3,134.5	4,163.2	5,529.8	7,343.9
50	64.463	84.579	112.80	152.67	209.35	290.34	406.53	573.77	815.08	1,163.9	1,668.8	2,400.0	3,459.5	4,994.5	7,217.7	10,436	15,090	21,813	31,515	45,497

APPENDIX 3

Present Value Interest Factor of a Lumpsum of ₹1 per Period at i% for n Periods, PVIF (i,n)

Period	1%	2%	3%	4%	5%	6%	7%	8%	9%	10%	11%	12%	13%	14%	15%	16%	17%	18%	19%	20%
1	0.990	0.980	0.971	0.962	0.952	0.943	0.935	0.926	0.917	0.909	0.901	0.893	0.885	0.877	0.870	0.862	0.855	0.847	0.840	0.833
2	0.980	0.961	0.943	0.925	0.907	0.890	0.873	0.857	0.842	0.826	0.812	0.797	0.783	0.769	0.756	0.743	0.731	0.718	0.706	0.694
3	0.971	0.942	0.915	0.889	0.864	0.840	0.816	0.794	0.772	0.751	0.731	0.712	0.693	0.675	0.658	0.641	0.624	0.609	0.593	0.579
4	0.961	0.924	0.888	0.855	0.823	0.792	0.763	0.735	0.708	0.683	0.659	0.636	0.613	0.592	0.572	0.552	0.534	0.516	0.499	0.482
5	0.951	0.906	0.863	0.822	0.784	0.747	0.713	0.681	0.650	0.621	0.593	0.567	0.543	0.519	0.497	0.476	0.456	0.437	0.419	0.402
6	0.942	0.888	0.837	0.790	0.746	0.705	0.666	0.630	0.596	0.564	0.535	0.507	0.480	0.456	0.432	0.410	0.390	0.370	0.352	0.335
7	0.933	0.871	0.813	0.760	0.711	0.665	0.623	0.583	0.547	0.513	0.482	0.452	0.425	0.400	0.376	0.354	0.333	0.314	0.296	0.279
8	0.923	0.853	0.789	0.731	0.677	0.627	0.582	0.540	0.502	0.467	0.434	0.404	0.376	0.351	0.327	0.305	0.285	0.266	0.249	0.233
9	0.914	0.837	0.766	0.703	0.645	0.592	0.544	0.500	0.460	0.424	0.391	0.361	0.333	0.308	0.284	0.263	0.243	0.225	0.209	0.194
10	0.905	0.820	0.744	0.676	0.614	0.558	0.508	0.463	0.422	0.386	0.352	0.322	0.295	0.270	0.247	0.227	0.208	0.191	0.176	0.162
11	0.896	0.804	0.722	0.650	0.585	0.527	0.475	0.429	0.388	0.350	0.317	0.287	0.261	0.237	0.215	0.195	0.178	0.162	0.148	0.135
12	0.887	0.788	0.701	0.625	0.557	0.497	0.444	0.397	0.356	0.319	0.286	0.257	0.231	0.208	0.187	0.168	0.152	0.137	0.124	0.112
13	0.879	0.773	0.681	0.601	0.530	0.469	0.415	0.368	0.326	0.290	0.258	0.229	0.204	0.182	0.163	0.145	0.130	0.116	0.104	0.093
14	0.870	0.758	0.661	0.577	0.505	0.442	0.388	0.340	0.299	0.263	0.232	0.205	0.181	0.160	0.141	0.125	0.111	0.099	0.088	0.078
15	0.861	0.743	0.642	0.555	0.481	0.417	0.362	0.315	0.275	0.239	0.209	0.183	0.160	0.140	0.123	0.108	0.095	0.084	0.074	0.065
16	0.853	0.728	0.623	0.534	0.458	0.394	0.339	0.292	0.252	0.218	0.188	0.163	0.141	0.123	0.107	0.093	0.081	0.071	0.062	0.054
17	0.844	0.714	0.605	0.513	0.436	0.371	0.317	0.270	0.231	0.198	0.170	0.146	0.125	0.108	0.093	0.080	0.069	0.060	0.052	0.045
18	0.836	0.700	0.587	0.494	0.416	0.350	0.296	0.250	0.212	0.180	0.153	0.130	0.111	0.095	0.081	0.069	0.059	0.051	0.044	0.038
19	0.828	0.686	0.570	0.475	0.396	0.331	0.277	0.232	0.194	0.164	0.138	0.116	0.098	0.083	0.070	0.060	0.051	0.043	0.037	0.031
20	0.820	0.673	0.554	0.456	0.377	0.312	0.258	0.215	0.178	0.149	0.124	0.104	0.087	0.073	0.061	0.051	0.043	0.037	0.031	0.026
25	0.780	0.610	0.478	0.375	0.295	0.233	0.184	0.146	0.116	0.092	0.074	0.059	0.047	0.038	0.030	0.024	0.020	0.016	0.013	0.010
30	0.742	0.552	0.412	0.308	0.231	0.174	0.131	0.099	0.075	0.057	0.044	0.033	0.026	0.020	0.015	0.012	0.009	0.007	0.005	0.004
35	0.706	0.500	0.355	0.253	0.181	0.130	0.094	0.068	0.049	0.036	0.026	0.019	0.014	0.010	0.008	0.006	0.004	0.003	0.002	0.002
40	0.672	0.453	0.307	0.208	0.142	0.097	0.067	0.046	0.032	0.022	0.015	0.011	0.008	0.005	0.004	0.003	0.002	0.001	0.001	0.001
50	0.608	0.372	0.228	0.141	0.087	0.054	0.034	0.021	0.013	0.009	0.005	0.003	0.002	0.001	0.001	0.001	0.000	0.000	0.000	0.000

APPENDIX 4

Present Value Interest Factor of an Annuity of ₹1 per Period at i% for n Periods, PVIFA (i,n)

Period	1%	2%	3%	4%	5%	6%	7%	8%	9%	10%	11%	12%	13%	14%	15%	16%	17%	18%	19%	20%
1	0.990	0.980	0.971	0.962	0.952	0.943	0.935	0.926	0.917	0.909	0.901	0.893	0.885	0.877	0.870	0.862	0.855	0.847	0.840	0.833
2	1.970	1.942	1.913	1.886	1.859	1.833	1.808	1.783	1.759	1.736	1.713	1.690	1.668	1.647	1.626	1.605	1.585	1.566	1.547	1.528
3	2.941	2.884	2.829	2.775	2.723	2.673	2.624	2.577	2.531	2.487	2.444	2.402	2.361	2.322	2.283	2.246	2.210	2.174	2.140	2.106
4	3.902	3.808	3.717	3.630	3.546	3.465	3.387	3.312	3.240	3.170	3.102	3.037	2.974	2.914	2.855	2.798	2.743	2.690	2.639	2.589
5	4.853	4.713	4.580	4.452	4.329	4.212	4.100	3.993	3.890	3.791	3.696	3.605	3.517	3.433	3.352	3.274	3.199	3.127	3.058	2.991
6	5.795	5.601	5.417	5.242	5.076	4.917	4.767	4.623	4.486	4.355	4.231	4.111	3.998	3.889	3.784	3.685	3.589	3.498	3.410	3.326
7	6.728	6.472	6.230	6.002	5.786	5.582	5.389	5.206	5.033	4.868	4.712	4.564	4.423	4.288	4.160	4.039	3.922	3.812	3.706	3.605
8	7.652	7.325	7.020	6.733	6.463	6.210	5.971	5.747	5.535	5.335	5.146	4.968	4.799	4.639	4.487	4.344	4.207	4.078	3.954	3.837
9	8.566	8.162	7.786	7.435	7.108	6.802	6.515	6.247	5.995	5.759	5.537	5.328	5.132	4.946	4.772	4.607	4.451	4.303	4.163	4.031
10	9.471	8.983	8.530	8.111	7.722	7.360	7.024	6.710	6.418	6.145	5.889	5.650	5.426	5.216	5.019	4.833	4.659	4.494	4.339	4.192
11	10.368	9.787	9.253	8.760	8.306	7.887	7.499	7.139	6.805	6.495	6.207	5.938	5.687	5.453	5.234	5.029	4.836	4.656	4.486	4.327
12	11.255	10.575	9.954	9.385	8.863	8.384	7.943	7.536	7.161	6.814	6.492	6.194	5.918	5.660	5.421	5.197	4.988	4.793	4.611	4.439
13	12.134	11.348	10.635	9.986	9.394	8.853	8.358	7.904	7.487	7.103	6.750	6.424	6.122	5.842	5.583	5.342	5.118	4.910	4.715	4.533
14	13.004	12.106	11.296	10.563	9.899	9.295	8.745	8.244	7.786	7.367	6.982	6.628	6.302	6.002	5.724	5.468	5.229	5.008	4.802	4.611
15	13.865	12.849	11.938	11.118	10.380	9.712	9.108	8.559	8.061	7.606	7.191	6.811	6.462	6.142	5.847	5.575	5.324	5.092	4.876	4.675
16	14.718	13.578	12.561	11.652	10.838	10.106	9.447	8.851	8.313	7.824	7.379	6.974	6.604	6.265	5.954	5.668	5.405	5.162	4.938	4.730
17	15.562	14.292	13.166	12.166	11.274	10.477	9.763	9.122	8.544	8.022	7.549	7.120	6.729	6.373	6.047	5.749	5.475	5.222	4.990	4.775
18	16.398	14.992	13.754	12.659	11.690	10.828	10.059	9.372	8.756	8.201	7.702	7.250	6.840	6.467	6.128	5.818	5.534	5.273	5.033	4.812
19	17.226	15.678	14.324	13.134	12.085	11.158	10.336	9.604	8.950	8.365	7.839	7.366	6.938	6.550	6.198	5.877	5.584	5.316	5.070	4.843
20	18.046	16.351	14.877	13.590	12.462	11.470	10.594	9.818	9.129	8.514	7.963	7.469	7.025	6.623	6.259	5.929	5.628	5.353	5.101	4.870
25	22.023	19.523	17.413	15.622	14.094	12.783	11.654	10.675	9.823	9.077	8.422	7.843	7.330	6.873	6.464	6.097	5.766	5.467	5.195	4.948
30	25.808	22.396	19.600	17.292	15.372	13.765	12.409	11.258	10.274	9.427	8.694	8.055	7.496	7.003	6.566	6.177	5.829	5.517	5.235	4.979
35	29.409	24.999	21.487	18.665	16.374	14.498	12.948	11.655	10.567	9.644	8.855	8.176	7.586	7.070	6.617	6.215	5.858	5.539	5.251	4.992
40	32.835	27.355	23.115	19.793	17.159	15.046	13.332	11.925	10.757	9.779	8.951	8.244	7.634	7.105	6.642	6.233	5.871	5.548	5.258	4.997
50	39.196	31.424	25.730	21.482	18.256	15.762	13.801	12.233	10.962	9.915	9.042	8.304	7.675	7.133	6.661	6.246	5.880	5.554	5.262	4.999

Index